ERSKINE CALDWELL

ERSKINE CALDWELL

The Journey from Tobacco Road

A BIOGRAPHY BY

DAN B. MILLER

Alfred A. Knopf   New York   1995

THIS IS A BORZOI BOOK
PUBLISHED BY ALFRED A. KNOPF, INC.

Copyright © 1994 by Dan B. Miller

All rights reserved under International and Pan-American
Copyright Conventions. Published in the United States by Alfred
A. Knopf, Inc., New York, and simultaneously in Canada by
Random House of Canada Limited, Toronto.
Distributed by Random House, Inc., New York.

Owing to limitations of space, all acknowledgments of permission
to use previously published or unpublished material will be found
following the index.

Miller, Dan B.
Erskine Caldwell: the journey from Tobacco Road:
a biography / by Dan B. Miller.
p.   cm.
Includes index.
ISBN 0-679-42931-X
1. Caldwell, Erskine, 1903–1987—Biography.
2. Novelists, American—20th century—Biography.
3. United States—Intellectual life—20th century.
I. Title.
PS3505.A322Z74   1994
813'.52—dc20
[B]   93-48924
CIP

Manufactured in the United States of America

First Edition

For Maurice Immerman,

my grandfather

CONTENTS

ACKNOWLEDGMENTS

A number of fine teachers have encouraged my work. I think first of Hugh Hawkins, Stephan Thernstrom, David Blight, the late Nathan Huggins, Elizabeth McKinsey, Daniel Aaron, and Larry Buell. My greatest debt is to David Herbert Donald, the adviser for the dissertation that grew to be this book. He responded with care and wisdom to everything I said or wrote, and he was critical when he needed to be. Most important, Professor Donald inspired me with his own biographical studies—graceful unions of lyrical prose, exhaustive research, imagination, and common sense.

The staffs of a number of fine libraries have helped me with my research. I have acknowledged them on the first page of my endnotes. Special mention is owed Phillip Cronenwert and his colleagues at Dartmouth College's Baker Library, who helped me mine the huge Caldwell collection located there.

For financial assistance I am grateful to the Jacob Javits Foundation, the Mrs. Giles Whiting Foundation, and the History of American Civilization Department at Harvard University.

Several Caldwell scholars who preceded me have been generous with their expertise. Professor William Sutton spent years working on Caldwell, and I have benefited greatly from his prodigious research. Professor Harvey Klevar has published a fine Caldwell biography and has been kind enough to speak with me on several occasions. I am most grateful for the generosity of Wayne Mixon of Mercer University, who is currently finishing an intellectual history of Caldwell. We spent a summer side by side at the dark tables of Baker Library, and I've counted on him for support, guidance, and commiseration ever since.

I am particularly indebted to three groups of individuals who granted me interviews over the last three years: Caldwell's college classmates who brought to life his years of wild rebellion and artistic awakening; elderly citizens who knew the young Caldwell and his parents in small towns across the South; and, most important, Caldwell's four children and two widows, who shared their memories, good and bad, in spite of very mixed feelings for my subject. To Virginia Caldwell Hibbs, I owe a special debt of gratitude.

My editors, Paul Schnee and Bobbie Bristol, worked hard on my behalf, as did my production editor, Melvin Rosenthal, and my agent, Elizabeth Kaplan. Good friends also took time to read my manuscript carefully—Joel Doerfler, Wendy Kohn, Michael Mann, Jeffrey Melnick, and Jim Totten. Joanna Feinberg was helpful with the final draft. My family offered unconditional support. My brother Matt and his wife, Tina, let me write for a summer in their New Mexico house. Maurice Immerman, my grandfather, taught me more about history than anyone; this book is dedicated to him.

D.B.M.

PREFACE

I first heard of Erskine Caldwell in 1989, when Dartmouth College announced that the author's voluminous papers—over seventy linear feet—had become available to scholars. His name did not ring a bell. I had never come across one of his novels in a bookstore, nor seen his name in an anthology, syllabus, or critical evaluation of American literature. Neither had most of my peers, although a few claimed to have heard of (but not read) a novel called *Tobacco Road*. An informal survey of friends and colleagues over the age of fifty, however, elicited a quite different response. All of them, it seems, had read Erskine Caldwell, and most shared the same guilty admission. A work by Caldwell was the first "dirty" book they had ever read.

Just for fun, I took a quick look in the card catalogue at Harvard University's Widener Library. I was amazed to see that between 1931 and 1976 Caldwell had published an enormous body of work: more than one hundred short stories, twenty novels, and ten books of nonfiction, including three photo-text collaborations with his wife, the well-known *LIFE* photographer Margaret Bourke-White. Intrigued, I pulled a few dusty volumes off the shelves. Caldwell, it was immediately clear, had been extraordinarily popular as well as prolific. A number of the book-jackets carried the eye-catching phrase "The World's Best-Selling Writer!" An index of American best-sellers confirmed that Caldwell's books had sold a staggering 70 million copies. Although most of this success had taken place in the late 1940s and the 1950s, one Caldwell novel, *God's Little Acre*, still ranked as high in total sales as any single work by Faulkner, Hemingway, Fitzgerald, or Steinbeck.

I drove up to Dartmouth and spent a day poking through the endless boxes of Caldwell's letters, interview transcripts, photographs, and scrapbooks. I spent another afternoon reading through his two autobiographies, whimsical and peculiar narratives written thirty-five years apart. As I flipped through the pages, the story of a remarkable man and a remarkable literary career unfolded. A biographer, I thought, could not ask for a better subject than Erskine Caldwell.

Born the son of an itinerant minister in 1903, Caldwell had lived in seven Southern states by the age of twelve. In his teens and early twenties he found work as a cotton-picker, bodyguard, semipro football player, and chauffeur. Caldwell never received a high school diploma, and when, at his parents' behest, he left home to further his schooling, he was kicked out of one college and dropped out of another.

Caldwell grew up to be a tortured, enigmatic man defined by his inconsistencies; he was drawn to the alluring glamour of Hollywood and Park Avenue, yet deeply attached to his modest, more provincial beginnings. While the sexuality and profanity in his own novels would eventually land him in court and earn him a great deal of money, he beat his children when they swore. He was abusive to himself as well as to his family. He drank heavily and was prone to violent mood swings. Tormented and withdrawn much of his adult life, he underwent psychoanalytic treatment for depression with the renowned psychiatrist Harry Stack Sullivan. Married four times, Caldwell had a number of extramarital affairs. Only in his later years, when his career was all but over and his children were long gone, did he find a measure of happiness in the company of a patient and devoted woman who was his wife for over thirty years.

THIS BOOK FOCUSES on Caldwell the man—his angers and regrets, triumphs and failures, virtues and tragic flaws. But while this is the story of his life, it is his extraordinary and largely forgotten literary career that justifies my interest.

From the beginning, Caldwell pursued the craft of writing with a maniacal single-mindedness, working for almost six years in abject poverty and complete obscurity before being "discovered" by the famed Scribners editor Maxwell Perkins. With the publication of *Tobacco Road* in 1932 and *God's Little Acre* in 1933, Caldwell attracted a following of distinguished literary critics. Malcolm Cowley was only one of many who ranked him alongside F. Scott Fitzgerald, William Faulkner, and Thomas Wolfe. Cowley once wrote that Caldwell "had a greater natural talent for telling stories than anyone else in his generation." Kenneth White of *The Nation* thought him more powerful than Hemingway; William Soskin, reviewer for the *New York Post*, compared Caldwell favorably to Mark Twain. Faulkner himself named Erskine Caldwell as one of America's five greatest novelists. Throughout the

1940s and 1950s, universities offered seminars on his fiction, and eager doctoral candidates analyzed every aspect of his thought. As late as 1960, Caldwell was under serious consideration for the Nobel Prize in literature.[1]

Caldwell's arduous struggle to achieve publication for his early work highlights the process by which the first generation of American modernists became established in the 1920s and 1930s. As with many other young authors, Caldwell's first success came in the so-called "little magazines." Even more than the New York publishing houses, a network of avant-garde publications—*Dial*, *This Quarter*, *Poetry*, and *Broom*, to name but a few—served to establish some authors and consign others to obscurity. Caldwell's relationship with these experimental journals and their editors (brought vividly to light in his correspondence) reveals an important but poorly understood process by which the American literary canon has developed.

Caldwell's closest ties in artistic circles were to the left-wing intellectuals centered in New York City in the 1930s. His correspondence with Michael Gold and Jack Conroy, for instance, offers new insight into their thought. Yet because Caldwell lived and worked in rural Maine rather than New York, his involvement in this world—and the role he might play in helping scholars understand it—has been largely overlooked by American literary historians. In Daniel Aaron's classic study *Writers on the Left*, for example, Caldwell's name appears only in a footnote.

Caldwell's role in the Southern Literary Renascence is also greater than has been previously recognized. Even a cursory examination of the reviews for *Tobacco Road* and *God's Little Acre* reveals that standard critical wisdom placed Caldwell at the forefront of the emerging Southern canon, a status that has been all but forgotten in current studies of the period. Many Southerners, to be sure, did not appreciate Caldwell's groundbreaking efforts to "tell the truth about Dixie," and the angry debates his work provoked among Southern thinkers represent a fascinating and stormy chapter in that region's intellectual history.

Caldwell's writing drew the loudest outcry from those who found his work obscene or pornographic. Outraged citizens picketed theaters that dared show his plays, and high-minded city councilmen found political capital in banning his books. Boston's "Committee for Decency" targeted "Erskine Caldwell, above all other writers, as America's chief purveyor of filth." When *God's Little Acre* was seized from bookstore shelves in New York and declared "obscene" by the New York Society for the Suppression of Vice, Caldwell took his complaint to court. With the help of testimony from such literary lions as H. L. Mencken and Sherwood Anderson, he won his case. The trial is a landmark in First Amendment litigation, and Caldwell's ongoing battles against censorship provide a glimpse into a less than flattering side of our nation's cultural history.

Caldwell's commercial success, however, overshadowed all the artistic controversies that surrounded him. As one of the first authors to be published in mass-market paperback editions, he is a key figure in the history of American publishing. By the late 1940s, Caldwell had sold more books than any writer in the nation's history, and by 1960, his sales exceeded sixty million copies. But it was the stage adaptation of *Tobacco Road* that first made him a household name. The play opened in New York in 1933 and ran for over seven years—then the longest run in Broadway history. As many as three road companies brought the play to sold-out houses in every corner of the country. Attendance figures confirm that during that time, more people saw *Tobacco Road* than any other American play.

Today, Erskine Caldwell has been virtually forgotten by popular readers and scholarly critics alike, and he surely represents one of the greatest disappearing acts in our literary history. Understanding his calamitous decline will necessarily be an important goal of this book. What is the role of a publisher or the academy in guaranteeing a literary reputation? How does popular success influence a writer's critical standing? What makes a piece of literature "timeless"? This biography seeks to illumine the forces that contribute to the ambiguous and sometimes fleeting phenomena of credibility, reputation, and fame.

Working steadily until the very week of his death at age eighty-four, Caldwell produced an immense body of work that is also exceptionally uneven. But the very best of it is quite remarkable. His satirical portraits of "po' white trash" are so compelling as to have become part of the collective American vocabulary. From "Snuffy Smith" to "Hee Haw" to "The Beverly Hillbillies," Caldwell's literary images have been projected to the level of popular stereotype. His writing is rich in the detail that makes good social history, and he is responsible for some of our most dramatic renderings of the Depression era's Southern poor.

Erskine Caldwell wrote books for many, many years; some of them were poignant, graceful, and stunningly powerful. If nothing else, I hope this biography will encourage new readers to explore the work of a forgotten American writer, or will remind one-time fans of what they appreciated years ago.

ERSKINE CALDWELL

Chapter One

THE LESSONS OF CHILDHOOD

T HE TRAIN RIDE FROM GREENWOOD, South Carolina, to Due West, South Carolina, seemed endless to Ira Sylvester Caldwell. The air in the coach was invariably hot and sticky, and the narrow benches were too small for his lanky, muscular frame. Simply sitting still was an ordeal. At ten-minute intervals Ira would bound from his seat and stride vigorously up and down the length of the car, a dark-complexioned man of twenty-five with intense brown eyes, angular features, and a shock of unruly black hair. His mother likened him to a young Abe Lincoln. With his rumpled black suit, his string tie, and a Bible clutched in his big right hand, he looked more like what he was: a disheveled country preacher.[1]

Ira had come a long way from the cotton country of central North Carolina, where he was born in 1875, the first of seven children. His large family had struggled to make ends meet on a small farm, and Ira never forgot the "indescribable ecstasy . . . of the small hunk of cheese and the piece of peppermint candy" that were his reward for a successful harvest. He and his brothers worked long days in the field and, when there was time, they attended classes at a nearby school. For Ira, these hours away from the farm were sweet relief from a crowded household and the unremitting toil of the cotton fields. Lost in the pages of Stevenson's *Treasure Island* or a Shakespeare play, he found an escape from the narrow world of the family farm. To his mother's delight, he also found time to read and study the Holy Bible.[2]

Ira's father, John Harvey Caldwell, had neither time nor patience for organized religion, but his mother, Rose Hunter Caldwell, adhered strictly to the tenets of the Associated Reformed Presbyterian Church. A splinter group from mainstream Presbyterianism, the A.R.P. Church was founded by sturdy Scottish "seceders" who had come to America in the late eighteenth century to practice a more rigorous form of the faith. "A.R.P.s" regarded "Sunday" as a pagan term, preferring the more Biblically correct "Sabbath." Shopping, socializing, or reading the paper were forbidden on this day, and in stricter A.R.P. homes, a child who whistled or skipped rope went without supper. It was said that a rooster daring to crow on the Sabbath would surely be cooked for Monday's dinnertime meal. Dancing, card-playing, and, of course, drinking were strictly forbidden. The church services were stern and serious affairs. Hymns were considered too "secular," and the music was limited to psalms set to joyless melodies. Outsiders often considered A.R.P.s clannish, pious, and judgmental—and in many cases they were. Yet within their closely guarded circle were also the tight bonds of community and the comforts of shared virtue.[3]

For Rose Caldwell, her husband's distance from the church was not only an embarrassment but a spiritual threat to the rest of the family. She looked to her eldest son as their means of redemption. Ira, in turn, saw the freedom from a lifetime of hard farm labor that might come with a career in the ministry. The local school was run by the A.R.P. Church, and while John Caldwell may have grumbled, he eventually allowed his son to attend full-time. When Ira graduated from high school in 1893, John bowed once again to his wife's desires and agreed to send the boy on to Erskine College in Due West, South Carolina. Named for Ebenezer Erskine, founder of the A.R.P. Church, the small religious school provided a rigorous college and seminary education under the auspices (and watchful eye) of the church. Sending a son to the "Holy City" was a crowning achievement for any A.R.P. family. For Ira, it meant a chance to continue his education and see more of the world.

Ira seemed to possess limitless energy. Within a year, he was a standout in almost every sport the college offered. With the strong hands of a farmer and astonishing stamina, Ira came to be one of the school's great athletes. He was also an extraordinarily gifted student. He worked hard at his studies, reading far outside the bounds of the narrow curriculum. In four years he received no grade below an A, and in his senior year he was elected president of one of the school's two literary societies. Ira was known to speak his mind, and a slight stutter did not prevent him from taking center stage in almost any debate. While friends praised his fervent commitment and admired his courage and directness, less charitable colleagues found him caustic and abrupt.

By his senior year, Ira was increasingly troubled by the A.R.P. Church's unstated but unmistakable aversion to confronting the social problems of the larger society. Many A.R.P.s felt that "worldly concerns" were an unnecessary distraction from a properly spiritual life. Ira disagreed. He worked hard as the president of a school YMCA branch, and sometimes missed mandatory chapel services if he was immersed in a community project. He closely followed national politics and greatly admired the vigorous nationalism and concern for the environment espoused by Theodore Roosevelt. When, after his graduation from Erskine College, he was accepted into the Erskine Divinity School, church elders worried a bit about his somewhat breezy disregard for serious theological debate. There were whispers that Ira ought to spend less time helping the poor in neighboring counties, and more in contemplation of church doctrine.[4]

I

ONE LATE SUMMER DAY, while returning by train from his parents' home to the campus in Due West, Ira found himself momentarily distracted from the book he was reading. As he sat on his narrow bench, uncomfortable in the sweltering August air, he noticed a young woman at the far end of the coach. She was meticulously groomed, with a carefully ironed blouse, a dark skirt, and black high-heeled shoes. She was not beautiful, but she had striking red hair pulled back from a high aristocratic forehead, and bright blue eyes that sparkled from her fair-skinned face. Her slightly pinched features and rigid posture indicated, Ira thought, the austere good looks of a schoolteacher. She was, in fact, an instructor at the Due West Women's College, the sister school to Erskine College.[5]

Born in 1872 in Staunton, Virginia, Caroline Preston Bell was extremely proud of her heritage. Her great-grandfather had fought under Lafayette during the American Revolution, and she frequently reminded people that all of her ancestors were "born on this side of the Atlantic since the . . . first part of the 18th century." She represented the tenth generation of an old, but slowly declining, Virginia family. Most of the ancestral land had been lost to the Union Army, the rest to bad management.[6]

Richard Henry Bell, her father, was an accountant for the railroad, and Caroline, her five sisters, and two brothers grew up in a comfortable middle-class home. The Bells were stately Presbyterians—unemotional, distinguished, and refined. They voted Democratic at election time and went to church each Sunday. Carrie, as she was called, showed an early interest in poetry and a love for all the arts.

She spent hours composing dainty verse and painting watercolors of the dogwoods that grew in the back yard of her family's roomy white house. Like all the Bell girls, she was prim and exceedingly ladylike. To some she seemed aloof.[7]

The Bell family could not afford to educate all of their eight children, and the boys were first in line. But with characteristic determination Carrie applied for, and won, a scholarship to the nearby Augusta Seminary. The Seminary, later Mary Baldwin College, was more than a finishing school for proper decorum and etiquette, although it dispensed a healthy dose of these. The school also offered ambitious young women the opportunity to pursue the equivalent of a college degree, a so-called University Program demanding proficiency in both an ancient and a modern language, as well as requiring advanced courses in natural science, mathematics, English literature, and American history. At her graduation in 1893, Carrie was one of only four students to have completed the requirements for a degree, and she was also awarded the Star Medal for outstanding scholarship. She had impressed instructors with her genuine love of learning and her thorough, meticulous work. No one was surprised when she announced her ambition to be a teacher.[8]

There is no indication why Carrie taught at three different schools over the next three years. Perhaps she was enjoying her independence, or perhaps her contracts called for only one year's employment. But it is quite likely that the jobs in Atoka, Mississippi; Pocahontas, Virginia; and Chatham, North Carolina, did not meet Carrie's exacting standards. She was both a perfectionist and quietly domineering, and she expected deference and respect as a matter of course. She would have found any school that placed restrictions on her teaching, or unruly students who tested her authority, entirely unacceptable.

Carrie was returning to work at her fourth school, the Due West Women's College, when she attracted Ira's attention on the train. She noticed him as well, and on their return to the small town—Ira to complete his senior year, and Carrie to resume her teaching duties at the college—they began a courtship that would last three years. It was a slightly awkward situation. Ira's freedom was severely limited by the strict rules of Erskine College, and Carrie, several years his senior, was keenly aware of the impropriety of a student-teacher relationship. Except for the occasional stolen walk along the path that surrounded the Women's College, their contact was limited to the exchange of notes and letters. The postmaster in the tiny town of Due West must have smiled in knowing amusement as he watched Ira and Carrie come daily to his small post office to carry on their romance through the mail.

In many ways, the strict social conventions of the A.R.P. community in which Ira had been raised blended nicely with the prudish Virginia Presbyterianism that had guided Carrie's upbringing. Neither swore, drank, or danced, and they had little patience for those who did. They shared a passion for the classics—for Shakespeare, Virgil, and the British Romantic poets. Both could recite reams of verse from memory, and both possessed a seemingly insatiable intellectual curiosity. If Carrie was busy teaching herself Greek, Ira was searching for arrowheads in nearby Allendale County; if Ira spent a week comparing translations of *The Odyssey*, Carrie consumed books on Renaissance architecture. And for both of them, teaching and education anchored a firm social conscience. Both Ira and Carrie eagerly followed the work of Northern progressive reformers who were striving to solve the problems of an industrial society at the turn of the century. While Carrie's social conscience was tinged with a sense of noblesse oblige that Ira did not understand, they shared common objectives of uplift and reform.

Yet in other ways, Ira and Carrie were a study in contrasts. Where she was fiercely meticulous and organized, he lived in a state of scattered and perpetual activity. Even dressed in his finest suit, Ira never lost the look of an unpolished farmer, his tie chronically askew, his hair in resolute disarray. And whereas he enjoyed the company of all sorts of people, Carrie was something of a snob. Ira mingled easily among sharecroppers or mill workers, while they made Carrie patently uncomfortable. She was a spirited and witty conversationalist and preferred the more genteel amusements of an afternoon tea or a card party—events that left Ira nervously bouncing his leg and shifting restlessly in his chair. Most significant, Ira was graced with a sublime and pervasive self-confidence. To some it appeared as gruff arrogance, but to most others it gave an impression of open and even-handed authority. Carrie's social and intellectual vanity, however, masked deep insecurities. To outsiders she seemed invulnerable and aloof, but those who knew her well found that she demanded constant reassurance and support.[9]

Despite these differences, the courtship continued as Ira graduated from Erskine College and entered his first year of divinity school. They both agreed that the marriage should wait at least until Ira was ordained and could find a pulpit. Carrie, in any case, was in no particular hurry to get married. She was enjoying her teaching in Due West and was deeply ambivalent about having children of her own.

Nonetheless, she was understandably dismayed when Ira decided to leave school to fight in the Spanish-American War—dismayed, though not surprised. Her fiancé's passion for "just causes" and his fascination with world affairs were well known to her. These qualities had worried college officials for years, but they were much of what she loved in Ira. In practical terms, the separation meant little more than a change in postmarks from "Due West" to "Havana." But even if she was reassured by the silver sugar spoon he sent from Cuba with the inscription "To Carrie, With Love," she was still terribly worried about his safety.

To everyone's relief, Ira returned from the war unscathed, having come no closer to combat than the sound thrashing he gave an imprudent tent-mate who mocked his nightly Bible study. He breezed through his final year at Erskine with flying colors and was ordained in the spring of 1900. At last, it seemed, nothing stood in the way of the patient couple.[10]

Carrie, however, was not quite ready. Ira's first assignment would be in White Oak, Georgia, a small village struggling to survive on the state's western frontier. She held deep reservations about sharing the grim and arduous life of an A.R.P. minister: the rigid strictures of life within the sect, the lonely, impoverished posts, and the nominal salary. Although she loved Ira deeply, she was simply not ready to leave her books, her painting, and her comfortable life in Due West for the uncertain pleasures of matrimony and motherhood. Disheartened, Ira left for White Oak alone, resigned to continuing the courtship by mail.

In later years, Ira would insist that he had known Carrie would be his bride from the moment he first saw her on the train. Carrie would maintain that had she been aware of such impudence she would never have married him. Nonetheless, after a year of lonely soul-searching and daily letters, she acquiesced. Her younger sisters had long since married, and her family worried that she might die an old maid. Perhaps Carrie could not bear the thought of the disorganized Ira fending for himself. On more than one occasion, he mailed her a completed sermon and found himself before an expectant congregation with nothing but a love letter in hand. The long-awaited ceremony took place in the Bell family home in Staunton, in October of 1901, and a few months later Carrie joined Ira in White Oak.[11]

II

ON THE NIGHT the Caldwells' first child was born, a cold winter rain pelted the roof of the weatherbeaten manse, and throughout Carrie's long and difficult labor, a steady flow of water trickled through gaps in the dilapidated roof. Not until late into the night of December 17, 1903, was the child born. He was big and healthy, with Carrie's red hair and eyes that held the faintest hint of her sparkling blue. They named him Erskine, not, perhaps, in honor of the founding theologian of the A.R.P. Church but for the college where they had met.[12]

The two years just past had been challenging ones for the young couple. White Oak, Georgia, was a town of less than two hundred people. The inhabitants eked out a minimal existence on small cotton farms, and they depended on their gardens to keep them alive. Most owned at least one dependable dairy cow and a few chickens, and a few of the more ambitious citizens grew corn. The nearest store was in Moreland, four miles away on deeply rutted dirt roads—a perilous trip by horse and buggy when rain turned the sandy soil into thick, slippery mud. A new plow blade, a dress pattern, or medical attention required a trip to Newnan, the county seat, almost ten miles away. Atlanta, thirty-five miles to the northeast, was a two days' journey.[13]

Carrie's heart must have fallen the first time she saw the tiny unpainted house she was to live in—a one-story structure of loosely nailed pine board set on a small dirt lot. Inside, the four cramped rooms were only partially divided and offered almost no privacy. The church community had precious little money to spend on furnishing their pastor's house, and consequently, the dark rooms remained bleak and impersonal. The manse was heated by a central wood fireplace, and in winter, icy drafts blew through the thin walls. In summer, the careless construction offered no challenge to voracious mosquitoes. There was, of course, no electricity or running water; the privy and the well were located out back at opposite corners of the yard.[14]

Ira hardly seemed to notice the primitive living conditions, for he was absorbed in his duties as the town's new pastor. His first responsibility was to the small congregation of thirty who came each Sunday to hear him preach at the sober little church. His direct, almost curt sermons were well received, as was Ira himself. Although the A.R.P. Church was known for its highly educated ministry, he was straightforward and unpretentious, and he understood a farmer's needs. On shaking Ira's hand after church, members of his congregation took note of the strong, callused grip of a man who understood hard work. While he opened and closed each sermon with a quotation from the Bible, he spoke largely about applying Christian ethics to his congregants' everyday lives, about helping one another through hard times and sharing what little wealth they had.

Almost immediately after his arrival in White Oak, Ira turned his energies toward improving the local system of education. The nearest school was located in Newnan, and many of the young people in White Oak had stopped going altogether. Those who did manage the daily trip did so only sporadically, and a teacher who insisted on attendance during harvest time could expect a very short career. Ira set to work building a school for the community that would operate on a regular academic calendar. Within a year, a modest structure had taken shape across the street from the church, and both Ira and Carrie became full-time teachers. By the time Erskine was born, the school had been divided into grades, and Ira had managed to persuade a growing number of his congregation to keep their children in school. Under Ira's guidance, the White Oak School became an accredited high school serving students from all across Coweta County. Many of the students went on to study at Erskine College or the Due West Women's College.

With the end of classes each day, Ira was off into the surrounding countryside on horseback. Often he paid visits to the impoverished farmers working on the county's poorest land. He inquired about their spiritual condition, but his chief concern was to distribute the food he brought in a large croker sack. On other days, he traveled to Newnan to preach to the convicts on the chain gang, or to nearby Moreland, where he was busy organizing an orphanage. Many times, he turned homeward in darkness and arrived long after Carrie had gone to sleep. For Ira, life in White Oak, though taxing, was extraordinarily fulfilling. He lived for the satisfactions of his work—for translating his theological training into practical use.[15]

Carrie, however, shared none of his enthusiasm. The drafty and desolate house made her long for the comforts of her rooms in Due West and for the spacious Victorian house where she had grown up. She felt trapped in a "barren, desolate wilderness" and surrounded by coarse and unsophisticated people. There was no one for her to talk to about books or poetry, and with Ira gone most of the time, she was terribly lonely. At night in the cold dark house she envisioned horrific disasters, and she was so terrified of being alone that she persuaded a

Civil War veteran who lived nearby to lend her his old musket. The smallest sound brought her cautiously to the door wielding the heavy, antiquated weapon in trembling anticipation.[16]

The family was exceedingly poor, and Carrie had to manage the household accounts alone. Although augmented by donations of food from members of the congregation, Ira's salary was less than three hundred dollars a year, and Carrie frequently had to remind him that the provisions he distributed in the countryside were critical for their own survival as well. And she knew virtually nothing about the practical demands of living in the country: growing a vegetable garden, milking a cow, coaxing eggs from ill-fed chickens—these were obligatory parts of life in White Oak, and she was left to struggle with them by herself.

The members of the small congregation did little to help her, for they held serious reservations about the new pastor's wife. To begin with, Carrie was not an A.R.P., and church adherents viewed interfaith marriage as a threat to the sect's very existence. Worse still, Carrie made very little effort to conform to their rigid way of life. On the sacred Sabbath she might walk to town, or pull weeds in the garden, apparently oblivious to her neighbors' disapproving looks. On several occasions she was late to Ira's sermon, and the congregation watched with disapproval as she slowly made her way to her reserved pew in the front of the church. If there was pressing work at the schoolhouse, she might even miss church altogether. Ira respected his wife's fierce independence, and he married her well aware of her reservations about the A.R.P. Church. His congregation, however, was far less forgiving.

And Carrie was simply difficult to get to know. With her rigid carriage and aristocratic tilt of the head, she appeared cold and arrogant. Her clothes were extravagant and ornate by the simple standards of White Oak, and her careful Victorian English and Virginia accent set her clearly apart. She had no patience for quilting bees or church socials, and she had trouble making small talk with the women of the church. To neighbors, Carrie seemed a "high-falutin, book-smart lady who put on airs." Her fumbling efforts in the garden or difficulties in handling a horse were met, not with the sympathy she so desperately needed, but with scorn. She was treated as an outsider and felt it very deeply. Carrie would never forget how she "suffered, bled, and worse than died" in her first years in White Oak.[17]

When Erskine was born, he seemed the one bright light in her desolate existence, a steady salve to her loneliness; even his plaintive cries were far better than the stony silence that had once filled the house.

To Carrie's surprise, little Erskine even brought support from the women of the congregation, who came to her aid during her difficult pregnancy. Her sisters made the long trip to Georgia to help with the infant's care, and Ira took a short break from his frenetic schedule to spend time with the mother and child. For the first time since her arrival in White Oak, Carrie was not alone.

Not surprisingly, Carrie was intensely possessive and appreciative of Erskine, pampering him shamelessly and smothering him with affection. She would clutch him close to her breast for hours and refuse to let anyone else hold him. She dressed him up in his finest baby clothes and endlessly combed his long reddish hair.

But as time went by, Carrie became increasingly resentful of the obligations of child care. More and more, her spells of intense affection alternated with periods of total exasperation. Within a year Carrie returned to teaching full-time, and Erskine spent his days under the watchful eye of an older woman in the congregation. Whenever she could, Carrie took long trips into Newnan—again leaving the child with neighbors. Often she would be in such a hurry to be off on her errands that she would neglect to send diapers along, and the baby-sitter would have to make do with a flour sack. On one occasion, a visiting member of the congregation was shocked to find the one-year-old Erskine playing outside in an icy rain without hat, gloves, or shoes. And during Ira's sermons, Carrie often seemed to forget Erskine was there, and he would crawl unrestricted among the legs of the seated parishioners until someone noticed him and carried him back to her pew. Perhaps most difficult for the fastidious Carrie was dealing with the messiness of a small child. At his christening, Erskine wet the front of her dress as they stood to receive the blessing. On this occasion, and in the future, she responded angrily and with disgust to the disorder Erskine brought into her life. Whenever possible, she left the feeding and changing of her son to baby-sitters.[18]

If Erskine's sense of security was undermined by such fluctuating attention from his mother, he was even more shaken by the string of mishaps that he suffered during his first three years. As a one-year-old he drank a dangerous quantity of kerosene; six months later, he nearly lost a hand from a severe cut he received from Ira's shaving razor. But the most serious accident took place soon after Erskine learned to walk. Carrie was cooking the evening meal and left a large white bowl of boiling sausage grease on the counter to congeal. Erskine, toddling around the kitchen, reached high over his head and pulled the bowl of sizzling fat down upon himself.[19]

Luckily, Janie Walthall, their closest neighbor, heard the screams—Carrie's were louder than Erskine's—and sent her son galloping off to Newnan to fetch a doctor. Meanwhile, she managed to calm the hysterical Carrie and examine the child, who was lying in the center of the kitchen floor wailing, his body in convulsions from the pain. The grease had been so hot that the buttons on his pajamas had melted into his skin, and there were terrible burns down his entire front. While Carrie sat sobbing in a chair, Janie rubbed a mixture of lard and chimney soot into the child's body. Although it was clear after a few weeks that Erskine would survive, the accident left him with lifelong wales and scars criss-crossing his body from neck to waist.[20]

But the deepest scars were psychological. Whether Carrie's negligence was responsible for this and the other accidents, is impossible to know. The little boy was deeply frightened and certainly disappointed by the person he trusted most in the world, and the anger Erskine felt towards his mother would never leave him. The radical pendulum swings of Carrie's affections and this series of traumatic injuries were two of the most potent lessons of his childhood.[21]

WHEN IRA ANNOUNCED in 1906 that he and his family would be leaving White Oak for a new post in Prosperity, South Carolina, his congregants were dismayed. But Ira was restless and impatient for new challenges. Carrie, of course, had been anxious to leave White Oak from the moment she arrived, and her reservations about the town were well known. Moreover, she still suffered from the effects of Erskine's difficult birth, and local doctors had suggested that she might need a hysterectomy—a procedure far beyond the capacities of the medical facilities in Coweta County.[22]

Nonetheless, it was an abrupt departure. Ira and Carrie took only a couple of days to pack their few belongings into heavy black trunks and load them on a neighbor's wagon. There were quick good-byes and a final dinner in the church. Almost before they knew it, they were on their way to the train station and their cheerless White Oak house was disappearing around a bend in the road.

III

ERSKINE NEVER FORGOT the mingled thrill and fear of his first train ride—"the thundering monster, looming bigger and more threatening each moment, that looked as if it would sweep us from earth," and the stationmaster who "pulled on the long chain of the red-painted semaphore board high above the station to signal the engineer to stop for passengers." The hard wooden benches of the waiting room reminded him of the pews in the White Oak church, and the "bottles of milk and a large sack of red apples" that Ira bought for their journey remained forever in his memory. For the three-year-old Erskine, the move was not only a grand adventure but the approximate beginning of his conscious childhood. He was no longer a baby; he was a little boy.[23]

Erskine's new home, Prosperity, South Carolina, was located in the central part of the state, thirty-five miles northwest of the capital city of Columbia and approximately sixty miles from the Georgia border—cotton country through and through. In spite of the town's name, its seven hundred inhabitants were simple, hard-working farmers, raising cotton and a little corn on modest parcels of land. Their soil was a bit richer than that around White Oak, and, consequently, their lives a little easier. Quite a few local farmers had accumulated enough acreage to keep several families of black sharecroppers hard at work growing their cotton, and good harvests were regular enough to support a small commercial center. Downtown Prosperity boasted its own post office, a general store that sold everything from bullets to calico cloth, a small grocery, two banks, and a mule trading stable. At the end of Main Street was a battered mill that ran day and night, crushing cotton seeds and shipping out the oil for use as a lubricant in the factories of the Northeast.[24]

But if the community seemed positively cosmopolitan compared to the barren settlement at White Oak, the Caldwells' new house was painfully similar. Ira and Carrie must have been disappointed in the dilapidated, unpainted structure that greeted them on their arrival. The one-story manse, with narrow porches front and rear, was built facing a small dirt road on a large, two-acre lot, halfway between the small A.R.P. church and the local cemetery. Out back was a two-seated privy with a rusted tin roof, a large vegetable garden, and, beyond that, an old peach orchard. Inside, narrow, listing hallways connected four small rooms inadequately heated by a central brick fireplace. The house had been unoccupied for seven years, and only a few days before the Caldwells' arrival church members had replaced the last broken window and repaired the leaky roof. Like their home in White Oak, it was gray, cheerless, and poorly furnished.[25]

Not surprisingly, Ira hardly spent enough time there to grumble about the uncomfortable house. His assignment in Prosperity demanded that he preach at four separate congregations within Newberry County. On rotating Sundays he conducted services at the Prosperity, Newberry, and Cannon's Creek churches before rushing off to deliver a sermon at the Excelsior schoolhouse a few miles outside of town. Weekdays were spent in the area schools, where Ira divided his time between teaching and working toward improving attendance and curriculum. As he had in White Oak, he urged farmers to keep their children in school, and he worked hard to gain accreditation for the local high school so that its graduates could go on to college. Before long, Ira drafted and successfully implemented a county law that channeled local farm taxes into the community school.

Ira also continued to minister to the needs of the county's poorest families. In Prosperity, he found the most grinding poverty among blacks—sharecroppers crowded into ramshackle cabins and millworkers who lived in the squalid shantytown on the far side of the town's railroad tracks. He became a familiar face in these communities, distributing provisions and urging the creation of schools and churches. To his all-white congregations he delivered blunt sermons on the brotherhood of man and the godlessness of prejudice, and he called for improved working conditions for farm and factory laborers alike. On one occasion, he paid a special visit to chastise a landowner notorious for his mistreatment of black tenants. Predictably, Ira's outspoken racial liberalism brought him into conflict with members of the community. There were grumblings in his congregation about a pastor who "took up for the goddam niggers."[26]

While Ira's schedule did not allow him much time at home with his wife and child, Carrie was spared some of the bitter loneliness she had experienced in White Oak. Soon after their arrival, her eldest sister moved to town with her husband, and the other Bell sisters became frequent visitors to Prosperity. Ira occasionally grew impatient with their girlish laughter and "incessant gabbing," but for Carrie their companionship was a sweet relief. The trains that stopped right in downtown Prosperity also offered an easy escape from the scrutiny and isolation of being an A.R.P. minister's wife in a small Southern town. Both the C.N.& L. and the Southern made daily runs to nearby Newberry and the capital city of Columbia. On any given day, Carrie could leave Prosperity behind to visit the Newberry Public Library, buy paints from the art supply store, or even attend a free lecture or play.

The trains also made the large city hospital in Columbia accessible enough for Carrie to undergo the hysterectomy that she had contemplated for a number of years. The surgery must have alleviated the physical discomfort that had been with her since Erskine's birth, and she did not regret her inability to have more children. She had found motherhood a profoundly mixed blessing. Although Erskine was too young to understand it, the implications for him were, perhaps, greatest of all. He would be an only child.

Carrie continued to blow hot and cold in her treatment of her son. Erskine was now old enough to be actively naughty, and Carrie responded to his misbehavior by refusing to talk to him—sometimes punishing him with silences of two or three days. As her son began to assert greater independence, straying farther from the house, and taking rides down the road on his blue bicycle, Carrie reacted with gestures of rather extreme possessiveness. She began to dress him in an outfit of her own design that would, she thought, set him apart from the local ruffians of Prosperity. For the rest of his life, Erskine could describe the hated apparel in detail:

> The clothing I wore consisted of a white linen blouse or jacket that was so long it hung halfway to my knees, and with that were knee-length, unbuckled pants of the same material. There was no necktie to be worn with the costume, but there was a wide, black patent-leather belt with a brass buckle and that drooped downward over my stomach as far as my crotch.[27]

Erskine never forgot the humiliation he felt dressed in this bizarre costume, while the other little boys in Prosperity played comfortably in cloth cotton overalls.

Carrie also refused to take her son to a barber, and throughout his early childhood Erskine's locks fell from his shoulders in luxurious, reddish-blond curls. Neighborhood boys teased him mercilessly, and he begged his mother for a haircut. To no avail; as Carrie saw it, her son's hair, like his dress, would distinguish him from the uncouth children of an uncouth community. When Erskine directed his entreaties to his father, Ira only shook his head. He left the raising of their son in Carrie's hands. Dressed in her elaborate costume, his hair long and beautiful, Erskine was still her little baby, and she was reluctant to let him go.[28]

Carrie also kept Erskine out of the Prosperity school, and tutored him at home instead; but, while he learned to read, write, and do simple math, he was denied the company of other children. Although Ira taught in the area, Carrie argued that a local education was beneath her son, and a dangerous breeding ground for coarse habits. She was adamant that her son speak without a thick Southern accent and without the use of slang or vile language; on occasion, she washed out Erskine's mouth with water and ashes for such transgressions. Isolated already by his status as a "preacher's kid" and by his unusual feminized appearance, Erskine was a very lonely child. Like any little boy, he longed to make friends. Carrie was unyielding, and Ira, as before, said nothing.[29]

Erskine was too young to realize that Ira placed a great deal of pressure on Carrie, both through his frequent absences and through his seeming unwillingness to set guidelines of his own. Quite unfairly, Ira emerged in Erskine's mind as an unblemished hero, while Carrie was held rigorously accountable for the strictures she placed on his behavior. Caldwell's resentment of his mother colored his entire life. Both his fiction and his adult personal relationships were characterized by a persistent hostility and mistrust of women. And throughout his career, critics took note of Caldwell's obsessive and almost fanatical assault on accepted standards of propriety and decorum—the very values that Carrie treasured most.[30]

With Ira absent much of the time and his aunts constantly in attendance, Erskine also grew up largely in the company of women. The relationships he might have had with other young boys were severely curtailed by Carrie's decision to keep him out of school. Certainly his fiction and personal life testify to a man with profound doubts about his own masculinity—a man almost consumed by efforts to prove his virility.[31]

Despite his mother's overbearing attentions, Erskine did manage to pursue some of the activities of an average Southern boyhood. He played catch and swam in the creek behind the house. Every year the carnival came to Newberry, and once, Carrie reluctantly allowed Ira to take him. Occasionally Ira treated Erskine to an excursion in his battered Ford coupe—the only car in the county—and they would drive to Newberry to buy cinnamon rolls still steaming from the baker's oven. On other days the two might spend a hot afternoon in the bleachers of the nearby ball park.

But for the most part, Erskine was still lonely. He spent long afternoons watching the trains pull in and out of the Prosperity station and hours riding his bicycle around the streets of the small town. Like many another only child, he developed extremely strong attachments to pets—a habit he would keep forever—and he was devastated when they died or ran away. Even as a grown man, he found it easier to express his feelings for animals than for the people he loved.[32]

His childhood continued to be marked by unpredictable calamities, somewhat more serious than the average scrapes and bruises of boyhood. One morning the five-year-old Erskine was playing alone in the peach orchard behind the house and threw a rotten peach into an old wooden crate. Without warning a bee shot from a concealed hive into his eye and stung him badly, leaving him with a partial blindness he would have for life. On another occasion, while he was watching a baseball game, a foul ball rocketed into the stands and struck him directly in the face. He was knocked off his feet by the blow, and the extensive blue-black swelling closed one eye.[33]

But these accidents were overshadowed by the house fire that nearly claimed the lives of the entire Caldwell family. Carrie was awakened one morning at two a.m. by a flickering reflection against the bedroom window. The dry pine boarding of the house was almost entirely ablaze and only minutes from collapse. Erskine was fast asleep when Carrie jerked him out of bed and dragged him from the inferno. By the time the Prosperity Fire Department arrived on the scene the house was virtually gone, and the three Caldwells were left shivering in their night clothes in the red mud in front of the manse. When the local doctor arrived later that morning, he found them still there, silent, "their eyes wide open and unblinking in a state of shock."[34]

The fire was a terrible blow. The few valuable belongings Carrie and Ira had managed to collect during their lean years together were destroyed, and they had no insurance. More tragically, the fire also claimed the mementos of their life together—photographs, beloved books, diplomas, Carrie's paintings. But Carrie and Ira did not dwell on their tragedy and were resolutely unsentimental. Carrie always boasted that when she and Erskine fled through the back door of the burning house, they took care to hop between the rows of newly planted vegetables. The family was taken in by a widow with a large house, and while Ira continued on with his duties, Carrie set to work drawing up plans for a newer (and much larger) manse.[35]

For young Erskine, however, the fire was deeply traumatic. He was most visibly upset by the loss of his dog, and years later he would recall the horror of the event in *The Sacrilege of Alan Kent*—in terms that reflected his perception of Ira and Carrie as well.

. . . my dog ran from window to window pawing the glass while the flames ate bare his skin. My father went back after him, but before he reached the door the roof fell in. I ran towards the house for my dog, but my mother jerked me back in her arms.[36]

Of the sudden catastrophes that had plagued Erskine's childhood, the fire was the most dramatic and terrifying—one made all the more frightening by his near-fatal experience with burns as a toddler. The world must certainly have seemed a dangerous place, and one beyond the control of a little boy—a place where tragedy and pain loomed unexpectedly, with devastating results.[37]

I V

WHEN ERSKINE WAS EIGHT, his father announced that the family would be leaving Prosperity. For a number of years Ira had been seeking a position within the A.R.P. Church that would allow him the opportunity to travel more widely, and in early 1912 he was appointed Secretary of Home Missions. As the official church troubleshooter, his job was to heal rifts in contentious congregations, sometimes intervening in situations where combative groups of parishioners sat in stony silence on opposite sides of the church. Often a local minister had been evicted, but no new one would step forward until harmony was restored.

The job suited Ira, for it required almost constant travel and boundless energy. The Home Secretary had to pick up and move at a moment's notice and find his night's sleep wherever he could—usually in the spare bedroom or front parlor of a generous parishioner. For periods ranging from one to nine days, Ira worked in the center of rather violent controversies before moving on again to yet another divided church. In three years he visited over one hundred congregations across the South, and he thrived on the erratic schedule, the hands-on problem-solving, the challenges that came with every new situation.

With Ira away so much of the time, Erskine missed him badly. He eagerly anticipated his father's all-too-infrequent homecomings. Years later, he still recalled the "tingling smell of the coal smoke" that clung to Ira's clothes after a long train journey. Shaking the cinders from his father's hatband and rubbing them between the palms of his hands, he would inhale the acrid smell and know beyond a doubt that—if only for a little while—his father had returned.[38]

For Carrie, Ira's new job offered one consolation. While he was in the field, she and Erskine stayed in the Bell family home in her beloved Staunton. Grandma Bell and Carrie's sisters were a great help with Erskine, and the house was bright, cheerful, and gracious. For Carrie, returning home to Virginia from the Deep South was a dream come true. Although she missed Ira, she had grown accustomed to his absences. Moreover, at least once a year he was needed by a congregation for a period of months, and Carrie and Erskine could join him while they waited for a new preacher to take his place. Over the next three years, the family managed to live together for extended periods on three occasions, with Staunton serving as an informal home base in between.[39]

Erskine's impressions of life from ages nine to twelve—of his homes in Timber Ridge, Virginia; Charlotte, North Carolina; and Bradley, South Carolina—were forever mingled in his memory. By now he was a good-looking boy with Carrie's red hair, blue eyes, and freckles and a suggestion of Ira's rugged frame. Whenever he could, Erskine escaped from the house and continued his habit of lonely roaming. In Staunton, he sometimes disappeared into the woods and stayed there all day, or stopped at the cemetery and watched the old grave diggers at work. In Timber Ridge, he was mesmerized by the work at the nearby stone quarry and would "sit on the edge of the open pit and watch the workmen drill and blast the blue-green rock below." He never forgot witnessing an accidental explosion and how close to him a workman's shoeless foot had landed. The congregations in these towns came to know him as a barefooted boy who rarely spoke and seemed to take everything in—an inveterate wanderer who might be found at the depot at any time of day, sitting and watching as the trains pulled in and out with comforting regularity.[40]

These were hours, of course, when most of Erskine's peers were in class. Soon after Erskine's arrival in Staunton, Carrie had agreed to let him attend the excellent local school, but when the family moved to join Ira in Bradley she kept him at home once again. In Charlotte, when a truant officer came to their boardinghouse in search of Erskine, Carrie lied that her little boy was gravely ill and could only be taught at home. She continued to tutor Erskine herself—with mixed results. He could read fairly well and wrote in a painfully neat cursive which, if not terribly graceful, was very legible. He was, and would always be, a terrible speller, and his mathematics skills were uniformly poor. To Carrie's satisfaction, his speech was rigidly proper—untarnished by contractions or slang—but she continued to wash his mouth with ashes and water after any serious slip.[41]

The quality of Carrie's homespun education was not the major problem. By keeping Erskine at home, she continued to isolate him from other children; and he never forgave her for this. Without brothers or sisters, where else could he learn to share, to communicate with his peers, to feel comfortable in groups? It is no mystery how parents as talkative as Carrie and Ira produced such a resolutely taciturn son. If he did speak, he often mumbled, and while he appreciated a good joke, he rarely told one. Erskine would always have great difficulty making conversation or making friends—in part, because he never learned how.

When he was twelve, Carrie gave Erskine permission to take odd jobs during his free time. She was worried, and perhaps embarrassed, by his growing reputation as a dreamer and a wanderer. By this time he was a good-sized boy and too old to spend his days in such idle pursuits. Both Carrie and Ira were firm believers in the value of hard work, and their son was approaching an age where too much free time seemed a dangerous thing. Erskine was equally anxious to find employment. Perhaps he was trying to emulate his hard-working father, whom he idolized, and certainly he was eager to be away from the house and Carrie's watchful eye. Most likely, a boy who had been jerked suddenly from place to place his entire life found satisfaction and comfort in making decisions for himself.

There was not much work open to a twelve-year-old, but Erskine showed remarkable initiative and determination. He was, and always would be, fascinated by strategies and schemes for making money. One summer, he collected old automobile tires and shipped them "express-collect" to a scrap dealer in Columbia. Usually he earned fifty cents, but once, to his great delight, he received an even dollar for a particularly large delivery. He scoured the streets for discarded cigarette packs, collecting the aluminum liners and packing them into orange-sized balls that he sold to the metal scrap dealer for a dime. On Fridays, he picked up copies of *Grit* magazine from the Greenwood station and delivered them to twenty-two subscribers on his route. He even started a small laundry bluing business, ordering five-cent packages of bluing powder through the mail and selling the packets to the black washerwomen behind the cotton gin—underselling the local merchants by fifty percent.[42]

All this hard work provided more than nickels and dimes for Er-

skine's ice cream sodas. His jobs exposed him to every segment of a
Southern town. Mondays were wash days in the black quarter of Bradley, and Erskine treasured the friendly waves and cries of "Here comes
Mr. Bluing Man!" that greeted him along his route. He was well known
in the black community, for in Bradley, as in Prosperity, Ira sometimes
brought his son with him on his rounds to the opposite side of the
tracks. Erskine noted the poverty of the black mill workers, but he also
took note of the respect that his father paid them.[43]

Despite his friendliness with the people he met delivering his papers
or selling his bluing, Erskine was never in one place long enough to
get to know them well. In the spring of 1915, Ira was directed to investigate reports of dissension in a large church in western Tennessee.
He arrived there to find a bitterly divided and intractable congregation,
and he sent word to Carrie and the twelve-year-old Erskine to join him
in the small town of Atoka. This move would be Erskine's fifth in four
years, and although Ira originally planned to stay for only a few
months, Erskine would be sixteen before they left.

Atoka was a sleepy little place on the Illinois Railroad in the extreme
southwest corner of Tennessee, only a few miles from the borders of
Arkansas and Mississippi. One general store, one bank, a post office, a
run-down pool hall, and Dr. Fleming's humble general practitioner's
office met the needs of the residents. They were cotton farmers for the
most part, and the First World War was pushing the demand for cotton
to new highs. Atoka farmers lived comfortably, if not lavishly, on their
modest plots. A few of the wealthier townspeople owned stores in
nearby Millington or Covington. One or two determined entrepreneurs
made weekly trips to Memphis, thirty-five miles to the south, to buy
stock for their stores. To Carrie and Erskine, Atoka was another home
like so many others before it—a quiet stop on the railroad in the heart
of a small cotton-farming town.[44]

In their drab second-floor apartment, the family fell into a fairly set
routine. Ira was struggling around the clock to heal the rifts in his
troubled congregation. Carrie began teaching and tutoring in the local
school, and Erskine, now almost thirteen, looked for ways to make
money. He worked long days picking cotton, earning forty cents for
every hundred pounds he could lug to the old steelyard scale. Farm-
hands made a dollar a day, and he spent a month behind a team of
mules preparing a neighbor's field for fall planting. He trapped rabbits
and sold their hides, delivered papers, mended fences. For a month he
lived at nearby Millington Army Base working as an officer's
chauffeur—sleeping in a tiny windowless room and taking his meals in

the enlisted men's mess. Ira and Carrie saw his work as patriotic, but young Erskine's contribution to America's war effort was not what they presumably imagined. He spent most of his time carrying personnel to and from the Memphis whorehouses.[45]

Surprisingly, Carrie put a stop to her son's diligent wage-earning and enrolled him in the local school. He was now a gangling, awkward adolescent—growing fast and grappling with the preoccupations of any thirteen-year-old boy. Erskine later recalled that the "unexpected swelling and insuppressible throbbing of the penis was as thrilling as it was mysterious." But for Carrie, the emergence of Erskine's sexuality must have been terrifying. She could no longer mother him or smother him with affection; nor did she care to speculate on his hours away from home. Perhaps school began to seem less threatening to her son's welfare than did the world of whorehouses in Memphis or the pool hall in downtown Atoka.[46]

Erskine always claimed that he was finally sent to school when his parents were confronted with his fledgling efforts to write fiction. Consumed with adolescent self-pity and the conviction that he was misunderstood, Erskine locked himself behind the door of his room and wrote the "story of a young boy who runs away from his home in the country to escape the harsh tyranny of cruel parents." When he showed Ira and Carrie his twenty-two-page effort entitled "A Boy's Own Story of City Life," their reaction was "swift and uncompromising." They sent him to school.[47]

In later years, Erskine related this incident in countless variations to countless reporters, though he always ended it with the frustrated adolescent author shredding his work and tossing it to the four winds. There is, however, no evidence that the account is true. Whatever the actual story, Carrie and Ira had good reason to be concerned about their son's education. A letter Erskine wrote to his Aunt Sallie in 1915 was riddled with every variety of punctuation and spelling error. He told of a dark night without a "latern," when he and a friend "camped out dors as far as from the top of the hill down there." His prose and penmanship had improved very little during the last four years of constant travel and upheaval. If Ira and Carrie did read an early piece of his fiction, they had no cause to be surprised, but every reason to be disturbed.[48]

Erskine made the half-mile walk to Robison School each morning for two years. With only three teachers for grades six through twelve, the instruction leaned heavily on rote memorization and recital; the children were expected to sit quietly with readers and grammar books for long, unattended stretches. This was surely a difficult transition for Erskine, and only with a great deal of help from Carrie did he manage to pass all of his seventh-grade courses. As an eighth-grader he did little better, having particular problems with mathematics—something Carrie had almost totally ignored. He was, however, fascinated with foreign lands, and he excelled in geography. On one occasion, he won a copy of Gibbon's *Decline and Fall of the Roman Empire* for outlasting the rest of his classmates in a "geography bee."[49]

Erskine's first concern was not academics but the intoxicating social arena that was suddenly open to him. He was a good athlete, played on the Robison basketball team, and with his size and open good looks he found people drawn to him. On weekends there might be an excursion to Rosemont to see a play, or a Boy Scout camping trip far up the Mississippi. And there were joyous days playing hooky, now in the company of other boys and girls. Sometimes after school he and a friend worked on Ira's Ford and were rewarded with an hour or two of car privileges. With Erskine at the wheel, they drove the dusty roads of the surrounding countryside at breakneck speed.[50]

His first social contact was marked by some conspicuous awkwardness, for his lonely past had left a mark. He longed to be accepted, but a few of the more popular boys were quick to point out that although "he tried to cuss like any other bad boy," he "used too good English." He sought out the company of his peers, but he was uncomfortable in a group. A cluster of boys around the campfire might suddenly become aware that Erskine had not spoken for hours, but had just been sitting, quietly listening, quietly watching. He circled around the edges, preferring to attach himself to louder and more boisterous youngsters who kept the spotlight focused on themselves. He was most comfortable with one person at a time. His closest friend was James Boyce, and the two spent hours together, fishing, buying cigarettes on the sly at the local pool hall, or playing catch. Often they hopped the slow moving train through Atoka and rode it far out into the country.[51]

He also spent time with Elise Strong, a pretty brunette of fifteen who lived just down the road. Before too long, everybody in Atoka "knew he was crazy about her," and he did his best to impress her. Once, he rigged the steering wheel of Ira's Ford with baling wire and drove noisily back and forth in front of her house while hiding out of sight in the back seat. Elise's next-door neighbor thought she was "as crazy as he was" if she went out with him, but the matron evidently missed the cumbersome charm of adolescent wooing. Erskine and Elise shared a carefully chaperoned and entirely proper young romance. On

Friday or Saturday nights, the two would sit and talk on the Strongs' porch swing, while Mrs. Strong peeped nervously through the curtains. Other times they attended box dinners at the church or walked hand-in-hand to a school dance.[52]

A driverless car may have helped Erskine win Elise's heart, but it was only one of a dozen pranks he visited on the people of Atoka. Taken singly, Erskine's escapades appear to be the typical shenanigans of any adolescent. Tearing along Main Street with the Ford's muffler removed, he rattled the windows and nerves of the sleeping town. On innumerable occasions, Mr. Boyce's chickens ended up in Mr. Simpson's yard, and the clapper from the town's bell was stolen more than once.

But many of Erskine's pranks were far from harmless, and less easily forgiven. Neighbors would rise on Sunday morning to find their outhouses tipped over or bags of feed slashed and spilling onto the ground. Windows got broken in Covington stores. On one occasion Erskine badly frightened a neighborhood boy by firing over his head with a .22 rifle; on another he drank so much moonshine whiskey that he passed out cold on a neighbor's porch. Driving recklessly, he once smashed the Ford headlong into a mule-drawn cart.

The people of Atoka had seen rebellious teenagers come and go, and generations of restless boys had stolen Mr. Boyce's chickens and gotten drunk on bootleg gin. But they were puzzled by the seeming grimness and joylessness of Erskine's mischief. His "pranks" did not have the feel of the sporadic and impulsive rebellion so common among adolescents—and almost expected from the children of preachers. They seemed relentless, unsmiling, and calculated. Most surprising, Erskine was completely indifferent to being caught, and in fact appeared to encourage it. Many concluded that "Erskine was just plain mean"; others, that he "was none too bright." He was, it would seem, crying out for attention, and for a clear expression of his parents' expectations and limits—something they had rarely provided him.[54]

Carrie and Ira were certainly concerned about Erskine's behavior, but they were preoccupied with problems of their own. The congregational dissension that had brought Ira to Atoka had blossomed into open and bitter conflict. Almost one-third of the congregation's 270 members were advocating a defection from the A.R.P. in order to establish a new church under the auspices of mainstream southern Presbyterianism. These were the congregation's wealthier and more socially ambitious members, people who found the A.R.P.'s strict moral codes and solemn, unemotional services embarrassing when among their friends outside the denomination. The more traditional A.R.P.s deeply resented the move, of course, but recognized that without the financial support of this most affluent third, the little church could not survive. It was a violent, ugly situation that divided friends and families in the small town.[55]

Ira, as the denomination's official representative, fought hard to keep the congregation intact, and he was disgusted by the social climbing that motivated the defection movement. In characteristically abrupt and forthright sermons, he castigated the dissenters for their opportunism and materialism.

He soon found himself under attack from a variety of quarters— from members of the dissenting group and from parishioners fearful that Ira's hard line was further dividing the congregation. And there were many in Atoka who used the controversy to voice grievances that had been festering since their preacher's arrival in 1915. Ira's continued commitment to poor sharecroppers, black and white, seemed to come at the expense of his own congregation. Too often an assistant conducted funerals or marriages while Ira was out in the field establishing a new country school or organizing food drives for the poor in Covington. Others were troubled by his efforts to educate the black sharecroppers and his "meddling" in their business contracts with white landholders. Almost everyone noticed that Carrie and Erskine rarely attended church at all.

As the controversy dragged on, Ira became a scapegoat for the congregation's mistrust and frustration. An increasing number of people refused to shake his hand or meet his eye on the street. On one occasion, his life was threatened. The local school board was hesitant about renewing Carrie's teaching appointment, and the Robison School was suddenly overcrowded and having trouble finding a place for Erskine in the ninth grade. The window of the Caldwell house was shattered by a rock. Once Erskine was waylaid and left unconscious by the side of the road; there were whispers that "enemies of Mr. Caldwell" were behind the attack.

After four years of almost constant turmoil and growing abuse, Ira resigned. Most of the seceding faction returned to the church, and a new pastor agreed to take over on the condition that the matter never be discussed again. Many of the relevant pages from the church records were torn out and burned.

The Atoka years were sobering and depressing ones for the entire Caldwell family, but they were not ashamed of their ignominious departure. Years later, Carrie would recall Ira's tenure in Atoka as a grand conflict of good versus evil, and it was this understanding that she passed on to her son.

"His life was a struggle," she wrote to Erskine years later.

His ministry was a warfare against those baffling powers of evil called indifference, weakness and inertia. If the story of his sacrifice, privations, hardships, heart-bruises and wounds of the spirit were written, it would read like a page from the book of martyrs.[56]

Erskine came away from the experience with a hardened conviction that Ira was, as Carrie said, "a noble warrior of the truth"—a man who stood up against the small-mindedness, bigotry, and cruelty he found in the small towns of his native region. As an adult, Erskine would make his father's causes his own, and in his writing he sought to honor and vindicate him.

V

THE CALDWELLS ARRIVED in Wrens, Georgia, on a steaming July day in 1919. As they pulled up in front of their new home in the heavily loaded Ford, their troubled stay in Atoka must suddenly have seemed far behind them. Trellises of blooming morning glories bordered three sides of the roomy, freshly-painted one-story house, and gracious porches extended the length in front and back. Lush willow trees offered shade for the small, sandy plot. Inside, there were five spacious rooms, each with its own coal fireplace. There was no running water, but Carrie was thrilled by the oak-wainscotted bathroom complete with a built-in tub. After more than fifteen years of living in the denomination's poorest accommodations, the comfortable house was a well-earned surprise.[57]

With a population of over one thousand, Wrens seemed to Erskine "like a great city compared to Atoka, Tennessee." Located in eastern Georgia, thirty-five miles south of Augusta, the town was one of many that sprang up along the route of the Augusta Southern Railroad as it extended south in the mid-1880s. The surrounding land was good for short staple cotton, and thick stands of Georgia pine dotted the tops of the sandy clay ridges. In 1919 cotton was fetching upwards of sixty dollars a bale, and the forests offered some of the best timber in that part of the state. The local economy was thriving, and on a hot summer

day the acrid fumes from a sawmill and a cottonseed mill wafted
through the unpaved streets of the town.

Downtown Wrens consisted of four or five groceries, three banks,
two barber shops, two drug stores, a hardware store, a post office, a
gift shop, a tiny jail, and a funeral parlor. At the end of Main Street
stood the crowded offices of the local paper, and just beyond, an ice
factory and small iron works hummed with activity the year round.
The train tracks ran right through town, and at 8:00 a.m. and 4:00 p.m.,
the Southern made stops on its daily run from Augusta to Tennille.
There was always a small crowd on the platform—a few businessmen
on their way to work, a housewife out for a day's shopping in Augusta,
a farmer in to buy seed or fertilizer. But most came simply to pick up
the mail and pass the time gossiping about the comings and goings of
their small community.[58]

To fifteen-year-old Erskine, Wrens seemed a place "alive with new
possibilities." He had grown into a lean, red-headed boy, with broad
shoulders, thick, strong wrists, and muscles hardened from his labors
in the cotton fields of Tennessee. But his boyish features and freckled
good looks were tempered by an almost perpetual frown and ramrod-
straight posture. His manner was most often one of detached and impassive amusement.[59]

He surely hid his nervousness on the first day of school in the fall
of 1919. The two-story, red-brick high school had only been completed
the previous spring, and it was a far cry from the small Robison School
in Atoka. Wrens High School boasted twelve classrooms, two labora-
tories, a wood shop, a music room, a library, and an auditorium. For
those students who planned on returning to their farms or sought sec-
retarial or industrial jobs in Augusta, the school provided a two-year
vocational course; but for those twenty or so youngsters each year
interested in going on to college—the children of the doctors, lawyers,
preachers, and businessmen for the most part—it offered a rigorous
four-year course of study. Erskine was enrolled as a senior, more by
virtue of his size and age than his academic preparation. Ira promised
the school superintendent that his son would work hard and could
manage the course load.[60]

Predictably, however, Erskine was a very poor student. In his first
year, he received a C in quadratic equations, a C in plane geometry, a
C− in Latin (his mother's class) with a terse note that he had not read
the required amount of Cicero. He managed a B in world history. He
received a C+ in English, where his poor grammar and spelling continued to plague him. He enjoyed some of the reading, however, and

worked through Macaulay's *Life of Johnson*, Shakespeare's *As You Like It* and *Hamlet*, and Dickens's *Tale of Two Cities* and "A Christmas Carol." Erskine read with intense concentration and hated to be disturbed. A number of visitors to the manse were offended when he opened the front door without any greeting and ushered them inside without looking up from his book.[61]

For the most part, however, he seemed indifferent to the world of academics his parents held so dear. The school principal grew accustomed to retrieving him from the banks of a nearby stream, where he daydreamed away the hours he should have spent in geometry or biology class. Before long, he had attached himself to a somewhat wild group of boys, and, as before, he gained a reputation as a conspicuously indelicate prankster. When the old school bell began to toll late one weekday night, the police chief arrived at the belfry to find Erskine tugging doggedly on the rope, as if waiting to be found. On another occasion, the boy pitched a rock through his math teacher's window, then waited calmly in front of the house until he was apprehended.

As in Atoka, Erskine traveled on the edge of his boisterous social group. Sometimes he would take other teenagers for wild drives through the country, saying little while his noisy compatriots whooped and carried on. Although often in the company of others, he seemed distant, and he was consumed with a sense of loneliness and isolation. Erskine found it extremely difficult to trust anyone, and he appeared mysterious, cold, and aloof. He was also painfully shy. When a little girl in his neighborhood began teasing him about his red hair, crying "Here comes Woody Woodpecker!," he walked blocks out of his way to avoid her.[62]

As he had done in Atoka, and as he would continue to do for the rest of his life, Erskine sought comfort and solace in romantic relationships. Sara Farmer was pretty and blond, with rounded features and a full figure. She was, that is, exactly Carrie's opposite. Erskine met her at a school dance, and he wooed her with an almost embarrassing ardor. People in Wrens soon grew accustomed to seeing them together, although in that strict A.R.P. community unmarried couples limited their romantic endeavors to carefully chaperoned Friday and Saturday nights. So while they may have kissed and held hands in the front seat of the car on an occasional stolen drive, the relationship was quite chaste. "Everyone in Wrens knew they were in love," but whatever Erskine may have told his confederates about his conquests, Sara's circle of friends knew better—she was a fiercely proper young woman.[63]

While he obviously cared deeply for Sara, he was also extremely

demanding. Growing up as an only child, Erskine was accustomed to
having his own way, and he reacted very poorly when he did not get
it. During a particularly passionate quarrel with Sara, he climbed out
onto the portico of the school's central doors and refused to come
down until she gave in. His behavior would have come as no surprise
to Carrie. She often related the story of her sixteen-year-old son refusing to get out of bed until she bought him a pair of purple socks to
wear to school.[64]

In what would become a lifelong pattern, most of Erskine's time
was spent not with the woman he loved or his family, but hard at
work. Soon after his arrival in Wrens he took a job driving and re-
pairing a rattletrap Ford for the local physician. On odd afternoons and
weekends, Erskine drove Dr. Pilcher to the far corners of Jefferson,
Glascock, and Burke counties. Tobacco had been grown in these areas
years before and a few abandoned "tobacco roads"—flat trails left by
the heavy hogsheads of cured tobacco as they were rolled from farms
to the Savannah River—were still to be seen on the crests of several
of the blackjack ridges. Later, the same sand-clay soil yielded good
cotton crops. But the farms Erskine and Dr. Pilcher visited were now
barren and desolate—the soil leached of minerals by years of single-
crop agriculture. Absentee landlords, living in relative comfort in Augusta, Louisville, or Wrens, had long ago given up on the marginal
property and on its struggling inhabitants.[65]

As he escorted Dr. Pilcher on his rounds, Erskine was exposed to
scenes of almost unbelievable deprivation. He saw families of fourteen
crammed into dilapidated tarpaper shacks and thirteen-year-old girls
(themselves with children of their own) bent and aged from the effects
of malnutrition. He observed the offspring of incestuous unions—tod-
dlers with blank stares and birth defects. Many of these people were
simply starving to death, and there was little Dr. Pilcher could do.
Often, he was reduced to leaving a dollar or two on the chair before
moving on to the next family.[66]

Erskine saw more of the same poverty on frequent trips into the
countryside with his father. As he had throughout his career, Ira
brought what food he could from the household pantry to the people
in direst need, and although Carrie fretted that "the family couldn't
afford to feed every poor family in Jefferson County," she often stowed
a few pieces of candy in his sack for the elderly and children. Driving
back into town, Ira would lecture Erskine on the shame and injustice
of a wealthy nation that allowed such poverty to exist. His temper
would rise as he warmed to his subject, driving faster and faster until

they were fairly flying along the deeply rutted road. "Those folks are like toads in a post hole!" he would lament. "They just have no fair chance at all."[67]

People in Wrens sometimes tired of hearing Ira's impassioned, stuttering sermons—harangues about the need for greater aid to the poor and the Christian responsibility of every individual for his fellow man. He was often disheartened by his parishioners' response. Too many seemed blindly indifferent or unwilling to face the enormity of a problem existing in their own backyard. Although one day Erskine reached an audience beyond Ira's wildest dreams, people in Wrens might have laughed when critics praised *Tobacco Road* for "blowing the lid off rural poverty." They had been hearing about it in church for years.[68]

Dr. Pilcher and Ira introduced Erskine to the county's most destitute whites, but his job at the local cottonseed oil mill familiarized him with some of the poor black citizens of Jefferson County. For almost a month, Erskine crept out the back door of the manse late at night to work the midnight-to-seven-in-the-morning shift, shoveling cotton seeds onto slow-moving conveyors. By punching out half an hour early he managed to return home undetected, just in time for breakfast. It was grueling work on little sleep, and when he finally nodded off at the morning meal, Carrie found out and put a stop to it.[69]

But his brief contact with black co-workers marked him deeply. He cherished the interracial relationships that sprang up in the cramped quarters of the mill. All his life he treasured (and embellished) the memories of "working side by side in the seed house" and "eating early-morning lunch together on the Railroad siding in fair weather and in the boiler room on rainy nights." He remembered the cottonseed mill as "the only completely democratic institution in town," where "there was no intimation of racial distinctions, and everyone, white or Negro, was entitled to express his opinion and his likes and dislikes on any subject he wished."[70]

Erskine held a patently romantic view of the mill. He failed to note that the task of carrying the two-hundred-pound bags of seed fell entirely on black workers, or that their pay was only half that of whites. Still, in the early morning hours at the mill, a teenage boy could at least glimpse an otherwise hidden world. In unguarded moments, he gleaned some small idea of how the black citizens of Wrens felt about their fellow whites. Sitting in the storage shed he overheard black houseboys, moonlighting at the mill, tell their stories—"some scandalous, some tragic, others humorous." He grew to better understand "the inherent anxiety of black people living in the shadow of white people."

Erskine's eavesdropping was only part of a continuing education. Only months before, Ira had been threatened by the Ku Klux Klan for his efforts to aid black sharecroppers. A black man accused of raping a white woman had recently been dragged through the streets of Wrens and lynched.[71]

The frank sexual discussions of workingmen late at night were also exciting for a sixteen-year-old boy. Growing up in Carrie and Ira's puritanical home, it was especially thrilling to hear adults so casually dissecting their latest romantic adventures. He was, after all, a rather sheltered minister's son, and the mill seemed "a seminar devoted to the theory and practice of male and female aberrant relationships." As his fellow workers passed the time on a rainy night, he received an excellent introduction to the underside of small-town life: to the "family feuds, secreted births, mysterious deaths, violent quarrels, desertions, infidelities, and scandalous love-makings." Erskine was an excellent listener.[72]

Unfortunately, Erskine's more formal education was not nearly so successful. Poor grades and even worse attendance ruined his chances of graduating from Wrens High School with the rest of his class in the spring of 1920. He participated in the ceremony anyway, taking his turn in the procession, and received a blank scroll when his name was called. The audience of friends and relatives may well have exchanged knowing glances, but they applauded politely as their minister's son took his turn. Many years later, Erskine would still deny that it had been an embarrassing day, but those sitting closest to the podium could not miss the blush that rose on his fair-skinned face. Carrie maintained her characteristic poise and stately posture, but she too betrayed some discomfort. A neighbor observed, somewhat unkindly, that "while Ira seemed calm and relaxed as always, she looked as if she might've just swallowed a green apple."[73]

Over the next few weeks, while his friends pored over their college catalogues, Erskine was studiously indifferent. He was, he proudly declared, a graduate of "the school of hard knocks," and he was anxious to "get the hell away from books and slide rules." He was equally anxious, no doubt, to escape the scrutiny of his mother and the small A.R.P. community. Moreover, the bustling town of Wrens that had once seemed so exotic now irritated him, and he ached for a change of scenery.

When his uncle in northern Georgia offered him a place to stay and a job as an assistant to a local stonemason, Erskine jumped at the chance. Carrie and Ira both liked the plan; they believed in the importance of hard work, but more, they were well aware that a bored, restless summer in Wrens would mean nothing but devilment for their rebellious son. They were surely relieved as they watched Erskine board a northbound train for the small piedmont town of Calhoun, Georgia, fifty miles south of Chattanooga.[74]

For the next two months, Erskine spent his days lifting granite blocks and carrying heavy hods of mortar up a steep ladder as he helped the stonemason construct a small Baptist church. Erskine was proud of his physical strength, and he thrived on the hard work. Beyond appreciating a job well done, he was minutely aware of every penny he earned. Letters to Carrie made only token mention of his aunt and uncle or his social life but included detailed accounts of his financial affairs: "Mother I have saved $50 in three weeks, and will stick it out three more weeks and make it an even $100. Am making $4.00 a day but only averaging $22.00 a week but some time work all day Saturday [*sic*] . . . If I save $100 this summer do you think that my vacation will be well spent?"[75]

While Erskine sought his mother's approval, he was in no particular hurry to see her. When Carrie proposed a visit in late July he instructed her, rather bluntly, "not to come here till the last of August, because you are not needed out here and it will be better for you to stay away as long as possible." Still, he was not quite ready to be on his own. Two weeks into his stay he realized that he had not planned thoroughly for his trip, and shot off a desperate letter to his mother: "Send me some underwear *poste haste*, pronto, quick, am out, totally."[76]

By the middle of August, the four walls of the granite church had reached rooftop level, and Erskine returned home. After two months away, he found it difficult to come back to the nest. A few years later, Erskine wrote a rare piece of autobiographical fiction entitled *In the Days of Our Youth*, which captured his feelings of frustration and helpless entrapment that August of 1920. The protagonist, a callow seventeen-year-old named Donald, is particularly impatient with his mother, who overwhelms him with "the things she wanted to tell me, the advice she wanted me to have, the love that she wanted me to remember her by, the concern she felt." His mother, young Donald laments, understood nothing about life and was resolutely blind to his newfound maturity: "What did she know? I was a man, I could take care of myself!"[77]

Moreover, Donald feels smothered by the grinding routine of his hot, dusty hometown. Wrightsville (an almost exact replica of Wrens) was "a place where nothing ever happens," where a young man could walk endlessly up and down Main Street searching for something to do and where "each hour seemed a useless waste." Donald was certain that in the world beyond the town "things were always happening . . . one right after another." For Erskine, this uneasy sense of stagnation was exacerbated by memories of his itinerant childhood. He had grown accustomed to frequent moves, and he bridled at his circumscribed fate—"anchored so early in life . . . like a rusting ship no longer seaworthy."[78]

Many of Erskine's friends were making their final preparations for college, and others had volunteered for military service and were pursuing unimaginable adventures overseas. Erskine desperately envied them. Unlike his parents, who had gone eagerly to school, excited by new ideas and the thrill of scholarship, Erskine came to view college as a means of escape—a means of moving beyond the tired patterns of life in Wrens, the watchful eyes of his mother, and an A.R.P. community that closely monitored the behavior of its minister's son.

Carrie had long dreamed that Erskine would attend the University of Virginia, but the tuition for out-of-state students was well beyond the family's means. Ira, not surprisingly, favored his alma mater in Due West. Aside from its sentimental appeal, the school held two very practical attractions for the sons of A.R.P. ministers: tuition was reduced, and applications were considered in a somewhat generous light. Erskine had completed fewer than four desultory years of formal schooling, and years later he would admit that "Erskine College was the only school that would take me." If he had mixed feelings about attending the "Holy City," he had precious few options. In the fall of 1920, he was on the move again. This time, he was on his own.[79]

Chapter Two

THE HOLY CITY
AND BEYOND

IT WAS AN EXHAUSTING, full day's journey from Wrens to the tiny college town of Due West, South Carolina. As he headed north, Erskine had to switch trains in Augusta, again in Greenwood, twenty-five miles inside the Carolina border, and once again at the depot in Donalds, South Carolina. The final leg of the ninety-eight-mile trip could be negotiated only on the "Dinky," a two-car train that made runs twice daily from Donalds to Due West. While this individually owned route was unusually short, the proprietor bragged that his four miles of track were as wide as any in the state.[1]

The crossroads settlement of Due West, was not, as the students snidely put it, "due west of nowhere," but it was, indeed, an isolated little town in the far western corner of South Carolina. In 1920, the surrounding countryside was dotted with small cotton fields, and as Erskine entered his freshman year, the farmers in the neighboring villages of Donalds, Shoals Junction, and Hodges were beginning to suffer as their crop fetched ever-decreasing prices at the local mills.[2]

But the fewer than two hundred townspeople of Due West were more concerned with the arrival of the students than the fluctuations in the cotton market. Due West was a college town, and it revolved almost entirely around the life of Erskine College and Due West Women's College. Jim Plaxco's Pharmacy and the few other stores that formed the single commercial block often closed during the hot summer months. Over Christmas and spring recesses the unpaved Main Street of the sleepy village was all but deserted.[3]

Founded in 1839 to train the ministers of the A.R.P. Church, Erskine College had changed very little since then. The school still provided a chaste, closely monitored environment for young men and hammered home a rigorous liberal arts curriculum rooted in Christian theology. The small student body came mostly from South Carolina, with a smattering from other A.R.P. outposts across the South. Few of the students were very poor, fewer still were wealthy. For the most part, the matriculants of Erskine College were earnest, religious, and serious-minded young men from middle-class families. Many were ministers' sons, and many were themselves headed toward careers within the A.R.P. Church.

Both the academic and the religious requirements of Erskine College were arduous and severe. Following mandatory daily chapel service at eight, students sat in classes all morning, coming back after lunch for part of each afternoon. More than half of the classes were strictly prescribed: all freshmen took Bible, mathematics, and English. The remaining course work could include either Greek, Latin, or German in fulfillment of a language requirement, and either American literature, English history, or science. Erskine College considered its graduates to be the trustees of their tiny denomination; classes were small and expectations extremely high, particularly for the children of A.R.P. ministers. Of the fifty students in Erskine's freshman class only thirty-nine returned to school after the Christmas exams.[4]

When Erskine, still three months shy of his seventeenth birthday, stepped off the train in Due West in the middle of September, his scant belongings fit easily in the two small suitcases he carried. Arriving at the college's single dormitory in the center of the tiny campus, he found the halls of the four-story red-brick building teeming with incoming students. Rooms were assigned without regard to class standing, and confident seniors shouted joyous greetings to one another amidst nervous, awkward freshmen making their first tentative introductions. Varsity athletes, resplendent in their letter sweaters—a bright scarlet E against a white woolen background—talked excitedly about the upcoming football season. A number of the boys had recently come back from military service overseas in the "Great War," and, still proudly in uniform, they regaled their awestruck classmates with stories of battlefield glory and exotic French women. Officers of the two literary societies discussed plans for the debate scheduled for the middle of October.

Still dressed in his best Sunday suit, with his hair parted severely in the center and slicked down against his head, Erskine stood quietly in his doorway watching the goings-on. A classmate walking by wondered at the tall redhead whose carefully guarded expression was "a kind of mixture of Mona Lisa and Mencken—enigmatic, and amusedly cynical. . . ."[5]

I

DURING HIS FIRST SEMESTER of college work, Erskine picked up where he had left off in Wrens. In a regimented atmosphere where attendance was taken extremely seriously and students were graded on their daily recitations, he was notorious for his frequent absences. "He cut class every chance he could," a friend recalled, and his grades reflected his lack of interest. His best marks came in Bible, history, and American literature, where he received three solid D's. He received a D— in German and "conditionally failed" algebra and English composition, receiving grades too low to allow credit but just high enough to allow a make-up course the following year.[6]

Over Christmas vacation, Carrie told her son that his poor showing, was embarrassing the family and hurting Ira's reputation in the Church, but Erskine continued to flounder in the spring of his first year. His algebra marks fell so far below passing that he was dropped from the class entirely and received a zero for the semester. Although he liked his German teacher, Professor Pressley, a man who "would talk to you about anything . . . baseball, aviation, books or anything," his grade dipped from a D to a "conditional failure." His D in English history fell to a D—.[7]

Erskine's work in Bible class was little better, and he finished the second semester with a D+. In a course designed to "begin with Genesis and go through Second Samuel," Erskine was annoyed by the strict and literal interpretation of the Old Testament. Most A.R.P. ministers, including those at Erskine College, were still violently opposed to Charles Darwin's theory of evolution and clung tenaciously to the Biblical explanation of the origins of mankind. While Carrie and Ira were not completely reconciled to evolutionary theory, they had encouraged their son to decide for himself. The professor of Bible, John Irenaeus McCain, however, was a staunch opponent of Darwinism and, as a classmate recalled, "he did not tolerate an argument from an undergraduate." Students disagreeing with his stern pronouncements were summarily dismissed from that day's lesson. In the pious religious environment of Erskine College and McCain's classroom, where "the highest justification of education is its Christian interpretation of life," Erskine professed a scientific rationalism that did little to further his academic career.[8]

Erskine was more successful in his English composition course. Also

taught by McCain, with fierce, unbending routine, the class was a methodical, no-nonsense review of usage and grammar. Students were
"urged to throw off careless habits in spelling, punctuation, and grammatical usage . . . and strive for mechanical excellence." Although Erskine had nothing but disdain for the professor, he put in long hours
with Canby and Opdycke's *Elements of Composition* in order to pass the
exams. He picked up a reasonable grasp of English grammar along the
way, and his letters to Carrie and Ira (though still far from perfect)
showed marked improvement.[9]

Of far greater interest than the dry grammatical exercises were the
frequently assigned essays. Professor McCain believed that the most
promising compositions focused on "the study of life . . . home and
fireside experiences, field and stream." Erskine was sufficiently involved
to turn in all the required writing assignments and to attend the bulk
of the classes—a level of commitment he had not even approached in
his other courses. Under McCain's scrutiny, Erskine made his first consistent efforts to write clearly and accurately. At the end of the semester
he earned a C, then considered a "fair" grade at Erskine College.[10]

Erskine's favorite class was a general survey of American literature.
Taught by Edgar Long, a young assistant professor fresh out of the
University of North Carolina, the class was the most relaxed and informal at the school. Long, whom Erskine considered "the best sport
here," had a contagious enthusiasm for American literature, and his
students tackled a wide range of classic American texts. Although Erskine would forever claim that he "was a writer, not a reader," he
enjoyed the fiction enough to do fairly well in Long's course. He received a D the first semester, but worked much harder in the spring
and earned an 82, or high C. This was the best mark he would ever
get at Erskine College, and it came at just the right time; combined
with his mark in English composition, it raised his yearly average to
73, assuring his place with his class for the following year.[11]

I I

YEARS LATER, Caldwell blamed his poor schoolwork at Erskine
College on the intolerant, closed-minded professors he found there. But
Erskine's difficulties were more a function of his priorities than of the
instruction he received.[12]

His first concern was making the football team. After a week of
grueling practices, however, it was clear that, while he was strong and

tough, he would not make the starting eleven. Fortunately, the team was too small to cut anyone, and he joined the squad as a backup center on offense and a linebacker on defense.[13]

Practicing every afternoon from four to six, Erskine earned a reputation as a hard-nosed, scrappy competitor. Day after day, he lined up against the older starting players, many of whom outweighed him by thirty pounds. He absorbed tremendous physical punishment without complaint, and on one occasion his nose was broken. The joyless, grim ferocity with which Erskine attacked the game startled some of his teammates. A senior on the team marveled at the "long-legged, shut-mouthed freshman" who in the most emotional and heated of contests "never uttered a sound." His quiet intensity also impressed the coach. When a starter was injured before the season's final game, Erskine was given a chance to play. A few upperclassmen groaned "when a damn Frosh took the field," but they need not have worried. Erskine, a teammate recalled, "made tackles from end to end and threw 'em for losses damn near every play."[14]

While Erskine exhibited a barely repressed, silent fury during practice, his teammates noted that his off-field demeanor was marked by transparent bravado. So notorious was his use of foul language that he was nicknamed "Cussin' Erskine"—a reputation he worked hard to maintain. His boasts of sexual conquest and a fascination with the scatological were matched, it seems, by a determined irreverence and irreligiosity. "Everything was 'goddam this' and 'goddam that,'" one classmate complained, and when the team clasped hands before a game to offer prayer, Erskine pointedly refused to participate. He found great satisfaction in offending the more pious of his teammates. On a football team where seven of the eleven starters were the sons of A.R.P. ministers, that was not particularly difficult.[15]

Although he happily spent his afternoons with the football team, Erskine was not comfortable socializing in such a large fraternal clique. His closest friend and almost constant companion was his classmate Andrew Murphy. "Murph" was short, dark, and vivacious, with a sparkling wit, an easy, mischievous laugh, and a taste for broad humor. Voted "happiest student" by his peers, he dominated conversations, filled the air with quips, and played the clown to tireless perfection. His antics offered a comforting shield for Erskine, who would always be most at ease in the role of bemused bystander. And like all of Erskine's close male friends throughout his life, Murphy was physically unthreatening and formed a stark counterpoint to Erskine's own size and good looks. The two became a familiar, if incongruous, sight as they made their way across campus: Murphy, sparkling and garrulous, Erskine—towering head and shoulders above his friend—nodding occasionally in sardonic amusement.

Erskine, soon to be known as "Red," Murphy, and a few others gained a reputation quickly as the "wild boys" of their class. In the sometimes stifling religious atmosphere of Due West, college pranks were raised to an art form, and Erskine found himself on familiar ground. With Murphy and Erskine in command, the group rigged the "Dinky" train's whistle so that it awoke the entire campus at midnight. They milked cows in the middle of the night and lifted chickens surreptitiously from unlocked coops. The clapper of the chapel bell vanished; the ice cream for the faculty picnic mysteriously disappeared; the windows to classrooms were nailed shut.[16]

More often than not, it was the irrepressible Murphy who was caught at these hijinks while the more savvy Erskine remained safely behind the scenes. Still, Erskine could not refrain from some adolescent swaggering, and he took great pride in the mischief he masterminded. In letters home to Wrens, it is clear that the ire his tomfoolery drew from college officials was not enough; Erskine still coveted the attention of his parents:

> We have been having *some* time the past weeks [he wrote Ira and Carrie]. . . . Thursday morning his [Professor McCain's] buggy was up in his class room and his horse spent the night in the Chapel Hall . . . also, on Friday morning every inside and outside door was nailed and every window was locked. Consequently, there were no classes at all Friday. I am not saying that I was, or was not in some of this, because the entire student body have done something with the exception of several that are too scared to turn over in bed at night.[17]

While Caldwell later claimed that he was miserably unhappy from the moment he arrived on "the trash-littered campus" of Erskine College, he and his peers were obviously enjoying the intoxicating freedom of college life. They established the "Night Hawkers Club"—a loose confederation of chicken thieves who met weekly "at the 'Fry'," whose stated aim was to "borrow the feathery dames," and whose chosen password was "poultry." Ignoring the college's rigid curfew rules, the boys would creep past the sleeping matron's room and out onto the campus green, where they indulged in illicit feasts of boiled chicken and bootleg gin that lasted all night. Safe in the gregarious Murphy's shadow, Erskine found a comfortable social niche among his class-mates.[18]

But while he moved within this small group, even his closest friends found his demeanor mysterious and, at times, a bit intimidating. One night, a fellow freshman bet Erskine a dollar that he could not swing a baseball bat and break the tip off the single light bulb that hung in the center of the room. Without comment, Erskine laid a dollar on the table, picked up a bat, and in the same motion knocked the tip off the bulb, plunging the room into darkness. When a new bulb was installed, Erskine picked up both dollars and sat down again without a word. Another time, Murphy observed Erskine among a group of inebriated boys singing their way down Main Street; his friend was walking calmly in the midst of the drunken carousing, his mouth set in stony silence.[19]

Erskine's reputation for aloofness increased that spring. Although students were explicitly forbidden to leave town during the semester, he and Murphy began taking short weekend trips beyond the confines of Due West. After a four-mile walk to Donalds, Erskine and Murphy would wait in the darkened freight yard and hop the 11:00 p.m. train towards Greenwood. Erskine, already an expert from his days in Atoka, knew to avoid the more closely guarded mail cars, and they had little trouble catching the slow-moving train as it passed by. Dropping to the ground after an eighteen-mile trip, the two would loaf around the deserted town of Greenwood and visit the all-night Busy Bee Cafe near the station. They passed the hours sitting in a dimly lit booth, sipping coffee, smoking cigarettes, talking, and listening to the surly dialogue of the drunks slumped heavily over the counter stools.

At 2:00 a.m. they returned to the freight yard to await the 2:30 for Atlanta, a train they rode as far as Abbeville, South Carolina. The historic Abbeville square, pitch black and utterly deserted, was a fine spot for a picnic. After a feast of smuggled dining hall food, the two would lie happily in the cool, thick grass, congratulating themselves on their adventure and relaxing before the final leg, a twelve-mile walk back to Due West; leaving at 4:00 a.m., they would arrive, exhausted but triumphant, just in time for mandatory chapel at 8:00.[20]

These weekend jaunts, designed primarily for sport, also offered a means of escape to two beleaguered freshmen. While hazing was strictly forbidden, according to the college handbook, it was a central part of the Erskine College scene. Freshmen, or "rats," were expected to attend weekly "rat meetings" where sophomores put them through a variety of ritual degradations. At any sophomore's whim, "rats" might be forced to lower their trousers and run through "pad-

dling lines" or form a circle and assume "ankle formation"—bending
over to receive a sharp smack on the backside with a heavy textbook.
"Rats" were also required to serve as messengers and delivery boys.
They might be summoned at any time to go for cigarettes, perform a
shoe shine, or fetch coal for a dying fire. If a sophomore poker player
got hungry in the middle of the night, it was a "rat's" responsibility to
raid the dorm pantry for provisions.[21]

Years later, Erskine denied the sting of these humiliations and maintained that he, among his peers, had "decided not to be one of those
freshmen who would meekly submit to abusive physical hazing, un-
buckling my pants and being swatted at will on my bare buttocks with
a paddle." In an effort to reclaim a masculine dignity that had been so
rudely compromised, he recalled that his "towering six feet of height
. . . and authoritative depth of voice" had won him an exemption from
the worst of the hazing. In truth, Erskine's size and impenetrable demeanor made him a natural target for sophomores bent on establishing
the pecking order. He walked with a slight swagger and sometimes,
one classmate recalled, "he wore a hat cocked jauntily and smoked an
arrogant cigar." Before long, he was a marked man. In one particularly
degrading incident, he was forced to simulate copulation with a tackling
dummy while a ring of sophomores cheered him on. Once he was
beaten so fiercely with a bed slat that he could not walk for days.[22]

In early June, Erskine headed back to Wrens for the summer, relieved no doubt that his "hazing year" was over. In typical fashion, he
made no effort to find his friends before he left. "He just left without
a word of good-bye to anyone," a classmate recalled. "One moment
Caldwell was here, the next, he had just up and left."[23]

III

IN THE HOT SUMMER of 1921, Erskine spent his days much as he
had as a high school student. His old sweetheart, Sara Farmer, had just
graduated from Wrens High School and would be heading off to Wesleyan College in Macon that fall. On many Friday or Saturday nights
the couple attended local dances and concerts at the church. Every
now and then they stopped by a box-lunch auction at the local school,
and Erskine and the other young suitors bid for a chicken dinner made
by their beloved's own two hands. Many of his old friends were also
back in town, and Erskine took Ira's car out of the garage and carried
groups joyriding through the countryside. There were illicit poker

games and some moonshine whiskey and smirking tales of "loose women" in the nearby town of Avery. On Saturdays, he sometimes played pickup baseball, fielding well at first base, but hitting poorly on a team of local boys that Ira had put together. His friends knew, however, not to count on his showing up. "If it was in his mind to play, he'd come," one teammate recalled. "If he was doing his own thing, which he often was, he just wouldn't be there when the game started."[24]

Erskine's first priority on his return to Wrens was finding a good summer job. He had very little luck. He shared his father's interest in journalism, and for a short while he worked for the local *Jefferson County Reporter* setting type, soliciting advertising, laying out pages, and running errands. He hoped to break a big story, but found little to report in the dusty streets of Wrens; he soon became discouraged. Friends of his remember that when Erskine was not drifting aimlessly along Main Street he was "sitting in the office all day with his feet on the desk smoking cigarettes and doing nothing . . . if in fact he decided to show up at all." Although Erskine would later claim that he quit work at the paper when the editor refused to pay him, in truth he was fired.[25]

Discouraged by the menial routine of a newspaper office, Erskine was still determined to see his name in print. He sent dozens of dispatches "reporting fires, accidents, and other newsworthy calamities" —some true, some apocryphal—to the big city papers in Atlanta. None was accepted. Working as an unofficial string reporter, he finally managed to place accounts of local baseball games in the Augusta paper without a by-line.[26]

Unemployed and unable to find another job in town, Erskine tagged along with his father, who continued to expose him to the region's hardships and injustices. That summer, the ravages of the boll weevil and a disastrous drop in cotton prices (from forty cents a bale to less than fourteen) conspired to push more and more poor sharecroppers near Wrens to the brink of starvation. Erskine spent long, hot days beside Ira in the old Ford as they traveled delivering food from one dilapidated hovel to the next. On Sundays, Ira brought Erskine with him when he preached to the shackled convicts on the county chain gang. The shuffling lines of gaunt men were a common sight near Wrens, and Ira took the opportunity to lecture his son on the exploitative evils of the Georgia penal system.[27]

Ira's horrified fascination with the more eccentric splinters of fundamentalist religion carried them far afield—to clay-eating rituals in a "tree-arbor" church near the edge of town, and a foot-washing ceremony far along the dusty back roads towards Augusta. They sat in the back of a church during snake-handling rituals and stared appalled as a preacher hit himself on the head with a mallet in an effort to get nearer to his God. They observed the almost orgasmic contortions of people "coming through" in a Holy Rollers service. Years later, Erskine recalled with cool disdain "looking through an open window of a country church during a revival meeting on a Saturday night, slapping mosquitoes all the time, while a middle-aged farmer writhed on the floor for about a quarter of an hour and slobbered as though he were having an epileptic fit."[28]

Often, Erskine could be found down at the train depot, a place whose mixture of regular routine and unseen adventure continued to captivate him. He spent countless hours hanging around the barbershop and pool hall listening to the stories and gossip of the men, mesmerized by their salty tales of scandal and violence. From time to time, he spent a night back at the cottonseed oil mill, visiting with his old friends, absorbing the talk, and picking up a dollar for eight hours of work.[29]

By early August, Erskine was impatient to get back to school. He missed the joyous liberation of college, and he missed Andrew Murphy, his closest friend. Most of all, he was anxious for football practice to begin. He had grown another inch, gained ten pounds, and at six feet and one hundred and seventy pounds, he hoped to earn a starting spot on the varsity squad.

Back in Due West, he threw himself into the afternoon practices with reckless abandon. Again, he impressed both his teammates and the coach with his ferocity and unrelenting determination. The Erskine College team of 1921 was to be the greatest in the school's history, and although he easily made the varsity squad, he was relegated to a backup spot. Nonetheless, he treasured his status as a varsity athlete, and wore his crimson-letter sweater with great pride.

After losing the first two games, the team went on to win its next five by impressive margins. In the season's final contest, it scored the greatest upset in the college's history. Led by all-conference halfback Dode Phillips, the tiny religious school defeated the mighty Clemson College Tigers by a score of 13 to 0. Numbering only thirteen players over the entire season, "the iron men of Due West" were hailed as young "Davids" in newspapers across the South. When the team arrived back in Due West, they were met by the entire student body and most of the town residents. After a rousing ovation, they were escorted on a torchlight parade down Main Street and around the entire campus, and finally deposited in front of the central dormitory breathless and triumphant.[30]

A season like this was bound to bring an anticlimax, and when it ended Erskine found it almost impossible to concentrate on his work. His attendance slipped, as did his grades, and by Christmas vacation he was once again teetering on the brink of expulsion. He managed C's in English literature and European history, but received D's in physics and trigonometry. His failing grade in Bible was "conditional," but he flunked German outright, having stopped going to class soon after the season was over.

Much of the novelty of college wore off for Erskine during his sophomore year. Aspects of the school that he had once simply ignored, like the somber religiosity, now began to irritate him. Even as a very little boy, Erskine had been free to do as he wished on Sunday mornings. Carrie often missed church to prepare her lessons, and Erskine was granted the same privilege. As a teenager, particularly following the turmoil in Atoka, Ira had allowed Erskine "free choice to do as he pleased," and organized religion had become "a matter for [him] to reject if that was [his] choice." By the time he was sixteen Erskine was calling himself an agnostic, and while most of his friends in Wrens had been churchgoers, Erskine usually spent Sundays escorting Dr. Pilcher on his rounds or passing the time with the convicts on the Louisville chain gang.[31]

Erskine College was no place for an agnostic. Most of the students were deeply religious and participated in the solemn spiritual life of the school without reservation. Aside from mandatory chapel each morning and a compulsory Bible course each semester, there were required Sunday services, daily Bible study, blessings before every meal, and frequent prayer meetings. The town of Due West also held strictly to A.R.P. doctrine. On the Sabbath, residents did not sit on their porches, cook, converse in "idle tones," or read the newspaper. Even window-shopping was strictly forbidden on the holy day, and storefronts were curtained. As the months passed, Erskine increasingly saw Due West and the college as "a medieval dungeon," with "religious symbols . . . everywhere he turned."[32]

For school administrators, a student's religious education was closely joined to his moral supervision. Dating was strictly forbidden, as was any unchaperoned interaction with a member of the opposite sex. Dancing was permitted at certain events scheduled with the Due West Women's College, but couples were carefully separated after every song. The "thrillingest event of the year" was the Junior-Senior Dance,

where lovebirds were allowed fifteen minutes of unchaperoned prom-
enading before a bugle blast mandated a change in companion.[33]

Informal interaction between the sexes could only be achieved
through the use of "wickets," secret, prearranged signals that a young
man used to express his affections. As a coed looked out her window,
she might acknowledge her suitor's subtle tip of the hat or casual left-
handed wave by fluttering a handkerchief or dropping a comb. Erskine
College students were not allowed on the women's campus and only
by "loafing forbidden"—wandering dangerously near the edge of the
Women's College grounds—could they effect their amorous gestures.[34]

While Erskine exchanged a few casual "wickets" and was known to
"loaf forbidden" now and then, he rarely participated in these quaint
courting rituals. The women of the Due West Women's College soon
discovered that he was hopeless at making casual conversation and
extraordinarily awkward in social situations. Erskine was still involved
with Sara and felt none of the pressure to meet a prospective spouse
that many of his classmates shared. More pointedly, he had nothing
but disdain for the restrictive social atmosphere imposed by the college.
Even as a young teen in Atoka he had been free to see Elise Strong
with only a minimum of supervision. And while Sara's uncle monitored
her evening drives with Erskine, they still spent a great deal of time
unchaperoned.[35]

Erskine's unhappiness at school deepened as his sophomore year
progressed. While he still spent time with Murphy and the boys, he
was increasingly alone. Classmates grew accustomed to seeing him sitting by himself on a campus bench, his head held in his long-fingered
hands, staring off into the distance. He became, in the words of a
classmate, "moody, somewhat melancholy, reserved, and indifferent."
He rarely changed his clothes, wearing a pair of blue serge trousers
and his letter sweater until his wardrobe became something of a campus joke. Although Erskine had enjoyed moonshine whiskey with his
friends in the past, now he sometimes drank by himself. One night he
became so inebriated on a concoction of lemon extract and moonshine
that a friend was forced to keep him in his room lest he incriminate
himself.[36]

The cheerful, impish pranks that had given Erskine so much pleasure
during his freshman year now seemed tiresome, and as the year wore
on, his transgressions of school rules became more flagrant and more
destructive. Soon after the Clemson game, Erskine, with help from
Murphy, covered the steps of the administration building with block
letters made of thick black tar. They spelled in huge capital print: "ER-

SKINE BEAT HELL OUT OF CLEMSON? SHE MUST OF DID, SHE DIDN'T LOSE."
Later in the fall, Erskine uncoupled an extra baggage car from the
"Dinky" train soon before its scheduled departure. When the train
reached a hill, the car broke free and careened backwards down the
track, stopping, only by chance, just before it derailed. On a train trip
with the basketball team, Erskine walked silently down the aisle, collected all the coffee mugs from his teammate's trays, and threw them,
without a smile or explanation, out the window. If Erskine was not
actively seeking expulsion from college, it is clear, as a classmate noted,
"that he didn't give a damn if he was."[37]

Late one night, he was caught stealing food from the dorm pantry.
Instead of taking away the food to prepare it in secrecy, Erskine chose
to cook in the dorm kitchen, and the smell inevitably woke the house
matron. The college demanded that he move out of the dorm, and
Erskine took up residence in a boarding house down the road. Here
too he offended his hosts with surly and impolite behavior. When his
landlady came in to clean his room, she found him reading in bed, still
wearing his muddy boots; he ordered her out. On her return she found
a terse note on the door: "Stay out unless you are invited in!"[38]

Although he had been particularly victimized by hazing the previous
year, Erskine became one of the sophomores most feared by the freshman "rats." He presided over a whole range of initiation rituals, without, it seems, the lightheartedness that separated good, clean fun from
mild sadism. "Go get me a pack a cigarettes," he snarled to one terrified
freshman; then almost in the same breath added, "You're not back yet,
goddam it?" He rarely smiled. When Erskine's second cousin arrived
in the freshman class he was mortified by his older relative's harsh and
persistent use of profanity. When he pleaded, "Please, Cousin Erskine,
stop swearing so much!," Erskine gained the nickname "Cousin Erskine," a name understood by all to be a pun on his previous one,
"Cussin' Erskine."[39]

Erskine's chief means of coping with his dissatisfaction was to escape.
Weekend after weekend he made the four-mile walk to Donalds to hop
a freight, sometimes to Greenwood, sometimes to Columbia, Anderson, or Spartanburg; once he went as far as Charleston. Often he traveled without any destination in mind, going wherever the open freight
car might take him and dropping off in the yards of small communities
along the way. After dark, he walked the streets of these deserted
towns, lingering at the train depots, bus stations, and cafes—the gathering places of a nighttime world. During the daylight hours he fre-
quented pool halls and barbershops or sat quietly in front of the general

store while the local farmers discussed the falling price of cotton in worried, angry tones. Predictably, Erskine's weekend forays from Due West were not viewed sympathetically by the school's student council, and on several occasions he was threatened with expulsion.[40]

Returning to Due West after Christmas vacation, Erskine knew that, between his abysmal academic record and his persistent violations of school policy, his standing at Erskine College hung by a thread. Overwhelmed by the unhappy prospect of another full semester of school, he planned a trip that far outreached any he had undertaken before; he convinced the reluctant Murphy to accompany him. In mid-January, Erskine and Murphy withdrew their combined savings of eighty dollars from the Due West bank, sneaked off to Donalds, and caught a Pullman car headed for the distant glamour of New Orleans.[41]

IV

YEARS LATER, Erskine boasted that after arriving in New Orleans he and Murphy worked on a gunrunner to Colombia, dodged pirates and whistling bullets, and mingled easily with the hardened sailors. In truth, when the two youths, without passports or experience, asked for work, members of the crew laughed them off the pier.[42]

Rejected in New Orleans, Erskine and Murphy decided to try their luck in the city of Bogalusa, seventy-five miles north. They were attracted to Bogalusa by announcements for the enormous wedding of a wealthy local entrepreneur. Special trains were running to and from New Orleans to accommodate the crowds. After mailing a box of pralines to Sara in Macon, Erskine and Murphy availed themselves of the free train trip (and a few complimentary cocktails), and before long, settled themselves into a cheap boarding house near the Bogalusa station. Their room was sparsely furnished, infested with bedbugs, and noisy. That night, they were kept awake by a tireless Victrola that droned the strains of "Tuck Me to Sleep in My Ol' Kentucky Home" over and over again.[43]

They thought of finding work in an oil field, but were discouraged by a man at the train station who warned them that his entire earnings there had only "bought one pair of goddam' boots." Bogalusa was a lumber town, and for a week they lined up outside the mill gates, only to see the scarce day jobs go to older, more experienced men. With their money running out and the novelty quickly wearing thin in the crude, comfortless room, Murphy returned to Due West. Erskine, however, found work selling magazines on commission to the local mill workers—something he had done successfully as a young boy—and he was not yet ready to go home.[44]

With Murphy gone, Erskine spent his days soliciting subscriptions and his nights exploring the sights and sounds of the small city. Bogalusa was on edge in the winter of 1922, convulsed by frequent outbreaks of labor violence. The local lumber company was bitterly determined to keep the I.W.W. from unionizing its workers, and labor leaders had been shot in the back by company guards. Local police were arresting and interrogating men suspected of union activities. A sign at the train station warned away "agitators of any kind."[45]

It was not a good time to be an unfamiliar face in town, and when Erskine's magazine boss skipped out of Bogalusa without paying him, he found himself unemployed and on the streets. As he returned to his boarding house one evening, his rent a week in arrears, Erskine was intercepted by two plainclothes policemen, dragged before the booking desk at the local precinct, and thrown unceremoniously into the city jail. He was officially charged with "unlawfully, maliciously and willfully loitering around suspicious places without being able to give a satisfactory reason theretofore." He was, in short, a vagrant, and, although his landlady had fingered him for his overdue rent, it was his gravitation towards the underside of the city and the haunts of workingmen that landed him in trouble.[46]

Erskine's actual experiences in the Bogalusa jail are difficult to reconstruct. In later years, he invented relationships with a black jailer and a black fellow prisoner in order to discuss the tragedy of Southern race relations. Sometimes, he recalled that he won his release by getting a passing child to send a message to his father. Whatever the exact circumstances, it is clear that for at least two days, Erskine was imprisoned in a squalid cell—his only food a plate of soggy turnip greens and fatback pushed abruptly through a slot in the prison door, his only convenience a single rusted bucket. Helpless, alone, and seemingly forgotten in a city jail far from home, the eighteen-year-old Erskine gained an understanding of victimization and oppression that he could never forget—a lesson that resonated with a sensitivity to injustice already imparted by his father.[47]

Before long, the local police realized that the lean, freckle-faced teenager was not a hardened union organizer but a college boy whose adventure had turned terribly sour. Erskine College officials had notified Carrie and Ira of their son's disappearance, and they, in turn, had pressured Sara into divulging Erskine's plan to visit New Orleans.

Ira managed to track his son to Bogalusa, and wired money for train fare through the local Y.M.C.A. After a shower and a free meal, Erskine was on his way back to Wrens to face his parents and another full summer in his quiet hometown.[48]

That spring and summer in Wrens passed with painful slowness. Erskine had split up with Sara soon after his return because she had revealed his whereabouts during the Bogalusa fiasco. Although it was information that occasioned his prompt release from jail, he would not forgive her for "betraying him." Few of his friends were left in town, and work was difficult to find. He still struggled to become a published journalist, and, again, his only success came as string correspondent for the local baseball team. He attended so many games that he was taken on as the club's official scorer. Through the long months of July and August he sat at the park recording hits and errors for semi-pro and town league games that were all the rage in Georgia that summer.[49]

As September approached, Erskine despaired at the thought of returning to the "prison" in Due West. With his mother's support, he sent a series of desperate—and unsuccessful—letters to the University of Virginia seeking a last-minute transfer. In the end, at Ira's insistence, he grudgingly agreed to head back to Erskine College. As he made the familiar train trip to Due West once again, he faced three more years in an environment he had come to detest. In early September of 1922, he settled, with heavy heart, into a boarding house at the edge of town.[50]

That fall, even the football team lost its luster. Many of the "iron men" had graduated, and although Erskine had the satisfaction of playing a bit more, the team did not win a game all season. His academic work remained on the same level. As usual, he had the most success in English class, where he received C grades, but his attendance was spotty and he studied very little. And while his escapades the previous spring had made him something of a legend among the younger students, he seemed not to notice and walked through the pretty campus "smiling his bemused and quizzical little smile, his face quite often a freckled mask." The few who knew him well were not fooled. They whispered among themselves that "his spirit was still Bogalusa-bound."[51]

Inevitably, Erskine's chronic dissatisfaction brought him once again into open conflict with the school administration. After the first baseball game of the season, the manager of the visiting team complained that their lockers had been ransacked during the afternoon contest. Before the next home game, two members of the student council stationed themselves above the locker room, where a large gap in the floorboards offered a clear view of the room below. Midway through the game, Erskine and a friend were caught red-handed as they rifled through players' clothes, removing watches, fountain pens, and wallets.[52]

The school administration had been remarkably patient with their incorrigible ward, but he had finally succeeded in pushing them too far. The student council and administration agreed that out of respect for Ira, Erskine would be allowed to finish up the year; but he was barred from returning to Erskine College in the fall.

For Erskine, this humiliating finish to his stay in Due West was surely freighted with relief. While he would miss the camaraderie of Murphy and a few others, he could not have stood another semester. He was aching and restless to move on, and he left Erskine College gratefully and without a backward glance. In his adult recollections, Erskine was unjustifiably cruel to the small religious college, if, in fact, he chose to acknowledge it at all. Frequently, "the medieval dungeon" became a convenient foil in long diatribes against intellectual repression in the South and the enervating conservatism of fundamentalist religion. But at the time, his problems stemmed more from a distinctly poor match of student and school. Erskine College—a conservative institution with a sometimes overbearing paternalism—was an inauspicious environment for an unhappy young man perpetually bent on testing the limits of authority.[53]

V

ERSKINE'S PARENTS WERE adamant that he finish college, and Carrie urged him to reapply to the University of Virginia. As a girl in the small, blue-blood town of Staunton, she had watched all the finest young men go off to "Mr. Jefferson's University," and she had always dreamed that her son would follow suit. But even with both parents working full-time at Wrens High School—Carrie as a Latin teacher and Ira as a history teacher and athletics coach in addition to his pastoring duties—they could not afford the out-of-state tuition at Virginia or the relatively high cost of living in Charlottesville.[54] With much of his congregation suffering from the depressed cotton market, Ira had forgone a large portion of his minister's salary.[55]

Through July and August, Carrie and Erskine spent their evenings combing through university brochures in search of a scholarship. Awards given for academic merit were clearly out of the question, so they were elated when they discovered a small grant offered by the United Daughters of the Confederacy to local descendants of Civil War veterans. The loyal women of the local U.D.C. chapter could hardly have known Ira's feelings about the "Southern die-hards who hung on the outdated glory of the Civil War," and they happily awarded his son money for a year's tuition. The benefactor of his grandfather's bravery sixty years before and of the notoriously lax admission standards of state universities in the early 1920s, Erskine was on his way to Charlottesville in the fall of 1923.[56]

Erskine had driven through Charlottesville many times on trips to and from Carrie's family home in Staunton, and he was quite familiar with the lovely, rolling campus near the foot of the Blue Ridge Mountains. The family had often walked across the elegant green, admiring Thomas Jefferson's carefully engineered grounds—the lush concourse framed on either side by the two long rows of stately pavilions and headed by the grand dome of the rotunda. They had picnicked in the shade of the famous undulating wall with Monticello just in sight atop a hill on the southern horizon, and admired the massive portico inscribed with Jefferson's forthright challenge to "Enter this Gateway and Seek the Way of Honor, the Light of Truth and the Will To Work for Man."[57]

Erskine's boarding house at 110 Fourteenth Street was distinctly less grand. The influx of veterans following the First World War had badly overtaxed the limited housing on the campus, and Erskine was lucky to find a room. The house was a slightly run-down, three-story clapboard structure with an unassuming facade and a patchy lawn. Miss Yeager's was a far cry from the plush establishments of Miss Hamilton or Miss Page where wealthier students lived in luxurious comfort and dined with silver cutlery on fine china plates. But the location was among the best in town. He was only two blocks north of The Corner—the central campus strip of bookstores, lunch counters, barbershops, and variety stores—and only a few hundred yards from the edge of campus. If he wished to venture into downtown Charlottesville, a bustling city of eleven thousand, the streetcar ran from dawn till dusk just a few hundred yards from his door. The university was firmly committed to an honor system, and the fifteen hundred undergraduates were free to come and go as they pleased. Far from the restrictive religious environment of Due West, Erskine began his second collegiate career with high hopes.[58]

Although he would never really get used to sharing his living quarters, Erskine got on well with Louis Ballou, his roommate at Miss

Yeager's. A cheerful, hard-working architecture student, Ballou spent hours over his sketch pad or in the studio. He fancied himself a ladies' man and was always impeccably dressed. Years later, Ballou recalled his "stepping out" ensemble with pride—from his "bell-bottom grey felt slacks," to his "wing-tipped, scotch-grained, tan leather-heeled shoes."[59]

That fall Ballou, vivacious and nattily attired, and Erskine, quiet and always rough-edged and awkward (no matter how hard he tried), together explored the possibilities of college life. On Friday nights, they often took a streetcar downtown to see a film, then walked back in the cool evening air, saving a nickel on the return fare. There were pickup football games on the lawn, and moonshine bought on the sly from the bootleggers at nearby Shiflett's Hollow. On occasion, they attended the free weekly dances held under the moonlight at Fry Springs—unchaperoned events where the young men of the university danced with girls who had come in from the women's colleges of Sweet Briar, Hollins, and Carrie's alma mater, Mary Baldwin. Under Ballou's tutelage, Erskine learned a few dance steps and even managed to improve his dress. Before long, he could brag of reaching the exalted collegiate status of absolute conformity, and in accordance with the university's unofficial uniform, was "never without a necktie from the time [he] dressed in the morning until [he] went to bed at night."[60]

However badly Erskine wanted to fit in, he also became increasingly aware that he had little chance of gaining access to the inner circles of college life at a "gentleman's university." The white-columned fraternity houses, set back on thick expanses of lawn, were the heart of the social scene at Mr. Jefferson's University, but they were clearly unencumbered by the founder's notions of egalitarianism and democracy. The fraternities were dominated by scions of FFV's, or "First Families of Virginia," and while Erskine's mother claimed such a heritage, he was still the son of a poor minister from rural Georgia. He had not graduated from one of the handful of prestigious "feeder schools" that had supplied the campus leaders for generations. He had not, in point of fact, graduated from high school at all.

The boys from Woodbury Forest, St. Christopher's, Virginia Episcopal School, or Shady Hill Academy possessed a sophistication and instinctive style well beyond him. They moved effortlessly in a world where groups of students greeted each other with the single word "Gentlemen," where failure to tip one's hat to an upperclassman was a major breach of protocol, and where, as one alumnus remembers, "the wrong-colored cravat could mean ostracism for a term." How could Erskine have known that wearing a varsity letter sweater was thought excessively "rah-rah"? Ballou, a Virginian with faultless manners, was right at home in the university's social set and was tapped by Theta Chi fraternity and asked to join the art staff of the yearbook. Erskine, his roommate, was studiously ignored.[61]

Many of Erskine's social woes stemmed, quite simply, from his poverty. The U.D.C. paid his tuition that year, but Ira and Carrie could spare him barely enough money to survive. He could not possibly afford the white-tie dances in the gym, where the day's big-band legends—Fred Waring, Guy Lombardo, "Sweet" Wayne King—played until all hours of the night. A weekend trip to a girl's college in Richmond or the appropriate style of hat or shoes was well beyond his means. Dinner dates and dress clothes had never interested Erskine before, but for the first time his relative poverty and provincialism set him apart. He watched with quiet envy while those around him indulged in a life-style that excluded him. With Ballou, his one real friend, preoccupied with his own broadening horizons, Erskine felt increasingly left out.

While many students had free time to loaf on the lawn or attend parties, Erskine spent long hours trying to earn enough money to get by. He found a job only days after his arrival in Charlottesville. At the far end of the Corner was Johnny LaRowe's Pool Room, and Erskine gravitated there first. LaRowe had been a world-class boxer before a war injury consigned him to a wheelchair. Heavily muscled, charismatic, and full of exotic stories of "the world," LaRowe was a living legend, and his pool hall the campus hangout. In the familiar, smoky environment, Erskine swept the floor, reglued broken cue tips, racked balls, and emptied trash cans from six o'clock until midnight, six nights a week. His pay was a dollar a night, and with tips he cleared a total of thirty dollars each month. As he waited on the carefree, polished fraternity boys who stopped into Johnny LaRowe's as part of their daily routine, Erskine's estrangement from the aristocracy of the university was hammered home.[62]

Later in life, Erskine denied that he suffered substantial humiliation that first year at Virginia. In *With All My Might*, he recalls a time of graceful nonchalance when he "had the satisfying feeling of being completely integrated in the life and environment" of the university. Yet his actions at the time betrayed a young man anxious to elevate his social standing and eager to impress those around him. Soon after his arrival in Charlottesville, he began informing people that he was born not in the back-country town of Moreland, Georgia, but in the more cosmopolitan city of Atlanta. That spring, he tagged along with a golfing party and regaled the foursome with tales of recent adventures on "the Continent." In his registration materials the following year, he listed Ira's occupation as "newspaper editor," betraying his embarrassment with the more modest title of "minister" that he had listed the year before. Most revealing of all was his decision to adopt a middle name—"Preston"—his mother's middle name, and one with clear bloodlines in the Virginia aristocracy.[63]

Carrie and Ira were far more concerned with their son's poor grades than with the equivocal genealogy they had imparted to him. Erskine tried to intercept his report card before his parents saw it, but the registrar informed him that until he was twenty-one his grades would be sent home to Wrens. He had registered for five courses—English Literature, Geology, Introductory Psychology, Introductory Spanish, and Physical Training—and failed three of them outright. In psychology he compiled a year's average of 55, and in Spanish he averaged just under a 70 for two trimesters before dropping out of class after Christmas vacation. The former football player and son of a part-time athletic coach managed only a 38 in physical training for his first trimester, and received no grade at all for the remainder of the year.[64]

On the brighter side, he managed to maintain a solid C all year long in a geology course. Archeology and geology had long been hobbies of Ira's, and Erskine had often accompanied his father on day-long hunts for Cherokee arrowheads buried near Wrens. The class at Virginia included field trips to the numerous caverns surrounding Charlottesville—just the sort of activity Erskine loved—and students had a close look at the wondrous displays of stalactites, stalagmites, and fossils hidden behind thick limestone walls. In addition to his interest in the material, Erskine appreciated the style of his young professor, a man renowned for his spirited, good-natured irreverence. There were lengthy weekend assignments accompanied by the admonition to "get twice as much work done on Sunday because you have the Lord on your side that day!"[65]

Erskine also did fairly well in a course on British literature. In addition to reading a number of Shakespeare plays, Erskine labored through a syllabus of eighteenth-century British essayists including Swift, Addison, Johnson, and Burke, and a small selection of "modern prose fiction" that featured Stevenson and Kipling. Taught by Professor Calvin Metcalf, a reserved, dignified Kentuckian who would later help establish the *Virginia Quarterly Review*, the course also offered the opportunity for some creative writing. There is no evidence that Erskine gave these assignments or the class any serious attention. Yet his regular attendance and his respectable final year average of 76 suggest a consistent, if superficial, interest and a growing facility with the English language.[66]

Nonetheless, Erskine finished his first year at Virginia several course credits behind. When a fellow student mentioned that the University of Pennsylvania was an excellent place to make up college credits during the summer, Erskine jumped at the idea. There, Erskine told Ira and Carrie, he might take courses in economics, a subject he knew they would approve of. Ira was fascinated with the macroeconomics of rural poverty, and Carrie viewed economics courses as a practical step towards a profitable career in business. Swallowing their reservations, they endorsed Erskine's plan to find a part-time job in Philadelphia and attend summer school at the University of Pennsylvania's Wharton School.

For Erskine, any practical benefits of the summer were surely secondary to his burning desire to see more of the world. He had never traveled north of the Mason-Dixon line and, aside from the few stolen days in New Orleans, had never spent more than half a day in a city. Even his time in college had been spent in the familiar environs of Due West and Charlottesville, places that seemed as much his parents' as his own. In early June, Ira and Erskine drove through the night to Richmond, where Erskine could catch an inexpensive train into the Thirtieth Street Station in Philadelphia. Sleeping uneasily in the back of Ira's rattletrap Ford, Erskine dreamed, no doubt, of the adventures, possibilities, and danger that lay ahead in an enormous northern metropolis far from home.[67]

VI

PREDICTABLY, ERSKINE FOUND his classes at Wharton far less interesting than the urban turbulence of central Philadelphia. Although he later claimed to have harbored "exciting visions of arbitrage, commodity futures, due bills, free ports, and demurrage," a letter to his parents a month after he arrived betrayed a more familiar pattern of interest: "Passed 2 courses and failed 1 at S.S. [summer school]. That gives me two units for the summer. So it wasn't wasted entirely." Erskine's attention, it seems, was elsewhere.[68]

Within a week, he secured a job at a cheap, cubbyhole lunch counter, where he worked the six-to-midnight shift as a short-order cook and counterman. Located just off lower Market Street, Nedick's Lunch served a working-class clientele in a seedy downtown neighborhood. Most of the steady stream of men who stopped to buy hot dogs and sodas were on their way to or from the Trocadero Burlesque Theater just down the block.[69]

He would not admit it in letters home, but the cold anonymity of urban life made Erskine homesick and afraid. Returning from work in the early morning hours, he lay in bed, kept awake by the noise of the city and troubled by thoughts of his own mortality. "I was always fevered by the thirst for knowing what men and women would do on the earth when I was dead," he wrote a few years later in a book titled *The Sacrilege of Alan Kent.* "Just before daybreak each morning but while there was still no light, I forgot about the people who would be alive and thought of my own self in that everlasting silence of darkness." He grew painfully nostalgic for the sights and smells of the farm country where he had been raised, and lamented an urban world where "men bathed themselves every day and the women sometimes bathed three or four times" but never "smelled as nice to me as the youngest colt or even the oldest horse."[70]

Although he was accustomed to the grinding poverty among the sharecroppers of eastern Georgia, Erskine was struck by the suffering and inhumanity he saw on the streets of Philadelphia. In *Sacrilege* he recalled the horror of seeing "a man become angry and beat a dog with a stick until it lay lifeless on the street." "I could never forget," he wrote, a still more vivid portrait in his mind, "the agony I saw on a woman's face while she stood in the doorway of her home. Her body was covered with the tired creases of labor and beneath her skin was the pain of hunger and love that gave it the texture of hopelessness."[71]

Toward the end of June, Erskine met a young Chinese student in a morning class, and he happily agreed to serve as an informal tour guide, translator, and bodyguard. Together the two immigrants—one from rural Georgia, the other from Shanghai—sat through double-feature Westerns starring the great screen cowboys Tom Mix and William Hart, or browsed through the aisles at the huge Wannamaker's Department Store. On more than one occasion they sat silently in the darkened Trocadero and watched the "hootchy-kootchy" dancers and listened to the comedians who, between the acts, sought to lighten the theater's grim, silent atmosphere. Erskine was fascinated by the audience as well as the performers. A few years later he wrote with mingled compassion and contempt of the "sad faces of men . . . who went in and out of all the moving picture shows they could find . . . but were afraid to feel the breath on a woman's lips and to caress the softness of her thighs."[72]

As a boy, Erskine had been forbidden to attend the local carnival, a spectacle Carrie considered "smutty" and "indecent." Watching the matinee show at the Trocadero or walking home from his night job through the spirited, erotic chaos of lower Market Street, Erskine was intoxicated by his freedom and self-sufficiency. And as the summer drew to a close, he bridled at the prospect of returning to Wrens. Throughout the month of August, letters from Ira and Carrie, sometimes as many as two a day, piled up unanswered on his desk. They wanted to know when he was coming home.

In early September, Erskine finally scrawled a long, sloppy reply to his parents' increasingly urgent appeals. Ostensibly a reasoned argument for his continued stay in the city, the letter represented Erskine's heavy-handed assertion of independence from Ira and Carrie. "Have decided the best thing to do this year is to stay here and work," he began bluntly. He was learning too much, he told them, to return to Virginia. Taking a patronizing tone, Erskine promised to send along a "big-city" paper so that his provincial parents might know what they were missing. "If either one of you see anything in the ads you want —tear the ad out and send it back and I'll get it. . . . Don't hesitate to do it." He ended the letter with the most clichéd of paternal directives, a closure that surely left Carrie steaming at her only son: "both of you," he instructed, "write soon."[73]

Erskine's decision to stay in Philadelphia represented more than a self-absorbed declaration of adulthood. He was also feeling extremely guilty about the financial burden he placed on his parents. Ira had fallen seriously ill that summer, succumbing to the stress of a work schedule that often exceeded eighteen hours a day. The U.D.C. had revoked Erskine's scholarship to Virginia when they received his spring grades, and Erskine knew that his father had been laboring desperately to raise money for tuition when he had become sick. Overwhelmed by the thought that he was responsible for Ira's poor health, Erskine informed his parents that he "could not go back to Virginia and take the money you both need." He beseeched them to "leave me entirely out of it for a year and see what I can do." "Don't overwork now because there's no need of it," he implored his father. "Better to slow up a little than have to slow up altogether."

Erskine knew that his parents would be unconvinced by his arguments for staying in Pennsylvania. "I'm not staying here to have a good time or to keep from going to school," he assured them. "I want to finish." That summer, for the first time in his life, he had "found out by experience and observation what an education means," and he assured Ira, and particularly Carrie, that one day he would parlay a degree into a high-paying job. By watching local Jewish businessmen —"and you know how they are about work and money"—he had, he told his parents, learned to "keep up with anyone."

Another three weeks passed before Erskine wrote his parents again, and once more he sent surprising news: He was no longer living in Philadelphia. The Kresge's Department Store in Wilkes-Barre had offered him a part-time position as an assistant stock manager, and Erskine had quit his jobs at Nedick's and the Trocadero Theater (where his frequent visits had landed him work sweeping up after the midnight show), moved out of his barren apartment in the tenement district, and boarded a train for the raw, coal-mining city one hundred miles to the north. With the help of another Kresge manager, he settled into a dreary, five-dollar-a-week apartment in a run-down building on North Main Street.[74]

More for Carrie's sake than his own, no doubt, Erskine registered for two morning classes at Lehigh University in nearby Bethlehem, Pennsylvania; but he had little time for school. His afternoons were spent at Kresge's frantically unpacking and cataloging enormous hogsheads of glassware, cotton goods, and toys in the drafty stockroom beneath the store. Hundreds of five- and ten-dollar orders arrived each afternoon at three, and it was Erskine's responsibility to have the merchandise delivered upstairs to the clerks by five-thirty. "It sounds easy," he complained, "but it's hard work." The pay was twenty-two dollars a week, and after paying for rent, trolley fare, and food, Erskine had very little left over.[75]

But while he was barely scraping by, Erskine took satisfaction in supporting himself without his parents' help. He indulged a conspicuous sense of martyrdom. "I don't mind it so long as I can live without taking your money when you need it so bad," he assured them. "So please don't worry about a thing; if I go broke or hungry it won't matter because I'm used to that now." And while he manfully struggled on in the city, he encouraged his parents to "take an occasional Saturday off and go to a movie in Augusta or to a good football game some place." For years Carrie had reminded him of sacrifices the family had made on his behalf, and there was satisfaction, as well as expiation, in reversing the roles.[76]

After three weeks in the Kresge's stockroom, however, Erskine began to tire of noble suffering. The weather was growing colder, and
he felt the bite of his first northern winter just around the corner. The
stockroom air was dank and stale, and before long Erskine developed
a bad cold and painful sore throat. Worst of all, he was hungry all the
time. Unable to satisfy his huge appetite on the meager wages he
brought home each week, he lost ten pounds. When a position as a
"short-order chef, waiter, cashier, and janitor" opened up at a restaurant in the Wilkes-Barre Union Railroad Station, he happily resigned
from Kresge's. The new job offered an irresistible benefit, and years
later Erskine could still relish the heaven-sent bounty of "ham steak,
sausage and eggs, apple sauce, cole slaw, Danish pastry, chocolate pie
and glazed doughnuts." Aside from fielding the customers' "minor
complaints about burnt toast and empty water glasses and failure to
keep coffee cups full," Erskine enjoyed the job immensely. The warmth
of a railroad depot on a frosty October night offered a reassuring,
familiar haven. And unlike the stale basement of Kresge's Department
Store, Union Station offered a matchless stage for the idiosyncratic, late-
night world that so beguiled him.[77]

Erskine looked for a weekend job to supplement his income from
the station. Soon after quitting Kresge's he tried out for the Wilkes-
Barre Panthers, the local semi-pro football team. Although the Panthers
had three former University of Pennsylvania stars on their squad, most
of the players were brawny coal miners looking for some extra cash.
Erskine soon found out that he was no match for the "hard-rock coal
miners" in the so-called Anthracite League. He was too light to play
on the line and too inexperienced to do much else. Erskine and his
publicists would one day celebrate his "career as a professional football
player," a "career" that was extremely short-lived: common sense and
a badly broken nose brought it mercifully to a close after only a couple
of weeks.[78]

When Erskine wrote to his parents in early November, the blustery,
smug confidence of his earlier correspondence was fading fast. "Will
owe $8 on the overcoat next Saturday," he lamented. Payment on his
one suit came due on the same day, and he wondered which essential
article to let go. He was sick with a cold, homesick, and lonely. In a
rare expression of vulnerability, he admitted that he had "found out
what it means not to have a home you can go to at night." He wanted
to return to the South before Christmas, before the first heavy snow,
and reestablish contact with the familiar world where he had grown
into adulthood.

Erskine calculated the train fare from Wilkes-Barre to Wrens at thirty to thirty-five dollars, and he very nearly begged for the money to come home. Carrie and Ira were only too happy to oblige. By early December Erskine was on his way to Wrens, and his family was pooling its resources to send him back to Charlottesville for the spring term.

Chapter Three

AWAKENINGS

WHEN ERSKINE BOARDED THE TRAIN for Charlottes-
ville in January, the people of Wrens may have noted that their
preacher's son had grown into a handsome young man. He was broad-
shouldered and rangy, six feet tall, with rigid posture, strong, well-
defined muscles, and large, powerful hands. He wore his sandy red hair
slicked back from his broad, freckled face and parted severely down the
middle. On rare occasions, the corners of his mouth curled in sardonic
amusement, and his light-blue eyes flashed. But for the most part, an
acquaintance recalled, "Erskine looked like a wooden Indian—expres-
sionless, cold, and somehow cruel."[1]

School was in full swing when Erskine returned to his cheap boarding house in the winter of 1925. The University of Virginia was alive
with the excitement and energy of the Jazz Age. Convertible Ford
roadsters jammed with laughing undergraduates roared through The
Corner on their way to "bathtub gin bashes" at the fraternities. The
first women had been admitted to the school the previous year, and
although there was considerable resistance on the part of some faculty
and students, coeds bedecked in university colors were a conspicuous
part of the giddy, joyous atmosphere on campus.[2]

But Erskine's homecoming to Charlottesville was not as satisfying as
he might have anticipated in his barren tenth-floor flat in Wilkes-Barre.
He had just turned twenty-two—older than most of the students
around him—and after six months of struggling to survive on his own,
the antics of college life seemed frivolous and inane. With money even
tighter than it had been the previous fall, Erskine went back to work
at the pool hall and guarded every penny. He spent hours alone in his
room, the gaiety of nearby parties serving as a noisy reminder of his
isolation.

I

IN HIS SEMI-AUTOBIOGRAPHICAL work *The Sacrilege of Alan Kent*, Erskine recalled the acute loneliness of his college years. The despondent prose captured a time when, above all else, he longed for a woman to love. In Wilkes-Barre he had sat alone by the window in his darkened room and watched with quiet longing as an unknown couple prepared for bed across a darkened alley. He was mesmerized by the sight of "a girl who stood like a piece of unfinished sculpture in the center of the room . . . reaching . . . with her arms and hands and fingers" for a man "who took off her clothes and folded them carefully on a chair." Walking home from the pool room through the darkened streets of Charlottesville, Erskine's melancholy only deepened. "I had no place to go and nothing now to do," he wrote in *Kent*. "Almost everybody else I saw had someone who loved him and they were happy together."[3]

But what kind of woman did he seek? The chaste, innocent relationships he had shared with Elise and Sara were part of Erskine's adolescence and would no longer satisfy him. In *Sacrilege*, he recalled with frustration "a girl who was clean and . . . wore an orange-colored ribbon around her head," but who did not respond to his desire: "She cried as loud as she could when she saw my hungry eyes and ran away." He dreamed of a sexual partner—a woman uninhibited by his mother's Victorian strictures—a woman who shared his intense carnal inquisitiveness and appetite.[4]

Erskine had first satisfied his sexual curiosity in his accustomed role of spectator. In Atoka, when he drove military officers to and from the whorehouse in Memphis, he was awestruck by the sight of the "high-heeled slippers," "becoming smiles," "bright-colored clothing," and "flashy beads and necklaces." In Wrens, he was fascinated by the lascivious banter of the mill workers and the sordid tales of the traveling salesmen who congregated in the pool hall. When alone, he spent hours studying an assortment of pornographic postcards—a collection his friends knew to be the best in town.[5]

But while Erskine was preoccupied with all the things his mother referred to as "smut," he was not yet ready to act upon his fascination. Following his freshman year in Due West, he accompanied a few older boys to a brothel in Augusta. While his companions went upstairs with prostitutes, the eighteen-year-old Erskine sat in the shabby, red-velvet lobby alone, watching the people and feeding dimes one by one into the player piano. He seemed, a friend remembered somewhat crudely, "to prefer watching to doing." He was, another thought, "too afraid to try."[6]

Eventually, Erskine mustered the courage to move beyond voyeurism. He lost his virginity with a prostitute, either in Augusta that summer, or during one of his many weekend jaunts from Due West. In *Sacrilege*, he recalled a series of prostitutes and strangers who satisfied his lust by night before disappearing with the coming of a new day. The trip to Bogalusa was marked in Erskine's mind by "a brown-limbed girl" who "warmed me at night . . . [and] even helped me lick my wounds."[7]

Not until he reached Philadelphia, however, did Erskine fully indulge his appetite for pornography and sexual adventure. On his frequent visits to the Trocadero, Erskine was immersed in a world of overt sexuality that would have horrified the Bell family women. "He had no interest in 'good girls,' " a friend recalled, and before long, Erskine developed a mad crush on one of the dancers—an older prostitute who took a liking to the handsome and inexperienced Southern boy. Predictably, the romance was a disaster. "I found a girl . . . and she took me home with her," he wrote in *Sacrilege*. "The next night . . . she came home late and she was drunk and the odor of whiskey on her breath when she kissed me made me cry. . . . She came home drunk every night." Worst of all, this woman preyed on Erskine's innocence. He awoke one morning to find that she had stolen both his wallet and his "biscuit-sized pocket watch."[8]

By the time Erskine returned to Charlottesville, he'd had his fill of the empty lust and feigned love offered by streetwalkers and burlesque dancers. He came to the painful realization that "there were lots of women who would lie down for a little while . . . ," but he might "never find a girl who would lie a long time" with him. "Sometimes I cried," Erskine wrote in *Sacrilege*, "because I could not find a girl who would let me love her as I wanted so much to love someone." As Erskine walked the Virginia campus that winter, he appeared to classmates as "a solitary figure, always in a hurry." He despaired of meeting a woman who was passionate but uncorrupted, a sexual being who was also educated and refined. His search for the lovely innocent whose "body throbbed with her eagerness like his own pulse-beat" is the central preoccupation in *Sacrilege*, and in the winter of 1925, it seemed to Erskine that he would never find her. "I knew," he wrote with acrid certainty, that "I would always be alone in the world."[9]

Louis Ballou skimmed through his thick black book and tried his best to find a companion for his troubled friend. But he had little luck. Erskine seemed bored by the nursing students and coeds whom Ballou brought by, and his dates complained that although the tall redhead was certainly good-looking, he was also cold, decidedly noncommunicative, and sometimes downright rude. Once, Erskine called for a very proper young lady an hour late with his breath reeking of corn whiskey.

Ballou, however, was a determined matchmaker. In February, he introduced Erskine to Helen Lannigan, a first-year graduate student in French literature at the university. Ballou had dated Helen on several occasions, and even though they had not gotten along particularly well, he guessed that she and Erskine might hit it off. He was right. "From the moment I introduced them," he recalled, "I was past history."[10]

Helen was enrolled in one of Erskine's English classes, and in an environment where the entrance of a coed at the start of a lecture sometimes brought on loud stamping and whistling, Helen's blond hair and curvaceous figure could not have passed unnoticed. Moreover, Helen was part of a well-known university family. Her father was the renowned "Pop" Lannigan, Virginia's beloved trainer and track coach, and one of the school's most colorful figures. Her house, called "The Chateau," was a campus landmark, a dark Gothic castle complete with a moat and drawbridge. The area just behind the house held its own notoriety. Here, two abandoned ice pits, known affectionately to all undergraduates as the "petting pits," served as the university's less-than-picturesque lover's lane—a place where the burgeoning sexuality of the Jazz Age encouraged "petting parties" that were popular across many college campuses in the mid-1920s.[11]

Helen thought the sexual adventures that went on outside her bedroom window were, in fact, unnecessarily prudish. She was an extremely confident and passionate young woman of eighteen, proud of her sexuality and well aware of her attractiveness. Of medium height, with long, wavy hair, her face was a gentle oval with small features and soft, fair skin. Helen had nothing but disdain for the pert, slim androgyny of the flapper. Her figure was rounded, even plump, and she was, as a friend recalled, "extremely proud of her bosom." She walked with a calculated, erotic sway. "I am completely liberated," she would brag, and she had lost her virginity to an older man when she was sixteen.[12]

Helen possessed the passion and sexual appetite Erskine craved, but she was a far cry from the "brown-limbed girls" or prostitutes of his past. In some ways, she was much like his mother. Helen's parents had pushed their precocious daughter to succeed, and she was an engaged and gifted student. She entered high school at eleven, and shortly before her eighteenth birthday graduated with honors from the College of William and Mary, with a major in English and a minor in both French and German. When Erskine met her, she had recently returned from the Middlebury summer school, where she had been perfecting her French; she was also nearing completion of a master's degree in French literature. Like Carrie, Helen was a knowledgeable admirer of classical music and English poetry, and she dabbled in painting and writing. She was extremely well read, in both the classics and contemporary fiction, and an accomplished actress as well. At the time of her first meeting with Erskine, she had the leading role in the campus production of Molière's *Cercle d'Odéon*.[13]

On their first date, Erskine and Helen attended a concert by the local orchestra. Years later, Helen would say that she "was seduced by Rachmaninoff," and not by Erskine's blunt expressions of desire. According to Helen, when they arrived at her front door after the performance, Erskine said abruptly: "I'd like to knock you on the head with a rock and fuck you." If he "hated good women . . . like his mother," as Helen came to believe, he was making sure that she knew it.[14]

Helen, however, was not put off by Erskine's violence or his crudeness. She was deeply moved by his quiet, burning intensity, his strong physique, and his handsome features. The polished college boys at Virginia bored her with their swank conservatism and sophomoric ardor. She longed for adventure and idolized the expatriates in Paris who, she imagined, lived in rough-edged, lusty experiment. She responded to Erskine's unmistakable physical energy and appetite for experience, and shared, perhaps, his fascination with the "obscene." Before long, they were lovers consumed by a passionate affair.

For Erskine, the combination of Helen's eager participation and undeniable refinement was the consummation of all his desires. "I fell on my knees and cried with joy because she had been made as she was," he wrote in *Sacrilege*. His confidence swelled as their affair blossomed. Eating lunch with a friend at a local diner he playfully ordered raw oysters; he strode across campus with new self-possession, his shoulders squared with pride. "We both knew now why God had made her with such passion and me a man," he rejoiced. With Helen, a woman "with all the eagerness he had ever hoped to find . . . he had the strength of a giant."[15]

Erskine reveled in his physical relationship with Helen, but he was also determined, as he put it, to "make an honest woman" out of her. Within a month of their first date, he proposed marriage. Helen thought it was too soon. "I didn't want to get married. Christ almighty, I didn't want to get married," she would later admit. Erskine, however, refused to use contraceptives—was not, in his own words, "going to use a God damn thing"—and Helen was afraid she might get pregnant. Very much in love, she reluctantly consented to the marriage, and the two made plans to elope.[16]

On March 3, 1925, Erskine, sporting a clean shirt he had borrowed from Ballou, met Helen at the Charlottesville station to catch a train for Washington, D.C. Helen had told her mother that she was wearing her best dress in order to attend the inauguration parade for President Calvin Coolidge, and indeed, the train from Charlottesville was crowded with tourists on their way to the capital city. With the streets of Washington filled with the joyous sounds of the festivities and decorated by a sea of cherry blossoms, Erskine and Helen were married in the dark parlor of their cab driver's pastor. Erskine recalled later that the driver and the "minister's weeping wife" were the only two witnesses in attendance.[17]

From Washington, the newlyweds headed to Baltimore, where they planned to spend their wedding night. In his second autobiography, Erskine described the charming difficulties of the couple conniving to consummate their marriage on a slow-moving train back to Charlottesville. In this apocryphal account of their honeymoon, both his virility and his sense of romance are finally satisfied in the cramped privacy of the train bathroom. In reality, the couple spent their wedding night under far less romantic circumstances. That evening, Erskine took Helen to five burlesque shows in the red-light district of Baltimore. Although Helen liked to think of herself as an "enthusiast," she was startled by the crude gyrations of the strippers and hurt by the crassness of Erskine's behavior. An act on the runway of the Gaiety Theater "really made [her] blush," and she was shocked when Erskine encouraged her to join in and be "led down the runway [to] do a strip-tease" herself. Once he had "made an honest woman out of Helen by marrying her," he was driven, it seems, to debase her.[18]

The honeymoon was an inauspicious beginning, but the couple was clearly very much in love when they returned to Charlottesville to face Helen's parents. Mr. and Mrs. Lannigan were not pleased. Helen's education was foremost in their minds, and there was little to recommend Erskine, whom they knew only as an extremely quiet, somewhat sinister young man with no money and an abysmal academic record.

Carrie and Ira were also upset because Erskine was not, as he had promised, rededicating himself to his studies. All four parents were understandably disappointed that the couple had chosen to elope.

Fortunately, both the Caldwells and the Lannigans had grown accustomed to their children's unpredictable behavior and, swallowing their disapproval, extended a helping hand to the newlyweds. Ira and Carrie sent a small wedding check, and Helen and Erskine moved into the Lannigans' house to save money on rent. While Helen continued on with her studies, Erskine resumed work at the pool hall, and before long, had taken on another menial job as well. That semester he had registered for two economics courses, a geology course, and an English course. He failed all four, attending so few classes in two of them that he received no grade at all. He didn't care. Erskine and Helen made love every night—they "never missed," Helen bragged. For the first time in his life, Erskine did not feel alone.[19]

II

THAT SPRING, it became increasingly clear to Erskine that no amount of conjugal bliss could mitigate the strain of living with his in-laws. Mrs. Lannigan's initial distrust had deepened into barely disguised animosity, and she had little patience for Erskine's silent, brooding manner. He smoked constantly, drank heavily on occasion with Ballou, and did not attend class. In Mrs. Lannigan's opinion, he was a poor excuse for a son-in-law. Erskine, for his part, made very little effort to pacify her. He rarely spoke, and would not meet her eyes when he did. The atmosphere in the damp, dimly lit house was increasingly unpleasant, and tempers flared.[20]

The situation improved a bit that summer when the family traveled north to spend a few months in the Lannigans' summer house in Mount Vernon, Maine. In the spacious, drafty retreat, there was room for Helen and Erskine to spend time alone—miles of trails for hiking and a lovely lake for fishing and swimming just in view from their second-floor room. But here too, Erskine was bothered by his lack of independence, and it hurt his pride to rely on his in-laws. When, in early July, Helen discovered that she was pregnant, Erskine's dissatisfaction in the Lannigan household was joined by an acute sense of responsibility, and he vowed to get a full-time job.[21]

Helen urged him to look for work in Charlottesville, where she could complete her master's degree, but Erskine decided that they should move to Atlanta. With his father's help he had secured a job as a cub reporter for the *Atlanta Journal*. In early August, Helen and Erskine moved into a charmless, unfurnished flat at 43 Currier Street, in a working-class neighborhood on the edge of downtown.[22]

Atlanta was a great place for a newspaperman in 1925. What ten years before had been a relatively small city of 100,000 had exploded into a bustling metropolis of over 230,000. Horse-drawn carts and streetcars were rapidly being replaced by Fords and Studebakers. While only six thousand Atlantans had registered cars in 1910, by 1925 there were over 47,000 on the road. Atlanta's tireless boosters worked night and day to make their city "the South's distribution point," and their successful publicity campaigns in the Northern press soon earned the state's capital such cumbersome nicknames as "The Big Hustle," "The Convention Center," and "The Office Branch Town." In 1925, the year Helen and Erskine arrived, the Florida real-estate boom was at its peak, and thousands of hopeful investors passed daily through Atlanta on their way south. Buildings went up at a staggering rate; stores were swamped with customers; dignitaries, great and small, fought for headlines in the three local papers.[23]

In this dynamic city, Erskine began his career as a reporter, walking each morning to the five-story, red-brick building that housed the disheveled, tempestuous Forsyth Street offices of the *Atlanta Journal*. The *Journal* was an afternoon paper and its main competition was the *Atlanta Georgian*. Both papers raced to get editions on the street and outdid each other with the boldness and size of their headlines. "Extra! Extra! boys" worked on commission to bring breaking news stories to as many readers as possible.[24]

Erskine never forgot his first encounter with the gruff city editor, Hunter Bell: "Now get busy and wind up that typewriter and phone all the undertakers in the city and take in fresh obits," Bell thundered. "I don't care how short your obit sticks are just so you fill up two columns of space every day. Now that's it, boy!" Bell assured Erskine that "people were dying all over town—and complaining like hell about not getting their names in the paper."[25]

After a few weeks of writing "farewell items," Erskine moved on to cover the weekly luncheons and banquets held by the city's numerous business and social clubs. While churning out short publicity pieces for Atlanta's avid entrepreneurs offered little intellectual challenge, Erskine knew that the weekly helpings of "chicken à la king and strawberry shortcake" that he received on assignment were the city editor's way of compensating his underpaid reporters. Still, Erskine was ill at ease among the polished glad-handers at these luncheons, and embarrassed by his "brown tweed coat with the threadbare cuffs and . . . baggy-kneed gray trousers." Erskine used most of his first week's pay to buy a derby hat and walking stick "to invigorate his psyche." But if his appearance improved, he still had little talent for writing the glib promotional plugs that guaranteed the paper's advertising. Sent to cover the inauguration of one of Atlanta's new luxury trains, he focused his story on the conductor's comic (and failed) efforts to board the fast-moving engine before it left the station. Not surprisingly, the piece was never printed.[26]

Hunter Bell and the other editors at the *Journal* were tough critics of Erskine's prose. Composing on an old upright Underwood typewriter—a habit he would never lose—Erskine struggled to write the crisp, dispassionate prose that would one day characterize his best fiction. Later in his career, Erskine credited Bell with teaching him to write. "He would begin his copy reading by whisking a soft-lead pencil over a three or four hundred word story about a fire, or a hold-up, or an accident until there were perhaps a dozen lines left," Erskine recalled, "and then he would hand it back to me and say he could use it only if I rewrote the story in half as many lines." "This," he remembered, "was a realistic course of instruction in writing, completely different from anything I had learned in English courses anywhere, and from that time forward I was glad something had prompted me to go to work on a newspaper."[27]

Like most new reporters, Erskine was eventually assigned to the police beat, and here he saw the underside of Atlanta's bustling commercial culture and chamber-of-commerce optimism. In the 1920s, Atlanta was convulsed by labor violence. Streetcar operators carried out numerous strikes, some of them successful, and bloody clashes between workers and police in the city's textile and paper mills were common. While Erskine sided with the mill workers in these conflicts, there was no room for his sympathies on the pages of the *Journal.* Inevitably, the paper's editorial board chose to overlook these blemishes on the city's image or supported management in their battles with "outside agitators" and "radicals."

Atlanta also had its share of racial violence. The city was strictly segregated, and the black community, sequestered in squalid "alley houses" in the worst part of town, worked hard to maintain its self-respect in a world where "Colored" and "Whites Only" signs delineated clear boundaries between the races. The blacks of Atlanta worked predominantly in menial jobs, and only a few held middle-class positions as teachers, barbers, waiters, or railroad porters. The Ku Klux Klan, which staged a massive national revival in the 1920s, was very active in the city, and racial intimidation of all sorts—from cross-burnings to lynchings—was part of daily life for the city's minorities. On more than one occasion, Erskine arrived at the site of a lynching "before the body had been cut down." But in a highly competitive newspaper market serving a largely white audience and supported by lily-white advertising, Erskine was forced by his editors to abide by the unstated journalistic truism that a "nigger murder wasn't news."[28]

Erskine's job also exposed him to the plight of the white underclass of Atlanta. In the first years of the 1920s, thousands of rural poor—chased from their farms by falling crop prices and the boll weevil—flooded into Atlanta to seek better lives in the city's paper mills and Coca-Cola plants. On one of his first assignments, Erskine was sent to investigate the death of a man in a dollar-a-night hotel. Erskine learned from the desk clerk that Monday mornings often brought suicides from "poor devils who've waked up stony-broke . . . and had a bellyful of it." Erskine returned to his desk at the *Journal* and wrote an effusive two-page tribute to the "discouraged, penniless, middle-aged man who felt that life had treated him badly and as a result had lost all desire to continue an existence in an unfeeling, unsympathetic, hard-hearted world." The city editor's abrupt reaction to the piece was predictable: "What are you doing—writing his five-dollar-a-copy biography? . . . No name, no home address, no story."[29]

III

ERSKINE AND HELEN had trouble making ends meet on his weekly salary of twenty dollars, and with a child expected in a few months, they were desperate to augment their income. A friend at the paper helped Erskine land a second job with the *Journal* as a book reviewer, and by early December he was making trips downstairs from the city room to pick up his review copies. Although the position paid no salary, he was allowed to keep the books, which he could resell to local book stores for a quarter apiece. Perhaps more enticing, Erskine was guaranteed a printed byline, something he did not receive writing the news, and an accomplishment he had dreamed of since his days as a string reporter in Wrens.[30]

Erskine thought that his reviews for the *Journal* might also be carried by other newspapers, and he wrote letters to book editors across the

South offering his services. Cora Harris of the *Charlotte Observer* responded immediately. She was "delighted to send books for review, and in fact was mailing half a dozen that same day." Soon the baseboard of Helen and Erskine's tiny flat was lined from corner to corner with brand-new review copies. Erskine hoped to make some extra money through book collecting, and he combed the local secondhand stores to improve their collection with first editions whenever he could. Unsure which books to keep and which to resell, he sent a letter to May Becker, book editor at the *Saturday Review*, asking her advice. "We are building up a library," he wrote. Could she recommend "some ten or a dozen recent publications suitable for a young man and his wife (both college graduates [sic]) . . . dealing with books of interest to collectors?"[31]

Erskine's book reviews first appeared in the *Journal* and the *Observer* in early November of 1925 and ran every week or two for the next six months. Without the strict editorial supervision that he received on his news reports, Erskine's prose was riddled with every manner of grammatical and stylistic gaffe, and it is clear that his authorial education was far from complete. In a review of *The Hunter's Moon* by Ernest Poole, Erskine explained that the characters were so realistic that "they could be very less plainer of met on the street [sic]." Trying to summarize the tangled plot in H. G. Wells's *Christina Albert's Father*, Erskine only made matters worse: "The father, we find is not the parental relative, which at first glance seems paradoxical; but the husband acquires a daughter, much to his apparent satisfaction." *The Selmans*, by V. R. Emanual, received a similarly haphazard summary: "Rhoda becomes a haven for David for awhile. Rhoda is exotic. She proves to be unreal just at the crucial moment, however."[32]

While Erskine's prose was still crude and disjointed, his literary taste was increasingly consistent. As he explained in a review of William Cumming's *Passion and Glory*, it was "the achievement of realism" that made a work "remarkable." Erskine was particularly impressed by Cumming's frank exploration of "unschooled passions . . . sensuality and brutality," and his decision to withhold the "customary happy ending." In a review of *A Modernist and His Creed*, Edward Mortimer Chapman's critical study of American fiction, Erskine took the author to task for doubting the sincerity of Sinclair Lewis and Theodore Dreiser. Quite clearly, these two writers, whose sometimes savage realism and uncompromising satire helped turn the romantic tide in American letters, were two of Erskine's literary heroes. "Are we to think that Mr. Lewis and Mr. Dreiser laugh up their sleeves at the muddled minded [sic] public who read them with all sincerity? There must be one or two faults in our lives if we can't let Lewis poke fun at us. . . . We read *Babbitt* and *Main Street* and were a bit angry at him, perhaps, but that was because the books smacked us in the face, not because we doubted his seriousness of purpose." Erskine went on to say that Dreiser "hands us pretty stiff doses of pornographic pictures; but we can't deny their authenticity."[33]

Erskine was frustrated that most Southern literature did not follow the lead of writers like Dreiser and Lewis and still sought to perpetuate a myth of "moonlight and magnolias" so at odds with his own critical perspective on the region. He had nothing but disdain, for example, for *Shepherds*, by Georgian novelist Marie Conway Oemler. "Sitting here upon a fence watching the new novels and their authors parade by, we unconsciously sit erect when someone from the South catches our eyes," Erskine began. But he was disappointed by Oemler's gentle romanticism. "There was a rumor in the air saying there was a new order just beginning to find voice," he wrote, referring perhaps to Ellen Glasgow, a novelist he much admired. "However, when we smelt for the bracing salt air of Savannah in 'Shepherds' and found it lacking, there was nothing left for us to do but climb back on the perch and wait patiently for the next one."[34]

Of the nonfiction Erskine reviewed, he reserved his highest praise for Newbell Niles Puckett's exhaustive collection of black folklore entitled *Folk Beliefs of the Southern Negro*. In his review of this huge volume—"644 pages for a thousand and one nights"—Erskine warned that "the old plantation negro is rapidly being lost in the background by the present-day industrial one," and that this rich folk culture was well worth preserving. In passing along some of Pucket's findings—"warts may be removed . . . by the breath of a child who has never seen its father"—Erskine refrained from the amused, patronizing tone that characterized other reviews of the book. "Those of us who live in the South," he suggested, could find in black folklore "our own lives and thoughts as well as our neighbors."[35]

Erskine's experience as a book reviewer makes a mockery of his lifelong boast that he was "a writer not a reader," an unschooled artist ignorant of literary trends around him. In the course of six months he read hundreds of books, reviewed the work of authors ranging from Robert Louis Stevenson to Fyodor Dostoevsky, and exhibited a considerable knowledge of a variety of American writers including Mark Twain and Sherwood Anderson, as well as Dreiser and Lewis.

But the education in letters he received as a critic was an exhausting one. Many nights Erskine stayed up well past midnight, ploughing quickly through the books stacked on his desk, then writing feverishly to meet a deadline. He awoke, bleary-eyed and exhausted at dawn, gulping down a quick breakfast before rushing to the *Journal* offices in time to receive the morning police reports.

With the birth of his son—also named Erskine—in February 1926, money and space were even tighter in the Caldwell home. Erskine became increasingly dissatisfied with his taxing work schedule and poor salary. And, no doubt, he was tired of having his stories about racial violence or exploitative labor practices returned to him by his editors. Helen was also fed up with Atlanta. Although she also wrote a few reviews for the *Journal* pages, she was lonely and bored. Stuck in the tiny book-lined apartment with an infant son and a huge collie that she had given Erskine for Christmas, she longed to go back to Virginia to see her friends and finish her degree.[36]

The final decision to leave Atlanta was Erskine's, and his primary concern was not the long hours, the low pay, the restrictions on his creative freedom, or his wife's unhappiness. In Charlottesville, he thought, he would have time to explore an interest that was fast becoming an obsession. He had decided to become a fiction writer.

IV

ERSKINE HAD MADE tentative efforts at creative writing before his stint at the *Journal*. Alone in his boarding-house room, he had spent hours writing poetry. For the most part, the work was flagrantly adolescent and painfully trite. "Streams are slow, they always flow," he wrote in "To a Lake." "Barking Dogs at Night" ended this way: "Barking dogs are singing dogs, And that's their way of making song." Many of the poems were directly autobiographical. In "One Day More," a work consisting of rhymed couplets, Erskine bemoaned his alienation from the smooth social elite at the university:

> They suck my blood and sap my life,
> My heart they cut as with a knife.

> O! Christ! They spit upon my face,
> And laughing still, increase their pace.[37]

Erskine transcended this technical and thematic crudity in only two poems. "Southern Nights," an ambitious saga of ten eight-line stanzas, chronicled the plight of a poor white sharecropper who has been pushed off his farm. Compelled by an informed empathy, Erskine wrote passable verse that had power, if little grace:

> *None would feed my wasting*
>   *Body, Unwanted*
> *My presence, my ragged clothes they*
>   *Said were haunted.*
> *Two willing hands a hungry body,*
>   *But all said No!*
> *Your unkempt face, your dirty*
>   *Rags, you are low!*

"Face Beneath the Sky" was the best of Erskine's poems. Like "Southern Nights," it drew authority from the author's striking social conscience and intimacy with the harsh realities of Southern life. Written in the shadow of Klan meetings held in Charlottesville churches and widely attended campus meetings of the Anglo-American Club of America, the poem is a remarkable testimony to Erskine's race liberalism:[38]

> *A gust of wind evoked a sigh*
> *From leaded willow branches hour on hour;*
> *A figure hung beneath the sky*
> *Its neck was crumpled like a faded flower.*
> *With glassy eyes he looked at me*
> *And asked the color of my skin and face,*
> *I told him White—he laughed with glee*
> *And loudly cursed his God-forsaken race.*
> *The man then told me how he died,*
> *They fought, he said, in anger for his ears;*
> *His blood they drew with gruesome pride,*
> *And took his hands away for souvenirs.*
> *His arm I grasped, and turned away*
> *From dusky death that hung from drooping limb;*
> *A fleeting glance at break of day*
> *Saw weeping willows sadly guarding him.*[39]

Despite these occasional glimmers, Erskine's year in Atlanta pushed him decidedly away from verse and towards prose fiction. Reviewing novels, particularly Southern ones, Erskine came to believe that he had something original to say; the more he read, the more he ached to try. Eventually, the work of other aspiring authors he met on the *Journal*'s staff gave him the courage to begin. He was particularly heartened by the methodical progress of Frances Newman, who was writing a novel she called *The Hard-Boiled Virgin*. Each day a friend of Newman's on the *Journal* brought Erskine a typescript page of the novel for him to read. "The finished page, so neatly typed and without corrections, always looked as if it had been written with ease and without laborious revision," Caldwell remembered. Even closer at hand than Newman was an "unusually attractive" feature writer Erskine had noticed around the office. She too was working on a novel, and although Erskine surely did not share her literary taste—she liked Sir Walter Scott—he "admired her for having enough confidence in herself to . . . write a book." This confidence, it turned out, was well founded. Ten years later "Peggy" Mitchell published *Gone with the Wind*.[40]

With book reviews to write until after midnight, Erskine worked on his first stories through a haze of fatigue. He longed to be published, and with Helen's assistance, worked hard to polish his grammar and spelling. It was no use. "No matter how many times I rewrote them," Erskine later recalled, his fledgling efforts received little encouragement from the New York magazine editors who read them. Before long, he had accumulated a number of "blandly worded rejection slips" and had pasted them neatly in a stamp collector's album. A few years later, when his writing had improved and his fortunes had turned, Erskine gathered up both the unappreciated stories and the editors' rebuffs and burned them.[41]

Erskine brought his determination to write fiction back to the Virginia campus in the fall of 1926, and for the first time in his life, he began to attend classes on a regular basis. He became deeply involved in a sociology course titled "Poverty and Dependency" taught by Associate Professor William Bean.[42] Widespread rural poverty in the early twenties had stirred interest in the study of local welfare systems on many Southern campuses. That year the university established the Institute for Research in the Social Sciences to focus attention on the state's problems. Professor Bean was a strong believer in the hands-on investigation of such problems, and on Saturdays he took his class to visit the county's insane asylums, prisons, hospitals, and old-age homes—excursions not unlike the ones Erskine had taken with his father in Wrens. Erskine approached his work like a journalist and wrote strictly factual reports of what he saw. Bean appreciated Erskine's dispassionate analysis and obvious conviction, and rewarded him with his first A grades.[43]

In Professor A. K. Davis's class on the nineteenth-century British novel, however, Erskine was frustrated and fell into his old habits of half-hearted involvement. Instead of joining the rest of the class around the room's small wooden table, he ensconced himself in the back corner; he rarely spoke and did little of the assigned reading. Erskine did not care for the "cold, objective, Oxfordian manner" of young Professor Davis, whose prominently worn Phi Beta Kappa key and dignified Virginian bearing better fit his mother's ideal of professorial deportment than his own. He had less patience still for Davis's written assignments, which seemed to him irrelevant and absurd. Years later, he still recalled his disgust with "such English course assignments as 'What Wordsworth Means to Me' and 'Humanity as Exemplified by the Lake Poets.' " He failed the class.[44]

But if Erskine was bored by the British novel, his composition course with Professor Atcheson L. Hench was the most influential in his long and checkered academic career. Professor Hench, a well-built, youthful man of thirty-five, with rugged good looks and an easy, relaxed style, was the only Northerner in the English Department. Hench had attended school in Pennsylvania before getting his Ph.D. from Harvard, and he had come to Virginia from Wesleyan University in 1925. He was a favorite among students from the very start—a faithful spectator at football games and a willing sponsor of events ranging from dances to political debates. Hench had no use for the formal distance and unapproachable dignity assumed by most Virginia professors; on a campus where the faculty expected tipped hats and deference as a matter of course, he encouraged his students to call him "Atch."[45]

Hench brought this same informality to his course in English composition. Limited to ten or so students whose writing samples indicated to Hench that "they had some skill in writing," the class met weekly around a large table in a sunny second-floor room. Most of the two-hour session was taken up by informal discussion of the class members' weekly essays, and Hench tried to create a gentle, supportive atmosphere for his budding writers. For Erskine, who would never be comfortable discussing his work, and was terribly sensitive to any kind of evaluation despite his unflappable demeanor, the environment was reassuring. He would later recall that "Atcheson Hench was more helpful, more understanding, more patient with my bumbling attempts to learn how to write than anybody anywhere at any time took the trouble to be."[46]

Erskine was thrilled to find that in Hench's class he was free to write on any subject he chose. His most impassioned work, Hench remembered, dealt with "the soil and people of humble origin or of the lower classes." Stories of the urban dispossessed or diatribes against the Ku Klux Klan—pieces unlikely to find publication in the *Journal*—enjoyed a warm reception in Atch's class. Drawing on material and impressions garnered on his trips with Professor Bean, Erskine wrote "God's Children," "The Promised Land," and "The Stench of Civilization"— essays and sketches dealing with poverty on the remote edges of Albemarle County. On a campus that was, as Hench later remembered it, "overwhelmingly lacking in anything remotely resembling a social conscience," he identified Erskine as a student "with the world upon his shoulders."[47]

Erskine's liberal convictions did not translate into graceful prose. Hench clearly had mixed feelings about the sparse, deadpan tone that was part of Erskine's evolving style. Commenting on the essay "Promised Land," Hench noted an "abnormal style of writing—strong but unpleasant and unlikable." He was bothered in other pieces by Erskine's "staccato style . . . that forces *too* much attention," a "leaden oversimplified style," and an "intentional drabness of the English." Explaining a grade of C that he awarded a story entitled "Florence," Hench anticipated the concern (and titillation) that would meet a good deal of Erskine's work. He wrote simply: "Sex too crude, it seems to me."[48]

Erskine's most successful piece for Hench's class was entitled "Georgia Cracker." Although Hench awarded it only a B+, the four-page essay was accepted for publication in *The Haldeman-Julius Monthly*, part of a series better known as the "Little Blue Books." Erskine wrote the piece as a rebuttal to an *Atlanta Journal* editorial by Harlee Branch, who had trumpeted: "No state in the union has a purer strain of Anglo-Saxon blood running through the veins [than Georgia]. . . . No state has a finer culture. . . . No state in the Union has produced a longer list of distinguished men and women."[49]

Erskine's portrait of his home state was far less flattering; it was, in fact, as passionate in condemnation as Branch (whom he labeled a "booster and windbag") had been in praise. Erskine was particularly vitriolic in his attacks on Georgia's more extreme fundamentalist sects. "Georgia suckles more Holy Rollers, Snake Charmers and the like, than any other state in the Union," he wrote, clearly drawing on his fact-finding tours with Ira. Erskine's description of a young woman at a revival, however, would have shocked his father into stuttering indignation, for it foreshadowed a lifelong preoccupation with the fusion of fundamentalist religion and primitive sexuality:

> There she was, clothed only in a scanty piece of underwear, using her stomach and hips to great advantage, but the bowed worshippers took no notice of her actions. The exhibition continued for more than fifteen minutes, during which she sported herself like a hoochy-coochy teaser, a contortionist, and an epileptic recovering from a fit. At last she ran out of the church into the arms of one of the male preachers who quickly carried her off into the darkness.[50]

Erskine augmented his attack on "bogus religionists" with a healthy dose of crude adolescent humor. For the rest of his career critics would argue over passages like the following, unwilling to accept that such broad satire was, as he claimed, a form of social protest:

> . . . one of the clergy-men told us to get down on the floor and roll our sins away. A buxom woman weighing not less than three hundred pounds was there on the floor beside us, and since she was apparently unable to make a complete revolution, I gave her a hand. Once started, she could not stop, and rolled with gaining velocity down the aisle in the direction of the two preachers, whose backs were turned. If the three had been football candidates, they could not have done better— the two apostles shot backward simultaneously, their heads cracking the uncarpeted floor. Those two men of God were familiar with more oaths than any laymen I ever heard, but possibly that was because they knew more of the words.[51]

The piece shifted quickly from this anarchic slapstick to an impassioned account of the "cruification [sic] of unruly convicts" and the brutal lynching of a feeble-minded black man. Erskine was not interested in balanced sociological analysis; he aimed to shock, and in the end hyperbole undermined his credibility. Yet, in publishing the piece, the editors of the Monthly acknowledged that Erskine's prose had a simple compelling power that overshadowed awkward construction and overblown imagery. Erskine closed with an unforgiving summary of life in his home state:

> So this is Georgia—whose inhabitants do cruel and uncivilized things; whose land is overrun with bogus religionists, boosters, and dema-

gogues; whose politics are in the hands of Klan-spirited Baptists; and yet whose largest city boasts of being the "greatest city in the greatest state in the world."[52]

The publication of "Georgia Cracker" and Hench's continued encouragement were a great boost to Erskine's confidence. "Nothing before or since," Erskine wrote Hench a few years later, "has given me the feeling I used to have when I walked into your classroom." Hench had indeed understood that Erskine's best writing would spring from a vigorous social conscience, and while he blanched a bit at Erskine's crudeness and violence, he had not discouraged him. Hench was the right teacher at the right time. In the fall of 1926, Erskine Caldwell was finally ready to learn; he was, in his own words, "a haystack on the verge of bursting into flame."[53]

V

THE UNIVERSITY OF VIRGINIA was a fertile environment for a would-be author. The members of the small, tight-knit Department of English, chaired by John Calvin Metcalf, shared a commitment to the development of Southern letters. Metcalf, a reserved Kentuckian of unshakable decorum, taught Shakespeare, but his passion was modern American fiction. He worked hard to bring prominent writers to the university, and in the fall of 1926 several literary celebrities, including Carl Sandburg and Sherwood Anderson, paid visits to the Charlottesville campus. Erskine was particularly impressed by Sandburg, whose sloppy dress and relaxed, unpretentious manner seemed to him the epitome of artistic nonchalance.[54]

The department's interest in modern literature inspired it to launch its own journal, and in 1925 the university's presses ran off the pilot issue of the *Virginia Quarterly Review*. James Southall Wilson, a noted authority on Edgar Allan Poe, became its first editor, with Metcalf serving in an advisory position. From the beginning, the *VQR* sought to steer clear of the sort of controversy that surrounded the University of North Carolina's *Journal of Social Forces*, a publication that had made a name for itself with searing critiques of Southern culture. The *VQR*, Wilson declared, "is in no sense a sectional publication; it is a national journal of discussion published in the South."[55]

Such tact assured alumni support, but it did little to impress those Southerners who looked to the universities for intellectual innovation.

"It fails," the *Baltimore Sun* complained, "to shake the dear old commonwealth from that delightful Bourbon trait of neither forgetting anything nor learning anything." A writer for Norfolk's *Virginia Pilot* better understood that the editors of the *VQR* were, above all, dedicated to the pursuit and criticism of the country's "belles lettres" and not to sociological or political debate: "[T]he editors at Chapel Hill wore galluses and overalls," while those in Charlottesville sported "spectacles and white collars. . . . To compare the two journals is like comparing the American Federation of Labor and the American Academy of Arts and Letters."[56]

If the *VQR* began timidly, it picked up steam under the direction of Professor Stringfellow Barr, who became editor the year Erskine returned to Virginia. While Barr held reservations about the ruthless criticism of Southern life leveled by North Carolina editors Howard Odum and Gerald Johnson, he bristled at the intellectual currents emanating from Vanderbilt University in Nashville, Tennessee. Barr had nothing but contempt for the so-called Agrarians, who sought to preserve traditional Southern values. This loosely joined school of Southern patriotism, whose credo found its most complete and powerful expression a few years later in the 1930 manifesto *I'll Take My Stand*, provoked Barr to uncharacteristic belligerence:

> The traditionalists, frightened by the lengthening shadows of the smokestacks, take refuge in the good old days and in what I have called the apotheosis of the hoe. They make a charming but impotent religion of the past, make idols of the defunct horse and buggy, and mutter impotently at the radio.[57]

Aside from the *VQR*, the university's Alderman Library housed an excellent collection of "little magazines." Dedicated to the development of fresh talent and new forms of expression, publications such as *Dial, This Quarter, transition, Poetry*, and *Broom* offered the first published venues for the writers who would shape the course of American literature. By the time Erskine returned to Virginia, these journals were publishing the work of Ernest Hemingway, James Joyce, Sherwood Anderson, T. S. Eliot, Ezra Pound, and Hart Crane—authors who, along with their literary peers, were shattering the Victorian decorum that had once guided American letters. In the pages of these magazines, the first full generation of American modernists honed their craft.[58]

In the fall of 1926, Erskine stumbled on the book-lined reading room in the rotunda library. Although "the names of the little magazines . . .

were," Caldwell recalled, "as unfamiliar to me were the names of the authors themselves," he was intoxicated by the violence, sexuality, and uncompromising realism he discovered. Erskine made a second home of the well-lit alcove nestled in the east wall of the rotunda and dreamed of the day when he might "become a part of this new world of writing." Metcalf had been particularly careful to stock the shelves with Southern periodicals, and Erskine must have been inspired by publications like the *Double Dealer*. A few years earlier, the editors of this New Orleans journal had prayed for a "clear-visioned penman to emerge from the sodden marshes of Southern literature" who might recognize that the "storied realm of dreams, lassitude, pleasure, chivalry and the nigger no longer exists." It was a challenge that would strike a chord in young Erskine Caldwell as he sat in the fading autumn light of the university library.[59]

Hench required his composition students to keep close track of what they read, and Erskine's carefully typed and tabulated records reveal the full extent of his appetite. He read scientific and sociological journals like *Scientific Monthly* and *Social Forces*, as well as journals of opinion and political debate like the *Nation, Forum*, and the *Independent*. As an aspiring writer of fiction, he devoured a wide range of literary criticism in the *New Masses*, the *London Bookman*, the *Yale Review*, and the *New Republic*. Mainstream journals like *Harper's Bazaar, Scribner's Magazine*, and the *Atlantic Monthly* were also part of the mixed fare, as were newspapers from across the nation.[60]

Although Erskine read voraciously, even indiscriminately, his tastes had not changed much since his days as a book reviewer. He admired Hemingway and Sherwood Anderson, but also lesser-known realists like the Danish immigrant Carl Christian Jensen. One Jensen story, "Life Is All a Variorum," was an unrelenting account of an immigrant's struggle to survive on the dockyards of New York. "I was a man, and stronger than most men," the story begins, and goes on to describe the longshoremen whose "eyes were wild with lust for work" and "a scaffold [that] gave way under a dozen men, who tumbled down with their barrels in a bleeding heap." Erskine also reserved high praise for D. H. Lawrence and, in particular, his erotic supernatural tale "Glad Ghost." While he surely did not appreciate the author's abstract imagery or elaborate prose, he could not resist the overt sexuality of Lawrence's work. In the margin of his reading list Erskine wrote simply: "It is an example of the author at his best—(Don't tell the censors)."[61]

In nonfiction, he eagerly followed articles dealing with racial issues and prejudice and was particularly impressed with Wilson Wallis's

"Race and Culture." Wallis, a professor at the University of Minnesota, took issue with the school of scientific thought resurgent in the 1920s that held the innate potential of blacks inferior to that of whites. Wallis concluded that there was no evidence to suggest that the "potential accomplishment of one physical type is above or below that of another." Repeating in scientific terms what Erskine's father had long espoused, Wallis declared: "There is no reason to believe that one race differs from another in innate psychic equipment."[62]

Ira would have had less sympathy, perhaps, for Carl Van Doren's "Why I Am an Unbeliever," another of Erskine's favorites. Van Doren's bold assertion that he did "not believe in any god that has ever been devised, in any doctrine that has ever claimed to be revealed, in any scheme of immortality that has ever been expounded," squared nicely with Erskine's own cynicism towards organized religion. As a determined "unbeliever" himself, Erskine admired Van Doren's courage in speaking his mind.[63]

He also appreciated the merciless satire of H. L. Mencken, and shared Mencken's notion that the South was inhospitable to a creative temperament. Mencken's influence is obvious throughout "Georgia Cracker" and, in particular, in Erskine's sneering at a literary milieu where "the presentation of nature and romance was raised to high art." Everyone in Hench's class would have read "Sahara of the Bozartz," Mencken's ruthless denigration of Southern culture; and on at least one occasion, Hench reprimanded Erskine for writing "too much like Mencken."[64]

Erskine also found courageous, if less weighty, inspiration in several iconoclastic student publications at the university. The *Virginia Magazine*, for instance, was denounced by University President Edwin Anderson for a frankly sexual narrative entitled "Mulatto Flair." The magazine's editor, fired by his own staff but lionized by many students, dropped out of school. The college humor magazine, the *Virginia Reel*, also came under attack, this time from the school newspaper editors who lamented the "vulgar obscenity which burst violently into the recent issue." It was just the kind of press a college humor magazine coveted most, and it seems likely that Erskine shared in the editor's satisfaction. He had been in the habit of slipping "decidedly off-color jokes" under the *Reel* office door to be published anonymously.[65]

Even had he wanted to, Erskine had little chance of playing a more prominent role on the *Reel* or other campus periodicals. Like the fraternities, the university publications were governed by a strict social hierarchy that excluded him. But Erskine did become part of a more informal literary culture that revolved around the New Dominion Bookstore in the center of Charlottesville. Gordon Lewis, the proprietor, was only a few years older than the ragged gang of would-be writers who congregated in the back of his shop to drink and discuss the latest issue of *Dial* or *Poetry*. Before long, Erskine had become a regular, if noticeably silent, visitor to the shop. In a group of spirited young men, eager to hear themselves talk, Erskine was remembered best as "the redhead who sat on the floor in the back of the store reading everything he could get his hands on." Some of the crowd at the New Dominion were working on fiction of their own and would read aloud from their manuscripts. Charles Wertenbaker, the furthest along of the group, had almost completed his novel about an interracial love affair between a Virginian aristocrat and a beautiful "octoroon." Published in 1928 to critical acclaim and horrified gasps across the South, *Boojum* was typical of the determined iconoclasm of all the New Dominion artists. James Aswell, Lewis, and of course Erskine, all went on to careers as published authors; all of them, like Wertenbaker, took great satisfaction in rattling the cages of conservative Southern opinion.[66]

Occasionally, Lewis persuaded more established writers to stop by the store to talk about their work. Erskine had the opportunity to speak with James Branch Cabell several times, but he was far more excited by the visits of Sherwood Anderson. Like many of his peers, Erskine greatly admired Anderson's *Winesburg, Ohio*, and he could not help comparing the dusty, claustrophobic streets of Wrens to those of Winesburg. Assembled on the steps of the store, Erskine and his friends listened in rapt fascination as Anderson regaled them with stories from his past and shared secrets of authorship. Only a few years later Erskine would insist that Anderson was "the best writer in America."[67]

Erskine enjoyed the informal lectures by Anderson, the fellowship of his peers, and access to Lewis's formidable collection of contemporary fiction, but he could never fully relax in such a communal setting. He longed to get on with his own writing, and he was impatient with the self-indulgence and bookishness of literary debate. Late one night, observing a particularly heated intellectual discussion in the bookstore's dimly lit back room, Erskine was overcome by frustration. Rising suddenly to his feet, he slammed his hand on the table, stunning the group into abrupt silence. James Aswell, his closest friend at the time, recalled Erskine's blunt challenge: "We can sit around here talking about it all day," he said, "but there is only one way to get to the top and that is to give up EVERYTHING but writing!" He strode from the shop without a backward glance.[68]

<h1 style="text-align:center">VI</h1>

HOUR AFTER HOUR Erskine sat, erect and brooding, in front of his typewriter. Because he was such a terrible speller, he stopped frequently to consult the dictionary that he always kept close at hand. He worked as if in pain, seemingly reliving the hardships and injustice that he described. Erskine was "possessed by an overwhelming obsession to write," Helen remembered, and everything he wrote "was like the conception of a child." Acquaintances were intimidated by his single-minded devotion and wary of him when he was working. "Erskine was always at his studies and typing, typing, typing," one friend recalled. He was increasingly unapproachable and remote.[69]

Erskine was so consumed by his work, in fact, that Helen had delayed telling him that she was pregnant again. With money tight, and Erskine already frustrated by the crying of one infant son, she feared he would insist on an abortion. To her relief, he did not, and that March, Helen gave birth to their second son. The addition of Dabney to the family, however, made the Lannigan house almost unbearably crowded, and the noise and commotion bothered Erskine most of all. During the day he escaped to the library, but at night he was constantly interrupted by the cries of the newborn baby. When Erskine became frustrated, he retreated into spells of icy silence or lashed out at Helen for failing to keep the children quiet. Helen felt that her husband's writing "mattered more to him than human beings by far." By the spring of 1927, the palpable tension in the household had reached the breaking point. The Lannigans suggested that Erskine, Helen, and the two boys move North into the Maine summer house, and Erskine readily agreed.[70]

Years later, he would remember only his acute restlessness and "the need to go as far away as possible." At the time, however, the decision to leave was extremely painful. While he relied less and less on Hench and the circle at the New Dominion Bookstore, they were still important sources of support. He also had mixed feelings about leaving his parents. In a poem entitled "The Countryside Says Goodbye," the narrative point of view was his parents'; clearly, Erskine still sought their approval and felt guilty for leaving them. And while pieces like

"Georgia Cracker" revealed a genuine hostility towards aspects of Southern life, Erskine's love for his family was mingled with an affection for the charms of his native countryside:

> *You'll become famous there*
> *And have a lot of friends*
> *But, Son, Don't you love*
> *The meadows, the creek, the hills?*
> *God bless you, Son*
> *I'll miss you*
> *Every minute.*
> *Do you remember*
> *When you picked blackberries*
> *And wild strawberries*
> *On Sunday afternoons in the pasture?*
> *God bless you, Son*
> *I'll miss you*
> *Every minute.*[71]

However compelling his attachments, Erskine could not resist the prospect of a quiet, rent-free environment in which to write. But his decision to leave was artistic as well as practical. Greater distance from his parents—both physical and psychological—would allow him to explore the full range of his creative impulses, free of the worry, for instance, that his explicit use of sexuality might offend them. Moreover, he sought an emotional distance from the very Southern life he so desperately sought to describe. His sole objective was to write, and Erskine hoped that life in the North would, he recalled later, offer a "revealing perspective of the scenes and circumstances" in which he had grown to manhood. If he could only "look back from a distance," he was certain he could "hold up a mirror to nature in the South."[72]

In the spring of 1927, Erskine, Helen, and the boys left Charlottesville and headed north towards their new home in Mount Vernon, Maine. Although they had few other possessions, the car was packed to overflowing with cartons of accumulated books, and Borzoi, the huge collie, had to ride with his head out the window. The week-long drive would be cramped and hot, and Erskine insisted on driving the entire way himself. Although he would come back to visit on occasion, Erskine would not live in the South again for forty years.

Chapter Four

APPRENTICESHIP

A FULL SEVENTY MILES northeast of Portland, the remote community of Mount Vernon, Maine, certainly offered little distraction for a would-be writer. The Caldwells' neighbors were small-scale farmers who worked depleted, rocky plots that had been in their families for generations. They lived austerely on the produce of their gardens and depended on the family cow to provide their milk. Most owned chickens as well, although only a very few had enough eggs to sell for profit. Some supplemented their income with part-time jobs at the nearby lumber and tanning mills or worked seasonally canning blueberries that grew in abundance in the surrounding countryside. In the summertime, salmon and bass from nearby lakes were staples; during the long winter, trapping and hunting were an essential part of survival.[1]

Built in 1745, the Caldwells' new home was a huge, sprawling colonial that had seen better days. Gray shingles hung askew or were missing altogether, and the white trim was peeled and cracked. Floorboards, both inside and on the broad front porch, were warped, and there were cracks in the enormous fireplace that dominated one entire wall of the living room. On rainy days, the line of regularly shaped bedrooms off the long upstairs hall gathered impressive puddles from leaks in the steeply gabled roof. For twenty-five years, the rustic, drafty house had served as an informal training site for "Pop" Lannigan's athletes; the carpets, needless to say, were badly in need of repair.[2]

In spite of its condition, the house retained a certain disheveled charm. Situated on one hundred acres of rolling, wooded land and just in sight of lovely Parker Lake, Greentrees, as the Lannigans called their ramshackle estate, was a charming place to spend the summer. Some years later, Caldwell was moved to rare nostalgia as he recalled the "enchanting world of softly unfolding shades of green" that greeted the family on its arrival. His initial reaction to the picturesque environs was more practical: "One could surely write in such a place," he thought, "if writing ever was to be done."[3]

I

EARLY EACH MORNING, Caldwell began work in the house's dark book-lined study. At noon he broke for lunch, then returned to his desk for the afternoon. While he wrote, Helen was expected to keep the two boys—both under the age of two—absolutely quiet. If crying disturbed the morning work, Caldwell might refuse to speak to Helen when he emerged for lunch. Pixie, as Erskine, Jr. came to be called, and Dabney learned to whisper when their father was at work. The study, with its heavy oak door, was off-limits, and the boys played outside whenever possible, regardless of the weather. Although visitors were scarce in the scattered Mount Vernon community, those who stopped by rarely came back. Caldwell refused to come out of the library, and Helen was afraid to invite people in, lest the conversation disturb him.[4]

Even with such draconian restrictions, Caldwell found the house too noisy, and during the summer months he moved to a small guest cottage on the edge of the lake. Working at the plank table in the rough-hewn log cabin, Caldwell virtually disappeared from his family for weeks at a time. They were forbidden to venture near during the day, and only rarely would Helen gather up the children and make the half-mile trek along the darkened path to spend the night with her husband. "He does not like to have anyone around him at all," Helen lamented to his parents. "He stays in the cottage all day and writes." Even suffering from a summer flu, Erskine remained holed up inside the tiny shack and ignored Helen's entreaties to come out. Only with the arrival of fall and the first frost did Caldwell return to work in the main house.[5]

From the time they could walk, Pixie and Dabney were expected to behave like little adults. They were not to call their father "Dad," but instead "Erskine" or "Skinny." Baby talk was forbidden, as was crawling, shouting, or laughing too loud. Mealtimes were particularly tense affairs, especially if the day's writing had gone poorly. Once Dabney vomited at the dinner table after being forced to finish his turnips—a vegetable he detested; Caldwell insisted that his son resume eating and remain seated until the entire family had finished its meal.[6]

Caldwell beat the boys frequently—at times savagely—from the time they were very young. Sometimes they were punished for making noise, or for using language that Caldwell considered slang or "obscene." Occasionally, he used a switch they had to cut themselves. More often, he whipped the boys with a razor strop kept in the garage. One of Dabney's most enduring memories was of his father battering him and his brother with a canoe paddle. A neighboring farmer often heard cries of "No! no! no!" from his house more than a half mile away. On a visit to Greentrees one summer, Helen's sister was stunned by Caldwell's "violent, brutal," and seemingly arbitrary punishment of her nephews.[7]

For the spirited and outgoing Helen, the chief trial of life in Mount Vernon was her isolation and loneliness. She missed her graduate-school friends in Virginia and was frustrated by the laconic, poker-faced farmers who were her neighbors. Erskine's rudeness had scared off any would-be visitors, and with the two boys and the house to look after, she was trapped in an endless round of chores. Before long, the Caldwells were considered village eccentrics—not merely outsiders, but reclusive, strangely intellectual, and decidedly unsuited to life in Maine. Helen, who had summered in Mount Vernon her entire life, was an object of pity in the community, and Erskine was almost universally disliked. Behind his back, people laughed at his peculiar ambitions and wondered at a man who spent the summer inside a small cabin with all the windows closed, instead of providing for his family.[8]

When Caldwell began cutting wood to heat the large house for their first Maine winter, his neighbors did not bother to inform him that while their own woodsheds were stocked with seasoned maple and other hardwoods, the soft birch and pine he so carefully piled in the yard would be exhausted before the brutal winter was even half over. Indeed, as November approached, and the first frost hardened into determined cold, the logs began disappearing from the Caldwells' woodpile at an alarming rate. The Mount Vernon house had not been used in winter for over a hundred years, and it was almost impossible to heat. Icy air whistled through gaping cracks in the walls and floors and around the loosely fitted windows. By December, only three rooms in the entire sprawling house—the kitchen, Erskine's study, and an upstairs bedroom—were habitable without hats, mittens, and scarves. A local farmer joked, rather cruelly, that he "would rather sleep in the apple orchard on a cold winter night, than in the Caldwells' 'barn.'" When the pipes inevitably froze, all running water was cut off, and the family relied on an outdoor privy that was little more than a shack. One of the Caldwells' rare overnight guests never forgot the trauma of "the trek outside through deep snow with lantern held high to visit the outdoor convenience."[9]

The poverty that confronted the family was as dire as the unrelenting winter. In summer, the garden had provided an ample, if monotonous, yield of turnips, summer squash, and potatoes; nearby blueberry and huckleberry bushes were laden with fruit. But by December, the last of this produce, like the firewood, was dwindling faster than anticipated, and the children grew weary of the uninterrupted diet of macaroni and cheese and boiled vegetables. None of the family had sufficient winter clothing, and the house was kept in near-darkness to conserve precious kerosene. In late November, things were bad enough that even Erskine, who took such pride in his stoicism, admitted that the hardships of their new life were taking a toll. "We are buried in snow and ice," he wrote sadly to his parents. "We shall have a rather lonely Thanksgiving—not even a football game or a chicken dinner."[10]

By February, Caldwell could take no more. The temperature outside had fallen to twenty below, and he had to wear a sweater, leather jerkin, and overcoat in the study where he wrote. Seated with a blanket wrapped around his feet, he was forced to stop every few minutes to blow on his fingers while he typed. The children had been sick all winter with colds and the flu; Helen was exhausted; they were out of wood; the last of the potatoes had been taken from the cellar bin. Loading up the old car, the family began the first of what would be a yearly flight south, first to Charlottesville to see Helen's parents, then on to Wrens.

II

ON THIS FIRST TRIP, Caldwell insisted that Helen drop him off in New York City while she and the children continued on to Virginia. He was desperate for privacy—he could not write without it—and he had no patience for Helen's protestations. Over the course of their marriage, Helen came to expect her husband's sudden departures from the household. She grew accustomed to receiving his brief businesslike letters from New York or flophouses near the Portland waterfront: "Dear Helen: I got here last night and found this place after an hour or two. . . . Send my mail here to this address until further notice," read a typical card. On one occasion, Caldwell disappeared to Baltimore for two weeks and lived on lentils while writing short stories in a bare room on Charles Street. More commonly, he found tiny, five-dollar-a-week basement flats in the marginal neighborhoods of Manhattan and nearly starved himself to death to pay the weekly rent. "I've only had two meals so far," he wrote Helen from a basement room on West 75th Street. "I'm eating doughnuts, rye rolls, or chease [*sic*] pie twice a day."[11]

Even in Wrens, where Erskine would eventually catch up with Helen and the children each winter, he could only stand a few weeks in the overcrowded manse. Ira, sympathetic to his son's desire for privacy, arranged the use of a friend's fishing shack where Erskine could write undisturbed. On several occasions over the next few years, Caldwell disappeared into the isolated cabin, surviving on pork and beans and writing for as long as sixteen hours a day.[12]

Ironically, the same writing that was pulling Erskine and Helen's marriage apart was also crucial in keeping it together. Late at night when the children were asleep, they read and debated literature in front of the huge Mount Vernon fireplace. They were both aroused by the stirring sexuality of D. H. Lawrence, and during the first month in Maine, they read all of his works. While Sherwood Anderson and Theodore Dreiser continued to be favorites, they also explored the newest American fiction in the "little magazines." Together, Helen and Erskine discovered less well known authors like Morley Callaghan—an artist who, like Caldwell, favored blunt, hard-boiled prose and violent, uncompromising realism.[13]

Helen also edited everything her husband wrote. Whenever Caldwell emerged unshaven and exhausted from the lakeside cabin or a weekend in the Portland YMCA, he brought his manuscripts directly to his wife. Aside from correcting the grammatical and spelling errors that still plagued his work, Helen rewrote sentences, restructured paragraphs, and deleted entire pages. Working with a large blue pencil, she dedicated herself to improving her husband's fiction, and he trusted her judgment absolutely. When they were apart for more than a few days, Caldwell mailed his work back to Helen for her criticism. Clearly, she provided psychological as well as editorial support. "When you read it again, write me the same hour and tell me what feeling it gave you," he wrote from New York. "I am depending on you . . . to tell me if the new part is fine enough." "Without your help I couldn't do anything," he admitted on another occasion. "I never know until you tell me."[14]

Once a short story had been carefully edited and rewritten, Caldwell sent it off to one of some two dozen magazines. If it was rejected, he mailed it elsewhere. After two rebuffs, he changed the story's title and tried yet again. Only after six or seven refusals did he "retire" a story. With the help of a large chart, Caldwell kept as many as ten pieces in circulation at a time. Explaining this ruthlessly pragmatic strategy to another young writer, he wrote: "Send what you have to . . . magazines as fast as they are rejected, the idea is to keep one's stuff in motion. . . . The mathematical law of probability will work in your favor eventually." "No matter what anybody tells you," he urged, "keep it up. Anybody who bangs away at anything long enough is going to ring the bell sooner or later." But in spite of his dedicated—near-maniacal —labor and Helen's unstinting assistance, the literary partnership was still unpublished after almost two years in Maine.[15]

Part of the problem was Caldwell's inability to sustain a narrative for longer than a few pages. His "stories" were really impressions, anecdotal sketches that captured a mood but contained little or no plot. There was no room for such work in *Century* or the *Saturday Evening Post*—magazines that wanted a well-told yarn to hold their readers' attention.

More important, most editors were simply not ready for Caldwell's graphic, and often awkward, treatment of violence and sexuality. *Vanity Fair* found his work "too rough," as did the editor at *Forum* who wrote simply that "Our stories must be clean." A few years later, John Hall Wheelock, an editor at *Scribner's*, complained of the "piling on of horror upon horror and brutality upon brutality," and worried about Caldwell's "grotesque overrealism." Like Wheelock, the editor at the experimental journal *London Bookman* thought that the work went beyond realism into the realm of superfluous atrocity: "We have no weakness for sweetness and light," he assured Caldwell, "but we have a distaste for sawdust and blood."[16]

By the late fall of 1928, with the weather ominously colder with each passing day, Caldwell was forced to admit that his fiction could not support his family through a second harsh winter in Maine. Another summer of writing in the isolated guest house had yielded only a mounting pile of rejection letters, and although the elder Caldwells and Lannigans both continued to send small checks when they could, Erskine, Helen, and the two boys lived in unremitting poverty. There was rarely enough to eat in their unvarying diet; their clothes were worn and full of holes; the children were frequently sick. Caldwell faced facts: he needed to find a job.

When Carrie's mother died in November, she offered to lend her son part of the modest inheritance. But she insisted that the money should not merely provide living expenses while he worked on his fiction. Carrie wanted Erskine to start a respectable business and provide for his family. In late November, Caldwell wrote his mother to inform her that he was willing to give it a try. "We are moving to Portland . . . into a small bungalow—very small but very inexpensive. We cannot afford an apartment." With his mother's money and a loan from a Portland bank, Caldwell organized a business, and there was not a penny to spare. But if he had reluctantly agreed to curtail his writing, this first entrepreneurial venture was a predictable compromise of interests. In early 1929, the Longfellow Square Bookshop opened its doors in the heart of downtown Portland.[17]

III

YEARS LATER, CALDWELL characterized the bookstore at 668 Congress Street as something of a lark—a no-lose proposition in which he casually sold off the volumes he had accumulated in his years as a reviewer. But Erskine entered into business with high hopes and a specific ideological agenda. In "The Bogus Ones," a painfully autobiographical (and never published) novel that dealt explicitly with his stay in Portland, Caldwell vented his outrage against the owner of the city's only bookstore, who "by deciding what to sell and not sell, was the literary arbiter of the entire city." In a particularly impassioned passage, the protagonist—a struggling writer whose short stories are continually rejected by New York editors—is taken to task by the bookstore proprietor for trying to buy a novel by D. H. Lawrence:[18]

> The man came out in the aisle and looked Fritz over from his hat to his shoes and began to berate him . . . saying that the particular novel was indecent and obscene, that all novels by the author were vile and impure, and that Lawrence himself was a moral lepper [sic] who should be imprisoned for life and not be permitted to write another line. Fritz took the situation as an insult not only to Lawrence, but to himself as well. . . . He thought of going to another bookshop but he remembered hearing that there was only one in the city.[19]

Caldwell envisioned his shop as a much-needed corrective and modeled it after his beloved New Dominion Bookstore in Charlottesville. His would be a place that celebrated the most recent literary trends and offered haven and inspiration to courageous would-be artists.

Caldwell's artistic and philosophical concerns were, as they always would be, joined by lofty financial ambitions. The cache of new texts accumulated in his reviewing days did, in fact, form a part of the store's inaugural stock. But Caldwell also had a scheme by which he hoped to make a fortune. Typically, retailers received their books from the publishers at a forty-percent discount. By then selling a book at its full cover price, they earned enough margin to cover their operating costs and take in a small profit. But Caldwell sought to win the business of libraries and universities across Maine by offering them a twenty-five-percent discount, thus underselling their wholesalers. "I am going out after some business," he informed his father. "I haven't got Bowdoin College yet and that is my first goal. After that there are about a dozen libraries I'm going to work for."[20]

Like most of Caldwell's business schemes, this one was hopelessly ambitious and destined for failure. Most institutions were either loath to trust such a small and untested distributor or had well-established loyalties to their wholesalers. Before long, Caldwell learned the hard way "that New Englanders are hard as the dickens to changing [sic] their habits of buying." Even had sales been good, the fifteen-percent margin Caldwell allowed himself could not possibly cover the expenses of his store through the ups and downs of an entire business year. Only a few months after he opened, Caldwell admitted to his father that "business had hit a soft spot in the road, and it was a hard pull to get out." Fate, of course, would deal the harshest blow. The year 1929 was a particularly inauspicious time to open a retail operation.[21]

The store also suffered from Caldwell's inconsistent management. Much of the time he left both the store and the two boys entirely in Helen's charge while he worked on his fiction in the small house they had rented in nearby Cape Elizabeth. Within a few months it was clear that Helen needed help, and Caldwell hired a young woman to work in the shop. Margaret Montgomery was a recent graduate of Smith College—blond, attractive, and forthright. She and Helen hit it off, and for weeks at a time the two ran the business smoothly and efficiently. But without warning, Caldwell would rush into the store with a host of complaints, berating Helen for her "sloppy bookkeeping," or angrily instructing her in the proper way to sweep. Sometimes he lambasted Montgomery for using too much wrapping paper. If he came in when business was slow, he castigated them for reading in their spare time. "I'm not paying you to read," he warned Montgomery. "I need to make some money. . . . If a customer is just looking, sell them a book, if they want one book, sell them two." After he stormed out, leaving as suddenly as he had arrived, Helen wondered aloud to Montgomery why "all laughter stopped when he entered a room."[22]

The atmosphere in the shop worsened when Caldwell began making advances to Montgomery. He flirted brazenly with his new clerk even when Helen was there, and as the months passed, his propositions became increasingly bold. Caldwell could muster a certain quiet charm, and Montgomery, torn between her loyalty to Helen and her attraction, in spite of herself, to Caldwell, eventually succumbed.

Caldwell's behavior in this first affair became a familiar pattern in his subsequent infidelities. With Montgomery, as with all the others that followed, Caldwell made no effort to keep the liaison a secret. In fact, he felt compelled to share the explicit minutiae of his sexual adventures with his wife. On one occasion, he detailed his seduction of a schoolteacher on a ferryboat into Portland. On another, he went out of his way to be caught in the act with another woman—Helen returned from shopping to find her husband *in flagrante delicto* with a Portland woman on the Mount Vernon swimming platform.[23]

Perhaps to salvage her self-respect, Helen encouraged Montgomery to sleep with Erskine and professed a belief in "open relationships." But the frequent infidelities took a dreadful toll on the marriage and the children. Several times Helen took the boys south and lived with her parents for months at a spell while Caldwell stayed behind in Portland or Mount Vernon. On one of these visits to Charlottesville, she too had an affair. Erskine, whose own behavior was a function of deep insecurity, was devastated by Helen's tryst. In a white heat, he banged out a letter that reveals at once a stupendous capacity for hypocrisy and, in its mangled syntax and near-incoherence, his acute distress. For all his own wandering, Caldwell was desperately afraid that Helen would leave him:[24]

[I]f you are going to keep that up like you did last winter, I may as well through the whole thing overboard now. I can't do a damn thing while I know that you doing something I wouldn't want you to do. If a person can't be honest he be fair and say he's not. There are too many goddam deceitful women in the world now for me to perpetuate the lot. I'd rather not having anything to do than kind of thing. If I can't trust a person behind my back, I shall certainly balk at trusting him in front of me. Capone attributed his success, you know, to the fact that he always put double-crossers on the spot. If you want to get out, go ahead; I myself do not. If I had not loved you I wouldn't have married you. I wouldn't live with anyone else. It's either you or *nobody*. [*sic*]²⁵

I V

WHILE THE MARRIAGE and the business stumbled along in Portland, life in Maine's largest city had some distinct advantages. Chief among these was the small but vibrant artistic community that had arisen on the fringes of this bustling town of sixty thousand. Painters, writers, and musicians, many of whom had traveled north to escape the stifling, puritanical atmosphere in Boston, comprised a lively, rebellious pocket near the city's grimy waterfront. Helen met dozens of these struggling artists, who naturally stopped by the Longfellow Square shop. She had been "lost in the woods" in Mount Vernon, she used to say, and was eager to share ideas and energy with people her own age. She hosted frequent teas and poetry readings in the store's back room, some of which Caldwell grudgingly agreed to attend.²⁶

At the center of this eccentric mélange of Portland artists was Alfred Morang. Two years older than Caldwell, Morang had dropped out of school as a teenager to pursue a career as a classical violinist. After years of moderate success touring small concert halls up and down the East Coast, Morang settled in Portland with his wife, Dorothy, and became interested in modernist painting. He still taught violin to pay the rent, but he was consumed with a desire to become an American Picasso or Duchamp.

Like Caldwell, Morang felt at odds with the more conservative citizens of Portland, and he went out of his way to shock and offend them. He was one of the city's notorious characters. Striding the downtown streets, Morang was a vision of self-conscious rebellion: his long, black, unruly hair flowed over the shoulders of a billowing cape; gold rings were stacked up on his fingers; he rarely bathed, his fingernails were outrageously long, and he was usually spattered with paint from head to toe. Morang was a vocal agnostic, a dabbler in leftist politics, and a formidable pontificator on any subject. Like Caldwell's college friend Andrew Murphy, the diminutive but electric Morang became a flamboyant counterpoint to Caldwell's quieter and more sullen iconoclasm. The two became close friends and disappeared together for days at a time, drinking in waterfront saloons or traveling to Lewisville or Augusta to watch a boxing match.[27]

Caldwell and Helen often stopped by the Morangs' shabby, expansive studio on Baxter Street. There, as many as a dozen young scruffy painters, writers, and musicians would sit and discuss their work; the Morangs' apartment was the gathering point for the city's disaffected intellectuals—a place where high-flown talk was endlessly exchanged over bottles of cheap red wine.[28]

At first, Caldwell, or "Skinny," as his new friends called him, seemed to take pleasure in the community of aspiring artists, and he and Helen spent long nights in Morang's drafty loft. After two years alone in Mount Vernon, they enjoyed the camaraderie, and, like his peers, Caldwell could find a sour satisfaction in lamenting the small-mindedness of the literary establishment that did not appreciate him. In Morang's apartment, he had his first real exposure to left-wing politics, listening to an endless assortment of dissent that ranged from impassioned theoretical diatribes against the capitalist system to unfocused harangues against the Hoover administration. Morang held forth on the moral bankruptcy of landscape painting and portraiture; writers argued about other writers, musicians about other musicians.

But although Caldwell enjoyed the company of the regulars who congregated in Morang's apartment, he was terrified by the example of their failure. Moreover, he could not shake the suspicion that talking about art was the worst form of laziness—a tempting diversion from the actual work of perfecting a craft. In the unpublished and unsubtly titled novel "The Bogus Ones," Caldwell's autobiographical protagonist begins to slip into a quicksand of ineffectual discussion, but in a sudden revelation, escapes the fate of becoming "just another pseudo-artist":[29]

They aren't artists, they are fools passing away the time—all of them! They were even making him one. The hell with them! He looked at himself in the mirror. What a damn fool I am! I thought I was getting ahead, and I come to my senses and find that I've been doing nothing. They act like artists and look like artists—that's as far they can go. None of them has anything inside that makes an artist. . . . Artists—ha, ha, ha! Long hair and dirty hands—smocks and no underwear! . . . All of them put together don't care enough about their music, and dancing and painting to work at it more than ten minutes a day.[30]

In the spring of 1929, Caldwell was increasingly disheartened by his failure to get published. "If I could get only one piece accepted by an important magazine or publisher it would be easier to have hopes," he confessed to his father. "Just now the one thing I do need is that kind of encouragement." In "The Bogus Ones," Caldwell revealed the anguish of a young man terribly afraid of failure, yet consumed by an artistic ambition he could not relinquish. Caldwell's fears and dreams are poignantly captured in the tortured ruminations of the novel's protagonist:[31]

> Why didn't he give up his fruitless ambition to be a writer? He should know by this time that he did not have the slightest chance in the world of breaking through. He should get a good job somewhere, stick to it and save money. . . . He was almost thirty years old. Soon he would not be able to get a job whenever he wanted one. He would be too old to start all over again as he had done a dozen times before. . . .
>
> But would he? Could he ever shake off this damnable desire to create men and women on paper and make them living, breathing creatures? He was beginning to believe he could not, but he still had hope that some day he would be hurled from this damnable cycle of his and find himself a massive star hovering above the world. . . . But once more he would try . . . to break himself off the whirling circle and find himself flung high over the world.[32]

As soon as the summer weather allowed, Caldwell moved back to the Mount Vernon house and resumed his quest. Helen remained with the children in Portland to mind the struggling bookstore, and only on weekends did she bring the two boys on the seventy-mile commute to Greentrees. From Monday until Friday, Caldwell lived and wrote in almost total isolation. His only personal contact was with the mailman, whose regular delivery of rejection letters made him a familiar, if unwelcome, face.

V

ONE MIDSUMMER MORNING, the mailman delivered something different, and Caldwell would forever after recall the missive in minute detail: "The letter was foreign. The shape of it was nearer square than oblong, and it was gray, and it bore French postage stamps." An experimental English-language journal published in France called *transition* had accepted a story entitled "July" for its June 1929 issue. There would be no payment for the piece, but this first acceptance brought joyous disbelief: "Fritz read the letter a dozen times before he fully realized just what had happened," Caldwell wrote in "The Bogus Ones." "He read the letter over some more. He could repeat it from memory, but the sight of it was worth everything else in the world. . . . He was being accepted among the modern writers!" When the initial shock passed, the neighboring farmers of Mount Vernon were treated to an unusual spectacle. In an uncharacteristic moment of abandon, Caldwell ran whooping and hollering back and forth across the broad expanse of Greentrees' lawn.[33]

Caldwell's feet hardly had time to touch the ground before another acceptance letter arrived. This one came from Alfred Kreymborg, an editor of the prestigious fiction yearbook *The New American Caravan*. Kreymborg and his co-editors, Lewis Mumford and Paul Rosenfeld, were anxious to print two Caldwell pieces—a prose-poem entitled "Tracing Life with a Finger" and the short story "Midsummer Passion." Unfortunately, Caldwell's reaction to Kreymborg's letter was necessarily tempered by consternation. In his constant remailing and retitling of manuscripts, an almost inevitable mix-up had occurred. The *New American Caravan* and *transition* had accepted identical stories for publication; "Midsummer Passion" was, in fact, a retitled version of "July." Luckily, the editors at both journals graciously excused the gaffe, and the *Caravan* agreed to print a different story.[34]

Given a choice, Caldwell would surely have dropped his submission to the slightly esoteric *transition* for publication in the *Caravan*. Inclusion in this renowned yearbook was a passport into the highest circles of the American literary fraternity. Editors of every fiction journal in the nation, critics, academics, and, of course, authors, waited anxiously for the *Caravan's* appearance, for it had a reputation for printing a broad spectrum of the best and brightest in American letters. In the October 1929 edition, Caldwell would appear alongside such diverse and established stars as e.e. cummings, Yvor Winters, Jean Toomer, Paul Green, Matthew Josephson, and John Gould Fletcher. Of the twenty-nine contributors to the volume, in fact, Caldwell was one of only three who had not published before.[35]

When the *Caravan* came out, Caldwell's two pieces did, indeed, catch the fancy of a number of prominent readers. Even the cranky John Gould Fletcher was struck by the simple, evocative grace of Caldwell's autobiographical prose-poem. "The best prose I have found," he wrote to Lewis Mumford, "was in Pearl Anderson Sherry's sketch and in

Erskine Caldwell's "Tracing Life with a Finger." F. Scott Fitzgerald read the *Caravan* in Paris, and although he thought he detected "the usual derivations from Hemingway and even [Morley] Callaghan," he felt Caldwell showed real promise.[36]

Lewis Mumford, the influential literary critic and historian who served as one of the editors at the *Caravan*, also praised Caldwell and the "strong, masculine appetite for life" he saw in his work. Mumford recognized and respected Caldwell's informed commitment to unearthing the crude realities of the rural poor. "Caldwell has a thorough familiarity with materials and modes of life that are outside the scope of the more urbane middle-class novelist," Mumford wrote soon after the pieces first appeared. "If a picture of proletarian life, without sentimentality, without false idealization or simplification is to come out of American letters," he prophesied, "it will come, as like as not, through Caldwell himself."[37]

With the recognition that came with his publication in the *Caravan*, the doors of the little magazines were suddenly wide open. Charles Henri Ford, the editor of *Blues*, not only accepted "Joe Craddock's Old Woman," a bleak vignette of a poor farmer's death, but also referred Caldwell to other editors who might appreciate his work. "Charles Henri Ford has told me about the work you are doing with a new magazine to be called *Pagany*," Caldwell wrote editor Richard Johns in Boston. In a characteristic mix of exaggeration and artless candor, he offered two stories for Johns's newly formed fiction journal. "You don't know me and neither does anybody else. I've been working for seven or eight years unsuccessfully, though several of my pieces are coming out this fall. . . . In case you should want to see anything else by me I'll be glad to send what I have that you would consider. That's about all I have to say."[38]

Johns was not put off by Caldwell's abruptness—he was, in fact, charmed by it—and accepted a story immediately. Caldwell was not averse to politicking—often awkwardly—on his own behalf, and his letters to editors hovered on the edge of transparent flattery: "It [*Pagany*] is the only magazine I read with enthusiasm, and when I don't see it, I am down in the depths," he wrote Johns. "Honestly, you have passed, as far as fiction goes, every magazine printed in the English language. There are no exceptions whatever."[39]

Before long, a number of other small fiction journals that had rejected his stories in the preceding few years accepted them. Many publications had seen enough Caldwell pieces to choose ones that met their tastes; others had not, and Caldwell worked hard to direct particular stories to the editors who he thought would appreciate a specific type of work. *Hound & Horn*, a fiction journal that avoided larger social issues, received and published "The Automobile That Wouldn't Run," a comic tale of a Maine woodsman. *Nativity*, a dour left-wing organ that promised to expose "America's political and social decline," printed "Saturday Afternoon," a brutal tale of a Georgia lynching.[40]

In most cases, even though these publications professed quite different philosophies, during the very early years of the Depression they were allied by a network of editors and authors that softened political or artistic differences. Caldwell had no problem placing pieces similar in theme and style in such divergent publications as the elitist *transition*, whose manifesto declared bluntly, "Let the plain reader be damned," and in *Pagany*, a journal that advocated "simple, native expression." By 1931, Malcolm Cowley, writing in the *New Republic*, concluded that Caldwell was a fortuitous "literary child" of eight quite different "foster parents: 'The New American Caravan,' 'Blues,' 'Front,' 'Hound & Horn,' 'Nativity,' 'Pagany,' 'This Quarter,' and 'transition.' "[41]

Some critics feared that such a parentage, however diverse, would have disastrous results. T. K. Whipple, writing in response to Cowley, worried that such "occult magazines" were "insidious poison" for an instinctive, forthright author. These "purveyors of caviar," he charged, would corrupt Caldwell's integrity with pretense and abstract imagery; he hoped that this untutored genius might be "delivered from the highbrows." Whipple's agenda, of course, was political as well as artistic. Caldwell's obvious sympathy for America's downtrodden was coupled with a prose style that made him an excellent prospect for Communist intellectuals looking for writers to carry their message to the masses.[42]

Caldwell was not ready to assume such broad obligations. Even had he acknowledged a fusion of art and politics in his work—an issue still very hazily defined in his mind—his first priority, after years of trying and failing, was getting published. He would not limit his opportunities on political grounds. "I do not write for a cause like Communism,— or propaganda for Single-Tax, the Pope, more sewers, bigger Buicks, or fewer babies," he assured a worried editor in 1930. The perfect magazine, he wrote Richard Johns at *Pagany*, "shouldn't be the mouthpiece of a group or a collection of groups. It shouldn't be Catholic or Methodist, Surrealist, Republican, Single-Tax, New England, or dogmatic."[43]

But if Caldwell was as yet unwilling to take on political responsibility, Communists like Whipple need not have worried about his becoming a "highbrow" author. As his extensive correspondence with Richard

Johns reveals, Caldwell's immersion in the fiction magazines of the early 1930s only intensified his commitment to simple, direct expression and his fascination with the underside of American life. After receiving the first issue of *Pagany*, Caldwell sent a long letter to the editor praising the journal for its "intelligible" contributions. "Experiment is sometimes necessarily unintelligible, in a shell like a green walnut," he conceded, "but any man who consciously covers up his work in difficult technicalities is robbing himself and his readers." The key to leaving "a deeper and more sincere impression on the mind," Caldwell advised Johns, was to reach the "reader's emotions."[44]

Of all the contributors to *Pagany*, it was William Carlos Williams who seems to have made the "sincerest impression" on Caldwell himself. As a favor to Johns, Williams had sent the new journal the opening section of his novel-in-progress *White Mule*. The graphic description of a newborn child's first hours embodied Williams's evolving literary philosophy—an emphasis on economy of style and intense emotional impact that he termed "super-realism." Like many readers, Caldwell was taken aback by the explicit biological detail that Williams—a physician—included, but he was drawn to the lean authority of the prose and the attention to violent, often repulsive, detail. "Williams gives me an inelegant [*sic*] puke with his White Mule but he's got *something* (God knows I don't know what it is) that nobody else has ever had," Caldwell wrote Johns. Not only was *White Mule* "a hell of a sight better though than the 'sweetness and light' the monthlies turn out," but, the work would, Caldwell predicted, "place Williams at the head of writers, where he belongs." The following year, Williams returned the compliment when he and his co-editor Nathanael West revived the defunct journal *Contact* in an effort to legitimize "American super-realism" by "attempt[ing] to cut a trail through the American jungle without the use of a European compass"; they solicited a piece from Caldwell for the inaugural issue.[45]

Caldwell, like Williams, also believed that some of the best new American fiction was rooted in the regional backwaters of the country. He was disappointed when Robert McAlmon, an author he admired, diverged from the small-town, midwestern settings of his early work. "I wish he would stick to USA," Caldwell complained to Johns. "There is culture in picking potatoes and binding wheat . . . perhaps a dramatic quality west of the Pecos that nobody else can explain." Caldwell went on to bluntly summarize his own artistic relationship with (and ambivalence toward) his native South: "It's a rotten country, but people live there, therefore there must be something to write about."[46]

As the Depression deepened, more and more young writers sought to combine their art with critiques of the American political and economic system. Some, like Michael Gold, worked from a well-articulated Communist ideology; others merely voiced an intuitive concern for the nation's underdogs. In 1930, it was these gritty and realistic, but less explicitly political, "proletarian writers" whom Caldwell most admired. "God, as long as you don't grind any axes, or let some scented paper drive you off your wheels, I'm with you," he wrote Johns. Although he felt that "ninety percent of the stuff written by women [was] junk," he had high praise for the vigorous, well-crafted short stories of Janet Lewis and Margery Latimer. Their straightforward prose was "well worth reading," Caldwell wrote Johns. "They can write as well as a man."[47]

VI

ALTHOUGH CALDWELL FOCUSED on short stories during his first years in Maine, he also composed two novellas between 1927 and 1929. On his trips to New York, he brought these manuscripts to publishing houses, both large and small, and was met with a decidedly unenthusiastic response. But while his publication in the *American Caravan* did little to entice the more commercial publishers, the stories gave him instant credibility at smaller, more artistic houses. In 1929, just as the first acceptances from the "little magazines" began to trickle in, he signed contracts for his longer works. In early 1930, eleven hundred copies of his first novella, *The Bastard*, were printed by a fledgling New York City art house called Heron Press. The following year, the equally tiny Rariora Press published a second book, *Poor Fool*.[48]

Given the quality of these two apprentice works, it is remarkable that they were published at all. Both books represent an amalgam of unwieldy prose (in a number of styles), labored dialogue, disjointed organization, transparent characterization, and preposterous narrative coincidence. Gene Morgan and Blondy Niles, the respective antiheroes of *The Bastard* and *Poor Fool*, are brutal, stupid, amoral men who live by a murky code of hard-boiled machismo and animal appetites. Caldwell awkwardly chronicles these parentless, conscienceless wanderers as they drift through the squalid fringes of American life committing a range of violent acts and sexual abuses that are as random as they are horrific.[49]

The failure of both novels can be attributed, in part, to Caldwell's unfamiliarity with his material. *Poor Fool*, the story of hard-luck boxer Blondy Niles, is set in the bars, flophouses, and brothels of the Portland waterfront. While Caldwell's explorations of the city's grimy underside gave him a cursory knowledge of this terrain, he was still an outsider to this northern, urban world. Similarly, while the most compelling scenes in *The Bastard* are set in a small Southern town—prefiguring the sensitive, powerful imagery he would eventually master—Caldwell begins and ends the novel with obscure evocations of a northern city. Most important, in the murderous, uneducated Niles and Morgan, Caldwell set out to create characters whom he in some sense admired but did not really know.

Without intimate insight into the characters or their environments, *The Bastard* and *Poor Fool* quickly devolve into hackneyed clichés and two-dimensional characterizations. In his days as a reviewer, Caldwell read countless books in the so-called hard-boiled school of American fiction made famous by writers like Raymond Chandler and Dashiell Hammett. This genre of violent urban crime stories offered a vehicle for Caldwell's fascination with human cruelty and was a perfect testing ground for the dispassionate, laconic tone that would later become his trademark. Both *The Bastard* and *Poor Fool* are informed by 1920s detective fiction, but the following passage from *The Bastard* makes it abundantly clear that Caldwell's application was so unskilled as to approach parody:

"Listen, kid," Gene began huskily, "I'm nothing but a bum, and I ain't got no family, and I ain't got no money—but I swear to god I want to marry you. . . . I'm busted on you, kid, and I'll work like hell for you and keep you like a queen. I ain't much on this high-class stuff but so help me God Almighty I'll treat you like the best there is. Jesus, kid, I never thought I'd fall like this for a she, but God knows I'm busted on you. You're the swellest little kid these old lookers ever looked at. Jesus, Kid! I'm plain nuts about you."[50]

The failure of *Poor Fool* and *The Bastard* cannot be blamed solely on Caldwell's uninformed and schematic approach, or his muddled experimentation with a variety of fictional forms. Both novels are an exorcism of the author's personal demons. Most remarkable in these two works is Caldwell's blatantly sadistic and dehumanizing portrayal of women in general, and mothers in particular. "When Gene Morgan had last heard of the woman who was his mother," *The Bastard* begins, she "was young no more, nor was she now beautiful as she once had been. But she was experienced in the ways of men and of money, and she possessed a formula for increasing the fee which men were always eager to pay for her knowledge." Caldwell constructs Gene's mother not merely as a whore in a traveling carnival's "hoochie-coochie tent" but as a would-be murderess who resented her little boy's existence from the very start:[52]

> She cursed all the time she was in labor and the roustabouts had to tie her to a trunk to keep her from killing the baby with a stakemallet [*sic*]. She would have killed him sooner or later if an old negro woman had not offered to raise the child.[53]

When Gene sees his mother next, she is working a Philadelphia burlesque theater obviously based on the Trocadero. He callously buys her services without revealing his identity, but, after committing this most heinous act of degradation (and incest), he feels rejected when "she did not know he was her son, or if she did know . . . didn't care."[54]

Known by a variety of names—"Norfolk Gertie–Denver Sal–Rose of Scranton–Big Butt Bessie"—Gene's mother is finally depicted by Caldwell as a vicious grotesque of an aging, degenerate prostitute. A passing stranger recounts her exploits with a "stunted pony" in a "pit about three feet deep and ten feet wide" and recalls that she "had twenty-seven men the Sunday night before." The man shows Gene a crudely styled photograph (much like the ones Caldwell himself had carried in high school) of a woman grossly disfigured by her random encounters with violent men—a mother whose reproductive system, he suggests, has been surgically excised and whose nurturing breast has been viciously defiled:

> There were the red and blue scars sinking into her hips, the long knife-slash furrowing her belly like a drain ditch cut through the Louisiana swamp, and there too was her left breast nippleless where some drunken horseman had severed it with his teeth.[55]

While Gene's mother is singled out for the greatest hostility and degradation, the following dialogue roughly summarizes Caldwell's treatment of the other female characters in *The Bastard*—a cast of prostitutes, lonely wives, and schoolgirls, all similarly ruled and debased by their slavish pursuit of sexual pleasure:

—"Have you got a wife?"

—"Sure, I've got a wife—only I don't call her that."

—"What do you call her?"

—"Call her lots of things, most of them dirty."

—"Is she dirty?"

—"She's rotten—stinks. She's a two-timer."

—"I got a clean one."

—"The hell you have!"

—"The cleanest one there is."

—"Say, there ain't no clean ones. All of 'em are dirty."[56]

In *Poor Fool*, the protagonist reflects Caldwell's misogyny intensified by his fear of women's castrating power. Blondy Niles is trapped in a house by a monstrous, horribly obese woman, aptly named Mrs. Boxx. Mrs. Boxx, who runs an abortion clinic designed to kill both mother and child, is also consumed by her desire to emasculate virile and independent men. For reasons Caldwell does not explain, she is determined to castrate Blondy Niles with a pair of sharp "snapping" shears, and this once-mighty boxer is powerless to resist her:[57]

> The power the woman held over him was stupendous. She could make him do anything she wanted him to do. If she had decided she was going to make him submit to that kind of operation she could make him want to have it performed. Blondy suddenly realized the extent of her domination over him and he was frightened. But he could do nothing about it.[58]

When Blondy is rescued at the eleventh hour by Mrs. Boxx's daughter, he is torn between his fearful loathing of this grotesque maternal figure and his guilt for deserting her: "What's it about your mother that she can make me do anything she wants? . . . I want to try and forget that God damn witch. I know she's your mother, but I can't help hating her like hell."[59]

Caldwell surely could not admit—or recognize—that *The Bastard* and *Poor Fool* expressed his own deep hostilities. An irrepressible, uninhibited writer like Thomas Wolfe could consciously transform his personal angst into lyrical art, but such a process was impossible for Caldwell. A fundamentally private and repressed person, his catharsis manifested itself in ferocious outbursts of rage and frustration that could only distort the texture of a narrative. He was well aware, however, that his grotesque, pornographic work would not please his parents. "The Bastard is coming out November 1st," he wrote a friend in Atlanta. "I still have time to stay away from a certain Presbyterian manse or parsonage."[60]

Caldwell could not hide, however, from the upright citizens of Portland, who reacted to *The Bastard* with outrage and disgust. No sooner had Caldwell set up his window display in the Longfellow Square Bookshop than the book was seized by the Cumberland County District Attorney, who deemed it "obscene, lewd, and immoral." Helen was threatened with arrest for selling the book; Caldwell was ordered to ship the remaining copies back to his publishers in New York or face prosecution in a Portland court for the dissemination of pornography. Without money to hire a lawyer, he had no choice but to accede, and his first published novel—a work he described to his friend Carl Van Vechten as the "book which is like a first love to me"—was removed from local circulation.[61]

Searching for some means to vent his fury and frustration, Caldwell printed and distributed a handbill he entitled simply "In Defense of Myself." In it, Caldwell made a passionate, if hyperbolic, case for his First Amendment rights. The banning of *The Bastard*, Caldwell seethed, was a "comedy of justice" orchestrated by the county attorney, who was representative of the puritanical fanaticism of the entire state of Maine. Caldwell was incensed that he had been denied "trial before a judge, or before a jury" and, in fact, had never been informed precisely which "word, or words" had been deemed "impure and obscene." The cumulative injustices done him and his work when it was "hustled out of town," left him, he concluded bluntly, with "an involuntary urge to vomit profusely."[62]

Part of Caldwell's rage stemmed from the feeling that the rejection of his book was also an indictment of the characters themselves. Even though *The Bastard* betrayed Caldwell's ambivalence about his underdog heroes, "In Defense of Myself" articulated the passionate loyalty he felt toward them as well. Many left-leaning writers of the 1930s claimed a kinship with the working class by exaggerating their impoverished childhood, or their year's labor in a coal mine. But Caldwell would always exhibit a degree of heartfelt identification and furious defensiveness, far beyond that of the slumming intellectual. If exaggerated and self-important, the closing paragraph of "In Defense of Myself" was far more eloquent than the novel it sought to vindicate:

I have an intense sympathy for these people. I know them and I like them. I have slept with them in jails, I have eaten with them in freight

cars, I have sung with them in convict camps, I have helped the women
give birth to the living. I have helped the men cover up the dead. . . .
I could not stand silent while the story of their lives was branded obscene, lewd and immoral; because this story belongs to them even more
than it does to me. I shall defend them until the last word is choked
from me. I cannot disown them.

The manifesto also articulated a link between poverty and sexual
degeneracy, one that remained muddled in *The Bastard*, but would become a central theme in Caldwell's later work. In Caldwell's view,
sexual activity was the only form of diversion available to the poor
man, for "he plays no golf, he has no club; the churches were not built
for him. He cannot read." And if his women characters were promiscuous, Caldwell argues that they too have been conditioned by their
indigence:

She works in a cotton mill. She is a lint-head. She earns eleven dollars
and fifteen cents from one Saturday to the next. . . . Neither her mother,
nor her father, if either she has, can afford to give her money to buy a
pair of stockings and a hat. Somebody else can. A man. . . . She gets
along the best way she can. We all do.

It was soon after the banning of *The Bastard* and the release of "In
Defense of Myself" that Caldwell churned out "The Bogus Ones,"
which took up the manifesto's themes in crude fictional form. In the
story, Ted, a brilliant but misunderstood painter, is forced to destroy
his greatest work when it is deemed "obscene" by polite Portland society and its corrupt district attorney. This "little Mussolini" and his
gang of "rabid neo-puritans, who think he or she is God himself," are
representative, Ted protests, of the entire New England region. "New
England isn't mountains and lakes and seashores," he proclaims, "but
an inhibited and repressed old wretch who is a witch if there ever was
one." The impassioned hyperbole mounts throughout the book, until
by the end, Caldwell has abandoned any effort to form a coherent
narrative and presents instead long-winded diatribes against intolerance
and the injustices done an artistic temperament:

Going around with your nose cocked for obscenity! Obscenity! You are
obscene! You are obscene New Englanders looking for something dirty
all the time. God didn't make you—God wouldn't have anything to do
with a bunch of dirty guttersnipes always looking for something dirty

. . . God wouldn't have anything to do with you—the devil made all of you![63]

Fortunately, *The Bastard*, *Poor Fool*, and "The Bogus Ones" seemed to provide a significant catharsis for Caldwell. Never again would his own emotional unrest so dominate (and distort) his fictional work. But the banning of *The Bastard* would always haunt him: not only had his first published novel been swept from the shelves, but Heron Press refused to pay him. "The bastards who published it vamoosed with all the copies and the money—a clever combination of Hungarian and Jew," Caldwell raged to Milton Abernethy, an editor at *Contempo*. The loss of the book and its revenue only reinforced Caldwell's deep-seated, lifelong fear that circumstances and individuals would conspire to cheat him of what was rightfully his. In years to come his obsessive attention to publication contracts and his excessive demands for guarantees would drive a number of excellent agents and editors to distraction. But Caldwell, a man always terrified of betrayal, would dedicate immense amounts of time and energy to ensure that he was never burned again.[64]

VI

PORTLAND'S ECONOMY RELIED on the distribution of consumer goods to the rest of New England, and by early 1930 the Depression had hurt commerce dramatically. With less disposable income at hand, those citizens of Portland who were not studiously avoiding Caldwell's shop on moral grounds could ill afford to spend their money on books. Trade in the store, never heavy, slowed to a trickle, and the Caldwells were once again reduced to living off the small handouts their parents sent from their own diminished budgets. Acceptances from small journals, however encouraging, did little to alleviate their poverty. *Pagany*, one of the higher-paying journals, offered twelve dollars per story, and Caldwell surely recognized that even a successful year of placing his work would net less than one hundred dollars.

When Caldwell received a note from Maxwell Perkins, the premier fiction editor at Charles Scribner's Sons, it was an answer to a prayer. "I was much impressed by your stories in the *Caravan*," Perkins wrote, "and I thought it possible you might be willing to send something to *Scribner's Magazine*." Perkins, as Caldwell well knew, had already made literary stars of F. Scott Fitzgerald and Ernest Hemingway, two writers the editor had discovered among the hundreds of authors writing in the "little magazines." Fitzgerald, in fact, who served as an unofficial talent scout for Perkins throughout their long friendship, had first directed the editor to Caldwell's work.[65]

Within a day, Caldwell had a humorous New England sketch on the way to New York. Perkins responded with characteristic promptness and tact. "The story impressed me in the way it was told, and in the quality of authenticity about it," Perkins began, but "in the superficial sense, which we do have to consider, it would seem too much an anecdote." Would Caldwell "give us another chance?" Gathering a handful of manuscripts, he and Helen took the next bus to New York. In the lobby of the building that housed the famed Scribner's offices, Caldwell informed Helen that she was too shabbily dressed to meet the great editor and should wait while he went upstairs alone. Once in the office, however, he was overcome with nervousness and left the satchel of short stories with Perkins' secretary before rushing from the room.[66]

Back in Maine, Caldwell waited by the telephone. He was desperate to call the editor in New York, but "the truth was," Caldwell admitted to the editor later, he was so certain of rejection that he "did not have the courage." But when the phone finally rang, the news was good. Perkins had decided to accept "The Mating of Marjory," a subtle evocation of a lonely New England woman and her search for a husband; a few days later, he accepted a second story, "A Very Late Spring," a farcical tale of a Maine farmer's infidelity and his forgiving wife.

Years later, Caldwell, always anxious to present himself as a backwoods *noïf*, professed to have mistakenly interpreted Perkins's offer of "three-fifty" as three dollars and fifty cents, when in fact he was to be paid the unimaginable sum of three hundred fifty dollars. But while his letters to Perkins reveal a glaring lack of social sophistication and painfully sycophantic flattery, Caldwell was in fact far from naïve about financial matters. Both Perkins and his colleague John Hall Wheelock immediately recognized the young author as a "cool cat" who "played it close to the vest." Caldwell well knew that acceptance into *Scribner's* placed him in the elite company of professional writers who could support a family by their craft.[67]

For the next few months, Caldwell bombarded Perkins with story after story, entering into what he later described as "a three month orgy of writing, the intensity of which I had never before reached and which I never equalled afterward." One by one the submissions were rejected. But while the editor might gently suggest that a story "did not quite come over," or that the two already accepted created "enough of an impression," he unfailingly encouraged Caldwell to continue his work. When he was informed of the trouble Caldwell was having with the suppression of *The Bastard*, Perkins, sensing Caldwell's frustration, responded with a long letter of sympathy. "The trouble is, few people . . . seem to understand that the *motive* for fiction, or the impulse from which it arises, is a serious one," Perkins counseled. "They think of fiction as having no value excepting that of amusing and passing the time;—and so it is impossible for them to understand why it could not just as well be pleasant and pretty." Caldwell should not be discouraged, Perkins wrote. "I should think you are bound to come out well in the end."[68]

Perkins's confidence in Caldwell was confirmed in May 1930 when the editor informed him that Scribner's was "ready to publish in 1931 a book composed of what stories you then have ready." Caldwell's deluge of submissions had convinced Perkins that in the next six months his new author could write a few new stories to round out a collection of his previously published work. Caldwell, of course, was overjoyed. Not only would the $300 advance help pay the year's expenses, but in Perkins he felt he had found a person whom he could trust. As was often the case, his enthusiasm moved him to rather overblown rhetoric. "When I saw you last winter I believe I told you how little faith in publishers I had," Caldwell wrote. "But now I know there is one that I shall always respect. The glib promises, the unkept promises, the deceiving lies—these must be confined to a class different from you. You see, I love the truth with all the passion that makes me hate a lie."[69]

With new stories to write and old ones to revise, Caldwell had no patience for the bookstore or his family. He worked irritably in the small lakeside cabin, and when the weather turned colder, he informed Helen that he would not be making the yearly pilgrimage south. Nor would he agree to remain in Portland. The $650 Caldwell received from Scribner's for two short stories and the advance for the book gave him an economic freedom he had never experienced, and he was determined to spend a few months as far from family and business concerns as he could get.

Packing his portable typewriter and cigarette rolling machine, he traveled first to New York to consult with Perkins, then boarded a Greyhound bus for California—a place he had dreamed of visiting his entire life. Caldwell found that he wrote well in the cramped seats of buses; with the endless stretches of countryside racing by, he labored constantly at the typewriter balanced precariously on his knees. He arrived in California, settled into a dingy Hollywood hotel at 1151 North Wilcox Avenue, and although he did not "think much of the ungodly country—mostly desert, no trees, no grass—nothing but sand and sage brush," he worked hard to finish work on the collection he had decided to call *American Earth*.[70]

The first section of the collection, "Farthest East," consists of stories that lampooned Caldwell's Mount Vernon neighbors. In "The Corduroy Pants," "Ten-thousand Blueberry Crates," and "John the Indian and George Hopkins," for instance, New Englanders outdo each other in their comic stinginess and thick-headedness. By detailing even the most absurd behavior in a completely detached and impassive voice, Caldwell achieved a wry, comically ironic tone that ranged from patient amusement to vicious satire. Perkins and his colleague John Hall Wheelock, however, both thought that the characters' oblivious hijinks in these pieces went overboard and urged Caldwell to tone them down. "Of course it is told in a light humorous way," Wheelock wrote of "Var-Monters," but "even so it is hard for the reader to accept intuitively the fact of a bride and groom, the former with no clothes on, married through the crack of a door by a minister who cannot see them—all because of the obstinacy, without any sufficient reason, of the groom." If Caldwell could "discipline yourself rigorously," Wheelock encouraged, "your natural talent for understanding of people and the inner relation of events [could] make you one of the really outstanding writers of our time." The editors hoped Caldwell would write more New England stories like "The Mating of Marjory," in which he sought to capture the pathos of lonely people isolated by their cold, impersonal culture in a still more frigid climate. Here Caldwell's stark prose underscored the hopelessness of his characters and the barren worlds in which they lived.[71]

Perkins recognized, sooner than Caldwell himself did, that these New England stories could not compare to those set in the author's native South. "I can't make up my mind over the problem of which place I should dig in, and concentrate," Caldwell fretted, but Perkins had no such uncertainty: "After reflection I am inclined to favor those of the South," he wrote to Caldwell. These works "went deeper than those of the North" and dealt "with fresher material." Unlike the New England stories, largely told in the detached third-person, many of those set in the South were told in the first person and conveyed a much more intimate and convincing sensibility. The best of this work concerned the emergence of adolescent sexuality, as in "The Strawberry

Season," a delicately written piece that drew the praise of such notable writers and critics as Ezra Pound and Malcolm Cowley when it first appeared in *Pagany*. Here, and in stories like it, Caldwell evoked the innocent stirrings and curiosities of a young boy by drawing him into sexually loaded situations that went just beyond his capacity to understand them.[72]

Although he treated such boyhood themes with charm and subtlety, in other stories Caldwell attacked the South's rural poverty and racial brutality with sledgehammer blows. In "Saturday Afternoon," the relentless, enervating heat of a midsummer day underscores the latent violence in a small Southern town. The story centers on the butcher Tom Denny, a horrifying grotesque who literally wallows in the blood of his work. When business is slow, he stretches out "with the cool hump of rump steak under his head," and dozes off in good-natured oblivion to the flies that feast at the corners of his mouth. Denny personifies the slack-witted, amoral cretins of a tiny Southern town who participate in a lynching as thoughtlessly as they would in an offhand conversation. The very casualness with which the townspeople carry out this atrocity, graphically but dispassionately recounted, underscores its deep roots in their small-town culture. The murder of Will Maxie, a prosperous black farmer who, in his upright morality and studious work ethic, is everything the white townspeople are not, indicates not only the festering resentment of a black man's success, but a mere diversion from a long "Saturday Afternoon." As Maxie's corpse sags from the tree, the weight of the bullets pumped into his body pulling his feet close to the ground, a little white boy celebrates the number of cold Coca-Colas he has managed to sell to the assembled crowd.[73]

Both Perkins and Wheelock were repelled by the unremitting, carefully detailed violence in this and several other stories, and the absolutely dispassionate tone Caldwell maintained throughout. "I think you perhaps bear down too heavily on the beastliness and brutality," Perkins advised. "The impression of such exaggeration," the editor worried, undermined credibility and "verged on burlesque." Wheelock shared Perkins's concern that an "over-emphasis on horror" and the "repetition and bearing a bit too hard on the point . . . mar the very impression you are seeking."[74]

Caldwell pleasantly acceded to the editors' criticisms of his more humorous pieces, but he stubbornly resisted suggestions to soften these more tragic stories. His resolve represented more than an undeniable fascination with "beastliness and brutality" or the joy he surely took in shocking his audience. In his barbarous grotesques, Caldwell ad-

dressed his long-standing frustration with romantic portrayals of Southern life; his characters were more horrible, more vivid, and thus more
memorable than real life. Similarly, Caldwell's use of repeated words
or phrases incanted mindlessly by his characters—a technique that
struck both Perkins and Wheelock as heavy-handed—was a calculated
fictional device. In "Saturday Afternoon," for instance, the deadening
repetition of simple phrases accentuates the almost hypnotic pursuit of
the lynching ritual, and mirrors the inexorable buildup of violence on
a hot summer day.[75]

The third section of *American Earth* was made up of the prose poem
Caldwell called *The Sacrilege of Alan Kent*. This autobiographical hodgepodge of images, narrative paragraphs, and single-line epiphanies was
unlike anything Caldwell had ever written before or would ever write
again. Both Perkins and Wheelock were moved by these terse, angst-
ridden musings and by the poetic prose, which was both graceful and
poised. Both editors, however, were adamant that Caldwell omit passages in the work that they felt were either too sexually explicit or, in
other cases, blatantly sacrilegious. The threat of book-banning was, as
Caldwell knew, a very real danger in 1930, and while Wheelock acknowledged that "such an episode may sometimes slightly increase the
sale of a book at the time," a Scribner's author did "not want to get
the reputation of being distinguished by this sort of thing." Such exposure would only hurt Caldwell's reputation and his career, Wheelock
explained, for although there was "a very small group of people capable
of understanding the honest, artistic motives behind difficult passages,
the general reader cannot and will not understand."[76]

Perkins and Wheelock did indeed have Caldwell's best interests at
heart, and it was characteristic of these two men to resist the tempta-
tion of short-term profits in favor of safeguarding their author's artistic
reputation. Moreover, both editors were protective of their firm's image as a respectable, highbrow publishing house, and they knew that
the firm's head, Arthur Scribner, was watching them carefully. At the
urging of Perkins and Wheelock, Caldwell deleted the most offensive
sections, for he had grown to trust these editors a great deal. "I appreciate the things you said," he informed Wheelock, "and after forty-
eight hours, I am fully convinced that my wisest course is down your
stream."[77]

VII

PERKINS WARNED CALDWELL that amidst the worsening depression, *American Earth* "wasn't a book for which one could expect a very large immediate sale." Both editor and author hoped, however, that the book would attract serious critical attention, and, as the first reviews trickled in during the summer of 1931, there was cause for celebration. "A significant thing about the reception of *American Earth*," William Soskin of the *New York Post* noted, "was the way the lions and the lambs gather together on its behalf," and indeed, the book engaged a wide range of political and artistic taste. Almost every major critic agreed that Caldwell's spare, unvarnished prose was powerful and effective; many thought it reminiscent of Hemingway or Sherwood Anderson.[78]

But if its style struck many reviewers the same way, the content of *American Earth* engendered no such consensus. Horace Gregory of the *New York Herald-Tribune* was one of a number of critics who did not recognize any larger social message in Caldwell's work but praised the author's natural talents as a storyteller. *American Earth* recalled for Gregory "the fantastic yarns told in smoking bars and at fishing camp firesides." A good-natured humorist, Caldwell was the literary heir of Mark Twain, and his characters were "the legitimate grandchildren of Tom Sawyer and Huckleberry Finn." Gorham Munson of the *New York Sun* echoed this view of Caldwell as a droll Southern storyteller. "Mr. Caldwell is a country store raconteur," Munson wrote. "Directly, simply, he relates the scandals of the neighborhood, and with a sunny humor, spins some tall yarns."[79]

Other critics, focusing their remarks on *The Sacrilege of Alan Kent*, also ignored the larger social message in the book, but regarded Caldwell as more a sophisticated modernist than a rawboned humorist. Writing in the *New Republic*, Malcolm Cowley applauded the "violent poetry, simple, romantic, arbitrary and effective," and declared that Caldwell had captured a "mood unique in American prose." While certain passages were so "trite and sentimental" as to move Cowley "to personal fury against the author," much of the section was so innovative that the critic could "forgive any amount of faulty writing." Vincent Wall, of the *Saturday Review of Literature*, saw Caldwell as a bold and innovative artist, who in *Sacrilege* had taken "the stream of consciousness technique . . . almost to the limits of its possibilities."[80]

The most passionate responses to *American Earth* came from various quarters of the literary left. T. K. Whipple recognized that while Caldwell "pretends to be the unsophisticated raconteur," his simplicity was misleading. The "picturesque, proletarian, peasant American . . . has appeared in literature but little," Whipple lamented. Yet because Caldwell "had a varied and extensive career among the people of whom—and like whom—he speaks" and wrote in their "own chosen mode of expression," he was an excellent spokesman for their culture. Like many other reviewers on the Left, Whipple was most impressed by Caldwell's proletarian "credentials" as presented on the book jacket—a biographical sketch that began: "Erskine Caldwell has been a farm-hand, a cottonseed oil mill and lumber mill worker in Georgia, a cotton picker and hack driver in Tennessee."[81]

Norman Macleod of the *New Masses* also recognized Caldwell's intimacy with the American working class, but found the author sorely lacking in political sophistication. Moreover, stories like "Saturday Afternoon" suggested that Caldwell believed the unrelenting heat of an August day to be as much to blame as economic exploitation for the South's racial violence. Such causality, a potent element in much of Caldwell's writing, could not be addressed by Communist solutions based on economic redistribution. "The proletarians of which Caldwell writes," Macleod complained, were "as unaware of Russia as any South Sea Islander." These "un-class-conscious proletarians in the sticks of America," Macleod went on, while "always on the verge of starvation, . . . [had] no perception of the class struggle or the economic forces operative in the United States which produce the conditions responsible for their poverty."[82]

Still more problematic for Macleod than Caldwell's political naïveté or crude determinism was the author's degrading portrayal of the nation's proletariat. For leftists like Macleod, it was difficult to reconcile their vision of an enlightened, dignified working class with the "primitives" of Caldwell's fiction—characters as much concerned with their next sexual adventure as with the upkeep of their farm. Macleod was only the first of many left-wing intellectuals to be frustrated by the strange mix of nobility and degeneracy that would typify most of Caldwell's characters. Not understanding that the author's own confused feelings of sympathy and disdain for his subjects would always guarantee such treatment, Macleod looked forward to a day when Caldwell would use his talents more effectively: "When he goes deeper into the life of the working class of the South, he promises to become one of our most significant writers in America," Macleod predicted. "We need writers like Caldwell. He should go left."[83]

On the whole, Caldwell had reason to be pleased with the reviews of *American Earth*, although he grew annoyed with the incessant comparisons to Hemingway and Anderson. There were also, to be sure, some outright dismissals, but these came chiefly from the sort of critic whom Caldwell took pleasure in incensing—reviewers like the one for the *Pittsburgh Courier* who were offended by "too much lingerie and not enough literature." Of the handful of Southern papers reviewing the book, only the *New Orleans Picayune* reacted defensively, demanding to "see affidavits to support one of the stories dealing with a lynching." Frank Daniel, Caldwell's old friend at the *Atlanta Journal*, wrote a favorable review, as did the critic at the *Macon Telegraph* who beseeched Georgians to "immediately stake out their claim to Erskine Caldwell . . . a genuine and excellent talent." The icing on the cake came from Edward J. O'Brien, the influential editor who each year assembled a yearbook of the nation's best short fiction. Three selections from *American Earth* made O'Brien's "roll of honor" and one, "Dorothy," was included in the prestigious *Best Short Stories of 1931*.[84]

Caldwell's confidence, growing steadily since his first acceptance in *transition*, soared to grandiose heights. He had "made up his mind to win a Guggenheim," he informed his parents. "I was determined to get in the *Caravan*, and after that *Scribner*. . . . I've got this far, and I've got to go further." Although he feared that the prize committee was "a bunch of professors," and he "was not in that kind of a boat," he was certain that "if the work [was] good enough it should carry me over." With the Guggenheim safely in the bag, his course of action would be clear: "After that," he told his parents, "I'm working for the Pulitzer Prize, so help me God!"[85]

By the end of 1931, Caldwell had begun a novel that would carry him closer to his dreams than he could possibly have imagined.

Chapter Five

TOBACCO ROAD

Before leaving for California, Caldwell had stopped in New York to straighten out publication details for *American Earth*. This time, he mustered the necessary courage to meet Maxwell Perkins face-to-face, and like most writers who entered Perkins's sparsely furnished office, he was struck by the editor's dignified, unpretentious charm. Sensitive to Caldwell's conspicuous awkwardness, Perkins filled the silence with reminiscences of his own boyhood in northern New England. As he moved stiffly about the office, occasionally looking down at the traffic below, Perkins gently turned his attention to Caldwell's literary future. Although Scribner's had rejected "The Bogus Ones," *Poor Fool*, and *The Bastard*, he urged Caldwell to try another novel, this time focusing his creative energy on a story with a Southern setting—the part of the country his young author knew best.[1]

After a quick meal at a stand-up counter, Perkins fairly hustled Caldwell out of town. New York, according to Perkins, was filled with pitfalls for young authors: high-flown talk, cocktail parties, and lavish publishers' lunches only took the edge off a writer's art and squandered his creative energy. "Flustered and confused," writers in New York "fluttered to their doom like moths to a flame," Perkins warned, and he urged Caldwell to steer clear. "Don't talk to anybody about a novel you are thinking of writing," he advised. "Talk, and you dissipate your enthusiasm and much of the spirit will disappear from what you write later."[2]

Although Caldwell lamented the skimpiness of the meal Perkins paid for—"cream cheese and nut sandwiches and two glasses of milk"—he shared his editor's convictions. New York, Caldwell wrote Richard Johns, was nothing but a "nest of bogus bohemians," and he was eager to get to the West Coast, where he could concentrate on his work.[3]

Once in California, Caldwell dedicated every moment he could spare from *American Earth* to the opening chapter of his new book. But while he felt that it was "inevitable that the novel was to be concerned with the tenant farmers and sharecropping families [he] had known in East Georgia," he found it almost impossible to get started. Try as he might—sitting hour after hour in front of his typewriter—he could not make narrative sense of his most powerful memories. And as the days passed unproductively, he grew increasingly frustrated. In the next two months, Caldwell wrote fifty pages, but he failed to find a coherent theme or workable plot. To his friend Frank Daniel, who inquired about the book, he responded testily, "Can't tell you the name of the novel because it isn't written yet." To Wheelock, who, along with Perkins, was anxious to know of his progress, he offered hollow boasts that the new novel was better than *American Earth*. More truthfully, he admitted, "at least in my mind it is better."[4]

After two months of frustrated effort, Caldwell made plans to leave the West Coast. He was unshakably committed to writing about the impoverished farmers of eastern Georgia, but it was painfully clear that he could not do so in California. With Christmas only a week away, Caldwell packed his bag and typewriter and settled his bill at the Warwick Hotel. By that afternoon, the landscape was once again speeding past through a bus window. This time, however, Caldwell was heading east, back to his hometown of Wrens, Georgia.

I

LIKE MOST SMALL Southern towns in 1930, Wrens was suffering terribly from the effects of the Depression. Cotton prices—always the barometer of the community's prosperity—had not rebounded after the frightening downward plunge that had begun nearly a decade earlier. Those farmers who had managed to hold on to their farms operated at a tremendous loss, and much of the best land had been turned over to subsistence crops like turnips and corn. Many smaller landowners, unable to pay their mortgages, lost their farms to the Augusta banks; these families often slid into marginal tenancy—exchanging their labor for seed, fertilizer, and a small share of a nearly valueless crop. Children left for Augusta or Atlanta seeking mill work in an impossibly tight job market. In Wrens, the cottonseed oil mill where Caldwell had worked in high school fired most of its day laborers; many merchants in town closed their doors; the lumber mill was quiet. The wealthiest citizens of Wrens tightened their belts; the middle class hung grimly on. The poorest townspeople—men and women who had once subsisted on handouts and odd jobs—now lived on the very edge of survival. And out in the countryside, on the fringes of Jefferson and Burke counties, those families that had barely maintained a primitive existence in 1920—the families that Caldwell had once visited with his father and the local doctor—were slowly starving to death.[5]

Helen and the boys met Erskine at the Caldwell home on his return from California, but he had little time for his family. Every spare moment was spent with his father. Ira had not slackened in his dedication to the impoverished farmers scattered along the sandy foothills near Wrens, and during the Christmas season he spent most of his time delivering food and medical supplies in his old Ford. Caldwell now joined his father on these missions, hoping to find inspiration and focus for his work.

December in Wrens was cold and damp, and the cotton fields were brown and stunted. As the two men drove along the sandy dirt roads, they confronted a grim and dispiriting landscape. Ten years later, Caldwell still shuddered at the memories of those bleak December afternoons and the horrors he found "in my own country, among clay ridges and barren sand hills, a land I had known all my life." Day after day he traveled with Ira into the countryside, becoming increasingly disheartened by what he saw inside the "shabby and dilapidated, two-room shacks with sagging joists and roofs"—appalled by the specter of "hungry people wrapped in rags, going nowhere and coming from nowhere, searching for food and warmth."[6]

In the past, Ira had simply lectured Erskine as they drove along the deeply rutted country roads, but now father and son talked more as equals. The two men's lives and interests had overlapped to a remarkable degree, and they closely identified with each other. After Erskine's acceptance into the University of Virginia, Ira had followed his son to Charlottesville and enrolled in a sociology class at the school's summer session. When Erskine decided to leave school, Ira helped his son land a reporting job at the *Atlanta Journal*; almost simultaneously, Ira launched his own career as a journalist, writing a weekly column for the nearby *Augusta Chronicle*. Ira fully supported his son's decision to become a writer, and parishioners grew tired of hearing their preacher boast of "his boy with the six-cylinder mind." Soon after *American Earth* was accepted at Scribner's, Ira wrote to Maxwell Perkins proposing to write a book of his own. "I am the father of Erskine Caldwell," Ira wrote Perkins proudly, "whose book [*American Earth*] you are about to publish." Might Scribner's be interested in another Caldwell's work?[7]

Erskine, in turn, paid particular attention to Ira's career as a small-town newspaperman which blossomed during the hard years of his own Mount Vernon apprenticeship. Beginning in 1926, Ira wrote a weekly column entitled "Let's Think This Over," which earned him local notoriety as a hard-hitting muckraker concerned with a wide range of issues. He railed against the "degrading influence of lynching," shocking and angering readers with his grisly account of "several thousand people watching a cringing, screaming man as his blood was licked up by the raging fire." He infuriated construction contractors with an impassioned polemic against the use of chain-gang labor, recounting the tragedy of an "eighteen year old boy with shackles on his legs who died of sunstroke on a Greenwood County chain gang." Lumber mill operators fumed when he lamented the "brutal depletion of Georgia Pines"; local bankers and seed merchants were not pleased with his criticism of high interest rates and his assertion that "the world would have been better off had the deferred payment plan never been invented."[8]

Ira's first priority was the plight of impoverished tenant farmers and sharecroppers. In graphic terms, he chronicled the problems of malnutrition, pellagra, hookworm, illiteracy, and incest which afflicted a class of people that his congregants disdainfully referred to as "po' white trash." The text of Ira's articles often doubled as his Sunday sermon, and indeed the pieces rang with the rhetoric of an impassioned preacher. Ira yearned to shake his complacent congregation and readership from their social apathy, and he did all he could to provoke them. At times, he was viciously sarcastic, mourning the "tragic" plight of landlords who were too busy barbecuing to help their starving tenants. Most often, he tried to capture the pathos of rural poverty in bluntly poetic terms that might awaken the conscience of his audience. "Out on the highway I sought solace from the hell that man has made," Ira wrote sadly, "but I saw strong-armed men flogging lean mules that were poorly harnessed and insufficiently fed. . . . My eyes wanted to see green trees and clinging vines, but instead they saw tumbled-down fences and ramshackle houses."[9]

In 1929, Ira engineered a social experiment based on his belief that a change in environment was the first step towards the uplift of the poorest members of society. He brought a family of destitute farmers from the edge of Burke county into Wrens. The clan was marked by illiteracy, incest, feeblemindedness, hookworm—all the attendant tragedies of grinding rural poverty. The children were put in school, the father was given a job at the local mill, new clothes and regular meals were donated by the community, and the whole family was encouraged to attend services at the A.R.P. church.[10]

The experiment was a depressing failure. Within a few months, the children had stopped attending classes, the father had quit his job, and the family had quietly moved back to their dilapidated hovel and barren farm. Most painful for Ira, his wards bitterly resented his efforts, blaming him for interfering with their lives. By the time Erskine returned to Wrens, Ira's chronic exasperation was slipping into hopelessness. Although he continued to work tirelessly to provide the basic necessities of life to the rural poor, he despaired at finding real solutions for their destitution. Families like the one he had attempted to save, were, as Ira often put it, "like toads in a post hole"—unwilling or unable to improve their lot.[11]

The ultimate expression of Ira's hardening pessimism came in a five-part article he wrote for the New York magazine *Eugenics: A Journal of Race Betterment*. In the piece, entitled "The Bunglers," the last installment of which was published just a few months before Erskine's return to Wrens, Ira presented the case study of the family he had tried so hard to rehabilitate. This investigation into the ancestry and lifestyle of the so-called Bunglers now justified a hesitant call for the sterilization of the nation's most destitute citizens. While effective birth control was limiting the number of the country's elite, Ira argued, the very poor—people he saw all around him—seemed to be multiplying at an alarming rate. Writing in the slightly hysterical tone that typified much of the eugenicist literature of the Depression, Ira warned of a "great army of delinquents" and the "swelling tide of inefficiency" that threatened the nation. "Ignorance, stolid stupidity, thick necks and low brows," Ira cautioned, "are the greatest perils of a republic."[12]

One of Ira's greatest frustrations was his inability to reach the "Bunglers" through his church. He had never been able to diminish their susceptibility to what he termed "bogus religionists" and "fakirs"—traveling preachers, revival exhorters, fire-and-brimstone evangelists—religious mercenaries who exploited poverty, hopelessness, and naïveté with promises of eternal salvation and graphic warnings of hell and damnation. Ira had no patience for "emotional" religion or any of its physical manifestations and saw "muscular dancing," "speaking in tongues," and "coming through" as "the earmarks of heathenism." Mustering the most extreme example he could to vent his disgust, Ira described a congregation completely bewitched by the "facility and smugness with which a preacher handled a large rattlesnake." "To the

unthinking Bunglers and their like," Ira wrote in dismay, "the fact that
he was able to stand in the pulpit and allow the snake to bite his
unsleeved arm was all the credentials needed . . . [and] was evidence
that he was under the immediate protection of God."[13]

But unlike many other contributors to *Eugenics* who blamed the
poor's misfortunes and mistakes on inferior genes, Ira clung to his belief
that immediate environment—as well as heredity—contributed to the
"dwarfed intelligences and lean souls that one sees in these humble
people." His thinking, more sympathetic than coldly analytical, was
roughly Lamarckian; he argued that the pathologies brought on by
abject poverty were passed from parent to child. "They have the failure
habit," Ira wrote. "It is a habit that is more than a century old. It is
handed down from father to son with crushing regularity." For years,
Ira had implored farmers to diversify their crops, and he had been
repeatedly discouraged by the "amazing lack of economic foresight"
that kept them planting cotton even after the soil was depleted of vital
minerals and crop prices had reached all-time lows. Yet Ira refused to
indict these people—as his wife sometimes did—for their stubbornness.
To queasy would-be reformers who were offended by the "fearful
stench of poverty"—the horrifying lack of sanitation, the incest, the
goiters and disease—Ira observed that "people can be so poor that they
cannot be decent."[14]

Ira's disappointment with the "Bunglers" never matched his frustration with the people of Wrens—many of whom were part of his
congregation—who would not acknowledge their impoverished fellow
citizens "hidden away in the hinterland of the country districts." The
rural poor of Burke and Jefferson county "were as politely disavowed
as the inhumanities of the slave system had once been," Ira wrote,
searching for the most provocative metaphor he could find. "No matter
how crass a civilization becomes there are certain tragedies it does not
parade before the public."[15]

> It is not at all pleasing to our vanity; it is not in keeping with our smug
> complacency to have these people paraded before the world . . . they
> make us think, and thinking is painful to people who are satisfied with
> themselves. Hence we keep the Bunglers and their type hidden away in
> the cellar of subconsciousness. . . . They are the drab, dull kind of
> tragedies . . . in which people can find no thrill. There is nothing
> magnificent in ignorant stupidity. There is no glamour about these trag-
> edies that are dragging themselves across the stage of life in Georgia
> today.[16]

The "Bunglers" article represents the most cogent expression of a hunger to expose and enlighten, to shock and confront, that had consumed Ira for over thirty years. He communicated this passion to Erskine over the course of his lifetime. And in the early months of 1931, as Erskine struggled with his novel, Ira passed the lesson along with greater urgency than ever before.

II

IN THE DREARY Christmas season of 1931, Erskine labored unsuccessfully to write in his parents' crowded house. Distracted not only by his family but by well-meaning neighbors who stopped by, Caldwell finally packed a few belongings and moved to a boarding house in Augusta. He renewed his work in isolation, but that seemed to make little difference. The pile of discarded, crumpled pages continued to mount on the floor by his feet. Caldwell moved yet again. Ira picked him up and, after provisioning Erskine with coffee and a few bare essentials, dropped him off at the abandoned fishing shack he had used in visits past—fifteen miles north of Augusta on the South Carolina side of the Savannah River.[17]

It was no use. In California, Caldwell had felt too removed from his material; now he was paralyzed by proximity. The tragedy of the people he sought to describe seemed overwhelming, and he was daunted by the responsibility of capturing the pathos of their lives. For the rest of his life, Caldwell recalled his agonizing impotence that winter—a time when "the austere meanings of written words" seemed grossly inadequate to capture "the mental images and emotional perceptions of humanity"—when "nothing put down on paper succeeded in conveying the full meaning of poverty and hopelessness and degradation."[18]

Most important, Caldwell was surely concerned that his fiction would disappoint his father. The rural poor of eastern Georgia had been Ira's life work, both in his ministry and in his writing; this material belonged to him, and Erskine was hesitant to appropriate it. Moreover, Erskine could not possibly reconcile the violence, sexuality, and coarse humor so central to his own creative vocabulary with Ira's strictly upright Presbyterian sensibilities. In order to make Ira's cause his own, Erskine would have no choice but to offend him, and the rebellious son could not affront his mentor face-to-face. With mingled feelings of liberation and betrayal, Erskine made plans to leave the South. In mid-

January, despite Maxwell Perkins's warnings, he caught a bus north for New York City.

As Wrens and Ira disappeared behind him, the title of the novel— something he had struggled to find—came to him. He would call it "The Old Tobacco Road." Before the Civil War, the term had referred to the sandy ridge-top thoroughfares that planters made by rolling heavy tobacco casks east from their Georgia farms to the Savannah River. Along these elevated ridges, wealthy landowners built estates to escape the heat and mosquitoes of their lowland plantations. By the 1920s tobacco was long gone, and so too were the grand estates. "To-bacco Road" came to hold a less savory reputation as a meandering strip of the poorest, most desolate lands in eastern Georgia. The barren farms scattered along the once-imposing highway were now owned by absentee landlords who had long since left them in neglect. It was along the "Tobacco Road" of Jefferson and Burke counties that Ira had found his "Bunglers" in greatest numbers.[19]

In a tiny bedroom on the fourth floor of a condemned brownstone on Fifty-first Street between Fifth and Sixth avenues, Caldwell sat at a small table and destroyed everything he had written in California and Georgia. He bought a fresh ribbon for his typewriter for fifty cents, spent a quarter on a box of water-stained yellow paper, and a nickel for two pencils. Far from his subject, far from his father, Caldwell began to write anew. Each morning he rose late, breakfasted on bread, cheese, and tap water, then worked steadily into the late afternoon. As the sun began to set, he left the apartment for a short walk, usually stopping at a lunch counter on Sixth Avenue for a bowl of lentil soup. Returning to his room by six, he worked late into the night, smoking cigarette after cigarette. Never before had he written so confidently, so steadily. "The story I wanted to tell was so vivid in my mind," Caldwell recalled years later, that he began each morning without a glance at the pre-vious day's labor. He was totally absorbed in his work and saw no one, making one exception in three months to attend a cocktail party held by the *American Caravan* publishers, where the chief attraction was the "well-provisioned buffet table."[20]

Through February and March of 1931, the typed yellow sheets piled up with comforting regularity. By early April, *Tobacco Road*—over two hundred carefully typed pages—was complete. "Me, I have finished the book I've been doing these long, sometimes hungry, most of the time painful months," he wrote to Richard Johns in the first letter he had sent to anyone since January. "I got to page 'the end' by working for

22 days, from 12 PM to 12 AM. That last month was hard, but the other nine were unbearable."[21]

Characteristically, Caldwell exaggerated. He had actually begun the project six months before in California, and completed the actual writing in only three months. But the process had been a grueling one and, understandably, it seemed much longer in hindsight. Caldwell was exhausted but proud, and he closed his letter to Johns with an unusually frank appraisal of his work: "I feel confident that Scribner's will want to publish it. It's not sensational, experimental, nor important; it is just human. Maybe it's not so good; but I have a sympathy for the people in it, and I have become attached to it. Enough."[22]

That sympathy, and the speed with which Caldwell wrote, are not surprising, for by the time Caldwell reached Manhattan, he had settled on more than a title for his novel. *Tobacco Road*, like Ira's piece in *Eugenics*, was the story of a single family devastated by abject rural poverty. The Lester family of *Tobacco Road* was, in fact, largely based on the very family Ira had vainly tried to integrate into the Wrens community—the very same people Ira had described in his articles only months before. Although he switched their first names, Dude and Jeeter of the Bungler clan became Jeeter and Dude Lester, the patriarch and son of *Tobacco Road*. Ellie Mae Lester, Jeeter's daughter, was based on another member of the family, but Caldwell gave her the appearance of a young girl Ira had helped in Atoka. Like Ellie Mae Lester of the novel, this daughter of a poor west Tennessee cotton farmer was disfigured by a severe harelip that her family could not afford to have corrected. Sister Bessie, the forty-year-old traveling evangelist who marries the sixteen-year-old Dude Lester in *Tobacco Road*, was an almost literal replication of Sister Bessie Rauss, a well-known character in Wrens whom Ira had described in the Bunglers piece as a woeful example of a "bogus religionist." Like the novel's Sister Bessie, Bessie Rauss spent her inheritance on a car that her young husband soon destroyed. Those members of the Lester clan who were not thinly disguised caricatures of the Bungler family were modeled after another destitute family Ira knew well and had described in his article. The Lesters' disintegrating hovel, rubble-filled yard, and barren farm were virtually identical to the Bunglers', complete with the rusting carcass of an automobile.[23]

Tobacco Road's similarity to Ira's Bunglers article, however, went far deeper than a shared cast of characters. Erskine had adopted much of his father's thinking as well. The Lesters are licentious, stubborn, painfully stupid, and amoral, and there seems no hope for their improvement. But in the novel, as in Ira's article, grinding poverty is always at the forefront, reminding the reader of the source of such incorrigible depravity. Jeeter Lester clings pitifully to the dream that one day he will again raise a crop of cotton, although it has been years since he has done so. "Captain John," the absentee landlord, has long since stopped advancing credit, and without seed or fertilizer Jeeter's plans can never advance beyond ineffectual scheming. In his absolute inability to modify his routine, to think or act constructively to change his lot, Jeeter is an archetypical "Bungler." Like the head of the real-life clan in Wrens, he has been reduced to living like "a toad in a post hole."

Like Ira, Erskine could not help but admire the tenacity with which the Lesters clung to the very land that had betrayed them. In spite of his thievery and infidelity, Jeeter never loses a certain unassailable dignity, for his spirit—his exuberance—is never broken. Jeeter's strength lies in his animated unwillingness to recognize his ineffectuality. Jeeter's wife, Ada, and his mother are also heroic figures, who achieve their dignity through stoic—literally speechless—endurance and resignation. They have been reduced to an almost-animal state, completely beaten down by years of toil, malnutrition, and childbearing. Yet they are as honorable as they are pathetic—redeemed by a grim, habitual determination. At one level then, *Tobacco Road* is the poignant story of a family's courage and character and a powerful indictment of the welfare and land policies that allowed such poverty to exist.

Tobacco Road was also a continuation of a long tradition of Southern writing that found humor in the lives of the region's poor. As far back as the 1729 work *The Secret History of the Dividing Line* by William Byrd of Westover, Southern authors had made gentle sport of the foibles, uncleanliness, amorality, and stupidity of "po' white trash." Antebellum Southern artists like George Washington Harris and Augustus Baldwin Longstreet had perfected this genre of comic degeneracy, depicting a world where ridiculous, chronic stupidity devolves into slapstick buffoonery. In many respects, Jeeter Lester is reminiscent of Harris's shiftless, conscienceless protagonist Sut Lovingood.[24]

But in *Tobacco Road*, Caldwell moved beyond the burlesque that characterized the fundamentally sympathetic ridicule of the "Southwest humorists," and it is easy to see why he had trouble getting started with his father so close at hand. Ira's exasperation and pessimism occasionally provoked him to reluctant humor at the expense of the "Bunglers," but Erskine's depiction of the Lesters and Sister Bessie betrays a hostile impatience that borders on repugnance. While the Lesters are certainly victims, in many respects they are also unspeakably loathesome individuals. In one memorable scene, for instance, Dude Lester backs over his grandmother in his automobile. She is left unattended on the ground for hours, her moans of pain casually ignored by the entire family, before Jeeter throws her—still alive—into a shallow grave. By setting the Lesters' absurdly unsympathetic antics within an environment of realistically articulated suffering, Caldwell ensures that their intractable stupidity is never laughable. One cannot fully enjoy Jeeter's bumbling, farcical efforts to steal his son-in-law's turnips, or chuckle forgivingly as he selfishly gobbles them up. Caldwell has already made clear beyond a shadow of a doubt that Jeeter and his family are starving to death.[25]

The unforgiving denigration of Southern culture that informs *Tobacco Road* had been central to Caldwell's thinking since boyhood, and as early as 1926, his "Georgia Cracker" piece revealed a virulent antagonism towards his home state. But Caldwell may well have found artistic validation for such sentiments in the work of other young Southern writers who were publishing at approximately the same time—writers who shared his disaffection from their native region and whose groundbreaking novels would soon be recognized as part of the Southern Literary Renascence. As an avid reader of all of Scribner's publications, Caldwell was acquainted with *Look Homeward, Angel*, Thomas Wolfe's damning dissection of life in Asheville, North Carolina, published the previous year. A few years later, Caldwell recalled his admiration for Wolfe's bold and aggressive assault on the "moonlight and magnolias" school of Southern literature and declared him "one of America's great literary figures."[26]

Caldwell was more directly influenced, it seems, by the work of William Faulkner. Although he once wrote that he could "not see with a telescope" Faulkner's convoluted structure and narrative density, and resented what he called the "scare-head ballyhoo" of the author's more melodramatic novels, a few years later he saluted Faulkner as a writer who "digs stories out of life with his bare hands." A number of scenes in *Tobacco Road*—most notably Sister Bessie's comic misadventures in an Augusta whorehouse—are quite similar to episodes in Faulkner's gothic and violent *Sanctuary*, a novel published just as Caldwell arrived in New York to begin writing.[27]

While both Wolfe and Faulkner were fascinated by human sexuality and were—for their time—shockingly forthright in its depiction, Caldwell's preoccupation with carnal degeneracy dominates his text. The opening scene of *Tobacco Road* sets the tone for a novel permeated with a strange mingling of frank eroticism, burlesque-show pornography, and farcical, libidinous humor. The book begins with a long, rhythmic description of Ellie Mae, with her gruesomely deformed face, dragging herself across the Lester yard in masturbatory excitement as she prepares to seduce her brother-in-law. This union takes place—as does all the sex in the novel—heedlessly in full view of a crowd of fascinated bystanders. Sex in *Tobacco Road* is devoid of love, even healthy passion. With mingled admiration, adolescent fascination, and disgust, Caldwell describes a world where people have sex with the thoughtlessness of animals—their almost reflexive couplings serving the community, as much as the participants, as a form of entertainment.

Caldwell's description of the Lesters' volatile sexuality reflected an unquenchable prurient fascination and a deep-seated urge to offend readers who shared his mother's rigid Victorian sensibilities. Yet, like his mother, he held a patronizing vision of the Bunglers—or Lesters—as simple, intuitive people, more in touch with their biological impulses and less restrained by societal norms. Erskine, however, did not condemn the Lesters for their excesses; in point of fact, he could not help admiring, even envying them, their freedom. Most pointedly, Caldwell had long shared his father's belief in the connection between abject poverty and moral degeneracy, and he viewed the Lesters' antics as an indictment of their degraded circumstances.

Tobacco Road is a novel of violent incongruities—between sympathetic admiration for gritty farmers and vicious ridicule of their faults; between images of dignified endurance and heartless sketches of outrageous buffoonery; between calls for social reform and testimony to hopeless depravity. Such contradictions reflect Caldwell's complex ambivalence toward his subject, yet they also represent the sophisticated manipulations of a novelist in full command of his material and his artistic goals. Caldwell was well aware that the fundamental dissonances in his novel made it uncomfortable to read. By wreaking havoc on a reader's expectations, Caldwell ensured that his novel—unlike most "protest" writing of the early 1930s—would not bring facile sympathetic tears and then fade quickly from memory. "The sympathy of a reader—in my mind—is won and held by the intense reality of a story, not by its pleasure-pain," Caldwell wrote Maxwell Perkins. "I do not believe the sympathy of any reader is worth holding therefore if the winning was not at first difficult; the ease with which friends are made is the index to their short life."[28]

In early April, Caldwell checked out of his New York boarding house and headed north to Mount Vernon. Helen and the two boys had spent the previous few months in Charlottesville with the Lannigans, and Helen, who had been ill most of the winter, hoped to remain there until she felt better. Caldwell, however, was adamant that she join him in Mount Vernon. He was anxious to send the novel on to Scribner's, but would not do so without her careful editing. By mid-April, the family was reunited at Greentrees and Helen and Erskine were hard at work polishing the novel. "I hope to have my new novel in shape for you to read in about a month," he wrote Perkins. "I'll send it to you as soon as I can pull myself away from it."[29]

III

IN SPITE OF CALDWELL'S UNCERTAINTIES, there was precious little editing to do on *Tobacco Road*. While his previous novels had rambled almost incoherently, experimented with a range of styles and settings, and been distorted by Caldwell's cathartic railings, *Tobacco Road* was tightly organized and controlled. Where the northern urban toughs of *Poor Fool* spoke in absurdly unconvincing clichés, the speech of Jeeter Lester and his family rang absolutely true. Dark saloons and wet pavement in *The Bastard* seemed more fantastical than authentic, but the dusty roads and broken-down shacks of Jefferson County were vibrantly and unmistakably real. Moreover, the intensive work on the short-story format that had shaped *American Earth* helped Caldwell tighten and define his prose. Helen trimmed a bit here and there and corrected spelling and some punctuation, but the bulk of the novel remained as Caldwell had originally written it. By May 1931, after less than a month of editing, another carefully typed manuscript—this one on white paper, not water-stained yellow—was on its way to Perkins. "I have finished the novel I was working on and it was sent to Scribner's Saturday," Caldwell proudly wrote to his parents. "The title is *Tobacco Road*. That should sound familiar to you. The story is about some people not far from Augusta."[30]

Once the novel was in the mail, Caldwell began to worry that Perkins would reject it, just as he had "The Bogus Ones" and *The Bastard*. While he was still quite sure that Scribner's was "anxious to get a novel," Caldwell confessed to his parents that "I do not know if this is the one they have been waiting for." Much of Caldwell's anxiety was desperately practical, for he urgently needed money. "Right now the financial life isn't so hot; it's pretty cold," he wrote Morang. "Have finished a novel though and hope to get it accepted and an advance out of it." All the money he had received from Scribner's for *American Earth* was long since spent in California and New York, and while the collection of stories had garnered critical attention, it sold very few copies.[31]

Caldwell worked feverishly to write new short stories and begged editors for payments past due. "Could it be possible (bluntly) to send me a payment for the story in Winter no. 5," he pleaded with Richard Johns at *Pagany*. "I wouldn't ask but I'm down on the bottom and can't see anything coming my way." He resumed his old practice of circulating dozens of stories at once, and, as usual, this led to confusion and sharp exchanges with journal editors. "I have allowed my short stories to get into a mix-up," he confessed to Johns after one such blunder, "and I don't know where most of them are now." He tried again and again to place another story with the high-paying *Scribner's Magazine*, but Perkins was unreceptive to the comic New England stories Caldwell sent him. Responding to a submission entitled "A Country Full of Swedes," Perkins resorted to uncharacteristic bluntness in hopes of stemming the tide. "I think it is one of those stories you have very much overdone, so that it has become burlesque. I am therefore sending it back."[32]

While Caldwell struggled to make ends meet in the early summer of 1931, the editors at Scribner's were embroiled in an acrimonious debate over whether to publish *Tobacco Road*. The frank sexuality and explicit language horrified several older members of the firm determined to protect the hallowed Scribner's name. Perkins had faced stiff opposition to the early novels of both Fitzgerald and Hemingway for similar reasons—works that were positively prudish in comparison to Caldwell's novel.[33]

Those editors willing to ignore the overt sexuality in *Tobacco Road* could not reconcile Caldwell's dark, violent, and vicious picture of the South with the genteel and romantic myths that had characterized most Southern writing for generations. The year before, the firm had hesitated before publishing Wolfe's *Look Homeward, Angel*, a book whose condemnation of the South was subtle compared to *Tobacco Road*'s. Moreover, the Scribner's vice-president in charge of the education department was convinced that the publication of *Tobacco Road* would devastate the firm's textbook sales below the Mason-Dixon line.[34]

Scribner's strongest objection to the book, however, was that it would not sell, and by the middle of June, Perkins admitted to Caldwell that the prognosis was not good for publication. "I'll tell you plainly that I think myself it is well-nigh perfect within its limits," Perkins wrote. "The difficulties on the sales account, however, are very great, and that side of the argument has gained great force on account of the Depression." Perkins and others at the firm worried that readers, themselves hard-hit by the Depression, would have little interest in Caldwell's cheerless tale of rural deprivation.[35]

Sales were even more problematic because the Lesters were preposterously unsympathetic characters, and those readers hoping to open their hearts to noble yeomen farmers would be sorely disappointed. "The people in the book are of such a nature that although they arouse your sympathy in a curious way (the humor that pervades the whole book is magnificent), they do not interest the reader in the ways usual in a novel," Perkins wrote Caldwell; "there is nobody any reader could possibly identify himself with with any sort of pleasure." Writing to a Scribner's overseas agent the following year, Perkins stressed that while "we think that from a literary point of view [*Tobacco Road*] is quite a remarkable performance . . . it is an unpleasant story—in fact one of the most unpleasant that I can ever remember."[36]

Some members of the firm may also have begun to doubt Caldwell's trustworthiness, although Perkins and Wheelock retained faith in their young discovery. Over the previous two years, Caldwell had entangled himself in a variety of conflicting publication agreements. When Heron and Rariora published *Poor Fool* and *The Bastard*, they also sold options to Harcourt, Brace & Company for the right to publish Caldwell's future novels. In addition, Caldwell negotiated independently with Harcourt, accepting a $150 advance in exchange for first refusal rights to his future work. As Scribner's began their final consideration of *Tobacco Road*, it became clear that Harcourt had equal claims to the novel, and that Caldwell had been far from forthright in disclosing these obligations. Arthur Scribner, president of the firm, had long believed that a writer's character, as well as his work, had to be considered before he became a "Scribner author." Caldwell's awkward and embarrassing machinations did nothing to help his cause.[37]

"The novel is having a hell of a time," Caldwell mourned to Johns. "Scribner's can't make up their mind: editorially, they say it is a masterpiece and all that rot: sales department, they say they can't make a best seller out of it, probably not a good seller." While Perkins had carefully explained the reasons behind Scribner's indecision, Caldwell insisted that it was the unmitigated reality of his tale that was causing the holdup—that Scribner's, like the people of Wrens, did not want to accept that such tragedy existed. "The real trouble," Caldwell insisted, "is that it is a story of a Georgia Family (10,000 persons) who are starving of malnutrition and pellagra because the absentee landlord has stopped giving them credit for food and seed."[38]

With his hopes for publication slipping fast, Caldwell desperately wrote Perkins to express his "keen disappointment" over Scribner's waffling. Appealing to the editor's well-known soft spot for the economic plight of young writers, Caldwell suggested that his family's very survival depended on an advance for the book. Although he did not "intend to have any influence upon your ultimate decision," he pleaded his case to the editor in offended tones: "If you had said the book was rotten, it would be a different matter; but since I know what of it was written, and the trueness of its people and story, I cannot bring myself to believe that it should be thrown away unread with the published trash of yesterday." Caldwell was particularly upset that the very originality of his approach—the calculated mixture of sympathy and disdain, and his uniquely bleak vision of the South—should work to his detriment. "I should hate to be disbarred from writing," he protested, "because I had made myself aloof from the 'tricks' of the hacks."[39]

As it turned out, Caldwell's desperate pleas were unnecessary, for at the strong urging of Perkins and Wheelock, the firm reluctantly approved *Tobacco Road* even as Caldwell's letter was in the mail. "This is just to tell you that we are for *Tobacco Road*, and we shall plan to publish it in the spring of 1932," Perkins wrote. "Within your intentions and the limits set by the nature of the subject, I think the book is extraordinarily fine." But in this and subsequent letters, he cautioned Caldwell to expect little profit from his book. "Maybe the book's salability is greater than I had feared, but the trouble is, you see, we are in this frightful depression," Perkins wrote. "If it were not for that, those qualities in the story which are the ones, of course, which are important, would have been enough to make us hopeful of good results. Anyhow, we shall try to get them mighty hard."[40]

While Scribner's advanced Caldwell $300, Caldwell had to turn half the money over to Harcourt, Brace & Co. for their rightful claim to the novel. Moreover, Scribner's, fearful of the damage the book might cause to the firm's reputation and textbook sales, had already decided to market the novel with extreme caution and restraint; *Tobacco Road* was guaranteed poor sales before it ever hit the shelves.[41]

But if Caldwell could expect but little profit from *Tobacco Road*, he took comfort in Perkins's kind appraisal of the novel. "I'm so glad that we're going to have *Tobacco Road*," the editor wrote Caldwell. "The book is done *right*." Both Wheelock and Perkins felt *Tobacco Road* could go to press almost immediately, and when the small printing of fifteen hundred copies rolled off the press in early 1932, the book had changed very little from the manuscript Caldwell had begun in New York just over a year earlier.[42]

One reviewer remarked that *Tobacco Road*'s book jacket marked a "new high in fatuous pomposity," but Scribner's was taking no chances with its carefully guarded reputation. The sparsely rendered cover depicted a dignified, even noble-looking Jeeter, while the blurb solemnly announced a novel that was "most definitely, not a shocker," but a "piece of genuine literature." Caldwell's dedication page surely pleased the Scribner's editors as well, for it unintentionally added the finishing touches to their attempts to window-dress this disturbing, idiosyncratic novel. It read simply "For My Father and Mother"—a sentiment far more complicated than they could ever have known. *Tobacco Road*, of course, was a work of rebellion as well as love.

I V

THE NOVEL MADE VERY LITTLE SPLASH outside of New York. Some Southern reviewers never received a copy of *Tobacco Road*; others expressed their disdain for Caldwell's novel by simply ignoring it altogether.

To Caldwell's surprise, however, many Southern papers carried favorable, albeit somewhat defensive, reviews of *Tobacco Road*. Most ignored Caldwell's artistic achievement, however, and focused on his sociological exposé of the region's poor. While Georgia papers in particular took pains—as did the writer for the *Augusta Chronicle*—to point out that the Lesters represented only a "pitiable small percentage of backwoods people," most grudgingly admitted that Caldwell had shed light on a problem too often ignored. The writer for the *Richmond News Leader* was one of many who saw the book as an "earnest appeal, a forceful sermon, a compelling argument for diversified farming." While the reviewer for the Gastonia, North Carolina, *Gazette* found *Tobacco Road* to be "the most uncouth, repulsive novel I have chanced on in many a day," he was nonetheless carried away by its powerful social message. "*Tobacco Road*," he wrote grandly, was "one of the greatest human chronicles of its kind that has ever been written in modern America."[43]

The Southern reviewers who engaged the novel on artistic grounds recognized it as an abrupt departure from the region's genteel literary tradition. The reviewer for the *Louisville Courier Journal* rejoiced that the Lesters were "far from possessing the noble characteristics assigned by sentimental tradition to those who live close to the soil." Invariably, Caldwell's bleak Southern landscape was compared, often favorably, to those of Wolfe and Faulkner. The *Baltimore Sun* felt Caldwell had already reached the forefront of the emerging school of Southern realists. Because "the people in *Tobacco Road* never cease to be human even in their lowest states of degradation," the *Sun*'s reviewer argued, Caldwell was not, as Faulkner was, "exclusively a merchant of horror." While *Tobacco Road* lacked the massiveness of *Look Homeward, Angel* or the originality of *Sanctuary*, it was "more graceful and orderly than either." If Caldwell's talent continued to grow, he predicted, "he may yet lead the triumvirate."[44]

One notable reproach came from James Southall Wilson, writing in the *Virginia Quarterly Review*. Wilson charged Caldwell, Wolfe, Faulkner, and other younger Southern novelists with being literary prostitutes and regional traitors, selling gruesome pictures of the South for the amusement of Northern readers. "An uneasy suspicion begins to stir," Wilson wrote, that these authors "consider duly what the publishers think more readers—who are not Southern—will buy." While Wilson acknowledged in Faulkner a "surprising experimentation" and "shocking fullness of detail of naturalism," there was "nothing he could honestly find to recommend" about *Tobacco Road* "except a sort of drab sincerity of narration." His indignation moved him to rather uncharacteristic sarcasm at Caldwell's expense. "Not even if some future young man attempts to 'novelize' the entire life of the critters under a rock," Wilson scoffed, "could living in the South be presented on a lower level than here."[45]

Northern reviews were generally positive, although beyond superficial comparisons to Wolfe and Faulkner, there was little consensus on how to classify Caldwell's novel. A good many critics, particularly those on the Left, read *Tobacco Road* as a straightforward indictment of the American economic system. "Caldwell has caught with photographic accuracy the illiterate and repetitive gibberish which reveals the seedy background, the scant hopes and the ineluctable vassalage of these poor whites," intoned Edward Dahlberg in *The New Republic*. The liberal critic for the *St. Paul Dispatch* was certain that *Tobacco Road* "had the justification of telling the awful truth. . . . It is as though Mr. Caldwell took the reader by the hand, led him to the scene of these dreadful happenings, and commanded: 'Look! Listen!'" Caldwell's novel, he suggested solemnly, "should be read aloud to everyone who has ever made a glib, ignorant generalization about the high standard of life in the United States."[46]

Some leftist critics, however, were disappointed with the decidedly ignoble proletariat of *Tobacco Road*, and Caldwell's unsympathetic depiction of their lives. Jack Conroy admitted that the novel was a "document of no small importance," but compared Caldwell to a " 'bored and bilious God' unmoved by his subjects' agonies." Edwin Seaver echoed this sentiment more eloquently in a piece he wrote for the *New York Sun*. "Of what earthly use," Seaver wondered, "is it for the artist to write of the disinherited, of the insulted and injured if he does not consent to become their voice, to utter their tragedy in words of pity and of wrath; if he does not suffer himself to permeate their darkness with his light?"[47]

Conroy also shared Seaver's frustration with Caldwell's failure to propose concrete economic reforms to meet the Lesters' needs. "Mr. Caldwell," Conroy lamented, displayed none of the "social understanding which [was] the life of revolutionary prose." Caldwell, Seaver added sadly, "insists that the reader remain bound and gagged suffering the agonies of a nightmare and powerless to act. . . . having observed his characters capering and jabbering from a sufficiently objective retreat, Caldwell complacently watches them go up in smoke."[48]

Many critics commented upon Caldwell's completely dispassionate, detached recounting of the Lesters' antics, an authorial distance one reviewer compared to "a man watching an anthill." Some praised Caldwell's "literary slyness" that "forces a sense of responsibility upon the reader by seeming to take none himself." Others, however, thought him unforgivably callous. "These poor-white Borgias commit every crime on the calendar of sin," the critic for *Forum* complained, "and Mr. Caldwell recites the orgiastic litany calmly and with a serene detachment . . . not likely to be shared by most readers, who, if they take the book seriously, will probably finish it—if they do finish it— with disgust and slight retching." The reviewer for the *Philadelphia Enquirer* was slightly more forgiving: "With the gift of pity, Mr. Caldwell would be a first-rate artist."[49]

A less socially conscious critic, Horace Gregory of the *New York Herald-Tribune*, saw *Tobacco Road*—as he had *American Earth*—as the work of a basically good-natured humorist in the tradition of Mark Twain or Bret Harte. In an influential review entitled "Our American Primitives," Gregory praised Caldwell's "charming boyish personality," "inarticulate naïveté," and "ability to tell lies engagingly, exaggerating a point here and a point there, but never violating the essential truth of a character or a situation." Gregory felt that the most salient characteristic of *Tobacco Road* was the "adolescent, almost idiotic gravity of Mr. Caldwell's characters" that "produces instantaneous laughter" and "the sexual adventures . . . treated with an irreverence that verges on the robust ribaldry of a burlesque show."[50]

The most ambitious critics struggled to reconcile Caldwell's ribald humor with his social conscience. The reviewer for *The Saturday Review* recognized that *Tobacco Road* was "too ludicrous for any free pity, too pitiful for any whole laughter," but beyond concluding that the novel was "strong meat," he could offer little explanation for the strange combination. Kenneth White of *The Nation* went further. Taking issue with Gregory's notion that Caldwell was a humorist, White argued that the "false notion" of Caldwell's naïveté or humorous intent "completely obscured the original, mature approach to the incongruities existing in a people who ignore the civilization that contains them as completely as the civilization that ignores them." While the Lesters "come into contact with other ways of American life only at its more amusing points," Caldwell's goal, White argued, was not to poke fun at the Lesters, but rather to "achieve pathos which is far from sentimentality."[51]

Caldwell had a healthy disdain for all critics, but he was extremely sensitive to any and every reproach. He was particularly defensive over charges—and there were quite a few—that the book was simply "obscene." *The Portland Express* (still angry over the publication of *The Bastard* two years before) voiced the feelings of dozens of smaller newspapers when it described *Tobacco Road* as an "animal book . . . built on the oozy, slimy, dark foundations of the mud of life . . . limited to the sordid, to disintegration . . . obsessed with sex, unhealthily so." While part of Caldwell relished shocking prudish readers, he bemoaned his fate at the hands of the provincial "hinterland" critics. "There," he wrote to Morang, "is where the fools begin." Morang and Helen grew accustomed to Caldwell's pat, outraged response to such reviews. "There is nothing obscene or dirty in the book," he protested to anyone who would listen (but with his parents surely in mind), "because the people in it did not live consciously obscene lives."[52]

Perhaps the most rewarding response to *Tobacco Road* came from Perkins, the man whose literary judgment Caldwell valued most of all. "Taken all in all, it is, I think, the finest thing, artistically, that you have done," Perkins wrote, and he agreed to recommend Caldwell for a Guggenheim Fellowship on the strength of the book. "Caldwell,"

Perkins wrote to the prize committee, "has shown an understanding of American character and conditions in the country which goes beyond anyone else. And he has expressed this with absolute artistic integrity in a way which flinches from none of the facts, however unpleasant or tragic." Although Perkins acknowledged that Caldwell "had a deep natural, human sympathy with his people, whatever was their condition," the editor respected his young author's unwillingness to become an explicitly political writer in the way Seaver or Conroy would have liked. Perkins genuinely admired Caldwell's refusal to "compromise his writing . . . by any sort of an alliance."[53]

But unbeknownst to Caldwell, Perkins, like so many other sympathetic reviewers, could not comfortably reconcile the conflicting elements within *Tobacco Road*. His rambling recommendation letter betrayed his confusion. "No other writer," Perkins wrote, struggling valiantly to define Caldwell's achievement, "has found these conditions and at the same time so fully and sympathetically understood the people that the reader pities, and at times feels revulsion from them, and yet feels with them, likes them, and realizes that what is wrong with them comes from their situation." With his letter becoming increasingly lukewarm as it went along, Perkins confessed that although he felt Caldwell's future work would "be of a very high order within the limit I have tried to describe," he was nonetheless "rather perplexed as to what his development may be."[54]

V

THE PEOPLE OF WRENS responded to the book less philosophically. Before long, dozens of copies were circulating around the small community, and clusters of citizens gathered in front of the train depot, barbershop, and general store to discuss the novel in angry whispers. The church-going, God-fearing community was deeply offended by *Tobacco Road*. Many could not believe that such explicit sexuality and filthy language were allowed in print at all—offenses all the more difficult to understand when they were committed by the son of a respected local minister. In the text, Jeeter Lester habitually begins sentences with the exclamation "By God and by Jesus!," and while Caldwell had probably enjoyed this tiny blasphemy each time he wrote it, the words moved many readers to livid indignation. In nearby Augusta, a community leader initiated an angry protest against the book and very nearly succeeded in banning it from the city library.[55]

But outrage was mingled with fascination. Although the book would not grace the shelves of the Wrens High School library for another twenty years, every teenager in town knew the particularly racy pages, and they took a smirking, illicit pleasure in reading these passages aloud. Dog-eared copies of the book went hand to hand in the boys' locker room and found a hiding place under countless adolescents' mattresses. But adults read the novel as well, and, as one resident recalled, *Tobacco Road* soon became a book that parents hid from their children, and children hid from their parents. Most readers were drawn into the game of matching the characters in the book with their real-life counterparts, and the less-than-sympathetic portrayals of *Tobacco Road* only validated many people's long-standing prejudices against their county's poorest citizens.[56]

But any guilty pleasure that the people of Wrens found in the novel was overwhelmed by the belief that Caldwell had held up both his hometown and his region to national ridicule. A few years later, Caldwell would lament that "the greatest error of my life was in not appending a preface to *Tobacco Road* stating that the story did not pretend to typify the entire South." At the time, however, provoking Southerners, particularly in Wrens, was very much the point—as it had always been his father's—and provoke them he did. The police chief made it clear to anyone who would listen (and most would) that Caldwell's presence would not be tolerated inside town lines, and that he would gladly, and personally, run him out on a rail. Others informed Caldwell of their displeasure through the mail. "There is some of the damndest fan mail here you've ever seen in your life," Caldwell happily wrote Morang. "Some of it would put a couple of people in jail for the rest of their lives."[57]

Caldwell may have found devilish satisfaction in Wrens's fury, but Carrie and Ira had to live with the fallout from their son's book. While they were surely dismayed by the explicit nature of *Tobacco Road*, both maintained a brave outer face. To neighbors who dared approach her, Carrie explained that her son was only a "missionary of the truth," and she bragged to her classes at the high school that some of his prose "was the most beautiful ever written." Carrie's sisters were far less indulgent, and they made her suffer for her support of her son. They felt that Erskine had "shamed the family name," and the eldest, Sallie, peremptorily cut off all contact with both Carrie and Erskine. Neighbors silently impugned Carrie's parenting and one went so far as to write her a letter suggesting that she "give your son a good spanking first time you see him."[58]

Ira was even more outspoken in Erskine's defense. Some Wrens residents, knowing of Ira's long-standing interests and research, assumed that he had actually ghost-written *Tobacco Road*. Passing Ira on the street, one particularly enraged citizen made clear how closely he identified Ira with Erskine's work. Under his breath he seethed, "Why don't you go back to Maine?" Members of his congregation felt particularly betrayed and indignant, and their thinly masked hostility was painfully reminiscent of Ira's bitter days in Atoka. But characteristically, Ira brusquely met his critics head-on. He stubbornly continued to preach on the shame of rural poverty. To the few people with the courage to confront him directly, Ira offered the same angry response: "I can take you to the scene and show you the facts!" Even fewer took him up on this offer, and his bluntness only fanned the flames.[59]

VI

BY THE TIME *Tobacco Road* was released, Caldwell realized that his own tireless efforts to make a living from his writing were a dismal failure; he had created confusion and ill will among editors and publishers and garnered little in the way of royalties to feed his family. When he was approached by a New York literary agent named Maxim Lieber, he dared not turn him away.

A slight man with a thick mustache and nervous, blue-gray eyes behind horn-rimmed glasses, Lieber had a growing reputation as an agent specializing in the work of left-leaning artists. Himself committed to leftist causes, he represented among others, such well-known American leftists as Richard Wright, Langston Hughes, and Albert Halper. He was also thought by many to be the man responsible for placing the work of Leon Trotsky in American journals.

Lieber's politics had never interfered with a hard-nosed business sense and a ferocious commitment to making money for his clients. In fact, one-upping large New York City publishing houses for the benefit of a starving proletarian artist represented the sweetest of successes. He was a tough, ruthless negotiator who contested every percentage point for the authors in his stable.[60]

Lieber's first assignment for Caldwell was a difficult one. In the months between completing the final revisions on *Tobacco Road* and the book's release, Caldwell hastily composed a short novel he described as the story of "present-day people in the cut-over pulpwood section of West-Central Maine." Like most of Caldwell's New England work, there was little substance to the novel "Autumn Hill." Much of the material had been lifted from incomplete short-story manuscripts, and the quality of the prose was as uneven as that in *The Bastard* and *Poor Fool*. Helen, always her husband's most forthright critic, recognized the work as merely "short stories sketched into a book," and both she and Lieber urged him to shelve the project.[61]

Although he was far from confident about "Autumn Hill," Caldwell resolutely ignored their advice. He badly wanted a new manuscript to arrive at Scribner's before the old one—*Tobacco Road*—reached the presses. As he made clear to Perkins, he had formulated a strict time-table that he was determined to maintain: "I had hoped to have the manuscript finished in time for publication this fall, as I have a volume of short stories almost ready to submit. As soon as these two are disposed of, I can then begin the new novel I have in mind." Making a living had eclipsed making art, as Caldwell readily admitted. "Writing is the only source of income I have," he reminded Perkins, "and I must keep everlastingly at it."[62]

Perkins sympathized with Caldwell's economic straits but quickly saw that "Autumn Hill" was a careless, poorly realized novel and could do no good for the reputation of either the firm or Caldwell. He was also well aware of Caldwell's fragile ego, and knew that his young author's insecurity could turn quickly to a sense of betrayal. "In a good many ways it seems to me magnificent," Perkins began, stretching to find a silver lining in the dismal manuscript. "But in other ways we feel doubtful about it. . . . It seems to us though, that the book calls for a great deal more development." Perkins knew that neither he nor Wheelock could accept the novel on artistic grounds, yet he implied that good marketing sense, rather than the quality of the manuscript, caused his reservations. "We may be all wrong," he kindly suggested, "but really, the publication of two novels in a year is very unusual, and perhaps injudicious."[63]

Ignoring Perkins's advice as he had Helen's and Lieber's, Caldwell submitted a revised manuscript a month later. He badly needed money; he was also desperately in need of Perkins's approval. The days passed with excruciating slowness in the Mount Vernon house as he awaited word from New York. "I may not be able to do another story for six months," he wrote melodramatically to Johns. "I can't do anything until this new novel is satisfactorily disposed of. Scribner's have made no decision yet." He badgered his editor with letter after letter. "Is there a prospect of a word about 'Autumn Hill' in the near future?"

he wrote Perkins. "I have been on pins and needles." As the days passed into May and June, the pressure in the house became almost unbearable, and Caldwell's anxiety was increasingly mixed with anger. "Nothing new here. Watching the mail for something to turn up," he complained to Morang. "They've been holding me up too damn long."[64]

In early June 1932, Perkins finally acknowledged what had been inevitable from the start. "I've got to write you now to say that we have decided against 'Autumn Hill,' personally disappointing as it is to do." As always, Perkins was marvelously gentle and supportive. "I believed in it," he wrote sadly, "and still more in you." As he had all along, Perkins tried to salve Caldwell's feelings. "The fact is that this depression compels a scrutiny of manuscripts from the practical point of view such as never was before required," Perkins wrote, "and it is very hard when confronted by the figures to resist the practical arguments. . . . I can't tell you how sorry I am."[65]

By turning down "Autumn Hill," Scribner's technically released Caldwell from any further obligation to the firm. Almost immediately, Lieber was hard at work looking for a new publisher. Years later, when Caldwell's relationship with Lieber had deteriorated and his publication fortunes were in decline, he blamed his agent for pushing him away from Perkins and Scribner's. In actuality, Caldwell agreed with Lieber's advice to leave the firm. Caldwell blamed Scribner's for the poor sale of *American Earth* and *Tobacco Road* and nurtured an ever-growing suspicion that they were not working hard enough to market his books. Moreover, Caldwell could not bear to have "Autumn Hill" and the three months of work it represented go unrewarded. "Can't get any satisfaction out of Scribner's about the next novel," he complained to Richard Johns. "It is falling through. . . . In the meantime, no book, no money, no nothing."[66]

More than the money, Caldwell felt betrayed by Perkins, a man whom he had come to see as a surrogate father figure, an older man on whom he could depend when he was away from home. "I had come to look forward to receiving letters from him," Caldwell later wrote in an uncharacteristic admission of vulnerability. "It was the first rejection I had received in a long time, and overconfidence had left me unprepared for it." Most disturbing of all, it was Perkins who had pushed Caldwell to write "Autumn Hill" to begin with, an experience the editor thought would clear his young author's mind of the intense emotional experience of writing *Tobacco Road*. Although Perkins had guaranteed him nothing, Caldwell held his editor responsible for his wasted time. Perkins had grown used to Caldwell's complaints that he had been treated "shabbily" by other publishers before his association with Scribner's; with the rejection of "Autumn Hill," Caldwell turned his anger against Perkins himself.[67]

Only two years earlier, Perkins had convinced Scribner's to take a chance on Caldwell by publishing *American Earth* and accepting two short stories for *Scribner's Magazine*. Perkins had introduced his young author to thousands of readers and to the country's most influential critics and scholars. The generous advances Perkins provided for this early work represented the first substantial payment Caldwell had ever received for his writing and allowed him to continue on after years of discouragement. As Caldwell well knew, Perkins had been his strongest advocate in the firm and his closest confidant; Perkins, along with Wheelock, was instrumental in the publication of *Tobacco Road*.

Sadly, Caldwell's rage did not allow him to see how much his editors at Scribner's valued—even liked—him. Both Perkins and Wheelock badly wanted to keep Caldwell in their literary stable and nearly begged him to give them another chance with his next manuscript. But Caldwell was far too bitter and wounded to consider it. "I'm out at Scribners," he wrote bluntly to Gordon Lewis in Charlottesville, his sense of injury obscuring the facts. "Had some words in command that I made good use of. Now I'm looking for a new publisher. . . . Perhaps I'll be a little more careful where I lie down next time."[68]

Caldwell's angry break from Perkins, and his conviction that the editor had treated him unfairly, represented a characteristic and tragic tendency to find betrayal where there was loyalty, to see conspiracy despite overwhelming evidence to the contrary.

Chapter Six

GOD'S LITTLE ACRE

P ERKINS'S DIRE FORECASTS for the sale of *Tobacco Road* proved to be depressingly accurate, and when Caldwell took his family south in the winter of 1932, he was not seeking artistic inspiration. Wrens, he sadly admitted, "was the one place he knew they could get a square meal." This was a terribly frustrating realization. Six hard years had passed since he had given up a secure career as a journalist in Atlanta. From the very start, Caldwell measured his success as a writer on his ability to earn a living, and by this standard he was a dismal failure. As the paltry royalty checks that trickled in from Scribner's made clear, critical acclaim could not feed his family, nor could it free him—at the age of twenty-nine—from financial dependence on his parents and in-laws.[1]

To make matters worse, the Longfellow Square Bookshop in Portland finally, and inevitably, went bankrupt. The banning of *The Bastard* had earned Caldwell a certain notoriety in Portland's artistic community, but his reputation as a "writer of dirty books" kept respectable citizens out of the store. The deepening Depression was a much more serious problem, and under Caldwell's sporadic, apathetic management, the Longfellow Square shop never really had a chance. "The book shop went sky high in Portland," Caldwell lamented to his old Charlottesville friend Gordon Lewis, trying to put a brave face on a dismal situation. "Did you hear the bang? Jesus, we came out with our clothes, and several (many) hundreds hanging over our heads."[2]

Helen and the boys saw best how deeply Caldwell was hurt by his failure to support them. He made his family suffer for the shame they witnessed and, indeed, blamed them more and more for the financial burden they represented. His moods darkened; his outbursts of ferocious anger became more frequent and more difficult to predict. Although as a writer he was increasingly notorious for the explicit sexuality and bawdy humor in his work, Caldwell reacted savagely to any use of obscenity or foul language in his own house. While the characters in his fiction carried on with bacchanalian exuberance, and he himself drank heavily on occasion, Caldwell demanded puritanical restraint from his family. "If I had ever taken a drink of alcohol," Helen recalled later, "he would have killed me." Caldwell continued to beat both boys for trivial offenses, responding viciously, for instance, when the six-year-old Dabney used the word "hockey" as a euphemistic synonym for excrement.[3]

Pixie, not surprisingly, was an increasingly angry little boy, and he took out his fury on other children. In a particularly telling manifestation of behavior passed from father to son, he often played a game of demanding a penny from other children for the make-believe sale of a newspaper; if they refused to pay him what he felt was his due, he became enraged. Where Pixie lashed out, Dabney became increasingly withdrawn; even as a four-year-old, he escaped from the house into the yard whenever he could.

In the spring of 1932, the family left Wrens and headed north again. But when they reached Charlottesville, Helen and the children stayed there, while Caldwell continued on to New York and then Mount Vernon. His family, no doubt, was relieved to see him go.[4]

I

DESPERATE FOR MONEY, Caldwell continued to cast about for ways to support himself while he wrote. Although he was painfully uncomfortable in the company of other writers, he sought admission to the prestigious Yaddo writer's colony in upstate New York. But even though Wheelock wrote on his behalf, Caldwell had little chance for admission. He already had a reputation in artistic circles as a determined loner, dour and withdrawn. The program's executive director wondered whether Caldwell could "adapt himself to a group of ten or twelve persons living under one roof. . . ."[5]

Another option fell through when the Guggenheim Foundation rejected Caldwell's proposal to write a novel about life in a Southern mill town. Caldwell was not surprised, for it was well known that the foundation strongly favored grants for foreign travel. But he was predictably bitter, and, as usual, he felt betrayed: "How about asking all the Guggenheim Fellows in creative writing for the past six or seven years what they have written and published since getting the money," Caldwell complained to editor Milton Abernethy. "[Thomas] Wolfe, no book; [Katherine Anne] Porter, no book; [Jonathan] Daniels, no book; [Hart] Crane went off the deep end. What the hell? There must be something wrong, somewhere."[6]

Eventually, Caldwell stumbled into some free housing from an unexpected source. In the fall of 1930, Nathanael West had been made manager of the Sutton Hotel, a relatively plush establishment on East 56th Street. West hoped to make the Sutton a cultural mecca for struggling writers, and in the early thirties, Edmund Wilson, Dashiell Hammett, Lillian Hellman, and James T. Farrell were only a few of the critically acclaimed but impoverished writers who benefitted from his generosity. The Sutton, like most hotels in the early 1930s, was operating well below its capacity, and West assured Caldwell that lighted windows would only encourage paying customers. There had been visits to New York when Caldwell slept in the armchairs of hotel lobbies, and once in the doorway of a Tenth Street tenement. West's was a difficult offer to refuse.[7]

Caldwell and "Pep" West got along well, and Caldwell even read drafts of West's work-in-progress, *Miss Lonelyhearts*. But Caldwell was put off by the host of other writers who buzzed around the halls discussing their work, and he was distracted by the constant activity at the Sutton. Moreover, even though Caldwell often enlisted Helen to beg rent money from her mother, he felt uncomfortable taking charity from another man. The free room at the hotel became only another reminder of his failure to earn a living, and he recoiled from the knowing glances of the Sutton's cashier. "Eating bread and cheese in one of the hotel's rich carpeted rooms was more than I could continue doing," he confessed some years later. "No matter how much water I drank, the food was increasingly difficult to swallow." After only a short stay at the Sutton, he packed his battered suitcase and left for the drab but familiar confines of a barren boarding-house room on the Upper West Side.[8]

Caldwell redoubled his efforts to place short stories anywhere he could. He continued to have success with the small, experimental journals, many of which were quite selective; but Caldwell was not satisfied with artistic prestige. While they could ill afford to pay him, he pressed editors for whatever they could spare. "Have to give most of my short stuff away," he hinted broadly to his friend Gordon Lewis. "I can give them away, yes; but who wishes to buy them, would you care to buy one?" To Richard Johns, he was even more direct: "I'm hard up, rather more so than ever, and I am in need of something to get along on. Anything you can do will be a great help."[9]

He accompanied his submissions with long lamentations about his poverty and showered potential editors with obsequious praise. He also continued his practice of submitting stories to a number of journals at once and continued to find himself in awkward situations. "If you will let me have it back, I promise never to do such a thing again," he begged Johns, after yet another such mix-up. He assured the editor—who knew better—that "it was the first time, and it shall be the last."[10]

Caldwell's self-esteem hinged directly on his ability to place his stories, and every rejection, however gently worded, shook his confidence badly. "Whatever the error is, I beg you to tell me," he wrote beseechingly to Richard Johns. "Perhaps it is something I would never suspect unless I was told. . . . The thing has upset me so much . . . that I cannot write with any clarity." More typically, he masked his insecurity with a transparent nonchalance. When *Hound & Horn* rejected a piece, Caldwell remarked casually to his friend I. L. Salomon that they were "missing a wonderful opportunity to publish better stuff" and wished "they would cut out the rolling of dead bones and get down to creative work." It was sad, he noted dryly, for "the current number [is] very weak tea."[11]

Even with the help of his new agent, Maxim Lieber, the more commercial magazines, including *Scribner's*, continued to reject Caldwell's submissions with clocklike regularity. Unlike such writers as F. Scott Fitzgerald, who could churn out pleasant, catchy stories to pay the bills, Caldwell found it impossible to conform his work to popular tastes. Most of his stories continued to be far too brief for publication in a commercial magazine. While some pieces offered lovely, subtle evocations of a mood or setting, they were usually closer to sustained vignettes than to short stories. Even the featherweight New England farces that came so easily to him rarely exceeded five or six pages. By the end of 1932, in fact, Caldwell had published over thirty short stories; only a handful of them exceeded ten pages in length.

Those rare stories with a sustained plot and compelling narrative drive were, almost without exception, painful and unpleasant to read. Usually, they were brutal and tragic, with any humor compromised by dire circumstances or violent farce. Frequently, the characters' sexual antics were explicit to the point of pornography. As Perkins had often noted, when Caldwell wrote well, he "repudiated the role of entertainer"; he was, in fact, exactly the opposite of what editors of commercial publications were looking for in the dark Depression days of 1932.[12]

The failure to make a living from his short stories only intensified the frustration Caldwell felt over the poor sales of all his published work. In early 1932, he enlisted Morang's help in an ill-fated effort to take matters into his own hands. With the cooperation of the tiny Bradford Press in Portland, Caldwell and Morang printed seventy-five illustrated pamphlets of two Caldwell stories—"A Message for Genevieve" and "Mama's Little Girl"—hoping, as Caldwell put it, to "reap a little coin." Book collectors in New York were willing to buy copies of *Poor Fool* and *The Bastard*; Caldwell hoped that such dealers would be interested in a special-edition pamphlet as well.[13]

Morang was in charge of illustrating Caldwell's stories, while Richard Bradford, the owner of the press, was to take care of layout and production. From the beginning, however, there was tension between Caldwell and the others. Morang and Bradford were uncomfortable with Caldwell's willingness to use stories that he had already promised to journals in New York. But when Bradford balked at printing "Mama's Little Girl," then under consideration by William Carlos Williams and Nathanael West at *Contact*, Caldwell had little patience for his concern. "If [Bradford] won't print them," he coolly instructed Morang, "bid him good-day, sir, and walk out." Both Williams and West had been more than kind to Caldwell in the past, but Caldwell was unmoved by any feelings of loyalty: "The story is my property, no matter who prints it," he indignantly lectured Morang. "Even if Williams does print it in CONTACT, there's nothing to keep us from doing the same thing. . . . The story is my property, no matter who prints it until I sign away the rights, and that is something I've never been fool enough to do yet, and I hope never. [*sic*]"[14]

The greatest source of friction between Caldwell and the others was his inability to adhere to his own plan of allowing each partner to work independently within his own area of expertise. Caldwell was not only intoxicated by the logistical minutiae of every aspect of the project, but characteristically, he was plagued by nagging suspicions that his friends were cheating him. He deluged Bradford with detailed technical instructions on layout, printing, distribution, and marketing until the printer threatened to quit. And while Caldwell made a pretense of urging Morang to "do whatever you like," he ran roughshod over the artist's excellent aesthetic judgment. "I am enclosing the drawing I should use if I were you," he directed his friend. "It's the one without the three people. . . . Don't you think the idea of not having the drawings peopled will be well to follow? I do." The final product, not surprisingly, was poorly put together—visually lackluster and carelessly printed. Seeing the pamphlets in a New York bookstore, the publisher Bennett Cerf thought them "unimportant little stories in overpriced and unlovely editions."[15]

The pamphlet scheme, quite predictably, was a flop. The printer had warned that $1.50 was too much to charge in the depths of a depression, but Caldwell had ignored his advice. Most citizens of Portland who could afford such an indulgence had a healthy dislike for both Caldwell and Morang and steadfastly ignored the pamphlet. In New York, collectors were unimpressed, and perhaps put off, by Caldwell's transparent profit-seeking. In the first month, only six copies were sold, and Caldwell woefully admitted that "the movement of the stories is damn slow." The price was cut to seventy-five cents, then to fifty. Eventually, Caldwell was reduced to sending the pamphlets to personal friends and begging, as he put it to Richard Johns, "for anything you think it's worth."[16]

Finally, Caldwell was forced to resort to reviewing books for money, an activity he had happily given up after his stint in Atlanta. Malcolm Cowley, editor of the *New Republic*, never forgot Caldwell's desperate foray into his office in search of work as a critic. Although he had spent a great deal of time in New York by then, Caldwell invariably struck urban intellectuals as out of place in the city—raw-boned, ungainly and unrefined. "He was six feet tall, with a big square-cut head, broad shoulders and enormous hands, but with little flesh on his bones," Cowley remembered. "His orange hair was cut short and lay forward close to his scalp, so that he looked like a totem pole with a blob of orange paint on top." Cowley was amused by Caldwell's apparently genuine annoyance that people mistook him for a humorist, and his solemn vow that "he had never intended to be funny." "Indeed," Cowley recalled, echoing most people's first impression of Caldwell, "he was as sober-faced as an Indian or a back-woods farmer." Cowley admired Caldwell's work and thought it represented a genuinely unaffected proletarian art. "Caldwell," Cowley remembered thinking, "had a greater natural talent for telling stories than anyone else in his generation and they seemed to come straight from life, without memories of how someone else might have written them." Unfortunately for Caldwell, Cowley thought such priceless naïveté could only be corrupted by writing reviews, and he refused him access to what he facetiously called his "Indigent Book Reviewers Fund." He instructed Caldwell that "he shouldn't make his talk self-conscious by writing critical prose." While Cowley was more than happy to take Caldwell out to lunch, this was as far as he would go.[17]

II

AS HIS PROSPECTS for making a living from writing dimmed, Caldwell's empathy for others suffering economic misfortune seemed to grow. Evidence of dire hardship was everywhere in the first years of the 1930s. In Wrens, Caldwell was haunted by the gaunt faces of sharecroppers struggling to survive on exhausted farms. In Mount Vernon, people dug in frozen soil for potatoes that might have escaped the fall harvest. Ice-fishing on Parker Lake took on a desperate, joyless determination, and dairy farmers took up hunting in hopes of securing some meat for their families. An elderly couple, weakened by lack of food, froze to death less than a mile from the Greentrees house. On his frequent trips into New York, Caldwell was confronted by other visions of despair—growing lines of unemployed shivering in soup lines, pale, poorly clothed children begging for pennies. Outside Nathanael West's hotel, where Caldwell still stayed on occasion, beggars reached such numbers that the city declared them a public menace.[18]

Caldwell, of course, was not the first American writer to be inspired by the suffering of his fellow citizens. Stephen Crane, Upton Sinclair, Jack London, to name but a few, had found art in the forgotten, sordid underside of American culture. But Caldwell was part of an entire generation of young artists who responded to the economic disaster that dominated the national landscape—who sought, as Malcolm Cowley put it, "to measure themselves by the stature of their times." Unlike the scattered voices of Dreiser or Sinclair, Caldwell and his peers united their art with a damning, systematic critique of America's political and economic culture.[19]

In search of answers, many writers began to view Communism as a realistic solution to their nation's seemingly incorrigible economic woes. As the United States stumbled toward hopelessness, the Communist U.S.S.R. appeared galvanized by a heady utopian optimism. The common workingman, so cruelly marginalized by his circumstances in the States, was, in Russia, elevated to mythic stature as society's most critical member. While bread lines, labor violence, homelessness, and chronic despair signified a languishing and corrupt American society, Russia boasted zero unemployment and camouflaged its hardships with imagery of a heroic proletariat laboring for the greater national good. By 1932, many writers increasingly shared the stark prognosis of Arthur

Koestler. "They are the future," Koestler wrote bluntly, "we, the past."[20]

For Caldwell, the pull of Communism was all but irresistible. His father's lifetime of work on behalf of society's underdogs had always been accompanied by a critical perspective on the American capitalist system. Ira was a fearless iconoclast by nature, and his sermons and newspaper columns did not shy from outspoken attacks on the concentration of wealth in the hands of a few citizens, or the corruption of "bloated industrialists." In Atoka and then in Wrens, Ira had tried to bring tenants together to farm cooperatively, and he had filled his sermons with apocalyptic warnings to a national government that ignored the plight of its disempowered. Erskine had heard Ira call for labor unions in cotton mills, attack exploitative interest rates charged by local banks, and argue for a tenant farmers' union. Throughout his childhood, Erskine had overheard whispers that Ira was a "Red."

Well before Communism spread among America's intelligentsia in the early thirties, Caldwell's writing exhibited a primitive but unmistakable class consciousness and a commitment to the nation's underdogs. The crude verse he penned at Virginia, the papers he wrote for Atcheson Hench, and the articles he submitted to the *Atlanta Journal* all display a fierce identification with the nation's poorest citizens and a spirited, if unfocused, condemnation of capitalist exploitation. In 1927, Caldwell wrote a letter to Oswald Garrison Villard, editor of the *Nation*, condemning Mrs. Calvin Coolidge for failing to attend the funeral of a distant uncle, "a poor man, a laborer, a man who lived by the side of the railroad in a rented house." In language that foreshadowed the strident, outraged tone of the *New Masses* of the thirties, Caldwell suggested that a first lady who "disowned her uncle because he was a laborer" represented a damning symbol of national priorities.[21]

Caldwell's first three novels are also infused with a nascent, if crude, political message. In *The Bastard*, the protagonist flails ineffectually against the cruelty of corrupt labor bosses, brutal working conditions, and heartless mill owners who greedily trade his health and safety for a few extra pennies. The down-and-out boxer in *Poor Fool* is manipulated by managers in a system he can't possibly understand. As a lone fighter in the world, he is courageous and noble, but powerless. "Let me give you a little advice," he is finally told. "You ain't got a chance by yourself. Why don't you get a gang together? . . . You got to have a bunch to get anywhere." While Caldwell eschewed such transparent metaphors in *Tobacco Road*, he interrupted Jeeter Lester's ineffectual schemings with lectures on the need for cooperative farming and the evil of exploitative interest rates foisted on the poor by greedy bankers and absentee landlords.[22]

Erskine's sympathy for the working class reflected his father's teachings, but his more formal political education came from his literary associates. Like many of the artistic set in Portland, Alfred Morang was a committed and well-informed leftist. While there is no evidence that he ever persuaded Caldwell to read Marx, he did lecture him (as he did anyone) on the finer points of Communist political philosophy. In New York, Caldwell was inescapably exposed to a whole range of left-wing thought, for by 1931 almost every writer he had admired in the "little magazines" in the late twenties was moving leftward. Many were dedicated Communists.[23]

Although he was uncomfortable in social situations, Caldwell could not refuse a free meal, and on several occasions found himself at publishers' cocktail parties or buffets in the *New Republic* offices. There again, he was bombarded by a range of leftist thought by critics who found him too political or not political enough, too realistic or not realistic enough; he rarely spoke, and it is hard to tell what sank in. Clearly, he enjoyed playing the role of the ham-fisted, hard-living anti-intellectual, a persona much in vogue in leftist circles, and one that came easily with his large frame, rugged features, and slow Southern drawl. Caldwell's patently absurd claim that "he was a writer not a reader," a backwoods everyman who decried sophistication of every variety, a purely intuitive artist who alternated writing with log-cutting and potato-planting, had its roots in the decidedly self-conscious anti-intellectualism of the early thirties.

By 1932, many of the editors at the "little magazines" were left-leaning, as were many of the nation's most influential literary critics and reviewers. Caldwell cultivated relationships with anyone who could help him, and he approached both his personal and his political associations with a shrewd eye to the advancement of his career.[24] But, desperately sensitive as he always was to criticism, he also gravitated naturally toward anyone who appreciated him. In the 1930s, he was flattered by the serious attention of such major leftist critics as Malcolm Cowley and Matthew Josephson. Josephson's intellectual and rather sophisticated political approach made little sense to Caldwell, but he was easily seduced by the kind review Josephson wrote of *Tobacco Road.* "The best critical mind, in my judgment, in America today," he raved to Morang soon after the review appeared, "is Matthew

Josephson." Cowley, too, operated on a level of political complexity entirely foreign to Caldwell, but his praise of *American Earth* nevertheless drew the author deeper into Communist circles.[25]

There is no doubt, however, that Caldwell found common ground with the blunt, violent speech and prose of Mike Gold. Gold, the son of poor garment workers on the Lower East Side, had knocked around left-wing circles since dropping out of junior high school. By 1926, he was the editor-in-chief of the *New Masses*, and, as Caldwell put it, the "thunder and lightning" of that central organ of American Communism. In the September 1930 issue of the *New Masses*, Gold had outlined his *sine qua non* of true revolutionary prose, a genre he called "proletarian realism." "Every poem, every novel and drama, must have a social theme, or it is merely confectionery," Gold announced. Looking, as Daniel Aaron later put it, for a "Shakespeare in overalls," Gold sought an authentic, primitive art form as uncorrupted and vital as the coal miners and steel workers who would produce it. "Let the bourgeois writers tell us about their spiritual drunkards and super-refined Parisian emigres," Gold sneered. "We must write about our own mudpuddle." Direct, angry literature, written by workers, of workers and for workers, would, Gold argued, generate the "revolutionary elan to sweep this mess out of the world forever."[26]

No other American leftist of the time was as committed or influential as Gold in the recruitment of artists to the Communist cause, and after the publication of *American Earth*, he did his best to bring Caldwell into the fold. While he shared the reservations held by other Communist critics over the grotesque buffoonery of Caldwell's characters, he recognized a great opportunity as well. Although Caldwell rarely admitted that he came from highly educated parents and had attended university three different times, it nonetheless paid off in his work. For unlike so many of the workingmen and -women Gold recruited for the pages of the *New Masses*, Caldwell offered more than real-life experience as a laborer: he wrote beautiful, compelling prose.

Gold was also drawn to Caldwell's particular familiarity with the Southern poor. In the early thirties, American Communists became increasingly interested in the Southern working class. Delegations of prominent writers visited striking coal mines and cotton mills and brought back horrified accounts of subhuman working conditions and a simple, proud yeomanry oppressed by ruthless millowners. Communist authors churned out novels glorifying the strike of mill workers in Gastonia, North Carolina, and when New York radicals traveled South to cover the arrest of nine black teenagers accused of raping a

white woman in Alabama (in what came to be known as the "Scottsboro Boys case"), the plight of Southern blacks became a *cause célèbre*
in the left-wing press.[27]

But unlike these well-intentioned voyeurs, Caldwell, as he affirmed
again and again, "was a Southerner by birth, a Southerner by inheritance, a Southerner by residence." And unlike Wolfe and Faulkner, the
two other most prominent Southern writers of the day, Caldwell focused almost exclusively on the poorest members of Southern society
and wrote in the simple, unvarnished idiom associated with "proletarian" fiction. Moreover, Caldwell's work dealt with the region's agricultural poor, a field of potential revolutionaries virtually untouched by
the many novels and poems that focused on the urban proletariat in
the South's cotton mills or coal mines.[28]

Many Communist intellectuals read *American Earth* and *Tobacco Road*
as the work of a sympathetic authority. By 1932, Caldwell's work had
already gone a long way toward establishing the image of the South
in northern liberal circles as a land of wasted yeomanry reduced to
hapless peonage by corrupt landowners; a place where honorable, virtuous Negroes were lynched at the slightest provocation with the
smirking complicity of a potbellied white sheriff. If Gold and some of
his colleagues at the *New Masses* were not wholly satisfied with the
books' political content, they took much of *American Earth* and *Tobacco
Road* as gospel truth.[29]

"Spent a lot of time with Mike Gold in N.Y.," Caldwell wrote
proudly to Morang soon after the release of *American Earth* in the summer of 1931. "He's a damn fine man. He doesn't think so much of my
Communism, though, and he devoted most of our conversation to a
harangue." Much of Gold's "harangue" was directed towards Caldwell's political apathy, and he urged his young writer to get more
involved. New York in 1932 was alive with Communist rallies, bookshop debates, political dance groups and theater, films, and mass
meetings—the city was, a bewildered Orrick Johns wrote, "as full of
dates as festas in Italy." With Gold's encouragement, Caldwell became
a sporadic participant at these events. He attended, for instance, a debate sponsored by the *New Masses* entitled bluntly "Capitalism vs. Communism." Inside the stuffy Mecca Auditorium between Sixth and
Seventh avenues, Caldwell joined hundreds of others to hear a debate
between Hamilton Fish, a ranking Republican congressman, and crowd-
favorite Scott Nearing, a Communist economist and author of the
anticapitalist tract *Must We Starve?*[30]

The 1932 presidential election was a litmus test for many leftist intellectuals, and Caldwell did not let Mike Gold down. He was among fifty-two artists who published an "open letter" in support of the Communist Party ticket of William Foster and James Ford for president and vice-president of the United States. Denouncing both the Republicans and the Democrats as "hopelessly corrupt," Caldwell and his fellow authors presented capitalism as a doomed system on the verge of collapse—"a house rotting away; the roof leaks and rafters are crumbling." A month later, Caldwell was part of the group that organized the League of Professional Writers for Foster and Ford, and he helped put together *Culture and Crisis*, the organization's manifesto:

> Very well, we strike hands with our true comrades. We claim our own and we reject the disorder, the lunacy spawned by grabbers, advertisers, traders, speculators, salesmen, the much-adulated, immensely stupid and irresponsible "business men." We claim the right to live and function. . . . We have acted. As responsible intellectual workers we have aligned ourselves with the frankly revolutionary Communist Party. . . . we think that you too should support the Communist Party.[31]

Caldwell's burgeoning political commitment was reflected in his literary tastes as well, and increasingly he judged novels by their revolutionary content. "What do you think of Dahlberg's new book [*From Flushing to Calvary*]: I've just finished reading it for the NEW MASSES," Caldwell wrote excitedly to Morang. "It struck me like a ton of bricks." Caldwell's review, entitled "Ripe For Revolution," barely touched on the questionable artistic merit of Dahlberg's rambling and overblown novel. After lambasting unfavorable reviewers as capitalist tools "filing a column or two of reading matter next to advertisements," Caldwell broke into a sustained homage to the "kind of story of which revolutionary literature is made." Sounding very much like Gold himself, Caldwell ripped into the "unhealthy, squalid, painful environment imposed upon America by the barons of coal and steel, wheat and cotton" and announced the need for Communism to "furnish . . . direction and leadership out of the slough of capitalism." Slipping into the melodramatic corporeal imagery favored by Communists of the day, Caldwell wrote that the time had come "for the gut-rotting disorganization of unplanned society to be thrown bag-and-baggage overboard:"[32]

> All this stench of Bensonhurst will continue to seep into the nostrils of men until our system of life is changed. Only a complete reorganization can erase the mean streets, the packing-box flats, the hamburger-and-

coffee meals, the body-crushing existence of four-fifths of America. . . .
Our cause lies there.[33]

Caldwell's intellectual debt to Gold and other Communists at the
New Masses was also evident in his Guggenheim proposal, writtenjust
after the acceptance of *Tobacco Road* at Scribner's. Wary of offending
the conservative prize committee, Caldwell carefully avoided the word
"Communism" in the application, but given the content of his essay,
this seems a wasted precaution. "My aim is to write a full-length novel
of proletarian life in the South," he began. "My sympathies lie with
the millions who do not know what to do. . . . Shall they continue a
precarious existence, living from hand to mouth, always in debt, uneducated, and solemnly waiting for a 'better day'?" He proposed to
"write the novel which would at least lay open the sore which is
spreading the germs to every man, woman, and child" and "point out
the direction the masses must take in order to keep from falling below the deplorable standard of living the Negro has already become
heir to."[34]

Like his father, Erskine was most comfortable discussing the problems of society in hyperbolic generalities. While he had campaigned for
Foster and Ford, he showed only superficial interest in political philosophy or the contentious debates over ideology and social strategy that
raged within the American Left. And like his father, Erskine took a
more emotional than intellectual approach—directed more toward ex-
posing society's hidden ills than in offering diagnoses for their redress.
When he finally sat down to begin his "proletarian novel of the South,"
he would adhere to no formula; the influence of Michael Gold and
other American Communists would be mingled with his own very
personal sensibility.

III

WHILE WAITING ANXIOUSLY for word from Scribner's about
"Autumn Hill," Caldwell had dashed off scattered notes to himself
about the novel he had outlined in his Guggenheim proposal. But he
would not allow himself to begin writing until Perkins had made his
final decision on "Autumn Hill," and he stowed away his sketches and
outlines in an upstairs closet. "During 1931 it took all the energy I could
command to let it alone," Caldwell confessed; but while he wrote very
little, in his head he rehearsed the scenes, characters, and narrative he

was bursting to put on paper. In June 1932, almost a year from the date Caldwell had first conceived of his "full-length proletarian novel of the South," he began work on *God's Little Acre*.[35]

God's Little Acre was written more quickly than anything Caldwell had done before or would ever do again. Starting as he always did, with a ritualistic purchase of a "ream of second-sheets and a new type-writer ribbon," Caldwell launched into the novel that had been ger-minating for so long. And as with *Tobacco Road*, the pages of *God's Little Acre* "twisted out of the typewriter and . . . fell on the floor" almost as quickly as Caldwell could type them. "The story of *God's Little Acre* was so close to the surface of my consciousness, and the characters so familiar to my mind," Caldwell recalled, that he wrote as if in a trance—breathlessly, eagerly, confidently.[36]

Only when he had a completed manuscript in hand did he resume contact with the outside world. "I've been working like hell for 30 days (though not at hard labor by order of court)," Caldwell wrote his friend I. L. Salomon. "It's done now, however, and I have a week or two in which to rest and read before starting something else." Typically, he did not discuss the specific artistic decisions that went into his book—narrative voice, length and focus of chapters, the structure of the novel as a whole—but despite Caldwell's claims that his eleven balanced chapters flowed spontaneously and without a thought, *God's Little Acre* is lovingly and painstakingly structured.[37]

Ty Ty Walden, the protagonist of *God's Little Acre*, like Jeeter Lester, is the irascible tragicomic patriarch of a poor family on an East Georgia dirt farm. For fifteen years he and his family have spent their lives in a tireless, exuberant, and futile search for gold, and their farm is a sea of giant, yawning craters. Ty Ty has designated one acre of his farm as "God's little acre" and has promised to set aside any riches he finds there for the church—a promise he happily and unconsciously com-promises by shifting the site carefully away from wherever he digs. Ty Ty's son-in-law, Will Thompson, is a mill worker on strike in nearby Scottsville, one of a dozen or so cotton mill towns just over the South Carolina border. Aside from a brief interlude in the city of Augusta, the action shifts gracefully between the crushing industrial world of Will Thompson's cotton-mill town and Ty Ty Walden's barren, deci-mated farm.[38]

The proletarian themes Caldwell sketched out in his Guggenheim proposal are most explicit in the mill-town segments of *God's Little Acre*, where the influence of Michael Gold and the Communist literary cul-ture in New York is unmistakable. The mill in Scottsville in Horse

Creek Valley has been closed for eighteen months—"barred against the people who starved in the yellow company houses"—people who "sat with contracted bellies and waited for the end of the strike." But while the workers are determined, they are unfocused and unable to advance their protest beyond sheer, stubborn resistance. "Here in Scottsville there was a murmuring mass of humanity," Caldwell wrote, "always on the verge of filling the air with concerted shout."[39]

Will Thompson is the man to harness this energy, and in many ways, he is an archetypical proletarian hero—virile, magnetic, and driven by a primitive understanding of economic injustice. "I'll be damned if I work nine hours a day for a dollar-ten," he snarls, "when those rich sons-of-bitches who own the mill ride up and down the valley in five-thousand-dollar automobiles." Will is the only person in Scottsville with the "will" to take matters into his own hands, and the town rallies behind him. "There are enough of us to get in there and turn the power on," he declares. "We can run the damn mill. We can run it better than anybody else. We're going down there in the morning and turn it on!" Afire with revolutionary fervor and the righteousness of the wrongfully dispossessed, Will is Caldwell's mythic working-class warrior. "You come over here and look at me in this yellow company house and think that I'm nothing but a piece of company property," he cries. "I'm as strong as God Almighty Himself now, and I can show you how strong I am. Just wait till tomorrow morning and walk down the street together and stand in front of the mill. I'm going up to that door and rip it to pieces just like it was window shade. You'll see how strong I am."[40]

With Will to lead them, passive and dispirited men who stood helplessly outside the ivy-covered mill walls "spitting their lungs into the deep, yellow dust of Carolina," become the noble mill-working heroes of Scottsville. They rip the fence from its concrete moorings, march to the once-forbidding walls, and fight "their way in silently, hammering at the narrow doors with their fists and pushing with their muscles, angry because the doors were not wide enough to admit them quicker." Caldwell's stirring, lyrical description of men, women, and children seizing control of the means of production—of a mass movement being born in a company town—is a classic Communist document of the age:[41]

> People passed the yellow company houses faster, all going swiftly in one direction. Women and children were among them. . . . The people were walking faster down the street, their eyes on a level with the sun-red

mill windows. Nobody looked down at the ground on which he walked. Their eyes were on the sun-bright windows of the ivy-walled mill. The children ran ahead, looking up at the windows.[42]

But like Joe Hill, the martyred victim of copper bosses so prominent in Communist iconography, Will Thompson is sacrificed to the cause —predictably shot in the back by hired guns of the millowners. As his body is carried away on the muscular, bare backs of his fellow workers, their impromptu eulogy might have graced any number of proletarian novels of the day. "They were afraid of Will," a nameless worker intones. "They knew he had the guts to fight back. . . . he was Will Thompson now. He belonged to those bare-backed men with bloody lips. He belonged to Horse Creek Valley now."[43]

Such formulaic Communist ingredients, however, are only part of *God's Little Acre*. Caldwell had spoken often to Morang and others of a growing distaste for "obvious" symbolism and transparent social messages in contemporary American literature—particularly proletarian literature—and *God's Little Acre* veered sharply from Gold's call for "clear form, the direct line, cinema in words." "To me it is not subtle enough," he wrote Morang. "When you overdo it . . . you cease to be an artist and become a salesman to the public." To I. L. Salomon he complained of short fiction where the "story's point or conclusion is in the bag, so to speak, from the start."[44]

Caldwell laced *God's Little Acre* with wild, fantastic imagery and obscure, often cryptic, symbolism. In its rich lyricism and strikingly erotic poetry, the novel was a return to the style of *The Sacrilege of Alan Kent*, the prose-poem that concluded *American Earth*. Significantly, such abstract writing particularly colored the more overtly political Scottsville sections, where, for instance, Caldwell evoked a mysteriously sexual relationship between the women of a mill town and their machinery:[45]

The machinery did not hum so loudly when the girls operated it. The men made the mill hum with noise when they worked there. But when evening came, the doors were flung open and the girls ran out screaming in laughter. When they reached the street, they ran back to the ivy-covered walls and pressed their bodies against it and touched it with their lips. The men who had been standing idly before it all day long came and dragged them home and beat them unmercifully for their infidelity.[46]

There is, in fact, a surreal, fantastical quality to *God's Little Acre* and the extreme, often bizarre behavior of its characters. Ty Ty and his family are Dionysian, larger than life, mythic; indeed, other than references to the loveliness of Griselda's breasts or hair, or the extent of Pluto Swint's girth, Caldwell gives the characters in *God's Little Acre* little physical detail, and they are defined only by their intensely comic, sexual, or tragic behavior.[47]

But while such abstract imagery and poetic style separated Caldwell from many Communist intellectuals, an artistic obsession with human sexuality distinguished him from almost every American writer of his time. A central theme of *God's Little Acre* is the tension between sexual impulse and societal constraint. Stirred perhaps by his own and Helen's infidelities, Caldwell increasingly believed that monogamy was in biological contradiction with human nature. "There was a mean trick played on us somewhere," Ty Ty Walden piously intones at the novel's end. "God put us in the bodies of animals and tried to make us act like people." In fact, much of *God's Little Acre* testifies to the harm that comes when natural impulses—in work or in play—are restricted. "God made pretty girls and He made men, and there was enough to go around," Ty Ty preaches. "When you try to take a woman or a man and hold him off all for yourself, there ain't going to be nothing but trouble and sorrow the rest of your days."[48]

Ty Ty's youngest daughter, Darling Jill, is defined by her reckless, exhilarated sexual abandon. She recognizes no boundaries of decorum or convention. She sleeps thoughtlessly and passionately with her brother-in-law in her sister's house, with her prospective fiancé in the next room; and although she is spanked when caught in the act, like a naughty child, she is immediately forgiven. "I like healthy people: men and women," Caldwell lectured Helen in a letter discussing sexual behavior. "I know it is more satisfying to be natural. That comes out of the earth . . . and it endures." Darling Jill's passion and sexuality are organic to her personality; her conduct is conscienceless, casual, matter-of-fact, and, as Ty Ty brags on a number of occasions, "She's just made that way."[49] Many years later, Caldwell wrote that "Darling Jill is the kind of girl a man would like to know," and it is clear that the character is also an exercise in extended fantasy. She gives spontaneous expression to the appetites Caldwell felt sure lay dormant in every female personality. "There's a little bit of Darling Jill," he wrote smugly, "in every woman."[50]

Ty Ty's daughter-in-law, Griselda, is Caldwell's symbol of the ultimately erotic and sexually magnetic woman. Confronted with her physical beauty, all the men of *God's Little Acre* are compelled to worship her. In a passage that is repeated almost verbatim three times in the novel, Caldwell presents a man's desire to perform oral sex as the ultimate paean to female beauty and a testimony to his helplessness:

> I reckon Griselda is just about the prettiest girl I ever did see [Ty Ty says]. There ain't a man alive who's ever seen a finer-looking pair of rising beauties as she's got. Why man alive! They're that pretty it makes me feel sometime like getting right down on my hands and knees like these old hound dogs you see chasing after a flowing bitch. You just ache to get down and lick something. That's the way, and it's God's own truth as He would tell it Himself if He could talk like the rest of us.[51]

Caldwell's description of men shackled by their libido, however, is quickly overshadowed by his more compelling interest in their power over women who slavishly pursue them. Caldwell's descriptions of Will Thompson's trysts with both Darling Jill and Griselda betray not only his characteristic misogyny but his fantasies of sexual power. Early in the novel, Darling Jill sneaks into Will's bedroom while her sister (Will's wife) steps out of the house to run an errand. Their dialogue represents the hokeyest sort of sexist, pornographic melodrama:

> "Don't do that so hard, Will. You hurt me."
> "I'm going to hurt you more than that before I get through with you."
> "Kiss me a little first, Will, I like it." Will drew her closer and kissed her. . . .
> "Take me, Will," Darling Jill begged. "Please Will, right now. . . . Take me, Will—I can't wait."[52]

In the novel's most developed scene, Will tears Griselda's clothes from her body piece by piece. Caldwell presents Will as the glorious, conquering man, raised to omnipotence by his virility.

> "Now!" he shouted at her. "Now! God damn it, now I told you to stand there like God intended for you to be seen! Ty Ty was right! He said you were the most beautiful woman God ever made. . . . He said you were so God damn pretty, a man would have to get down on his hands and knees and lick something when he saw you like you are now. . . . And I'm going to do what I've been wanting to do ever since the first

time I saw you. You know what it is, don't you, Griselda? You know what I want. And you're going to give it to me. But I'm not like the rest of them that wear pants. I'm as strong as God Almighty Himself is now. And I'm going to lick you, Griselda."⁵³

Griselda, intoxicated by Will's domination, is reduced to breathless, mesmerized subservience:

> "Stand up Griselda," he said calmly. She stood up immediately, rising eagerly at his command. She waited for anything he might tell her to do next.
> "I've waited a long time for you, Griselda, and now is the time." . . . Griselda stood before him. Her eyes were closed and her lips were partly open and her breath came rapidly. When he told her to sit down, she would sit down. Until then she would remain standing for the rest of her life.⁵⁴

As in *Tobacco Road*, Caldwell's assault on sexual proprieties represented more than an exercise in literary fantasizing, or a personal rebellion against Victorian standards. Caldwell challenged polite images of gender and sexuality as part of a larger confrontation with standard fictional portraits of his native region. "I'm starved for a damn good 'Southern novel,' " he wrote Milton Abernethy, the editor of *Contempo*, later that year. "But none of your goddam Harvey Allens, DuBose Heywards, [Ellen] Glasgows, [James Branch] Cabells. I swear I'll ship it back to you via freight collect if it's by one of those sires." As he wrote *God's Little Acre*, Caldwell's impatience with authors who he felt romanticized Southern life reached new heights. "God, how I hate that Richmond-Charleston School!" he ranted to Abernethy; their "attitude is enough to puke a cat." As he made clear in the Guggenheim proposal for the novel in 1931, the sexual antics of *God's Little Acre* were inseparable from larger artistic ambitions. "There has already been too much of 'romance,' of 'magnolia blossoms,' of 'Negro dialect,' " Caldwell wrote. "It is time someone really wrote about 'life.' "⁵⁵

In *God's Little Acre*, Caldwell's artistic assault on Southern literary stereotypes dovetailed nicely with his burgeoning political sensibilities. "There is horror and drabness in the Worker's life," Gold wrote in his 1931 directive to new proletarian writers. "But we know that this manure heap is the hope of the future." Caldwell was particularly fascinated by the South's "manure heap," and like *Tobacco Road*, *God's Little Acre* presented a vision of Southern life that was brutal and grotesque.

In his review of Dahlberg's novel for the *New Masses*, Caldwell argued that hopelessness, not hope, should characterize good proletarian fiction; that such fiction should serve as a sermon, a testimonial to the results of capitalist exploitation. Written just as he finished *God's Little Acre*, Caldwell's analysis of Dahlberg's novel summarized his own artistic agenda:[56]

> Dahlberg's people lift their voice and sing, America, you've made us what we are today. . . . There is no quarter given, no feeble excuse offered . . . what they are, is sufficient reason to indict the environment in which they were forced to exist. It is an unhealthy, squalid, painful environment. . . . Everybody in the story will lose in the end, just as we have done so far. . . . [They] have no contact with growth, either social or economic; they are in the backwash of America. . . . These people can't do a thing, not because they are incapable of direct action, but because they do not know what can be done with their lives . . . they all lose in the end.[57]

Like the Lesters of *Tobacco Road*, Ty Ty Walden and his family "all lose in the end." The final scene of *God's Little Acre* finds Ty Ty back where he began the novel—in a deep, deep hole, looking vainly for his salvation in gold he will never find. Likewise, the people of Scottsville return meekly to their hopeless lives after Will Thompson's death. "The men with the blood-stained lips who carried him down to his grave," Caldwell wrote, "would some day go back to the mill to card and spin and weave and dye."[58]

The ribaldry, violence, and degradation in *God's Little Acre*, like that in *Tobacco Road*, also revealed Caldwell's hostility towards his subjects. Although he was unable to articulate (or acknowledge) such an ambivalence, the Waldens, like the Lesters, were based on people Caldwell had grown up with, and he treated them with a malicious, detailed satire bred in familiarity—a viciousness strikingly absent from his portraits of the mill workers he knew far less well. Ty Ty's irascible lechery, for instance, is broadly comic, but also destructive; eventually, his drooling soliloquies about his daughters' beauty incite a fatal rivalry among his sons. Likewise, Ty Ty's brutally indifferent treatment of his starving black sharecroppers and his kidnapping of an albino to serve as his slave are a clear indictment of the racism among poor Southern whites. Pluto Swint, the obscenely obese and incorrigibly lazy candidate for sheriff, was a ferocious caricature of the Wrens police chief, a man

Ira had impugned for his stupidity for as long as Erskine could remember.

Caldwell had begun *God's Little Acre* as a "proletarian novel," but
his hostility towards its rural protagonists was just another way in
which he compromised such a vision. His preoccupation with sexual
themes, the poetic surrealism of the prose and imagery, the unique mix
of slapstick passion and grim tragedy, all defy easy artistic or political
categories. Caldwell had been a loner his entire life, and his art reflected
his independence.

I V

CALDWELL SOON DISCOVERED that it was far easier to leave
Scribner's than it was to find a new publisher—especially in the midst
of the Depression—and Lieber struggled to place "Autumn Hill" and
the completed manuscript of *God's Little Acre*. When the sympathetic
critic Matthew Josephson lobbied his friend, Alfred Harcourt, of Harcourt, Brace on Caldwell's behalf, the raspy-voiced editor responded
simply that "new novelists aren't selling nowadays." Lieber met a similarly disheartening response at Simon and Schuster. "Money is getting
more scarce each day with me," Caldwell lamented to Morang. "I'll
rob a bank some day, though, and be rich for a change." Rare guests
to the Mount Vernon house were instructed to bring their own food
or go hungry, and the Caldwells survived on the lean produce of their
front yard garden.[59]

Finally, in mid-September, almost two months after the break with
Perkins, Lieber managed to interest Marshall Best and Harold Guinzburg at Viking Press. "Maxim Lieber has had a nibble," Caldwell wrote
excitedly to Morang. "When it becomes a bite, he says he's going to
pull up a contract!" Viking was noncommittal about "Autumn Hill,"
but they offered a one-hundred-dollar advance for each of Caldwell's
next two novels. Although he had been advanced three times as much
for *Tobacco Road* the previous year, he signed the Viking contract without complaint. Having burned his bridges at Scribner's, Caldwell was
in no position to quibble with any reasonable offer. "We'll be able to
give the wolf the ha! ha! for a while yet," he wrote grimly to Morang.
"That will be something to put fat in the soup, anyway. God knows,
it has been lean long enough."[60]

Caldwell was relieved, if not overjoyed, by his new affiliation with
Viking, and his spirits gradually rose as he reflected on the firm's rep-

utation for high sales. "I'm hoping this won't be my last year," he wrote playfully to Morang. "If I can stave off starvation, I'd love to live many more years. The Viking Press can sell books if anybody can; maybe we'll live off the fat of the land yet."[61]

Ironically, Viking turned down "Autumn Hill" much more quickly than Scribner's had. But by this time, Caldwell had all but given up on the novel. "The book Scribner's and myself got sore about is laid aside temporarily, and Viking's publishing in March a novel called *God's Little Acre*," he wrote Morang. Much of the sting was salved by the unanimously rave reviews all seven Viking editors gave the new novel. "Viking seems to be nuts about the book," Caldwell wrote joyously to Abernethy. "Lieber says everyone says it's good." Caldwell could not help but compare this enthusiastic vote of confidence with the contentious debate that had raged at Scribner's over the publication of *Tobacco Road*. He was understandably flattered and encouraged that while Viking offered some "damn good" suggestions, "they said they thought so highly of the book that they would publish it whether I made the revisions or not." And indeed, the first manuscript Caldwell submitted was very similar to the final product. His infrequent, block-lettered corrections on the galleys reflect no serious rethinking of the original manuscript that had flowed so smoothly from his typewriter.[62]

God's Little Acre was a far more sexually explicit novel than *Tobacco Road*, yet this raised nary an eyebrow in the Viking editorial offices. In 1933, Viking Press was more aggressively commercial than Scribner's, more liberal, and less invested in protecting an image of dignified propriety. No editors wrote Caldwell to suggest he "soften" passages or omit segments of dialogue, as John Hall Wheelock had routinely done. And certainly, nobody at Viking took as personal and assertive an interest in Caldwell's work as Maxwell Perkins had. Caldwell had once appreciated such attention, but after the rejection of "Autumn Hill" and what he saw as Perkins's betrayal, he was relieved by Viking's more hands-off approach. "I'm beginning to think that Scribner's was a mistake to begin with," he wrote Abernethy. "Viking is much more decent about everything."[63]

With Viking's enthusiastic endorsement, Caldwell's confidence in his new novel soared, and he anxiously awaited the publication date of early February 1933. "I know you are going to like it, if you liked TR, because it's a much better book," he boasted to Abernethy. To Johns, he was even more direct. "It's called *God's Little Acre*, and it follows *Tobacco Road* in many respects, but a damn sight better." Although the first printing of the book would be only fifteen hundred copies—as it was for *Tobacco Road*—Viking had assured him that a second printing would follow shortly. If Caldwell was disappointed with the austere, white, yellow, and green cover, he was surely pleased with Viking's highly flattering jacket blurb, and its description of him as an author who defied comparison—"a *sui generis*—a writer who sees with a new eye."[64]

Lieber also managed to sell a short story to the *Yale Review*, and that, added to the advance money from the novel, allowed Erskine and Helen to put some money in the bank for the first time in over a year. In part to escape the −10° temperatures in Maine, in part to celebrate the upcoming release of the new novel, Helen and Erskine traveled south, dropped the two boys in Wrens, and continued on to spend a week relaxing at the Florida beach house of their old friend Gordon Lewis. The Caldwells had not taken a vacation together in years, and after the challenges of the past twelve months, they badly needed one.[65]

But Erskine's thoughts never strayed far from New York; even as he did his best to relax at Lewis's rustic cabin, he was well aware that in that first week of February 1933, critics were receiving their review copies of *God's Little Acre*.

V

ALMOST EVERY MAJOR CRITIC, North and South, shared Caldwell's belief that *God's Little Acre* was an advance over *Tobacco Road*. Most praised Caldwell for broadening his canvas to include the industrial as well as the rural poor and applauded the graceful prose. Jonathan Daniels of the *Raleigh News and Observer* thought the novel "one of the finest studies of the Southern poor white which has ever come into our literature." Louis Kronenberger, writing in the *New York Times Book Review*, asserted that "no more original novel has appeared in America for a long while." The reviewer for the *New Republic* felt that Caldwell had produced "among the most powerful of recent novels."[66]

God's Little Acre was a more light-hearted novel than *Tobacco Road*, and many critics stressed Caldwell's pervasive and Rabelaisian sense of humor. Without the backdrop of absolute, unremitting physical destitution that characterized the earlier work—the characters in *God's Little Acre* enjoy abundant meals, feast on fresh watermelon, drive a smoothly running car, and eat peach ice cream on the front porch—more reviewers than ever before shared the opinion of the *New Republic* critic who found "more humor in *God's Little Acre* than in any other recent novel"; the critic for the *Forum*, who had so disliked *Tobacco Road*, attributed the improvement to "the fact that the author has stressed that element in which he is at his best: poor white rural comedy." "No one writing today," he rejoiced, "can equal Mr. Caldwell in this peculiar variety of gusty humor."[67]

Many reviewers, however, had trouble reconciling Caldwell's earthy humor with the violence and deadly earnestness of the mill-town segments of *God's Little Acre*. They were particularly disturbed by the final third of the novel, which dealt in rapid order with the storming of the mill, Will's death, and the subsequent fratricide on the Waldens' farm. Kronenberger, and many others, felt betrayed by Caldwell's efforts to address more serious social concerns and, perhaps, by the tragedy that soured their laughter. The reviewer for the *New Republic* suggested that Caldwell's political sympathies were to blame for his error. "The tragedy seems unreal and slightly grotesque, out of key with the rest of the book," he noted, "as if Caldwell wanted to bring a specific social criticism into his world, and had not found an entirely successful way of doing so." James T. Farrell, writing in the *New York Sun*, contended that when Caldwell moved from "excellent slapstick humor" to "a description of deeply rooted feelings, he kill[ed] his novel."[68]

To Edward Dahlberg of the *Nation*, there was nothing at all funny about *God's Little Acre*, and he viewed the book as a heavy-handed political tract. Clearly unmoved by Caldwell's glowing review of his own novel just a year before, Dahlberg felt that *God's Little Acre* was disastrously compromised by Caldwell's association with the New York Communists. Dahlberg only scoffed at Caldwell's ideological agenda and described the people of Scottsville as "disincarnate specters moving in a quasi-Marxian haze ten thousand feet above Georgia and Carolina." Dismissing the book as "less a novel than an expanded short story, with little to recommend it aside from a few highly amusing and picaresque touches," Dahlberg concluded that Caldwell and other proletarian artists were "left-wing band-wagonists who encourage . . . pogroms against literature." "One would expect after a reading of these 'proletarian novels,'" Dahlberg sneered, that "it must be a bourgeois fault to be able to write well."[69]

American Communists, however, were among the novel's sharpest critics. Edwin Rolfe, in a review for the *New Masses*, made clear that while he had forgiven Caldwell's shortcomings in the past in the hopes of better things, his forbearance was nearly exhausted. While Rolfe conceded that "inclusion of the mill scene in *God's Little Acre* marks a

definite increase in Caldwell's social awareness," he had no patience
for the novel's abstract imagery or poetic language. He dismissed the
entire Scottsville section as "fantastic, disconnected, unbound to any
semblance of reality, artificially grafted to the rest of the book" and
sadly concluded that it "neutralizes the very growth that its presence
in the book indicates." Rolfe was disgusted with Will Thompson's
larger-than-life, mythic qualities, which he thought belittled the gritty
day-to-day dignity of the American workingman. Had Caldwell engaged
in "a more thorough investigation into the causes of the Southern
industrial struggle," Rolfe suggested disdainfully, "he might have created a character more firmly built of flesh and blood."[70]

Like Communist critics of both *American Earth* and *Tobacco Road*,
Rolfe was also distressed by Caldwell's unwillingness or inability to
articulate an explicit political agenda. Rolfe, and others at the *New
Masses*, found the political naïveté of Caldwell's characters particularly
unforgivable considering Caldwell's own recent involvement with the
Foster and Ford campaign. "He is surely aware of the class conflicts
raging throughout the country and of the crisis in which not only
American, but world capitalism finds itself," Rolfe scolded; he warned
that Caldwell's "logical development as a writer must begin to parallel
his development as a social being."[71]

Rolfe's final complaint was shared by critics of every political hue,
for, predictably, he was affronted by what he called "Caldwell's preoccupation with sex as a theme." Aside from including an astute comparison to the work of D. H. Lawrence, Rolfe limited his critique to
vague and ominous warnings against the book's "decadent possibilities." Dozens of other critics from papers across the country were also
offended. Many felt, quite simply, that Caldwell was a pervert. The
Springfield Republican complained that "the unbridled passions of the
characters seem to be the sole motivation, and they merely wallow in
their own actions." The *Chicago Daily News* thought Caldwell had attempted to write "the great epic of sex." In a letter to Allen Tate, John
Peale Bishop was far more crass: "Erskine Caldwell," he declared, "has
written a book glorifying cunt-lapping."[72]

A few months after the first rush of reviews, Carl Van Doren struggled to make sense of the wildly disparate responses to *God's Little Acre*
in an article he wrote for the *Nation*. Van Doren marveled at the range
of labels that Caldwell had attracted—from "left-wing band-wagonist"
to political ignoramus; from depraved pervert to good-natured humorist; from photographic realist to surrealist poet—and sympathized with
a young author taken to task from so many sides. "Life for Erskine

Caldwell has lately been a kind of chronic tap day," he observed. "One coterie after another has expected him to join it, and he has even been claimed as a member already of this or that society." Seeking, in part, to atone for the gratuitous nastiness of Dahlberg's *Nation* review, Van Doren finally concluded that the difficulty in defining Caldwell was the highest form of compliment. And indeed, his appraisal seems closest to the truth. "A writer who attracts a variety of readers with a variety of qualities," Van Doren suggested, "does it not because he is himself a miscellany but because he is something single and impenetrable, and arouses curiosity."[73]

VI

CALDWELL WAS NOT NEARLY so philosophical about the range of criticism he received, and he responded to the reviews with anger and disgust. He was particularly sensitive to reviews that focused on the humor in his work. Acquaintances like Malcolm Cowley assumed that such disavowals were merely disingenuous red herrings, but people close to Caldwell saw his genuine rage and marked defensiveness at being described as a "humorist." Once, he walked angrily from the room when a fan innocently praised the humor in his work. He lost his temper again when old acquaintances in Charlottesville laughed out loud during a reading of *Tobacco Road*.[74]

Although cruel humor was clearly one of Caldwell's creative objectives, he would never acknowledge such a purpose. In part, Caldwell's reaction reveals his protectiveness of the very people he lampooned. Moreover, he felt guilty for his satire, and his shame engendered a significant degree of denial. But Caldwell worried most that his serious social message was lost on many of his most enthusiastic readers. "What peeves me right now," he raged to I. L. Salomon, echoing remarks he made to all his friends, "is the way so many readers and reviewers went blah-blah about what they said was comedy, and not a word about the theme of the book."[75]

Caldwell was sure that critics had intentionally ignored the meaning of his work. He was certain that his vision of the South was too bold, for instance, for James Branch Cabell. "I presume by way of silence that Cabell threw up his hands in horror," he wrote Milton Abernethy. "What else could the little man do? A man has to be man-sized to get that book. B. Cabell is rather runtish." Other reviewers, Caldwell suspected, were afraid to acknowledge either the social and economic criticism in his novel or his thinly veiled argument for sexual liberation. "Christ! Can't they read?" he complained to Salomon. "Or after reading are they afraid to report what the thing was really concerned [with]?" Having lectured everyone he knew on the need for thematic subtlety, he felt betrayed by critics who had "missed the point." "Next time," he vowed to Gordon Lewis, "I'll not make the theme as prominent as a wart on the end of your nose; I'll make it a boil under the seat of your pants. That'll make them stand up."[76]

"The only review so far (out of the hundreds I've seen) that gets what I drove at in *God's Little Acre*," Caldwell wrote Milton Abernethy, "is William Soskin's in the *New York Post*." In a review entitled "D. H. Lawrence and Erskine Caldwell: An Unusual Association," Soskin argued that the treatment of sexuality in *God's Little Acre*—as in the work of Lawrence—represented a conscious challenge to the accepted standards of propriety and sexual decorum, and that "back of all the Waldens' comedy and back of their hilarious antics one senses an essentially ominous note." Diverging from most of his literary compatriots, Soskin noted judiciously that Ty Ty Walden was "something more than a clown." Soskin read Ty Ty's search for gold as a metaphor for man's search for spiritual discovery—"his own emotional urge that will not be denied"—and Caldwell seemed to support that interpretation.[77]

Caldwell was hurt and worried that American Communists did not share Soskin's appraisal, and he took special pains to write to Mike Gold in defense of his left-wing credentials. Not a registered Communist himself, Caldwell's strident proclamations of party loyalty do not ring true. "Revolution needs numbers," Caldwell wrote Gold. "But it is also important that the members of the revolutionary movement be whole-heartedly supporting. The guts of the loyal ones will see that the flag is carried high." Caldwell fairly begged Gold for another chance. "My own work so far has been slow to reach what I am striving for," Caldwell lamented. "I may never reach the status of a revolutionary writer. . . . If that is to be the case the fault will be mine and not the material's." Caldwell promised Gold that he would do better next time. "There is revolution in the whites and blacks of Georgia," he assured Gold. "The trouble I find (which I try to show in what I write) is that the masses have been damn near killed by the lack of education and starvation. The two forces together make a situation where protest against hunger and mistreatment is without a voice. . . . There are millions in Georgia (four out of every six) who think that hunger, illiteracy, cruelty and oppression are the natural laws of nature."[78]

But while Caldwell sought to justify his status in the Communist camp and was anxious to reassure Gold of his political agenda, to Morang he self-righteously declared his independence. Indeed, by the time Caldwell had finished *God's Little Acre*, it was obvious to him that he could not possibly adhere to Gold's—or anyone else's—formula for his work. He cautioned Morang, and perhaps himself, that "a serious writer can never be anything more than an echo once he begins listening to somebody else."

> A man knows what he feels, and since that is the basis of his art, he's a fool to take second handed mouthings no matter how earnest or well intentioned the advice may be. . . . Writing is an individual act, like going to the bathroom, or kissing your wife. All else is 100% bunk.[79]

"The thing to do," he advised Morang, "is to go your own way . . . even though the American Soviets say otherwise."[80]

However drawn he was to Communism, however flattered he was by the attentions of left-wing intellectuals, however beneficial such affiliations seemed for his career, Caldwell was not, and would never be, a joiner of anything. Like his father, he thrived on antagonism and felt stifled by consensus. "A fellow still has to do his own writing—no matter what his politics are," he raged to Morang. "That's why I say to hell with anybody other than yourself." Morang probably knew that Caldwell's promise to "some day . . . join the Party if for no other reason than to be able to say, and say proudly, that I am a Communist," was one he would never keep. Caldwell, as he admitted in a more self-aware moment, was "a lone Wolf."[81]

VII

ONLY MONTHS AFTER the first wave of reviews died down, Caldwell's self-righteous anger and feelings of persecution were given new life. In April 1933, the New York Society for the Suppression of Vice, one of the country's best-known moral watchdog agencies, took Caldwell and Viking Press to court, claiming that the sale of *God's Little Acre* represented the dissemination of pornography. According to John Sumner, the society's legal counsel and fire-and-brimstone secretary, the sale of the novel was a violation of Section 1141 of the New York Penal Code, which forbade the sale of literature that was "obscene, lewd, lascivious, filthy, indecent or disgusting." Hoping to initiate a national test case, Sumner cleverly bought the novel directly from the publisher's office, thus making Viking Press—rather than a single retailer—the defendant in the case.[82]

Harold Guinzburg, president and one of the founders of Viking Press, answered the challenge directly and hired noted litigator Wolfgang Schwabacher to argue the case. In early May, Schwabacher and Sumner presented their briefs to Judge Benjamin Greenspan of the New York Magistrates Court in Manhattan. "As far as I know, down here Down East, it's a toss-up between Sumner and us," Caldwell wrote nervously to Milton Abernethy. "I've been assured that he can't win his case, but I'm pessimistic." Caldwell had reason for concern, for the case hinged on the single issue of whether a book could be deemed pornographic on the basis of isolated words or paragraphs, or if it needed to be considered in its entirety. While New York State courts had considered the issue before, no definitive ruling had been made. With the memory of the successful banning of The Bastard still fresh in his mind, Caldwell took to heart Sumner's assertion that the Society had "a water-tight case."[83]

In the first sentence of his ruling, Magistrate Greenspan made clear that Caldwell's worries were unfounded. He was unwilling to judge God's Little Acre—or any piece of literature—on the basis of selected passages. "In order to sustain the prosecution," Greenspan wrote, "the court must find that the tendency of the book as a whole, and indeed its main purpose, is to excite lustful desire and impure imaginations. . . . Although some paragraphs standing by themselves might be objectionable, so might a similar selection from Aristophanes or Chaucer or Boccaccio or even from the Bible." His dislike of Sumner and the society overwhelming his careful legal prose, Greenspan warned that "those who see the ugliness and not the beauty in a piece of work are unable to see the forest for the trees."

Greenspan's decision was also a significant statement on the type of evidence legally admissible in defense of literature. As soon as charges were brought, Lieber had formed the "God's Little Acre Protest Committee" and marshaled the support of a remarkable cross section of the New York intellectual community. Over sixty authors, editors, and literary critics from every major newspaper and book club in New York sent testimonials or signed a manifesto to "protest vigorously against the action of the New York Society for the Suppression of Vice in attempting to suppress God's Little Acre, by Erskine Caldwell, which we consider an honest and sincere work of imaginative literature." Aside from long-time supporters like Malcolm Cowley and Lewis Mumford, a galaxy of other writers rallied to Caldwell's cause. Sherwood Anderson, Sinclair Lewis, and H. L. Mencken headed a list that included Thomas Beer, V. F. Calverton, Henry S. Canby, Max Eastman, Clifton P. Fadiman, Lewis Gannett, Harry Hansen, Granville Hicks, Louis Kronenberger, Dorothy Parker, Burton Roscoe, Edwin Seaver, William Soskin, Carl Van Doren, Ella Winter, and Alexander Woollcott.[84]

Sumner argued that such testimony was legally inadmissible and morally unsound. Writers and intellectuals had a vested interest in pornography, Sumner hinted, "and had no interest in public welfare." It was the court's job, Sumner declared, to represent "the whole people and not only the literati." Sumner contended that Lieber's petition was invalid by virtue of a previous decision that had ruled "that these matters must be decided by normal people and not the abnormal." "Substitute the word 'literati' for the words 'abnormal people,' " Sumner sneered, "and we have an exact explanation of the letters, reviews, and other favorable comments presented on behalf of this book and its author."[85]

Magistrate Greenspan, however, took his cue from H. L. Mencken, who dismissed Sumner as an "enemy of common sense and common decency." After reading all the major reviews of *God's Little Acre* and the extensive testimonials, "the court is of the opinion," Greenspan wrote, "that this group of people, collectively, has a better capacity to judge the value of a literary production than one who is more apt to search for obscene passages in a book." In allowing the testimony of literary figures to serve as evidence in defense of obscenity charges, Greenspan established a second critical precedent for the defense of artists' First Amendment rights.[86]

Caldwell was relieved with the decision and understandably gratified by the widespread support he received from other writers. Telegrams received from, among others, editors John Hall Wheelock and Marshall Best further encouraged his belief that he was a noble warrior against the dark forces of suppression and small-mindedness. Best also pointed out that the case, and the extensive newspaper coverage it received, would certainly benefit Viking's and Caldwell's financial standing. Sales of the book were brisk, and Viking quickly issued another edition of the novel with a copy of the judge's decision appended to the back. Although Caldwell continued to gripe about Viking's initial printing of fifteen hundred copies, he was cheered by the fact that over five thousand books had been sold since the original publication five months earlier.[87]

Indeed, Caldwell's fortunes had taken a dramatic turn for the better by the spring of 1933. To Caldwell's surprise, H. L. Mencken's *American Mercury*, one of the commercial journals that had consistently spurned him, accepted a story. *Vanity Fair* followed suit a few months later. A young playwright contracted for the dramatic rights to *God's Little Acre*, and Scribner's finally succeeded in placing *Tobacco Road* with a British publisher.[88]

But the biggest boon of all came just after Sumner's well-publicized assault on *God's Little Acre* hit the New York newspapers. MGM pictures, always a close observer of who was hot on the New York literary scene, approached Caldwell with an offer to write a screenplay on location in Louisiana. William Faulkner, whom they had hired for the job, was angry, unhappy, and sometimes drunk. Caldwell, the writer to whom Faulkner was most often compared, seemed the perfect replacement.

Caldwell accepted the offer immediately and presented his decision to Helen in characteristic fashion. After the preliminary hearing in New York, he returned to Mount Vernon and simply handed her a copy of his train ticket. She never forgot the shock of reading the printing which stated clearly: "Boston, to Akron, to St. Louis, to New Orleans." Helen had taken care of the two boys single-handedly many times before, but this, only the latest of her husband's abrupt departures, came at a particularly bad time. Helen had become pregnant in August 1932 with the hope that a new child might buoy the struggling marriage and keep Erskine closer to home. In May 1933, she was eight-and-a-half months along and terrified at being left alone in the remote Mount Vernon house. Caldwell had little patience for her concerns, or his growing responsibilities as a father. "I have a job," he declared bluntly. "I'm going to replace William Faulkner for Metro-Goldwyn-Mayer, and I'm going to leave tomorrow."[89]

Chapter Seven

FAME AND GUILT

Throughout their tempestuous and often unhappy relationship, Erskine and Helen remained desperately afraid of losing each other. Sensing that this latest separation brought their marriage very near the breaking point, they strove to salvage it through the mail. They wrote one another obsessively—once, twice, sometimes three times a day. But even in prose, they fell into the familiar patterns of behavior and response that had plagued them from the very start.[1]

From the moment he began writing, first from New Orleans then from California, Caldwell's letters were filled with detailed instructions—marching orders really—that revealed his characteristic obsession with detail and his need for total control over Helen. A typical letter began bluntly: "Buy fertilizer . . . the garden won't grow without it, even if it costs $5 a sack. Have the hot water fixed, of course. Don't let the lawn and the garden get ahead of Clifford [a neighboring workman]. Grass grows fast when it starts to grow." Another concluded: "Replace stone walls in small cellar, put large stones under the water tank, plug drain hole of the tank, paint the wooden window in shed, put new locks on the shed door."[2]

Sometimes Caldwell warned his pregnant wife not to "overdo it," but even his concern was couched in the form of angry directives.[3] "Don't be foolish and kill yourself," he commanded. "It's silly to cripple yourself for life just to do a few days wash." In the very next paragraph, Caldwell returned to the detailed enumeration of chores, shamelessly treating Helen as his servant. "Send 25 cents to the Sat. Review for two copies," he wrote. "Have one sent direct to me, and the other to you. I suppose it's on sale here somewhere, but it's too hot to get out and look."[4]

Caldwell extended his endless instructions to the raising of the children. On May 24, 1933, Helen delivered a baby girl—Janet—in the Mount Vernon library with the help of a neighbor, and Erskine wasted no time in providing detailed coaching on how the child should be treated. "The trick now is to change her sleeping time around," he wrote Helen. "You can do that by gradually keeping her awake during the day so she will sleep at night. You can train a kid to do anything, just as you do a puppy to do some things. And the younger they're trained, the sooner will they learn." In another typical letter, Caldwell ordered Helen to give the baby "all the milk she can eat, and all the sunshine she can stand. Sun will do more good now than later; there won't be any sun after September, and you should keep her outdoors and let her store it up for the next six months to come."[5]

Building up physical toughness in his children was essential to Caldwell, and he lectured his wife on the need to keep the boys, as well as the baby, outside as much as possible. "How's the new kid? Why not hang up a basket in the front yard under the tree like we did for Dabney?" he suggested when Janet was ten days old. Because the boys were expected to be tough, rugged, and independent, he did not allow them shirts or shoes until well into the fall. "Make Pixie and Dee [Dabney] stay in the sun when it's warm enough," he wrote several times that spring. "They should not wear a shirt or sweater except on cold and rainy days and at night. If they start getting tanned now, they'll be in fine shape within six weeks."[6]

Without their father in the house and his terrible demands for silence, Dee and Pixie became increasingly unruly. Caldwell was aware of this, and he commanded Helen to maintain strict discipline over the two boys. "They can go wild in a couple of months if turned loose," he wrote worriedly. "The idea is not to let them tear up the place and burn it down." Caldwell insisted that Pixie begin acting more like an adult, and he instructed Helen to inform their elder son—now seven years old—that he "was the man of the house and to run things right."[7]

Caldwell continued to worry over the boys' moral education. Although he frequently drank in the Greentrees home and both his sons knew it, he was furious when Helen took the boys for a visit to a family that served alcohol in their house. "I hoped you had woken up to those bogus people by this time so you won't take the kids down there," he raged. "There's no sense in trying to raise the kids to one way of thinking, and then take them to places where they learn just the opposite." He arranged for Ira and Carrie to visit the Mount Vernon house for the summer while he was away, knowing that they would serve as moral guardians of his children.[8]

Caldwell's need to control Helen was most evident in the way he managed their money. The MGM contract guaranteed a salary of $250 a week for three months, more than Caldwell had earned thus far in his entire career as a writer. "You know why I came here, and you know what I'm going to do," he assured Helen. "I'm trying to get some money for you, and I don't give a damn about anything or anyone else." But as the weeks progressed, Caldwell kept the bulk of the paychecks to himself, and Helen became increasingly desperate. She wrote again and again and begged for help with the grocery and doctor bills. "Don't worry about the money," he repeatedly consoled her, but he continued to release funds in dribs and drabs—a check for ten dollars one week, for fifteen dollars the next. Only after Helen provided a careful documentation of her expenses would he relent. "Figure out how much you will need between now and June 15," he wrote. "Subtract what you now have on hand, and send me the figures for the net balance." When Helen planned a visit to California, he disbursed the money with characteristic penuriousness:[9]

> The check will be for everything except train fares. Out of it you are to buy all materials, pay wages a week in advance [for yard work], pay travelling expenses. . . . I have not determined yet what amount to send, but I have your expense sheet at home and I'll figure it all out tonight. Your expense account amounts to $120 (carried over from last week—which has been taken care of with the sixty-five I sent.) This leaves you some eight bucks over the amount, as I am sending two hundred. You should arrive here with something out of that. Meals will be the biggest expense, and they will probably average $1.50 per person.[10]

Aside from the humiliation of having to beg for every penny, Helen and the children were in very real financial straits. While Caldwell matter-of-factly detailed his own new purchases, including a third new suit in two weeks ("The two [new] seersuckers are too light for this climate, except in the middle of the day, and I can't be jumping up to run home to change"), his family continued to survive on garden vegetables and handouts from Helen's mother. Eventually, Helen was forced to charge some of their local expenses. When Caldwell received the bills he was absolutely furious, seeing her behavior as an attack on his authority:[11]

> I've tried to make it plain to you that you've been a damn fool, and that you ought to behave with some sense. How much money do you owe on your bills? I wish to Christ you would try to pay them up instead of trying to cover them up. . . . I don't think you were born with much

sense. But if you'll listen to me I'll teach you some, and you'll pay all that you owe by August first. And if you ever charge another dime I'll wring your neck off. Or else insert a no-responsibility ad in the paper.[12]

I

CALDWELL'S CONTROL OF HELEN in financial matters compensated for his dependence on other fronts. Perhaps most difficult for him to accept was his continued reliance on his wife's editorial involvement in his fiction. Caldwell was extremely insecure about his spelling and punctuation and embarrassed by the frequent gaffes that still plagued his prose. He counted on Helen to catch the worst of these blunders before manuscripts were sent out to publishers.

Helen also passed final judgment on the literary value of everything Caldwell wrote. When Marshall Best, Caldwell's editor at Viking, sent him a report on the collection of stories they were planning to release in late 1933, Caldwell immediately passed it along to Helen. In a striking shift from his typically didactic pronouncements, he pleaded with his wife for guidance: "Do you think they should be left out? If you know any reason why they should be in, please tell me—and write him your reason, too, if you wish." When Viking demanded the final galleys a few months later, Caldwell was worried that Helen had not reviewed them in their final form. "I can't find much wrong with it, but I have no doubt that you could find plenty. I wish you could have read it at least once before it goes to press."[13]

The strongest bond in Helen and Erskine's marriage, however, was their powerful, if twisted, emotional dependency on each other. Caldwell often revealed how much he needed Helen's approval and expressed his vulnerability in almost childlike terms. He was, in fact, terrified of losing her. "Write to tell me how everything is and if you still love me," he wrote forlornly. "When you discover that I care a hell of a lot more for you than you do for me, you won't be questioning my faith any longer. Don't forget that." If a day went by without a letter, he became morose and angry. "Write soon," he begged her. "It's pretty bad sitting here all day and again another day, and not getting a letter from you. If I didn't hear from you, I couldn't stay here five hours."[14]

Occasionally, Caldwell even admitted his fears of sexual inadequacy.

"The only trouble," he wrote in his typically blunt, awkward way, "is that I'm at a disadvantage: you are not constituted so that you are handicapped, while I have to be able to go in and that's not possible all the time." But he compensated for such expressions of vulnerability with abrupt outbursts of machismo, and within single sentences or paragraphs he mingled confessions of sexual insecurity with crass declarations of sexual domination. "If I'm not good enough for you, then you won't wish me to have you, will you?" he began sadly. In the next sentence, however, he was moved to violent boasting: "All I can say is that I'm going to keep it up as long as it stays big enough; and if you know how to make it get stiff enough to go in again, in you it's going." On another occasion, he fretted that when he finally saw Helen he "wouldn't be able to keep up," but concluded his letter by pronouncing that "the only thing I can do to you is fuck you, and I'll do that as long as I'm able, but whatever you do will be what I wish."[15]

Helen was worried that her husband was cheating on her, and, indeed, he sometimes was. But while Caldwell went through the motions of reassuring her, he also seemed intent on keeping her in suspense. He discussed at great length, for instance, the physical attributes of the nubile dancing girls on the MGM lot who walked by his window wearing "only a pair of slippers and a chemise." He made matters worse with frequent demands that his wife lose weight. "You ought to weigh between 140 and 145—not a pound more, not a pound less," he told her. "You'd better not refuse to step on the scales when I say I don't believe it." And while he repeatedly rebuked Helen for her jealousy and feelings of inferiority, he usually catalogued her merits—especially her physical attributes—in crass comparison to other women. "There may be fifty million other girls in the country," he informed her, "but none of them has a pussy as good as yours." "I'd be a fool to like anybody but you," he wrote on another occasion. "It would take 100 girls to equal you—and I couldn't afford that expense."[16]

More than once, Caldwell suggested that he was destined to find other women. "If at any time I should like somebody other than you," he wrote, "it would mean not that I am going off you, but that it was my nature to like somebody else." He often claimed to be a helpless slave to his biological impulses and therefore blameless for his infidelity. "You know damn well the only reason I ever liked anybody else (momentarily) was because it was the contrast. . . . I couldn't help being a fool about anybody (no matter whom) with what you lacked. Call it round breasts, firm legs, or mental or physical agility." As a form of consolation, Caldwell promised Helen that the only other woman he could now imagine sleeping with was a prostitute:[17]

> And I wouldn't take anybody unless I asked or told you first, and gave you a chance to forbid it. And the only kind of girl I would take—no matter if you did say I could have the other kind—would be a prostitute. . . . I couldn't take any other kind of girl because she would be too much like you—and I'd be dissatisfied. . . . Maybe you'd better sign an order for one intercourse with a professional prostitute, good only for one time, and void on and after August 5th [the date of Helen's visit]![18]

Caldwell used these veiled threats of his infidelity to keep Helen in line; he was desperately afraid that she too would be unfaithful again. But characteristically, he took no responsibility for the strains in his marriage; he blamed Helen for his own affairs and placed the burden of holding the marriage together squarely on her shoulders.

> I'm not that kind. You seem to forget that I don't care about anybody else and . . . as long as you don't let me down, I don't try to fool you. . . . As it is, everything is up to you. . . . You can depend on me as long as you are the kind I think you are. It's up to you to know if you are to be the kind I've counted on your being. Nobody else has ever been anything to me while I had you, and it could never happen in the present or future unless you let me down.[19]

Caldwell had a remarkable capacity for feeling betrayed or wronged; he made demands on his wife and children he could not conceive of living up to himself, yet was unable or unwilling to acknowledge any such double standard. Helen grew accustomed to her husband's terrible insecurities. She also understood that for all his violent hypocrisy, mistrust, and fear, he needed her badly. She still loved him in spite of his abusive behavior and in spite of her own best judgment, and he—in his own dark, angry way—loved her, too.

I I

CALDWELL WAS in good company as he made his way westward, first to New Orleans and then to Hollywood, in May 1933. The Depression had reduced book sales and royalties for all but a very few authors, and many publishing houses had cut their advances in half. Hollywood, on the other hand, offered salaries to well-known writers that ranged from $250 to $1,500 a week. In places like the Garden of Allah, a Beverly Hills hotel on Sunset Boulevard, literati of every artistic and political hue crowded together in stuccoed bungalows. F. Scott Fitzgerald, Nathanael West, William Faulkner, Lillian Hellman, Dashiell Hammett, Robert Benchley, Dorothy Parker, and John Dos Passos were among the luminaries who had swallowed their artistic pride to reap quick profits from the Hollywood studios. In the early 1930s, *Fortune* magazine noted sarcastically that "MGM employed more members of the literati than it took to produce the King James Bible." Some of these writers returned to their work as novelists, playwrights, and poets; others, seduced by the quick money, or simply unable to pay their bills any other way, stayed on for years.[20]

From the very beginning, Caldwell was ill at ease on the West Coast. "This country is not a fit place to live," he wrote Helen the day after he arrived in Culver City from New Orleans. "There is no soil, nothing to put your feet on." A few days later he wrote again: "God did not intend for people to live here in this desert. What I miss is honest-to-goodness dirt underfoot, and real rain in the air. All this dry sand gets on my nerves." The unfamiliar surroundings intensified Caldwell's ever-present fears of impending calamity. He worried that earthquakes would topple the run-down brick hotel he had settled into, or that a fire would strand him inside. "The building in which I work has wooden fire escapes," he wrote anxiously to Helen. "I could not imagine a worse footnote on Hollywood than that."[21]

The shifting sands of southern California underscored Caldwell's insecurity with the movie business as a whole. He was terrified that the almost unimaginable windfall of weekly checks would somehow be cut short, and he badgered Maxim Lieber to verify the terms of his agreement with MGM. The moment Caldwell received the contract he mailed it to Helen and commanded her to take it to the bank and lock it up without delay. "And don't lose the key!" he lectured. "It's the only piece of paper in the world that binds the company to pay." Even with the contract safely stowed away, he fretted constantly that something would go awry and he would be sent home. Caldwell sought to reassure himself with false bravado. "Only a calamity or an act of God can stop my pay," he blustered. "I'll collect, or somebody will be sorry." In rare vulnerable moments, he gave voice to his fears. "I would not be surprised to see the movie business blow up here some day," he wrote nervously to Helen. "There is no stability."[22]

Caldwell thought the people he met in the studios were unreliable as well. Co-workers at MGM seemed to follow an endless round of boisterous partying, and Caldwell was decidedly uncomfortable around the witty, garrulous, and self-consciously intellectual writers who met each night after work. "Somehow, I can't enter into the spirit of Hollywood," he wrote to Helen. "I stay [at the studio] all day; go home about six, eat supper, go back to the room and read until it's time to go to sleep." On the infrequent occasions that Caldwell did go out, he went to Hermosa Beach—a place where he did not have "to drink, dance, and do all the other insane things the picture mob does." Other writers soon regarded him as a dour and severe loner. "Most of them think I'm a 'funny' person because I won't fall in with the crowd," he wrote. "I suppose most of them think I'm half, if not wholly, cracked."[23]

Caldwell was also offended by the contrast between the decadence and extravagance of the people he met in the movie business and the poverty of the rest of the community. He was painfully aware that only a few miles from the back-lot fantasies of the studios, swarms of homeless waited anxiously at the city dump for the latest load of incoming garbage; dozens of beggars wandered beneath the stately palms of Sunset Boulevard. He vowed not to be sucked into the dissolute immorality of the movie business. In office meetings, he created a stir by demanding a chair with a hard seat and straight back, and as he proudly told Morang, he quickly earned a reputation as a frugal Puritan. "The 90 dollar tailors are shocked because I won't let them in my office," he bragged. "The crowd is speechless because I refuse to buy a car, rent a four-room apt. in Hollywood, and keep a couple girls. And to knock them completely speechless, I only have to add that I drink nothing stronger than beer." On another occasion, he remarked more honestly: "It's not my pie. I couldn't get any fun out of acting and thinking like a 12-year-old with 10 times too much money."[24]

Caldwell's biggest complaint with Hollywood was with the demands of being a professional screenwriter. Studio producers preferred to shuttle scripts among teams of writers; some groups brainstormed for plots, others wrote dialogue, still others specialized in creating "continuity" in the script. Typically, a screenplay passed through six or seven stages, and it was extremely rare for a writer to follow one project through to completion. Most artists who came west found this process frustrating and confusing, but for Caldwell it was absolutely intolerable.

He had determinedly followed his own personal visions to conclusion for his entire career, and he was fiercely goal-oriented. "I'd thank god for a chance to complete a story," he wrote Morang desperately. "But it seems that is not the way things are done in the racket." Every time a script was taken out of his hands he took it as a personal insult which only heightened his fear that he would be fired.[25]

Caldwell's insecurity was aggravated by the uncomfortable feeling that he was but a tiny cog in a huge process that operated beyond his control. Screenwriters were low men in the movie business's hierarchy, and they rarely knew what became of their work. Completed screenplays were routinely discarded or radically altered without their knowledge even after weeks or months of labor. Usually, writers had no idea who would star in the pictures they wrote, who else had worked on them, or when, if ever, they would be filmed. "Just try to find out something!" Caldwell wrote in exasperation to Gordon Lewis. "Don't ask me anything about the picture—it's a mess. MGM bought a play script from somebody; the director and studio hack rewrote it; and now my job is to rewrite that, with sound. I don't know a damn thing about it, and neither does anyone else."[26]

Caldwell had little patience for collaborating with other writers, another staple of the Hollywood system. Indeed, there could not have been an author on the MGM payroll more temperamentally unsuited to working as part of a team. On his first picture, Caldwell was paired with Jim Sprague, a screenwriter who soon disgusted him by keeping the hours of a typical Hollywood writer. "Sprague is lazy as hell," he raged to Helen. "He never gets up until 10 or 11, and I have to wait for him every morning to talk over the work with him before I go ahead." When Sprague—or whomever he happened to be teamed with—did arrive, Caldwell was usually sullen and quiet. He had always been hesitant to discuss works-in-progress, for he firmly believed that discussion bled the intensity from good fiction. The endless deliberations over screenplays, he told Helen, guaranteed that "if anyone ever had a good story, it would be talked to death before it could be put down on paper." Predictably, Caldwell's collaborators warned him that he would have to moderate his appetite for graphic violence and sexuality—advice he had little patience for. "Picture business is pretty hokey, and my stomach may turn any day," he complained. "There are so many taboos (1,000s of them), and five or six people have to be pleased instead of myself alone."[27]

Screenwriters dissected one another's work with brutal honesty, and they learned to save their pride by approaching everything they wrote with a detached cynicism. Caldwell could never manage this critical separation, and his hurt feelings only hardened his natural stubbornness and egotism. "I've been listening for two days to a story that has not yet been written," he wrote disgustedly to Helen. "The main concern seems to be to invent something new for it every half hour. . . . I've listened but have not agreed to anything so far, and when it does get to the point where it is to be put down on paper, I'll either be so repelled by it that I'll say so, or else, vomit right on the floor in the 'conference.' "[28]

The sporadic rhythm of work also bothered Caldwell, for he was accustomed to following a strictly regimented schedule when he wrote. In Hollywood, there were frequent spells of inactivity, and during these lulls Caldwell paced nervously around his studio office like a caged animal, damning his sentence in the "Hollywood prison." Suddenly, however, demands for plot synopses, dialogue, or narratives would pour in from the studio executives, and the office would erupt into a frenzy of activity. Caldwell, whose creative imagination was plodding and methodical, was not by nature adept at brainstorming, nor did he really understand the fluffy, fantastical vocabulary that propelled Hollywood pictures in the 1930s. "This thing of pulling a story out of the blue sky is enough to do up the best of men in a tight knot," he wrote anxiously to Helen. "It's impossible to explain the rush they put a person in. It's the phone ringing every half an hour, asking if you've got another page done. Or else sending a messenger for it, and then trying to write a decent script at the same time. It's a hell of a way for a man to earn a living."[29]

The erratic rhythm of the work was underscored by the chaos of the studio offices, and Caldwell had a terrible time concentrating. He missed his old typewriter, the carefully stacked pads of yellow paper and neatly arranged pencils; most of all, he missed the quiet of the tiny lakeside cabin in Mount Vernon or a barren New York City apartment. To Helen, who was painfully aware of her husband's desperate need for silence when he wrote, Caldwell described a scene of unrelenting bedlam:

Joan Crawford was in the next room for three hours practicing voice lessons with a teacher. She did nothing but run the scale for three hours. If you don't think that will drive you crazy, add on top a crying girl in the same room with you (a rejected actress who got axed by the producer) . . . Up here in the writer's building there was nothing to bother me, though; 20 or 30 typewriters, half a dozen phones ringing, and a stuttering writer across the hall."[30]

Caldwell might have suffered the uncertainty and dissatisfactions of the screenwriting process more easily had he believed in anything he was assigned to write. On his first picture, he was asked to produce dialogue for a group of New Orleans fishermen. After some research, Caldwell discovered that they spoke a colorful blend of French and English, and he worked hard to capture the rhythm of their speech. The movie's producers, however, felt that "a sort of dog-Spanish" would be both more entertaining and more marketable. "I refused to do a damn fool thing like that!" he wrote in exasperation to Helen. "Who with any sense would? . . . I was there and I heard them speaking French just as plainly as we did in Quebec! . . . Nobody can make me, even for $250 a week, write dog-Mexican dialogue when the people are speaking French." The producers took him off the picture. Soon afterwards, Caldwell was assigned to a film set on a small farm. By the time he was brought in, most of the footage had been shot, including a scene where a colt was tied securely to a stake while its mother roamed freely about the farm. Oblivious to director King Vidor's exalted reputation in the film industry, Caldwell bluntly informed him that such a scene was absurd: "a colt would never be tied up on a farm because they always stay near their mother." Vidor stared at him blankly and did not respond. Caldwell was reassigned to another film. Slowly, he came to see—but not accept—one of the more cynical truths of a writer's status in Hollywood. "I've learned that as long as a writer says 'yes' he is kept on a picture; but if he answers 'no' to any director he is immediately taken off and given another assignment. I have yet to say 'yes.' "[31]

Caldwell was most distressed by Hollywood's unapologetic failure to address the real social problems confronting the nation. Studio executives wanted their films to serve as a distraction from the hardships of the Depression, not as a reminder, and indeed, this was what audiences seemed to demand. Caldwell, however, was aghast at the featherweight romances and comedies served up by Hollywood and watched with bitter resignation as one after another of his story ideas was rejected. He worked long and hard on a screenplay for director Howard Hawks, only to be told that it was "too realistic." "It won't make any difference," he wrote acidly to Morang. "Ninety-nine out of a hundred stories they manufacture here are tripe anyway . . . formulas on new backgrounds. Christ!" For a while, he found hope in a different King

Vidor picture entitled *Let the Hurricane Roar*. "I've found one that I'm
standing up for," he wrote Morang excitedly, for Vidor's liberal political
convictions were quite similar to his own. "It has genuine life in it—
none of this goddam' tripe of [romantic] triangles and such." While he
acknowledged that the "odds against us are 100 to 1," he was determined to "hold out for it to the last ditch." Predictably, the project
was shelved, and Caldwell's repugnance for Hollywood only deepened.
He worked to salve his disappointment in the usual way: "But what
the hell! That weekly check comes in every Saturday morning on the
stroke of 11," he wrote Morang. "And I should worry if they never
read what I write."[32]

Caldwell's frustration intensified when film proposals for *Tobacco
Road* and *God's Little Acre* made the rounds of the major studios without
a nibble. "All the directors and supervisors turned thumbs down on
[*Tobacco Road*]," Caldwell wrote angrily to Morang. "I did not see the
synopsis, but someone told me the reader had given this comment:
'Too Brutal.'" Caldwell, of course, was proud as well as angry that he
was considered too "brutal" for the movies. "They can't quite see 'TR',
they can't quite see me, and they don't think anything I write is movie
material, which does not make me cry." Nonetheless, he was irked
when his friend Nathanael West sold the rights to *Miss Lonelyhearts*, a
novel he liked but thought far less important than his own. Unaware
of any irony in his statement, Caldwell complained to Morang that
West had succeeded only by virtue of the strong sexual elements in
Miss Lonelyhearts. "This business goes so far away from reality that most
pictures even attempt to deny a man his stomach," he wrote angrily.
"Have you noticed that in the pictures people as a rule don't eat? But
sex, sex, sex."[33]

But in spite of his fierce attacks on "everything Hollywood," Caldwell found himself mesmerized by it as well. He was helplessly fascinated by the fantasy and glamour of the set, and he stared
open-mouthed at stars, naming the ones he saw in long lists. "The
studio cafe is the place to see everybody," he wrote Morang breathlessly. "You can go in to eat lunch and look up and see a Barrymore
perched on a stool across from you; while beside you will be a clown
or an Indian eating soup. The next day you'll be eating your apple pie
and a corn-fed [girl] who has been running all morning from the 'villain'
will come to get a sandwich before going back to the set to be
seduced."[34]

For the first time in his life, Caldwell had a little cash in his pocket,
and he took a long, considered look at the freedom wealth could bring.

"All this easy money, no hard work," he confessed to his wife, "would appeal to anybody who was out to make money by writing." He noted the cut of men's suits, and began to dress a little better himself. While he began the summer disgusted by writers who spent their paychecks on new cars, at the end of July he bought the latest Ford roadster, had it delivered to Mount Vernon, and began swamping Helen with detailed instructions on the proper way to wash it.[35]

Caldwell even worried that Hollywood's lack of social conscience might undermine his own cherished artistic agenda. He wrote long, guilt-ridden letters reassuring his writer friends—and himself—that he would never become a "literary whore." "I have not gone Hollywood. I can assure you of that," he wrote to I. L. Salomon. "I thought when I left there might be danger, but since being here three weeks, I know damn well it's not my pie. I'm disgusted, dissatisfied, and disgruntled." He was a "serious writer," he repeatedly pledged, and it would be "suicide" to stay more than three months. Over and over, in increasingly hysterical tones, he proclaimed his loathing for a culture where "it's not what you write, but how much money you make"—a place where writers "churned out tripe for cash."[36]

Many of Caldwell's left-wing friends back east saw Hollywood as the ultimate expression of American capitalist decadence, and he saved his most urgent affirmations of integrity for them. He railed passionately against "capitalistic" screenwriters who made him "sick at his stomach"—men who "would not admit that people in their own country were starving." His financial straits left him no choice, Caldwell pleaded to Morang, for "what in hell can a man do in this capitalistic society but try to earn a living?" Painfully contrite, he promised "never again [to] try to make a dollar above what I really need."[37]

Caldwell depicted himself—and believed himself to be—a Hollywood rebel unwilling to compromise his social principles or take orders from the crassly mercenary studio heads. "By God, they soon found out here that I wasn't another of the yes-men school of NY writers," he crowed. His guilt inevitably led him to blustery proclamations of his manhood and independence. "They'll fire me before I'll be their monkey," he stormed. "I don't give a damn about any of them."[38]

In reality, however, Caldwell saved most of his brave rebellion for his letters home, and this surely intensified both his guilt and his anxiety. While he admired writers like Laurence Stallings, who walked out on assignments for political and artistic reasons, he was never so bold. He complained enough to be shuttled from one picture to the next, but he was careful not to overstep his bounds. His most substantial film credit, in fact, was as a screenwriter for an episode of the decidedly conservative series *Crime Doesn't Pay*. Caldwell also steered safely clear of the labor dispute then raging between writers and the major studios. While the complaints of the fledgling screenwriters' union were almost identical to his own, he made no effort to join their struggle. To Helen, he admitted that his chief worry was that the writers might initiate a strike that would cut into his pay. Caldwell was too desperate for the money to be a troublemaker, too much of a loner to join them. "I'm getting mine," he admitted to Morang, "and then getting out."[39]

As the end of his summer approached, Caldwell poured out complaints about Hollywood so obsessively that Helen and Morang surely tired of his desperate efforts to convince himself of his deep, unending enmity for the movies. "It would the lowest degree of hell to be stopped Friday and told that the option had been taken up for 6 months," he assured Morang, although MGM had never suggested such a deal. "I'd do murder right then and there." Caldwell was terrified of the pull he felt—of the mingled lust and loathing he had for Hollywood and the compromises it demanded of his personal and artistic values. "By God they'll never get me," he wrote, almost hysterically, to Helen. "Each day I thank God that I've got one day less to stay in this factory."[40]

Caldwell left Culver City at the end of August and returned east to Mount Vernon. Artistically, the summer had been an unproductive one, as he proudly told Milton Abernethy: "I've only completed two scripts in all my three months. One an original story (which no one after about two months has read), the other an adaption [*sic*] for a two-reel short about crime-doesn't-pay, or some such hoke. I turned down seven assignments, was taken off three, and completed two. That's my record."[41]

Financially, however, the summer was a windfall. In addition to buying his first new car, Caldwell settled two gnawing debts that were psychological as well as monetary. First, he bought the Mount Vernon house from Helen's mother, finally silencing her complaints that her ne'er-do-well son-in-law lived off her charity. Even more satisfying, he paid off the Portland bank (an institution he equated with the conservative element in the city that had banned *The Bastard* three years earlier) for the money it had lent him to open the Longfellow Square Bookshop. "I'll have squared myself with your Portland sons-of-bitches," he wrote fiercely to Morang, his anger and humiliation still very much alive. "They can now, one and all, go straight to hell and roast there."[42]

To be out of debt, with money in the bank, seemed almost too good to be true, and Caldwell bragged about his good fortune to everyone he knew. "I'm back at scratch again. I don't owe nothing, and I ain't got nothing; but I'm even with the world. Thank God!" he wrote joyously to I. L. Salomon. "For the second time since 1903," the future looked bright and full of promise, and Caldwell was moved to uncharacteristic optimism. "The debts are paid off, by God, and we'll have about three hundred clear," he exulted to Abernethy. "We can live off that till kingdom comes if necessary!"[43]

III

BEFORE LEAVING for Hollywood, Caldwell had been approached by a likable young playwright named Jack Kirkland. Kirkland considered *Tobacco Road* one of the great books in American literature, and he begged Caldwell for permission to write an adaptation of it for the stage. After checking with Lieber to ensure that the project would cost him nothing, Caldwell gave Kirkland the go-ahead, and promptly forgot about the matter.[44]

Meanwhile, Kirkland moved overseas and struggled to write a script. "I went around with the book in my pocket," Kirkland remembered later. "Soon I knew it by heart. I cried over it. There wasn't a pub in the West End or a bistro on the Left Bank that didn't know my tears." Kirkland's tears were ones of frustration as well as ones of sympathy for Caldwell's characters. Much of the power of the novel lay in the static, on-going lethargy of the Lesters; Kirkland was stymied trying to transform Caldwell's idiosyncratic novel into an "active dramatic tragedy." Stranded in Majorca with his money dwindling, he finally hit on an idea, "and when the answer came," he remembered, it was deceptively simple. "In the book Jeeter loved his land, but there was never a question of losing it," Kirkland realized. "Wouldn't that loss, then, be the beginning of tragedy?" Kirkland introduced the character of the dastardly, heartless banker—already becoming a caricature in Depression era literature—and made him the villain; the fight for the farm provided the compelling dramatic theme he was looking for.[45]

Caldwell read Kirkland's adaptation in Hollywood and was not particularly impressed; nor was he optimistic that it would ever see the stage. Even when Nathanael West's sister informed him—incorrectly, as it turned out—that Kirkland had interested a producer, he was unenthusiastic. "I don't like the play as it is now," he wrote grumpily to

Helen. "But that's probably the last we'll ever hear of it." Caldwell was very nearly correct, for Kirkland was having no luck finding a producer willing to risk money on a play about a group of starving sharecroppers living on a dirt farm in Eastern Georgia. In a theater season when even the most light-hearted dramas were failing by the score, *Tobacco Road* seemed a poor bet. Only after promising to put up six thousand dollars of his own money did Kirkland manage to interest Sam Grisman, a well-known Broadway producer in New York.[46]

In late October 1933, the play went into rehearsal in New York, but Caldwell remained skeptical. "If it ever reaches the boards, I'm sure it will be a fizzle," he wrote Morang. When Kirkland asked him to come to New York to help with staging, he was annoyed at the imposition. "I'll go down when I am sent some travelling expenses but not before," he wrote testily. "I hope something happens to it so it will be better, but I don't see much hope."[47]

As opening night approached, however, Caldwell was reluctantly caught up in the excitement of seeing his work come to life on the stage. While Kirkland had softened some of the grimmer reminders of the Lesters' poverty, he had not shied from the overt sexuality or the bawdy humor, and he had successfully re-created the Lesters' rich vernacular that Caldwell had so brilliantly captured in the book. Kirkland worked hard revising and tightening the script, and Caldwell noted with satisfaction that when the play was finally completed, it "followed the novel from beginning to end just as it was written." Two weeks before opening night Caldwell conceded that while he still worried about a "slip-up" in the acting and directing, he thought "Kirkland has made a tight drama." "It surprised me a lot," he admitted to Morang. "I was looking for a mess."[48]

On December 5, 1933, two days after his thirtieth birthday, Caldwell drove with Helen and the Morangs from Mount Vernon to New York for opening night. The roads were so icy that they arrived at the Masque Theater after the play had already started, and they slipped into the darkened auditorium halfway through the first act.

Caldwell's first disappointment was the number of empty seats, for the theater was only a little more than half full. More disturbing than the poor attendance, however, was the audience's reaction to the play. As Caldwell watched, trying to concentrate on the action, the silence around him was punctuated with outbursts of laughter. Caldwell still had difficulty recognizing or acknowledging the humor in his work, and he was fiercely protective of his characters' dignity. Moreover, as the play progressed, Caldwell became convinced that the loud guffaws he heard were ones of derision—not only for the Lesters, but for the play as a whole. At the final curtain he stormed out, certain that *Tobacco Road* was a dismal failure. With Helen and the Morangs in tow, he burst onto the street, only to find it jammed with a boisterous crowd, their mood starkly at odds with his own. That same evening, national Prohibition had been repealed, and mounted police were having trouble maintaining control over the drunken revelers.[49]

Caldwell's grim appraisal of the play seemed to be confirmed by the first wave of reviews in the New York papers the next day. On the bright side, every reviewer had high praise for Henry Hull's characterization of Jeeter Lester. Percy Hammond of the *New York Tribune* thought Hull's "searching impersonation of the squalid and lazy dust-eaters of 'Tobacco Road' " was "as thorough a deed of acting as I have seen in forty years of professional playgoing." Brooks Atkinson raved that "as Jeeter Lester, Henry Hull gives . . . a character portrait as mordant and brilliant as you can imagine." Atkinson also called Caldwell "a demonic genius—brutal, grimly comic and clairvoyant."[50] Although he thought the play "reels around the stage like a drunken stranger to the theater" and was one of "the grossest episodes ever put on the stage," Atkinson saw "spasmodic moments of merciless power when truth is flung into your face with all the slime that truth contains." "*Tobacco Road*," he concluded, "left a malevolent glow of poetry above the rudeness of his statement."[51]

Most critics, however, outdid one another seeking snide ways to pan the play. Walter Winchell characterized *Tobacco Road* as yet "another of those familiar plays about Southern imbeciles, who never bathe, rarely eat and are generally disagreeable. For the most part," he wrote dismissively, "the play is blabby and uneventful." John Mason Brown thought it a "resolutely squalid yarn," that was "as feeble as it is unpleasant." Even Henry Hull's performance, he wrote, could not "save the play from itself or from the deadening weight of the livestock it chooses to parade as men and women." Richard Lockridge of the *New York Sun* thought *Tobacco Road* was "rather loosely strung together in a lagging drama which quite frequently achieves the repulsive and seldom falls below the faintly sickening."[52]

Not surprisingly, ticket sales for the play were slow, and it struggled along to half-empty houses. While Caldwell insisted that "it is a good play . . . regardless of how long it runs," he unsubtly reminded friends that he "didn't have a thing to do with it, except furnish the novel." Kirkland and Grisman, however, refused to give up easily. The play, while not meeting costs, was inexpensive to stage and was losing money very slowly. The costumes were little more than hand-me-down rags, and the most expensive component of the set was the two-foot layer of topsoil heaped onto the stage (a prop, some reviewers derisively noted, that caused the actors to raise clouds of dirt as they moved around). The play struggled on for a month, losing a little less each week, before the Masque Theater finally kicked it out. Undeterred, Kirkland and Grisman secured the 48th Street Theater and staged the play again.[53]

This time, their stubborn belief in *Tobacco Road* was rewarded. New reviews, far more favorable, were scattered in the press. While unable to resist categorizing the play as part of the "Caldwell-Faulkner 'Howdy Lecher!' School," the critic for *The New Yorker* saw "a certain quality about the play . . . which brings one up just short of giggling. It has the strange disheveled dignity of sounding true." A number of papers carried letters from playgoers who passionately endorsed the play. The *New York Times* printed an eloquent testimonial from a woman annoyed by the "squeamishness" of Walter Winchell's opening night review. "Personally," she wrote, "I think it would do the delicately natured among us good to crowd up to see 'Tobacco Road.' They would see some superb acting and they might have something to think about." The biggest boost for the play came from an editorial in the *New York Post*, the first of the New York papers to sense the changing tide of opinion and endorse the play. "It is savagely humorous in spots, but its high notes are pity and terror and the elements of great tragedy," the anonymous critic wrote. "To us, *Tobacco Road* seems grand entertainment; also a disturbing commentary on life in the United States."[54]

Within a week of its late January move to the 48th Street Theater, the play's ticket sales doubled. "The play is now running well and it looks as if both of us were right. It *is* a good play," Caldwell wrote Morang. "It looks as if it will run another month, maybe two." Ten days later, Caldwell reported that "the play is going like wild fire," and noted with some satisfaction that "out of 26 plays that opened in December, 'Tobacco Road' is the only one now running." In late February 1934 the play was ninety-nine performances old, and still the crowds continued to grow. "They were standing four rows deep," Caldwell bragged in early March, and by month's end *Tobacco Road* was selling out eight weeks in advance.[55]

Caldwell carefully followed the New York papers, and watched with vindictive pleasure as the critics who had initially panned the play scrambled to recant their first reviews. "That play is going to give

Walter Winchell piles yet!" he wrote joyously to Morang. Character-istically, Caldwell even considered reviewers like Brooks Atkinson, who had always liked much of *Tobacco Road*, to have been part of a con-spiracy of critical censure. When Atkinson wrote a follow-up to his initial piece, Caldwell described him as "only the latest to masticate his review."[56]

In spite of this early success, Caldwell, Kirkland, and Grisman could not have predicted just how popular their play would become; as the months went by, *Tobacco Road* thrived beyond their wildest dreams. A year after opening, the play sold out its six-hundredth straight perfor-mance; another year later it was still going strong and nearing Broad-way's rarely achieved mark of one thousand straight shows. Tickets continued to sell, and the play crept up the list of Broadway's longest-running plays. By October 1935, it was third, behind *Lightnin'* and *Abie's Irish Rose*—two plays that had achieved their remarkable runs during the 1920s, an era when theater attendance had reached unprecedented highs. In December 1936, three years after opening, *Tobacco Road* took over the second spot by selling out performance number 1,292, and still its remarkable popularity continued. In late 1939, almost five years after opening at the Masque, the play passed *Abie's Irish Rose*. In a decade when a theater ticket was a costly indulgence for most New Yorkers, *Tobacco Road* became the longest-running play in Broadway history.

During this remarkable run, what the *New York Times* called the "oath-begarnished, eighth wonder of the theatrical world" became an established part of the glittering landscape of New York. Each anniver-sary of opening night brought retrospective features reporting such crucial data as the number of auto fenders that had been dented, the quantity of turnips eaten, and the pounds of dirt that had covered the stage. The lore that inevitably grew up around the play was bandied about at fashionable cocktail parties: Dude had thrown his rubber ball against the house twenty-five thousand times without a miss; real spi-ders had spun real webs on the set; the cast planted a garden in the stage dirt and harvested their own crop of turnips. The actors—wave after wave of them—became celebrities, and many of them parlayed their stage fame into lucrative Hollywood careers. Hirschfeld drew car-icatures of the cast members, and gossip columnists followed their every move. Caldwell, Kirkland, and Grisman were besieged by re-quests for interviews, and novice playwrights and aspiring producers hung on their every word. Celebrities as varied as Eleanor Roosevelt, Mae West, and J. Edgar Hoover raved about the play; Harpo Marx asked to stand in for a night, Ira Gershwin began work on a *Tobacco Road* opera, and James Thurber became so obsessed with his impersonations of Jeeter Lester that his friends begged him to stop.[57]

The play garnered serious critical attention as well. Such literary notables as Theodore Dreiser and Carl Van Doren recommended *Tobacco Road* for the Pulitzer Prize in drama. Dreiser thought it "the best play I have seen for some years . . . a rare and moving drama." *Tobacco Road*, he wrote, was "honest and forceful reality" that "constitutes a valuable contribution not only to the stage but to general enlightenment." Van Doren felt that the play exhibited an "essential veracity and striking literary skill" and thought it "one of the most powerful, moving, and salty pieces of comedy ever produced in the United States."

In spite of such endorsements and Lieber's determined lobbying, *Tobacco Road*, while in the running for the prize in 1934, was passed over by the Pulitzer committee in favor of Sidney Kingsley's *Men in White*. "The play doesn't need the prize to my way of thinking," Caldwell wrote Morang in a huff. "I think it will be a better play in spite of it." No one who knew Caldwell was fooled by such disclaimers. Critic Percy Hammond offered his sympathy to "the messenger who bears to Erskine Caldwell, author of *Tobacco Road*, the news that his play was judged unfit for the Pulitzer." Hammond knew that Caldwell was "easily irritated" and "apt to be hard to handle." Caldwell, at least, had the grim satisfaction of watching each year's Pulitzer recipient drop by the wayside while *Tobacco Road* continued to draw full houses. "No prizes," Grisman commented sardonically—"only dividends."[58]

Tobacco Road's popularity outside of New York was as stunning as its success on Broadway. During a time when most producers considered it financial suicide to send shows on the road, two, three, and sometimes four productions of the play crisscrossed Depression America simultaneously, breaking attendance records wherever they went. In California, cities usually considered too far west to embrace a New York show, drew crowds in record numbers. Hull received a twenty-three-minute ovation in L.A. on opening night, and the play's run was extended from four to eight weeks to accommodate the demand. In San Francisco, ten curtain calls marked the beginning of an unprecedented eight-week engagement. America's heartland also poured out to see the play. Columbus, Indianapolis, Cleveland, and Cincinnati all hosted *Tobacco Road* six times between 1933 and 1939. From Syracuse to San Antonio, Provo to Pittsburgh, Tulsa to Tucson—in almost every city in every state outside the South—people flocked to see the play year after year after year. In the late thirties, the producers ventured tentatively into the Deep South as well, playing more cosmopolitan cities like Memphis, Atlanta, and New Orleans; the performances sold out. By 1939, every state in the Union save seven had hosted *Tobacco Road*.* Never in the history of American drama had a play been so popular for so long in so many different places. Conservative estimates suggest that on the road and in New York, over seven million people saw *Tobacco Road* between 1934 and 1940.

The reasons behind such immense and unprecedented popularity are difficult to pinpoint, and as *Tobacco Road* became a legend—a phenomenon—its success became self-perpetuating. People flocked to it as they would to Niagara Falls or the Empire State Building; everyone had to see it once. Caldwell was asked to explain the play's success in literally hundreds of interviews and appearances. When feeling loquacious, he usually offered the theory that Americans were morbidly fascinated with the Lesters because the debased sharecroppers indulged their own worst instincts and allowed theatergoers to confront their darkest impulses. "The ideal of books and plays and novels is to mirror life. We see our good sides and our bad sides," Caldwell explained to the reporters clustered around him at the St. Louis or Toledo airport. "When people laugh at the antics of Jeeter Lester, they're only trying to cover up their feelings. They see what they might sink to." When he was in a hurry, or not in the mood to speak to reporters—which was frequently—he said more simply: "Well, everybody sees something of himself in it."[59]

Many people came to see *Tobacco Road* because the play made them laugh. Henry Hull—the first Jeeter—never let his character's buffoonery and incorrigible lechery become undignified, but the second Jeeter, James Barton, had been trained in musical comedy and, as reviewer Robert Benchley noted, he was "more comic and less sophisticated." Barton was the first of many Jeeter Lesters who found that playing the part for laughs was far easier than seeking to communicate Jeeter's honor or reminding audiences of the character's spiritual as well as physical starvation. As the years passed, Jeeter evolved into a slapstick hillbilly, a portrayal audiences seemed never to tire of.[60]

Part of the laughter was prompted, as Caldwell suggested, by the uneasiness the play evoked. People laughed because they were embarrassed by the sexuality, or by their attraction to it. Others laughed to

---

* The seven states were Maine, New Hampshire, Vermont, Rhode Island, Mississippi, Florida, and North Dakota.

hide the pain the Lesters' suffering caused them. But the characters of *Tobacco Road* also vindicated—and perpetuated—the non-Southerner's smug notions of Southern degeneracy. The gleeful convulsions that rocked audiences were, in part, a crass expression of regional enmity and prejudice, and the hilarity came at the Lesters' expense. As a result, while upper-class Southerners could find humor in the antics of their "country cousins," audiences below the Mason-Dixon line were usually less amused.

There was an undeniably serious side to Kirkland's adaptation, but the play's reminders of rural poverty were not, as the producers originally feared, so depressing as to deter playgoers from seeing *Tobacco Road*. To Caldwell's disgust, many audiences found the Lesters' degradation so extreme that they dismissed it as staged hyperbole and enjoyed the show. Other viewers recognized that the Lesters were on the brink of starvation but viewed the clan's verve and spark (however licentious and depraved) as an inspiring testimonial to the resiliency of the human spirit. And many playgoers undoubtedly found something comforting about the Lesters' plight; the poverty of *Tobacco Road* was abject enough to make almost anyone feel wealthy by comparison. There were, of course, many people who watched the play with solemn concern and applauded Caldwell's illumination of a serious social problem. But as Southern journalists were quick to point out—particularly to New Yorkers—shedding tears for the denizens of *Tobacco Road* served as a convenient distraction from the grinding urban poverty in one's own backyard. A trip to the theater could satisfy a playgoer's appetite for social concern without ruining his day.

But what drew the millions to *Tobacco Road* was not primarily the social message, nor was it the humor; it was sex. Most of the play's notoriety sprang from what came to be known as "the scene"—the segment in the first act when Ellie Mae masturbates against the ground and eventually seduces her brother-in-law in the Lesters' dirt yard. While played with varying degrees of explicitness by different actresses, in all its forms it was beyond anything Broadway had seen before, and certainly more explicit than the usual fare in Toledo or Dubuque. Add to that Jeeter's sacrilegious exclamation of "By God and by Jesus!"; Lov Bensey's complaints about the frigidity of his twelve-year-old bride; and a middle-aged woman minister's public seduction of a sixteen-year-old boy, and playgoers were privy to the bawdiest Broadway hit in history.[61]

Considered titillating and outrageous in New York, such subject matter proved absolutely explosive on the road. In the play's first tour, the play stopped in Chicago, and the firestorm of controversy that broke out became national news. *Tobacco Road* was in its seventh week of sold-out performances when the Irish-Catholic Mayor Edward Kelly finally attended; he was mortified. "It is an insult to decent people," Kelly stormed to reporters. "That show is not interesting nor artistic. It is just a mess of filth and degeneracy without any plot, rhyme, or reason for producing it except filth." Worrying about the play's impact on "women and impressionable young people," Kelly ordered the show closed that very night.[62]

With the future of the entire tour in jeopardy, the producers of *Tobacco Road* took Kelly to court. Five years after the banning of *The Bastard* in Portland, and only two after the vindication of *God's Little Acre* in Boston, Caldwell was embroiled yet again in a fight to save his work from censorship. The Catholic Church mobilized its powerful lobby in an effort to ban the play, and local civil liberties groups fought to save it. Caldwell and Kirkland toured Chicago's literary clubs and universities to drum up support. "It's terrible that an honest, truthful expression of this kind is forbidden by men in power," Caldwell told reporters. "*Tobacco Road* is," he said, in a refrain he had taken to using during the *God's Little Acre* trial, "no more obscene than the truth."[63]

Letters both for and against Mayor Kelly's decision poured into the Chicago papers. Many agreed with the man who demanded to know "what qualified Edward F. Kelly to be monitor of Chicago's morals? . . . Do we have to yield to the arbitrary dictum of this one-cylinder, self-appointed Legion of Decency?" Others, however, felt that Kelly had rightfully taken a stand against the "decadence of New York's muck-rakers and keyhole pornographers." "I'm with the mayor in his war on theatrical filth," one outraged Chicagoan wrote. "A city can be liberal without being downright insane in its acceptance of dirt."[64]

With the national and local press following every move, *Tobacco Road* was eventually vindicated in the local circuit court. A restraining order against the city was issued, and the play was finally allowed to go on. "That three-week junket to Chicago just about ordered my coffin for me," Caldwell wrote Morang. "Fighting the Catholic Church is like sticking your head in a cannon." But Caldwell, Kirkland, and Grisman were extremely pleased with the outcome of the case. The legal fees were high and the play had lost money while the ban was in effect, but the publicity *Tobacco Road* received was stupendous. Ticket sales, already brisk, skyrocketed in every city where the play was booked. In New York, where the hot summer weather had thinned out the crowds, the Chicago case brought them flooding back.[65]

Wherever it was staged, the play prompted an open forum on civil liberties and artistic freedom, and the hotter the debate, the faster tickets sold. Over the next five years, *Tobacco Road* was taken to court thirty-six times and banned in cities across America. The mayor of Detroit labeled the play "a conglomeration of obscenity, filth, putrescence; in short, a garbage pile of indecent dialogue and degenerate exhibitionism." Usually, however, town officials stopped short of legal action. Some were philosophically opposed to artistic censorship, but more could simply not turn away the revenue the play represented to local economies hard hit by the Depression. In exchange for forbearance, Caldwell and the producers often agreed to soften the play's more offensive elements. At the behest of church groups, "By God and by Jesus!" frequently became "By Gad and by Judas!" Ellie Mae's sexual contortions were toned down. Cast members grew accustomed to seeing plainclothes policemen dutifully writing down each obscenity in small black notebooks and comparing them to the list approved by the mayor's office.[66]

As the court victories and ticket sales mounted, Caldwell feigned indifference about the storm of controversy that followed the play. "The cops in Albany, Buffalo, Utica, and Syracuse have been raiding Tobacco Road, but that's not news any longer," he noted drily to Morang in 1936. But behind his nonchalance, Caldwell felt every effort to suppress *Tobacco Road* as a personal attack, and he eagerly and self-righteously rose to its defense. Although the well-publicized efforts to ban the play contributed mightily to its popular success, the censorship battles hardened Caldwell's conviction that he was being persecuted— that his greatest successes inspired the greatest efforts to silence him. He logged thousands of miles defending *Tobacco Road* and became recognized as one of the nation's leading advocates of artistic freedom. And with the rise of fascism in Europe, he began to liken his trials to the struggles for liberation going on around the globe. "Maybe it will keep the little Hitlers from causing so much trouble," he wrote to Frank Daniel after a drive to ban the play failed in Atlanta in 1938. "As long as we are able to tie tin cans to the little ones, there is not much danger of a big one getting a grip on America."[67]

In March 1941, *Tobacco Road* closed on Broadway after its 3,180th performance, over 900 more than any other play in American history. While road companies sputtered along throughout the early forties, America's entrance into the Second World War marked the end of the play's popularity. With the economy on the mend, and people absorbed in the spectacle on the world stage, Southern sharecroppers and rural poverty seemed increasingly irrelevant. There is also some truth to Kirkland's explanation for the end of the play's remarkable run: in eight years, traveling productions of the show had permeated the nation's population centers so thoroughly that most of the people who had ever wanted to see *Tobacco Road* had finally done so.

IV

EVER SINCE THE TURMOIL surrounding the publication of *God's Little Acre* in early 1933, Caldwell had struggled to find time to write. Working in fits and starts between trial dates in New York, after long, frustrating days "with the Hollywood idiots" on the West Coast, and finally between rehearsals and performances of the play, Caldwell managed to work on a new novel. In early 1934, as the play took off at the 48th Street Theater, he completed the draft of a work he titled *Journeyman*.

Journeyman is the story of Semon Dye, a corrupt, lecherous, and hypnotically persuasive itinerant minister who seduces and swindles the poor white farmers of a small Georgia town. In the course of Dye's brief stay at Clay Horey's farm, he cheats him out of his land, his car, and his wife. He wields a gun, shoots a virtuous black man, swills white lightning by the gallon, rolls dice with expertise, seduces fifteen-year-old girls, and at the end of the novel, skips town as suddenly as he arrives. The focal point of the novel is Dye's revival meeting, which Caldwell depicts as a violently passionate ordeal where the religious ecstasy is inseparable from the sexual, and where Dye presides over what amounts to—as Caldwell vividly and explicitly describes it—a communal orgasm.

Like *Tobacco Road* and *God's Little Acre* before it, *Journeyman* is characterized by a startling mixture of burlesque humor, stark violence, sexual abandon, and social criticism. The novel addresses a lifelong interest Erskine shared with his father—first expressed in the "Georgia Cracker" piece written for Professor Hench's class—in "the effects of bogus religion and bogus preachers upon the character of the Southern people." *Journeyman*, Caldwell wrote critic Brooks Atkinson (in language he might have taken directly from one of Ira's articles) "is the story of 'pseudo-ministers' . . . who are perched like vultures on fence posts in the South, waiting to claw and devour the flesh of ignorant people."[68]

Both *Tobacco Road* and *God's Little Acre* were written during sustained bursts of consuming creative effort. But *Journeyman*, composed in bits and pieces, was less carefully crafted and less sophisticated than his previous novels. The characters are devoid of the contradictions and subtlety that make Jeeter Lester and Ty Ty Walden so compelling, and they exist without dignity or composure. In their evil and stupidity, their childishness and sexual interests, the characters of *Journeyman* read like caricatures of work Caldwell had done before.

When Lieber presented the novel to Marshall Best at Viking, the editor was distinctly unenthusiastic. "You and Erskine both know that we don't think that *Journeyman* is as good a novel as *Tobacco Road* or *God's Little Acre*," Best told Lieber. "It is our opinion that it will not advance his reputation or his position in the book field." Best also felt that the book, which was even more sexually explicit than *God's Little Acre*, was "definitely dangerous, particularly in view of the renewed activities of the censor." Unlike *God's Little Acre*, which he thought was "a fine book and an important contribution to literature," Best did not think *Journeyman* could be defended on artistic grounds. While he stressed that "I believe in Caldwell as a writer," he hoped Lieber could convince his author to "put the book aside or at least rework it." If Caldwell was adamant that the book be published, Best agreed only to put out a limited edition, with a small initial printing that might be reviewed in the New York papers but would not enter widespread trade distribution.[69]

Caldwell was both hurt and outraged by Best's response to the novel. "I can't help being shaky all over from it," he admitted to Helen. "I wish to god I knew about the book. I think it is good, and feel it is, but how can you be sure?" "But what the hell!" he wrote Morang. "Maybe it's as rotten as that after all." Typically, he mingled such admissions of insecurity with angry boasts and outrage over his impotence. "What the hell can I do? A publisher has got you, no matter which way you turn. I told them to go to hell before I'd change it, and I don't know what is to be done."[70]

Lieber felt no such indecision. He immediately put out the word that Caldwell was interested in talking to other publishers. With the success of *Tobacco Road* on Broadway, Caldwell was an increasingly hot property, and before long, Bennett Cerf at Random House and Patricia Covice at Covice-Friede made him offers for *Journeyman* and his future books. But negotiations with Random House stalled when the firm's lawyer read the novel and insisted that its publication would entangle Random House in a long and costly legal battle with the censors; Covice also backed off after reading it. With their options slipping away,

Lieber tried to pressure Best into making a better offer by grossly exaggerating Random House's interest in *Journeyman*. The publishing community in New York was a small one, and Best easily saw through Lieber's and Caldwell's fumbling chicanery. He coolly reiterated the firm's original offer for a limited edition. Bitter and resigned, and no doubt embarrassed, Lieber and Caldwell accepted. In 1935 Viking printed 1,475 handsome, sparely decorated copies of *Journeyman*, a printing small enough, they hoped, to escape the attention of the moral watchdog agencies that had pounced on *God's Little Acre*.[71]

The book was reviewed by most of the New York papers and magazines, and except for a thoughtful analysis by Kenneth Burke in the *New Republic*, the response was largely negative. Quite a few critics, like William Troy at the *Nation*, were simply bored by what they saw as an obsession with sex at the expense of literature. "One may inquire," Troy wrote disdainfully, "whether Mr. Caldwell, in so limiting his own interest in his characters, does not also limit the possibility of very much future interest in his writing." Many other reviewers felt that Caldwell was merely repeating an old formula without finesse or inspiration. "There have been times when reading Mr. Caldwell that I have felt he has almost exhausted the soil from which all his writings have sprung," Hamilton Basso wrote later in *New Masses*. "I felt it most strongly in *Journeyman*." James T. Farrell described the novel as "just another monster hastily rolled off Caldwell's typewriter." By this time Farrell had grown tired of reprimanding Caldwell for his lack of political sophistication, and he summarized his criticism in the simple damning conclusion that *Journeyman* was nothing more than "the same article but with a lessened impact." Even faithful Caldwell advocates like Horace Gregory of the *New York Herald Tribune* admitted worriedly that if "Caldwell were a few years older . . . the present tendency to repeat himself would indicate the end of his career."[72]

V

CALDWELL WAS BADLY SHAKEN by the harsh critical reception of *Journeyman*, but his disappointment was softened by his ongoing success in writing and publishing short stories. In the early 1930s, he had continued to place his work in the nation's most prestigious literary journals, and as his reputation grew, in wider-circulation magazines such as *Vanity Fair*, *American Mercury*, *Esquire*, *Redbook*, and *Atlantic*

Monthly. Soon after the publication of *God's Little Acre*, Viking collected twenty "brief stories" in a volume titled *We Are the Living*.

The twenty short stories—some brutally violent, some absurdly comic, many dealing with sexual themes—were deeper, more evocative, and more sophisticated than any Caldwell had written before. Critics of every political and artistic school recognized that the book marked a clear advance over *American Earth*, the collection Caldwell had published with Scribner's two years before. While many reviewers noted that the stories were peopled with characters they had come to know well in Caldwell's previous work, most recognized a maturation in his prose and a greater willingness to express sentiment and emotion. The almost uniformly positive reviews for *We Are The Living* marked Caldwell as one of the nation's most highly regarded short-story writers. Six pieces were named to O'Brien's prestigious Roll of Honor, another was included in O'Brien's *Best Short Stories of 1934*; yet another, "A Country Full of Swedes," won the *Yale Review*'s 1933 award for fiction and appeared in the *O. Henry Memorial Award Prize Stories* collection for 1934.

In the two years following the publication of *We Are the Living*, Caldwell's hectic schedule encouraged a continued focus on short fiction. His work steadily improved, and in 1935 Viking brought out a second collection called *Kneel to the Rising Sun and Other Stories*. More explicitly political, more considered, more sympathetic and humane, the pieces in *Kneel To The Rising Sun* were the best Caldwell would ever write. "Erskine Caldwell's sun is rising," wrote Charles Wagner in the *New York Post*. "It is a rising sun running blood, to be sure, but Caldwell's mastery of words and his instinct for drama turn the gory to a glory of short story achievement that will be heard from in our literature." Caldwell, wrote Lewis Gannett of the *New York Post*, was "the most profoundly tragic writer on contemporary America," whose "quick emotional intensity" and "subtle atmosphere" placed him "unquestionably in the front rank of American writers." The sadistic broad burlesque that had often clashed so conspicuously with Caldwell's social message was less pronounced in the collection, and many critics now embraced him as the nation's most powerful social realist. "There is no question of humor here," wrote the *New York Times*'s Harold Strauss, previously one of Caldwell's sharpest critics. "There is no question of humor in the timed, smashing strokes of a steam hammer." For Caldwell, who was certainly deeply disturbed and guilty about the comic archetype he had unintentionally created in Jeeter Lester, such a response was sweet absolution.[73]

Many leftists felt that Caldwell had finally arrived. Writers like Hamilton Basso, Matthew Josephson, and James T. Farrell expressed their enthusiastic approval of the stark social landscape presented in the collection and praised Caldwell's depiction of a world where economic exploitation undermined human decency. Basso was only one in a chorus of voices who felt that the title story—"Kneel to the Rising Sun" —was "by any critical standard whatsoever, one of the finest short stories any American has written."[74]

The forty-page story was longer, more sophisticated, and more developed than any Caldwell had attempted before. Even Helen, always her husband's toughest critic, wrote I. L. Salomon that "Kneel" was "the best . . . Erskine has ever done, or anyone else for that matter." Years later, Caldwell himself picked the story as the one he "would select if faced with the choice of taking only one to that desert island and leaving the other ninety-nine behind."[75]

Caldwell wrote this tragic tale of a biracial friendship between two sharecroppers in late 1933. The story—which includes a scene in which one character is eaten alive by hogs—had been rejected by virtually every major magazine in the country on the grounds that it was too explicitly and gruesomely violent. "Lee Harman of *Harper's* has a bad case of intestinal grippe and a fever of 100 plus after reading 'Kneel to the Rising Sun,' " Lieber wrote Caldwell. "His voice over the telephone was all weak and quavering as he told me that this story was 'too cruel and sadistic and had made him sick.' " But in early 1935, after a year of failed efforts to find a magazine willing to publish it, Caldwell— pragmatism overriding his lingering resentment—allowed Lieber to take "Kneel to the Rising Sun" to Maxwell Perkins at *Scribner's Magazine*. Perkins exhibited characteristic editorial courage, as well as a refusal to let past disagreements with Caldwell stand in the way. He accepted the story.[76]

The response to "Kneel to the Rising Sun" was overwhelming. Letters poured into the *Scribner's* offices, some praising the story's power and vicious critique of Southern farm tenancy, others expressing disgust at the violence of the tale. A number of readers wrote to cancel their subscriptions; a great many more sent renewal checks. *Time* magazine reprinted the story and was deluged by letters. "I closed my eyes and wept! And I almost never shed a tear," a college professor from Montana wrote. A housewife in Chicago urged that the story "be reprinted and broadcast over our land until we are all quickened into action against these horrors." Others, however, shared the opinion of a woman from New Haven, who thought Caldwell was "revolting, irritating and depressing." Editors at both *Time* and *Scribner's* recognized that "Kneel to the Rising Sun" generated more publicity and more heated discussion than any short story in recent memory. With this notorious tale as its centerpiece, the collection soared to the fourth spot on the national best-seller list.[77]

VI

WHILE CALDWELL'S STAR was rising in most parts of the country, throughout the South he was widely and enthusiastically despised. Even before the play made him famous, Caldwell had received a small but steady stream of angry letters from Southerners who felt he had slandered his native region. But Caldwell's books had not sold enough copies to attract widespread attention, and for the most part, these angry protests came from the reviewers at small Southern papers or from citizens who lived in or around Wrens.

The success of the play, however, made Caldwell a household name and carried his violent and vivid portrayal of Southern degeneracy into every corner of the nation. The image of "po' white trash" was not a new one, but never before had it been captured in such a compelling package and so widely distributed. Other Southern writers had disparaged their native region; but the number of readers who waded through one thousand pages of Thomas Wolfe's *Look Homeward, Angel* or the abstract stream-of-consciousness of Faulkner's *The Sound and the Fury* could never match the millions who attended performances of *Tobacco Road*. While Caldwell's original characters were far more dignified and complex than the two-dimensional hillbillies who cavorted on stages across America, this was a distinction lost on most audiences; for many Americans the lecherous, amoral, shiftless Lesters became the most resonant impression of the South. To Southerners protective of their regional image, Erskine Caldwell was Public Enemy Number One.

The most widely celebrated Southern protest came from Braswell Deen, a U.S. congressman from southeastern Georgia. When the touring company of the play came to Washington in 1936, he brought his outrage—and that of his constituents—into the chambers of the United States House of Representatives. "I open my mouth and resent with all the power of my soul this untruthful, undignified, undiplomatic and unfair sketch of Southern life," Deen raged. "There is not a word of truth in it. I denounce it and resent it." In the fiery oration, which was reprinted in newspapers nationwide, Deen declared that while he "knew families of 22 children . . . they were all refined, God-fearing citizens." Through his effort to ban the "infamous, wicked, and damnable play," Deen hoped to vindicate "the thousands of sharecroppers and their families who are not in the nation's capital to defend themselves against this infamous, vile, and wicked web into which they have been woven by those who would commercialize upon them."[78]

As Caldwell's notoriety grew, he received hundreds of letters a year that ranged in tone from matronly reproofs that "he should be ashamed of himself," to chilling death threats. Many considered Caldwell a "regional traitor" who catered to Northern prejudices with a mercenary zeal. "Any man who seeks to make his native state ridiculous merely for money holds no claim on the respect of the people of that state," a typical letter read. "We have read worse books than *Tobacco Road*, but none that were more intrinsically rotten, inane and vapid." The most angry and defensive letters invariably came from Georgians, and a number of the state's citizens begged Caldwell to stop admitting that he was born there. "Why do you traduce Georgia and Georgia people with abominable books such as you write?" one man asked. "I had rather go down in poverty, unhonored and unsung, than to write such ignoble literature as you have about your native state." Under a headline that proclaimed "Erskine Caldwell is the Personification of an Earthworm," a journalist in Gainesville, Georgia, summarized the sentiments of his readership. "To turn against one's family is bad enough," he wrote angrily. "But to turn against one's own state and section, holding it up to scorn and ridicule, is terrible. Phooey on Erskine Caldwell!"[79]

Many Southerners felt that the brutal deprivation Caldwell described was a figment of his twisted imagination, and they swamped him with defiant challenges to "prove" or substantiate his work. Many letters began: "I have known countless sharecroppers" or, "I grew up in eastern Georgia" and then went on to denounce Caldwell's depictions as vicious calumny. "I wonder if you wrote them while drunk," the wife of a sharecropper began. ". . . How much better for the world, had you never learned to read or write!"[80]

Many letter writers were so incensed that they insulted Caldwell any way they could; some questioned the integrity of his parents, others even took swipes at his appearance. A woman from Tennessee was sure that Caldwell's evil showed clearly in his face and concluded solemnly that, before long, he would "be able to sit for a picture of the devil." An irate North Carolinian informed Caldwell that he would "be prouder to claim Jesse James or John Dillinger as fellow citizens than you," and that "thousands of other people in Georgia and the South feel the same way."[81]

A disturbing number of letters were more difficult to dismiss, for they contained ominous and quite solemn threats on Caldwell's life. One Georgia man wrote: "White trash like you should die a thousand deaths. And maybe you will. I hope so." "Understand this you SON-OF-A-BITCH," another man wrote. "Write and talk fast, for when the time comes only the one you doubt will be able to save you." References to "stringing Caldwell up," or "beating the tar out of him," were commonplace.[82]

There were, of course, exceptions to this general climate of hostility. Caldwell received scattered letters like the one from a man who assured him that he "was one person born and raised in South Georgia who doesn't resent your writings and holler that it is not true." Liberal journalists like W. J. Cash wrote on Caldwell's behalf in the *Charlotte News and Observer*; and his friend Frank Daniel continued to defend him in the pages of the *Atlanta Journal*. A few newspapers in the upper South and in more metropolitan cities like Memphis and Birmingham mourned the tragic neglect of poverty in rural areas and thanked Caldwell for drawing attention to the problem.[83]

In Wrens, Ira continued to defend his son on the street and from the pulpit. While many of his congregants cringed, he consistently reiterated that his son's fiction was based on simple, undeniable truths, and he happily led tours to the worst-afflicted areas of Jefferson and Burke Counties. While in private Carrie might admit that she was distressed by the sexuality and profanity in her son's work, to the town of Wrens her rigid carriage and proud turn of the head deterred most people from ever broaching the subject. When pressed, she resorted to a well-worn line: "My son is a missionary of the truth."

Caldwell also had the satisfaction of noting that however violently people profaned him below the Mason-Dixon line, his books moved briskly in and out of the Southern libraries and bookstores that carried them. And while the play toured far less extensively in the South than it did in the rest of the country, theaters that did stage *Tobacco Road* drew sold-out houses. Many Southerners hated Erskine Caldwell with a fierce passion—for his godlessness, for his pornography, for his defamation of their native region—but most could not resist finding out what all the fuss was about.[84]

VII

IF CALDWELL'S FIRST STINT in Hollywood finally cleared his
debts, the success of the play made him—almost overnight—a wealthy
man. In early 1934, Caldwell was harassing Lieber to collect $10 and $15
payments from tiny literary journals; two months later royalty checks
ranging from $300 to $500 were arriving like clockwork every week. At
its peak, the play was grossing over $10,000 a week in New York and
almost $20,000 on the road. From the spring of 1934 until early 1940,
Caldwell could count on an income of at least $25,000 a year from the
play alone. The placement of stories in popular magazines, and the
success of *Kneel to the Rising Sun and Other Stories*, raised his income
another $3,000 or $4,000 a year.[85]

Caldwell viewed himself as a simple laboring man who understood
hunger and hardship. He took great pride in his proletarian credentials,
and in many ways, his poverty. Having always scoffed at American
writers who accepted money from patrons or lived in relative comfort,
he struggled now to reconcile his wealth with a deep-seated conviction
that money undermined artistic integrity. To friends—particularly
Communist ones—he steadfastly minimized his income and continued
to act and speak in public as if he were still living from the potatoes
in his Mount Vernon garden. "I don't know what prosperous means,"
he wrote a friend in a typical letter. "Maybe it's hustling, because I
have to hustle like hell to keep enough wood cut to keep us from
freezing in this sub-zero climate." He no longer slept in doorways or
hotel lobbies on his visits to New York, but continued to frequent tiny
boarding houses and to eat sparingly at dilapidated coffee counters.
Though his suits were no longer worn through at the elbows, in press
conferences he took care to present himself as the same raw-boned
country boy he had appeared to be a few years before.[86]

But for all his pretenses to poverty, Caldwell could not deny his
fascination with financial matters and an obsessive interest in making
money. His mother had always encouraged him toward a career in
business, and Caldwell would forever share her social and monetary
ambitions. From the moment the first royalty checks came in, he became an avid and knowledgeable—if somewhat secretive—investor in
the stock market. He followed the progress of his portfolio intently and
spent long hours poring over financial digests. While he usually invested in solid and well-established companies and his return was al-

ways conservative, he was intoxicated by the game and calculated percentage points to the last decimal. He drove two separate brokers to distraction with daily calls and constant transactions. If his public persona remained one of the simple farmer, in the secrecy of his Mount Vernon study, he wheeled and dealed with the appetite and enthusiasm of a Wall Street banker.[87]

The tension Caldwell felt between his social conscience and his new-found wealth only intensified in the late spring of 1934 when Hollywood came calling yet again. MGM offered him a second summer screen-writing contract, and Caldwell agonized over the decision for two months; in the end, he could not resist the money. Well aware that the success of *Tobacco Road* on Broadway increased his marquee value, Caldwell coolly pushed the studio into doubling their original offer from $300 to over $600 a week. MGM assigned him to *Wicked Woman*, a picture directed by Charles Brabin and starring Mady Christians—a film that studio heads thought would be well suited to Caldwell's reputation in the literary field.[88]

Caldwell had felt guilty about "going Hollywood" the summer before, and he felt even worse accepting MGM's offer while the play boomed on Broadway and the royalty checks were arriving regularly in the Mount Vernon mailbox. In letters to friends back East, he insisted that he simply could not afford to turn MGM down. "But if the bread-box gets empty again . . . what can a fellow do?" he asked Frank Daniel, hoping for reassurance. "I held out against them two months this time, but what could I do in the face of gold?" To Morang, who knew better, Caldwell insisted that if only he "could afford to take their 600 dollar checks and choke them with the things I'd be on my way home instead of writing letters about it."[89]

As he had the summer before, Caldwell assuaged his conscience by being as uncooperative as he dared, and he went about his work with undisguised disgust. To his great satisfaction, he was pulled off the *Wicked Woman* project and moved to something else—a testimony, as he saw it, to his incorrigible independence. "But at least they can't force you to write the stuff," he wrote defiantly to Morang. "I listen to them raise hell, but keep on writing my own way just the same." As the summer progressed, and his bank account continued to swell, Caldwell's professions of independence and artistic integrity became increasingly grandiose. "They can't break me on the Hollywood water-wheel, no matter how hard they try," he wrote. "They can fire me, and black-list me, but I'll be damned if I let them break me as they try to do every writer that has ever come out." For all his swaggering, he finished up his contract.[90]

Caldwell's convictions went too deep to be entirely appeased by such hollow boasts, however. As his material situation improved, his fiction writing became a means of expiating his guilt; his work became more sober and more explicitly sympathetic to its down-and-out characters. His involvement in left-wing causes in New York intensified during these early years of his sudden fortune, and the short stories he wrote during the periods following both the first and second Hollywood stints were among the most solemnly political in the *Kneel to the Rising Sun* collection.

When the *New York Post* proposed that Caldwell write a series of articles chronicling the plight of sharecroppers in the Deep South, he leapt at the chance. He was exhausted by writing stories, and the vicious reviews of *Journeyman* dimmed his enthusiasm for attempting another novel. Most important, the assignment offered him an opportunity to answer the critics, particularly Southern critics, who doubted that poverty anywhere could be as grim as it was in his fiction. Although he would never acknowledge it, Caldwell knew that he was partially responsible for the doubts of his readers, aware that he had mingled his depictions of rural deprivation with absurdly comic burlesque and vicious satire. And while Caldwell was not solely responsible for the way in which the play had turned the Lesters into the nation's greatest laughingstock, he had nonetheless played a part in stripping the people they represented of their dignity and pathos. The assignment from the *Post* was an opportunity to redeem them.

Three years had passed since Caldwell had spent extended time in the region that had inspired his best fiction. He would need a guide on his trips into the Georgia backcountry, and a guide back to the deeply sympathetic convictions that had molded his best work. His father was only too happy to oblige.

Chapter Eight

"KIT"

IN DECEMBER 1934, Caldwell left Helen and the children in Maine and returned to Georgia to revisit the familiar, sandy byways of "Tobacco Road." Since his last extended stay, the Depression—two years of rock-bottom cotton prices and depleted soil—had taken a dreadful toll on the farmers near Wrens. Even more landowners had lost their land to Augusta banks, becoming renting tenants or share-croppers who traded half their crop in exchange for fertilizer and a place to stay. Those who could no longer cover their yearly expenses slipped ever deeper into debt. A cycle of peonage took hold, exploitation deepened, and the number of farmers suffering malnutrition, disease, and desperation reached all-time highs. Caldwell had always written about East Georgia's most extreme cases of deprivation and degradation; that winter, likely subjects for his work were more abundant than ever.

The Roosevelt administration recognized that America's farmers were suffering terribly and that the country as a whole could not be revitalized with forty percent of its citizens living in a state of chronic destitution. During the first months of the New Deal, the President signed into law the Agricultural Adjustment Act to reverse the economic decline of farmers that had begun in the early 1920s. The AAA represented a hodgepodge of farming legislation proposed in the previous fifteen years, but it operated on one very basic principle: if farmers grew less, their goods could command higher prices. In an effort to reduce cotton production across the South, the Agricultural Adjustment Association purchased land outright and let it lie fallow, offered incentives to landowners who switched from cash crops to subsistence crops like corn or soybeans, and paid farmers to plow under part of their crops.[1]

For all its good intentions, the AAA was hastily composed during the heady rush of legislation that defined Roosevelt's first term. The

Act failed to take into account that the South's poorest farmers were not landowners at all, but rather renters or sharecroppers. For every acre a landowner took out of production, then, there was a sharecropper or tenant farmer whose labor was no longer needed. And while the tenants and croppers who managed to stay on the land were legally entitled to a share of their landowner's compensation for reduced acreage, they rarely received it. Few understood their rights, and most were afraid to ask anything of their landowners for fear of being evicted. Those with the courage to complain found that the AAA had placed the administration and supervision of funds in the hands of the landowners themselves. Before long, a growing multitude of displaced farmers were traveling from farm to farm begging for a day's employment. They worked at anything and anywhere for as little as twenty-five cents a day and lived in abandoned shacks on run-down farms. For most farmers the AAA seemed to make a desperate situation worse. By the time Caldwell traveled South to research his pieces for the *New York Post*, over seven thousand sharecroppers had already written Washington to complain about the effect of crop reduction plans or the failure of the Federal Emergency Relief Administration to distribute funds appropriated by Congress.[2]

The plight of the Southern sharecropper and tenant farmers was not entirely unknown to Northern readers in December 1934. Indeed, Caldwell had played a large part in this education through his fiction and the dramatic adaptation of *Tobacco Road*. A few nonfiction monographs on farm tenancy had been published, and journalistic coverage of the plight of sharecroppers had trickled into the Northern press. While the bulk of reporting on the Southern poor still dealt with striking cotton workers or coal miners, left-wing publications like the *Daily Worker* and the *New Masses* carried scattered accounts of the "agricultural masses," and more mainstream national publications ran a few pieces as well. As Caldwell left for Georgia, correspondent Hugh Russell Fraser journeyed South for the Scripps-Howard chain and began an investigation of the "Peonage of 8,000,000 sharecroppers in the South." When a Southern Tenant Farmer's Union was formed in Arkansas, the *New York Times* was only one of a number of papers that covered the story.[3]

But Caldwell's series in the *New York Post* represented the boldest, most extensive piece of investigative reporting dealing with the South's poorest citizens. Written by the nation's foremost expert on the subject and carried by the most colorful mass-circulation paper in New York, the story garnered nationwide attention when it was picked up and reprinted by *Time* magazine. Caldwell's first foray into investigative journalism was both an impressive and a timely one.[4]

I

OVER FOUR CONSECUTIVE DAYS in mid-February, Caldwell bombarded *Post* readers with gruesome stories of rural poverty and attacked the state and federal government's flawed efforts at relief. He scornfully censured Georgia Governor Eugene Talmadge—"the dictator of three million people, who exercises more power than Huey Long"—for failing to distribute federal money allotted to his state; he criticized the shortsightedness of the AAA and described the suffering of tenant farmers put off their land when the "government plowed them under." Relying on poignant case studies rather than statistics, he conveyed the pathos of evicted sharecroppers "unable because of old age and illness to work out their crop"; he told the tragic tale of a four-year-old girl who "died in January 1935 from the effects of malnutrition, her body twisted and knotted by rickets and anemia."[5]

Caldwell took time to explain the differences between a sharecropper and a tenant farmer to his Northern readers, and he made an effort to detail the logistical flaws in the FERA and AAA. But he was at his best when his passion moved him to impressionistic panoramas of the rural poor:

These are the unknown people of 1935, the men, women, and children who hide their nakedness behind trees when a stranger wanders off the main-travelled roads. Here are the deformed, starved, and diseased children born since 1929. Here are the men who strip leaves off trees, dig roots out of the earth, and snare whatever wild animal they can. These are the people who were forced off the tillable land, these are the women and the children the urban residents deny that exist. . . . There is hunger in their eyes as well as in their bellies. They grasp for a word of hope. They plead for a word of advice.[6]

In part, Caldwell had undertaken the *Post* assignment to answer criticism that his fictional portrayals were too brutal to be true. But while he struggled to maintain a reasoned tone in his journalism, his hunger to shock and his obsession with the grotesque undermined his credibility yet again. "In parts of Georgia human existence has reached its lowest depths," Caldwell wrote in the opening paragraph of the four-part series. "Children are seen deformed by nature and malnutrition, women in rags beg for pennies, and men are so hungry that they eat snakes and cow dung." As the pieces progressed they became more and more fervent, until by the fourth and final article of the series, Caldwell was bludgeoning his audience. He described a scene inside a sharecropper's cabin that received more attention than the rest of the articles combined:

> On the floor before an open fire lay two babies, neither a year old, sucking the dry teats of a mongrel bitch. . . . The dog got up and crawled to the hearth. She sat on her haunches before the blazing pine-knots, shivering and whining. After a while a girl spoke to the dog and the animal slunk away from the warmth of the fire and lay down again beside the two babies. The infants cuddled against the warmth of the dog's flanks, searching tearfully for the dry teats. . . . The dog got up and shook herself and lay down several feet away. The babies crawled crying after her.[7]

"What Will Good People of Jefferson County Say of This?" asked a headline in the *Augusta Chronicle* on the day Caldwell's pieces were reprinted in *Time*. Deeply embarrassed by their native son's latest insult to their good name, local residents filled the pages of the *Chronicle* with letters, editorials, and articles impugning Caldwell's honesty, intentions and research methods. "Until now," proclaimed Thomas J. Hamilton, the *Chronicle's* editor in chief, "no one has taken the trouble to call Caldwell's hand, but I think it is now high time to do so." Prominent local officials, many of whom worked with the relief programs Caldwell roundly condemned, jumped to their county's defense. A FERA case worker for Burke County swore that "she had personally investigated every needy family in her district" and found nothing to substantiate Caldwell's findings. The chairman of the Jefferson County Board of Commissioners thought that Caldwell was merely "endeavoring to commercialize on a possible instance of poverty in a community at the expense of humiliating a majority of good citizens."[8]

There were, however, a few brave local residents who wrote to the *Chronicle* in Caldwell's defense. "I am very glad indeed that the matter has been brought to the attention of the public," one man wrote. "Let us thank Erskine Caldwell for an effort to open our eyes, and now instead of criticisms, let's do something about it." Others wrote to testify to the existence of the people Caldwell described, for indeed, many residents of Wrens knew them by name; and while no one was sure of the people involved, the horrifying story of the suckling babies had been passed around Wrens for years. A number of readers saw Caldwell's work as compelling support for the selective sterilization law then awaiting approval by the Georgia legislature. "There is no use being sentimental about it," one man wrote. "If a patient has a cancer, cut it out. These people are a cancer on society, a menace to themselves and the state."[9]

The controversy that raged so hotly in Wrens was projected onto the national stage when both the *Post* and *Time* began printing some of the deluge of impassioned mail they received. Although Caldwell had carefully targeted a "strip of America twenty miles wide and a hundred miles long" near Augusta, his passion had moved him to write more grandiose defamations of the state and region as a whole—a tendency underscored by the *Post*'s typically sensational headlines. "Georgia Land Barons Oust Starving Man and Dying Girl," read one; "Starving Babies Suckled by Dog in Georgia Cabin," announced another. In the words of *Time*'s editors, Caldwell's articles "met with wide hostility throughout the South," but Georgians led the protests. "Erskine Caldwell has grossly erred and *Time*, in playing up such far-fetched tripe, has reflected on the integrity of the people of a great state, and should hide its face," a typical letter read. Another began: "I have never seen anyone eating cow dung, but perhaps Mr. Caldwell is referring to his own experience. . . . Such silly stuff as he writes about will make excellent copy for Russian newspapers."[10]

The *Post* and *Time* also received many letters in support of the articles, and in much of the Northern—and particularly left-wing—press, Caldwell's depiction of starving sharecroppers was accepted almost without reservation. For Caldwell, the most gratifying endorsement surely came from poor farmers who wrote in broken sentences to thank him for making their story public. "I cannot remember but two or three times in all my life when my hunger was fully appeased," a sharecropper from Millen, Georgia, wrote. "Why can't we get some sort of a break? I am not married (thank god), for I would not be a party to bringing more unfortunates like me into this world."[11]

As usual, Caldwell did not focus on the sympathetic responses to his work, but lashed out at his critics like a man betrayed. Most of his anger was directed at the *Chronicle*, and the paper became a foil for his frustration with Georgia as a whole—a state that was "so busy telling the world about its natural assets and tricky golf courses that it has neglected to look into the mirror occasionally." In a letter carried in the *Post*, Caldwell issued a forthright challenge to the *Chronicle*'s

editor in chief to leave "his swivel chair for two weeks, and with
reporters and photographers, find out what has happened to the country and the people during the last five years." Caldwell promised that
if, after a tour of the region, "the conditions are not as acute as I have
described," he would "let the editor of the Augusta Chronicle hang
me, with a suitable inscription pinned to my coat tails, on the highest
pole in the city." His prose became increasingly powerful as his indignation rose:

> I could tell of families thrown out of their houses plodding along the
> public highways of Georgia and dragging their possessions on the ground
> behind them. I could tell of men, with tears in their eyes, begging fruit-
> lessly while their children starved. I could tell of teenage girls without
> job or home, offering "french-dates" for a quarter on the streets of the
> editor's own city. I could continue these items until he hollered
> "Enough!"[12]

Ira shared his son's fury. Knowing that citizens in Augusta were
swamping *Time* with angry denunciations of Erskine's work, he sent a
blunt telegram of his own:

ERSKINE CALDWELL'S STORY ESSENTIALLY TRUE. NO INVESTIGATION
MADE, EFFORTS BEING MADE TO COVER UP FACTS. NEWSPAPER PROP-
AGANDA IS BEING SENT IN EFFORT TO HIDE FACTS IN CASE. PEOPLE
NOT ON GROUND DENOUNCE THE STORY AS FALSE.[13]

To its credit, the *Chronicle* admitted that "the controversy over the
Caldwell articles had reached such an intense stage" that a full investigation was warranted. With the assistance of Ira and Dr. Pilcher—
the men who had served as Erskine's guides during his boyhood—two
reporters from the *Chronicle* ventured into the worst sections of Jefferson, Burke, and Richmond counties. In mid-March the paper printed
a four-part series and, given the climate of opinion among its readership, its conclusions were courageous. While issuing endless guarantees
that most citizens of the area were upstanding and well provided for,
the paper also grudgingly admitted that "there is some basis for the
writings of Erskine Caldwell. While we did not observe the details of
what he said in his writings," they wrote, "we did observe the conditions under which depicted events could have happened."[14]

Father and son took great satisfaction in the *Chronicle's* admission,
although Ira complained that the paper "counted the unfortunate by

tens when they ought to have been counted by hundreds or thousands." Erskine also had the satisfaction of seeing the national press take note of his victory. "Charges of undue exaggeration against him may now be dropped," a writer for the *New Republic* wrote. "There are Jeeter Lesters in the world and something should be done to remedy the conditions under which they are forced to live."[15]

Delighted by the controversy brought on by Caldwell's articles, the *Post* encouraged him to travel South again for another four-part series. Caldwell happily obliged, for he too had reveled in both the attention and his vindication. In this second series, he focused even greater attention on the failings of the AAA and extended his reporting to cover the rural fringes of Alabama and Mississippi as well as Georgia. Caldwell illustrated the articles with an assortment of crude photographs that he took himself and accompanied them with a selection of provocative blurbs. The captions seemed to express the unspoken thoughts of the bleak, starving faces in the grainy photos. Under a picture of a malnourished nine-year-old boy was the caption "Dark Future"; under one of a tired couple on a dilapidated front porch was the single word "Hopeless."[16]

Caldwell also included a number of first-person testimonials from the villains and victims in the tragedy he described.

GEORGIA LANDOWNER: We know how to treat the blacks like they ought to be treated. . . . I jumped on that nigger and gave him the worst beating he ever got in all his life. He was in bed a week, he was so beat up. The next time I saw him he was as meek as a scared kitten.

GEORGIA TENANT: My children had one meal of meat sometime before last Christmas. I brought home four pounds of liver, and they grabbed the bag and ate up every bite of it before my wife could get hold of it long enough to cook it.

ALABAMA TENANT FARMER: All my life I worked for the landlords, and now when I'm all broken down from hard work, I can't get a mite of help from anybody. I went to the relief office and told them my foot is broken and the doctor says it won't ever heal, and that I've got a stomach cancer and piles and fainting spells. They told me they couldn't do nothing for me. Me and my wife don't know what to do except wait to die.[17]

The second *Post* series, like the first, stirred up angry responses, particularly from Southerners. South Carolina Senator Ellison D. Smith, a large landholder himself, spoke for many when he wrote the *Post* to decry Caldwell's "vicious propaganda and gross exaggeration." But Caldwell received wider praise for the second series than he did for the first. Violent treatment of the Southern Tenant Farmer's Union by landlords and local law enforcement agencies only confirmed Caldwell's pictures, and articles on the embattled union and on the plight of tenants and sharecroppers began to appear in the *New York Times, Time,* the *New Republic,* and the *Nation.* Only a month after Caldwell returned from the South, Henry Wallace wrote an article entitled "The Dangers of Tenancy" for the *New York Times Magazine*; a few months after that, in May 1935, Cecil Holland published a widely read piece entitled "The Tenant Farmer Turns" for *Survey Graphic* in which he noted that sharecroppers were "now in the national spotlight." In the following months, sharecroppers were the heroic, beleaguered subjects of documentary films, newsreels, and even a Rockwell Kent commemorative stamp. Caldwell's *Post* series had played a central part in making the Southern sharecropper the most visible symbol of Depression woes. "Beginning in early 1935," the Southern writer Oren Stephens complained, "the word 'sharecropper' was appearing regularly in lurid newspaper headlines in cities where neither the editors nor the readers had a very clear understanding of what a sharecropper really was."[18]

II

CALDWELL'S INTEREST IN socially conscious journalism and leftist causes continued to grow in the mid-1930s. Although he still did not join the Communist party, he was increasingly involved in its activities. He joined the organizing committee for the leftist periodical *Anvil* and the executive board of the New Theater of Action, a drama company committed to revolutionary works. He lent his name to mastheads, helped raise funds for Communist candidates, and attended rallies. He donated the rights to the short story "Daughter" to the Workers Laboratory Theater, which staged an adaptation to raise money for the *Daily Worker.* His short stories appeared alongside those by John Dos Passos, Clifford Odets, and Langston Hughes in *Proletarian Literature in the U.S.*, a collection edited by well-known radicals Michael Gold and Joseph North and published by the Left-Wing Book Union. In May 1935, the *New Masses* extended a "call for an American Writers' Congress" to all "writers who have achieved some standing in their respective fields; who have clearly indicated their sympathy to the revolutionary cause; who do not need to be convinced of the decay of capitalism, of the inevitability of revolution." Caldwell signed the "call," attended the congress, and had the pleasure of hearing papers recognizing him as one of America's best revolutionary writers.[19]

Caldwell also authorized the left-wing Phalanx Press to reissue his *New York Post* series in a pamphlet entitled *Tenant Farmer*. Described by Phalanx as a story of "Human Wreckage in the South" and "A First-Hand Account of Southern Misery," *Tenant Farmer* received a great deal of attention and solidified Caldwell's position as America's best-known spokesman for the Southern sharecropper. Ella Winter described it as a "shocking booklet, beautifully written," and many agreed with her assertion that even though "Caldwell is a novelist, he will never write a novel that merits the thanks of Americans more than this thirty-page, twenty-five cent pamphlet." Ezra Pound, who wanted Roosevelt's Works Progress Administration to fund regional presses, thought *Tenant Farmer* to be "precisely the kind of work which needs region-wide distribution and national consideration."[20]

Not everyone shared such enthusiasm for the pamphlet. W. T. Couch, the liberal editor at the University of North Carolina Press, bridled at Caldwell's fascination with the grotesque and his penchant for lurid, sensational detail. Although Couch had often challenged his own writers to produce passionate criticism of the region, he felt Caldwell had set out to make money—and perhaps, have fun—at his subjects' expense. "No amount of charity, of government aid, no change of system, revolutionary or otherwise, can rehabilitate people so improvident, irrational and idiotic as those Mr. Caldwell has chosen to describe in his works, and which he seems to regard as typical of the lower strata of Southern society," Couch wrote angrily. "Whether he is interested primarily in reform or royalties, it is certain that he has achieved only the latter."[21]

Caldwell continued his forays into journalism despite such criticisms, and for the first time, he began thinking critically about life outside his native South. He took a commission from *Fortune* magazine to live with a family of textile workers in New Bedford, Massachusetts, and write about their life. Soon afterwards, he traveled to Oklahoma and wrote about the "Okies" who were being driven West from their family farms by drought and foreclosed mortgages.[22]

In May 1934, only months after he finished the second *Post* series, Caldwell flew to Detroit to describe life on the automobile assembly lines there for the *Daily Worker*. "My journalistic bent won't stay down," he explained to Frank Daniel, his friend in Atlanta. "I'm off to

Detroit to see if I can do a five-part newspaper piece for a New York editor who sees the world through Marxian eyes."[23]

Caldwell's piece, "Detroit: Where America Died," was old-fashioned investigative muckraking that angrily described assembly line speed-ups, company spies, on-the-job injuries, starvation wages, blacklists, union-busting scabs, greedy bosses, and callous foremen. None of this was new to the readers of the *Worker*, but Caldwell imbued the articles with his own distinctive style. The third piece, for instance, was made up entirely of workers' testimonials—some partly fictionalized—that combined Caldwell's understanding of the situation with a creative imagination that imparted drama and pathos.[24]

Caldwell also indulged two of his particular fascinations: physical mutilation and sexual exploitation. His second article, entitled "Detroit: The Eight-Finger City," described the fate of workers who lost fingers when they could not keep up with the ever-accelerating assembly lines. A multitude of unemployed, eight-fingered men was a memorable image, and predictably, Caldwell could not resist pushing it past the limits of credibility. "The Hudson plant, and every other motor products plant in metropolitan Detroit," he proclaimed, "is littered with fingers, hands, arms, legs and crushed bodies." He was similarly dramatic in describing the fate of young girls who were forced onto the streets to feed their families. "In the empty houses and dark apartment buildings," he wrote grimly, "they are taught to circumvent their age for pennies, nickels and dimes. In back-room beer joints they strip off their clothes, go through a few childish motions of dance routine, and reap a fistful of copper money from the floor." Caldwell told his *Worker* readers that the name of Henry Ford (who personified the evil robber baron in a good deal of Communist literature) "has been inscribed on the cornerstone of The School of Whoredom."[25]

Caldwell enjoyed his forays into the rest of the country. He loved to explore, he loved to travel, and he was endlessly fascinated with the customs, appetites, and folklore of regional cultures. He decided to record his observations about America as a whole—to write a travel book that gauged the nation's character and mood in the midst of the Great Depression. The book was, in fact, an easy one to complete; the long articles for the *Post* that became *Tenant Farmer* and the auto industry pieces in the *Daily Worker* made up almost half of the finished manuscript. In the summer of 1934, he drove across the country from California to Maine, leaving Hollywood in June and making his way slowly eastward as he gathered material to round out the work he called *Some American People*.[26]

The book's new material consisted of twenty-four vignettes set in small towns, farms, and urban ghettos across America. Caldwell sought out a range of people who represented to him the "real" Americans— the gas-station owner in Spokane, the dump scavenger in Omaha, the amateur philosopher near Springfield, Illinois, the hobo barber who cut hair for the vagrants on the Pacific Northwest Railroad. For each character and each locale there was a story with its own vernacular, its own regional joke, its own mood. Although the book was billed as Caldwell's first full-length work of nonfiction, the dialogues and slice-of-life scenarios in *Some American People*, like the voices and testimonials of his earlier journalism, mingled a smattering of factual data with extended imaginings that, to Caldwell, captured the "truth."

Many of these stories were sad ones—tales of failed businesses in Madrid, Oregon; elderly panhandlers in Fargo, North Dakota; worn-out, lonely coal miners in Scranton, Pennsylvania. The Depression and the failed policies of the New Deal hovered behind all the human dramas. But while the articles for the *Post* and the *Daily Worker* were unremittingly depressing and bleak, Caldwell sprinkled *Some American People* with some of the most optimistic and patriotic images of America he had ever created. At points, the narrative echoed his mother's frequent endorsements of good old American values. He suggested, for instance, that hard work, not handouts from the Roosevelt administration, was needed to save the country. "It's not like it used to be at all," one of Caldwell's farmers complained. "People as a whole appear to be getting a little soft."[27]

Some American People's complex evocation of American character and broad geographical scope set it apart from the smattering of other travel books written to investigate the lives of everyday Americans during the early 1930s. Most of these either focused on a specific regional culture, or, like John Spivak's *Americans Face the Barricade*, shared stories of tragedy in order to substantiate a damning critique of American capitalism. In a decade when most Americans were both fascinated and concerned with their national problems, but still not ready to give up on their capitalistic heritage, *Some American People* struck just the right note of mingled sympathy and anger, pride and shame. By the time Robert McBride and Company published the book in October 1935, the advance sales of "Erskine Caldwell's new book" had surpassed all others on their fall list.[28]

More patriotic or nationally defensive critics were offended by the grimmer vignettes and the sections on sharecroppers and auto workers in the book. Quite a few shared the opinion of the *New York News* reviewer who thought that "the book reads too much like Mother India to be entirely credible." Louis Haloff of the *Atlanta Constitution* thought that "Caldwell, not the American people, should hang [his] head in shame," for he had "tried his hand at insulting the intelligence of our great nation." But many more reviewers praised Caldwell for his "strong medicine for a complacent society" and for his complex evocation of Depression America. Ernest Sutherland Bates, writing for the *New York Herald Tribune*, thought that "the scenes, the people, their ways of speech, their modes of living and dying are merged in well nigh perfect pictures, . . . are almost unbearably poignant," and "should have their permanent place in American literature of this type."[29]

The greatest tribute to *Some American People* was the flurry of other "I've seen America" books that followed in its wake. Nathan Asch noted that when Caldwell's travelogue appeared, it "was so unusual that it [was] a sensation." But by the following summer, a slew of authors were crisscrossing the country evaluating the American character. In the next four years at least six such books appeared. Although Caldwell had never intended to be a trendsetter, he had clearly become one.[30]

III

CALDWELL'S FATHER had illustrated his article for *Eugenics* magazine with his own grainy photographs, and fifteen years later Erskine did the same thing for the *New York Post*. Below his pictures he added captions that articulated his subjects' despair and degradation; the combination of words and text was powerful, and Caldwell was fascinated with the possibilities of the technique. But, as he was the first to admit, the photography in his work "was decidedly the work of an amateur." In order to extend and polish the medium he had so crudely engineered, he needed someone else to take the pictures. Soon after the publication of *Some American People*, Caldwell swallowed his natural aversion to collaboration and told Lieber to be on the lookout for a photographer to help with a photo-text study of the Southern sharecropper.[31]

Lieber did not have to wait long for a suitable candidate. In early January 1936, he was approached at a cocktail party by Margaret Bourke-White, one of the country's most famous photographers. Bourke-White had first attracted national attention in the mid-1920s with her stunning, elegiac portraits of industrial America—exquisite shots that dramatized the grandeur of the nation's steel mills and auto plants. Connections with big business led Bourke-White into a lucrative career as a commercial photographer. By the end of the decade, her signature black-and-whites were scattered in the nation's magazines as the most compelling feature in dozens of successful advertising campaigns.[32]

In 1930, *Time* founder Henry Luce created *Fortune* magazine, a photographic monthly celebrating America's business and industry. Impressed by Bourke-White's startling ability to transform the shadows and steel of machines into poetic tributes to their power, he signed her on as the magazine's premier photographer. She did not disappoint him. With Bourke-White's pictures dominating the pages, *Fortune* became the nation's best photographic journal and pioneered a trend in magazine journalism that allowed pictures, more than text, to communicate the central message. *Fortune*—and Bourke-White's fame—flourished during the early years of the Depression, at a time when most magazines and photographers were struggling to survive.[33]

Margaret Bourke-White combined her creative genius with a sparkling personality and an uncanny ability to market herself. A charismatic, effervescent, and attractive woman in a field dominated by men, she became something of a media darling. She had a natural flair for the dramatic, and was herself very photogenic. Pictures of Bourke-White perched precariously on narrow ledges or dangling from a speeding aircraft in search of the perfect shot contributed to the growing legend of a fearless beauty. "This Daring Girl Scales Skyscrapers for Art" read a typical headline in 1930; "Daring Woman Genius Braves Many Hazards to Obtain Photographs," read another. She traveled into coal mines hundreds of feet below the ground; she had her photo taken, camera in hand, perched on the wind-swept gargoyle of the swaying Chrysler Building. By 1934 Bourke-White was advertising coffee on the radio, was listed in *Who's Who*, and was followed breathlessly by a pack of reporters who carefully noted her latest sartorial ensemble and speculated on which celebrity bachelor might be her current beau.[34]

Caldwell's project offered a perfect opportunity for Bourke-White to broaden the scope of her work. Like so many artists of the day, Bourke-White was feeling the tug of a newly awakened social conscience. In 1934, *Fortune* assigned Bourke-White to bring back pictures of the Dust Bowl, and her experience with the staggering tragedy of the midwestern farmer triggered a crisis of conscience. Soon after her return she had a horrifying nightmare in which the automobile subjects of her commercial photography turned against her, "their giant hoods raised in fanged alarming shapes." She vowed to turn her talents away from the glamour of big business, now so tarnished by its failure, and towards the ever-deepening hardship and sorrow of the Great Depression.[35]

The sharecroppers of the rural South were among America's most visible victims of Depression woes, and Caldwell was their most celebrated champion. Caldwell gave Bourke-White's quest for social significance an immediate credibility she could not possibly have attained on her own. He was, in fact, something of a national celebrity himself—"America's most banned writer" and author of the notorious *Tobacco Road*. With her instinct for the public appetite, Bourke-White recognized that two well-known and attractive artistic celebrities working together would make for excellent publicity.[36]

Caldwell was flattered by Bourke-White's eagerness to work with him; he had admired her pictures in *Fortune* and was surely well aware of the attention her name would attract to the book. He asked Lieber to convey his enthusiasm. "I would give anything to work with Margaret Bourke-White, because I know we could produce a worthwhile book," he instructed his agent to tell her. "If she is stung with the idea, nothing would please me more than to try to do my share alongside her."[37]

Bourke-White was elated. Perhaps aware of Caldwell's reputation for moodiness and insecurity (and adept at working with men who might be threatened by her fame and talent), Bourke-White went out of her way to begin the partnership on the right foot:

> This is just to tell you that I am happier about the book I am to do with you than anything I have had a chance to work on for the last two years. If I had a chance to choose from every living writer in America I would choose you first as the person I would like to do such a book with. And to have you drop out of a clear sky—just when I have decided that I want to take pictures that are closer to life—seems almost too good to be true.[38]

It did indeed seem a match made in heaven, and Viking Press sanctified the alliance by offering them one thousand dollars in advance to cover expenses for the trip south.[39]

Unfortunately, the giddy optimism that surrounded the beginning of the partnership in January evaporated as the departure date drew near. Caldwell wanted to leave in June when the "heat of summer" made "the Southern climate at its best for such observations." Bourke-White agreed. As the date approached, however, she called several times to move the starting time back. She was swamped with commitments and had underestimated the time she would need to straighten out her affairs. Aside from closing up her studio and finishing up advertising obligations, she was immersed in the early days of *Life* magazine, America's first photographic news weekly. The starting date for her book with Caldwell had been set nearly six months before, but she assumed that he would be flexible.[40]

She was badly mistaken. Caldwell was extremely rigid about his schedule. He saw any engagement as a binding obligation and any broken date as a betrayal. He often set the exact time and place of meetings a year or more in advance, or wrote to people in January to arrange lunch at a New York restaurant in May. When Bourke-White called him in Wrens in mid-July to ask for a few extra days, he abruptly canceled the project. "I considered it the final straw," he wrote Helen in disgust. "I hate to see the trip broken up, but I think it was the wisest thing to do under the circumstances."[41]

Bourke-White was shocked by Caldwell's sudden change of heart, but she was not easily discouraged. She took the first available plane to Augusta and checked into the Richmond Hotel. Unable to arrange a telegram to the tiny town of Wrens, she hired a messenger to carry her impassioned plea to Caldwell on a bicycle—a distance of thirty miles. "It seemed to me that this work that you and I had planned is so important that I couldn't bear to see it hopelessly lost," she wrote. "If you judge the future by these last several days it isn't fair to me or fair to this important thing we plan to do." Although Bourke-White had only met Caldwell once, she seemed to sense that he responded well to flattery. "I know you do not question my sincerity about my admiration for your work and my happiness at having a chance to work with you," she told him. "I am sure you understand my deep desire to use my photography in ways that are more socially useful. I shall be waiting here in the Richmond Hotel to hear from you."[42] Caldwell drove to the hotel, and Bourke-White (who was not above staging tears) convinced him to give her one last chance. "Margaret came down Saturday after I told her not to come," Caldwell wrote Helen. "But she begged and cried and promised to behave and so we are going to start the trip!"[43]

The mood was somber as Caldwell and Bourke-White made final preparations for their journey. They were accompanied by an assistant, Ruth Carnell, whom Caldwell had brought along to manage the finances and logistics of the trip. Carnell, who had been Caldwell's secretary during his second Hollywood stint, took an immediate dislike to Bourke-White, who often did not get along well with other women. The car was overflowing with equipment and baggage, and Carnell was relegated to the badly cramped backseat. The temperature was nearly one hundred degrees, and the air was intensely humid. As the three headed off from Augusta to begin what would be a thirty-day driving tour of the Deep South, tempers were extremely short. Just before they set off, Bourke-White opened the trunk to check on a collection of praying mantis eggs that she had brought along to photograph as they hatched. As she bent over, the trunk door fell heavily and banged her on the head. Caldwell laughed out loud. Bourke-White later remembered it as the first time she had seen him smile.[44]

As the first days passed, and the three drove west across Alabama and into Mississippi, the atmosphere was so unpleasant that Caldwell was on the verge of canceling the trip yet again. Predictably, he was not enjoying the give-and-take of collaboration, and he was having particular problems taking advice from a woman. He doubted the depth of Bourke-White's social conscience and felt "like a tourist guide just showing someone around." Perhaps most disturbing, Caldwell was beginning to think that Bourke-White was not paying her own way—an offense he could not tolerate. Bourke-White was also unhappy; she was unfamiliar with the territory and unnerved by Caldwell's grim, sometimes forbidding demeanor. With Carnell, frustrated and resentful, rounding out the threesome, the trip went from bad to worse.[45]

"This is the worst trip I have taken so far," Caldwell wrote to Helen.

We had a scrap in Montgomery that could be heard for miles around —naturally she cried—but promised to follow my suggestions. She had another spasm the next afternoon near Meridian, Mississippi, and then we had a second big scrap that night in Jackson. Yesterday Ruth had one with her and I don't know what will happen. If I get so I can get along without her, I may have to let Ruth go home. She asked this morning if she could leave. I don't know what would happen if I were left alone. The trouble is Bourke-White is in the habit of getting her own way—and so am I—what happens when we fall out is all that can be imagined. The whole thing is on a day to day basis now, and it may be called off at any minute during the next week. . . . If Bourke-White and I could get along together there might be a book—but as things are going I'll be doing well to get back with a sane mind.[46]

There is no doubt that Caldwell was having trouble working with the temperamental Bourke-White, but this letter to Helen was, in fact, a remarkable and shameless piece of sophistry. He knew very well "what would happen" if they were to be left alone, and he was perfectly happy to let Carnell leave. In fact, the friction between Caldwell and Bourke-White had turned to passion; they had just become lovers; and Carnell had already angrily left the hotel without a good-bye.[47]

Throughout his life, Caldwell had initiated his romantic affairs, but this time the woman made the first move. "She seduced him," was how Ruth Carnell described the couple's first tryst. Maxim Lieber was more crude: he concluded bluntly that "she raped him." Bourke-White's romantic inclinations may have been—as they had sometimes been in the past—at least partly inspired by practical considerations. She felt that the work with Caldwell would place her at the forefront (and in the limelight) of America's burgeoning movement in documentary photography. Moreover, she had come to view the book as a vehicle of personal and artistic metamorphosis—a means of redefining her art, reordering her priorities, expiating her guilt. Terrified that Caldwell's commitment to the project was slipping away, she may well have seduced him when all other forms of persuasion failed her.[48]

But Bourke-White, like many other women, was also physically attracted to Caldwell. At thirty-three, he was an extremely handsome man. He had filled out his broad frame, his hair was a bit more carefully combed, and his clothes were a little better tailored. Bourke-White was drawn to his boyish freckles and almost innocent features and was intrigued by the striking contrast they presented to the violence and passion of his fiction.

> I could hardly believe this large shy man with the enormous wrestler's shoulders and quiet coloring could be the fiery Mr. Caldwell. His eyes were the soft rinsed blue of well-worn blue jeans. His hair was carrot —a subdued carrot. The backs of his hands were flecked with cinnamon freckles—cinnamon which had stood long on the kitchen shelf. His whole appearance suggested that he was holding himself ready to step back at any moment and blend into the background, where he would remain, patient and invisible, until he had heard what he wanted to hear or experienced what he wanted to experience.[49]

Perhaps most attractive to Bourke-White was Caldwell's intense, single-minded pursuit of his work, something she understood well and admired. Also, like many of her previous lovers, he was married. Bourke-White was drawn to men whose personal and professional commitments kept them from demanding or expecting too much in return.[50]

Caldwell certainly did not resist her advances; in fact, he had been attracted to his traveling companion from the moment he met her. Thirty-two, athletically built, with sparkling brown eyes and a glorious smile framed by silver-streaked brown hair, Bourke-White radiated an unmistakable sexuality and sublime self-confidence. After an unhappy first marriage she had avoided any serious emotional commitments, moving easily from affair to affair. She took great joy in the company of many men, from heads of industry to flying aces, and she left a trail of frustrated suitors behind her. Bourke-White was a sensual and passionate person, and by the time Caldwell met her, she had a reputation as one of New York's most sought-after women.

Like Helen, Bourke-White combined keen intellect with a healthy, unrepressed sexual appetite. But Bourke-White also had something that Caldwell, in spite of himself, could not resist: she was glamorous. She hobnobbed with heads of state and foreign diplomats, famous athletes and great musicians. She dressed like a fashion model and went dancing with Arthur Murray. Where Helen was plain, Bourke-White glittered; where Helen represented his past, his poverty, and his Southern roots, Bourke-White embodied the future, the lure of Hollywood, and the ache for fame and wealth that had always been with him.

IV

FOR THE NEXT MONTH, Caldwell and Bourke-White, or "Kit," as he called her, traveled a thirty-five-hundred-mile loop through the Deep South. Under what Caldwell described as a "steamy canopy of July heat," they drove slowly westward across Alabama, Mississippi, and Arkansas, rambled south through Louisiana, then angled north again into Tennessee and South Carolina. In his second New York Post series, Caldwell had covered similar territory, and he had a rough idea of where he wanted to go. He navigated with a simple objective: to find the poorest, most tragic citizens, the "struggling souls, living on tenant farms which are only clay deposits and sand dunes . . . the million and a half families . . . being bred and crushed in a land without hope."[51]

Locating suitable subjects for the book was easier than gaining their confidence. Bourke-White noticed that the rural poor "were generally suspicious of strangers . . . afraid we were going to try to sell them something they didn't want and fearful we were taking their pictures only to ridicule them." But Caldwell, who was awkward and unsure in New York social circles, had a remarkable gift for setting these farmers at their ease. He picked up the subtle intonations of the local accent almost immediately and could mimic it perfectly—something that critics had long noted in his fiction, and a skill that earned him an immediate degree of trust. Bourke-White remembered watching from the car while Caldwell established rapport with a poor sharecropper. "Erskine would be hanging over the back fence, and the farmer would be leaning on his rake," she recalled. "The two engaged in what I suppose could be called a conversation—that is, either Erskine or the farmer made one remark every fifteen minutes." Bourke-White saw that Caldwell's taciturn style was conscious and effective. "He was interested not only in the words a person spoke but in the mood in which they were spoken," she recalled. "He would wait patiently until the subject had revealed his personality, rather than impose his own personality on the subject."[52]

Caldwell's quiet respect for his subjects, his informed sympathy, and his humility worked wonders. Sometimes, he and Bourke-White were invited inside ramshackle hovels to meet an entire family. More often than not, Caldwell managed to learn a great deal about each farmer he met, and they shared with him the very personal and painful stories of their lives.

Caldwell's rapport with the people they met allowed Bourke-White the freedom to set up her shots. She was an extremely patient, precise, and savvy photographer. As Caldwell talked, she moved unobtrusively in the background with a small handheld camera until her subjects forgot her. As they relaxed, she gradually moved closer and closer, taking pictures all the time. Interior photographs required a tripod, a larger camera, and exploding flashbulbs. Well aware that people would be uncomfortable sitting before such daunting and obtrusive equipment, she developed a means of capturing them unexpectedly. After Caldwell and her subject had begun to chat she focused and framed her shot. Then she moved away from the camera with a remote-control button in her hand and waited. "It might take an hour before their faces or gestures gave us what we were trying to express," Bourke-White recalled. "But the instant it occurred the scene was imprisoned on a sheet of film before they knew what had happened."[53]

Bourke-White made no effort to bring back objective images. Like

Caldwell, she was motivated more by passion and a sense of drama than calculated or objective sociological method. And as the trip progressed, she seemed to absorb Caldwell's rage as well. Above all, she sought the graphic and the poetic in the poor farmers she photographed. By using a series of flashes for her indoor shots rather than a single bulb she achieved sculptured portraits fraught with emotion and pathos. Outside, she would wait an entire day to get the proper lighting to add drama to a single shot. Her orchestration and calculated use of lighting reminded Caldwell of a movie director, albeit an extremely tactful one, "in charge of everything, manipulating people and telling them where to sit and where to look and what not."[54]

Usually Caldwell supported her methods, so unlike his own hands-off approach. He saw that her charm and contagious warmth seemed to "help people be themselves" without undermining their dignity. But sometimes he thought her manipulation went too far. He criticized her, for instance, for rearranging the possessions on a poor black woman's bureau in order to achieve a certain effect. "After we left," Bourke-White recalled, "Erskine spoke to me about it. How neat her bureau had been. How she must have valued all her little possessions and how she had them tidily arranged *her* way, which was not my way. This was a new point of view to me. I felt I had done violence." Bourke-White later credited Caldwell for helping her find a balance between social empathy and an aesthetic quest for the perfect photograph. "I was learning," Bourke-White wrote, in words that might easily have been spoken by her traveling companion and lover, "that to understand another human being you must gain some insight into the conditions which made him what he is. The people and the forces which shape them: each holds the key to the other. These are relationships that can be studied and photographed."[55]

As the trip wore on, some of Bourke-White's most impressive pictures were taken spontaneously, without careful preparation or manipulation. Since the critical attacks on *Journeyman*, Caldwell had been anxious to obtain a photographic record of a white revivalist church service. Highly emotional religion among blacks was widely acknowledged in the North, but few had believed Caldwell's description of poor whites in the throes of "coming through" or "speaking in tongues." In rural South Carolina, Caldwell found a congregation of very poor whites who held such services. One Sunday, Caldwell and Bourke-White hid outside the window of the dilapidated church, peeked through a small window, and waited. When the service reached a fevered pitch, they climbed into the church and Bourke-White began snapping photographs while Caldwell passed her bulbs from his pockets. "Women were careening about in their cotton print dresses, and several times they nearly threw me off my feet and all but knocked my camera out of my hands," Bourke-White remembered later. "The worshippers were running the whole gamut of religious frenzy from exaltation to torpor. . . . Both men and women began rolling about on the floor, chanting their 'Amens' in voices fading from hoarseness." When the hallelujahs began dying away, and the congregants seemed spent of their religious ecstasy, Bourke-White and Caldwell quickly exited through the window they had entered by, and drove away.[56]

They were similarly ingenious in gaining pictures of a Georgia chain gang. Ira had been complaining about this brutal penal system for twenty years, and his son shared his disgust. When Caldwell located a gang working on a dusty back road in Georgia, the overseer forbade Bourke-White to take pictures, emphasizing his point by waving his rifle and shooting at the car's tires as Caldwell drove hurriedly away. That afternoon, Caldwell wangled an official-looking document from a friend in the county commissioner's office in Augusta. When they returned to the gang, the captain, who could not read but was intimidated by the fancy credentials, angrily allowed Bourke-White to set up. She snapped the long line of emaciated, haggard men in striped uniforms, each with his sole possession—a tin spoon—tucked in the cuff of his ankle chain; she took a close-up of a young black prisoner sleeping, his face innocent and childlike, surrounded by the tangle of arms and legs of fellow prisoners chained beside him. She photographed the obese overseer from behind as he looked down the line of workers in the roadside ditch, his huge girth barely contained in a pair of dusty overalls and a shotgun balanced casually on his shoulder.[57]

Caldwell and Bourke-White wrote captions to accompany each full-page picture, similar to those Caldwell had used in his second *New York Post* series. They wrote these blurbs together to represent their "own conception of the sentiments of the individuals portrayed." Many of the captions were stark echoes of the tragedy represented in the photograph. Under the exhausted, hopeless face of an elderly sharecropper woman were the words "I've done the best I knew how all my life, but it didn't amount to much in the end." An equally weary man, his face blank with the stupor of extreme poverty, said simply, "It ain't hardly worth the trouble to go on living." Other captions were bitterly ironic, and suggested—much as Caldwell's tragicomic fiction often did—a deprivation so severe that the subjects were unaware of their abject state. An ancient sharecropper with a moronic toothless smile was an oblivious victim of exploitation: "I get paid very well. A dollar a day when I'm working"; a grinning boy with gruesomely deformed teeth says brightly, "School is out for spring plowing and Pa said I could go fishing."[58]

Several picture-text combinations spoke to the dignity of the Southern laborer and revealed Bourke-White and Caldwell's respect for the farmer's love of his land. A proud woman with powerful hands and arms stands over her plow and says, "We manage to get along." Beneath a gauzy profile shot of a farmer plowing beneath a dramatic sky appeared the words, "There's lots of things easier to do, and pay more money, but plowing the land and harvesting the crops gives a man something that satisfies him as long as he lives."

Caldwell also wrote six short essays that separated the full-page photographs into groups of eight to ten. A comprehensive and emotional critique of the Southern sharecropping system, these pieces represent the best nonfiction prose of his career. With Bourke-White's irrefutable images to support and vindicate him, Caldwell was able to resist the pull of sensationalism that had undermined his credibility in the past. In a remarkably graceful union of journalistic and semi-fictional techniques, he combined explications of the mechanics of credit exploitation with poetic contemplations on the psychological impact of deprivation.

Caldwell's month-long immersion in the lives of the Deep South's poorest citizens also expanded his understanding of their problems. As he spoke with farmers they spelled out the concrete process by which they had lost hope. With their voices still ringing in his ear, Caldwell ended each essay with a fictionalized, first-person testimony from a range of characters in the tragedy of the Southern rural poor. Caldwell's sympathy was joined by a good command of facts—from hourly wages to interest rates for seed and fertilizer loans. Such specific information made his case studies, once impressionistic, far more convincing. And while Caldwell was still guided by a crudely Marxist paradigm of evil "landlords who accumulate wealth" and the "ten million persons now living under their yoke," he did not turn sharecroppers, as many left-wing commentators on the South did, into a uniform phalanx of proletarian warriors, heroic and enduring. Nor, as he had done many times in the past, did he exaggerate the moral failings of the poor for comic effect or as an outlet for his own disgust and hostility.[59]

Caldwell and Bourke-White arranged the photographs, captions, and essays to provide an overview of Southern rural poverty. The book focused on the story of the most tragic victims, the black and white sharecroppers of the Deep South, but it also featured prominently the villainous banker, the racist landlord, and the exploitative fire-and-brimstone preacher who passed the collection plate before skipping town. The pictures were carefully chosen to represent an equal number of men and women, an equal number of blacks and whites. The photographs and text covered a range of moods as well, presenting evidence of resiliency and courage as well as of hopeless deprivation; both photographs and text alternated emotionally fraught images with moments of detached, objective observation. At Caldwell's suggestion, they called the book *You Have Seen Their Faces*.

By 1937, most people had indeed seen photographs of sharecroppers before. The photographic arm of the Resettlement Administration (later called the Farm Security Administration) under the direction of Roy Stryker had begun sending talented photographers like Walker Evans and Dorothea Lange south in 1935. Their dispassionate, unemotional images of the poor appeared regularly in the nation's newspapers. *Fortune* and *Life* had also carried images of the rural poor, and the grim documentary newsreel films of Pare Lorentz had reached thousands of moviegoers.[60]

But when *You Have Seen Their Faces* was published in 1937, it caused an immediate sensation. The book was visually spectacular and beautifully laid out. Bourke-White's close-up shots of people with goiters, withered limbs, and blank stares were more daring and frankly evocative than those brought back by the FSA. She had insisted that Marshall Best at Viking use the highest-quality paper for printing, and the images jumped from the page. Caldwell's essays were also eye-catching. They were elegantly typeset, with large print and ample spacing. No book had ever combined artists of their fame, had achieved this powerful balance of photography and prose, had spoken so eloquently on a topic of such immediate and pressing relevance. A small collector's edition selling for $7.50 sold out immediately, as did Viking's first trade printing of 15,000 copies. A paperback edition came out almost immediately; sales were brisk, and *You Have Seen Their Faces* hovered briefly near the top of the national best-seller list.[61]

Reviews only spurred the book's popular appeal. Northern newspaper critics shared the opinion of Herschell Brickell of the *New York Post* who thought *Faces* to be "the most graphic account of the tenant farmer problem in the South ever produced." In fact, almost all the leading papers in New York, Boston, and Philadelphia carried extremely favorable reviews praising the lean authority of Caldwell's prose and the drama of Bourke-White's photographs. "I don't know that I've ever seen better photography," Robert Van Gelder wrote in the *New York Times*, "but Mr. Caldwell, a powerful single-tracker, pretty much makes the book his own by main force and conviction." The critic for the *Philadelphia Record* was only one of a number of reviewers to compare the reformist power and influence of *Faces* with Harriet Beecher Stowe's novel *Uncle Tom's Cabin*. The *Nation*, *New Republic*, and *Time* all included the book on their list of the year's best.[62]

Many left-wing and Communist critics embraced Caldwell's descriptions of evil landlords and exploited laborers. They praised his tentative call for "collective action by the tenant farmers themselves, or government control of cotton farming" and were relieved that he had refrained from humor at his subjects' expense. Indeed, Caldwell's argument that the moral turpitude of the indigent was purely the fault of an exploitative economic system seemed to allow leftists to reassess his earlier fiction in a more sympathetic light. "I am so anxious for you to be with us now that I have grown to understand your work with some degree of thoroughness," Edwin Seaver wrote him. "When I first read *Tobacco Road* I had to overcome a lot of ingrained resistance." Seaver told Caldwell that "I consider *You Have Seen Their Faces*—even considering only the captions for the pictures—an example, for sheer writing, unsurpassed by anybody in our time."[63]

A scattering of liberal Southerners commended Caldwell and Bourke-White, as Frank Daniel of the *Atlanta Journal* did, for offering "reality and strength and articulateness to a humble class of southern people of whose existence many southerners scarcely knew." Professor Hudson Strode of the University of Alabama sent a letter to the *New York Herald Tribune* advocating that the "eloquent collaboration . . . should go into the house of every Southerner incorrigibly in allegiance to King Cotton and to outdated romantic feudalism." Caldwell also received letters from other Southern authors like Lillian Smith, who thanked him "for the beautiful book you and Margaret Bourke-White have given us. It is unforgettably real and poignant. . . . There is an understatement there which increases the force of its truth."[64]

Bourke-White and Caldwell were particularly gratified by critics who not only praised the book, but recognized the unique power of their carefully combined photographs and text. Malcolm Cowley, one of the nation's most influential critics, wrote in the *New Republic* that *You Have Seen Their Faces* "belongs to a new art, one that has to be judged by different standards." Bourke-White recalled later that "this was just what I had hoped . . . through the fusion of words and pictures, we would create something new."[65]

The harshest criticisms of *You Have Seen Their Faces* came from the South, and they were directed almost exclusively at Caldwell. Countless Southern book reviewers (who by this time had developed a Pavlovian response to the mere mention of Caldwell's name) assailed his commercialism, his regional disloyalty, his overzealous imagination, his obsession with the least favorable elements of their region, and his blind eye towards the problems in the urbanized North. The *Memphis Commercial-Appeal* labeled Caldwell a "quack of social diseases"; the *Dalton North Georgian* ran its review under the headline "Selling One's Birthright"; another enraged critic ended his scathing review with the simple declaration, "Fie on Erskine Caldwell!" Letters from enraged Southerners flowed into the Viking Press offices.[66]

Serious intellectuals across the South, both liberal and conservative, also took note of, and criticized, *You Have Seen Their Faces*. W. T. Couch continued the attack he had begun in his review of *Tenant Farmer*. Writing in the *Virginia Quarterly Review*, Couch supported Caldwell's effort to raise consciousness and sympathy on the sharecropper's behalf, but was frustrated that Caldwell offered nothing new in the way of solutions. It seems also that Couch, like so many Southern liberals, was not yet ready to accept Caldwell's powerful attack on Southern racism, and he pointed defensively to the "substantial array of facts to support the argument that better relations exist between black and white in the Southern United States than between peoples of such widely different colors and heritages anywhere else in the civilized world." Couch predicted that "if we ever pass out of the present era of sentimental slush, or undiscriminating sympathy on the one hand and of merriment over psychopaths on the other, Mr. Caldwell's works will be forgotten."[67]

The angriest Southern intellectuals, however, were far more defensive of their region than Couch. Donald Davidson's article in the *Southern Review* expressed the opinion of a number of members of the so-called Agrarian movement—a group of Southern patriots who championed their region's distinctive agrarian culture and history. Caldwell's description of the South as "a retarded and thwarted civilization" and "a worn-out agricultural empire" was taken as a direct attack. While Davidson managed to find in Bourke-White's photographs "strong, irregular [faces,] often beautiful with a wild and touching nobility," he thought Caldwell to be a treacherous, traitorous propagandist who had "turned state's evidence" against his native land. He railed against Caldwell's "highly colored account," his "errors and distortions of fact," and his "nonchalant exclusion of testimony." Consciously linking Caldwell to a legacy of the South's worst enemies, Davidson described *You Have Seen Their Faces* as "Olmsted, Garrison, John Brown, Thad Stevens, Charles Sumner, with modern trimmings." Like many Southern conservatives, Davidson blamed Caldwell's "libelous and malicious proceedings against [the South's] character" on the author's leftist affiliations. "As a student of farm tenancy in the South," he wrote sarcastically, "Mr. Caldwell would make a splendid curator of a Soviet park of recreation and culture."[68]

Caldwell and Bourke-White also received criticism from the photographers and writers who experimented with the photo-text medium in the wake of *You Have Seen Their Faces*. Most of these artists were critical of Caldwell and Bourke-White's emotional and somewhat melodramatic reporting. They also resented their commercial success. In 1938, H. C. Nixon, a Southern academic and one of the original Agrarians, published *Forty Acres and Steel Mules*, a book dominated by photographs of smiling, robust sharecroppers. Underneath the pictures was a pointed caption: "Have You Really Seen Their Faces?" Dorothea Lange and Paul Taylor's 1940 photo-text study of the Dust Bowl entitled *American Exodus* included an unsubtle jab at the fictional "quotes" in *Faces*. "Quotations which accompany the photographs," Lange and Taylor wrote snidely, "report what the persons photographed said, not what we think might be their unspoken thoughts."[69]

The success of *Faces* particularly angered Walker Evans and James Agee. At roughly the same time that Caldwell and Bourke-White traveled across the South in the summer of 1936, Agee and Evans were studying the Southern sharecropper for a book they would call *Let Us Now Praise Famous Men*. Agee and Evans had also planned to publish in 1937, but Caldwell, Bourke-White, and Viking Press beat them to the punch. The phenomenal popularity of *Faces* helped discourage the publication of *Famous Men* for another four years.[70]

Aside from their understandable jealousy, Agee and Evans held philosophical reservations about *Faces*. Agee, deeply intellectual in his approach, was determined to avoid sentimentalizing the poverty he described. Such emotional reporting was, he felt, a form of exploitation, and Walker Evans's photographic style was guided by the same philosophy. In his work for Roy Stryker, Evans developed an aesthetic that was far more objective, impartial, and aloof than Bourke-White's. When *Faces* was published to such wide acclaim, Evans recalled later that he and his partner felt "outsmarted by an inferior motive." They thought Caldwell and Bourke-White's work was a "double outrage: propaganda for one thing, and profit-making out of both propaganda

Caldwell's mother, Caroline Preston Bell, c. 1901. *Courtesy of Virginia Caldwell Hibbs, and Dartmouth College Library*

Caldwell's father, Ira Sylvester Caldwell, c. 1895. *Courtesy of Hargrett Library, University of Georgia*

Erskine and his mother, in Prosperity,
South Carolina, c. 1907.
*Courtesy of Virginia Caldwell Hibbs,
and Dartmouth College Library*

Erskine on his tricycle in
Staunton, Virginia, c. 1910.
*Courtesy of Virginia Caldwell
Hibbs, and Dartmouth
College Library*

Caroline and Erskine, probably in Staunton, Virginia, c. 1911. *Courtesy of Hargrett Library, University of Georgia*

From the 1923 Erskine College Yearbook: Erskine in his football uniform. *Courtesy of Erskine College Library*

Ira Sylvester Caldwell, c. 1930. *Courtesy of Hargrett Library, University of Georgia*

Caldwell, his son Dabney, and the family dog, Mount Vernon, Maine, 1928.
Courtesy of Becky Gooding Laskody

Caldwell, 1931.
Courtesy of Becky Gooding Laskody

Caldwell's first agent, Maxim
Lieber, early 1930s.
Courtesy of Mrs. Minna Lieber

Caldwell's friend Alfred
Morang, c. 1955.
*Courtesy of Dartmouth
College Library*

Erskine and Helen in Burbank, California,
1934. *Courtesy of Virginia Caldwell Hibbs,
and Dartmouth College Library*

Caldwell, 1939. The inscription is to Frank Daniel, Caldwell's friend from the
Atlanta Journal. *Courtesy of Hargrett Library, University of Georgia*

Caldwell and Margaret Bourke-White on a research trip in the South, late 1930s.
Courtesy of the Margaret Bourke-White Estate and Syracuse University Library

"We manage to get along." From *You Have Seen Their Faces*, 1937. *Courtesy of the Margaret Bourke-White Estate and Syracuse University Library*

"I get paid very well. A dollar a day when I'm working." From *You Have Seen Their Faces*, 1937. *Courtesy of the Margaret Bourke-White Estate and Syracuse University Library*

. . . . your heart, and your pocketbook.

Erskine Caldwell   Margaret Bourke-White

White Sea, 1941

A Christmas card from Caldwell and Bourke-White. The photograph was taken on their return from the Soviet Union, 1941. *Courtesy of the Margaret Bourke-White Estate and Syracuse University Library*

Caldwell's third wife, June Johnson, 1951.
Courtesy of Dartmouth College Library

Covers from some of the mass-market editions of Caldwell's novels. Their lurid nature and strong sexual overtones did little to help his declining critical reputation.

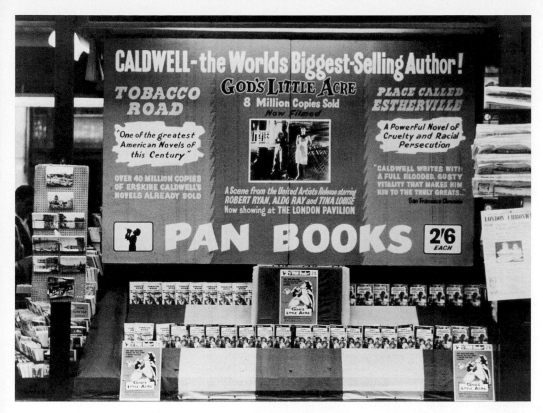

London kiosk featuring Caldwell's books, with *God's Little Acre* as the central attraction, 1958. *Courtesy of Dartmouth College Library*

Picketers of the movie version of *God's Little Acre*, c. 1958. *Courtesy of Dartmouth College Library*

Erskine and Virginia, his wife of thirty years, 1963. *Courtesy of Virginia Caldwell Hibbs, and Dartmouth College Library*

Caldwell surrounded by the jackets of various editions of his works, c. 1975.
Photo by Charles S. Sinks, Esq. Courtesy of Dartmouth College Library

Erskine Caldwell in the early 1980s. *Courtesy of Virginia Caldwell Hibbs, and Dartmouth College Library*

and the plight of the tenant farmers." Agee and Evans were particularly galled that so many readers and social activists saw *Faces* as "*the* nice thing to do, the *right* thing to do. Whereas we thought it was an evil and immoral thing to do. Not only to cheapen them but to profit by them, to exploit them—who had already been so exploited."[71]

Caldwell and Bourke-White's "exploitation" was, as Evans acknowledged, largely unconscious. Caldwell's taste for violent melodrama had guided his writing long before it made him a wealthy man; Bourke-White followed his lead and allowed herself to indulge the theatrical and emotional impulse that had also been ever present in her work. *Let Us Now Praise Famous Men*, today considered one of the great achievements of the time, proved to be too cerebral, too imagistic, too ambitious, and too difficult to fit the tastes of the passionate, angry decade in which it was written. *You Have Seen Their Faces*, today largely forgotten, was a perfect match.

V

THE EIGHTEEN MONTHS between the completion and publication of *You Have Seen Their Faces* were the most emotionally turbulent of Caldwell's life. During that time, the affair with Bourke-White that had begun so casually in a Southern hotel became a consuming relationship.

On his return to Maine he first tried to hide the affair from Helen, then to minimize its importance. But he quickly dropped the charade. He traveled to New York whenever he could and, when he was in Mount Vernon, he corresponded passionately with "Kit." He no longer slept with Helen, and, although she threatened to divorce him, he was too much in love with Bourke-White to care.

"Dearest Girl in All the World," he wrote to Bourke-White from Maine. "I love you. That's little enough to say, and it does not fill much spaces, but it is what I feel. I love you. I love you. I love you. I love you." Each letter was more ardent than the last. "You must know that I love you so deeply that living does not hold any promise without you in it," he wrote. "The trouble now is that I want to share everything with you—every minute, every look, every step. . . . I go to sleep every night holding you tight in my arms, and when I wake up, you are still there. And all day long it is the same way. I want to see you, talk to you, feel you every minute."[72]

Bourke-White returned his passion, and her physical attraction to him grew stronger every day. Once she sent him a cable that read, "MY PUSSY GROWS COLD FOR YOU." In New York, the two walked everywhere hand in hand, and observers were struck by the intensity of their love. When Malcolm Cowley saw them together at a party he thought that they were "radiantly in love so that their presence transformed the crowded room." Bourke-White and Caldwell dedicated *You Have Seen Their Faces* to Patricia, a person that none of their acquaintants had ever heard of. "Patricia" was their code word for the child they would one day have together, and in their letters they referred to her often.[73]

Bourke-White, however, was not yet ready to let a child alter her fast-lane New York lifestyle or compromise her soaring career. *Life* magazine was taking off in early 1937, and she was its star photographer. She flew west to Montana to photograph the magazine's first cover, a magnificent shot of Fort Peck, the world's largest earth-filled dam. She caught the last plane into Louisville, Kentucky, on an hour's notice to shoot the story of an Ohio River flood that injured nearly eight hundred people. She went to Washington, D.C., to do a portrait of the Supreme Court, then to Muncie, Indiana, to complete a story on the town that had inspired Helen and Robert Lynd's classic sociological study *Middletown*. In July 1937, she flew to the Arctic Circle to record the adventures of His Excellency Lord Tweedsmuire, the Governor-General of Canada, as he explored the Arctic in an old wood-burning steamer.[74]

As her photographic fame grew via the pages of *Life*, Bourke-White was swept up in the whirl of social life she so enjoyed. She embraced and encouraged publicity—endorsed cigarettes, wine, and the burgeoning airline industry. She displayed her work at the Museum of Modern Art. A photographer herself, she was followed by paparazzi; an investigative journalist, she was interviewed time and time again.

When Bourke-White was in New York, Caldwell traveled south from Mount Vernon to stay with her in her East Side apartment. For a while they lived together in the Mayflower Hotel, and later in the Beekman Towers apartment building. But these periods of relative domestic stability did not last long. Although Caldwell begged her to stay with him, to marry him, to make Patricia real, she steadfastly refused. *Life* was calling, and she was unwilling to turn it away.

Her hesitancy only fed Caldwell's insecurity and need to possess her. Each time she left him he was tormented by the "awful feeling that I will not see you again . . . a terrified feeling of our drifting apart." He worried that her hectic career and her history of short-term affairs indicated that he was "merely another customer coming into your house on a schedule." He begged "for a chance to make you happy—

to take care of you, to brush your hair, to wash you, to hang up your clothes for you, to undress you and everything else in the world that I can do for you." He signed letters, "Yours, if you want me," or "is there any hope?," and he wrote with a poetic sentimentality that he rarely indulged in his work. "I still have that extraordinary feeling I had when I first came to know you," he wrote.[75]

> . . . I was waiting for you to say, come into my arms and stay as long as you wish to, and stay forever if you want to. And even now I still believe you will say it, either this time or the next, or the next. . . . I have your pictures, your touch, still resting on me, your kisses: I have all these things with me day and night, and they seem to be a sort of promise. If they were not that, I would not even be able to write letters to you . . . look forward to you asking me to come to see you, to come in a hurry.[76]

"God only knows how much I love you, Sweet Kit—you will always be my dream and my love. I am yours as long as I live—if you want me—Do You? And when?"[77]

Bourke-White resisted Caldwell's endless pleas to "belong to each other 100%, night and day, 12 months a year." Aside from the demands of her very busy life, Bourke-White had serious reservations about his personality. She was most troubled by his shifts of mood from almost adolescent ardor to oppressive, brooding silence. These "frozen moods," as Bourke-White called them, seemed to her "to have no traceable cause in the world of reality," and they descended suddenly and without warning. On several occasions, Caldwell severely embarrassed her by having one of "his great freeze-ups" during a dinner or cocktail party, staring silently and grimly ahead while guests struggled to make conversation around him. Worse still, when he insisted on coming with Bourke-White on her photographic assignments, his moods sometimes undermined the quality of her work.[78]

Bourke-White also realized, as Helen and the children had long ago, that Caldwell's "unfathomable silences" often ended in outbursts of violent temper. Evidence suggests that he struck her, and once he gripped her so tightly by the arms that he caused deep bruises. Immediately afterward he was consumed with guilt and shame. He showered her with affection and filled letters with apologies and pleas for forgiveness. "Please help me," he wrote after one such outburst. "I want to be able to make up a hundred-fold for what I have done." Bourke-White always forgave him, but she never really trusted him either. "I never knew when the white curtain would fall," she wrote later. "He became absolutely impossible; a frigid, violent person."[79]

The more cautious she was, the more desperate he became. When Bourke-White traveled, he entered long periods of depression, unable to fall asleep, unwilling to get out of bed in the morning, or eat properly. "Sitting here trying my best to convince myself that you have not left me and that you won't leave me," he wrote. "What I fear now is that you will go away and be gone. . . . What? When? Where? I miss you so much it hurts going to bed, trying to sleep, and getting up is a twenty-four hour nightmare." She tried to reassure him, but Caldwell was inconsolable. "Kit, try to understand," he wrote desperately. I'm afraid I'm cracking up. I can't stand it much longer." He often made veiled threats of suicide, telling Bourke-White that life had no meaning without her. "Without you," he wrote on many occasions, "I'm not much interested in whether I'm living or dead."[80]

His anxiety increased when his mother and father found out that his marriage to Helen was in trouble. Carrie knew nothing about Bourke-White, and she immediately blamed Helen for everything; she considered her daughter-in-law's jealousy to be nothing more than "false impressions [that] grew into obsessions." But if she faulted Helen, she ruthlessly pressured her son to make things right. "I cannot think straight or write very intelligently," she wrote frantically from Georgia. "I am hoping and praying that you and Helen will consider the children before anything else in the world. I am appalled when I think of what would in all probability be their fate if they should be deprived of the close companionship and supervision." She advised Erskine that it "requires a great deal of sanity, strength of character and some sacrifice for people to live harmoniously under the same roof." More pointedly, she reminded him that his father was often sick, and in order to recover "he must avoid emotional shock."[81]

In the late summer of 1937, Bourke-White briefly broke off the relationship. On a trip out West she told Caldwell that his dark moods, his intense neediness, and his jealousy of her career were too much to bear. Years later, she recalled his agonized pleas for another chance. "You can't leave us, Kit," he begged her. "You can't leave *us*." She waffled, then relented on one condition. She insisted he visit a psychiatrist.[82]

By the mid-1930s psychoanalysis was very much in vogue among the New York intelligentsia and upper crust, and the relatively new field of Freudian analysis was seen by its supporters and practitioners as an almost magical cure for personal problems large or small. Bourke-

White had been in analysis sporadically for years, and she arranged for Caldwell to begin treatment with Harry Stack Sullivan, one of America's most renowned therapists.

Caldwell tried for Bourke-White's sake, for he would have done anything to please her. "If I thought you did need me, I'd see seven doctors, have 2,000 x-ray pictures taken, go to the hospital and stay until I could come out well," he promised. He began seeing Sullivan and even claimed to be making progress. "He has been working on me overtime," Caldwell assured Bourke-White. "I feel a lot better. I have eaten for the first time in a week, and hope to be able to sleep tonight for the first time in eight days." But Caldwell was a poor candidate for psychoanalysis. He hated to talk about himself, rarely took responsibility for his behavior, hated spending the money, and was motivated only by a desire to please Bourke-White. He stopped after a few months.[83]

Sullivan, who was a personal friend of Bourke-White's as well as her therapist, urged her to end the relationship. He warned her of "possible violence to you from him in connection with his failure to dominate you completely." Sullivan felt that Caldwell was not interested in real love but only "one-sided domination and submission." Sullivan reminded Bourke-White that "it is a very strange love indeed that resorts to physical violence in dominating the alleged love object." While Sullivan acknowledged Caldwell's "outstanding merits and attractive attributes," he thought that he "shows a fundamental lack of consideration that cannot be expected to improve" without extensive psychoanalysis. He advised Bourke-White against "heroic measures" in trying to salvage the relationship.[84]

But Bourke-White was torn. When things went well, she felt deeply in love with Caldwell. Her letters were frequently as ardent as his, and she was very attracted to him physically. She called him her "sweet, freckle-faced country boy," carried his letters in her breast pocket next to her heart, kept his picture by her bed, and signed her own letters "all my love to you my own darling." He could be remarkably gentle and romantic. On her Arctic trip he had sent telegrams addressed to "HONEYCHILE, ARCTIC CIRCLE, CANADA BOURKE-WHITE" that found their way to her in every port of call. He memorized her itinerary down to the minute, and when she changed planes in Chicago on a trip from the West Coast to New York, the public address system was blaring: "Paging child bride! Will child bride kindly step to the ticket counter!" When she arrived there was a telegram. It read: "WELCOME, WELCOME, WELCOME, WELCOME." He filled her apartment with pastel balloons, deluged her with flowers. He certainly seemed to need her, was devoted to her, appeared willing to die for her. And so, despite Sullivan's warning, the relationship lurched onward, sometimes giddy and passionate, at times bogged down by Caldwell's silences and violent outbursts. She continued to put her work first, to travel, to keep him at a distance; he continued to beg her for marriage, a child, and commitment, and to slide in and out of depression when she refused them.[85]

VI

WHENEVER BOURKE-WHITE went abroad or seemed to back away, Caldwell reached for Helen. For almost a year and a half, she responded.

"Needless to say, I miss us (you and me) more all the time," he wrote his wife from Bourke-White's apartment. "Maybe it will get so that the tide will turn the other way, and then there won't be any question at all anymore." But he took no responsibility for the affair. "It's something like being given a term on the chain gang," he explained. "I don't think I'll be on the gang for life, so just try to give me a chance to escape, or serve out the sentence. That's all I can say now. I don't wish to say too much. Anyway, I love you. And I miss what we should be having now."[86]

He promised to return to Maine if Helen would just be patient. "I just wish you to know that what I want most is for us to get back where we belong," he assured her.

> But if you are willing to stick it out with me until something happens, I'll be the most grateful person on earth—and I'll spend the rest of my life trying to repay you for being the finest person in the world . . . just try to let the thing run through of its own accord, and then when the day comes when we both know it is over, we'll have plenty of time to celebrate. I owe you a lot, and God speed the day when I can repay you—with interest plus a bonus. . . . You can write this down in the book. *I do love you.*[87]

More frequently, Caldwell implied that Helen was responsible for the separation. "I'd like to let you know at this time that your stock has gone up a lot from its low, and that means there is quite a spread between the high and the low," Caldwell wrote, using one of the financial analogies he had grown increasingly fond of. "I believe the long term, if not the near term, trend is definitely upward." But when Helen pressed him for a promise to leave Bourke-White, he responded with unsubtle threats: "Don't worry about anything in the meantime," he warned, "because we wish to keep the stock going up."[88]

Caldwell's heavy-handed financial metaphors were particularly cutting because, as always, Helen was completely dependent on him. Although Erskine's income from the play and books was now considerable, he continued to demand detailed accounts before meting out money. When Helen pressed for more, he ignored her, or even reprimanded her for being selfish and shortsighted. "Good intentions won't buy clothes and food for three of the best kids in the world," he scolded. "I'm interested in the future more than you may suspect from my past and present actions. I live for the future, because I look forward to the time when you and I get straightened out." Such cold assurances could not heat the Mount Vernon house, and during the first winter of Caldwell's affair Helen took the children south and moved in with her mother. In the summer they moved back to Maine, and Helen checked the mailbox every day hoping for a check from her husband.[89]

Helen also had emotional ties to Caldwell that were difficult to break. For ten years, his career had been her career, and she found satisfaction and self-esteem in his hard-won success. She could also justifiably claim a measure of credit for his triumphs as a writer. At great personal cost she had allowed him the freedom to work as he wished, acceded to his exorbitant demands for flexibility and privacy. Her careful editing, sage counsel, and excellent aesthetic judgment were evident everywhere in his best work.

In fact, even as his relationship with Bourke-White deepened, Caldwell continued to depend on Helen's editorial advice. "I have just finished the four stories, and I am sending them to you in another envelope," he wrote her from New York. "If you are satisfied with them, correct them and send them to Lieber right away." She did; she always had. When he asked her to help with the galleys of *You Have Seen Their Faces* while Bourke-White was in the Arctic, she traveled to New York and worked on the materials in the very apartment Bourke-White and Caldwell were then sharing. While she bitterly noted the black silk sheets on the large double bed and the opulence of the apartment, she worked through the project to the end.[90]

Helen could not, in spite of her better judgment, stop viewing Erskine as a victim. She was moved to pity by her husband's emotional turmoil and spells of debilitating depression, even though they were caused by his love for another woman. And she hung desperately on his promises for the future. In the summer of 1937, when Bourke-White broke off the relationship for a few months, Helen was frightened by her husband's desperate sadness—a state of depression so severe that Sullivan later referred to it as an "invalid state." When Caldwell phoned her from New Mexico saying he was unable to get back on his own, she drove two thousand miles each way and brought him home to Mount Vernon. When Bourke-White relented once again, Caldwell moved back in with her in New York, while Helen stayed in Maine.[91]

Helen eventually reached the limit of her love and her patience. She had hoped to save the marriage for the children's sake as well as her own, but he continued to be a poor father. Sometimes he remembered birthdays, many times he did not. It became increasingly obvious that Caldwell's commitment to his family was directly proportionate to the degree of Bourke-White's indecision, and his insensitivity and dishonesty seemed to know no bounds. When he moved into an apartment in the Beekman Towers with Bourke-White, Helen did not know until the bank called her thinking she was the "Mrs." of the Mr. and Mrs. Erskine Caldwell listed on the lease. He wrote her letters of reassurance using *Life* stationery and instructed Helen to request money through Bourke-White's secretary. When Helen checked into a New York hospital for treatment of an edema in her lung, Erskine spent the visit, as Helen remembered it, giving her "a blow-by-blow account of what happened in bed the night before."[92]

In January 1938 Helen finally filed for divorce on the grounds of "cruel and abusive treatment," and in April the papers went through. She retained possession of the Mount Vernon house, and Caldwell was required to pay her $2,500 a year and an additional payment of $12,000 to be paid in four installments over the next twelve years. A $25,000 trust was set up in a New York bank as a guarantee that Caldwell would make the payments on time. She also retained custody of the children, now aged twelve, ten, and five, although Caldwell could see them on visits and for one month each summer.[93]

Soon after the divorce Helen married Norman Cushman, a solid, dependable Mount Vernon handyman who had been devoted to her and the children for years. He gave them the security, stability, and unstinting devotion they had never had. Helen remained in the Maine house for the rest of her long life, and the children all attended school nearby. In time, Helen become one of the community's most beloved citizens. Generations of children came to know her as the "green ghost"—the town's official storyteller. She taught at the local schools and even wrote some stories of her own. Although Cush, as her new husband was known, was not wealthy, he was steady, and they settled into comfortable lives as longtime residents of rural Maine.[94]

Caldwell never dwelled on his failed marriage. "The world isn't going to stop turning," he wrote simply from Europe only months after the divorce. "For, after all, people have always had to buck the world." But Helen grew increasingly bitter as the years passed. She came to see more clearly the sacrifices she had made on Erskine's behalf, and she grew tired of writing to him for additional money when the children needed braces or school tuition. He traveled the world with Bourke-White, yet Helen, who had always been the more cosmopolitan and sophisticated of the two, remained in Maine. His standard of living was improving all the time, while hers remained painfully modest. "You can certainly afford to go to Europe, Hawaii, or Lima—theaters, plays, expensive house and deluxe entertaining," she wrote in one of her frequent requests for financial assistance. "But any sacrifice of your personal comfort for the kids, or to keep your word to them, you will not make. You owe all of them more than you can ever repay. For self-gratification, you wrecked their home, their life and mine, as well as your own creative genius."[95]

Chapter Nine

TROUBLE IN JULY

WHEN CALDWELL AND BOURKE-WHITE returned from a European jaunt in the summer of 1938, they were met at the pier by a swarm of eager reporters. The press, having discovered that the two celebrities had booked passage as Mr. and Mrs. Caldwell and berthed in adjoining cabins, swarmed the deck of the liner armed with tape measures to gauge the exact distance between the bedroom doors. They snapped photo after photo of the elegantly attired Bourke-White, complete with lap dog, and Caldwell, dour and dignified in a tailored blue suit. Bourke-White assured the assembled reporters that she was still single: "No, no. . . . We certainly are not married. I don't even want to be married. . . . I want to be single, and that's all there is to it." The press breathlessly reported every word but disagreed over whether the two celebrities were telling the truth. The sensational *New York Post* headlined their story "By Gosh and by Hector We're Not Married!" while the more staid *New York News* queried gently, "Is it Miss or Missus?" Even famed columnist Walter Winchell got into the act. "Miss Bourke-White," he urged in his column, "go ahead and marry the guy."[1]

Bourke-White's resolve was indeed weakening. Her love for Caldwell remained strong, and he seemed determined to change for her. He escorted her to formal dinners in a tuxedo and struggled to make small talk at cocktail parties. She loved to dance, and he agreed to take lessons so he could accompany her. Caldwell also began to see a psychiatrist again, although sporadically, and he worked hard to control his moods and temper. The more attention Bourke-White gave him the more secure he felt, and the happier they were together. Soon after their return from Europe they bought and decorated a house together in Darien, Connecticut, close enough for Bourke-White to commute to the *Life* offices in New York, and isolated enough for Caldwell to concentrate on his writing.[2]

They continued to talk of children they could someday have together and of honeymoons in Hawaii. When Bourke-White traveled on assignment, he addressed telegrams to "Miss Lalani Bourke-White" and signed them "Skinny (Hawaii or Bust) Caldwell." "Honolulu Chamber of Commerce is placing orders for March sunsets and wishes to know your preference," he wrote her. "County Clerk of Reno wishes your autograph. I don't want much myself. Just one prepaid word spelled YES."[3]

In her memoir, Bourke-White speculated that "a woman is most strongly drawn to the man who needs her most." In February 1939 she reluctantly accepted Caldwell's proposal, thinking that marriage would "lighten the burden of insecurity which he seemed unable to cast off"; but she was unsure of this to the end. On the flight to Nevada where they planned to be married, Bourke-White made Caldwell accept an unusual prenuptial agreement. Chief among the stipulations were his guarantees to treat her friends with respect and courtesy, make no attempt to limit her photographic assignments, and, as she later put it, "attempt to realize and control his fluctuating moods." He did not hesitate to sign.[4]

Caldwell also happily indulged Bourke-White's taste for theatricality in choosing the location for the wedding. After securing a license in Reno, they hired a cab and drove east into the ghost town of Silver City, Nevada, stopping on the way to pick up a minister in Carson City. Among Silver City's deserted buildings, they found a tiny, dilapidated church perched high on a bluff above the surrounding mesas and desert. With the cab driver and the local tobacconist serving as witnesses, Bourke-White and Caldwell were married as the setting sun streamed through the window. It was a shot only Bourke-White could have composed. The next day they headed west again for their long-awaited honeymoon on the beaches of Waikiki.[5]

I

THE MONTHS IN CONNECTICUT after the wedding were the happiest and most serene Caldwell and Bourke-White had ever spent together. They took long walks, entertained, saw plays, and attended rallies in New York. They made love every night, sometimes outside under the stars. They named their new house Horseplay Hill, a private joke on the owners of the grandly named mansions nearby and a reference to the joyous time they spent together.[6]

But Caldwell and Bourke-White's bliss was soon shattered by the
world events of 1939. Madrid had finally fallen to the Fascists in the
spring; Mussolini was on the march in Albania. In late August, Germany
and Russia signed a nonaggression pact, and a week later, Hitler blitzed
into Poland. On September third, England declared war.

Life was America's preeminent photo magazine, and as its marquee
photographer, Bourke-White was needed overseas. Fearless and exhilarated by adventure, she sailed for Europe in the middle of October
for a six-month assignment to cover the war. Before boarding, she
prepared her cameras in case the ship was stopped and searched by the
Germans; her only worry seemed to be that the light would be wrong
for recording the event. At the pier, where Caldwell saw her off with
a huge bouquet of roses, a reporter from the *Post* noted snidely that
"Miss Bourke-White did much better with the stiff upper lip than did
her bridegroom."[7]

When Bourke-White left for Europe, she and Caldwell flooded one
another with letters and telegrams that sought to maintain the giddy
passion of the marriage. She was, he told her again and again, "a model
of all earthly and heavenly perfection," and his telegrams met her in
every stop on her trip. In one, he simply wrote the words "I LOVE
YOU" twenty-seven times. "I'm so crazy about you and love you so
dearly, that nothing in the world can ever come between us," he told
her. "We have a lot of living to do the minute you get back. We are
going to be so close and do so much together that the whole world
will marvel at our love."[8]

She seemed intent on matching his ardor. "I just adore you, darling!"
she exclaimed. "It is so beautiful to be as happy together as we are.
My perfect husband, I love you." She addressed him as "the dearest
sweetest most loving most lovable most adorable most adored most
handsome freckled irresistible most precious companionable incompa-
rable most appreciated most worshipped husband." She signed her own
letters from "your infatuated adoring, eternally-loving, devoted wife."[9]

Caldwell continued to pressure her into having his child, for he felt
this was the best way to cement their relationship and bring Bourke-
White home to stay. He sent her an advertisement for babies' room
furnishings with the name Patricia written in. He begged her to tell
him when she would break down and "do the wifely thing." Their
child Patricia was waiting, he told her again and again. "She has inherited her mother's persistency. She asks for her every night, what
should she be told?"[10]

Bourke-White was torn. When Caldwell's three children visited the

Connecticut house, she smothered them with attention, let them help her with photographic assignments, took them out, and dressed them up. On occasion, she promised Caldwell that a child "will happen in our family too, sweet thing." "Patricia," she assured him, "is knocking at my heart too." But she was not willing to make the professional sacrifices a child would demand; with a war raging, having a baby was a poor choice for a photojournalist. Instead, she channeled her maternal impulses into the pets she and Caldwell bought for the Darien house. In her letters, the cats—Suzy, Fluffy, Johnnie, and Lottie—took the place of the family she was not yet ready to have. Bourke-White often referred to the animals as her children, and Caldwell as their "Papa." In a letter she signed "Your Devoted Mama," Bourke-White instructed the cats on how to behave as perfect children:[11]

> Suzy, you must keep on helping him write books as that is the most important thing in the world to Mama, Johnnie, you must try not to be sick and you must try not to do anything naughty in the house, and you *must* keep Papa good company in the car and stay awake when he is driving. . . . And Lottie, your job is the most important of all because you are learning to make your way in a new life. You must learn to climb trees because this amuses Papa. And you must learn to catch mice because that will make Papa feel you are a useful citizen, and you must wash that white vest of yours once in a while because that will make Papa very proud of you. But most of all you must grow older realizing that Papa is your Ideal, and that he is the most wonderful man in the world. . . . Take care of Papa, all four of you. Your devoted Mama.[12]

But the longer Bourke-White was away on assignment, the more reluctant she was to have a child: She was increasingly involved in her work, and Caldwell became more and more threatened by her independence. As the months wore on, his love letters came, once again, to be dominated by neediness, jealousy, and frustration. When an acquaintance teased Caldwell that Bourke-White had forbidden him to accompany her to Europe, he was thrown into a frenzy of insecurity. In letter after letter he begged her to come home and "show the world" that they were married, and badgered her for the exact date of her return. "Surely you can see daylight by now," he wrote. "Won't you tell me something like that to keep me from being so despondent and give me a time to look forward to?" After years of completely dominating Helen, he found it impossible to believe that Bourke-White refused to do his bidding.

What am I to do, take charge of you, or let you go your own way? If you thought you could trust me with your life I think it would be a very good thing for us if you would let me take charge of you. But if you are not sure you wish to trust me, then it would be better to keep on as you have. I believe I know a little about how to live, and once you tried it, I believe you would be glad we turned you over to me. Bring Kit home to us.[13]

Bourke-White was not a woman to "turn her life over" to anyone, and she was not nearly ready to come home. Caldwell slipped deeper into the depressions that had plagued him before the marriage, and he did not hesitate to dramatize his unhappiness in an effort to bring his wife back. "I can't hide it," he told her. "Everywhere I go, I'm told I look lonely. I am. I'm very lonely. I don't think I could live without you. I wouldn't want to live. . . . It's like marking off the days in prison—every day is an achievement and the marking off is a ceremony—a day's victory. I couldn't stand it if there were more than a day over six months of this. . . . I love you more than life itself."[14]

Bourke-White still maintained that psychoanalysis offered the best answer to Caldwell's unhappiness. When he agreed to visit the analyst Clara Thompson in New York, Bourke-White was overjoyed. "I care so much about having things right with us. They must be right with us. They must be right. We can have such a wonderful future together," Bourke-White wrote to him. "It means so much to me that you are doing something to make our future life perfect. I just couldn't begin to tell you how much it means to me."

But you must do something to yourself first. You must do those important things about those sides of yourself you don't know about— You must must must! I love you so much. But I love the good side of my husband. (I must love the other sides too, or I couldn't have put up with them so long. But the image of my husband in my mind is my big, adorable, sweetheart whose life I share and who shares mine. Please, sweet, see how earnest I am about this, because getting these things fixed, and realizing that they have to be fixed, will make all the difference in the kind of a future life we want to have, with Patricia, and all those things.[15]

Clara Thompson, like Harry Stack Sullivan before her, recognized that Caldwell was merely going through the motions of therapy in order to please Bourke-White. Both doctors had been interested in helping him deal with his wife's independence and absences, but Cald-well continued to fixate on the need for her to give up her career and raise a family with him. Only when Bourke-White finally returned from her six-month trip to Europe in April 1940, did he regain a fragile peace of mind. Inevitably, when new assignments took her away, he slid back—silent and brooding, unable to sleep, unwilling to get out of bed, and without appetite or enthusiasm. And as before, he used his misery as a leash to try to keep her close. "This time," he telegrammed her in Canada, "ask you hurry as never before—out of mind with worry and need you . . . can't describe what this means to me but ever since you left like nightmare. . . . Remember every minute I love you dearly."[16]

II

BOURKE-WHITE SEEMED to invigorate and inspire Caldwell's work in spite of the emotional turmoil she caused him. He continued to be involved with left-wing causes, and in particular, in the struggle of Spanish Loyalists against Franco in Spain—a civil war that was, by 1937, a preoccupation of most American leftists. Always drawn to tales of underdogs, Caldwell viewed the Loyalists "like 'Tobacco Roaders' everywhere . . . [with] unrest boiling out of hunger and submersion." He and Bourke-White donated the manuscript of *You Have Seen Their Faces* to an auction benefiting the Medical Bureau to Aid Spanish De-mocracy; they attended parties and fundraisers, donated food and money for the Loyalists, and spoke out in the press against the dangers of Hitler and the evil of Franco. Caldwell even donated a story—for him the most sincere form of generosity—to a pamphlet series that celebrated the bravery of the Spanish resistance.[17]

Caldwell also continued attending the American Writers' Congresses, gatherings still very much under the auspices of the American Com-munist Party in the late 1930s. He had been gratified by his invitation to the first Congress in 1935 and the serious consideration by leftist critics he received there. He happily accepted a post as an honorary vice-president to the 1937 Congress, held in Carnegie Hall, and joined other writers in damning international fascism. In the summer of 1939, he attended yet again.[18]

The *Daily Worker* recognized Caldwell's role as one of America's most influential writers during the angry decade of the 1930s—an artist whose conscience was formed "out of events like the Gastonia textile strike, the miners' strike in Harlan, the organization of sharecropper unions and unemployment relief demonstrations." Although he had come under attack from members of the Left for a variety of reasons through the years, his commitment to uplifting America's underclass was now beyond dispute. Caldwell was, the *Worker* wrote respectfully, "an artist in uniform."[19]

Caldwell also stepped up his nonpolitical activities in the late 1930s, and it seems that Bourke-White was instrumental in forcing him out of his social seclusion. He joined panel discussions on the future of American letters with other well-known writers and appeared on radio programs like *Author Author* where, in his quiet Southern drawl, he shared his ideas on the state of American fiction. He gave a few lectures, agreeing to speak to the Columbia University Writer's Club, in spite of that university library's much-publicized ban of *Tobacco Road* a few years earlier. He even tried his hand at teaching, offering a weekly lecture course entitled "Farm Tenancy and the Negro in Transition" at the New School for Social Research in New York City.[20]

Caldwell also spent time monitoring the international publication details surrounding *Tobacco Road* and *God's Little Acre*, his two most famous literary properties. Both works were appearing in translation around the world, and he badgered Lieber constantly for updates on royalties, options, and translation rights. Caldwell was particularly popular in Eastern Europe, and he kept close track of the rubles, zlotys, and other currencies that he was accumulating. The stage adaptation of *Tobacco Road* was just getting started in many places overseas as well. In Spain it was *Camino del Tobaco*; in Sweden, it opened at the National Theatre of Stockholm as *Tobakksveien*. Hollywood was also interested in the film rights to *Tobacco Road*, and Caldwell, Kirkland, and Lieber were kept busy sorting out the various offers.[21]

Caldwell continued to spend a great deal of time playing the stock market and seeking other profitable investments. His most ambitious effort and most dramatic failure was a stage production of *Journeyman* for Broadway. With the crowds for *Tobacco Road* finally on the wane, Caldwell hoped to find the magic touch again. Unfortunately, most critics simply saw the play as a cheap rip-off of the first play. The sexuality, far more explicit than that in *Tobacco Road*, fell flat without any dramatic motivation to justify it. The characters were without the dignity and underlying pathos of the Lesters, and seemed nothing more than crass caricatures. During the preview performance, the night before the formal opening, the audience rose en masse and hissed the play so loudly that the actors had to shout their lines. "Aimless, Shoddy,

Sickening, and Very Childish" read the headline in the *Brooklyn Citizen*; "Journeyman a Dirty and Noisy Bore" trumpeted the *New York Evening Journal*. "Journeyman," wrote Robert Coleman of the *Daily Mirror*, was "reminiscent of the literary efforts of adolescents trying to be smart with crayons on a blank fence." After forty-one performances at three different theaters, the play closed, forcing Caldwell to give up the hope that *Journeyman*, like *Tobacco Road*, was merely off to a slow start. He lost seven thousand dollars, and Bourke-White four thousand more.[22]

Caldwell also continued writing short stories between 1935 and 1938, most of which Lieber easily placed in large circulation magazines. In 1938, Viking came out with a new collection of Caldwell's short fiction called *Southways*, almost all of it published previously. Although the initial printing was only three thousand copies, the book—dedicated to Margaret Bourke-White—was widely reviewed.[23]

The stories in *Southways*, mostly short and grimly tragic, came closer to ennobling the victims of poverty than Caldwell ever had before. Coupled with his outspoken support for the rebels of the Spanish Civil War and his involvement in the Writers' Congresses, this more conspicuous compassion earned him support in leftist circles. While a few Communist critics, such as Arnold Shukotoff of the *New Masses* were still frustrated by his lack of political sophistication and failure to advocate revolution openly, a broad range of the left-wing press, including Robert Goldsmith in the *Daily Worker*, Otis Ferguson in the *New Republic*, and Dorothy Van Doren in the *Nation*, embraced him.[24]

In mainstream journals and newspapers, Caldwell's place at the front rank of American short-story writers was secure. There were still many who bridled at his penchant for violence and overt sexuality, many who felt his portraits of poor Southerners were merely Jeeter or Ty Ty in different settings. But most acknowledged the grace of his prose and the undeniable power and urgency he brought to stories of injustice and exploitation. Many reviewers grouped him with Hemingway, Steinbeck, Faulkner, and Wolfe. Lewis Gannett of the *New York Herald Tribune*, one of many critics disturbed by Caldwell's grotesques but stirred by his "raw, naked intensity of dumb emotion which is sheer genius," felt that *Southways* "confirms Mr. Caldwell's position as one of the most distinguished and exasperating writers in America today."[25]

The most significant aspect of the reviews of *Southways* was the continued confusion over how to categorize Caldwell's work. After nearly ten years, there was still no consensus, as William Soskin of the *New York Times* pointed out in frustration, on whether Caldwell was "a comic satirist, an amoral sensationalist, a social propaganda writer, a plain realist, or—since his home ground in Georgia lends itself to all these categories—just a writer with the South in his mouth." He was, of course, all of these things—a politically conscious writer with no interest in political dogma; a social realist with a strong taste for the surreal and grotesque; an instinctive and uncalculating artist well versed in current American literature and literary theory.[26]

Caldwell and Bourke-White also collaborated on a second book that was published in February 1939, the same month they were finally married in Silver City. The previous spring *Life* had sent Bourke-White to Czechoslovakia and Spain to chart the rise of fascism in Europe. Viking paid Caldwell to accompany her. Both the ominous international scene and the 1939 World's Fair would, Viking knew, create interest in international travel literature. The firm hoped that Bourke-White and Caldwell, still basking in the glory of *You Have Seen Their Faces*, might strike it rich again.[27]

North of the Danube, as Caldwell named the collaboration, was an impressionistic depiction of Czechoslovakia, a country on the verge of annihilation at the hands of the Nazis. The book followed the same basic structure as *Faces*, alternating series of photographs with selections of short essays, but this time, Bourke-White, who had been to Europe many times before, plotted the route and Caldwell followed along. They traveled a meandering path from east to west, from Uzhgorod, the capital of Carpathia Ruthenia, through tiny farming villages like Uzok near the Polish border and on to České Budějovice in the southwest part of the country.

The world press had thoroughly covered the political situation in Central Europe; Caldwell and Bourke-White wanted to capture the character of the Czech people. Caldwell related the plight of villagers starving for bread, told folksy tales of a proud laborer and his dog, described a long afternoon he and Bourke-White spent with a prosperous vineyard owner, and related conversations with farmers laboring in their fields. The pictures and the text in *North of the Danube* presented a world of dignified simplicity and ordinary citizens who showed courage in the face of adversity.[28]

The book also sounded a clear warning against the encroaching evils of fascism. All that was good in Czechoslovakia was threatened, Caldwell and Bourke-White explained, by the ominous cloud of the expected Nazi invasion. Caldwell wrote a powerful vignette of a smug German couple humiliating a Jewish woman in a train as her fellow passengers looked on, and the book closes with a searing portrait of an unctuous Nazi propagandist deriding the stupidity of the native Czech culture.

Caldwell had never been overseas before, but the high culture of Europe held very little interest for him; in Paris and London, when he and Bourke-White weren't working, they spent their time at sporting events and nightclubs. But the trip through Hungary and Czechoslovakia touched Caldwell deeply. The peasants of Vzorod reminded him of the poor farmers of the American South. He wrote home to Morang of people "who live entirely on oats and potatoes . . . [and] have not had enough money to buy salt for 2 or 3 years." The cities were equally depressing, with the fear of impending disaster darkening the atmosphere. Budapest, he wrote to Morang, was "sad-eyed as a calf," because "what the Germans haven't done to that part of the world hasn't been thought of yet." He was particularly horrified by the sight of gas masks for sale in a local bookstore. "Hungaria is a terrible place," he wrote Morang. "The Green Shirts will probably take over the country before long, and Budapest will have a coating of ashes sifted over it just as Vienna had!" A few months later, he admitted to Frank Daniel that working on *North of the Danube* was a "heartbreaking task"—"one day I write about a place there, and the next day Germany takes it."[29]

Bourke-White's aggressive and fearless pursuit of photographs attracted a great deal of attention from the local military police, then under Nazi control. She and Caldwell were followed, and, on several occasions, roused from deep sleep on overnight trains to be interrogated. Once, they were held in custody for hours at the German-Czech border. "After dealing 1st with the German Brown Shirts and now with the Hungarian Green Shirts, I've perfected the Nazi salute so well that I can give it like one of them," Caldwell wrote Morang. Caldwell realized that his blond hair and blue eyes, more than his salute, were the most useful deterrent to suspicion. "They probably would have made it tougher for us if we had looked a little more non-aryan," he wrote to Morang. "The thing is, they suspect everybody of trying to smuggle money out of the country for the Jews." By the end of the trip, although Caldwell could hardly believe it himself, he was homesick. "Funny how a fellow can miss a place like Georgia so much, isn't it?" he wrote to Frank Daniel. "I'll be pretty glad to get back to America too. I guess I'll stay there for a while once I get back."[30]

Viking's timing for the publication of *North of the Danube* was brilliant—or very lucky. Czechoslovakia was still a sovereign nation when the book was written, but by the time it was published in February 1939, Hitler had dismembered it. Caldwell's and Bourke-White's ennobling portraits of peasants and proudly independent laborers were all the more poignant. The book sold briskly at three dollars a copy.[31]

The reviews were sensational. Caldwell and Bourke-White clearly remained king and queen of the new photo-text medium. "Both are at their best here," Bertram Gale wrote, "and nobody denies that at their best they are unsurpassed." Maurice Hindus of the *New Republic* called *Danube* "one of the most extraordinary travel books I have ever read." Even a government minister of war-torn Czechoslovakia, Vladimir S. Hurban, sent congratulations via Viking to the authors for "representing a proud and hard-working people whose indomitable will shall triumph over the tragedy that has beset them."[32]

Despite *Danube*'s critical and financial success, however, Bourke-White and Caldwell were not entirely satisfied with it. Bourke-White knew that the photographs in *Danube* were not as intimate or evocative as the ones in *Faces*. She blamed Caldwell for this. Uncomfortable in the foreign environment, and unhappy following around after his wife, he had slipped frequently into dark moods. On several occasions, he had created awkward situations with his rudeness, and Bourke-White was unable to establish warm relationships with her subjects. Caldwell, in turn, recognized that his ignorance of the culture and language severely limited his ability to create a sophisticated narrative. Unable to decipher the vernacular or the humor of the people he met—two elements that had given so much depth to his essays on Southern sharecroppers—Caldwell replaced the fictionalized quotations that had enhanced the photographs in *Faces* with simple factual descriptions. Two months before its publication, Caldwell admitted to his parents that while *North of the Danube* was timely, he felt it was incomplete. "I am not sure that it is as good as the other book," he wrote worriedly. "We spent . . . months [in Czechoslovakia], while I felt as though I spent a lifetime in the South." A lifetime of experience, Caldwell well knew, was his most important resource as a writer. He was ready to return to more familiar terrain.[33]

III

CALDWELL HAD NOT attempted a novel since *Journeyman*, more than five years earlier, and there was increasing pressure for him to try again. Both Viking Press and Lieber wanted him to capitalize on the popularity of the stage adaptation of *Tobacco Road* and the success of *You Have Seen Their Faces* and *North of the Danube*. Caldwell was riding a wave of popularity that almost ensured excellent sales for his next novel. There was also pressure from the critics. In the reviews of *Southways*, many suggested that Caldwell needed to write a new novel to prove his place among America's preeminent fiction writers. They questioned Caldwell's ability to produce a book that could transcend the power and artistry of either *Tobacco Road* or *God's Little Acre*. "It should soon be time for him to give us a steady view," wrote the critic for the *New Yorker*, "more severe and dignified, less ramshackle and eccentric, than his previous ones." Lewis Gannett, Otis Ferguson, and Charles Poore agreed, and they urged him to put nonfiction and short stories behind him.[34]

The most compelling pressure came from his father. Ira felt that Erskine had strayed too far from his roots of late, writing about the Northwest and West in *Some American People* and then Central Europe in *North of the Danube*. "It occurs to me that it is time you were undertaking a great Southern story," Ira wrote him. "You can write about the South better than you can of any other section. At the same time you are not well enough acquainted with the South. You will inevitably make mistakes until you get better acquainted. I suggest that you come down here while Margaret is away and make a careful study of things Southern." When Caldwell finally began work on a new novel, he chose a subject close to his father's heart—a subject he had studied since boyhood.[35]

Erskine had been aware of Southern racism as long as he could remember. During his earliest years in the rural villages of White Oak, Georgia, and Prosperity, South Carolina, his father preached racial tolerance from the pulpit and waged a constant struggle to make a congregation of white farmers treat their black sharecroppers more humanely. Ira took Erskine with him on his long rides into the countryside to visit poor farmers of both races and pointedly treated black and whites with equal respect. In tiny railroad towns, he brought his son to the black shantytowns on the far side of the tracks to visit the sick and elderly, and lectured him on the shame of inequality in a rich democratic nation.[36]

Years later, Caldwell recalled with pride his father's treatment of a black man who did janitorial work for a tiny A.R.P. church in South Carolina. Moses Coffee had suffered a lifetime of violence, and he bore scars on his face and neck from the blows of a chain delivered by a white landowner. As a boy, Coffee had been unfairly charged with the theft of a pocket knife and had served two years of hard labor on a county chain gang. Erskine noted that Coffee often stuttered and trembled badly when he was in the presence of whites he did not know; Ira once had Erskine shake the black man's hand, and Coffee—unaccustomed to such intimacy from a white person—pulled away in fear.[37] Ira always treated Coffee with respect. While the previous pastor had made the elderly man sit in an unheated back room while waiting to clean the church after services, Ira urged him to occupy an empty pew. He knew that Coffee's presence would anger members of his church, but he did not care; when they complained and threatened to cut his salary, Ira ignored them. When Coffee died, Ira attended the funeral, and again, drew the ire of congregants who thought it unseemly for their pastor to attend a "nigger burial."[38]

When the Caldwells moved to Wrens, Georgia, in 1919, the state was suffering a period of intense violence towards its black citizens. The Ku Klux Klan had opened a new headquarters in Atlanta a few years earlier, and the organization grew so powerful and influential that a Klan member, Clifford Walker, was elected governor in 1920. Between 1919 and 1921, a state commission found over 135 examples of "atrocities," many of them lynchings, committed against Georgia's blacks. In 1923 a state civil rights group secured twenty-two indictments against lynchers. While only four were convicted, this was considered a significant victory for racial justice. In the previous thirty-seven years there had been just one indictment.[39]

Jefferson County, where Wrens was located, saw its share of racial violence as well. As in many cotton-growing areas in the South, there were instances of blacks held in peonage, tricked into unfair labor contracts, exploited at company stores, and intimidated into obedience. In Covington, Georgia, a case of particularly grisly abuse brought national attention when a white landowner named John Williams murdered eleven blacks on his farm rather than let them testify before an investigatory commission.[40]

Erskine had a close-up view of such brutality. Ira once took him to visit a wealthy parishioner, a man Caldwell later described as a "cigar-smoking, florid faced 250-pound landowner." Erskine and his father were sitting in the man's office when a black sharecropper was disciplined for buying a cow and fencing land for a pasture without the landowner's permission. Caldwell never forgot the horror he witnessed:

Clamping the cigar tightly in the corner of his mouth, the flush-faced landowner took a heavy black leather strap from the wooden peg on the wall, ordered [the man] to take off his shirt and drop his overalls to the floor, and then he was told to get down on his hands and knees. . . .[41]

Caldwell saw tears of frustration, helplessness, and rage in his father's eyes. When they returned home, he remembered his father trembling as he told him that "there'll be that kind of cruelty in our part of the world until people like that man in the plantation office become enlightened enough to be ashamed of their meanness." Ira did what he could. When a landowner battered a sick tenant for going home from the fields early, Ira tended to the injured man's wounds and then publicly criticized the owner for his cruelty.[42]

The Georgia chain gangs were notorious for their racial brutality, and Ira was an outspoken advocate of abolishing them. After delivering the morning sermon to his A.R.P. congregation on Sunday, he traveled to nearby towns to preach to the gangs who worked there. Erskine often accompanied his father on these trips. Years later, when he was working on *You Have Seen Their Faces*, he knew just where to look to find the long lines of shackled convicts for Bourke-White's camera.[43]

Caldwell never actually witnessed a lynching, but several took place near Wrens while he was living there. On one occasion, a black man accused of raping a white woman was dragged through the streets of the town behind a speeding automobile. The town sheriff did nothing to stop such actions, and he too was a familiar target in Ira's sermons. In a piece Ira wrote for the *Augusta Chronicle* titled "Civilization Is Only Skin Deep," he described a lynching so graphically that readers wrote in to complain. Not surprisingly, the Klan was also unhappy with Ira's outspoken race liberalism. A neighbor of the Caldwells overheard plans to "run the goddam' nigger-lovin' S.O.B. outa Jefferson County" because his generosity and kindness were "ruin'n every black bastard in the county." Such threats seemed to have no effect on Ira's behavior, and his courage was a powerful lesson to his son.[44]

Caldwell continued to see racism when he left Wrens for Due West and Erskine College. There were several lynchings in the neighboring town of Abbeville, one of which made national news. The victim, Mark Smith, had been acquitted of a crime and was leaving town when he was waylaid by four white men. His body was later pulled from the Savannah River, hacked almost to pieces, with the head and legs cut off. A few years later, when Caldwell spent a year in Atlanta as a reporter for the *Journal*, he arrived at the scene of a lynching, "before the body was cut down."[45]

Caldwell's writing had included attacks on racial prejudice and violence from the very beginning. At the University of Virginia, his best poem, "Face Beneath the Sky," included the powerful stanza: "They fought . . . in anger for his ears/His blood they drew with gruesome pride/And took his hands away for souvenirs." Caldwell's first published work, "Georgia Cracker," described the vicious disciplinary methods used on the shackled convicts who plodded along the roads near Wrens. He detailed, for instance, the "crucifixion of unruly convicts by stretching their arms against a fence and fastening their wrists with ropes . . . in such a position that the knees are drawn forward and the prisoner hangs by his heels and wrists." He recounted the lynching of Willie Dixon, an insane black man accused of killing his white nurse in a state sanatorium in nearby Milledgeville. Dixon was carried from the hospital, tied to a tree, and beaten to death with a pick handle by a band of angry whites. "Nothing was done by the State in this case," the twenty-two-year-old Caldwell wrote in disgust. "Nor will any steps ever be taken in the case. And indeed, the number of citizens who are ashamed of the fact that their brothers will lash a demented person's head with a pick handle is so small as to be negligible."[46]

Some of Caldwell's best short stories were based on incidents of racial injustice that he had witnessed or heard about while growing up. In most of these stories, it was the very virtue of black citizens that spurred their poor white neighbors to violence. He wrote of powerful black men brimming with life, sexual potency, and goodwill, cut down by whites threatened by their power and autonomy. In the best of these, "Candy-Man Beechum," a black man of mythic strength and vitality, is indifferently murdered by a small-town policeman when he refuses to be incarcerated without cause. Such stories of racial oppression were spare and tragic, without the humor or absurdity that leavened so much of Caldwell's fiction about poor whites. Although they verged on melodrama—callous, evil whites who viciously victimize honest, hard-working blacks—the lean prose and subtle evocation of dialect made them the most powerful and most widely praised pieces Caldwell ever wrote.[47]

Fiction with racial themes also allowed Caldwell to explore his fascination with violence. Typically, he detailed scenes of brutality with a studied indifference that accentuated the almost-casual viciousness of his white characters. "In the fall after all the crops had been gathered," he wrote in a story that became part of *The Sacrilege of Alan Kent*, "men lynched a negro boy. When they were ready to go home they cut off his ears and fingers and toes and put them into their pockets. One man wanted to take both of his arms, but they were too hard to cut off." In "Savannah River Payday" two cretinous whites knock the gold teeth from the head of "some nigger" killed in a mill accident. "Red took the stick and pushed the lips away from the teeth," Caldwell narrated. "Jake choked the monkey-wrench halfway and tapped on the first tooth. He had to hit it about six or seven times before it broke off and fell." In the course of the story, the corpse is carted around in the back of the car while the men casually attempt the rape of a black field worker, get drunk on moonshine whiskey, and play pool in town. When the town marshal reminds the boys to take care of the body before it "stinks the whole town up," Jake and Red are outraged. " 'Say,' Jake said, falling against one of the tables, 'you go tell that marshal that I said for him to take a long runnin' start and jump to hell—Me and Red's shootin' pool!' "[48]

In the novels, the marginal black characters are as dignified and decorous as the poor whites are licentious and depraved. In *Tobacco Road*, for example, a group of blacks look on in detached amusement while Ellie Mae and Lov couple openly and grotesquely in the Lesters' front yard. Caldwell was particularly sensitive to the dilemma of blacks who felt a moral superiority to their poor white neighbors but had to hide their judgment. In *God's Little Acre*, Ty Ty's black sharecroppers recognize the family's moral turpitude, incest, and stupidity, but they express themselves carefully, in the coded messages of the "dozens"— offering caustic, guarded commentary on the Waldens' hijinks in the guise of a rhymed song that Ty Ty cannot understand.[49]

Caldwell makes it clear that nothing can make Southern blacks safe from the capricious and often violent impulses of whites. When Dude and Sister Bessie go driving, they carelessly crash into a black man and his horse-drawn wagon. The man is thrown into a ditch, but they do not stop to help. "When we drove off again, he was still lying in the ditch," Dude comments absent-mindedly. "The wagon turned over him and mashed him. His eyes was wide open all the time, but I couldn't make him say nothing. He looked like he was dead." Jeeter is entirely unconcerned. "Niggers," he notes distractedly, "will get killed, looks like there ain't no way to stop it."[50]

Caldwell brought his interest in racial themes to his nonfiction work as well. Mob violence had died down in the late twenties, but the Depression brought a resurgence. In 1930, there were twenty-one recorded lynchings in the South alone, and the Northern press, particularly on the Left, took notice. In late 1933, while Caldwell and Helen were in Wrens, there was a series of lynchings in the nearby town of Bartow. Caldwell investigated, then wired a story to the *New Masses* office in New York. The magazine carried his story with the lead: "Erskine Caldwell, the noted author . . . has just stumbled into a season of terror in the backwoods of Georgia."[51]

During the gruesome Bartow lynchings, a white mob killed three blacks, severely beat five others with lead pipes, and burned down fourteen houses. One of the corpses was thrown down a well, another was left mutilated in a cotton field. Although the murderers were well known in town, they remained unpunished and, as Caldwell wrote, "walk the streets in heroic strides" and "boast of their crimes." The coroner's and police reports came back, as Caldwell reported it, with the simple phrase "Death at the hands of parties unknown"—the headline he used for one of his articles.[52]

Caldwell spent a number of days in Bartow asking questions, poking around, and sending dispatches back to New York. Along with a graphic account of the lynchings themselves, he described the ironic quaintness of the little Southern town. "Bartow," he wrote pointedly, "was as calm as any Georgia town at midnight. Georgia was as peaceful as any Southern state in January." He sarcastically pointed out that Bartow was a religious community with four churches, "two Baptist, two Methodist," for a population of only four hundred. More pointedly, he described men "who butcher hogs with more humaneness than they kill Negroes" and sneered at the local newspapers who had ignored the story entirely. Reporters in Georgia operated by a simple dictum; he wrote, thinking, no doubt, of his days at the *Atlanta Journal* as well: "If a white man is murdered, telegraph it in; if a Negro is murdered, mail it in."[53]

Before long, threats were made on Caldwell's life, and the *New Masses* reported that "Erskine Caldwell . . . is in danger. His personal safety is seriously threatened." One concerned local citizen warned the paper's editors that "if Caldwell sticks to his post and continues to fight, something will happen to him." Caldwell ignored the threats to his life, so similar to the threats that had been made to his father in the past. "I came pretty close to getting my neck stretched in Georgia," he wrote proudly to Morang. "But I got the story I was after anyway." Caldwell's pieces for the *New Masses* brought other reporters into the tiny town of Bartow, and an independent investigation from the Commission of Interracial Cooperation corroborated his findings.[54]

When Caldwell traveled south to write his stories for the *New York Post* the following year, he continued to focus on the problems facing

Southern blacks. He described how landlords exploited their black tenants through intimidation and trickery to keep them working their
farms at starvation wages. He included testimonies from blacks designed to bring their hardships alive for his Northern readership.

> The last time I tried to move off, the landlord said he's going to beat
> me with a stick if I ever mention it again. I don't owe him a single
> dollar, and he won't say why he's keeping me here.[55]

Caldwell, with Bourke-White's assistance, furthered his investigations
in *You Have Seen Their Faces*. While the reviews generally described the
book as a treatise on the plight of poor whites, it was far more ambitious than that. Fully one half of the photographs in the collection were
of blacks, and Caldwell reserved some of his most pointed prose for
his evocations of racial injustice. He lambasted Southern whites for
creating a "retarded and thwarted civilization:"

> The Negro tenant farmer is the descendant of the slave. For generations
> he has lived in mortal fear of the white boss in cotton country. He has
> seen his women violated and his children humiliated. He himself has
> been discriminated against, cheated, and whipped, and held forcibly in
> an inferior position. Every white face he sees is a reminder of his broth-
> er's mutilation, burning, and death at the stake. He has no recourse in
> law, because he is denied the right of trial before his peers. The Negro
> tenant farmer on a plantation is still a slave.[56]

Bourke-White's stark photographs only echoed this tragic tableau of
poverty, economic exploitation, and physical intimidation. There were
pictures of young black convicts on the chain gang in Hood's Chapel,
Georgia, and of grossly overcrowded schools in Scotts, Arkansas. One
of the book's most poignant photos was of a wide-eyed black child
and his dog standing in the doorway of a broken-down hut. The walls
of the shack were plastered—as were many black houses in the vicin-
ity—with advertisements for all the shiny material goods its residents
could never afford. The caption to a photograph of a black classroom
in Arkansas read: "And so the fairy godmother in the storybook
touched the little white girls with her wand and they were all turned
into little princesses." Beneath the image of a sleeping convict—a boy
still in his early teens—Caldwell wrote: "I reckon I was naturally born
a black boy in the white man's country." Beneath another he added,

"They can whip my hide and shackle my bones, but they can't touch what I think in my head."

During the research for *You Have Seen Their Faces*, Caldwell and Bourke-White passed through the town of Kelley, Georgia, and witnessed an angry mob searching for a black man accused of raping a white prostitute. Caldwell did not discuss the incident in the book, but he did not forget it; he already knew that it would serve as the centerpiece for the novel he was more than ready to write.[57]

IV

SINCE THE CIVIL WAR, civil rights activists had fought for federal antilynching legislation to protect blacks; in 1922, the so-called Dyer Bill came close to passing before being defeated by a Southern-led Senate filibuster. By the end of the decade, however, the number of lynchings had dropped and so did interest in new legislation. In the early thirties, Southern blacks were again the frequent victims of mob violence; efforts to pass antilynching laws were renewed, and Caldwell's work became an important part of the body of evidence supporting the new drive. As he began work on his new novel, an angry debate raged in Congress. A series of vicious lynchings (culminating in a mob attack in Duck Hill, Mississippi, in which two blacks were tortured with a blowtorch) spurred the passage of a bill in the House of Representatives in April 1937. But as in the past, Southern senators dug in their heels and filibustered the bill to death. Louisiana's Allen J. Ellender spoke for over six days, punctuating his remarks with promises to "preserve the white supremacy of America." Theodore Bilbo of Mississippi presented a plan for recolonizing American blacks in Africa.[58]

Caldwell's new novel, written in the shadow of this national debate, was called *Trouble in July*. Superficially, the novel was, as a number of critics pointed out, a typical Southern melodrama based on familiar clichés of victims and villains. Sonny Clark, an innocent, upright black boy, is accused of rape by a promiscuous white girl in search of attention; he is lynched by a vicious mob while an obese and lethargic sheriff looks on. Like much of Caldwell's short fiction dealing with racial injustice, *Trouble in July* was not infused with the absurdity, surrealism, and violent burlesque of *Tobacco Road, God's Little Acre,* or *Journeyman*. In many ways, *Trouble in July* was the most straightforward and conventional novel Caldwell ever wrote.

But the book was also far more sophisticated and ambitious than many critics recognized. Caldwell's black characters may have been simple and virtuous—uncomplicated foils for white brutality—but he drew on his experience in Bartow to portray the various ways in which a lynching resonated throughout their community. In the *New Masses* articles, he had described a reign of terror that drove blacks from the street and behind locked doors and tightly shuttered windows. Such a climate of fear hangs over every black character in *Trouble in July*. Well before the mob catches Sonny Clark, the entire black population disappears from sight. "There was not a glimmer of light to be seen in any of the houses," Caldwell wrote. "All of them looked deserted. The solid wooden blinds were closed tightly over windows of every building . . . all the doors were locked."[59]

The most ambitious and unusual aspect of *Trouble in July* was Caldwell's careful depiction of his white characters, all of whom are conflicted and complex. Sheriff Jeff McCurtain goes fishing whenever a lynch mob gathers in his county, and he permits the murder of the innocent Sonny Clark in order to protect his own political standing. Yet he is far from the archetypal villain, leering and grunting with sadistic pleasure. McCurtain is torn by guilt and confused emotions. When the mob takes another black man hostage, to be held until they find the accused rapist, McCurtain snaps out of his characteristic lethargy to save him. He confesses that "Sam Brinson is a sort of special friend of mine, even if he is a colored man." When he is accused of being a "nigger lover," McCurtain justifies his decision to save Brinson's life by pointing out that "there are brother whites in this county a heap meaner than any nigger I ever saw." And when a local white woman complains about a Bible depicting a black Jesus, McCurtain reveals an imagination far beyond that of the stereotypical Southern sheriff. "It looks to me like the niggers has got just as much right to say Christ was black as the brother whites has to say he was a white," he tells her angrily. "There ain't no way of proving it either way."[60]

The farmer who finds and turns in the accused Sonny Clark is also tormented by his conscience. "It was difficult for him to make up his mind," Caldwell wrote. "First he would tell himself that he was a white man. Then he would gaze at Sonny's black face." While he craves the praise of the "hunt-hungry mob" who will "slap him on the back and praise him," he knows he will "probably hate himself as long as he lived." In the end, the farmer cannot look Sonny Clark in the eye. "I hate like the mischief to have to do it, Sonny, but this is a white-man's country. Niggers has always had to put up with it, and I don't know nothing that can stop it now. It's just the way things is, I reckon."[61]

Many on the Left viewed poor whites as puppets of the white ruling class in the South. They argued that upper-class Southerners intentionally fueled race hatred to undermine any potential alliance between the poor blacks and whites who worked for them. Moreover, the argument went, poor farmers were exploited by a cotton market far beyond their control or understanding, and racial hatred was merely one more symptom of their economic subjugation.

A few years before, Caldwell had angered a number of leftist critics by downplaying the economic and class issues surrounding a lynching in his story "Saturday Afternoon." But *Trouble in July* reflects Caldwell's immersion in leftist thought in the early to mid-thirties. The protagonist, Sheriff McCurtain, is controlled by Judge Ben Allen, a sinister and calculating patriarch who lives in the grandest house in town. Uninterested in the welfare of the poor, whites or blacks, in his county, concerned only with his own political power, Allen pulls strings as he wishes, inciting or quelling potential violence as the political winds dictate. It is on his orders that McCurtain goes fishing whenever racial violence threatens. Caldwell makes clear that the slow-witted McCurtain has the potential to be a good sheriff and a good man, but that his instincts are undermined by Allen and the pressure he brings to bear. "McCurtain felt sorry for the little Negro boy, Sonny Clark," Caldwell explains. But when he considers intervening, "a feeling of helplessness came over him." As Richard Wright described it in a *New Republic* review, McCurtain is merely "a damp rag in the face of a whirlwind."[62]

Caldwell also shows that the personalities of his poor white characters are contorted by the bleakness of their lives, and that their extreme poverty reduces them to the level of animals. The struggling farmers of Andrewjones, Georgia, depend precariously on the vagaries of the cotton market. When Caldwell introduces the members of the lynch mob, they are talking, as they always do, about the price of cotton. "If the price dropped under eight cents a pound, it meant that a lot of them would have to live on short rations for the next twelve months," Caldwell wrote. "Day in and day out, the price of cotton was the most important thing in their lives." Helpless, fearful men, Caldwell's characters crave power and find it where they can. Their anger is directed against the most visible reminder of their own failure.

It was getting about time to clamp down on a nigger again, one of them said. 'A week ago I was in a store in Andrewjones, and I'll be damned if a black buck didn't come in with more money in his pocket than I've had in mine all summer long. That made me good and sore, seeing a nigger like him better off than I was. . . . Hell, this is a white man's country! Ain't no nigger going to flash a bigger roll of money than I can, and me not do nothing about it. It ain't right.[63]

In spite of his willingness to offer such explanations for Southern racial violence, *Trouble in July* also manifests Caldwell's ever-present anger toward the poor Southern whites he wrote about. He was widely considered their most eloquent and impassioned champion, and his work had brought their plight into the national limelight. But lynch mobs embodied Southern whites at their very, very worst, and Caldwell simply could not forgive them. Without the narrative devices of satire or burlesque humor that had provided an outlet for Caldwell's hostility in earlier works, *Trouble in July* conveys Caldwell's antagonism directly. The *New Masses* viewed lynchers as innocent pawns in an exploitative class system, but Caldwell details their brutality, their sadism, and their inhumanity in excruciating and angry detail. The white characters in *Trouble in July* emerge not merely as victims; they are villains as well.

V

TROUBLE IN JULY was the first piece of fiction Caldwell had written without Helen's careful editing. And even though he had relied on her less and less as his grammar and spelling improved, he badly missed her reassurance. He tried to get Bourke-White to take Helen's place, but she was, as usual, away on assignment for *Life*. "I wish to goodness I had the benefit of your valuable help in correcting galley proofs of the new book," Caldwell wrote Bourke-White. "This is the last chance to make changes in Trouble in July—your book! The first novel I've done under your spell—and I want it to be perfect."[64]

Unfortunately, Harold Guinzburg and Marshall Best at Viking Press thought the manuscript far from perfect. Over the past five years, Caldwell's relationship with his publishers had become increasingly strained. Angered by Viking's tentative marketing and printing schedule for *Journeyman*, he blamed them—not the devastating reviews—for the novel's poor sales. His frustration mounted when *North of the Danube* was published late, a few months after its scheduled release, then sold fewer books than expected. Caldwell was also convinced that Best and Guinzburg were pushing other authors in their stable harder, advertising them better, and paying them higher advances. He was particularly threatened by John Steinbeck, whose *Grapes of Wrath* became one of Viking's best-sellers the same summer that *North of the Danube* was released. His suspicions were unfounded, as even Lieber admitted. "I am in complete sympathy with you and you have never known me to favor the publisher against the author," he assured Caldwell, "yet I must give the devil his due." Viking had actually spent as much on the promotion of *North of the Danube* as they had on the hugely successful *Grapes of Wrath.*[65]

For their part, Best and Guinzburg were disappointed that Caldwell had spent so much time and energy on nonfiction, work that brought little profit to the house. They also grew impatient with his constant complaints about pricing, printing errors, and advertising strategy. Indeed, his persistent paranoia was bothersome and difficult to understand. On a trip to San Francisco, Caldwell could not find copies of *North of the Danube* in the bookstores, and he accused Best of sabotaging his sales; Best pointed out with some annoyance that the book had not even been released yet on the West Coast.[66]

Unlike Maxwell Perkins, who realized immediately that Caldwell needed very gentle treatment, Guinzburg and Best refused to coddle him—they were, in fact, unnecessarily blunt. It soon became obvious that they were perfectly happy to let Caldwell take his future work elsewhere. At a conference to discuss publication plans for *Trouble in July*, Guinzburg tipped back in his chair and casually remarked, "I suppose we'll have to publish this new item." Lieber and Caldwell were outraged, and thought Viking was treating *Trouble in July* "like a gross of stockings or a side of bacon." When Caldwell pressed Lieber to ask for a more lucrative contract from Viking, they were turned down flat.[67]

Caldwell's troubles with Viking were magnified by his tightening financial situation in the late 1930s. The stage adaptation of *Tobacco Road* was finally declining in popularity, both in New York and on the road, and while the nonfiction work had solidified Caldwell's critical reputation, it paid very little. *You Have Seen Their Faces* sold well in both hardcover and paperback, but *Danube, Tenant Farmer,* and the pieces in the *New Masses* and *Daily Worker* hardly covered expenses. Only occasionally did Lieber sell stories to high-paying magazines, and Caldwell's short-story collections, like most anthologies, brought critical attention but little in the way of royalties.

Most important, Caldwell's cost of living had skyrocketed. The failed adaptation of *Journeyman* cost him almost seven thousand dollars, and the divorce settlement with Helen cut deeply into his yearly income. He sent money to his parents too, mailing off monthly checks to help with car repairs, doctor bills, and trips north to visit the grandchildren. Life with Margaret Bourke-White was also extremely expensive; back from assignment, she favored black-tie dinners, five-star restaurants, and limousines. She loved expensive clothes, and she demanded that Caldwell improve his wardrobe as well. Under her influence, his own tastes grew more extravagant. He replaced the solid Ford roadster with a flashy convertible and stayed only in the very best hotels when he traveled. The biggest new expense was Horseplay Hill, the house and property in Darien; it had cost twenty thousand dollars, and property taxes were steep. It was decorated lavishly to meet Bourke-White's tastes, and the grounds required constant upkeep. The Mount Vernon house that Caldwell had bought from his mother-in-law for a song was heated by a wood fireplace, and Caldwell had chopped the logs himself. In Darien, the oil bill alone amounted to nearly two hundred dollars every winter.[68]

When a brand-new New York publishing house called Duell, Sloan & Pearce offered to buy out Caldwell's Viking contract and the rights to all his past and future works, the timing was perfect. Viking was happy to let their troublesome author go, and Caldwell was more than ready to leave.[69]

Charles Duell, Samuel Sloan, and Charles ("Cap") Pearce had worked at some of New York's most prestigious publishing houses. DS&P, as the firm came to be called, wanted to specialize in American authors and topics, and they were eager to make Caldwell the star of their new stable of authors. They offered him a guaranteed salary of twenty-five hundred dollars a year for three years and even agreed to pay off all the unearned advances that Caldwell had accumulated at Viking. They scheduled publication of a complete collection of Caldwell's stories, and they promised a new edition of *Tobacco Road*, something Caldwell had wanted for years. They even encouraged him to pursue another photo-text book with Bourke-White, an idea Caldwell liked because it guaranteed him time alone with his wife. Most important of all, DS&P flooded Caldwell with kind words and support, and promised "heavy and consistent promotion" for his new novel, *Trouble in July*. "I think," he wrote Bourke-White, "it is a fine thing to change publishers now."[70]

DS&P was well aware of Caldwell's reputation as a "difficult author," and the firm did its best to forestall his complaints. Bob Hunt, the firm's promotional officer, put Caldwell to work advertising the new novel and kept him up-to-date on every aspect of the marketing. He easily persuaded him to attend book signings at big New York City bookstores, do radio advertisements, and address book clubs. DS&P also encouraged Caldwell to buy stock in the new publishing house, thus making him a partial owner of the firm, and entitling him to attend stockholder meetings. Caldwell, who remained suspicious of betrayal, found his new relationship with DS&P full of reassurances. Although his actual power to influence decisions regarding the sale and promotion of his books was negligible, DS&P's warm welcome seemed to make all the difference. He would stay with the firm for almost thirteen years.[71]

VI

DS&P WAS AS GOOD as its word, and they released *Trouble in July* with an advertising blitz in February 1940. Bookstore window displays around New York carried the boldly lettered edition with the full-size photograph of Caldwell—a broad smile illuminating his square, handsome features—on the back.

Almost immediately, Caldwell began to receive angry letters from Southerners. Most complained that once again, Caldwell was slandering his region in exchange for money and fame. "Please don't try to be another Harriet Beecher Stowe," one woman wrote. "One was quite enough." A number of letters, as well as reviews in Southern papers, pointed out that racism was not merely a Southern phenomenon and that Caldwell's picture of the region's race relations was unfair and inflammatory.[72]

Over the years, a disturbing number of letter writers questioned Caldwell's loyalty, not to his region, but to his race. Letters from Southern whites lambasted Caldwell for "stepping out of line," "stirring up race hatred," and being a "negro-loving Bastard." One irate white supremacist sent Caldwell a flyer warning against "integration, amalgamation, and miscegenation" and the loss of "something priceless . . . the purity of race." On the bottom was scrawled: "You sold your soul to the devil a long time ago—you cannot recall the dirty books you sired."[73]

Negative reviews of the book in the New York press sounded the same themes that had greeted *Journeyman* five years earlier. "The author has done this sort of thing, has produced these same grim-comic effects before," wrote Clifton Fadiman in the *New York Times*. "There is no doubt that he is beginning to repeat himself . . . the book seems tired, like a Georgia drawl." Harold Strauss in the *Nation* went one step further. "*Trouble in July* represents not only no further advancement in Caldwell's art," Strauss wrote, "but a definite falling off." While Strauss acknowledged that "all of his fine craftsmanship is still in evidence," he thought the characters in *Trouble in July* were "the same people, moving in the same patterns and motivated by the same forces, about whom he has been writing for years."[74]

But most critics felt that Caldwell had produced a carefully crafted and powerful novel. A number of reviewers recognized that *Trouble in July* was more subtle and restrained than any of his earlier works. "No longer do we linger over the antics of poor whites in order to relish how hopelessly crazy life is in the South," wrote Edwin Berry Bergum in *Newsweek*. Because Caldwell's "delight in the ridiculous" had been "driven into the background by a more objective style," Bergum declared that *Trouble in July* was Caldwell's finest novel to date.[75]

Although Caldwell's contact with other American authors was still sporadic, he received support from a number of literary admirers. Perhaps the most gratifying applause came from Richard Wright in a review that appeared in the *New Republic*. Wright, who had explored the horrors of Southern racial violence from the perspective of the black community in his 1938 short story collection *Uncle Tom's Children*, admired Caldwell's efforts to understand the mindset of Southern whites. "In language as simple, melodious and disarming as the drawl of his outlandish characters," Wright wrote, "Caldwell depicts the bucolic tenderness and almost genial brutality that overtakes a Southern community." Wright's social and political sympathies were similar to Caldwell's, and he was one of the few reviewers to pick up on the economic argument implicit in *Trouble in July*. "Hovering grimly in the background of the lynching," observed Wright, "is King Cotton, an inanimate character whose influence is as fatal as that of any living being, and whose rise and fall on the commodity market set the narrow channel through which the political, social, and even the personal destinies of the other characters flow." Wright felt that parts of *Trouble in July* were "some of the most laughable, human, and terrifying pages Caldwell has ever written."[76]

Wright ended his review with a reminder that the character of Narcissa Calhoun was not an unrealistic one. He pointed out that her plan to force the return of American blacks to Africa was a direct reference to Mississippi senator Theodore Bilbo, and his proposal of just such a plan in Congress in January 1938. Most reviews, in fact, saw *Trouble in July* as part of the larger debate over federal antilynching legislation that sputtered on and off in Congress in the late thirties. Walter White, executive secretary of the NAACP and a leading player in the debate, was one of the novel's most outspoken proponents. At a hearing of the Senate Judiciary Committee, White submitted a statement that read: "If the members of the Committee and of the Senate are sufficiently interested and concerned about these conditions to want to find out what the atmosphere is, in a town where lynchings are possible, let me urge to them a reading of a novel soon to be published by the famous and distinguished novelist Erskine Caldwell."[77]

Caldwell thought of *Trouble in July* as the first book he had written "under the spell" of Margaret Bourke-White. But when the reviews came out, he was, as was often the case, alone in the Darien house. He received only a short telegram from his wife. "Thrilled," she wrote, "that critics appreciate our Trouble."[78]

Chapter Ten

ALL OUT ON THE ROAD
TO SMOLENSK

T HE WAR IN EUROPE kept Bourke-White hard at work and
away from home. In April 1940, Germany invaded Norway. The
Netherlands and Belgium fell in May; France surrendered in June. Germany occupied Rumania in October; Italy invaded Greece. By fall, only
Britain and its remarkable air force held the Nazis at bay. On the other
side of the world, Japanese aggression intensified, and in September
Japanese leaders signed a three-power pact with Germany and Italy.

Only a year before, in September 1939, Roosevelt had promised the
American people that the U.S. would "remain a neutral nation." But
his resolve—and the resolve of the nation—slowly eroded. In August
1940, Congress authorized induction of the National Guard into federal
service. In September, only two months before he was reelected to an
unprecedented third term, Roosevelt transferred fifty U.S. destroyers to
Great Britain. Later that month, the first peacetime draft was approved
by Congress, and men began to register for military service. American
isolationists, who had once prevailed in public opinion, were slowly
losing ground to those favoring a more aggressive campaign of aid to
the European democracies.

Caldwell himself was unsure where he stood. On his trip to Central
Europe, he had been horrified by the Nazi encroachment, and *North of
the Danube* contained a powerful attack on Hitler and German anti-
Semitism. He and Bourke-White had worked hard to raise money for
Spanish war relief, and both spoke often about the evils of Franco and
other fascist regimes. And in spite of Caldwell's cynicism about his
government's domestic policies, he had been raised to believe in the
importance of American leadership in world affairs. Ira had proudly
volunteered for the Spanish-American War, and he had made a point
of sending Erskine to work at an army base during World War I.

But Caldwell was also influenced by those on the Left who saw the
war as yet another imperialist struggle waged by capitalist nations. Only

six months before the Japanese bombing of Pearl Harbor, Caldwell, Richard Wright, and several others were elected as vice-presidents of the League of American Writers. At a conference in New York, Caldwell signed a strong antiwar statement that described the conflict as a "brutal, shameless struggle for the re-division of empires—for profits, territories, [and] markets."[1]

Most important, Caldwell's thinking was dominated by the writing projects he conceived, and no matter how hotly the war raged, his attention never strayed far from problems of poverty, racism, and injustice within the United States. With Bourke-White once again covering the war in Europe, Caldwell turned his back on world affairs and began work on his next project.

I

UNLIKE VIKING PRESS, which had pressured Caldwell to focus his energies on writing novels, DS&P urged him to follow *Trouble in July* with whatever sort of book he liked. Caldwell had nurtured a lifelong interest in regional cultures—in the accents, folklore, humor, and history that defined various areas of the country. He asked DS&P to introduce an entire series of books, each dealing with a specific region, each to be written by an author familiar with that culture. He proposed to edit the series himself. DS&P agreed, and the American Folkways Series was born.[2]

The project appealed to Caldwell for a variety of reasons. Alone in the sprawling Darien house, he missed Bourke-White badly, and her absence brought on bouts of depression or intense anxiety. Managing the Folkways Series offered a challenging diversion from his loneliness. The job demanded extensive travel, and beginning in 1940 Caldwell traversed the United States—usually by car—visiting potential authors, monitoring their progress, even accompanying them on field research. On the road, he was happily distracted by the endless logistical details of his meticulously organized itineraries. He also loved to explore, and he was inspired and comforted by the beauty he found in areas of the country he had never seen before—the Sangre de Cristo mountains near Santa Fe and the Catalina foothills outside Tucson. Perhaps most appealing, Caldwell was finally free from the painful vulnerability he had felt at the hands of his own editors. For the first time, he was on the other side of the desk, and he relished the control.

Caldwell was, in fact, an extraordinarily successful and conscientious editor. For years he had harbored grievances—most of them imagined—against editors and publishing houses, and he wanted to be supportive, flexible, and understanding for his own authors. He read drafts promptly and thoroughly and provided detailed comments for his authors. If editorial changes were required, or manuscripts overdue, he delicately framed his remarks with compliments and encouragement. "You know far more about the writing of any book than I could possibly suggest," he wrote one author, "and I now leave the matter in your hands." His authors appreciated the effort. "Caldwell is a wonderful editor to work for," one informed Charles Pearce at DS&P. "I haven't had anyone spur me on to my best effort in the way he does since H. L. Mencken was editing the *American Mercury*."[3]

Although Caldwell sought some famous authors for the series, including Robert Frost and Willa Cather, for many of the writers invited, the contract with DS&P helped launch a career or revitalize one that was fading. Caldwell offered one of the first contracts of the series to a twenty-four-year-old who had never published a book, but whose work he had noticed when judging an essay contest for *Direction* magazine. He also made a point of finding qualified women authors or those whose talents he felt had been too long overlooked. Many of the artists were colleagues who had enjoyed little commercial success but who shared his interest in local working-class culture. One of the series' finest books, *North Star Country*, set in the Great Lakes region, was written by Meridel Le Sueur, an author whose proletarian fiction Caldwell had admired in the early thirties.[4]

Caldwell's interest in developing new talent, his tenderness, his sympathy for the financial and psychological battles of aspiring writers, even the format of his editorial letters, were all reminiscent of the man who had given him his own start. Maxwell Perkins was the editor whom Caldwell ultimately remembered most fondly, and the severance of their relationship still caused him deep regret. His goal, and his achievement, was to give the authors of the Folkways Series something of what Perkins had given him.

The Folkways Series comprised twenty-four books published between 1941 and 1954, that spanned the geographic regions of the country, and were written in a wide range of distinctive styles. Each book told, as Caldwell put it, "the colorful story of America . . . through its own galvanic medium, the customs of the people." Otto Ernest Rayburn wrote *Ozark Country*; Edwin Corle described Death Valley in *Desert Country*; Herbert Croy wrote *Corn Country* about the Nebraska plains; Jean Thomas wrote *Blue Grass Country*; and Clarence Webster, a professor at Brown University, wrote *Yankee Country*. A good many volumes were indifferently reviewed and dropped quickly from sight. A number of others, including Le Sueur's *North Star Country* and Gertrude Atherton's *Golden Gate Country* became regional classics. Harvard University was only the most famous of the schools that used the series' books as part of its curriculum in folklore studies.[5]

Caldwell's fascination with American folk culture continued to inspire his own writing as well. Since the publication of *Some American People* five years earlier, travel books attempting to explain the "American character" had become increasingly popular, and in 1940, *Life* agreed to finance Caldwell and Bourke-White in yet another such project. Bourke-White returned from Europe, and they set out on a round-trip traversal of the continent from Vermont to California. In two and a half months, they traveled nearly ten thousand miles by car, as well as scattered distances by plane, passenger train, and at least once by slow-moving freight.[6]

Caldwell was determined to avoid what he felt were the glib generalizations that characterized so many other "see America" books—books written by overeager artists who "tore over mountains and prairies day and night, stopping spasmodically to inquire of filling-station attendants the current state of the nation." He told a pointedly sarcastic—and certainly apocryphal—anecdote of stopping at a gas station in Missouri, where the attendant simply looked at him and handed him a card that read:

I am 36 years old. I smoke about a pack of cigarettes a day, sometimes more and sometimes less, but it evens up. I take an occasional drink of beer. I am a Baptist, an Elk, and a Rotarian. I live with my own wife, send my children to school and visit my in-laws once a year on Christmas Day. I wear No. 9½ shoes, No. 15½ collar and No. 7¼ hat. I shoot a 12 gauge shotgun and have a 27 inch crotch. I like rice, sweet potatoes and pork sausage. I vote for FDR, pull for Joe Louis, and boo Diz Dean. I wouldn't have anything against Hitler if he stayed in his own back yard. I don't know any Japs, but I've made up my mind to argue with the next one I see about leaving the Chinese alone. I'm in favor of the AAA, the CCC, the IOU and the USA. If I have left anything out, it's an oversight. My business is selling gasoline and oil. If you want your tank filled, just nod your head. If you don't want anything, please move along and give the next fellow a chance. I thank you. Hurry back.[7]

Caldwell envisioned his own project as an aggregate of the intense regional explorations that were being written one book at a time in the Folkways Series. He and Bourke-White traveled great distances, but focused their attention on the few locales that they thought, as Bourke-White put it, gave "the impression and feel of America." They lingered in Pretty Prairie, Kansas, with a group of Rotarians, and in Bryon Lake, South Dakota, where they discovered a religious colony called the Hutterians. They spent time in Texarkana, Texas, watching the horse auctions and in St. Johnsbury, Vermont, where skilled craftsmen still made wooden pails by hand.

Caldwell prided himself on his ability to win the trust of ordinary Americans, and he was indeed a remarkably good listener: his broad, freckled face struck his subjects as trustworthy and honest, and his simple, unaffected manner was a perfect complement to Bourke-White's effervescent charm. Together, they were able to settle quickly into remarkably intimate relationships with a wide range of people.

Like *You Have Seen Their Faces*, the new book contained pointed criticisms of the national character. Underneath a Bourke-White photograph of a tiny all-black school in Mississippi Caldwell wrote: "They wonder sometimes why the white children ride in big yellow buses to the big brick school where there are swings and big, hot stoves, while they have to trudge along the best way they can." There were also glimmers of the leftist rhetoric that had dominated his journalism a few years before. "This America," he warned, "is a jungle of men living in the extreme of good and bad, heat and cold, wealth and poverty." Bourke-White took pictures of indigents outside an employment office in New York and of a weaver hunched over his loom in Lowell, Massachusetts.

But like many of the other travel books of the late thirties and early forties, Caldwell and Bourke-White's work also extolled the distinctive virtues of America. They applauded ethnic diversity, individualism, integrity, and small-town quirkiness—features so notably absent in the fascist regimes overseas. And with the United States economy and the fortunes of its citizens improving every day, the fury that characterized Caldwell's nonfiction several years earlier was now tempered by an unmistakable nationalistic pride. He flirted with a more optimistic view of the country's destiny; he was beginning to see beauty and promise, and his prose reflected this awkward fluctuation between critic and patriot. "In a certain light, America's cheeks look gaunt and the seat of its pants is sometimes threadbare," Caldwell wrote. "But," he admitted in one of the book's many Whitmanesque passages, "the rest of the time it is a healthy, rip-snorting, slam-bang America slinging freight trains across the country a mile a minute." Similarly, Bourke-White, who had begun her career celebrating the power and grace of American industry, once again revealed pride in the factories humming with wartime contracts and wheat fields ripe with grain.

Caldwell and Bourke-White's conflicted message drained the new book of the polemical ardor that defined *You Have Seen Their Faces.* Although *Life* had dutifully paid the trip's expenses, it never ran the material. But DS&P had promised Caldwell a photo-text book, and they published the collaboration in the summer of 1941 with the title *Say, Is This the U.S.A.?* Their timing was good, even if the title was bad. In a climate where Americans were eager to proclaim a national character that distinguished them from the war-torn nations of Europe, sales were brisk. Patriotic reviewers merged their evaluations of the books with testimonials to American greatness. "It reflects the plain earnest, expressive face of the country we all know," wrote Ralph Thompson of the *New York Times.* The critic from the *Boston Herald* thought it "an unparalleled record of this land of liberty . . . a sweeping and panoramic picture of our land and of the people who make it what it is." For a week in July, *Say, Is This the U.S.A.?* was a national best-seller.[8]

Caldwell was in the national spotlight again when the film version of *Tobacco Road* was released in February 1941. An adaptation of the book had been under consideration for more than seven years, but the producers of the play had been reluctant to divide their audience with Hollywood. By 1940, however, road companies were beginning to lose money, and Caldwell allowed Lieber to make a deal. Hollywood studio heads who had always balked at the sacrilegious profanity, overt sexuality, and grimness of Caldwell's novel were now amenable. The success of the film versions of *The Grapes of Wrath* and *Of Mice and Men* proved that rural tragedy could sell, and the sensational success of *Gone With the Wind* had made the South a hot subject.[9]

Lieber and Caldwell began to receive calls from Warner Brothers, Paramount, and Twentieth Century–Fox, each anxious to cash in on the marquee value of both Caldwell and *Tobacco Road*—"the longest running play in Broadway history." In February 1940, the *Hollywood Daily Reporter* noted that "every studio in town is bidding for the rights to Tobacco Road," and Darryl Zanuck referred to Caldwell's book as "the most valuable property the industry has ever known."[10]

Zanuck and Twentieth Century–Fox had produced *The Grapes of Wrath*, and eventually they won the bidding war for *Tobacco Road* as well. Zanuck did all he could to ensure that his new property would be as successful as its predecessor by immediately hiring John Ford to direct the movie and Nunnally Johnson to write the screenplay—the very same team that had adapted *The Grapes of Wrath*. When Zanuck could not convince Henry Fonda to play the part of Jeeter Lester, he hired Charles Grapewin instead, the actor who had played Tom Joad's father in *The Grapes of Wrath*. A good deal of Twentieth Century–Fox's preliminary advertising implied that *Tobacco Road* was the unofficial sequel to *Gone with the Wind*, a crass exploitation of that film's success that only stopped when Margaret Mitchell's attorneys threatened to file suit.[11]

Zanuck, Ford, and Johnson soon discovered what Jack Kirkland had learned years before. *Tobacco Road* was an extremely awkward novel to adapt, and certainly far more challenging than *The Grapes of Wrath* or *Gone with the Wind*. The Lesters had neither the nobility and courage of the Joads nor the compelling romanticism of Scarlett O'Hara. Although Ford and Johnson struggled to capture the peculiar mix of humor, depravity, and violence in Caldwell's novel, they could not bring it off. The ribald sexuality that provided so much of *Tobacco Road*'s power could never have passed the industry censors, and the Lesters' behavior was simply too unsympathetic to fit any Hollywood convention. Ford and Johnson's adaptation slipped gradually toward sanitized, sentimental farce.

At Zanuck's insistence, the character of Ellie Mae, whose aggressive sexuality and grotesquely deformed face set the tone for the novel, was played in the movie by the glamorous Gene Tierney. Tierney's only concession to her character's less lovely aspects was to rub a bit of stage dirt into her arms and legs before shooting. Ford and Johnson hoped at least to retain the novel's tragic ending, but when Zanuck saw the final cut, he ordered them to redo it. As the credits rolled, Jeeter and his wife joined arms and headed happily into the sunset toward the poorhouse.[12]

Twentieth-Century Fox staged a massive advertising campaign featuring the slogan "At Last It's on the Screen," and generated tremendous anticipation for the film's release. The Roxy Theater in New York held screenings for twenty-four hours straight, and its optimism was rewarded when huge crowds greeted the premiere on February 20, 1941. At the 3:10 a.m. show over eleven hundred people lined up for tickets. The movie also fared well in the rest of the country, briefly earning more than any other film in America and eventually grossing Twentieth-Century Fox over eleven million dollars.[13]

Although Caldwell was pleased with the thirty-five thousand dollars he received from the studio, he hated the movie. "Hollywood," he told an interviewer, "murdered *Tobacco Road*." Film critics who had any regard for the novel shared his disgust. *Time* complained that Hollywood had given *Tobacco Road* "a moral scrubbing, a bath of pathos and a sort of happy ending," that "rubbed off its sharp edges of character and depraved psychology." But many other reviewers were relieved that Caldwell's work was finally available in a more wholesome format. They seemed to relish the straightforward buffoonery Johnson and Ford offered up and were grateful to be spared the violence and tragedy of the novel. The critic for the *New York Herald Tribune* called the film "a masterpiece . . . a hundred times better than its theatrical prototype— a challenging reminder of the screen's vast potentialities as well as fascinating entertainment."[14]

Unlike either *Gone With the Wind* or *The Grapes of Wrath*, whose film adaptations eventually equaled or even eclipsed the reputations of the novels that inspired them, the movie version of *Tobacco Road* soon faded from sight. In the ensuing years it was screened less and less, and before long it appeared hardly at all—and when it did, usually (and ironically) as the second bill before showings of *The Grapes of Wrath*.[15]

II

IN MARCH 1941 Stalin and Hitler were still bound by the non-aggression pact they had signed in 1939. But many observers, including some of Stalin's closest advisors, knew that the truce could not last long. Wilson Hicks, Bourke-White's photo editor at *Life*, concurred, and he wanted his star photographer in Russia in time for the invasion. She was overjoyed with the assignment.[16]

Bourke-White asked Caldwell to come with her to collaborate on another photo-text book, and when *Life* agreed to pay his passage, Caldwell agreed to accompany her. He had been dreading the prospect of yet another long separation, and as he later remembered it, her enthusiasm was contagious. "It's the thing for us to do," she told him. "It'll be an exciting experience for you and me—for both of us. We'll be together all the time." When he reminded her that war was on the horizon, she responded, "Of course! That's it exactly. Now, don't you want to go, Skinny? Please say you do!"[17]

Constantin Oumansky, the Soviet Ambassador in Washington, did not share Bourke-White's zeal, and he did all he could to discourage her. With Europe in the hands of the Nazis, she and Caldwell would have to cross China and enter Russia from the east. China, however, was at war with Japan, and existing travel routes were remote and treacherous. Oumansky warned them that they might easily be stopped and interned for the duration of the war, or shot down by Japanese planes. He also reminded Bourke-White that a government decree banned foreigners from taking photographs inside the Soviet Union.[18]

Bourke-White was an expert at cajoling reluctant diplomats, and she had made a career of circumventing official decrees. When Oumansky realized he could not dissuade her, he reluctantly agreed to send instructions to the Soviet ambassador in Chungking. If they could get that far, his government would issue a Soviet visa. Within a month, Caldwell and Bourke-White were on their way. After dropping off the manuscript of *Say, Is This the U.S.A.?* at the DS&P offices, they flew to Los Angeles. Along with an extensive wardrobe, Bourke-White insisted on bringing more than five hundred pounds of camera equipment. On March 20, 1941, they boarded the SS *Lurline* for Honolulu.[19]

The passage from Honolulu to Hong Kong was supposed to be the easiest leg of the journey, but squalls and typhoons stretched the trip to eleven days. Things only got worse. The Chinese National Aviation Company in Hong Kong was unenthusiastic about transporting a quarter ton of camera equipment to Chungking, and it took all of Bourke-White's charm (and some extra cash) to get reservations. They finally flew out on a rickety cargo plane at 4 a.m. in heavily overcast skies in order to avoid Japanese fighters. The only seats available were on top of stacked bales of newly printed nationalist currency en route to the wartime capital.[20]

From Chungking, Caldwell and Bourke-White planned to fly to Hami in the Sinkiang province of China, where they would catch a connection into Alma-Ata, the capital of the Soviet region of Kazakhstan. But when they finally arranged a flight after an eight-day wait, their ancient German-made plane—apparently too old for wartime use—developed engine problems and was forced to make an emergency landing in the desolate settlement of Lanchow. A flight to Hami was arranged after another week of waiting, but this plane was also forced to land when it was hit by a violent sandstorm over the Gobi Desert. When they finally touched down at a remote Mongolian airfield, soldiers rushed the unmarked plane with drawn bayonets, and the passengers were marched single-file into the military barracks. Caldwell was reminded of Oumansky's dire warnings of internment, but the next morning they were released—as inexplicably as they were detained—and they were on their way again.

The delay in Mongolia caused them to miss the weekly connecting flight from Hami to Alma-Ata, and they spent another long, frustrating week waiting before catching a flight into the Soviet Union. When their departure from the eastern region of Kazakhstan to Moscow was delayed by only four days, they considered themselves fortunate. Caldwell and Bourke-White had been traveling in fits and starts for over a month.

Once in Moscow, things improved dramatically. A number of Caldwell's books had been published in Russia, and along with Jack London and Ernest Hemingway, he was one of the nation's literary heroes. His simple, blunt prose made his work perfect for translation, and his critique of capitalist society reached a highly sympathetic audience. Caldwell was a bona fide celebrity; people recognized him on the street—something which rarely happened in America—and Soviet officials fell over themselves extending courtesies and invitations.[21]

The state publishing house had also kept careful track of Caldwell's accumulated rubles. After a jubilant vodka-soaked reception, he was awarded his cash in carefully stacked piles. He later claimed to be "unprepared for such a windfall," and that the "means of luxurious living were thrust" upon him; actually, he had been planning to use the interned currency well before he left. Still, he and Bourke-White were surprised by the luxury of their huge suite at the National Hotel—a place where, he wrote later, "it seemed foolish . . . to ask the waiter not to bring caviar and champagne for a midnight snack." A few weeks after their arrival, he wrote Bourke-White's secretary and asked her to "please inform my parents . . . that we are well and living on the fat of the land."[22]

Bourke-White had been to Russia twice and had shot very flattering photographs of the country's people and burgeoning industrial sector. Along with her status as the wife of the "great Erskine Caldwell," her reputation as a sympathetic observer allowed her to take pictures in spite of the official ukase. She took her camera everywhere, even into a church where she photographed religious services in progress—something most Americans thought strictly forbidden in Communist countries. Eventually, she managed one of the greatest coups of her career when Stalin himself posed for a portrait.[23]

Caldwell and Bourke-White were afforded an unusual freedom to bring back a terrific story, and world events played right into their hands. On June 22, 1941, Germany attacked Russia. Together with Finnish and Rumanian troops, the Nazis invaded Russia along a two-thousand-mile front that stretched from the Arctic to the Ukraine. They conquered the territory with brutal efficiency. The Russians lost more than eighteen hundred planes on the very first day of battle, and within two weeks, over half a million Russian soldiers were prisoners of war. The Red Army seemed overmatched, and foreign experts doubted they could last a month. By summer's end, the Nazis controlled the entire Ukraine; by September they reached Leningrad; by mid-November Sevastopol was under siege; and German troops were on the outskirts of Moscow.[24]

Caldwell and Bourke-White were traveling in the Ukraine collecting material for their project when the invasion began, and they rushed to join the throngs of Soviets catching overcrowded trains back to Moscow. They reclaimed a corner suite at the hotel, and Bourke-White gained permission to photograph the war; their balcony afforded sweeping views of Red Square and the Kremlin—lovely scenery that she knew would be prime targets for German air raids. The American ambassador begged them to leave. They refused. On July 19 the bombs began to fall on Moscow.[25]

Russian officials demanded that everyone in the city seek shelter in the cavernous subways below the streets during air raids—a rule most citizens followed without complaint. But Bourke-White was determined not to miss her opportunity; after two frustrating nights below ground, she stole away to the American embassy to take pictures from the roof. Over the following weeks, she and Caldwell stayed in the hotel suite during the air raids and were afforded a spectacular view of the action from the balcony. When wardens came to bring them down, they hid in the closet or behind furniture. With a camera in her hand, Bourke-White was oblivious to danger, and she loved the drama and spectacle of wartime photography. Once, she was very nearly killed, ducking back into a room in the American embassy only seconds before a bomb hit the roof. Undeterred, even exhilarated, she continued taking pictures, most of which she developed herself in the huge hotel bathtub. Her pictures of the night sky ablaze with flares, exploding bombs, and anti-aircraft fire are the best and most dramatic record of Moscow under siege.[26]

Because Caldwell was the most famous of the handful of American writers sealed inside wartime Russia, he was hounded—via telegram—by American papers and magazines eager to retain him as their exclusive reporter. But Caldwell refused to be tied down by a single contract.

He agreed to write not only for *Life*, which had paid for his and Bourke-White's trip, but also for the North American Newspaper Alliance (NANA), which agreed to pay him a thousand dollars a month. When *PM* magazine offered him twice that to join their staff, he agreed. With Bourke-White's prints developing in the tub, and piles of his notes and research materials accumulating on every surface, the suite, Caldwell wrote later, "was soon in such disorder that it looked more like an untended newspaper office than a Louis Quinze bedroom-and-parlor."[27]

The Soviet authorities also made the extraordinary concession of allowing Caldwell to conduct live radio broadcasts for CBS, although they had not allowed any transmissions, live or recorded, to leave the country in two years. Desperate for American aid, the government recognized the huge and sympathetic audience Caldwell would attract. But while the government trusted him more than any of the other American journalists, his work was still censored extensively. The press office allowed stories of Russian heroism or high troop morale to pass through easily; tales of hardship or food lines, retreats or casualties, were disallowed. Caldwell did not like being censored, but he was more than willing to cooperate. Before long the government trusted him enough to give him two daily time slots—one at 3:00 p.m., and one twelve hours later at 3:00 a.m. Caldwell's success opened the door for other journalists: a few days later a reporter for NBC was also allowed to broadcast after three years of failed efforts.[28]

Caldwell had an armed chauffeur to take him to the studio, but it was still an extremely treacherous commute. Once, as they drove with no headlights during a bombing raid, the car became tangled in an iron fence. Caldwell and his driver were forced to free the car while shrapnel pelted the walls of nearby buildings. Occasionally, if the chauffeur could not get through to the hotel, Caldwell was forced to walk the blacked-out streets during the raids. Years later, he still recalled the "eery [sic] whizzing sound" of steel cables shot loose from their moorings and clinging to chimneys as spent fragments of the antiaircraft guns fell to earth. On several occasions, bombs exploded within a block of where he stood; he saw "buildings and streets rise into the air," and he dove under parked cars or into doorways to avoid the "shower of brick and mortar flying all around." Once, his press pass was challenged by an air raid warden, and he was interrogated in a dimly lit room below a blacked-out apartment building before being released.[29]

The quality of Caldwell's broadcasts were mixed. Initially there were technical problems, and the first reports were so faint they were unintelligible. But even when the transmission problems were ironed out,

Caldwell's radio style was less than dynamic. His slightly nasal Georgia drawl was quiet, even hesitant, and he certainly possessed none of the dramatic flair, timing, or timbre of great broadcasters like Edward R. Murrow, then reporting live each night from London. Caldwell was, after all, an amateur. Occasionally, his mouth was too close to the microphone, and his voice became muffled. On the night of his first broadcast, Bourke-White stood by him in the booth with a stopwatch in one hand and a pencil in the other, signaling her nervous husband to slow down or speed up.[30]

Regardless of how it was told, the story of the Russian people and their fight to survive was absolutely spellbinding to American audiences. The technology of mass destruction had changed since World War I. Tanks, antiaircraft guns, and massive bombings were terrifying and mesmerizing new developments. And if Caldwell was a mediocre reader on the radio, the prose—in both his broadcasts and his stories for *PM* and *Life*—was characteristically clear, direct, and evocative. His first-hand accounts of people passing time during a nighttime air raid, or of the sound that bombs made just before impact were compelling. American audiences were particularly fascinated by the tank battles, and although Caldwell was unable to obtain permission to visit the front himself, he accumulated many "eye-witness accounts" from returning soldiers. *PM* wrote headlines to match the text: "Clash of 700 Nazi-Soviet Tanks Sounded Like End of World, Eyewitness Tells Erskine Caldwell: Rammed Tanks Reared and Buckled, Houses Toppled Like Duckpins in Battle Lasting Through Day."[31]

Like many of his leftist associates stateside, Caldwell dropped his isolationist stance the moment Hitler attacked Russia. With the full support of the beleaguered Russian government, Caldwell laced his articles with pleas for U.S. assistance. His reporting, in fact, was more wartime propaganda than objective journalism; it was dominated by tales of Russian heroism and Nazi cowardice, Russian integrity and Nazi avarice. There were stories of German planes brought down by Russian rifle fire, and of courageous Russian pilots who rammed German planes in mid-air—stories of plucky volunteers who put out rooftop fires, and headlines in *PM* that declared "Nazi Soldiers Cried When They Lost."[32]

In part, Caldwell's reports were shaped by the government censor board, but, always attracted to the underdog, he was also swept up in the struggle of the overmatched Russian army. He was comfortable with propaganda in which passion was translated into simple models of good and evil, victims and victors; and like his wife, Caldwell was electrified by the sheer drama and spectacle of war. His descriptions of

the Russian air force and the German air raids exhibited his characteristic intensity: "The sky was filled with Zenith gun bursts that looked
as if every star were disintegrating over and over again," he wrote.
"Flaming onions tore through the night with a ferocity that was breath-
taking; tracer bullets zinged upward out of sight; machine gun rattle
came from every direction; and the deafening bang of anti-aircraft ar-
tillery made the air tremble." He eagerly conducted interviews with
Red Army generals, German prisoners of war, and factory workers and
reported their stories with breathless excitement.[33]

Caldwell had an enormous capacity for hard work, but after nearly
three months of writing for *PM* and *Life*, as well as doing two broadcasts
a day for CBS, he was exhausted. So too was his supply of rubles.
Bourke-White's secretary had mailed him a bundle of short stories that
he sold quickly to Russian magazines, but such exchanges were in violation of copyright laws and difficult to transact with the vagaries of
wartime mail service. While his paychecks from *Life*, *PM*, and CBS were
accumulating back home, he could not get them until he returned. Nor
could he contact his Folkways authors, monitor the movie grosses of
Tobacco Road, or question Lieber about foreign editions and royalties.[34]

Caldwell and Bourke-White were also well aware that with more
and more reporters finding their way into Russia each day, their ad-
vantageous position in the country was slipping fast. They wanted to
capitalize on their expertise while it was still unique and while their
fame in the U.S. was at its peak. American agents, publishing houses,
movie studios, magazines, and lecture bureaus agreed, and barraged
them with offers to come home.[35]

On September 23, Caldwell and Bourke-White took passage on a
British convoy ship—one of twenty-two vessels escorted by a cruiser
and two destroyers—and began the cold journey across the Arctic to
the Firth of Clyde in Scotland. Several ships had been sunk by German
submarines along the same route, but after their misadventures through
China, they gladly took their chances. From Scotland, they took a train
to London, then to Bath, and then finally traveled by plane to Lisbon.
Before they left Portugal, Caldwell wired Bourke-White's secretary to
prepare a feast for two homesick travelers: "ARRANGE SUNDAY DINNER
WITH BOTH STEAK AND FRIED CHICKEN ALSO ALL KNOWN FRUITS AND VEG-
ETABLES BOTH IN AND OUT OF SEASON." With stops in the Azores and
Bermuda, they completed their around-the-world journey in New York
in November 1941. They had been gone over seven months.[36]

III

UPON ARRIVING IN NEW YORK on the second of November, Caldwell and Bourke-White hit the ground running. Both had signed contracts with lecture agencies while still in Russia—Bourke-White enthusiastically, Caldwell reluctantly—and chambers of commerce, women's clubs, synagogues, and universities across the country were eagerly awaiting their appearances. Bourke-White left for St. Louis the very same day she arrived home. Two days later Caldwell was on his way to Detroit for his first lecture. In the next few weeks he traversed the country, making appearances in Spokane, Los Angeles, Chicago, Charleston (West Virginia), and New York City.[37]

Unlike his ebullient wife, Caldwell hated public speaking, and he was not very good at it. He mumbled shyly through a prepared script, tugging nervously at his necktie and rarely looking up at his audience. "Margaret is crazy about lecturing," he explained to his parents, "but I certainly am not. I don't know why I got talked into doing them." The honest answer was the easy money: Caldwell was paid almost four hundred dollars plus expenses for each hour-long talk, and he could lift the text directly from work he had already done.[38]

But even his poor delivery could not obscure Caldwell's heartfelt adoption of the Russians as his new underdogs and new cause. Many Americans were sure that the Russian army was near collapse and that Stalin might renegotiate another truce with Hitler; many more had heard the stories of ruthless collectivization, purge trials, and famine and were reluctant to support a Communist regime. The lectures—entitled either "I Saw Russia in Action" or "What I Have Seen in Russia"—were designed to override these prejudices. Taken mostly from the *PM* pieces and the radio scripts, they were filled with melo-dramatic yarns of Russian heroism and sacrifice and touching anecdotes that brought home the personal tragedies of the embattled country.[39]

Caldwell continued his crusade with frequent—and lucrative—radio appearances. On his first day in New York he was rushed onto CBS's "We the People" program where he told stories of "children fighting for the honor of putting out fire bombs," and old women surrounding a German parachutist with pitchforks. "The Russians," he promised, "would never give in." In between lecture dates, he appeared with Rex Stout on the "Speaking of Liberty" broadcast and chatted with Margaret McBride on NBC. He gave interviews to Warren Bowen on his "Reader's Almanac" program and Edwin Seaver on WQXR.[40]

When, a month after Caldwell's return, the Japanese bombed Pearl Harbor, and a state of war with Germany and Italy quickly followed, America and the Soviet Union entered into an alliance of convenience. With his wartime experience, his strong belief in the Russian cause, and his fame, Caldwell was a perfect spokesman for the new partnership. The U.S. government now joined the line of those vying for Caldwell's time and expertise. The letter he received from a publicity officer of the Treasury Department was typical: "Please do not forget me," she wrote. "I really have been counting on a Caldwell script for our extremely successful program." The same department's director of press and radio asked for a piece that "compared the contributions of the Russian people to their national war effort and the participation of Americans in our own war financing campaign through the purchase of bonds." Caldwell always honored these requests, donating manuscripts to fundraising auctions and writing publicity shorts for magazines; and he spoke at rallies and on the radio: "Buy bonds," he exhorted, "and be glad you can lend your money to our Government, and not be forced to give it to the Japs. Buy *extra* War Bonds today."[41]

Caldwell had witnessed the power of the Nazi juggernaut firsthand, and following Pearl Harbor, he became one of the country's most outspoken gadflies for wartime preparedness. In the magazines and newspapers that clamored for interviews, he did his best to awaken Americans to the power of the forces now arrayed against them: "A rolling army like Hitler's can swallow nations in a few hours," he warned. "We think of 1943-4. They think of 3 pm to 5 pm." While most Americans agreed with the need for greater government involvement in the economy, Caldwell urged Roosevelt to become a "temporary dictator" and place the country "under complete military control." Typically, he was unafraid—even pleased—to offend people who he felt were too "lackadaisical." "We are being beaten every day and we might as well face it," he told reporters. "We are five years behind both Germany and Japan." He warned of imminent invasions, humiliating defeats, and marauding German and Japanese armies closing in from both coastlines.[42]

Caldwell also continued to write, and he saw his role as an artist very clearly. "Propaganda is mightier than the sword; and the best propaganda is the truth and expression of a creative mind. . . . The crying need is for American writers to get on the spot at the action

points of the world" and bring home the stories of the Allied forces—
to do, that is, just what he had done.[43]

The audience and the immediate profits for such timely work were,
as Caldwell well knew, enormous. "I've called various other editors,
and there's no getting away from it," Maxim Lieber gleefully informed
him. "You must submit to being lionized. After all, not many people
have been in the Soviet Union in these recent months, and certainly
none have yet come back, except the Caldwells." He also continued to
write for *PM* and received a generous salary ranging from $250 to $450
a week. There were hastily arranged appointments at *Collier's* and lunch
invitations from "the whole New Republic office," who were "dying
to have a chance to talk with Caldwell and Miss Bourke-White about
what is going on in Russia." The *Herald Tribune* bought his melodramatic and maudlin account of a young boy finding his dead parents
amidst the wreckage of their bombed-out house; *Redbook* paid him
$1,000 for a piece called "On the Russian Front."[44]

In spite of his hectic schedule of lectures, radio broadcasts, editorial
lunches, journalistic assignments, and continued work on the Folkways
Series, Caldwell managed to churn out three nonfiction books within
four months of his return. On the journey home, he and Bourke-White
used their stay in England to whip together *Russia At War*—a collection
of Bourke-White's wartime photographs with a brief essay tacked on. He
spent three hectic days editing his journals and research notes and sold
them to a British publisher in the form of a wartime diary entitled *Moscow Under Fire*. Back in the States, he spent an additional three weeks re-
shaping the same material into a narrative format, and DS&P rushed it
into print under the title *All Out on the Road to Smolensk**—a glossy black-
and-red edition billed as "the first real book out of wartime Russia . . . the
eyewitness story of famous American novelist Erskine Caldwell."[45]

Although the DS&P publicity department marketed *All Out on the
Road to Smolensk* as "the first uncensored work . . . the untold story"
of the Russo-German war, there was not much in the book to provoke
Soviet censors. Caldwell had, in fact, seen relatively little of the uglier
sides of war. Like all journalists, he was not allowed to leave Moscow
after the invasion, and his interviews with soldiers and Red Army
officers were carefully arranged and orchestrated by the government.
Most residents of Moscow—including the reporters—had little idea of
the horrifying battlefield carnage taking place at the front, or the crush-

---

* Smolensk was the farthest outpost on the Moscow-Leningrad line of defense.

ing military setbacks suffered by the badly overmatched Russian army. Citizens gathered around state-operated loudspeakers to hear a steady diet of propagandistic platitudes and vague assurances that "the Nazis were being engaged on all fronts."[46]

But if Caldwell had to rely on secondhand information for news from the front, he was well aware of the breadlines, the draconian rationing, and the devastation wrought by German bombings in Moscow. Yet such hardship was almost invisible in the books he wrote after he left the Soviet Union. The bombing raids depicted in *All Out On the Road to Smolensk* seemed to be almost festive occasions, with volunteers dancing niftily along the rooftops putting out incendiary bombs, with shrapnel and bomb fragments whistling through the air with cartoon-like ineffectiveness, with stoical Soviet citizens sleeping soundly through the worst of the German raids, and with Caldwell's car teetering farcically on the edge of giant bomb craters without falling in.

Most critics praised the book as part of their patriotic duty. Although no one treated it as serious literature, many were drawn to the colorful storytelling, and Caldwell's knack for bringing to life the sights and sounds of war. The *New York Herald Tribune*'s reviewer, for instance, seemed unbothered that Caldwell's descriptions of the battlefield came secondhand. He thought *Smolensk* contained "the most realistic account of a modern tank battle that has yet been written." Edwin Seaver declared that *Smolensk* brought the reader "about as close as it is possible to get to feeling that you were actually in Moscow during those first few months of the war." Even those who recognized that Caldwell had passed off propaganda in the guise of journalism admired his style. Lillian Smith scolded Caldwell for being a "whopping candidate for the Southern Liar's Bench" but admitted that she couldn't put *Smolensk* down. A soldier wrote from his barracks in New Jersey, urging Caldwell to "keep up the good work."[47]

Ironically, Caldwell's pro-Soviet book drew its harshest criticism from American Communists. Caldwell aimed *Smolensk* at the American mainstream, and he did not want politics muddying the clear propaganda value of his writing. For longtime leftists who saw the bravery and military successes of the Soviets as vindication of a Communist economy, the apolitical nature of *All Out on the Road to Smolensk* was extremely disappointing. Samuel Sillen of the *New Masses* was one of a number who complained that the book was "frequently amateurish, contradictory, and unconvincing."[48]

Left-wing critics were more enthusiastic, however, about the novel that Caldwell wrote soon afterwards—his fourth wartime book in less than a year. On their way out of the Soviet Union, Caldwell and Bourke-White had been granted a brief visit to the front, and Caldwell had been inspired by the stories he heard of Soviet resistance fighters who worked behind the advancing German lines. As soon as *Smolensk* was completed, he holed himself up in the Darien house and churned out *All Night Long*—a melodramatic tale of Russians who take up arms as guerrilla warriors. Lieber quickly sold the serialization rights to *Redbook* for nine thousand dollars, and DS&P published the book in November 1942.[49]

All Night Long is an old-fashioned potboiler, whose protagonist, Sergei Korokov, is a virtuous farmer with a beautiful young wife. When the Nazis overrun their village they are separated, and he becomes a resistance fighter, wreaking havoc on German outposts, supply depots, railroad bridges, and troop trains. He bands with others, each of whom—having been victimized by the Nazis—lives to avenge the tragedies that have befallen him, his family, and his country. "We'll follow them over every inch of ground, killing them one by one if that's the only way," Sergei declares in a typical monologue. "For every life they take, we'll take two of theirs." The book is full of action-packed raids and theatrical platitudes uttered by dying men. "They will kill me, too, someday," proclaims Fyodor Smirnovich, a man whose pregnant wife has been raped and murdered by the Nazis. "But another Fyodor will take my place. They can't kill all the Fyodors in Russia. That's why they can never defeat us. There will always be a Fyodor to destroy them."[50]

Critics expecting sophisticated literature were predictably disappointed. William DuBois of the *New York Times Book Review* noted that the plot was "as simple as a series of recruiting posters," with Nazis "going down like ducks in a shooting gallery." But most reviewers, like Howard Fast in the *Nation*, recognized that Caldwell was not interested in sophisticated art: "It isn't a great book, but you can't rip a novel out of the guts and blood of this hellishness and make it a masterpiece. . . . *All Night Long* is something else; it's part of a war effort." Fast suggested that "a million copies of Caldwell's book, paper bound, would cost less than a battery of anti-aircraft guns, and stowed, each in a soldier's knapsack, would do more good than a new cruiser." Sterling North was one of a number of critics who compared the book favorably to Hemingway's classic of the Spanish Civil War, *For Whom the Bell Tolls*.[51]

All Night Long sold very well. The subject matter could not have been more timely, and DS&P mounted an enthusiastic publicity campaign. *Publisher's Weekly* advertised the novel on its cover; the Book League of America selected it for special sale to its members, and the government's Council on Books in Wartime selected it as "imperative" reading for American citizens. Caldwell also did his part promoting the book, traveling the country to visit bookstores, give readings, and sign autographs. So much discussion and excitement preceded the book's release that publishing industry journals considered the novel "a sure bet for the best seller and best renter lists" a month before it reached bookstore shelves. *All Night Long* raced through a first printing and within a year it had sold more than 175,000 copies.[52]

Not surprisingly, Caldwell's new book caught the eye of Hollywood producers, as eager to profit from public interest in Russia as Caldwell was himself. In the early forties the film industry—with the full support of the U.S. government—cranked out a number of pro-Soviet films as part of a goodwill campaign towards the United States' new and unfamiliar ally. Before the first rough draft of *All Night Long* was even completed, the major studios began making tentative offers, and two weeks after Caldwell finished the book, Lieber sold the rights to MGM for fifty thousand dollars. Joseph Manckiewicz started work on a screenplay, and Hollywood gossip rags began speculating on whether Pierre Aumont, Spencer Tracy, or Wallace Beery would play the lead.[53]*

No sooner had the deal with MGM been sealed than Caldwell signed on with a rival studio, Warner Brothers, to work as a screenwriter. He accepted a contract of twelve hundred dollars a week to adapt *Mission to Moscow* by Joseph Davies—a chronicle of Davies's two-year stint as U.S. ambassador to the Soviet Union in the late 1930s. The book was clearly part of the U.S. propaganda effort, and F.D.R. himself took a close interest in the project. Stalin was presented as a stern but benevolent ruler whose acts of brutality were justified and whose notorious "purge trials" had been a harsh but necessary means of weeding out Nazi infiltrators and sympathizers. Given the pro-Soviet posture of his own books, *All Out on the Road to Smolensk* and *All Night Long*, Caldwell was a logical choice to bring the book to the screen.[54]

At first he was satisfied with the work. He was in sympathy with the goals of the studio and the government—both of whom kept a close eye on the project—and he enjoyed the challenge of transforming the rather dry, static memoir into a cinematic form. He plunged himself

* By the time the film was completed, the war was over and U.S.–Soviet relations had cooled. *Vengeance of the Earth*, as MGM called the film, was never released.

into Davies's notes and private diaries and began formulating a workable plot line. Recognizing, for instance, that the five purge trials in Davies's memoirs were too attenuated, Caldwell condensed them into one for the film. He introduced new characters and began writing dialogue.[55]

But his enthusiasm for the project did not last. He was irked by Davies's rather self-aggrandizing tone, complained to Bourke-White that "the guy is certainly crazy about himself," and described the former ambassador as "Ego #1." He also seemed resentful of Davies, perhaps because *Mission to Moscow* had far outsold *All Out on the Road to Smolensk*. Within a month, he was referring to the memoirs as "Davies' little squib."[56]

Much of Caldwell's frustration stemmed from the difficulty he had in adapting Davies's memoir to the screen. There was almost no narrative momentum or linear plot, and Caldwell soon realized that he "would have to write what amounts to an original story." He tried to compensate for the lack of drama by throwing in a huge range of well-known characters. "I've put everybody in it from Roosevelt to Stalin," he only half-joked to Bourke-White, "and that includes Hitler, Hess, Goebbels, Trotsky, Molotov, Voroshilov, Tukhachevsky, von Ribbentrop, Shigemitsu, Matsoaka, Timoshenko, Rykov, Bukharin, Yagoda, Vyshinsky, and Henry Shapiro." To make matters worse, he also introduced a number of characters who were stock characters in his own fiction, but whose relevance to the plot was tenuous at best. There was a pontificating Southern congressman, "a representative of the old school," who complained about sending ambassadors to "Rooshia," and a black shoeshine boy who delivered such folksy testimonies as "I declare. Those Russian folks sure must be up-and-doing people!"[57]

After completing a rough adaptation and nearly one-third of the dialogue, Caldwell was fired by Warner Brothers and replaced by Howard W. Koch, who had no familiarity with Russia, but knew how to concoct a Hollywood-style melodrama. He had written the script for Orson Welles's famous 1938 *War of the Worlds* broadcast, and only recently had put the finishing touches on *Casablanca*. While Koch kept some of Caldwell's suggestions for the development of the story line, he discarded virtually all of his dialogue. When *Mission to Moscow* was finally released in the spring of 1943, Caldwell's name did not even appear in the credits.[58]

In spite of his disappointing failure with *Mission to Moscow*, Caldwell remained in California to advise on several other films with Russian settings. He was encouraged to stay on by the State Department, which

wanted him to help raise sympathy for the Soviet Union. "The government has, in its casual way, given me to understand that it would
be best for me to work on war pictures," he proudly told Bourke-
White. "I take that to mean that it's more of a command than a request." Caldwell spent this latest stay in Hollywood with far fewer
complaints than before, because, for the first time, he felt that the
movies might serve some useful social purpose. Speaking with a group
of filmmakers and producers on a radio forum, he argued that there
needed to be "a striking difference between Hollywood pictures in war
and pictures in peace." Hollywood's job was to boost morale, he argued, for "a people without morale soon become the helpless victims
of superior forces." With the proper encouragement, he promised,
"Americans will stand up and cheer, and then go forth to fight as only
Americans can." Although he flirted with the idea of volunteering for
military service himself, at age thirty-nine he would serve his country
as a writer.[59]

I V

CALDWELL'S CONTRIBUTION to the war effort paid very, very
well. His failed efforts on *Mission to Moscow*, for instance, earned him
more than twelve thousand dollars in ten weeks. In 1942, Caldwell's
income tax alone was over thirty-three thousand dollars.[60]

Maximizing his profits remained an obsession. He continued to sub-
scribe to stock market journals and invest carefully and frequently. He
badgered Lieber with requests for royalty updates on every book in
every country where they were published. Road companies of *Tobacco
Road* continued to sputter along, and he was in frequent contact with
producers to check attendance and gate receipts. The DS&P editors
knew that he was always willing to visit bookstores or retail conventions if he thought it would boost trade, but that he would hound them
for explanations of poor sales or limited advertising budgets.

Caldwell's mercenary ambitions sometimes verged on the unethical.
He frequently cut corners on his income tax, and several times in the
late 1930s the I.R.S. questioned his returns; at least once he was forced
to pay penalties for filing inaccurate or incomplete information. In 1940,
for instance, he was caught for deducting the entire cost of his car and
telephone as work-related expenses.[61]

Maxim Lieber suffered the most from Caldwell's rapacity. Lieber had
been a tireless and patient worker on Caldwell's behalf for ten years,

yet Caldwell did not hesitate to betray him when it was profitable to do so. Several times, he tried to circumvent his agent's commission by submitting a manuscript directly to a publisher (as he did successfully with short stories in Russia), and when a Hollywood agent named Al Manual offered to negotiate his film deals, he agreed, even though Lieber was already hard at work on the same thing. Caldwell, in fact, did not notify either Manual or Lieber that the other agent was working simultaneously, and so while Lieber was submitting *All Night Long* to the studio offices in New York, Manual was busy fielding offers on the West Coast. Lieber spent weeks negotiating a good deal for Caldwell, but when Manual came up with a better one, Caldwell snapped it up and engineered a means of bypassing his commitment to Lieber. "My idea," he told Manual, "is to tell him . . . that I'm going to take the novel to Hollywood myself and try to place it. That will take the picture sale right out of his hands completely." When Lieber wrote saying he hoped Caldwell wasn't "selling [him] down the river," Caldwell replied sharply: "I suppose you were joking about the Warner deal. As you know, it was something I handled myself."[62]

A number of critics who had closely followed Caldwell's career felt that greed and opportunism had entirely undermined his artistic integrity. Some were gentle; Burton Roscoe of the *New York World Telegram* chided, "Erskine Caldwell has had more fun out of this war than anybody else has had or is like to have." Others, particularly in the South, saw the wartime books as just another example of Caldwell exploiting hardship for his own gain. "Mr. Caldwell has made a great deal of money in writing about the *Tobacco Roads* he finds wherever he goes," wrote the angry reviewer for the *Lynchburg Virginia Advance*. "He spends most of his time in the U.S. where he can buy what he wants with all that money he made writing about people who have no money." Margaret Marshall of the *Nation* was perhaps closest to the mark: "One can't help suspecting," she wrote, "that, quite aside from the war, Mr. Caldwell has been seduced, perhaps unwittingly and certainly to an unnecessary degree, by the 'outer world of telegrams and anger'—of journalistic action, global scoops and easy emotional excitement . . . he has completely lost his bearings as an artist and has landed in a dismal swamp of crude propaganda, fake realism—and Hollywood contracts."[63]

Caldwell, whose financial ambitions were always at war with his social conscience, was stung by such remarks. He could never acknowledge that he was a wealthy—and at times greedy—man. Small losses in the stock market or other investments loomed large in his mind, and he worried constantly that his fortunes would decline and leave him destitute. He continued to assure Morang that he was "living on bread and water," and that his latest Hollywood excursion was only a necessary evil required to pay his debts. Guilt and denial prompted him to make statements that must have struck those who knew him as patently ludicrous. "I do not write for money," he told a reporter. "Of course I want enough to eat and a place to live, but that's all. I don't write for fame—in fact, I'd rather not have it."[64]

But Caldwell had a more meaningful reply to those who doubted his integrity than these hollow declarations of poverty and virtue; for he had to satisfy himself as well as his critics. His writing had invited accusations of crass commercialism; his writing, then, could exonerate him.

V

IN 1937, Caldwell had written a deftly crafted and good-natured short story entitled "The Night My Old Man Came Home" for *The New Yorker*. The piece related the comic escapades of a young boy, his parents, and their black handyman on a small Georgia farm, and it rang with the pointed humor, caring, and veracity that characterized Caldwell's very best light fiction. Over the next few years, Caldwell was preoccupied by other work, including the novel *Trouble in July*, but he returned sporadically to the outlines and character sketches that shaped "The Night My Old Man Came Home." By the time he left for Russia, he had published five more stories with the same cast and setting, and an almost identical comic tone.[65]

Throughout his entire wartime adventure, from the long, perilous journey through Asia to his dealings with the Hollywood studios, Caldwell spent every spare moment working on what he called his "This Old Man" stories. During the long delays in China he secluded himself in tiny hotel rooms, embassy suites, and airfield barracks and wrote with the same consuming concentration that had forged *Tobacco Road* and *God's Little Acre*. During his first weeks in Moscow, he could not bring himself to leave the hotel, and he exasperated Bourke-White by staying at his desk while she roamed the streets with her camera. His wife was dismayed by his single-mindedness and accused him of "barricading himself against new experiences . . . making a retreat to Tobacco Road." She noted, quite perceptively, that the farther Caldwell strayed from his roots, the more compelled he felt to write about them.[66]

Although the bombing of Moscow and his journalistic assignments held up the project for a while, he wrote throughout the journey back and whenever he found a moment during his hectic schedule in the States. As his stint in Hollywood drew to a close, he began to incorporate his stories into a collection. Lieber had already placed six of the fourteen pieces in various national magazines; eight had never been published. Taken together they would offer both Caldwell and his critics a significant aesthetic counterweight to the hastily written and superficial wartime work. He titled the collection *Georgia Boy*, a reference to the stories' adolescent narrator, and, no doubt, a reaffirmation of his own literary roots.[67]

Georgia Boy, like *Tobacco Road* and *God's Little Acre*, revolves around a charismatic patriarch whose personality dominates the text. Morris "Pa" Stroup is the "old man" of the stories, and like Jeeter Lester or Ty Ty Walden, he is eccentric, amoral, irascible, feckless, sometimes lovable, and capable of horrific acts that are carried out with good-natured obliviousness to their consequences. He is incorrigibly lazy, but on occasion is possessed of spurts of energy that allow him to concoct hare-brained money-making schemes; his tireless libido leads him guiltlessly to flirtations and affairs; he steals and cheats, and he sleeps all morning with his mouth wide open.[68]

But unlike *Tobacco Road* or *God's Little Acre*, *Georgia Boy* was not burdened by the tragedy, explicit sexuality, or poverty that mixed so discordantly, yet potently, with the humorous moments in much of Caldwell's work. Usually, Pa Stroup's misdeeds and buffoonery are harmless and their consequences benign. In "The Day We Rang the Bell," Stroup gets a job as the bell-ringer for a wedding and mistakenly tolls a funeral march. In "My Old Man's Political Appointment," he is hired as the town dogcatcher at a salary of twenty-five cents per stray and walks the street with a hunk of raw beef until he has packed the pound with dogs. Unlike Jeeter Lester or Ty Ty Walden, he is an almost purely comic character; he lacks their sporadic dignity, and he is utterly devoid of the values and pathos that complicate and deepen them.

Taken separately, the stories are charming and well crafted, but carry little weight. Taken together, however, they are far more meaningful. Because Handsome Brown, the black handyman, and Mrs. Stroup are so much more virtuous and intelligent than the good-for-nothing Pa Stroup, their exploitation at his hands provides a gentle commentary on the plight of blacks and women in the Deep South. The upright

Mrs. Stroup is forced to take in laundry to keep the family afloat while her husband steals eggs to trade for chewing tobacco. Ma Stroup's frustration with her husband's idiocy builds throughout the collection, until by the final tale she enacts her revenge by baking his favorite fighting cock into a pie and watching him eat it. Similarly, the abuse of Handsome Brown, which in individual stories is leavened by its comic absurdity, becomes more painful to bear as the outrages mount up.

Although the stories were written over a number of years, Caldwell also achieved a remarkable consistency in tone and style that gives the collection the cumulative weight of a novel. *Georgia Boy* invites readers to carry knowledge and understanding from one story to the next, deepening their commitment to the material and adding layers of complexity to the relationships he describes.

Caldwell's editors at DS&P were pleased with *Georgia Boy*. Charles Pearce, who had taken on the responsibility of coddling the firm's prize author, was particularly effusive. "It is really a swell job," he assured Caldwell, "and so altogether entertaining and well done that I would be hard put to say which chapter I liked best. . . . Boy are we pleased with our old man." In subsequent letters the editors told Caldwell that he was the "greatest American humorist since Twain," and that *Georgia Boy* was "a honey, a natural, a smash." DS&P billed the book as a novel and published it in April 1943. "You have read *Tobacco Road, God's Little Acre*, and *All Night Long*," the book notices announced. "But you haven't read Caldwell until you've read *Georgia Boy!*"[69]

The critical reaction was more tempered. Like other authors who produced a very influential novel early in their career, Caldwell was frequently taken to task by reviewers who measured everything he wrote against *Tobacco Road*. Although *Georgia Boy* was a far different book in both style and intent, its Southern setting invited comparisons. "Mr. Caldwell goes back to the vein of his familiar 'Tobacco Road,'" wrote Stanley Walker of the *New York Herald Tribune*. "Compared to that famous study of repulsive white trash, the present effort seems a trifle pale." "There was a time when it seemed possible that Caldwell might grow into a kind of Breughel in prose, that out of the grotesque miseries of our submerged populace, he might develop a genuine and individual satire," Mark Schorer wrote in the *Yale Review*. "That has not happened. . . . Here are all the familiar Caldwell qualities, and nothing more and nothing new."[70]

Most critics, however, saw that *Georgia Boy* was a less angry, and less politically aggressive, book than any of Caldwell's earlier Southern works. Some were disappointed at his levity; *Time* described the stories as "featherweight," and Diana Trilling of the *Nation* characterized *Georgia Boy* as "an innocuous collection of extended anecdotes." But most enjoyed the humor in the collection, and recognized that Caldwell had written with unusual restraint and uncommon self-assurance. "Morris Stroup is Jeeter Lester with the psychopath burned clean away—as disarming a no-account as you will meet in a month of Sundays," wrote William DuBois of the *New York Times*, only one of a number of reviewers who compared Caldwell with Mark Twain, and the narrator of *Georgia Boy* with Huck Finn. Even Southern papers enjoyed the affectionate humor in *Georgia Boy*, and a number recognized Caldwell's mastery of the dialect and vernacular of his characters. The reviewer for the *Atlanta Journal* described *Georgia Boy* as "hilariously entertaining, unerringly accurate, warmly amiable."[71]

The most perceptive reviewers recognized the book for what it was: a self-conscious retreat from world affairs, commercial projects, and Hollywood. Caldwell was roundly congratulated for returning to familiar material. "Welcome home from Russia, Georgia Boy," one wrote. "Stay put Down South!" Caldwell hoped to oblige him, for indeed, he had found his return to Southern terrain extremely satisfying.[72]

Once again he had managed to find a balance for his aggressive greed and ambition with a project that verified his cherished artistic identity. Once again, the people of "Tobacco Road" had allowed him to return his warring personae of social reformer and literary mercenary to their fragile equilibrium. For both Caldwell and his fans, the wartime books could be seen as an understandable diversion in the heat of world events. *Georgia Boy* was a return to the integrity of Caldwell's best work.

Chapter Eleven

TRAGIC GROUND

ALTHOUGH CALDWELL'S WORK had often spawned angry debate, by the end of World War II even critics and literary scholars who disliked his books recognized him as one of America's most important writers.

The reading public still knew Caldwell best for *Tobacco Road*, but much of his critical reputation rested on his short fiction. He had written more than one hundred stories since the beginning of his career, and in 1940 he picked seventy-five of them for publication in a large collection called *Jackpot*. This 756-page volume offered reviewers a chance to evaluate the full range of his creative imagination, and the response was overwhelmingly favorable. "I thought I wanted to write a review of this 75-story omnibus," Edwin Seaver wrote in *Direction*, "but then I thought: what's the use? Might as well try to applaud the sunset—or condemn a rainy day because it doesn't get up to standard." Milton Rugoff of the *New York Herald Tribune Books* agreed that the book was a "conclusive kind of proof that Erskine Caldwell is, among modern short-story writers, a natural."[1]

Caldwell also sent copies of *Jackpot* to a number of authors whom he admired, and the letters he received in return were extraordinarily gratifying. "The stories are shot through with understanding, sympathy and humor," Theodore Dreiser wrote. "Somehow, in a prose way, they remind me of the *Spoon River Anthology*, which is forever an American classic. And this book of yours is another—full of the stupidity and aspiration of man. I like, admire, and love as I go along, each one that I read." Waldo Frank thought it "splendid to have in one volume so rich a variety of the great art of story-telling. I've liked your work from the beginning, but it has grown," he told Caldwell. "I am glad of this opportunity which you give me to express to you my real admiration for your work." H. L. Mencken, John Steinbeck, Carl Van Doren, and Sinclair Lewis all sent enthusiastic testimonials. Even William Saroyan, known for his stingy praise of his contemporaries, described Caldwell as one of America's five best living authors.[2]

Dozens of editors paid tribute to Caldwell by requesting one of his stories for their own anthologies, and because there was still no consensus on how to categorize his work, he was included in a wide range of collections. Bernard Smith put a story in *The Democratic Spirit*, an assortment of proletarian work celebrating "the ascendancy of the common man." He was part of Bucklin Moon's *A Primer for White Folks*, a collection of black and white authors who "present Negroes and whites as they were, are, and may become." Anthologies celebrating the work of the "little magazines" included him, as did more thematic collections like William Blake's *Modern Women in Love* and David Greenberg's anthology of "farm stories" entitled *Furrow's End*. When *The New Yorker* selected sixty-eight stories to represent the best fiction of their first fifteen years they included a Caldwell piece; Arnold Gingrich put a story in his *Bedside Esquire*; Somerset Maugham selected one for *Great Modern Reading*, a collection of "the one hundred best short stories from the world's literature of the last century." Even Southern patriots Allen Tate and John Peale Bishop accepted a Caldwell story—albeit one with a Northern setting—for *American Harvest*, their selection of the best short fiction written between 1920 and 1940.[3]

Although he had written *Journeyman* and *Trouble in July* since the early thirties, Caldwell's reputation as a novelist still rested largely on *Tobacco Road* and *God's Little Acre*. "Great books" lists compiled at the end of the 1930s usually included at least one of these two, and literary analyses of the period rarely failed to discuss Caldwell's contribution. In examinations of contemporary Southern literature, he was often ranked alongside Faulkner and Wolfe as leaders of the Southern Literary Renascence. Frequently, he was favorably compared to Hemingway for the blunt simplicity of his prose, or to Steinbeck as America's best writer on the rural poor. "As late as *The Grapes of Wrath*," Malcolm Cowley once wrote, "it seemed to me that part of Steinbeck's dialogue was patterned on Erskine Caldwell instead of being patterned on life." Carl Van Doren characterized the 1930s as the "decade of *Tobacco Road*; the twenties made 'Main Street' a proverbial term," he wrote, "and the thirties did this with *Tobacco Road*." In 1940 the *Nation* commented that "Erskine Caldwell is generally accepted by critics as one of the most important novelists now writing in the United States." The National Institute for Arts and Letters agreed, and elected Caldwell as a member in the Department of Literature in 1941.[4]

If Caldwell was widely appreciated by critics in the United States, he was virtually lionized overseas, embraced by critics and readers alike in Poland, Italy, Great Britain, Portugal, and Spain. He was widely acclaimed and widely read in Russia; in Latin America, only Richard Wright and Steinbeck were as popular.[5]

Caldwell received the most thorough and sympathetic consideration in France, where, beginning with the appearance of *God's Little Acre* in 1936, his works met a critical response verging on veneration. Caldwell was fortunate to have the support of the renowned literary scholar and translator Maurice Edgar Coindreau, who not only produced sensitive and careful versions of his work in French, but boosted his reputation with adulatory essays in the country's leading literary journals. Other French literary scholars followed suit, and throughout the 1930s Caldwell was championed by many of the nation's most influential intellectuals. Albert Camus staged a production of *Tobacco Road* in 1938; a few years later Pablo Picasso offered to illustrate a version of *The Sacrilege of Alan Kent*. André Gide, Jean-Paul Sartre, and André Maurois all sang his praises, and they took American detractors of Caldwell to task for failing to acknowledge a genius within their midst.[6]

By the mid-1940s, Caldwell had achieved a rare combination of critical and popular success, both in America and abroad. His best work in every medium—novels, short stories, journalism, and photo-text collaborations—accorded him an international standing as an original and important artist. At the same time, the movie and play adaptations of *Tobacco Road*, his marriage to Margaret Bourke-White, his well-publicized battles against censorship, and his wartime exploits had all made him something of a celebrity as well.

It was a remarkable balancing act, but a fragile one. Forces in his personal life were already working to upset it.

I

DURING THEIR STAY IN RUSSIA, Caldwell and Bourke-White's marriage continued to fluctuate between periods of giddy, passionate ardor and violent unhappiness. Romantic evenings in the hotel suite with caviar and champagne alternated with fierce quarrels.

The relationship was still plagued by Caldwell's sudden descents into unfathomable, brooding silence. Social situations in which he had to share his wife's attention brought out the worst in him. Bourke-White tried to head off his dark moods by smothering him with attention and reassurance, but this did not always work. Alice-Leone Moats, who traveled with the couple on their trip into Russia, remembered Bourke-White hovering over Caldwell's shoulder exclaiming "Splendid, Skinny darling, simply splendid! What a great writer you are!" as he composed telegrams or routine correspondence. Another acquaintance was shocked by her obsequious attempts "to be the sweet wife," in order to placate his moods. For the headstrong, self-confident Bourke-White, such posturing was exhausting. In time, she complained to her lawyer that a "disproportionate amount of my attention went into worrying about whether someone was in a good mood or not, whether he would be courteous or forbidding to others, whether day-to-day life would be livable at all on normal terms." In her own notes she confessed that she "didn't like the kind of person I am growing to be, in this marriage."[7]

Perhaps most disturbing to Bourke-White was the fact that Caldwell's unpredictable behavior continued to interfere with her own work. Her charisma and social graces were a crucial part of her professional arsenal, often gaining her entrée to picture opportunities denied other photographers. At his best shy and awkward, and at his worst downright rude, Caldwell often got in the way. And while she was a precise and extremely methodical photographer, Bourke-White needed to be relaxed and spontaneous in order to achieve her best results. Tension in the marriage had, she felt, adversely affected the quality of her work in both *North of the Danube* and *Say, Is This the U.S.A.?* Such difficulties were frustrating even in a collaboration; for her own career, they were proving intolerable.[8]

Caldwell, for his part, also had complaints. He could not understand his wife's seemingly unquenchable desire to be in the public eye. She dragged him to parties and gala fundraisers and arranged countless dinners with out-of-town guests; she loved to have her picture taken and give impromptu press conferences, while such attention still made him painfully ill at ease. Photographs of them together invariably showed a beaming, glamorous Bourke-White with Caldwell standing uncomfortably beside her.[9]

Caldwell had upgraded his wardrobe since the marriage, but he never got used to his wife's determined efforts to improve his appearance. Lieber recalled his discomfort in a new suit Bourke-White had picked out for the opening night of a play: when she left the room for a moment, Caldwell pleaded for Lieber to "get me out of this damn harness." For the trip to Russia, Bourke-White picked out ensembles for her husband that were so elaborate and detailed they prompted a traveling companion to note sarcastically: "he presented a picture of such sartorial perfection that he took my breath away." Caldwell, of course, thought his wife spent altogether too much money on clothes and on everything else as well, and her expensive tastes and notoriously poor management of finances were a constant aggravation.[10]

Although he would not admit it, Caldwell was also threatened by Bourke-White's success. She was as adept at her craft—and more famous—than he was. In the reviews of both *North of the Danube* and *Say, Is This the U.S.A.?* a number of critics compared the quality of the photographs with that of the text. Some implied that Caldwell was riding his wife's coattails, and he was angered by such remarks. Bourke-White was frequently recognized on the street; she was profiled frequently in magazines, and she endorsed products on the radio and in magazines. Much less charismatic than his wife, Caldwell rarely received such public recognition or exposure. While he was undeniably an important writer, Margaret Bourke-White was one of the most famous photographers in the world. Although they both lectured for money, she commanded a fee twice that of her husband's.[11]

To his credit, Caldwell usually kept his ego in check. He was proud of his wife, and he gracefully conceded the spotlight to her. But the unspoken competition between the two came into the open when they began work on *Moscow Under Fire*, their collaborative study of the war in Russia. Bourke-White refused to contribute her best photographs because she was reserving them for a photo-text book that she wanted to assemble—and write—on her own. When the couple returned to the United States, Bourke-White's secretary saw immediately that Caldwell was "hurt, angry, threatened, and betrayed" by his wife's decision. During work on the book, the tension in the office was so thick that the couple refused to speak, walking wordlessly past each other and communicating by passing terse notes through the secretary.[12]

To the outside world, however, they still appeared to be one of America's most glamorous couples. *Redbook* magazine described their life in an article entitled "Dream Jobs—Margaret Bourke-White and Erskine Caldwell: A Marriage on the Run." If Caldwell was occasionally piqued that his wife garnered first billing, he was far more frustrated by the fact that his was a "marriage on the run." His greatest disappointment with Bourke-White was, of course, her continued unwillingness to settle down and raise a family.[13]

Bourke-White was tempted. She still talked about Patricia, the daughter they both dreamed of having, and continued to treat their pets as if they were part of a close-knit family. She told friends that she badly wanted a baby and once sent a letter to an expert on child development seeking advice. Caldwell wanted her to leave the East Coast with him and raise a family in the lovely Catalina foothills outside Tucson, Arizona—an area they had fallen in love with during their research for *Say, Is The U.S.A.?* He thought they could live in the Southwest and commute to the West Coast to fulfill lucrative screenwriting deals. When he negotiated his Hollywood contract for *Mission to Moscow*, he arranged a deal for Bourke-White as well. MGM was willing to pay her $5,000 a month. She went so far as to co-sign on the mortgage of a new house, but in the end, she was not ready to move. When Caldwell traveled to Hollywood to work on *Mission to Moscow*, Bourke-White stayed east to give lectures, take small assignments from *Life*, and think things over.[14]

Caldwell did not give up easily, and he began a desperate campaign through the mail. He appealed to her love of glamour by listing the movie stars he saw each day in Hollywood. When she canceled a weekend visit, he wrote to tell her that Bette Davis had been particularly disappointed by her absence. He sent long descriptions of the new Arizona house sitting empty and urged her to buy whatever she wanted to decorate it. He even promised his wife that he would resume psychoanalysis if it would help to change her mind.[15]

Years before, Helen had written to him in Hollywood begging for reassurance. Now, it was Caldwell who needed support. "You are my wife, and I want to take care of you," he pleaded to Bourke-White. "When are you going to begin staying instead of going? I think it's about time you began staying. Life isn't much without you around. Maybe you can't understand that, but that's exactly the way it is." He complained constantly that his wife did not "write half enough often enough," and he wondered what she did and where she went. Embarrassingly, his misery was even picked up by the wire services, and a number of newspapers nationwide carried a story that began: "Erskine Caldwell has given up trying to keep track of his wife."[16]

As always, when Caldwell sensed that Bourke-White was pulling away, his letters became urgent and almost childlike. "I hope you will stay close to me no matter where you are," he wrote. "There is no finer thing in the world than having someone close to you and that's the way I feel about you. No matter where you are, you know you can always feel that I am as close to you as if we were the same person. That's what I mean when I say I love you—and I do." Bourke-White was moved by his ardor, but not enough. As she wavered, Caldwell grew more and more despondent. "Wish you would be definite about many things," he wrote plaintively. "Among them no provision for little Kit. That hurts more than you will ever know."[17]

By the middle of the summer, Bourke-White revealed that she was ready to be more "definite," but her decision did nothing to ease Caldwell's loneliness. Although she had not told him, for months she had been talking with her *Life* editors about an assignment overseas. She wanted to be where the action was, and the action was on the European front. "My feeling is this," she told a radio interviewer, perhaps hoping that her husband was tuning in. "We're going through a vital phase of history, and why not be willing to have your life disrupted so you can be part of that vital phase of history?" In August 1942, Bourke-White left for England to photograph a top-secret American airfield. "In a world like this I simply cannot bear being away from things that happen," she told her friend and lawyer Julius Weiss. "I think it would be a mistake for me not to record the march of events with my camera when I have such remarkable opportunities, and when my work is put to such good use."[18]

Caldwell could easily have found work as a war correspondent, and Bourke-White tried to persuade him to join her. He refused. She thought he was wasting his talent by writing for the movies and could not understand his desire to stay home when world events called. In the end, Bourke-White—who was herself largely responsible for introducing Caldwell to the finer things in life—blamed his decision to stay on a fascination with wealth. "Erskine has become interested in such different things lately," she complained to Weiss. "I do not understand his passion for big houses and comfortable living." Years later, she described the Arizona property and Hollywood as "golden chains." It was an apt description. Caldwell was interested in both the "gold" and in keeping his wife "chained" to his side. Although Bourke-White sometimes thought she could live out the domestic fantasy her husband envisioned, in the end, she would later admit, "I just couldn't."[19]

Caldwell tried to take her departure in stride. He wrote her warm letters addressed to "Honeychile," the nickname he had used during her previous trips. When she complained that she didn't have time to eat, he playfully mailed her a can of chipped beef. He told her again and again how much he loved her.[20]

But he soon began to worry. It was difficult to get letters to her in wartime, and he was frustrated, as always, that his wife did not respond more frequently. Within ten days of her arrival in England, he complained that it "looks as if I just don't hardly ever hear from you. . . .

You could write to me, too, you know." "About twice a week would be just about right. I've received only two letters since you left, and only two cables."[21]

He poured his energy and his love for his wife into decorating her house, and he kept her up to date with every detail from the "doe skin radio-phonograph automatic combination" to the "black ebony topped dining table with straw-wood base." He also took pains to remind her that each item conformed with her exact wishes. "The master bedroom is as you planned it . . . the guest room is Mexican, as you planned it"; the chairs were "upholstered with the black and yellow material you selected." When he bought a silver tea service, he reminded Bourke-White that "some day you can give it to our daughter." More and more, the house became a challenge for her to return and an ultimatum. He was waiting; their child was waiting; when was she coming home?[22]

In October, the house was finished and Caldwell moved in. He sent Bourke-White a long letter describing "Casa Margarita"—a place of unparalleled beauty and peace, a castle lacking only its queen. "There is a screened porch facing south which looks out over Tucson and into Mexico," he told her. "At night the lights of the city and air bases are spread out for miles." But for all its beauty, he could not be happy there alone. Nor, as he pointedly told Bourke-White, could he concentrate on his work. "I can't get much good writing done without you here. I need you around to put me to work. I seem to do better books when you are here, so I guess if you want me to do a good one, you should come home." She had another decision to make then: it was her career or his.[23]

Bourke-White was far too immersed in her work to consider coming home. She photographed Winston Churchill and the Emperor of Ethiopia, Haile Selassie. She chronicled the inaugural runs of the "Flying Fortresses," huge bombers raiding military targets in Germany. Although she could not obtain permission to go on an actual mission, she spent time at airfields and was honored by an invitation to christen one of the planes. Even with the grueling hours and spartan living conditions, Bourke-White could not have been happier. "In the last few weeks I have been doing a good deal of work out at one of the airdromes, where I have officer's quarters," she wrote excitedly to Julius Weiss. "When I come into that narrow cell with its tiny cot and little coke stove and wash stand, I think that this is all I want in the way of luxury—that it's the best in the world—as long as I am doing work I want to do."[24]

Bourke-White was so wrapped up in her assignments that she might not have noticed when Caldwell's letters trickled off in early October. But in November, a telegram arrived that shocked her to attention:

HAVE REACHED MOST DIFFICULT DECISION OF LIFETIME. DECIDED THAT PARTNERSHIP MUST DISSOLVE IMMEDIATELY SINCE PRESENT AND FUTURE CONTAIN NO PROMISE OF ULTIMATE MANIFEST—stop —NO SINGLE FACTOR OR COMBINATION COULD RECTIFY UNTENABLE SITUATION—stop—BELIEVE ME WHEN EYE SAY EYE AM TRULY SORRY AND UNCONSOLABLE.[25]

Bourke-White cabled back immediately, demanding an explanation, and asked if another woman was involved. He replied: "EYE HAVE WAITED FOUR YEARS FOR SOMETHING BETTER THAN THIS AND THE PRESENT AND FUTURE HAVE BECOME DISMAL APPARITIONS—stop—SUCH IS LONELI-NESS." Again, Bourke-White asked him to explain himself. "SUCH IS LONELINESS AND SUCH IS POETRY," she cabled, "BUT SUCH IS NOT AN AN-SWER TO DIRECT QUESTION—stop—THEREFORE CAN DRAW ONLY ONE CON-CLUSION AND SORRY YOU COULD NOT TELL ME OPENLY." This telegram received no reply.[26]

Clearly, something had snapped inside Caldwell in the month be-tween his long letter describing the house and his sudden demand for a divorce. Perhaps he simply realized that the war was dragging on, and that after this war there would only be other wars, other assign-ments. He was a perceptive man, but love and need had blinded him to a truth that even a poor judge of character could plainly see. Bourke-White could never be happy living in the isolated Catalina foothills, or anywhere else that took her from the flashpoints of the world scene. She thrived on danger, on excitement, on the spotlight. She had reached the peak of her profession, and Caldwell had given her no room for compromise.

There is also circumstantial evidence that Bourke-White had an abor-tion sometime after her return from Russia, and that she had not told Caldwell before leaving for Europe. If so, he may have found out during her absence, or perhaps had known of the abortion all along and, left to himself, had sunk into a spell of depression that triggered his anger. Years later, a friend overheard Caldwell say that "it was the worst thing she ever did when she got rid of that child." And indeed, he was so desperate for what he called the "ultimate manifest," the ultimate proof of her loyalty and commitment, that he could never have forgiven such an act.[27]

Bourke-White was shocked by the suddenness of Caldwell's telegram, but she recognized that his decision was rooted in years of disappointment. She also knew that her husband was prone to sudden and overwhelming feelings of betrayal; it was just such a paranoid epiphany that had, for instance, prompted his split from Scribner's. Part of her had been expecting such a rupture, even hoping for one; but she had not been ready to initiate it on her own. "I suppose by all the rules governing what is considered proper for a lady in these circumstances I should have felt desperate and devastated," she later admitted to her lawyer. "But my one feeling was relief." If Bourke-White felt any loss or regret, she drowned it in the excitement of her work. "I feel so *right*, somehow, that nothing, not even personal considerations are going to interfere," she told her photo editor Wilson Hicks in New York. "The work has always been first with me as you know. But now it is FIRST FIRST."[28]

The divorce was handled via businesslike, unemotional telegrams, for both wanted it done quickly. "The only thing that troubles me about this business is the mechanics of it," Bourke-White told her lawyer. "The minute I step off that clipper on my return . . . I shall be hurried to a lecture platform, which I shall not be off until the middle of April. Then I may want to rush right back abroad for the Great Offensive, and even the wishes of an ex-husband could hardly stop me." Indeed, only a few weeks later, she was in the thick of things again. On her way to North Africa to cover the Allied invasion there, her ship was torpedoed by a German submarine. Although she was one of the fortunate survivors who clambered aboard a badly overcrowded lifeboat, she would later recall that she "could think of nothing but the magnificent pictures unfolding before me which I longed to take and could not."[29]

Caldwell also worked to shut down any emotional turmoil he was experiencing. "I'm mighty glad I did what I did," he wrote Morang, "because now I'm feeling right for the 1st time in my life. I'm sorry it didn't happen sooner." Bourke-White also had been right in suspecting that Caldwell had found a woman who was willing to fulfill the domestic role that she would not. As a favor to an acquaintance, he had spoken to a creative writing class at the University of Arizona. In the front row was a young woman named June Johnson who admired Caldwell's work a great deal. He invited her to a party, then to his house—Casa Margarita—for horseback riding and swimming. She was in awe of him and attracted to him; she hung on his every word; eventually, she began to spend nights there.[30]

Caldwell closed out his marriage to Bourke-White and picked up his shattered vision of domestic harmony in a most dramatic fashion. On December 21, 1943, only two days after the divorce, he married twenty-one-year-old June Johnson in the office of a Phoenix minister.[31]

II

NEWSPAPERS AND MAGAZINES nationwide noted the marriage and assembled hasty biographies of the unknown college girl who had replaced Margaret Bourke-White as the wife of "the author of *Tobacco Road*." Under the headline "Meet the New Mrs. Caldwell," *PM* offered a thumbnail sketch: She was five feet six inches tall with hazel eyes and brown hair. A graduate of Phoenix Union High School and Phoenix Junior College and a member of Pi Beta Phi Sorority at the University of Arizona, June was an aspiring author. The previous summer she had written radio scripts for a local radio station, and she was expected to graduate with her class in only a few months. As the accompanying photographs made clear, she was strikingly beautiful and strikingly young next to her husband, who stood beside her, distinguished and prosperous-looking in a charcoal-gray, pin-striped suit. Even *Stars and Stripes*, the overseas newspaper for American servicemen, carried a story. Only by chance did Bourke-White see a copy, and in this way learn of her ex-husband's speedy remarriage.[32]

Caldwell had signed a contract for a lecture tour to begin in early January, but he canceled it when his Hollywood agent arranged another lucrative studio deal on the West Coast. Within two weeks of his marriage, Caldwell, with June in tow, moved to Beverly Hills and began his fifth stint as a screenwriter. He worked on a number of war pictures for Twentieth-Century Fox and drew weekly salary checks ranging from $1,250 to $1,500. As usual, he did unmemorable work and was shuttled from adaptation to adaptation without receiving any screen credits.[33]

Caldwell still felt guilty working for the movies, and he wrote Morang with his usual contrite declarations of financial woe. "Taxes soak up half of it to begin with," he complained, "then there's agent's commission, abnormal cost of living in Beverly Hills, and what not." But Caldwell's complaints were far less strident than they had ever been in the past, and he grew increasingly comfortable with life in Hollywood. In 1943, his salary was at least five thousand dollars a month and he and June lived very, very well. They spent the first few months in the luxurious Beverly Wilshire hotel, and eventually rented a house on the beach in Malibu. They bought a car, employed a full-time maid, and ran up large bills at fashionable clothing stores. June shopped at the Beverly Hills branch of Saks Fifth Avenue, and Caldwell seemed determined to replace the wardrobe that Bourke-White had assembled for him during their years together. Although he had always contended that three months was the maximum a writer could stay in Hollywood before he became a "hack," this time he and June remained almost nine.[34]

They returned to Tucson in the fall of 1944. June was extremely homesick for her friends and parents, and Caldwell, as he told Morang, was "pretty sick of other guys' stories." The lovingly furnished Casa Margarita had been sold, and Caldwell and June moved into a new home. At last, he had his own house and a wife by his side to share it. "A lot of money has been spent for a place to live," he admitted to his parents. "But I think it is worth it, if only for the fact that at last, and for the first time, I feel that I have a place to live in that I am satisfied with."[35]

Even though his screenwriting contracts paid extremely well—over $50,000 in 1944 alone—Caldwell never stopped searching for new ways to make money. Since the success of *Tobacco Road* on Broadway, he and Lieber had been approached by dozens of eager playwrights and producers who wanted to try their hand at adapting other Caldwell books for the stage. Caldwell himself was intoxicated by the potential windfall of another smash Broadway run, although he had lost a bundle on the failed production of *Journeyman* a few years before, and there had been a number of botched attempts to produce *God's Little Acre*. In early 1943, with *Tobacco Road* bringing in next to nothing in sporadic road engagements, he was eager to try again. As Lieber put it, "we had better hurry up and fill the void." They extended an option for *Georgia Boy* to Jed Harris, one of Broadway's leading producers and directors.[36]

Caldwell immersed himself in every detail of the production, from the set designs to the casting—from the failed efforts to extract a workable script from Nunnally Johnson to the speculation that Lillian Gish might play Ma Stroup. He flew back and forth to New York to negotiate deals and pressed Lieber for detailed explanations of every development. Caldwell did all he could to re-create the magic formula that had produced *Tobacco Road*. After a number of dramatists bowed out, he hired Jack Kirkland to write the script and even signed on Henry Hull, the original Jeeter Lester, to play Pa Stroup.[37]

When *Georgia Boy* finally made it to the stage, the production was an unmitigated flop. The play opened in Boston, where crowds and reviews were so poor that the run was shortened from two weeks to one. *Georgia Boy*'s backers all lost their money, and Caldwell was fortunate that, aside from enormous amounts of wasted energy, he had invested only three thousand dollars.[38]

He squandered a good deal more time and money as the manager and owner of four small-town Southern newspapers. Caldwell had been thinking of buying a paper since 1938, and at one time made serious inquiries into purchasing the *Augusta Chronicle*. Ira had always dreamed of being an editor, and Caldwell wanted to provide his father with the opportunity. In 1943, Ira attended a local bankruptcy auction and paid (with Erskine's money) a modest down payment toward the purchase of the *Allendale South Carolina Citizen*, the *Hampton County South Carolina Guardian*, and the *Jasper County South Carolina Record*. "I have always wanted a newspaper," Ira wrote joyously to his son after the sale, "and now I have newspapers a plenty." Soon afterward, the Caldwells added a fourth struggling paper, the *Beaufort South Carolina Times*, to their chain. Ira and some family friends set up offices and went to work.[39]

The venture proved far more complicated and expensive than they had anticipated, and although all the papers had tiny circulations, the difficulties seemed endless. Ira still had a remarkable capacity for hard work, but he was now sixty-eight years old, and his eyesight, always poor, was so bad that he could barely see the typewriter keys to write his editorials. His associates, Kathleen and Lawton Maner, while equally hardworking and dedicated, had virtually no experience in the business. Erskine had hoped to keep his involvement to a minimum, but he could not refuse his father's pleas for advice and assistance. Before long, he had acceded to Ira's wish to "accept the presidency of the Caldwell-Maner Publishing Company."[40]

Erskine was soon enmeshed in the intricacies of advertising and distribution strategies and puzzling over the thousands of other problems that arose. The woman in charge of the office wrote him to complain that "the typesetter is a liquor head," and indeed, the man had to be bailed out of jail on numerous occasions. There were labor disputes when Ira brought in a black veteran to operate one of the presses. What should be done about balancing farm news with more cosmopolitan topics? Should the format expand from four pages to eight, and how should the pages be folded? And of course, there was the need for constant financial backing—small checks to repair machinery and larger checks to keep things afloat when advertising was scarce. Although Caldwell poured his energy and money into the newspapers, they did not turn a profit.[41]

"All I have to worry about," Caldwell told Morang, "is doing another book, running four weekly newspapers in South Carolina, and such odds and ends. And of course, making a living." While he still insisted that he was "free of Movietown for all time," he was extremely reluctant to give up the security of the hefty Hollywood paychecks he had received ever since returning from the war. Caldwell even tried (although unsuccessfully) to negotiate a long-term contract that could bring him back to Hollywood for six months of every year.[42]

A decade after the publication of *Tobacco Road*, Caldwell expressed a resigned belief that "a writer's career was only ten years long." He had once put his work before everything else in his life; now he seemed ready, even eager, for diversion.[43]

III

CALDWELL'S INTENSITY and his focus had diminished, but he was still a writer. Between two Hollywood contracts and the arrangements for the new house; between letters to Ira concerning the struggling papers and flights to New York to check on the dramatization of *Georgia Boy*; between continued editorial work on the American Folkways Series and persistent inquiries into investment opportunities in Tucson, he wrote *Tragic Ground*, his eighth novel. "I am a storyteller, nothing more," he had always said, and he was not ready to give up.[44]

The pressure to write came from other people as well as from himself. Lieber, the editors at DS&P, and Caldwell's Hollywood agent, Al Manual, all bombarded him with pleas to produce new work. They flattered him with eager anticipation, asked for chapters-in-progress, and begged for hints about the story line he was pursuing. For all three, Caldwell's career was of paramount interest; he was the chief author —the chief royalty earner—in their stables, and his work was important to their financial survival. While they wanted him to produce quality work, they also wanted him to hurry. Lieber spoke for all of them when he told Caldwell that he "frothed and foamed at the mouth" waiting for a new novel.[45]

Everyone who knew Caldwell recognized that he was extremely vulnerable to promises of financial gain. Manual stressed the film possibilities of any new Caldwell novel and the huge windfall that a sale to a major studio could represent. "I'm very anxious to know something about your new book," he wrote as part of a long barrage of letters. "I hope you can understand my feelings in this matter and that you will cooperate to the best of your ability." Lieber complained that he had "not seen a Caldwell manuscript in God knows how long and it would do my heart good to get one soon." He reminded his author that serializations were highly lucrative and tempted him with possible sales to the *Atlantic* or *Redbook*. He informed Caldwell that even a sub-par novel could make money. "You might be very much surprised," he hinted, "at what popular magazines will take these days." While Lieber began letters with promises that "I for one, would never encourage you to write a single word that would detract from your stature as a writer of unimpeachable integrity," he also suggested that Caldwell write a piece for the "Dramas in Real Life" or "The Most Unforgettable Character I Ever Met" features in *Reader's Digest*. DS&P joined the chorus. "Recipe for how to torture a publisher," Charles Pearce wrote. "Tell him that in about three weeks he will either have his prize novel of the fall or he will have no novel at all. Don't prolong the agony; we're beginning to show the strain." He could afford to keep the tone light; Caldwell was a stockholder in the publishing company and his self-interest provided the greatest carrot of all.[46]

In June 1944, Caldwell put a momentary stop to the deluge of letters from Lieber, DS&P, and Manual by sending all of them the manuscript of *Tragic Ground*. Within a few months, Lieber was investigating the possibilities of a musical version of the book, Manual was peddling copies to all the major studios, and DS&P had it on bookstore shelves. "For all who regard Tobacco Road as one of the great classics of our time," the DS&P flyers read, "Erskine Caldwell has written this new novel."[47]

Tragic Ground is the story of Spence Douthit and his family, a clan of poor Southern farmers who migrate to an urban center on the Gulf Coast to take high-paying jobs in the wartime munitions factories. When the factories close, they are stranded: their country has lured them from their farms, their familiar way of life, then abandoned them without support. Trapped in a dismal shantytown called Poor Boy, the Douthits and their neighbors are unable to find work and unable to raise enough money to return home.[48]

As the book begins, the poverty and the squalid, hopeless environment of Poor Boy have beaten the Douthits down so that, like the Lesters of *Tobacco Road* and the Waldens of *God's Little Acre*, they are reduced to an almost animal state of primitiveness, amorality, and unthinking stupidity. Spence Douthit is quite similar to the patriarchs in other Caldwell novels—shiftless, conscienceless, incorrigibly lecherous, and possessed of a childlike innocence that blinds him to the ramifications of even his most heinous behavior. His wife is a hideous grotesque who lumbers around naked, shrieks obscenities, and lives only for her next dose of Dr. Munday's Miracle Tonic. Douthit's youngest daughter Mavis, age thirteen, has run away to become a prostitute; his oldest daughter has also left home. Around the Douthits are a cast of sketchily drawn satellite characters: a sadistic neighbor who sells marijuana for a living and whose seduction of Mavis sends her on the road to ruin; Spence's best friend, whose young daughters are being lured by the street, and who ultimately commits murder in a hopeless attempt to save their virtue; and two social workers who spout out-of-touch truisms about "the complex pattern of modern life" and try to save the Douthits by sending them back home to their farm.

Like other Caldwell novels, *Tragic Ground* is characterized by a violent mixture of burlesque, sexual preoccupation, absurd narrative coincidence, and vivid images of human suffering. Through these competing strains, a powerful social criticism emerges. With most of America caught up in the giddy, self-congratulatory patriotism of the war, Caldwell focused attention on the national disgrace in the inner city. He chronicled the historical processes behind the creation of an urban slum as well as the emotional and spiritual toll such an environment took on its residents. "With all its bawdy humor and vicious realism," observed the critic from the *New York Post*, "the novel is written with a purpose. It has pity and a sort of echoing hysterical rage at a society which can countenance such degradation." Jack Conroy, always one of Caldwell's most loyal fans on the Left, thought the story "pathetic, ominous and terrifying."[49]

Unfortunately, the multitude of distractions and mercenary incentives that surrounded the creation of *Tragic Ground* were also clearly evident in the final product. The book lacks the tight control and careful organization of Caldwell's best work. The dialogue, while retaining some of the vernacular verve evident in *Tobacco Road* and *God's Little Acre*, seems hastily composed and often canned. Almost everything, in fact, about *Tragic Ground* seems rushed and awkwardly contrived. The secondary characters are so featherweight, facile, and clichéd that Caldwell himself seemed to forget who they were. Introducing the young social worker on page 34, he noted that her "dark brown hair was carefully combed." Forty-five pages later he described "her blond hair . . . piled on top of her head in a mass of curls and waves."

In his best work, Caldwell had maintained a disquieting but provocative balance between his social commentary and burlesque humor, between sympathy for his characters and obvious disdain. In an influential review entitled "The Two Erskine Caldwells," Malcolm Cowley argued that this tension between "the sociologist and reformer, and . . . the wild humorist" was the fundamental characteristic in all Caldwell's work. As William Kupferberg of the *Weekly Book Review* confessed, he was "never certain whether to laugh at or weep for these ludicrous and pitiful people."[50]

A number of reviewers recognized that this uneasy balance was badly out of kilter in *Tragic Ground*. The weight of the bile and vicious satire that Caldwell heaped upon the Douthits degraded them to the point where, as Samuel Sillen of the *Daily Worker* put it, "they lose the power to compel either pity or indignation." Jonathan Daniels's complaint in the *Southern Review of Literature* that Caldwell "had found modern pay dirt in comedy at the expense of the half-wit and the deformed" was not a new one; this time, however, there was less in the text to contradict it.[51]

Tragic Ground might have been improved by careful revision or meaningful criticism. In the past, Helen, then later, to a lesser degree, Margaret Bourke-White, had edited Caldwell's work. But June was far too young and too much in awe of her husband to be so bold. Al Manual, who was now one of Caldwell's closest acquaintances, never commented on the quality of the manuscripts Caldwell sent him. He simply went about the business of trying to place them with the studios. The editors at DS&P also declined to provide Caldwell with substantial editorial advice, although they were concerned enough about *Tragic Ground* to make a few gentle suggestions. Pearce asked Caldwell if he might find a "thread of affirmation" to weave into the story, and "balance the hopelessness of the Douthits and the other people of Poor Boy."[52]

But the editors were too wary of offending Caldwell to press any pointed criticisms, and their first concern was rushing his novel into print, regardless of its flaws. "Whatever you decide to do, brother, my hat's off to you," Pearce assured him. "We'll be proud to publish TRAGIC GROUND without a change if you say so." Sloan also soft-pedaled his critique. "We hang on your word as to what you decide to do in this case," he wrote. "Anyway, we'll be cheering for you." When Caldwell agreed to make some minor changes, both editors fell over themselves in appreciation. "What a man, what a man!" wrote Pearce. "I couldn't be more delighted than I am with your reaction to our suggestions. I know you'll work out that main point of thread of affirmation in a masterful fashion." Sloan enthusiastically concurred. "The schedule you set is absolutely okay, as is your whole plan of procedure," he raved. "Better than okay, it's wonderful."[53]

Lieber was the only person close to Caldwell who was willing to be honest about *Tragic Ground*. As soon as he read the manuscript he sent Caldwell a detailed and incisive critique. Lieber thought that "the actual story is rather slight," with "a faulty dramatic structure," but his real concern was the lack of "a certain balance between good and evil, between justice and injustice." He reminded Caldwell that the Douthits were "not unicellular amoebae, but rather human beings prone to a variety of reactions, to a variety of impulses, and even to the suggestion of improvement." He presciently warned Caldwell that "many of your readers will regard these people you depict as grotesque caricatures and figments of your imagination," and suggested that Caldwell rework the book to give the Douthits some of the dignity he had given Jeeter Lester or Ty Ty Walden.[54]

Caldwell responded angrily and defensively to Lieber's bitingly accurate appraisal of *Tragic Ground*. He felt that his agent was out to hurt his feelings or repay him for some past grievance. Lieber was surprised—although by now he should not have been—by Caldwell's sense of betrayal and his immediate assumption that the criticisms were made "with vengeance to even some mythical score." Although Lieber reassured Caldwell of his "warm and loyal friendship," he also learned a lesson. He never offered such candid evaluation again.[55]

Caldwell did make a token effort to address Lieber's suggestions. In the final version of the book, Spence Douthit's oldest daughter and her new husband rescue him and his wife from Poor Boy and return them to the farm. But as many reviews made clear, this rather unbelievable twist of plot did little to alter the overall tone of the book or shore up the facile characterizations. *Tragic Ground* was far inferior to Caldwell's best work, and last-minute revisions would not save it.

Caldwell predicted that the novel "would probably be panned all over the map," but he was disappointed and angry nonetheless. In particular, he was defensive of charges that he had intentionally written a "dirty" book—a charge that gained credence when *Tragic Ground* was banned (then cleared) in Boston a few months later. In Caldwell's mind, he had only exposed the unsavory realities of slum life; he was simply unable to acknowledge either his hostility, his taste for the grotesque, or the scatological obsessions that were clearly evident in his work.

Sure, [*Tragic Ground*] is dirty in the sense that people are dirty [he protested to Morang]. They grunt and they groan in an effort to win an
existence, and it is not always pleasant to watch or to hear about. You
could say I tried to make it dirty, because I did try to make it real. . . .
I am merely trying, in this book and others, to reveal life.[56]

In spite of his protestations, Caldwell knew that *Tragic Ground* was
badly flawed. "The new book isn't so much," he wrote sadly to Morang, the one person he seemed to trust. "At least it's not as much as
I'd like for it to be." For over ten years he had pummeled his friend
with heavy-handed wisdom; now he wrote seeking solace and advice.
"Maybe after you read it you would be able to tell me what's wrong
with it. I know something's wrong with it, but I can't quite put my
finger on it."[57]

Two years before, Caldwell had told Bourke-White that the most
productive phase of his career was drawing to a close. *Tragic Ground*
seemed to bear out this prophecy, and indeed, there was a poignant
resignation in Caldwell's thoughts about his latest novel. Gone was the
blustery disdain and prickly egotism that had formed his shell against
critics in the past. He seemed confused, tired, vulnerable, and unsure
of what he had left to offer as a writer. Acknowledging his growing
alienation from his craft and the sense of fatigue which was turning
his once-passionate pursuit of fiction into a dreary chore, he wrote to
Morang:

Maybe, after all, the best that can be done is to plug along, doing the
best you can, writing one book after another, and then, God willing, at
the end of fifty years, maybe one book of the lot [will] be worthwhile.[58]

Such sadness and fatalism reflected more than Caldwell's solemn appraisal of his artistic career. In August 1944, just two months before the
publication of the *Tragic Ground*, Ira Sylvester Caldwell passed away.

IV

CALDWELL HAD REMAINED CLOSE to his father throughout
the turmoil and excitement of the previous ten years. However busy
he became, he still wrote his parents and visited Wrens often. Ira and
Carrie made regular pilgrimages north as well. They were very close
to Pixie, Dabney, and Janet, and they grew so fond of Margaret Bourke-

White that Caldwell once confessed to her that he "wouldn't be surprised if they loved you more than they do me."[59]

But Ira's first interest in life was, and always would be, his son. As Erskine became famous, he happily and proudly played the role of "Erskine Caldwell's father." He defended the veracity of the novels from the pulpit, in the pages of local papers, and face-to-face with his neighbors. Northern tourists anxious to see the "real Jeeter" or "real Tobacco Road" sometimes stopped by the house, and Ira usually indulged them with a quick tour of the area. When production crews for the film version of *Tobacco Road* came to Wrens for their location shooting, Ira served as an unpaid consultant and tour guide. When DS&P issued a limited edition of *Tobacco Road* with illustrations by a young Colorado artist named David Fredenthal, Ira took him along the same rutted byways that had formed so much of his son's education years before.[60]

By 1941, the years of long hours and overwork had begun to catch up with Ira. He suffered at least one "spell" that was probably a mild heart attack, and his eyesight grew steadily worse. "I can see objects but not details," he confessed. "I can see people in the church, but I cannot tell who they are." Erskine implored his father to relax, and as an incentive he steadily increased his financial support. More and more of Erskine's letters took on a parental tone. "Under no circumstances must you think that it should be saved," he commanded after sending a check for $1,000. "This particular sum is to be earmarked for a trip and nothing but a trip." When he traveled himself, Erskine worried about leaving his parents alone and about the anxiety he knew he was causing. He instructed Bourke-White's secretary to keep an eye on them. "Assure them they are to have anything they may wish," he wrote before leaving for Russia; "write them any news you think they may wish to hear—but nothing of a startling or sensational nature."[61] While Erskine was away, Ira sat on the front porch and listened to his son's broadcasts; when the transmission schedule changed, he was up at the crack of dawn. During these hours he brooked no interruptions, and neighbors and parishioners kept their distance.[62]

Erskine wanted his father to retire. He offered to buy his parents a newer and more comfortable house in Augusta, and he continued to send checks. Notoriously stingy all his life, Caldwell spared no expense when it came to his parents. "I should think that when the war is over you should seriously consider giving up school work, so both of you can have time to do some traveling," he wrote. "As it is, I hope both of you will let me present you with a six months trip to Europe. It will certainly be worthwhile, and I can easily afford the cost. . . . That is a promise as far as I am concerned, so please consider it seriously."[63]

In spite of his son's pleading, Ira was far too involved with his beloved newspapers to slow down. While Erskine supplied much of the money for the venture and a great deal of advice, it was Ira who worked eighteen-hour days to keep the papers afloat. He wrote the lead editorials every week, solicited advertising, agonized over layout, and bailed the drunken typesetter out of jail. "The job ahead of us is both large and hard," he wrote Erskine happily, "but I think we can make it a success." He viewed his growing infirmity as an inconvenience that merely required some practical adjustments. "I am hoping that when I go to the doctor Monday I will be able to get glasses that will make it possible for me to see," he wrote matter-of-factly to Erskine. "My left eye has not bled in nearly four weeks." Moreover, when a doctor diagnosed a blood clot on his coronary artery, Ira decided it would be better to "tuff it out" rather than have surgery. He grudgingly admitted that the condition was "very painful," but he refused to let it slow him down. "When the pain strikes, I can stop work," he explained to Erskine, "and if that does not stop the pain, I can take a tablet of nitroglycerine, and this stops the pain immediately."[64]

In August 1944, Ira acceded to Carrie's wishes and went to Johns Hopkins Medical Center for further testing on his heart. Although he hated to stop work for even a few days, he had never lost his love of travel, and looked forward to the trip. He sent Erskine a characteristically upbeat letter in transit. "We ate supper on the train," he wrote good-naturedly. "We had a great array of dishes, a meager amount of food, and a large beer." At the hospital, he was more interested in the "great array of maimed, halt [sic], and blind" that he saw than he was in his own ill health. Only as an afterthought did he mention to his son, "I'm going back tomorrow to see a specialist, and I hope that good will result."[65]

The prognosis, however, was grim, and the end came more swiftly than expected. On the train back to Georgia, Ira suffered a massive heart attack and died.

In the days following the funeral, hundreds of letters and telegrams of condolence flooded the Caldwell home. Testimonials—from former students, parishioners, and poor farmers both white and black—came from every town where Ira had served. Many letters were written in broken English that could not obscure the sentiments they contained. "We would have been at his burying Sunday if we would have known it," one man wrote from Atoka. "Reverend Caldwell was a good man, a useful man, and will be greatly missed." Margaret Bourke-White, who had stayed in touch since the divorce two years earlier, wrote Carrie that "Father's passing away is a loss to all whose lives he touched. He was one of the finest men I've ever known. People like Father really helped to leave the world a better place. The partnership between you two was always so close that my heart goes out to you in this loss."[66]

Caldwell, however, did not show any emotion when he heard the news; he did not cry, or reminisce, or lose his temper with June. Unable to get to the funeral because of wartime flight restrictions, Erskine simply retreated into a room in the back of the Hollywood house where he and June were living, and sat in silence for hours on end.[67]

With his father's death, Caldwell lost his greatest inspiration: the man he most admired, had most wanted to please, and the one person whose love and loyalty he had never questioned. Erskine Caldwell also lost something most dear to him as a writer—something he could never replace. He had lost his muse.

V

CALDWELL DID NOT EMBARK on any new writing projects in the aftermath of his father's death. Instead, he embraced a wide range of entrepreneurial distractions, each more disastrous than the last. He signed a lucrative contract to adapt Thomas Wolfe's *Look Homeward, Angel* for the movies, but while he greatly admired the novel, he worked on the project so sporadically that he was eventually fired. He tried to arrange a musical-comedy version of *Tragic Ground* for Broadway and signed on Agnes DeMille and Aaron Copland to do the choreography and the score. But there had been too many failed adaptations of Caldwell books since *Tobacco Road* to attract any investors; the production never reached the stage. Perhaps most painful for Caldwell was the demise of Ira's beloved newspapers. Although he continued to pour money and advice into them for another two years, they were sold for a loss.[68]

There was, however, one cause for optimism amidst all this depressing news. In 1945, the American wing of Penguin Books published a paperback edition of *Trouble in July*. Although Caldwell did not know just how popular the book would become, this twenty-five-cent edition marked the beginning of a decided improvement in his fortunes, and the beginning of a remarkable odyssey that would make him a central figure in the so-called "Paperback Revolution."[69]

Paperback publishing had a long and checkered history in the United States. Some of the country's first books—almanacs, religious or political tracts, and speeches—appeared in soft-cover editions. As printing technology improved in the early 1800s, so-called "supplements," cheap editions obtainable through the mail for as little as twelve cents per copy, offered competition for hardcover retailers. Later in the century, softcover pulp fiction editions known as "dime-novels" brought tales of violence, intrigue, and sensational romance to thousands of Americans. By the end of the Civil War, one publisher had brought out more than four million copies in such editions. Because there were no international copyright laws until 1891, cheap pirated versions of European books were also reprinted in paperback, and in the 1870s and 1880s, they were mass-produced on the newly developed (and very cheap) groundwood paper. Perhaps the most successful paperback venture was E. Haldeman-Julius's Little Blue Books series. Haldeman-Julius printed a wide range of fiction and nonfiction titles, and by the early years of the twentieth century his mail-order pamphlets had sold nearly 60 million copies. Caldwell's very first published work, his 1926 "Georgia Cracker" essay, appeared in a Little Blue Book.[70]

But while a number of paperback endeavors flourished for a short period of time, persistent fiscal dilemmas brought most to bankruptcy. Because a paperback's success depended on its low cost, and the books were more economically produced at high volume, huge numbers of copies needed to be sold to ensure a profit. Such large runs courted disaster if the book did not prove popular. And while technology for speedy, inexpensive printing methods was improving all the time, there was, as yet, no reliable way to distribute or sell books on such a large scale. Most important, there remained a deep-seated belief among American readers that "real books" needed to be bound in "real" covers—an impression reinforced by the less-respected "abridged editions" and the pulp fiction that most paperback publishers relied on for survival.

In 1939, Robert Fair de Graf launched a revolutionary new publishing program called Pocket Books. De Graf's plan was to reprint hardcover best-sellers in unabridged form and sell them for twenty-five cents a volume. Among his first ten titles—each chosen to appeal to a wide range of readers—were a best-selling self-help book, *Wuthering Heights* by Emily Brontë, an Agatha Christie novel, and Thornton Wilder's Pulitzer Prize–winning *The Bridge at San Luis Rey*. By reducing the margins and using a new type of lightweight paper, he made the books 4¼ by 6½ inches—smaller than most previous paperback editions, and de-

signed to fit conveniently in a person's pocket. Careful to distinguish
his volumes from the more lurid dime-store novels of the past, de Graf
hired excellent artists to produce colorful but dignified covers. De Graf
also solved the problem of distribution by selling his books as if they
were magazines—at drugstores, supermarkets, newsstands, and cigar
stores—as well as bookstores. On the day his first ten titles were released, De Graf ran a full-page ad in the *New York Times* that stated:
"Out Today—The New Pocket Book That May Revolutionize New
York's Reading Habits."[71]

De Graf's prognosis was not far wrong, but even he underestimated
the size of his eventual market. Within hours, bookstores were selling
out and reordering; a small cigar store sold 100 copies in a day and a
half; Macy's sold almost 7,700 copies before its staff completed the
window display. Three months later, half a million copies of the ten
titles had been sold and distributed to cities and towns across the country. The "Books and Authors" columnist for the *Times* noted that "it
begins to look as if the publishers of Pocket Books have what the public
has been looking for." De Graf's insignia, a lovable glasses-wearing
wallaby named Gertrude, was soon recognized by millions of Americans. Pocket Books, which started with an initial investment of $30,000,
was sold for $3,000,000 five years later.[72]

The phenomenal success of De Graf's venture encouraged other
publishers to launch competing lines based on the same sales principles.
A few months later, Allen Lane, founder of Britain's Penguin Books
announced that his firm was coming to the United States. Other publishers followed soon afterwards. This new wave of paperbacks radically
changed America's book-buying habits. In the past, Americans of modest means—clerks, writers, teachers, salesmen—did most of their reading from library books. Within two short years, however, they were
buying the majority of what they read in paperback form. More important, huge numbers of Americans who had never read for pleasure
at all were being drawn into the market by the glossy covers and
reasonable prices.[73]

America's entry into World War II created another outlet and audience for pocket-sized books. The U.S. military commissioned more
than 35 million copies of well-known titles to be distributed overseas
to members of the Armed Forces. Bound by staples and printed on
magazine presses, the so-called Armed Services Editions were the first
books (other than a Bible) that many soldiers had ever owned. "The
books are read until they're so dirty you can't see the print," one soldier
wrote. "To heave one in the garbage can would be tantamount to

striking your grandmother." Caldwell was honored that a number of his works, including *Tragic Ground*, a volume of short stories, and *God's Little Acre* were sent to the troops.[74]

In spite of the phenomenal popularity of paperbacks and the Armed Services Editions, many American critics, literary scholars, and publishing executives continued to deride paperback books as an inappropriate medium for "serious" literature. Some objected on aesthetic grounds; others were threatened by the obvious danger to hardcover sales. As a result, many authors would not allow their work (and critical reputation) to be sullied by a paperback cover and a mass audience. Caldwell, however, had no such elitist reservations. He relished the idea of thumbing his nose at the literary establishment and was electrified by the potential profits represented by mass-market books.

Throughout the war, Caldwell had hounded Lieber and DS&P to investigate the possibilities for reprinting his work. "We are all most interested to hear you express your ideas about the cheap edition business and the future of books," Sloan patiently assured him. "Every few days we make one sort or another of good effort in the direction of Caldwell cheap editions. We'll try to make it every day from now on."[75]

Under Caldwell's constant pressure, DS&P sold reprint rights for his more popular books, including *Tobacco Road, God's Little Acre*, and *Journeyman*, to a number of different paperback publishers. Between 1943 and 1945, they signed a flurry of contracts with Avon Books, Random House, Grosset and Dunlap, World Publishing Company, Pocket Books, Garden City Publishing Company, and the Canadian publisher White Circle, and made tentative plans with a number of others. But while print runs for these editions were as large as fifty thousand copies, none of the titles was extraordinarily successful. Most publishers had simply not worked out the complicated process of marketing and distributing the huge numbers of books that they printed. Many houses went bankrupt or withdrew from the paperback field to concentrate on hardcover editions. A few years later, Lieber admitted that the frantic efforts to "get every type and sort of reprint distribution" in the first days of the paperback bonanza had allowed "some mistakes to creep in."[76]

DS&P and Lieber made up for all the "mistakes" in a single stroke when they sold the rights for *Trouble in July* to the American branch of Penguin Books. Although the company had survived by printing light fiction and murder mysteries during the war, Penguin was determined to reprint books of lasting literary value. Under the direction of Victor Weybright and Kurt Enoch, the firm followed the lead of Allen Lane, who had already reprinted work by such writers as D. H. Lawrence, John Dos Passos, and Sherwood Anderson in Great Britain. Years later, Weybright recalled surveying the American paperback offerings in 1945 and noting with excitement that, along with Caldwell, there was still "not a trace of Faulkner, Farrell, Hemingway, Fitzgerald, Lewis, Wolfe, Cather, Joyce, Proust or James." The field was wide open.[77]

Weybright and Enoch were a perfect team to run a successful paperback venture in the States. For while both editors were dedicated to proving the viability of serious literature in a paperback format, they also embraced the challenges of marketing and distribution that had stymied the industry from the start. In order to get the huge printings into drugstores, bookstores, and train stations across America, Enoch and Weybright contracted with Fawcett Publications, a well-organized magazine distributor. By grafting paperback distribution onto the back of the pre-existing Fawcett machine, they gained immediate and convenient access to the 125,000 retailers that Fawcett already supplied. Together, Penguin and Fawcett also solved the lingering problem of how best to display a paperback book. They developed the "Spin-it" rack, and filled it with dozens of Penguin titles in a wide range of genres.[78]

Visual presentation was very important to Enoch and Weybright. Although British Penguin still insisted on maintaining its staid, unillustrated cover with the orange borders, American Penguin hired the talented painter Robert Jonas to develop a style of cover art that balanced the flashy charisma of the dime-store covers with a dignity befitting more serious fiction. *Trouble in July* was Jonas's first cover for Penguin, and he took a great deal of time and care creating an image of somber and symbolic power. Against a blood-orange sunset background appeared a cutaway figure of a hanged man. Inside the cutaway, Jonas painted a stark outline of a tree with a rope descending from the lowest branch. On the border of the cutaway another rope led from the man's neck to a stylized courthouse on the left side of the cover.[79]

Within days of its publication in December 1945, Fawcett's distribution machine placed *Trouble in July* and Jonas's vibrant cover in Spin-it racks across America. Caldwell, Lieber, the editors at DS&P, and of course, Weybright and Enoch, all watched the sales anxiously, for in these early days of paperbacks, it was difficult to know which authors would appeal to the suddenly enlarged market of American book buyers. Within weeks, they had their answer. Sales were excellent—stunning, in fact, compared to anything Caldwell had ever released in hardcover. The book sold 350,000 copies in less than six weeks, more than the combined total for all of Caldwell's other books.[80]

The success of *Trouble in July* encouraged Penguin to bring out a second Caldwell title, *God's Little Acre*. Sales were sensational from the start, and within a year of the novel's April 1946 release, Enoch and Weybright were hosting a party at the Hotel St. Regis in New York to celebrate their first million-copy seller. Caldwell flew in from Tucson to attend the festivities. Six months later he was back again for another celebration, when the two-millionth copy was sold. *God's Little Acre* was the fastest-selling paperback in the country, and Caldwell was beside himself with surprise and satisfaction. "Just got back from New York," he wrote Morang after yet another victory party the following year. "Penguin had a five-day spree celebrating the sale of the 4 millionth copy of God's." Within five years of its initial printing, the story of Ty Ty Walden's search for gold had sold nearly six million copies. It was, by far, the most successful book Penguin had ever published. Caldwell was the first American author with real literary credentials to become a blockbuster best-seller.[81]

The stupendous popularity of the paperback edition of *God's Little Acre* (like that of the play version of *Tobacco Road*) defies simple explanation. Part of the success was due to cover artist Robert Jonas, who once again created a visual package that was both eye-catching and original. The beautifully painted cover featured a peephole in a weatherbeaten wood fence. Through the hole was an arresting tableau of rural deprivation—a small sharecropper's cabin set in a desolate landscape of abandoned cars, barren soil, and scrub pines. This "peephole" design promised a voyeuristic glimpse into a hidden, and perhaps illicit, world. Jonas's design was so popular that cover artists from every major reprint house were soon copying it. By the late 1940s, keyholes, torn curtains, and gaps in fences were gracing the covers of virtually hundreds of paperback books.[82]

Fawcett's distribution machine was also humming along with ever-increasing efficiency. As paperback sales continued to mount in the postwar years, the company poured more and more money into expanding its markets. Sales representatives equipped with fully stocked Spin-it racks brought Penguin books into every corner of the United States. While the number of bookstores remained relatively constant, the number of card shops and cigar stores was virtually limitless. Everyone was paid by commission—from the store owner to the salesman, to the distributor, to Penguin, to the authors themselves. Distributors and store owners worked hard to keep the hot merchandise on the shelves, and Caldwell's titles, the hottest merchandise of all, rewarded their efforts.[83]

Like most great sellers, *God's Little Acre* was a well-known book before it was released in paperback. The best publicity came from returning servicemen, who had read the novel more than any other on the Armed Service's Editions list. But many other Americans also knew of the book—not from G.I.s or from the literary scholars and critics who had praised it—but from the various censor boards and Legions of Decency that had attempted to ban *God's Little Acre* from bookstore shelves for more than a decade. Since its most widely publicized clash with John Sumner in 1933, the book had been in the news dozens of times. In the mid-1930s, Detroit forbade the sale of the book, as did Boston, and the entire continent of Australia. In the early forties the novel was banned from the mail in the U.S., and the American Library Association stopped distributing the book to British libraries. Each censorship struggle brought news coverage—angry accusations of indecency and smut, and statements in defense of the book from liberal-minded citizens, Caldwell's publishers, or from Caldwell himself.[84]

Because paperbacks were inexpensive enough for children and teenagers to buy, and small enough for them to hide, the books threw new fear and energy into America's moral watchdog agencies. Like efforts to ban the dramatic adaptation of *Tobacco Road*, however, efforts to suppress paperback editions of *God's Little Acre* only fed its popularity. The controversy ensured exposure and publicity better than anything the marketing division of Penguin could have generated on its own. When the Mayor's office in St. Paul, Minnesota, for instance, declared the book "lewd and obscene" and banned it from the bookstores, the story was picked up by the Associated Press. The Fawcett distribution agent for the region could not have been more pleased. He ordered ten thousand copies for neighboring Minneapolis, and within days he had to order ten thousand more to meet demand. Other cities had no better luck than St. Paul. When Denver enacted a ban of the paperback the following year, demand for the hardcover skyrocketed. The paperback editions were also available illegally, although the book now fetched a market price of five dollars a copy.[85]

There was more to the success of *God's Little Acre* than the promise of a cheap thrill; indeed, the book's more prurient aspects paled in comparison to a number of available (and far less successful) paperbacks. *God's Little Acre* was a novel that appealed to a wide range of potential book buyers. For the literati, the socially conscious, scholars, and students, the novel was an unmistakably ambitious and complex literary achievement. But the book was also clear and direct enough for anyone to read and enjoy; the prose was simple and evocative, the story was compelling, the characters were memorable.

When Penguin released other Caldwell novels in the wake of *God's Little Acre*, they, too, sold extraordinarily well. Before *Tobacco Road* was even released, Penguin had orders for 450,000 copies, and they sold one million in the first year alone. *Journeyman*, critically panned in hardcover, sold three quarters of a million copies when it came out in 1947; *Tragic Ground*, released the following year, sold twice that number in the same period of time. For Weybright, Enoch, and the burgeoning paperback industry, Caldwell offered a perfect fusion of high literary standing and mass appeal.[86]

During the early years of the Caldwell boom, there was increasing strain between the American branch of Penguin and its British sponsor Allen Lane. Weybright and Enoch disagreed with Lane on a number of issues, including their wish for more aggressive marketing and the use of illustrated covers. Most disruptive was Lane's outspoken disapproval of his American division's best-selling author. Lane felt that Caldwell hurt Penguin's dignified image and once snidely suggested that Weybright and Enoch "have a pornographic imprint detached from Penguin—perhaps 'Porno Books'—for such material." Weybright, who was in charge of the editorial decisions, bridled at such remarks. He had a deep and long-standing admiration for Caldwell, whom he later characterized as having a "natural artful genius related to that of Dickens, Mark Twain or Balzac." A Southerner himself and born the same year as Caldwell, Weybright saw his prize author as a kindred spirit and a close friend.[87]

Weybright and Enoch also knew that Caldwell's phenomenal popularity underwrote the success of their American operation. Indeed, during the first five years of their tenure, DS&P's top four sellers were Caldwell titles. In 1948, Weybright and Enoch negotiated a split from Allen Lane, renaming their operation the New American Library of World Literature, or NAL. Caldwell's remarkable sales helped Weybright and Enoch pay off their debts to Penguin and firmly established NAL (and their Signet and Gold Medal imprints) as one of the premier paperback houses in the world.[88]

The huge sales filled Caldwell's pockets as well, although not as fully as he would have liked. Profits had to be shared among his hardcover publisher (who owned the rights to the books), his agent, NAL, Fawcett distributors, salesmen, and the store owners themselves. On average, Caldwell made between 1 and 1½ cents for every paperback sold. Naturally, he was annoyed by what seemed a pitifully small royalty, and he frequently wrote Lieber, the editors at DS&P, and Victor Weybright to complain. But the pennies did add up: for every one million books, he received approximately $12,000. In 1946, he received royalties of $13,000; the following year he made $33,000, and the year after that $58,000. In 1949, at the height of Caldwell's popularity, he earned the staggering sum of $95,000. Over the next three years, sales tapered off, but his royalties still averaged almost $63,000 a year. Caldwell was earning more money than he had ever dreamed of, and he had not written a single new word.[89]

More than a decade before, the stage adaptation of *Tobacco Road* had also garnered unexpected riches and astounding popular support. The success of his paperbacks, like that of the play, provided Caldwell with more than wealth and fame; it brought him a profound sense of vindication. For years he had protested that his critics were simply too removed from "real life" or too squeamish to appreciate his work. Now he had his proof. The millions of everyday Americans who lined up to buy *Tobacco Road*, *God's Little Acre*, or *Trouble in July* represented the unequivocal popular endorsement he had always sought. For these books, it was an endorsement he well deserved.

But Caldwell also took the same satisfaction in the huge sales of books like *Journeyman* and *Tragic Ground*. Here, his sense of triumphant vindication was misplaced. He would not acknowledge that the marketplace was an unreliable barometer of literary worth. The popular success of his indisputably inferior novels offered an unfortunate smokescreen to a man too eager to avoid the truth and a financial incentive to a man too eager to respond. In the next few years such self-delusion and greed contributed to an increasingly mediocre literary output.

Chapter Twelve

SLOWING DOWN

IN HIS SECOND AUTOBIOGRAPHY, *With All My Might*, Cald-well remembered the last half of the 1940s as a time when writing became secondary to other "irresistible causes and appealing choices" in his life. Indeed, as he and June became more settled in Tucson, Erskine's attention was not focused on his work.[1]

In the wake of Ira's death, Caldwell seemed determined to become closer to his own children. Although Pixie, Dee, and Janet had all visited their father sporadically over the years, they viewed him with mingled mistrust and resentment, proud of his success, but unable to forgive him for abandoning them, or for his treatment of their mother. They had, in fact, served as Helen's witnesses in both the divorce trial and her subsequent attempts to renegotiate the settlement. While all three were extremely fond of Margaret Bourke-White, they were upset by Caldwell's marriage to June Johnson—a woman closer to their own age than his. By the time Caldwell moved to Arizona in 1942, Pixie was sixteen, Dee was fifteen, and Janet was nine; they knew their father hardly at all.[2]

Pix had never lost the wild, angry streak that governed his behavior as a young boy. He had been an indifferent student in high school, and dropped out at sixteen to join the Marines. After the war, he was married briefly to a lounge singer, bounced around from job to job, and had a few minor brushes with the law. In his early twenties, Pix ended up in Hollywood, where he dreamed of being a writer, and quit a string of low-paying jobs. He was a handsome and dissatisfied young man.[3]

Perhaps remembering his own wild youth, Caldwell was patient with his son through these difficult years, and he tried to support him; know-ing that Pix's pride prevented him from asking for help, Caldwell sent a steady stream of checks through his Hollywood agent, Al Manual. Manual became a liaison, keeping Caldwell informed of his son's whereabouts, and passing along both money and assurances that Pix could come to Tucson if, and whenever, he wished. Eventually, Pix remarried and settled down, and his deep anger toward his father lost some of its edge. "One thinks he has everything figured out . . . when the bottom falls out of all one's dreams and plans so carefully made," he once wrote his father. "Words could not express my appreciation of the kindness and understanding that you so generously show and always at the time that it is needed the most."[4]

Dabney escaped childhood with less hostility than his older brother. He had been a quiet but contented child who found his peace of mind alone, camping and exploring the outdoor wilderness near Mount Vernon. He was an excellent student and ultimately pursued a doctorate in geology at Harvard—a career choice he credited to Ira, who had often taken him on long trips into the mountains to look for arrowheads and fossils. Dabney looked a great deal like his father, with pale blue eyes, reddish hair, and a large frame. Like Erskine, he was taciturn; but his moods were lighter, and his mischievous laugh (also like his father's) came more easily.

Dabney's relationship with Erskine was less intense, and much less emotionally charged, than Pixie's. Still, as even his joking letters implied, he would never forgive his father entirely. "It's the truth, Skinny," he wrote at age nineteen. "You don't look a day older than the first time I can recall your face—the day when you beat the daylights out of Pix and me in the wood shed." Over the years, he kept his father informed with matter-of-fact notes that rarely touched on his personal life. When he decided to get married, he merely sent a letter requesting twenty-five dollars for a new suit. Such petitions for money, in fact, made up the bulk of his correspondence. "Wish this could be avoided but must pay rent Monday," he wrote in a typical note. "Mistake in bookkeeping leaves me with no funds. Please wire $50."[5]

Caldwell was unfailingly responsive to such requests, although he liked to receive an exact accounting of where each penny was going. He paid for Dabney's graduate school without complaint and bought him plane tickets to Europe for his honeymoon. Monetary gifts would always be the form of affection Caldwell felt most comfortable with, but he tried hard to make more personal gestures as well. Although he hated disrupting his established domestic routine, Caldwell arranged for Dabney to stay in Tucson for a summer after the war. In his typically meticulous and thorough way, he arranged good seats for football games or plays and organized dinners at fine restaurants. Conversation between father and son never flowed easily, but as time went by, their relationship steadily improved.

While Erskine thought that the boys were best left alone to make their own decisions, he showed less restraint with Janet. He was very involved in her choice of colleges—much more so than she wished—and later sent her letters telling her what courses to take. Although his own problems as a student softened his attitude towards Pixie's spotty academic career, he had no such empathy for his daughter. When she considered dropping a Bible course, he reprimanded her and wrote the college president, asking that he speak to her. After so many years of sporadic attention, Janet found such involvement overbearing, as well as hypocritical. She had inherited her mother's fiery temperament, and was not afraid to assert herself. She stood up to her father, dropped the Bible class, and arranged for a transfer to a college she preferred.[6]

In spite of such clashes, Erskine's relationship with Janet was also warmer than with either of the two boys. "Don't let it be such a long time between letters," he wrote, his words a strange echo of his letters to Bourke-White a few years before. "I worry about a lot of things when I don't hear from you." When Janet informed him at age seventeen that she was planning to get married, he was supportive. "If you have made the decision, that's the way it will be, and you can always be certain that you have my love and blessing," he told her. "Don't ever feel that you can't write to me about your troubles or your happiness, and as long as I live you can be assured that I hope it will be little of the former and much of the latter." While Janet still resented her father and was angered by his intrusiveness, she appreciated him as well. She named her first son Guy Erskine in his honor.[7]

Caldwell's rededication to his family was most evident in his treatment of his new son, Jay, born only a few months after Ira's death. The desperate and single-minded passion to write had made him a poor father in his first marriage. But with his creative intensity on the wane, so too were the vicious outbursts of temper and the constant demands for absolute silence. Although he still disappeared into the study when he was trying to work, he made a concerted effort to spend time with his new son. As Jay grew older, Erskine took him to baseball games and carnivals and played games with him on the living room rug. Further, he seemed much more willing to let his little boy be just that; while he had insisted that Pix, Dee, and Janet call him by his adult nickname, Skinny, to Jay he was always Papa. Caldwell had the pleasure of watching his youngest son grow to be an extremely happy and self-confident boy.[8]

Caldwell completed his role as benign patriarch by bringing his mother to Tucson after Ira's death. Carrie was as proud, stern, and judgmental as she had ever been, and she could be a trying neighbor. She criticized her son's and daughter-in-law's parenting techniques and their decision not to attend church, and she demanded a good deal of attention. But Caldwell was remarkably patient with his mother and unfailingly courteous. Many of her more annoying qualities—her extreme meticulousness and frugality, for instance—made perfect sense to him, for he had inherited them. But he also learned to tolerate her social snobbery and elitism, traits that bothered him a great deal. He never felt the reverence and love for Carrie that he had for Ira, but he remained devoted to her until her death in 1968.[9]

Caldwell also worked hard to please his young wife. Like Bourke-White, June was a far more outgoing person than her husband. She loved to attend parties and to entertain, and she was eager to make new friends; after the marriage, she became active in the Tucson Junior League, where she met many of the city's leading socialites. Caldwell, of course, was simultaneously intrigued and repulsed by high social status. With June's—and his mother's—encouragement, though, he indulged himself as never before. He and June became charter members of the highly selective Old Pueblo Country Club, and they joined the rounds of champagne dinners, dances, and cocktail parties of Tucson's high society. Caldwell was still uncomfortable in social gatherings, but he did his best, smiling gamely and making small talk with guests who were fascinated by his exotic life as a writer. Typically he jingled his pocket change nervously during such exchanges, drank large quantities of bourbon, and looked shyly at the floor. But he did not "freeze up" or storm off as he had in years past. He was polite, if not scintillating, and he was thought to be a quiet, dignified, and pleasantly enigmatic member of the Tucson upper crust.[10]

Soon after Ira's death, Caldwell also became one of the chief sponsors of the Tucson Press Club, an informal group of newspapermen, radio newsmen, and local authors who gathered around rickety tables and strong drinks to play poker and shoot pool. Caldwell was extremely comfortable with these men; he enjoyed his status as the most famous member in their midst, but he felt no pressure to impress them. He was known as a quiet man with a twinkle in his eye and a wry sense of humor—a man able to hold a huge amount of liquor and willing to play cards until dawn. After formal evenings at the country club, a late night with the boys restored his precious self-image as a regular working man. Although the Press Club was constantly teetering on the brink of financial collapse, Caldwell made sure it survived. When fur-niture was needed, he bought it; when members' dues could not cover expenses, he made up the difference. Twenty years earlier, he had spent time with aspiring artists in Alfred Morang's Portland studio, only to withdraw when the camaraderie interfered with his work. Now, he seemed willing to leave his writing behind.[11]

Throughout his marriage to Bourke-White, Caldwell had begged her to settle down, to raise a family, to establish a consistent and steady life with him. By the final half of the 1940s he seemed to have found all the stability he craved. June adored him and seemed perfectly con-tent to be his doting wife. If Erskine wanted solitude to write, she brought him meals on a tray and disappeared from sight. If he was sick, she was there to take care of him. Although he would always worry about money, the paperback editions of his work and the low cost of living in Tucson afforded him the greatest financial security of his life. A maid came daily to clean his luxurious house; there was a gardening service to maintain the flower beds and a full-time secretary to handle correspondence.[12]

It was an incongruous life for an author who relished the sordid details of America's most deprived citizens—an author driven by rage and empathy. Caldwell's complacency did not bode well for his future as an artist.

I

LATE IN 1945, Caldwell joined a group of investors building a new radio station in Tucson. He later described his participation in the venture as a reluctant fulfillment of civic duty. But at the time, Caldwell was far from reluctant, and his ambitions were strictly financial.

The project got off to a rocky start. Although the Federal Com-munications Commission approved the petition for a broadcast license, they also granted permits to three other competing groups. Most of Caldwell's fellow investors backed out, and he was advised to do the same. Instead, he bought his partners' shares in the venture, put to-gether a new group of investors, and became the majority stockholder and president of the Catalina Broadcasting Company. With nearly $50,000 of Caldwell's money behind it, KCNA received its charter in May 1946 and went on the air the following April.[13]

Although the board of directors hired a station manager to run the day-to-day affairs of the station, Caldwell was involved with every detail of the operation. He helped choose the design of the building, consulted with electricians over the width of the cables, negotiated with the FCC, discussed programming and target audiences, sold advertising, and hired the building's janitor. "I've worked on it for a solid year now, and I think I must know close to all there is about getting a station started and on the air," he wrote Morang in April 1947. "It is a headache but I'm glad I got into it." He enjoyed the work so much, and was so optimistic about his investment, that he soon bought shares in several Phoenix stations as well.[14]

KCNA was a time-consuming venture and caused Caldwell a great deal of anxiety. Inevitably, his inability to trust the running of the station to the people he hired caused problems. There were disagreements over staffing, programming, and marketing strategies and arguments about whether the station should increase its wattage. To make matters worse, ratings were consistently mediocre. In the first two years, KCNA did not turn a profit, and Caldwell—who already owned more than half of the company's stock—had to deepen his investment to keep things afloat. By the time the station began to break even, television, not radio, represented the future of entertainment.

Although KCNA never became the windfall Caldwell had hoped for, it managed to survive in the Tucson radio market. Caldwell was fortunate that his partners were more able businessmen than he. When he finally sold his interest in the station in 1956, he recouped his original investment, but ten years of anxiety and obsessive involvement never produced a single dividend check.

Caldwell's chief source of income was still the paperback editions of his books. NAL's publicity department routinely asked him to fly to Chicago, or San Francisco, or Washington, D.C., to meet with sales representatives or attend book-signing fairs. "I am hopeful," read a typical request, "that some arrangement can be made to have your assistance when we kick off . . . into the sales season at Biloxi Mississippi." Could Caldwell "say some flattering words" to a group of wholesalers in Colorado Springs? Could he autograph a few dozen copies of *God's Little Acre* with the inscription "for the best wholesaler in Little Rock"? Would he mind flying to New York to have his "picture taken with some of the Fawcett Distributing Company executives and generally say hello to the boys?" How would he feel about posing (with his dog) for a Calvert Whiskey advertisement as a "Man of Distinction"? Aside from the three hundred dollars and the case of Calvert whiskey he would receive, Caldwell was reminded that such exposure would be "a good publicity gag."[15]

Caldwell agreed to all these requests and suggested more of his own, embarking on cross-country tours, stopping in book stores in small towns, and meeting with Fawcett distributors in big cities. He posed for photographs, autographed books, attended cocktail parties, and gave three-minute speeches to selling agents. The executives at NAL and Fawcett recognized that no American author of Caldwell's stature toiled as hard to market his work. "From my own experience," wrote a Fawcett sales manager, "I can tell you that no other author is as well known or has met, personally, the many important wholesale distributors you have. This is most beneficial to our cause."[16]

Caldwell worked just as hard to further his sales overseas, where his books continued to be very popular. In the years when Caldwell paperbacks were taking off in America, foreign-language editions were also becoming available worldwide. Russia, France, Italy, and Great Britain still led the way in both sales and critical appreciation, but Caldwell's popularity continued to grow in other parts of the world as well; translations of most of his books could be found in Central and South America, Scandinavia, Egypt, Switzerland, Australia, Turkey, Hungary, Japan, Poland, and Czechoslovakia. By the early 1950s, Caldwell titles had been translated into twenty-three languages and were available in twenty-eight countries around the globe.[17]

The publication of these international editions provided Caldwell with an almost endless variety of details to fret about. Sales in India, Albania, South Africa—Caldwell wanted to know the figures for each. "You're not really worried about Egypt, Turkey, and Switzerland, are you?" Lieber asked him. Caldwell, of course, was worried about everything. He was particularly concerned that many of his books were published in pirated editions without his permission and thus did not earn him royalties, or were printed in countries that would not release the currency. If Caldwell wanted to spend his sizable accumulation of Polish zlotys, for instance, he had to visit Poland. "The contracts continue to flow in in an endless stream," Lieber remarked. "But I doubt if we can draw blood from a turnip . . . the funds are tied up endlessly. No one seems to have gold except Uncle Sam."[18]

After the war, Caldwell began taking regular trips abroad to root out pirated editions, spend frozen currencies, and help his foreign publishers sell more books. He stayed in the best hotels, but he did not waste time sightseeing during these trips. He moved rapidly from city to city—from Stockholm to Helsinki, Copenhagen, Warsaw, Rome, and Naples—rarely spending more than two days in a single place. Every stop was scrupulously organized. During a typical twenty-four hours in Helsinki, he conducted a radio interview through a translator, lunched with his Finnish publisher, autographed books at a bookstore, went to a tea for the Young Finnish Authors League, and ate dinner with an official from the Office of Cultural Affairs. When Caldwell and June conducted a whirlwind tour of Central and South America in 1946, she found the pace exhausting as well as exhilarating. Between meetings with translators, interviews with reporters eager to profile the author of the famous *Camino del Tobaco*, and heavy lunches with publishing executives, there was almost no time to relax. Caldwell did not want to relax. He was looking after business.[19]

II

"IT'S A HELL OF A LIFE to be a writer and be so dumb you can't do anything else," Caldwell once complained to Morang. "Writing is like smoking," he said on another occasion, "I'm addicted to it. It's my hobby, my vocation, my life." Writing had become a joyless pursuit, but dogged perseverance still drove Caldwell forward. In the years following Ira's death, he lived by a rigid schedule that freed his summers for business travel and left his evenings open for social obligations and work on the radio station. The days were reserved for writing. For ten months each year, he entered his study at nine in the morning, worked for three hours, ate lunch, and returned to his study from one until five. "I'm in the middle of the grind again trying to do a new book," he wrote grimly to Morang in 1945. "I've been at it for about three months, and should get out of it in about two months more, God willing." When one book was finished, he took two months off, then moved determinedly on to the next. "No matter what else I try, I always like to get back to writing for myself," he told Morang. "It's the only way."[20]

Between 1945 and 1950, Caldwell churned out five novels in five ten-month stretches. At the end of each summer he mailed off a completed manuscript to Duell, Sloan & Pearce; each fall he geared up to begin the cycle again. *A House in the Uplands*, *The Sure Hand of God*, *This Very Earth*, *A Place Called Estherville*, and *Episode in Palmetto* were all set in the South, and after finishing the first two, Caldwell began to describe them as part of "step[s] toward the ultimate completion of the cycloramic depiction of Southern life that I have been writing in many novels for many years."

While Caldwell tried to link these later books to *Tobacco Road*, *God's*

Little Acre, and *Trouble in July*, even the best of them fell far short of this earlier work. Each novel contained flashes of power and clarity, and a number of the characters were memorable. All the novels addressed such serious social issues as racism and racial violence, the oppression of the rural poor, and the dissolution of the nuclear family. But none sustained a compelling narrative for very long. They were freighted with melodramatic clichés, hackneyed dialogue, and predictable turns of plot. The organic and provocative sexuality of *Tobacco Road* or *God's Little Acre* was replaced by a cumbersome, gratuitous crudity, and the trenchant humor had lost much of its edge. Caldwell's great discipline as a writer kept the sentences short and clean, and the paragraphs well organized and direct; but his prose, as one critic later wrote, seemed to "sleepwalk" through these books. While his best fiction crackled with energy and razor-sharp dialogue, these five novels seemed, to various degrees, exhausted, ponderous, and uninspired.[21]

Part of the problem was Caldwell's attempt to broaden the scope of his fiction. Tired of critics who had accused him of re-creating Jeeter and Ty Ty in various guises, he sought to tell the stories of people and places he hardly knew. *A House in the Uplands* chronicled the crumbling fortunes of the Southern aristocracy; *The Sure Hand of God* was the story of an aging prostitute; *This Very Earth*, like *Tragic Ground*, had an urban setting. *Episode in Palmetto* centered on the sexual misadventures of a beautiful schoolteacher in a small town. The best of the books, *A Place Called Estherville*, dealt with racial prejudice—a topic Caldwell felt comfortable with, but even in this novel he seemed to have lost touch with his subject matter. This was not surprising; he had not visited the South since his father's death.[22]

Caldwell, in fact, was fairly removed from anything going on outside of Tucson. While he had always claimed to be "a writer not a reader," for the first time he seemed to take this favorite expression to heart. Once fascinated by world events, now he barely skimmed the headlines of the local paper; he read no fiction and had no interest in keeping up with current literary trends. Lieber felt that Caldwell's unwillingness to read was partly to blame for the stultification of his work, and he was constantly suggesting novels he thought his author might enjoy. Caldwell rejected them all. If his editors at DS&P asked him to write a cover blurb for another of their authors, he skimmed the book as quickly as possible. On his two-month trips abroad, Caldwell did not bring along a single volume except a dictionary, which he occasionally perused in his hotel room or airport lounges.[23]

But the central obstacle to Caldwell's progress as an artist was his vision of literature as a commodity and not a form of art. "The major impetus to most successful writers is economics," he told an interviewer a few years later. "You know you have to make a living. . . . It's like digging ditches or anything else. . . . It's the only job I've got and I have to work at it full time just like a doctor or a lawyer." Caldwell's agents and publishers were happy to encourage this pragmatic approach to authorship. Lieber and Al Manual continued to tempt him with the idea that a smash Broadway play or Hollywood film—a new *Tobacco Road*—was just around the corner. Caldwell agreed, and although he would never openly admit it, all five novels seemed written with film or theater adaptation in mind. He rushed off his finished manuscripts to Lieber and Manual, then badgered them constantly about their negotiations with Hollywood studios or theatrical producers.[24]

Caldwell also felt pressure from DS&P, who signed him to a five-year contract in 1945 with the understanding that he would write five books. "That's the day I am going to retire," Caldwell told Morang, "if I can hold out that long. Right now I feel as if I could quit and live on a rich wife, if I had a rich wife." Although they kept the tone jovial, his editors constantly reminded him that they were depending on him to produce. Caldwell's novels never seemed to sell as well as expected, but they all turned a profit. More important, DS&P earned excellent revenues when they sold the reprint rights to the New American Library. While many hardcover houses waited at least two years for this exchange in order to protect their authors' literary reputations, DS&P —which, by the late forties was beginning to struggle financially—did so almost immediately.[25]

Victor Weybright and Kurt Enoch, Caldwell's editors at NAL, also encouraged him to write quickly. Indeed, there was no incentive not to, since his books sold in huge numbers regardless of their quality. Much of this popular success was a result of NAL's marketing strategy, which, judging from the covers they chose, could be summarized simply as "sex sells." Robert Jonas's dignified and abstract cover art was replaced by garish depictions of buxom women in strategically torn dresses, who were variously fondled, ogled, and threatened by salacious farmers or corrupt businessmen. On the cover of *The Sure Hand of God*, one of Caldwell's most explicit late-forties novels, a curvaceous blond woman in a revealing dress lies supine at the feet of a circle of scowling men. One man's crotch is positioned directly above her head, another man is in the process of unbuttoning his fly. This edition sold 1.4 million copies in its first year alone. The cover of *This Very Earth* pictured a voluptuous brunette staring forlornly over a fence with a leering man behind her. The back cover featured such excerpts as, "I talk as I damn well please to high-yellow wenches. Now strip off to your skin and quit answering me back." While the hardcover sales of the book were so slow in New York that Macy's returned four hundred of the five hundred copies it purchased, the garishly covered paperback, with the carefully chosen quotations on the back, passed the one-million mark in under ten months.[26]

Such a trend sent a clear but unfortunate message to both Caldwell and his publishers. Any Caldwell book containing a healthy dose of graphic sexuality would make money if marketed accordingly. A number of critics pointed out that in the late 1940s, Caldwell's work seemed to be tailor-made for the mass market—either melodramatic, violent, sexual, or broadly comic. All five books, in fact, were similar in length, as well as quality and tone. The shortest, *A House in the Uplands*, was 238 pages long; the longest, *This Very Earth*, ran 254. Side by side on a bookshelf or on a drugstore rack, it was obvious that they were cut from the same mold.

Lieber and the editors at both DS&P and NAL continued their chorus of fawning and toadying and urged Caldwell to keep the manuscripts coming. After reading *This Very Earth*, Pearce wrote to say "I can only repeat that there is only one Caldwell and that he seems to get better all the time." Victor Weybright concurred. "We rise to cheer! It's wonderful to know that the old maestro has delivered another great book in the series of novels." Lieber was no less effusive, having learned his lesson after responding honestly to *Tragic Ground* in 1944. He likened the characterization in *The Sure Hand of God* to the "perfection of a Bach Fugue," and even found kind words for *Episode in Palmetto*, perhaps the worst book Caldwell ever wrote. Pearce passed along the remarkable conclusion that this terrible novel was "the most finished Caldwell performance to date."[27]

III

HIGH PAPERBACK SALES and sycophantic praise could not protect Caldwell from the critical evisceration that greeted the publication of each successive novel. Attacks came from all quarters. Hamilton Basso, one of the leftist critics who had always had mixed feelings about Caldwell, called *The House in the Uplands* "the most disastrous piece of feeble pretentiousness [he had] ever read by an author of presumably serious intentions." Joy Davidman of the *New Masses* felt that "the only thing worth discussing about it is how a writer of Caldwell's distinction and power came to produce such a book . . . this novel is remarkably bad." Like many reviewers who had once admired Caldwell's potent social criticism, Davidman felt that the cause of his decline was his willingness to write "according to a special formula." She noted sadly that "the social criticism has shrunk almost to the vanishing point" and had been replaced by a gratuitous mixture of sex and violence.[28]

More mainstream reviewers were no gentler. The critic for the *American Mercury* concluded that *The Sure Hand of God* was "dreadfully written, is completely devoid of insight, and sets a new low in dullness even for Caldwell—which is to say, it sets a new low in serious contemporary literature." *Time* magazine titled its review of *This Very Earth* "Caldwell's Collapse," and likened the novel to the "uncoordinated performance of a once-talented dancer who still remembers all the steps . . . but has forgotten how to dance." Reviewing *Episode in Palmetto* a few years later, V. P. Hass wrote: "Not since the sub rosa of my college days have I read so shameless a piece of literary pandering. . . . I do not, believe me, exaggerate either the dirtiness or the silliness of this novel. . . . it's cheap, sleazy, and tasteless. I would hate to have it on my conscience."[29]

The most damning summation of Caldwell's critical decline came from James Baldwin in his 1947 review of *The Sure Hand of God*. Along with gratuitous nastiness—the piece was titled "The Dead Hand of Caldwell"—Baldwin offered a brutal but accurate characterization of the listless, uninspired work that Caldwell had written in the years following Ira's death. "Caldwell's knowledge of the scene has become mechanical, and his passion . . . has died," Baldwin wrote.

> The work is curious because of its effortless tone and absolute emptiness. Mr. Caldwell, it would appear, knows these people so well that he is no longer even interested in them. He sets them up and they strut their stuff and go back into darkness until it is time for another book. . . . He has not written a single sloppy sentence (nor a single interesting one) nor created (within his own familiar framework) a single unlikely character. This must be fun for Mr. Caldwell and there is no reason why it could not go on forever.

"Unless we hear from him again in accents more individual," Baldwin concluded, "we can leave his bones for that literary historian of another day."[30]

Occasionally, Caldwell received kind reviews from old acquaintances or gentle letters from fellow authors. Over the years, Caldwell had generously contributed book-jacket blurbs to young writers, and a number of them repaid his kindness with letters of support. "The review in the *American Mercury* made me so damned mad I sat down and wrote them a long letter," wrote James Aswell, one of Caldwell's acquaintances from the days at the New Dominion Bookstore in Charlottesville. "I don't see how anyone could fail to see that *This Very Earth* is a sharp advance over *Tobacco Road*." Most faithful of all was Alfred Morang, who wrote long letters full of grandiloquent praise, comparing his old friend to Picasso, and invariably assuring him that the latest book—whichever one it was—was "his best book to date."[31]

Caldwell's editors urged him not to worry about the "hatchet work" or the "negative tide of critical opinion" as long as his books continued to sell. "The reviewers seem to be swinging their tomahawks in your general direction," Pearce wrote Caldwell after the release of *The Sure Hand of God*. "But the book sellers and public don't seem to agree with the reviewers any more than I do." Indeed, by 1950, Americans had bought 22 million paperback copies of Caldwell's novels and short-story collections. This popular endorsement was the only comfort Caldwell had left. By the end of the decade, the mounting wave of critical condemnation had virtually dismissed him from the canon of American literature.[32]

Caldwell was deeply disheartened both with his novels and with the disastrous impact they had on his reputation. He lashed out at the critics, who he felt were merely envious of his popular success, but occasionally, he admitted his disappointment to Morang. "Things have been so-so with me," he once wrote. "There hasn't been anything seriously wrong but there have been ups and downs. One or two things have kept me in a stew, and I can't see daylight yet." When *Episode in Palmetto* was published in 1950 and met with the predictable din of critical censure, Caldwell seemed to have had enough. Although he began another book precisely on schedule after a two-month lay-off, he did not attempt another novel. Instead, he began work on an autobiography he titled *Call It Experience*.[33]

Not surprisingly, Caldwell's memoirs were short on personal revelation. Helen, June, and his four children went unmentioned, and while he recognized Bourke-White's work on *You Have Seen Their Faces*, he failed to note that they had ever been married. The book was a sometimes fanciful, sometimes honest, often self-aggrandizing account of his journey from boyhood to literary eminence. He wrote eloquently of his scattered education, his experiences as a newspaper reporter, his long Mount Vernon apprenticeship, and his father. There were detailed descriptions of the hardships he overcame, the success of his early novels, the stage play of *Tobacco Road*, and his adventures in the Soviet Union.

But while *Call It Experience* was published in 1951, the five novels Caldwell wrote between 1945 and 1950—his most recent work—were discussed in a single sentence. At the age of forty-nine, Caldwell was ready to sum up, even eulogize, his career, and he wanted to be remembered for the best—not the worst—of what he had done.

IV

IN 1951, MAXIM LIEBER closed his literary agency and moved to Mexico. He had been in poor health for a number of years and had recently suffered a second heart attack. *Call It Experience* was the last Caldwell book he worked on.

But it was politics, more than ill health, that forced Lieber out of business and out of the country. In the 1949 trial of Alger Hiss, Lieber was called a "secret Communist" spy by the chief prosecution witness, Whittaker Chambers. Following the trial, many of Lieber's writers— fearful for their careers—left for other agents. Friends in the publishing world shunned him as well. When Lieber left for Mexico to escape prosecution, the literary stable he had developed over more than twenty years was in ruins.[34]

Caldwell's publishers were happy to see Lieber go. Since the mid-1940s they had worried that his politics might hurt Caldwell's reputation (and the sales of his books) and, in a number of subtle ways, they had suggested that he might be better served by a new agent. But Caldwell always stood by Lieber; after twenty years together, he trusted him almost completely, and he knew that Lieber worked extremely hard on his behalf. And while Caldwell had drifted out of leftist circles with the onset of World War II, he still believed in many of the same causes. In 1947, Caldwell joined Joseph North (then editor of the *New Masses*) as co-chairman of the Progressive Writers Group, an organization designed to protect authors' First Amendment rights. When Howard Fast was arrested and sentenced to three months' imprisonment for failing to "cooperate" with the House Un-American Activities Committee, the group organized petition drives on his behalf and helped raise money for his bail.³⁵

But Caldwell was torn between his loyalty to Lieber and his abiding concern for his publication fortunes. Toward the end of the forties, as anti-Communist hysteria rose ever higher, he began to shy away from any actions that could be construed as "subversive"—a category that was growing more inclusive every day. When Lieber and Howard Fast urged Caldwell to sign an open letter in the *New York Times* supporting Henry Wallace for president in 1948, he refused. Caldwell also stopped Lieber from placing one of his stories in the new magazine *New Masses-Mainstream*, although Lieber tempted him with the reminder that "the magazine was read by a large number of literary and cultural people who, I assume, would represent a potential market for your books." Caldwell, it seems, was more convinced by the arguments of Charles Pearce, who told him simply that such an association could be "a kiss of death."³⁶

After the Whittaker Chambers testimony, Caldwell further distanced himself from his agent. Although he continued to give Lieber full rein over the management of his books, he excluded him from any further involvement in negotiations for dramatic adaptations or film deals. Even though Lieber was then trying to place several Caldwell novels with stage producers and was beginning to investigate the television possibilities of several short stories, Caldwell forced him to stop. He wrote Lieber a gentle letter informing him that only Al Manual could pursue such negotiations. With all of Broadway and Hollywood terrified of being blacklisted or labeled "Red," Caldwell knew that Lieber's name could kill any potential deals for his work.³⁷

In 1950, Lieber pressured NAL to issue a paperback edition of *All Night Long*, Caldwell's novel about Russian resistance fighters. The book was painfully out of step with the current anti-Communist hysteria, but that was precisely Lieber's point. Weybright and Enoch were horrified by the potential damage *All Night Long* could do to Caldwell's (and NAL's) reputation, and they stepped up their campaign to convince their prize author that Lieber would ruin his career. "We would greatly deplore it," Weybright wrote, "if, through your misguided friends, no matter how well-meaning they may be, you and your work were to be smeared by some of your critics and some of our competitors as pro-Communist." He reminded Caldwell that he was "a favorite author in Russia and the Iron Curtain countries," and already under suspicion by the American government. Indeed, NAL had needed to lobby aggressively to keep Caldwell titles from being struck from the list of books approved for Marshall Plan countries in Europe.* Weybright, who made such a great fuss about his authors' artistic integrity, proposed that Caldwell rewrite *All Night Long* with a Greek or Korean setting so that the resistance fighters could represent the forces of freedom against an oppressive Communist regime. Caldwell ignored this ludicrous idea, but he also dropped his efforts to reissue the book.[38]

Lieber's heart attack and flight to Mexico gave Caldwell the excuse he wanted to sever his ties with him. Still, it was a difficult decision. In a letter to Lieber's wife, who was still living in New York, Caldwell admitted that he felt "lost in a world of confusion without his help and advice." Other than Morang, Lieber was as close to a friend as Caldwell had ever had. His agent had been with him through three publishers, three wives, lean times, censorship battles, and through each and every tantrum Caldwell had thrown in the last twenty years. Perhaps most important, Lieber was Caldwell's only remaining link to his past of angry, passionate dedication and political involvement; he was the last tie to the social conscience that had informed his best writing.[39]

Caldwell, however, was no romantic. He quickly hired a new agent more suited to the tenor of the times. James Oliver Brown was young, well-bred, highly educated, and conservative. Al Manual and Caldwell's editors at NAL were overjoyed with his choice. "It must be a great relief," Weybright wrote (although it was he who was most relieved), "to have someone to cope with the details as well as the promotion of your best interests, who is young, vigorous, well-connected—and unpolitical." The following year, Lieber wrote to Caldwell from Mexico to request permission to use a Caldwell story in an anthology he was assembling. Brown advised Caldwell to ignore him. "I hope Maxim in his boredom does not attempt to build up a correspondence with you," Brown wrote coldly. "I see no reason for acknowledging this letter, although you may want to." Caldwell may have "wanted to," but he did not. He and Lieber never spoke again.[40]

V

CALDWELL'S SPLIT FROM LIEBER coincided with a growing estrangement from his wife as well. By the late 1940s, small strains in

---

* The Marshall Plan was an American program of economic aid to European countries designed to stop the spread of Communism after World War II.

the marriage were becoming significant points of conflict. Predictably, the twenty-year age difference between Caldwell and June caused problems. While he had committed himself to socializing more, he could not (as he could not with Bourke-White) match June's desire to entertain and go out. She was, after all, still in her early twenties, and Caldwell's friends at the Tucson Press Club and his business associates at the radio station were all forty or older; many of them, in fact, had children who were June's age.[41]

June also found it difficult being "the wife of Erskine Caldwell." While her husband's fame was initially gratifying, it also had its share of drawbacks. When they traveled together, she often felt invisible. While reporters clamored for interviews and well-wishers greeted him on the street, she was completely ignored. On several occasions, June felt insulted when she was mistaken for Margaret Bourke-White. On the trip to South America, Caldwell arranged for the State Department to wire ahead to embassies to warn the reception committees that June was "NOT, REPEAT NOT, MARGARET BOURKE-WHITE"—a phrase that became something of a joke in embassy circles.[42]

In the early years of the marriage, June had channeled her energy into her husband's career. She helped him answer the constant flood of correspondence from prospective authors, and ironed out the details for new Folkways editions. She sent long letters to critics she felt had misunderstood her husband's works, and she corresponded with overseas translators. She sent her own marketing suggestions to DS&P and wrote NAL to make sure that Caldwell's dedication "For Helen" was removed from new editions of *God's Little Acre*. June was embarrassed by Caldwell's growing reputation as an author of "dirty" paperbacks and mortified by the cover art used in the novels of the late forties. She began a heated correspondence with the publicity department at NAL and DS&P. Although they promised to "satisfy June 100% this time," the editors knew that Caldwell's first concern was sales. The covers did not change.[43]

As the years passed, however, June longed for a career of her own. She grew tired of taking care of Jay while Caldwell worked doggedly away in the study. Her life was circumscribed, and her legitimate talents as an artist and writer seemed to be wasting away. June began visiting a psychoanalyst and became more and more convinced that she needed to emerge from Caldwell's shadow. But even as she began working on her own fiction, and submitting her stories to magazines, she could not escape the feeling of being "Erskine Caldwell's wife." An editor at *The New Yorker*, for instance, rejected one of her short stories, then closed the letter with the request: "Please tell your husband that it seems a very long time since we've had the pleasure of reading one of his short stories." Other magazines were equally insensitive, as were other writers who often viewed June as her husband's secretary. "Your husband has a very great talent," one wrote. "Be extra sweet to him and help him fulfill himself continually in work and life. He will live a long time in our letters. I am proud to have known him."[44]

June cast around for other ways to assert her independence. She sought work as a French translator, audited courses at the University of Arizona, took singing lessons, and briefly enrolled in law school. She was fascinated by current events and wrote long letters to political candidates or government officials, including Ralph Bunche and Barry Goldwater. She also became more deeply committed to her psychoanalysis and increased her visits to three or four times a week. Most important, June began to curtail her involvement in Caldwell's career. She let his secretary handle almost all of the correspondence, and she stopped writing letters to NAL or DS&P. She also refused to accompany Caldwell on his promotional tours around the country or overseas. She did not want to disrupt her psychiatric treatment, and she was tired of tagging along while her husband pursued an endless round of press conferences, business meetings, and publicity events.[45]

Predictably, June's growing independence troubled Caldwell a great deal. While he encouraged her writing projects, he was extremely threatened by her psychoanalysis, which he began to view as a means of "willfully burdening [him] with debt." With his own writing going so poorly in the late 1940s, he badly wanted June's support just as she found it most difficult to give. He started to drink more, spent more hours with the newspapermen at the Tucson Press Club, was increasingly annoyed by June's social calendar, and traveled—now always alone—to promote the sale of his books at home and abroad.[46]

By the end of the decade, the marriage, like Caldwell's fiction, was nearing the bottom of a steady decline. "Don't rush into getting married too soon—there are too many women in the world who have too little to offer," he wrote in frustration to Morang. "It's a lot better to wait it out until the right one comes along."[47]

Caldwell's brusqueness masked grief as well as bitterness. He had tried to be a good husband and a good father and had succeeded to a greater degree than ever before. Still, his marriage was failing. He responded to June's growing independence, as he had to Bourke-White's, with an almost desperate neediness. But while such dependency had sometimes appealed to his second ex-wife, it had the opposite effect on

June. The harder he tried to keep her close, the more determined she became to be independent.

In 1952, Caldwell checked into the hospital for surgery to repair a severe stomach ulcer. The night before the operation he wrote June a plaintive letter, seeking reassurance and another chance to somehow save their marriage. "I love you and want your love more than anything else in the world," he wrote. "You may have reasons why it has to be like this but I don't understand them and maybe I never shall."

> It may be that you have grown to have different feelings or something but I have the same feelings for you that I've had all the time since I first knew you. I wish you could return to that and let us be happy together because that is all I want in life. I love you very much, Skinny.[48]

Not long afterwards, June asked for a separation. Caldwell packed up a few belongings and moved to Phoenix. He tried to convince June to reconsider and flooded her with letters. She was unmoved. "Being terribly sorry that I haven't been able to convince you myself and after having give the whole matter much thought," June wrote early in 1954, "I am asking David Watkins [her lawyer] to institute divorce proceedings for me."[49]

VI

ALTHOUGH CALDWELL AND NAL were enjoying financial success in the late 1940s, DS&P struggled to stay afloat. They trimmed office staff, reduced salaries, and cut corners on advertising. Once (in a remarkable reversal of the traditional author-publisher relationship), the firm even asked Caldwell for a short-term loan. Part of DS&P's financial woes stemmed from their heavy reliance on one author— Erskine Caldwell—and the disappointing hardcover sales of his books. They were partly to blame for this. They had spent less and less on advertising, and produced unattractive editions. Moreover, DS&P had granted reprint rights to NAL far too quickly. Readers wanting a new Caldwell title were well aware that NAL's less expensive Signet edition would soon be on the way. "The trouble is," Caldwell's new agent wrote to Al Manual, "that DS&P have been more interested in raking in their large slice from reprints than in trying to maintain a proper level of sales and a proper level of prestige for Caldwell's titles."[50]

But Caldwell's recent hardcover publications were not the only ones selling poorly. When Grosset & Dunlap published a series of hardcover editions of Caldwell's most famous novels, they found, as DS&P had, that Caldwell's paperback sales had undermined the marketability of everything else. Between 1948 and 1951, hardcover sales of *Georgia Boy* plummeted from 4,300 copies a year to 48; *Tobacco Road* from 1,700 to 550; and *Tragic Ground* from 2,000 to 200. In all, Grosset & Dunlap sold 24,000 copies in 1948, but saw hardcover sales fall to 5,000 by 1951. Caldwell had become, undeniably, a "paperback author" at a time when such a sobriquet was still a negative one in literary circles.[51]

In late 1951, DS&P was bought out by the Boston-based publishers Little, Brown & Company. Arthur Thornhill, president of the firm, and Caldwell's new agent, James Oliver Brown, were determined to resuscitate Caldwell's reputation. They promised him that subsequent novels would be marketed in a dignified and serious manner, and that NAL would have to wait before they could flood the nation's cigar stores with the softcover editions. They urged him to embark on a new work of fiction that would signal his critical resurrection.[52]

Caldwell, however, was not ready to produce a novel. Daunted by the viciousness of the reviews over the past five years and embroiled in the dissolution of his third marriage, he seemed unwilling—perhaps unable—to write anything new. He responded to his creative paralysis as he always had in the past: by trying to find new ways to cash in on things he had already written. When NAL had balked at the publication of *All Night Long*, he had immediately begun campaigning for the publication of *A Lamp For Nightfall*, a manuscript written under the title "Autumn Hill" twenty years before. The novel had been one of the irritants in his split from Scribner's, and over the years it had been rejected by Harcourt, Brace; Simon and Schuster; Viking; and most recently, DS&P. Caldwell urged James Oliver Brown to pursue serialization possibilities, and before long, the manuscript was also turned down by *Collier's, Redbook, Woman's Day, Country Gentleman, The Atlantic,* and *Cosmopolitan.* Little, Brown and NAL did not want *A Lamp For Nightfall,* either, for they knew the novel would do nothing to help Caldwell's tattered critical reputation, but Caldwell pushed them until they relented. The book was released in 1952, was harshly reviewed, and disappeared quickly from sight.[53]

Caldwell also lobbied for the publication of anthologies of short stories he had done years before. Between 1948 and 1950, he put together four profitable collections of old stories for publication with three different paperback publishers. *Where the Girls Were Different, Midsummer Passion and Other Stories, A Woman in the House,* and *A Swell-Looking*

Girl appeared only in paperback and were marketed (and obviously titled) to capitalize on Caldwell's reputation as a "dirty writer." Although many of the stories in these volumes dealt with starving share-croppers or stubborn Maine farmers and had very little sexual content, the covers and titles seemed to do their job; *A Woman in the House*, for instance, sold 1.4 million copies in its first year.[54]

In the early fifties Caldwell encouraged Little, Brown to publish several more hardcover anthologies. Although Arthur Thornhill insisted on more decorous and less misleading titles, they issued *The Humorous Side of Erskine Caldwell*, *The Courting of Susie Brown and Other Stories*, and a huge volume titled simply *The Complete Stories of Erskine Caldwell*. None of these collections contained new work, although a few titles were changed. *The Humorous Side of Erskine Caldwell*, for instance, had a piece called "A Sack of Turnips," a condensation of the first four chapters of *Tobacco Road*; another story titled "Gold Fever" was a combination of the first two chapters of *God's Little Acre*; and another called "The Doggone Douthits," was merely a joining of the second halves of Chapter 13 and Chapter 14 of *Tragic Ground*.[55]

The occasional new stories that Caldwell wrote in these years were not particularly good, and James Oliver Brown had a difficult time placing them. Editors at the better magazines were either afraid of Caldwell's reputation as a pornographer or Communist, or simply shared the current critical wisdom that dismissed him as a hack. When Caldwell's old friend James Aswell wrote a profile on Caldwell for *Collier's*, the magazine decided at the last minute not to run it. They informed Aswell that their readers no longer had any interest in Caldwell, for he had not "really written a good book in a long time." Editors at a number of other national magazines agreed, and Aswell dropped the project. "To hell with the bastards," Aswell wrote Caldwell. "All of them."[56]

By the early 1950s, the only editors who consistently expressed interest in Caldwell's new work were those working at what James Oliver Brown called "girlie magazines." *Cavalier* published a story called "A Gift for Sue" under the less-than-charming title "Just a Quick One." *Manhunt* published three stories as well. A few years later, in a burst of activity, Caldwell wrote eight new stories; six of them appeared in *Playboy*, *Cavalier*, *Dude*, *Swank*, and *Gent*. Although Lieber and then Brown occasionally warned him that such publications further damaged his reputation, Caldwell had a ready response. "I wish, selfishly perhaps, to have my work published while I am alive, and don't care particularly about it when I'm dead," he wrote bluntly in 1951. "It would be foolish

of me not to consider any reasonable offer directed toward the publication of my work. I live to write, and writing is my living."[57]

The royalties from NAL paperbacks still comprised the bulk of Caldwell's income in the early fifties, and as long as sales were good, he
and his editors at NAL got along well. James Brown gleefully informed
Caldwell that when he visited the publishers' offices in November 1951
"the reaction of the whole staff was that God's representative had arrived." Weybright and Enoch bent over backward to keep their star
writer happy. They agreed to publish all of the anthologies Caldwell
wished, and extended a series of long-term contracts in order to keep
his insecurities at bay. When attempts to ban his books were made—
and Caldwell was NAL's most victimized author—the publishers paid
all the legal fees. They also granted him huge advances against the sales
of his future works. Indeed, there seemed to be no reason not to.[58]

By 1952, however, Caldwell's paperback sales had begun to slip. In
1953, they fell further still. In 1951, 250,000 people had bought *Tobacco
Road*. The following year, sales dropped to 31,000. In 1953, a book that
had once sold a million copies in ten months sold a mere 10,000 copies.
Sales of *God's Little Acre*, which had averaged over 500,000 copies a year
since the record 2.1 million mark in 1947, also plummeted. The book
sold 23,000 copies in 1953. The rest of Caldwell's titles followed a similar
trend. "The bottom," Brown wrote Caldwell in alarm, "has fallen out
of the reprint market."[59]

There were many reasons for the precipitous decline. Paperback
readers held very tenuous loyalties to authors, and Caldwell's failure
to produce a new novel since his 1950 *Episode in Palmetto* broke the
momentum created by his early success. Moreover, many Caldwell
readers had been disappointed by the anthologies, which carried exciting titles, but turned out to be nothing more than a rewarming of old
material. It is also possible, as some sales representatives suggested,
that Caldwell's best and most popular novels had simply saturated the
reading public; everyone who wanted to read *God's Little Acre* or *Tobacco Road* had already done so.

But much of the problem stemmed from NAL's miscalculation of
demand. The publishers continued to print Caldwell's books in record
numbers even as sales slowed, and they inadvertently flooded the market. Stores began to return the extra books to wholesalers, some in
response to a wave of censorship efforts sweeping the country. Wholesalers, in turn, were forced to keep the books in ever-mounting piles
in their warehouses, and such stockpiles were a potent discouragement
to salesmen working on commission. As Fawcett wholesalers began to

lose faith in Caldwell's marketability, they stopped pushing his titles. Without their energetic promotion, retailers began filling their sales racks with newer authors.[60]

The sudden plunge in sales left Caldwell with an enormous unearned advance from NAL. By August 1954, he had received more than $50,000 not covered by the sales of his books. When Caldwell and Brown asked for another contract and another advance for 1954, Weybright and Enoch turned them down. Although he did not have to repay this money immediately, Caldwell would not receive any further royalties until his debt was cleared. When Arthur Thornhill wrote Weybright on Caldwell's behalf, Weybright responded bluntly. "The more we reflect upon and discuss the Caldwell situation, the more convinced we are that someone other than NAL will have to cope with Skinny's present financial crisis. I regard Skinny as a friend and as a genius, but I think it very unreasonable of him or James Oliver Brown to get the idea that we are the Ford Foundation instead of the NAL."[61]

The abrupt cessation of NAL royalty checks left Caldwell, always terrified of poverty, without any income. Most of his money was tied up in the radio stations or real estate in Tucson, and his hardcover sales were bringing in next to nothing. In late 1954, Caldwell's divorce from June was finalized. She received the large house and thirty-nine acres of valuable land, as well as alimony and child-support payments totaling $600 a month. When Caldwell nagged his agent for financial updates and pressed him for solutions to his monetary distress, Brown responded simply that he was "at a loss to know where to go for money."[62]

Caldwell was not. He scrambled to finish up a novel—the first he had written since *Episode in Palmetto* three years before. Entitled *Love and Money*, the hastily written book chronicled the trials and tribulations of a lovesick writer. Reviews were predictably mediocre, as were hardcover sales. Caldwell knew, however, that NAL's paperback edition would help recoup at least part of the money he owed them. He quit the expensive Tucson Country Club and found a small apartment in Phoenix. He made a deal with another paperback publisher to bring out new editions of *The Bastard* and *Poor Fool*; he accepted a commission to read the work of other NAL authors and provide cover comments like "I couldn't put this book down!"; he looked into the possibility of writing a syndicated newspaper column.[63]

Caldwell found some solace in travel, as he had throughout his life. In November 1954, he was invited to a Congress of Soviet Writers in Moscow. He badly wanted to go, for the trip would return him to a

country where he was still appreciated, take him far away from his
failed personal life, and, perhaps most important, allow him to live off
some of the rubles he had accumulated there.

With the U.S. still racked by the Cold War and anti-Communist
hysteria, James Oliver Brown and the editors at Little, Brown and NAL
urged him not to go. Caldwell had dodged a bullet when Lieber left
for Mexico, and they did not want him to attract the suspicion of red-
baiting forces. Sales of his books were slow enough already. "Our advice would be emphatically to stay away," warned an executive at
Little, Brown. "Unfortunately," Weybright added, "Communists are
known to be devious and their motives very often concealed and cun-
ning." Brown pointedly mailed Caldwell a clipping about the great
singer Paul Robeson, whose career had been nearly destroyed by anti-
Communist forces in the U.S. Brown's warning was prescient. When
Caldwell applied to have his passport approved, he was turned down.
A State Department inquiry had raised too many questions about his
political sympathies. Caldwell, in fact, had been under surveillance by
the F.B.I. since 1943.[64]

Caldwell was also targeted by several civilian organizations dedicated
to rooting out dangerous subversives. *Firing Line*, the official publication
of the American Legion, carried a long harangue that specified his past
affiliations with "14 organizations that are cited as subversive and Communist by the United States Attorney General and the House Committee on Un-American Activities." The article warned that Caldwell's
radio station was compelling evidence of "the left-wing influence into
the radio and television industry." The Cincinnati-based Protect America League also issued a detailed list of Caldwell's subversive activities.
It organized a ban of his novels from newsstands in order to "forewarn
against the possibility of accepting Communist propaganda and distortions that undermine our form of government and are detrimental to
our American way of life."[65]

Caldwell's career was never really damaged by these scattered reports, because he and his editors carried out a strident campaign of
denials. "We want to keep in step," Weybright wrote, "and not permit
such a snide attack to go unchallenged." Caldwell agreed, and by the
mid-1950s he completely and frequently disavowed any interest in any
left-wing causes then or ever. "I have no interest whatsoever in advancing the Communist cause; on the contrary I would do anything I
could to hinder it," Caldwell wrote the State Department at the time
of his failed bid to visit the Soviet Union. He pointed proudly to his
awards for "patriotic cooperation" that he had received from the Trea-

sury Department for his bond drives during the war, and his "esteemed citizenship" citation from the secretary of state of Arizona. He assured them that his contact with leftist organizations or individuals during the 1930s was merely a calculated effort to get published. The F.B.I., in fact, soon realized that Caldwell had very little interest in politics, and it could not refute the truth of his declaration that he "was not, nor had ever been a member of the Communist Party."[66]

Quite possibly, Erskine Caldwell did not seem important enough to warrant serious harassment. By the 1950s, his well-earned reputation as one of America's harshest social critics had been overwhelmed by his status as a "popular author"—a writer of bestsellers, a writer of "dirty books." In fact, the people interested in undermining Caldwell's fortunes could easily see that their assistance was not needed. His career as an important writer was already over.

By the mid-1950s, Caldwell's disappointments threatened to overwhelm him. His drinking became habitual, determined, and debilitating. He consumed up to a fifth of bourbon a day, and although he never appeared drunk, he moved in an almost-perpetual haze. Once, on a trip to Poland, he packed, along with one suitcase of clothes, two suitcases of Jack Daniel's whiskey. His physical appearance began to deteriorate. His weight ballooned from 185 pounds to over 230. There were dark circles under his bloodshot eyes; his face aged dramatically. He developed a skin condition on his scalp and began to comb his short hair straight forward in a strange, unflattering style to cover it. While he stubbornly maintained his ramrod-straight posture, he seemed listless, tired, and sullen.[67]

With June and Jay gone, Caldwell was alone most of the time. Occasionally, he drank and played cards with the newspapermen at the Phoenix Press Club. He took weekend trips to Las Vegas now and again with Al Manual, or traveled dutifully to New York to meet with James Oliver Brown or the editors at DS&P and NAL. He was tortured by his financial decline, and bitter about the huge alimony settlement with June. He slept poorly, ate poorly, and had no enthusiasm for his work.

At the depth of his despair, Caldwell flew to Minneapolis alone and checked himself into the Mayo Clinic. He did nothing but sleep and read newspapers, but after a week he flew home, as tired and disappointed as he had been when he left.

Since the publication of *Tobacco Road* thirty years earlier, Erskine Caldwell's personal life and his career had careened constantly and dramatically—from fiction to nonfiction to film; from novel to short story to documentary; from wife to lover to wife; from publisher to publisher to publisher to publisher; and from state to state. He had dipped and climbed from triumph to great unhappiness; from giddy passion to dark melancholy; from vindication to crashing disappointment. But there had always been change. Now, at the age of fifty, Erskine Caldwell seemed to have come to rest in a furrow of his own making.

Chapter Thirteen

WITH ALL MY MIGHT

W RITING," CALDWELL ONCE SAID, "is as harsh and
demanding as the stomach is for its daily food."

And once the writer begins to try and satisfy the hunger, from then on
he endures on faith, and might as well stop complaining about his allotted affliction and learn to live with it as best he can.[1]

Caldwell's relentless determination—his "endurance on faith"—had
carried him through the vagaries of a long literary career. Such blind
resolve drove him forward in spite of his despondency.

In 1954, Caldwell began to write short stories again, the first he had
attempted since the end of World War II. He worked slowly and half-
heartedly, but he worked. That year, he wrote one story; in 1955 another three; in 1956 he wrote six; and the following saw seven more.
James Oliver Brown sold all of them to mediocre (often X-rated) journals, and eventually the pieces were collected in two anthologies published by Little, Brown. Caldwell rewarded himself for each finished
draft with a weekend trip to Las Vegas, where he often sat alone at
the blackjack table and ordered bourbon after bourbon. But after a few
days of such heavy drinking, he always returned to work. Caldwell also
wrote a short novel entitled *Gretta* in the melodramatic, mildly pornographic vein of his worst late-forties work. Like the anthologies, the
book sold very poorly in hardcover. Reviewers, once angry or disappointed, were by now hardly interested. A typical critic thought *Gretta*
had "little to recommend it except a certain lasciviousness." Caldwell
was beyond caring about reviews or hardcover sales. Graced with lurid
covers, both the anthologies and the novel sold well enough in paperback to help him pay off his unearned advances to NAL. Caldwell was
still unhappy and alone, but he was once again earning a living from
his craft.[2]

I

IN LATE 1949, Caldwell had attended a cocktail party in his honor at Victor Weybright's house in Maryland. One of Weybright's guests was an attractive and vivacious twenty-nine-year-old woman named Virginia Moffett Fletcher. She had come to the party reluctantly, expecting Caldwell to be loud, opinionated, and certainly foul-mouthed. But when she arrived, she was surprised to see the guest of honor standing shyly in a corner mumbling awkward thanks to the steady line of well-wishers eager to meet him. She found him very attractive —a "Georgia country boy" with disarming appeal. When they spoke, Caldwell, in turn, was charmed by Fletcher. Like June and Bourke-White, she was dark-haired, bright, and extremely easy to talk to. At the end of the evening the two exchanged addresses, and they began a sporadic correspondence. As Caldwell's marriage to June fell apart, the letters to Virginia grew bolder and more intimate; occasionally, he met her in New York when he came to the city on business.[3]

In 1953, Virginia and her teenage son by an earlier marriage moved from Florida to Arizona for a change of climate, and, in part, to be near Caldwell. In 1956, when his secretary left, Virginia took over the job. Like Caldwell, she was meticulous to the point of fanaticism. Gradually, she educated herself on every aspect of his career—all his foreign editions and translations, the dramatic adaptations being staged worldwide, the hardcover sales at Little, Brown, and the paperback sales at NAL. She went to the stationer's to buy his preferred brand of pencils and made sure that he had a fresh supply of his favorite paper.[4]

As the months passed, Virginia spent more and more time at Caldwell's house and less at her own. They went swimming together in the large backyard pool, and Caldwell grilled hamburger suppers for them to eat outside. They grew increasingly relaxed around each other, and she became accustomed to his shy, sardonic manner, and his willingness to sit for hours without speaking a word. He grew to expect and enjoy her long narrative descriptions of her day and the detailed, excited accounts of her son's latest activities.

Virginia saw how unhappy Caldwell was, how much he drank, how often he disappeared to Las Vegas, and how, on his return, he locked himself in his study. She saw that his moods ranged from tranquil shyness to dark and angry brooding; she knew that he worried that his agents and publishers would cheat him; she recognized that he was hurt by the snide book reviewers who casually demolished each new story collection or novel. Virginia got to know Caldwell at his very worst—at his most disheartened and difficult—yet she gradually grew to admire him and his dogged perseverance. She wanted someone to take care of; he was badly in need of her attention.

When Virginia moved to Phoenix, Caldwell was torn by his desire for company and attention and a profound fear of being hurt. But Virginia gradually earned his trust. She made absolutely no demands on him. She did not reprimand him for his drinking, nor did she seem disappointed by his absences or his self-centeredness. When he wanted company she arrived, sunny and attentive; when he wanted silence, she disappeared. At one minute after midnight on New Year's Day, 1957, Caldwell and Virginia were married in Reno, Nevada.

II

CALDWELL'S MARRIAGE TO VIRGINIA coincided with a marked improvement in his financial status. Because *Love and Money* and *Gretta* had sold well in paperback, NAL extended another—albeit more modest—contract. The glut in the Caldwell market seemed to have been absorbed, and new editions of his early classics began to move more quickly from the drugstore racks. By the time of *Gretta's* second printing, Weybright and Enoch were once again optimistic about Caldwell's (and their own) fortunes. They distributed flyers to their Fawcett wholesalers with a cartoon of Caldwell sitting atop a cash register. Below the drawing was the caption: "Undisputed king of all paperbound novelists . . . Largest-selling author of modern novels . . . over 37 million sold." On the other side was a promise: "Unconditionally Guaranteed . . . Sales Profits for All."[5]

In 1957, the Hollywood windfall that Caldwell had dreamt of for years came through when Al Manual closed a deal for a film version of *God's Little Acre*. Caldwell received relatively little in advance for the sale of what NAL called the "best-selling novel in history," but he did retain artistic control of the project and a 25 percent share of all the profits. NAL released a new edition of the novel with a photograph of a passionate love scene on the cover to coincide with the movie, and Caldwell embarked on a 10,000-mile, 38-day, 54-city promotional tour to boost book and ticket sales. When director Anthony Mann's polished, farcical film starring Tina Louise as Griselda, Fay Spain as Darling Jill, Jack Lord as Buck, Buddy Hackett as Pluto Swint, Robert Ryan as

Ty Ty, Vic Morrow as Shaw, and Aldo Ray as Will Thompson was released, the reviews were sensational. So were the lines at the box office. A month after its release, the film was the top-grossing movie in the country and was chosen as an American entry in the Venice Film Festival. Aside from the accolades and the satisfaction, Caldwell received royalty checks of between four and five thousand dollars a week for almost an entire year.

With censorship codes beginning to loosen in the late 1950s, Manual also sold the rights to *Gretta*, and although the film died in production, Caldwell received $25,000. In 1957, Caldwell wrote another novel, *Claudelle Inglish*, described accurately by one reviewer as "a slick melodramatic novel about a Southern country girl, who, after her fiancé has jilted her, goes about seducing every man in town." Although the book was abysmal, the success of *God's Little Acre* enticed Warner Brothers to outbid three other studios and pay Caldwell $45,000 for the story.[6]

By 1960, Caldwell's resurgent popularity brought his sales figures to ever-more staggering heights. Between anthologies, novels, travelogues, and other nonfiction monographs, he had published thirty-eight books, and his domestic sales had reached fifty-five million copies. The preponderance of these books were NAL paperbacks, with *God's Little Acre* leading the way with more than seven million copies sold. Caldwell's popularity abroad also continued to flourish. His work sold best in England, France, and Italy, but by 1961, it had been translated into dozens of other languages, including Bengali, Hungarian, Serbo-Croat, Slovak, Slovene, Turkish, Turkoman, Danish, Icelandic, Hebrew, Japanese, Korean, and Dutch. Official sales abroad were listed at over four million, but hundreds of thousands of pirate editions were also printed each year. When Virginia took on the awesome task of tabulating all of Caldwell's sales, foreign and domestic, hardcover and paperback, in early 1960, she emerged with the remarkable tally of over sixty-one million copies. Caldwell truly was, in the words of the NAL publicity department, "The World's Best-Selling Author!"[7]

Virginia had money of her own, and with Caldwell's paperback sales and movie deals, they were well off. Soon after the marriage they moved to San Francisco, and over the next few years, they lived in a series of houses overlooking San Francisco Bay and the Golden Gate Bridge. Although Caldwell continued to worry about money, they dined out more and more and even bought a new car.

Virginia was so unstinting in her support, so selfless, and so unfailingly optimistic that Caldwell gradually grew to trust her as he had never trusted anyone before. Although she did not push him to socialize, as June and Bourke-White had, she gently persuaded him to go out more, attend concerts and plays, and relax by the pool—things he had not done since the late 1940s, when his marriage with June began to unravel. She sent letters to his children on their birthdays and arranged family reunions at their house. When he slipped into dour moods, she thought of ways to cheer him up. If he began to sulk during a meal or retreat into silence, Virginia flashed him a smile that seemed to soothe him. Caldwell's children marveled not only at their stepmother's patience and dedication, but at her uncanny ability to make their father laugh.[8]

Virginia shared Caldwell's passion for travel, and for the first decade of their marriage, they were away from home three to six months of every year. They took several car trips of over ten thousand miles, maintaining a staggering pace as they traveled across the country. Every day, sometimes twice a day, they stopped at colleges, or libraries, or bookstores, for Caldwell to give a lecture or promote his latest book. Although the publicity department of NAL often set up the itinerary, Virginia took charge of the details, from parking fees to dinner reservations and driving routes. They also voyaged extensively overseas. In 1958, they were in Venice for the film festival where *God's Little Acre* was being screened. The following year they visited London, Madrid, Paris, Lisbon, Rome, Istanbul, and Moscow. In 1960, they were in Japan and the Far East; in 1961, they traveled through Scandinavia from Copenhagen to Stockholm before moving on to Helsinki, Milan, Paris, and London. One year they toured Australia, China, and India; then, six months later, embarked on another ten-country tour of Central Europe.[9]

Although Caldwell and Virginia stayed at the best hotels and dined at the most expensive restaurants, the focus of these trips was still business. Caldwell, with Virginia always by his side, met with agents, translators, publishers, and book retailers in city after city. Some trips —particularly those to Eastern Europe—were designed simply to find a way to spend accumulated currencies. When the Cold War finally abated enough for them to visit Russia in 1959, for instance, they found rubles worth over $20,000 in the state bank. Other tours were arranged by the United States Information Agency, which paid Caldwell's air fare in exchange for his lectures at universities or foreign embassies. Although Caldwell continued to be a poor public speaker, in many foreign countries, particularly in Japan, Russia, Poland, and France, he was met by wildly enthusiastic fans who lined up for hours afterward to receive an autograph or to shake his hand.[10]

III

CALDWELL ALTERNATED THESE TRIPS abroad with his ha-
bitual stints of plodding, self-disciplined work. For five to eight months
a year he retreated to his study and worked eight-hour days, six days
a week. Between 1961 and 1973 he wrote eight new novels. None of
them was very good, and the critics who deigned to review them
shared the appraisal of the St. Louis *Globe-Democrat* writer who thought
they "swim along as smoothly and effortlessly as a comic strip, and at
about the same level." After Caldwell's 1973 novel *Annette* appeared,
the critic for the Chicago *Daily News* wrote sadly, "Poor Annette. Poor
reader. Poor novelist who, having once written well, doesn't know
when to stop." NAL continued to bring out the books in paperback,
and while by the mid-1960s sales had slowed down considerably, they
still earned a profit.[11]

Caldwell and Virginia also collaborated on two travel books, the first
of which followed an almost identical route that Caldwell had taken
with Margaret Bourke-White years before for *Say, Is This the U.S.A.?*
Virginia added lovely line drawings to Caldwell's observations on the
American character made during two nine-thousand-mile car journeys
—the first in 1964, the second ten years later—across the United States.
Caldwell also wrote two children's books, one about a rabbit, the other
about a deer. These works received scattered, politely supportive reviews, although a number of critics who remembered Caldwell's violent grotesques of the 1930s could not help but comment on the strange
phenomenon of such Caldwell titles as *Molly Cottontail* and *The Deer at
Our House.*[12]

There were two exceptions to Caldwell's tide of mediocre work.
The first, published in 1965, was *In Search of Bisco*, a provocative, imaginative, and timely investigation of racial prejudice in the South. In the
1930s, Caldwell's involvement in social issues had inspired his very best
work. Now, thirty years later, the raging civil rights movement engaged
his passionate interest once again. The book told the story of Caldwell's
warm childhood friendship with a black boy named Bisco, and his
efforts to find him again fifty years later. Bisco was probably a fictional
character, but Caldwell's "search" for him in small towns across the
South provided an excellent vehicle for his close observations about
the interaction between Southern blacks and whites. His slow driving
tour through his native region was the first real trip home that he had

made since his father's death twenty years before. When he returned to San Francisco, he wrote a book full of grace and caring, a book that rang with the conviction and energy of his best work.[13]

There was a second flash of bygone quality the following year in a semi-autobiographical work called *Deep South*. Originally titled *In the Shadow of the Steeple*, the book contained smoothly written essays on the history and evolution of white and black religious life in the twentieth-century South. But objective analysis was not Caldwell's first priority. *Deep South* was clearly an expression of his respect, his pride, and his love for his father. He celebrated Ira's conflicts with fundamentalists, with racists, with religious demagogues and con artists, and vindicated him in every battle he had joined during his long ministry. The book was a testimonial, a tribute, and an expression of gratitude. Caldwell had been unable to attend his father's funeral twenty-five years before: *Deep South* was an artistic eulogy for the man who had most inspired him.[14]

IV

BOTH BOOKS RECEIVED GOOD REVIEWS, and Virginia hoped they might spark a revival of critical attention for her husband. They did not. In the 1940s and 1950s, critics had expressed disappointment, even anger, at the mediocrity of Caldwell's post–World War II writing, but by the time *Bisco* and *Deep South* were published, he was rarely mentioned at all. New anthologies of twentieth-century American fiction frequently ignored him, as did critical overviews of twentieth-century authors. While college classes in American literature had once contained a Caldwell story or novel as a matter of course, he was now rarely found on reading lists.[15]

The most striking feature of Caldwell's disappearance from the critical canon was not the scorn and disinterest that met his undeniably mediocre books, but the dismissal of his best—and once highly acclaimed—work as well. Few literary scholars, book reviewers, or academics seemed to share the sentiments of William Faulkner, who in a 1957 seminar at the University of Virginia said, "I think that the first books, *God's Little Acre* and the short stories, that's enough for any man."[16]

Caldwell himself was partly to blame for the critical amnesia. *God's Little Acre, Tobacco Road*, his early anthologies, *You Have Seen Their Faces*—these were the anchor to his standing, but their reputations could not resist the tide of mediocre work that came in their wake. Caldwell was a victim of his own creative idiosyncrasy as well. His best work had been widely praised, but it had also engendered a remarkable degree of critical confusion. Was he a humorist, a social realist, a leftist? What comfortable category might ensure his inclusion in textbooks, anthologies, or college courses? How could he be remembered if he could not be described?

Reputations are created as well as earned, and at the end of his career, Caldwell did not have a hardcover publisher with a long-standing interest in his critical reputation. He did not have an editor who cared enough—had invested enough—to seek retrospective reviews from famous critics, to suggest profiles, to reissue his best work in uniform editions. Maxwell Perkins at Scribner's might have supported and promoted him, but Caldwell had switched to Viking; from there he moved to DS&P and then to Little, Brown. In the sixties, he left Little, Brown for Farrar, Straus & Giroux. Roger Straus and editor Robert Giroux believed in Caldwell, encouraged him, and were instrumental in bringing out *In Search of Bisco*. But when they asked for serious revisions in the manuscript of *Deep South*, Caldwell moved on to another publisher yet again. Virginia was aware, although Caldwell was not, of the painful irony: he spent a lifetime searching for a publisher he could trust, only to alienate those who cared most about him. When he needed help, there was no one there.

Caldwell's pioneering status as an author and promoter of mass-market paperbacks was the most potent ingredient in his critical decline. As Victor Weybright pointed out, "The massive multi-million sales of Caldwell's books gave fastidious critics . . . a hypocritical reason to aver that Caldwell was too successful to be really good." Caldwell first encountered this snobbery in 1948 when he attended a round-table discussion on contemporary American literature at the University of Kansas. On the way to the conference, Caldwell had taken the opportunity—as he almost always did when he traveled—to host a publicity event for NAL in a local drugstore. When he reached the university, he noted an "unmistakable aloofness and coolness" among the participants, who included such eminent critics as Allen Tate and his wife, Caroline Gordon. Caldwell was informed that one of the literature professors at the conference felt that he was "bringing disrepute . . . to the profession of authorship by engaging in an undignified publicity stunt." Another academic thought it was "humiliating to all participants at this conference for one of them to autograph books in a drugstore—and the books being twenty-five cent paperbacks makes the affair even more disgraceful and shameful." Two years later, in *American Writing in the Twentieth Century*, Willard Thorp summarized this broad critical disdain when he noted that "for every American who has read a novel by Eudora Welty there are 10,000 who read Erskine Caldwell."[17]

There was little Caldwell could do about what Weybright termed "the reverse snobbery of critics," for indeed, it was his very best work—*Tobacco Road* and *God's Little Acre*—that sold the most copies for NAL, and not his later novels. But he was indeed complicitous in the NAL marketing campaign that cemented his reputation as a "dirty writer." Although NAL and their artists designed the covers, Caldwell had the right to reject them. He chose not to. *Trouble in July*, the story of a lynching, was, judging from its NAL cover, the story of a rape; *Tobacco Road* and *God's Little Acre*, complex stories of rural deprivation, appeared in many editions to be nothing more than smutty tales of incest and hillbilly hijinks. After World War II, Caldwell wrote novels that almost did justice to their tawdry appearance. Gradually, the difference between the good novels and the bad, the early work and the post–World War II work, was blurred in a sea of lurid covers, provocative blurbs, and record sales figures. In an article for *College English*, Carl Bode lumped *God's Little Acre* with "the rest of Caldwell's hot and shoddy novels." Bode casually explained Caldwell's popularity with the simple conclusion that "sex did the job."[18]

As the years went by, Caldwell watched his mass-market appeal disappear along with his critical reputation. His sales at the New American Library gradually but steadily dwindled, and his rank as America's best-selling author slipped every year. Books about sharecroppers had little meaning to a generation of readers who came of age after the Depression, and the works had no critical reputation to ensure their timelessness. Moreover, the millions who had bought Caldwell's books for their heated sexuality could now find a wide range of far racier titles to choose from. In 1960, James Oliver Brown informed Caldwell that he could no longer afford to represent him. Caldwell's constant demands took up over half of Brown's time, yet the royalties no longer even covered expenses. One by one, his titles fell out of print, until by the mid-1970s only *Tobacco Road* and *God's Little Acre* were still available. Even these classics were issued in ever-smaller numbers, until by 1980 sales were so slow that Virginia did not even bother keeping track of them. There were occasional reissues of anthologies, and one or two commemorative editions of *Trouble in July* and *You Have Seen Their Faces.* "I hate to go to the bookstore any more," Caldwell admitted ruefully. "I hate to see how many of my books aren't there."[19]

Many American writers of high critical standing have lived to see their work fall out of print or their literary reputations decline. Most of Caldwell's left-wing contemporaries suffered such a fate. Many more authors of paperback best-sellers watched as their titles disappeared from the drugstore racks. Caldwell, who had achieved the rare combination of critical acclaim and popular appeal, had the unfortunate experience of losing both.

V

IN THE EARLY 1970S, Caldwell's health began to fail. Fifty years of smoking two packs of cigarettes a day and fifteen years of heavy drinking began to take a toll. In 1973, around the time of his seventieth birthday, Caldwell was diagnosed as having cancer and emphysema, and half of his left lung was removed. Less than a year later, cancer was discovered in his right lung as well. Although doctors wanted to operate right away, Caldwell insisted that he and Virginia finish the work they were doing on their second travel book. Only after completing the 10,000-mile drive did Caldwell check back into the Mayo Clinic for the removal of half his other lung.[20]

Caldwell's doctors were amazed at his stoicism and determination to recover. He never complained about his discomfort or his difficulty breathing, nor did he take the pain-killers they prescribed. He maintained a bitter sense of humor at his own decline. "If I had more lungs," he told one physician, "I'd probably have more cancer." Although the withdrawal was severe, he quit smoking completely and reduced his alcohol intake to one glass of wine a day. His only request was that he be allowed to check out of the hospital as soon as possible so that he could resume his writing.[21]

Caldwell and Virginia left San Francisco and moved to Dunedin, Florida, where the climate would be easier on his lungs. Although he was easily fatigued, Caldwell was soon back at work. He secluded himself in the study and completed the text for the travel book that Virginia was illustrating. When this was completed and the manuscript had been accepted at Dodd, Mead publishers, he found other things to do. There were still books in print overseas, sporadic interest from television or film producers, commemorative issues of *God's Little Acre*, and new stage productions of *Tobacco Road*. Caldwell watched over every detail, as he always had. He wrote letters to his new agent, made copies of old manuscripts for possible publication, and answered the sprinkling of fan mail that he still received. Although the doctors advised against it, Caldwell insisted on taking several trips abroad, where he and Virginia made their familiar rounds of foreign publishers, editors, and translators.

Caldwell's physicians told him that he would be fortunate to live for five years after his second lung operation, but with every checkup they revised their prognosis. Each year that he lived, Caldwell was rewarded with flashes of critical appreciation and acknowledgment. Abroad, where critics had always been kinder, Caldwell was honored with several awards for lifetime achievement. In 1981, he was accorded Poland's highest mark of literary achievement, the Order of Cultural Merit. Two years later on the other side of Europe, France bestowed the prestigious rank of Commander of the Order of Arts and Letters. In 1982, he was invited to Japan—where twenty of his books and ninety-five of his short stories had been translated—to address the inaugural meeting of the Erskine Caldwell Literary Society.[22]

In the early 1970s, a writer for the *Atlanta Constitution* began an article with the words: "Erskine Caldwell. There. We've said it. Not so very long ago any Georgian pronouncing that name might have been run out of the state on a rail. If he were lucky." By the mid-1970s, Caldwell was witness to a remarkable softening of attitudes in his native region. The University of Georgia and the University of Virginia, which had ignored—and been embarrassed by—Caldwell's work for forty years, now fought to claim him as their own. In 1977, the library at the University of Georgia bought a huge collection of his books and commemorated the event by staging a production of *Tobacco Road* on campus. The following year, the University of Virginia sponsored a seventy-fifth birthday party for Caldwell, and the alumni association finally acknowledged his attendance at the school. "Not only can he go home again," wrote a reporter for the *New York Times* in an article entitled "Caldwell Rehabilitated," "but he is also urgently sought." The University of Georgia produced a documentary, "In Search of Caldwell's Georgia," for public television, and in May 1985, he and several other Georgia authors were honored at the university's "Roots in Georgia" literary conference. Although the citizens of Wrens old enough to remember the publication of Caldwell's work in the 1930s never forgave him, younger residents greeted him warmly when he visited the local library. In Moreland, Georgia, plans were begun to save the house where Caldwell was born for a museum dedicated to their most famous citizen.[23]

Caldwell also lived long enough to see glimmers of a growing critical appreciation in the academic community. His sales were still terrible, and most of his books were out of print, but by the late 1970s, enough time had passed since his mediocre output of the two previous decades to allow some clear-eyed appreciation of his best work. The first monograph on Caldwell's complete body of work, *Erskine Caldwell*, was published in 1969, but although the author, James Korges, made an excellent case for Caldwell's lasting value, little scholarship followed in its wake. Between 1979 and 1984, however, a collection of essays, a short critical biography, and a flurry of academic articles appeared. A manuscript for one complete biography was nearing completion and another was begun. *Pembroke Magazine* released a commemorative issue dedicated to Caldwell, and the first bibliography of Caldwell's short fiction was published. He was increasingly in demand at writers' conferences, many of which he attended, and he was greatly honored when Dartmouth College invited him to serve a brief term as a writer-in-residence.[24]

In 1978, Caldwell and Virginia were invited to the White House by Jimmy Carter. A few years later in Arizona (to which the Caldwells had recently returned), Governor Bruce Babbitt declared November 1982 Erskine Caldwell Month. The most significant and most gratifying honor came in 1984 when Caldwell was elected (along with Norman Mailer) to the American Academy of Arts and Letters. In his induction tribute, John Hersey compared reading Caldwell to "diving deep into a vivid dream" and described his work as "balanced on a razor's edge between hilarity and horror . . . told in a quiet conversational voice, which speaks in the rhythms of truth."[25]

In 1982, Virginia began making plans for Caldwell's eightieth birthday party. Without her husband's knowledge, she sent notes to a wide range of authors and asked them to share their thoughts about Erskine Caldwell. Although Virginia had suspected that many of the writers she contacted had been influenced by his work, she was still astonished by the response.

Norman Mailer wrote that Caldwell was one of his "first literary heroes and always one of the best." William Styron described Caldwell as a "great creative presence whose wise, funny, sad, revealing books are an inspiration to the writers who have followed." John Updike recalled that he had read *The Sacrilege of Alan Kent* at the age of fifteen and that Caldwell's books "popped my eyes wide open . . . and lent courage to all of us who would like to describe life in America as it is." There were other moving testimonials from Ralph Ellison, Kurt Vonnegut, Edward Albee, and Art Buchwald. Vonnegut told Caldwell that he had "used your writings all my life as if they were wise and amusing and strong words from an encouraging older brother." He credited Caldwell for helping to "pull off a revolution in American literature as liberating and radical as what the cubists did for painters at the turn of the century." Saul Bellow included a note to Virginia saying. "I thought your husband should have won the Nobel Prize. A great many readers would have rejoiced at such an award."[26]

Caldwell never expressed emotion easily. But as he flipped through the pages of the two-volume scrapbook on the eve of his eightieth birthday, his hand shook, and tears welled in his eyes. He did not say anything to Virginia, but he held her gaze for a long, long time.

VI

IN 1985, ERSKINE CALDWELL began work on an autobiography that he knew would be his final book. He was eighty-one years old, and age and ill health had taken their toll. Although no new cancer had been found in his lungs, his emphysema continued to make breathing difficult. Occasionally, he ran very high fevers for no apparent reason, and his blood chemistry continued to worry his doctors. His blue eyes had lost their spark, his hands trembled continuously, and when he was in the presence of anyone but Virginia, he kept them clasped self-consciously in his lap.

Yet Caldwell wrote as he always had—with a relentless and determined regularity. At nine o'clock each morning he entered his study, sat down at the immaculate desk, and scrolled a piece of yellow paper into the typewriter. With a dog-eared Webster's dictionary at hand, he began to write, laying each completed page on the floor by his feet. He emerged at noon to eat lunch, and an hour later he was back at work, not breaking again until dinner was served at six. At the end of each day he placed a neat pile of typed manuscript pages in the top right drawer, returned the dictionary to its appointed space on the shelf, and swept the desk clear of any accumulated dust. This was a formula that had produced over fifty books and one hundred short stories. Age and illness could not alter the habits of a lifetime.

The phone never rang and people rarely visited, because Caldwell occasionally made scenes when his work was interrupted. Sometimes

Virginia made quick trips to the grocery store, but otherwise she did not leave the house. Caldwell had trouble writing when she was gone for even a few minutes; over the previous few years he had grown terribly afraid, for no good reason, that she would never come back.[27]

Caldwell worked on the manuscript through the summer and the following fall. After ten months of determined labor the book was completed and he titled it, appropriately, *With All My Might*. He sent it off to the publishers, and in July he and Virginia took a well-deserved vacation in Florida.

A few weeks later, Caldwell developed a bad cold that turned into pneumonia. He and Virginia flew home to Phoenix, where Caldwell checked into the hospital for six days until his temperature came down. His physicians suspected that his cancer had reappeared, but the first chest X rays were negative. A second set of test results in September, however, was not. Caldwell was diagnosed with oat cell carcinoma, a virulent and inoperable form of lung cancer. Virginia was in the room with him when his doctor said bluntly, "This time you've got a bad one. It goes like wildfire."[28]

Caldwell's first response was frustration that his illness would interfere with his plans to visit Paris where *With All My Might* was scheduled for release. But within days, Caldwell had begun chemotherapy, sometimes at the hospital, where the staff put a cot in the room for Virginia, other times in the office of their family physician.

Lung specialists estimated that Caldwell would live a month. But as the days went by, they revised their prognoses. A stubborn, stoic pride kept Caldwell going. When Virginia offered to bring him breakfast in bed he refused. "If you stay in bed one day," he told her, "then it's going to be the next day, and then you won't get up again." He moved about the house slowly but steadily, breathing through a long plastic oxygen tube connected to a rolling tank. He continued to keep up with his bills and publication contracts, and when his hands became too shaky to write, he rolled checks painfully into his typewriter. He insisted on dressing and shaving himself; he continued to reject the painkillers that were prescribed for him.[29]

Although he was self-conscious about his diminished appearance, Caldwell granted interviews with reporters. Wearing a stocking cap to cover his balding head, but sitting proudly in a jacket and tie, Caldwell spoke with Charles Truehart of the *Washington Post* and another reporter from *USA Today*. Both men were moved by the incredible will of the man they saw before them. "The voice was still strong, gruff and inflected with the grit of his East Georgia childhood," Truehart later wrote. "But the blue eyes were pale and watery, the weathered hands trembled in each other's grip, from time to time Caldwell's head sank to his chest in weary distraction."[30]

In March, Caldwell received a huge and final dose of chemotherapy. He lost the rest of his hair and grew too weak to walk on his own; although he insisted on getting out of bed every morning, Virginia's son Drew had to carry him to the wheelchair. Caldwell maintained his wry, macabre sense of humor in spite of the indignities of his condition. When Virginia asked him if wished to be cremated, a choice he had expressed years earlier, he said no. "Probably," Caldwell told her, "the best thing to do would be to find a shovel, find a dead-end street, and dig a hole." When she responded "A dead-end street?" he replied smiling, "Well, isn't that appropriate?"[31]

For a while in late March, it looked as though the chemotherapy had been effective and the cancer's growth stopped. "We actually got happy for a while," Virginia recalled. "We thought we were beating it." They drank champagne and toasted his recovery. But three weeks later, Caldwell's fever, his coughing, his shortness of breath returned. On a Wednesday morning in early April, Virginia dressed and shaved him and wheeled him to breakfast. After a few minutes he looked at her in amazement and said, "I'm going to have to go back to bed." Two nights later, Virginia went to him in the middle of the night. His fingers and toes were turning blue, but he was burning with fever. Virginia called their next-door neighbor, a physician, and said, "I'm frightened, I think Erskine is much worse tonight." When Caldwell saw the doctor enter the room, he mumbled something unintelligible. The man bent down to hear better, and Caldwell said, "What are you charging for house calls?"[32]

The next day, April 11, 1987, Virginia sat with her husband of thirty years while he tossed and turned with fever and pain. As his strength was ebbing she said, "I truly believe there is a heaven, and, with the good you have done with your writing, that you're going to be there." She asked him if he believed her, and he nodded yes. As his wife held his hand, Erskine Caldwell died at the age of eighty-three.[33]

EPILOGUE

WITH ALL MY MIGHT was published in France by Belfond and in the United States by a small Georgia press, Peachtree Publishers, Ltd.[1]

Like most autobiographies, the book is a study in selective and creative remembrance and represents a lifetime of wishful thinking hardened into fact. Most of the chapters steam along under their own cheerful, rose-tinted momentum. Caldwell's lonely, hardscrabble childhood seems somehow charming, as do his dogged efforts to be published and the personal failures that accompanied them. He writes contentedly of the critical acclaim that came with the publication of *Tobacco Road* and of the Broadway adaptation that brought him notoriety and sudden wealth. The exhausting censorship battles over *God's Little Acre*, his marriages to Helen, Margaret Bourke-White, and June, the years in Hollywood, the incredible paperback sales that made him the "World's Best-Selling Author!"—they all seem part of a merry, rollicking journey. *With All My Might* is written by a stubborn, proud old man, who pointedly reminds the reader that Erskine Caldwell, son of a poor Southern minister, had once been a very important person.[1]

But Caldwell's tale loses momentum as it crosses a hazy line in the late 1940s. He does not acknowledge the decreasing quality of his work, or the critics and fans who came to scorn and finally ignore him. For how could this part of his life be reconciled with the tumultuous, surprising, and ascendant marvel of his early career? Indeed, how could he relive the excruciating process of losing eminence, of losing confidence, which marked his final forty years?

From the first bright rays of dawn to the shade of evening, the day is done. . . . I accept my own failings together with the knowledge that my writings and I must exist with all our imperfections to the end of my time.[2]

As he wrote these final words in his final book, Erskine Caldwell surely marveled at his remarkable, careening odyssey. His career, he well knew, was a story of bright, stunning success and slow, agonizing decline. But if Caldwell was painfully aware of the "imperfections" in his life and work, he also was proud—and rightfully so—of what he had achieved.

NOTE ON SOURCES

An author who writes not one, but two, autobiographies would seem to provide an embarrassment of riches for a prospective biographer. Unfortunately, both *Call it Experience* (New York: Duell, Sloan and Pearce, 1951) and *With All My Might* (Atlanta: Peachtree Publishers, 1987) are obviously the works of an author of fiction. I have used them cautiously and only in conjunction with other, independent evidence.

More useful to a biographer is Caldwell's 1968 book *Deep South* (New York: Weybright & Talley, 1968). Designed, ostensibly, as an investigation of evangelical religion in that region of the country, the work makes only a token effort at serious historical analysis. It is largely a tribute to Caldwell's father—a minister for fifty years, and his single greatest inspiration. While the book suffers from an understandable personal bias, it sheds a great deal of light on the author's childhood and the roots of his social conscience.

Very little of Caldwell's fiction is manifestly autobiographical. His most significant protagonists are indigent farmers and dispossessed mill workers, and a biographer is spared the dilemma of separating narrative invention from fact. There is one notable exception. In 1930, Caldwell finished the "prose-poem" entitled *The Sacrilege of Alan Kent* (Portland: Falmouth Book House, 1936). Written in elegant, abstract language by an as-yet-unknown author, it contains passages of chilling and heart-wrenching honesty. No other source, published or unpublished, better conveys the overwhelming loneliness that pervaded Caldwell's early life.

Such evocative, lyrical work offers, by its very nature, little in the way of hard biographical fact. Here, I have relied heavily on the enormous collection of Caldwell material housed in The Baker Library at Dartmouth College. The last of over seventy linear feet of primary material was deposited upon the author's death in 1987, and I was fortunate to enjoy complete access to this remarkable collection. It

represents a lifetime of accumulated paper in every imaginable form—
from the most intimate love letters to the dry miscellany of canceled
checks and shopping lists.

Caldwell employed a clipping service from almost the moment of
his first publication to the week of his death. The accumulated press
accounts (including reviews of all his work) fill forty scrapbooks and
provide an invaluable overview of his long and checkered career. These
too are housed at Dartmouth. The collection also contains much of
Caldwell's work in both manuscript and final form, although there is
precious little difference between the two.

The Dartmouth papers are less useful in understanding Caldwell's
life before he was a published artist. The Ira Sylvester Caldwell papers
at the University of Georgia in Athens contain letters from Erskine to
his parents that are a great help in this regard. The Atcheson L. Hench
papers at the University of Virginia in Charlottesville supply a candid
look at Caldwell's erratic and undistinguished career at that institution.

For information surrounding the publication of Caldwell's books, the
papers of his second literary agent, James Oliver Brown, located in
the Butler Library at Columbia University, are extensive and detailed.
The New American Library collection at the Elmer H. Holmes Bobst
Library at New York University shed light on Caldwell's relationship
with New American Library—an association that brought him untold
riches but may have helped ruin his critical reputation. A far more
wholesome partnership is revealed in Caldwell's correspondence with
Maxwell Perkins and John Hall Wheelock housed in the archives of
Charles Scribner's & Sons in the Firestone Library at Princeton
University.

The Margaret Bourke-White collection at Syracuse University provides a complete picture of Caldwell's steamy and tumultuous relationship with that eminent photographer. Bourke-White's autobiography,
Portrait of Myself (New York: Simon & Schuster, 1967), although not
nearly so revealing as her papers, is surprisingly generous in her remembrances of a "fascinating, gifted, difficult man . . . whose insecurity
finally acted as blind against the world." The best portrait of Margaret
Bourke-White is Vickie Goldberg's *Margaret Bourke-White* (New York:
Harper & Row, 1986).

Cataloguing the published works on Caldwell himself is far too easy.
Professor William A. Sutton of Ball State University spent three years
in intensive research on Caldwell, from 1970 to 1973. Of greatest value
are the interviews and correspondence he conducted with Caldwell's
friends, family, and business associates, many of whom are now de-

ceased. His frank discussions with Caldwell's first wife, Helen Caldwell Cushman, are the best single source on that remarkable woman. Professor Sutton has generously donated both his research materials and his unpublished eight-hundred-page manuscript to the Special Collections Library at the University of Illinois at Urbana-Champaign.

Professor Harvey Klevar of Luther College in Decorah, Iowa, has published *Erskine Caldwell: A Biography* (Knoxville: University of Tennessee Press, 1993). Professor Klevar has kindly donated some of his research material to the collection at Dartmouth. Although I have not read his completed work, I have benefited from his research.

There is only slightly more published material on Caldwell's work. James E. Devlin's *Erskine Caldwell* (Boston: Twayne Publishers, 1984) is a useful introduction to the basic outlines of Caldwell's life and works. James Korges' pamphlet "Erskine Caldwell" (Minneapolis: University of Minnesota Press, 1969) is a perceptive, if slightly adulatory, analysis. The racial theme in Caldwell's fiction is treated in William A. Sutton's *Black Like It Is/Was* (Metuchen, N.J.: Scarecrow Press, 1974). A compendium of critical essays, *Erskine Caldwell Revisited* (Jackson: University Press of Mississippi, 1990) first appeared as an issue of *The Southern Quarterly* (Spring, 1989). Scott MacDonald's *Critical Essays on Erskine Caldwell* (Boston: G. K. Hall & Co., 1981) is extremely useful as well. Edwin T. Arnold has edited a collection of Caldwell's interviews— varying only in their degree of misdirection—entitled *Conversations with Erskine Caldwell* (Jackson: University of Mississippi Press). Sylvia Cook's *Erskine Caldwell and the Fiction of Poverty* (L.S.U. Press, 1992) provides the first full-scale critical monograph on Caldwell's enormous body of writing. The most complete listings of critical articles—the best of which were written before 1941—can be found in the appendixes of Cook's and Devlin's works mentioned above.

There is no comprehensive bibliography of Caldwell's work in print. The most complete is Scott MacDonald's "Erskine Caldwell" in *First Printings of American Authors* (Detroit: 1978). Both the University of Georgia and Dartmouth College have generated exhaustive computer listings accessible to interested scholars. An excellent listing of Caldwell's short fiction is provided by Scott MacDonald's "An Evaluative Check-List of Erskine Caldwell's Short Fiction" (*Studies in Short Fiction* 15 [1978]: 81–97).

Perhaps the best source for understanding Erskine Caldwell lies in the memories of those who knew him. The finest collection of this interview material—both on tape and in transcript form—is located in the William A. Sutton Collection at the University of Illinois at Urbana-

Champaign. I have augmented (and sometimes duplicated) this remarkable collection with over two hundred additional interviews
conducted in person, by phone, and through the mail over the last two
years. From his first baby-sitters to the physicians who sat at his death-
bed, from literary agents to clandestine lovers, I have attempted to
better understand this complicated man.

NOTES

ABBREVIATIONS USED IN NOTES

MA	Milton Abernethy, editor of *Contempo* magazine
MA-UT	Milton Abernethy Papers, The Harry T. Ransom Humanities Library, University of Texas, Austin, Texas
ALH-UVA	Atcheson L. Hench Papers, Alderman Library, Special Collections Department, University of Virginia, Charlottesville, Virginia
HLC	Helen Lannigan Caldwell, Erskine's first wife
ISC	Ira Sylvester Caldwell, Erskine's father
ISC-UGA	Ira Sylvester Caldwell Papers, Hargrett Rare Books and Manuscripts Library, The University of Georgia Libraries, Athens, Georgia
CPC	Carolina Preston Caldwell, Erskine's mother
EC	Erskine Caldwell
EC-DC	Erskine Caldwell Collection, Special Collections, Baker Library, Dartmouth College, Hanover, New Hampshire
EC-UVA	Erskine Caldwell Papers, Alderman Library, Special Collections Department, University of Virginia, Charlottesville, Virginia
VC	Virginia Caldwell Hibbs, Caldwell's fourth wife
FD-EU	Frank Daniel Papers, Special Collections Library, Robert W. Woodruff Library, Emory University, Atlanta, Georgia
JOB	James Oliver Brown, Caldwell's second literary agent
RJ	Richard Johns, editor of *Pagany* magazine
RJ-UD	Archives of Pagany Magazine, Special Collections, The University of Delaware Library, Newark, Delaware
JJ	June Johnson Caldwell Martin, Caldwell's third wife
GL	Gordon Lewis, owner of the New Dominion Bookstore in Charlottesville, and a close friend
GL-UVA	Gordon Lewis Papers, Waller Barrett Collection, Alderman Library, Special Collections Department, University of Virginia, Charlottesville, Virginia
DM	Dan Miller (used for private correspondence and interviews with author)
AM	Alfred Morang, Caldwell's close friend in Portland
AM-HU	The Alfred Morang Papers, Houghton Library, Harvard University, Cambridge, Massachusetts

NAL-NYU   The New American Library Papers, Fales Library, Elmer Holmes
           Bobst Library, New York University, New York, New York
MP   Maxwell Perkins, one of Caldwell's editors at Scribner's
EC-PU   The Erskine Caldwell letters; published with permission of the
           Manuscripts Division, Department of Rare Books and Special
           Collections, Princeton University Libraries, Princeton University,
           Princeton, New Jersey
ILS   I. L. Salomon
ILS-LOC   I. L. Salomon Papers, Collections of the Manuscript Division, Li-
           brary of Congress, Washington, D.C.
WS   William Sutton, previous Caldwell biographer
WS-UI   William Sutton Collection, Rare Books and Special Collections, the
           University of Illinois at Urbana-Champaign, Urbana, Illinois
JHW   John Hall Wheelock, one of Caldwell's editors at Scribner's
MBW   Margaret Bourke-White
MBW-SU   Margaret Bourke-White Collection, Syracuse University Library,
           Department of Special Collections, Syracuse University, Syracuse,
           New York

Phillip Cronenwett and his fine staff at Dartmouth College's Baker Library helped
me mine the huge collection of Caldwell materials located there. I am grateful to a
number of other libraries as well: The Harry T. Ransom Humanities Library, University of Texas, Austin, Texas; Hench-Caldwell Collection (#9150), Manuscripts Division, Alderman Library, Special Collections Department, and the Atcheson L. Hench
Oral History (RG-26), University Archives, University of Virginia, Charlottesville,
Virginia; Ira Sylvester Caldwell Papers, Hargrett Rare Books and Manuscripts Library, The University of Georgia Libraries, Athens, Georgia; Special Collections Department, Robert W. Woodruff Library, Emory University, Atlanta, Georgia; Special
Collections, The University of Delaware Library, Newark, Delaware; Houghton Library, Harvard University, Cambridge, Massachusetts; Fales Library, Elmer Holmes
Bobst Library, New York University, New York, New York; Firestone Library, Princeton University, Princeton, New Jersey; Collections of the Manuscript Division, Library of Congress, Washington, D.C.; William A. Sutton Collection, The Rare Books
and Special Collections Library, The University of Illinois at Urbana-Champaign, Urbana, Illinois; Syracuse University Library, Department of Special Collections, Syracuse University, Syracuse, New York; James Oliver Brown Papers, Rare Books and
Manuscript Library, Butler Library, Columbia University, New York, New York.

PREFACE

1. Malcolm Cowley to EC, 3 June 1970, EC-DC; William Soskin, *New York Post*,
    12 February 1932; Kenneth White, "American Humor," *Nation*, 6 July 1932;
    Baltimore Sun, 20 February 1932.

CHAPTER ONE: THE LESSONS OF CHILDHOOD

1. Interview with Miss Mary Maner, 24 January 1991; interview with Mrs. Hen-
    rietta Boyce, 25 January 1991; interview with Mr. C. W. Stephens, 15 January
    1991. Almost everyone I spoke with commented on Ira Sylvester Caldwell's
    restlessness and energy. A similar portrait is offered in Erskine Caldwell, *Deep
    South* (New York: Weybright & Talley, 1968). The best photographs of Ira
    can be found in "Photo File," EC-DC.

2. *Augusta Chronicle*, 7 September 1931. Erskine's father wrote a daily column for the *Chronicle* for a number of years. This is the only one that makes a direct autobiographical reference. For biographical information on Ira Sylvester Caldwell I have drawn heavily on a letter from CPC to Robert Cantwell, 23 August 1950, EC-DC. See also Erskine Caldwell's *Deep South* for a useful if sentimental treatment. For insight into Ira's personality, I have benefited greatly from an interview with Miss Mary Maner, 17 January 1991, and a letter from Mary T. Cochrane to DM, 28 December 1990.

3. I have received a great deal of help from both ministers and members of the A.R.P. Church. The following have provided particularly useful correspondence; Thomas Stewart to DM, 6 November 1990; Kate Stewart to DM, 4 January 1991; Mrs. Mary T. Baker to DM, 16 January 1991. I have also benefited from interviews with theologians at Erskine Theological Seminary, particularly Dr. Benjamin Farley, chairman of the Bible Department, 15 January 1991; Dr. Lowry Ware, professor of religious history, 15 January 1991; and Dr. Raymond King, professor of religion, 15 January 1991. For the best published history of the A.R.P. Church, see Ray A. King, *A History of the A.R.P. Church* (Charlotte: Board of Christian Education of the A.R.P. Church, 1966). Excellent discussions of the cultural milieu of the denomination are found in Kate Stewart, "Little Benjamin Goes West: A.R.P. in Drew County," *Drew County Historical Journal*, 1990; Benjamin Farley, "Erskine Caldwell: Preacher's Son and Southern Prophet," *Journal of Presbyterian History*, Fall, 1978.

4. Transcript and registration material for Ira Sylvester Caldwell, Erskine College Registrar's Office, Due West, South Carolina; CPC to Robert Cantwell, 23 August 1950, EC-DC; *Erskine College Yearbook*, 1897, Erskine College Library. For information on Ira's college activities I am also grateful to Dr. Lowry Ware of Erskine College. Interview with Dr. Lowry Ware, 15 January 1991.

5. The story of Ira and Carrie's meeting was widely known in the A.R.P. community of White Oak, Georgia, Ira Sylvester Caldwell's first post. Interview with Miss Janie Walthall, 21 January 1991; interview with Miss Nancy Bowers, 21 January 1991. For photographs of Erskine's mother at this age, see "Photo File," EC-DC.

6. CPC to Robert Cantwell, 23 July 1950, EC-DC.

7. I have assembled a portrait of Erskine's mother from a variety of sources: CPC to EC, July 1952, EC-DC; J. Roy McCracken to EC, 15 December 1944, EC-DC; Mary Maner interview with Professor Wayne Mixon, 25 May 1990, tape in EC-DC; Family tree of the Bell family, undated, ms 1156, ISC-UGA. I am indebted to Miss Mary Maner for further information on the Bell family genealogy.

8. Mrs. Fannie Strauss to WS, 4 November 1970, WS-UI; A. L. Booth to WS, 15 October 1970, WS-UI. These two letters provide an excellent overview of the curriculum at Mary Baldwin College. Carrie's Star Medal for excellence is located at the ISC-UGA.

9. I have read countless letters from Erskine's parents to their son that have contributed to my understanding of their personalities. I have also benefited from the following interviews: Miss Mary Maner, 21 January 1991; Miss Janie Walthall, 20 January 1991; Mrs. Henrietta Boyce, 23 January 1991; Mr. Ralph Stephens, 15 January 1991. Erskine Caldwell's *Call It Experience* (New York:

Duell, Sloan & Pearce, 1951) and *With All My Might* (Atlanta, Peachtree Publishers, 1987) provide useful character sketches of his parents. For a more impressionistic portrait, see Erskine Caldwell, *Sacrilege of Alan Kent* (Portland: Falmouth Book House, 1936).

10. Later in life, Ira complained of a war injury that limited the flexibility in his right wrist. There is no other evidence that he was ever wounded.

11. Mrs. W. J. Wren to WS, 20 August 1970, WS-UI; Mrs. June Johnson Caldwell to DM, 9 January 1991; WS interview with Mrs. Lucille Josey, 2 November 1990, transcript at WS-UI; WS interview with Erskine Caldwell, 19 December 1971, transcript at WS-UI. The silver sugar spoon is now in the possession of Mrs. June Johnson Caldwell.

12. Interview with Miss Nancy Bowers, 21 January 1991. Miss Bowers's mother served as midwife for the delivery. There has been some disagreement over the year of Erskine's birth. I have relied on the oral testimonies of citizens of White Oak who swear he was born in 1903. A Georgia census for the year 1910 indicates that this is correct.

13. For life in White Oak at this time, I have relied heavily on interviews with Miss Janie Walthall, 21 January 1991; Miss Nancy Bowers, 21 January 1991; Mr. Lamar Lewis, 25 January 1991. See also L. B. Walthall to EC 21 January 1965, EC-DC; Blanche Bowers Hemphill to EC, 25 May 1950, EC-DC.

14. The manse is still in existence, though it has been moved to nearby Moreland, Georgia. I am indebted to Winston Skinner at the *Newnan Times-Herald*, who showed me photographs of the manse from that period. For a full description of the manse and the efforts to restore it, see *Newnan-Times Herald*, 25 May 1990.

15. For the official summary of Ira Sylvester Caldwell's early career, see *The Centennial History of the A.R.P. Church* (Charleston: Walker, Evans and Cogswell, 1905). See also CPC to Robert Cantwell, 23 August 1950, EC-DC; Blanche Bowers Hemphill to EC, 10 October 1958, EC-DC; CPC to EC, 25 May 1958, EC-DC; Mrs. W. J. Wren to WS, 20 August 1970, WS-UI.

16. CPC to EC, 25 May 1958, EC-DC.

17. Interview with Miss Janie Walthall, 21 January 1991; CPC to Robert Cantwell, 23 August 1950, EC-DC.

18. Interview with Miss Janie Walthall, 21 January 1991; interview with Miss Nancy Bowers, 21 January 1991. See also Mrs. H. A. Phagan to WS, 11 October 1970, WS-UI; Miss Mary Stephens to WS, 30 December 1970, WS-UI; Virginia Caldwell to WS, January 8, 1971, WS-UI. For an excellent series of interviews with citizens of White Oak who remember Erskine's birth and early childhood, see *Newnan Times-Herald*, 6 July 1978. Of particular value are the recollections of Miss Eunice Chesnutt, who was Erskine's babysitter when he was one to three years old.

The psychological insights contained in this chapter are of such a broad and intuitive nature that I have cited no particular text. I have benefited, however, from the expertise of a number of psychologists specializing in early childhood and adolescent development. I am particularly indebted to Dr. Gail Hornstein, professor of Psychology at Mount Holyoke College, and Dr. Margaret Miller.

19. Virginia Caldwell Hibbs to WS, 6 September 1970, WS-UI; June Johnson Caldwell to DM, 9 January 1991; Blanche Bowers Hemphill to EC, 10 November 1950, DC-EC.

Carrie was manifesting a long-standing ambivalence towards motherhood (only intensified by her painful experience with childbirth) in these alternating waves of overprotectiveness and apparent indifference. It seems that these mixed messages were not lost on the toddling child. Throughout his life Erskine Caldwell fought the suspicion that those closest to him were destined to betray him; that he could not depend on the people whom he loved to be there when he needed them. It is also no wonder that through three painful divorces he manifested a particular mistrust of women.

20. There are numerous accounts of this tragedy. Everyone in White Oak remembers the event well, but I am particularly indebted to Miss Janie Walthall, whose mother nursed the injured child. For the most graphic account, see *The Sacrilege of Alan Kent*, p. 8. See also, Virginia Caldwell to WS, 8 January 1971, WS-UI.

21. WS interview with Helen Caldwell, 4 July 1970, WS-UI. Caldwell's first wife had excellent insight into her husband's childhood. I am particularly indebted to Dr. Margaret Miller for her expertise in the psychological ramifications of early childhood and adolescent trauma.

Though there is no direct evidence, any child who suffers such a remarkable number of accidents must be considered a possible victim of intentional abuse. In any case, it is clear that Caldwell harbored deep feelings of resentment and rage towards his mother.

22. JJ to DM, 9 January 1991. Carrie made a number of references to the "women's problems" that followed Erskine's birth.

23. *With All My Might*, p. 8.

24. I am indebted to two long-time residents of Prosperity, South Carolina, for their memories and photographs. Interview with Mrs. David Bedenbaugh, 10 February 1991; interview with Mr. Dove Connelly, 12 February 1991. For Erskine's own description of the town of Prosperity, see *With All My Might*, pp. 9–10.

25. I am indebted to Reverend Gary L. Pierstorff, current pastor of the Prosperity A.R.P. church, for the use of his photographs, and access to the records of that small congregation. See also Erskine's own description of the manse in *With All My Might*, p. 11. It is remarkably accurate.

26. Mrs. Dallas Caldwell to CPC, undated 1944, ISC-UGA, box 2; Reverend Gary L. Pierstorff to DM, 24 January 1991; June Johnson Caldwell to DM, 9 January 1991; Mrs. Wilson C. Brown to WS, 9 December 1970, WS-UI; Dr. Hattie Mae Carmichael to WS, 31 December 1970, WS-UI. For the official account of Ira's career during these years, see *The Sesquicentennial History of the A.R.P. Church* (Clinton, S.C.: Jacobs Brothers Press, 1951).

27. Interview with Miss Mary Maner, 21 January 1991; *With All My Might*, p. 13.

28. Helen Caldwell interview with Harvey Klevar, 28 June 1978, EC-DC; Helen Caldwell interview with WS, 4 July 1970, WS-UI; Mary Maner interview with Harvey Klevar, 21 January 1979, EC-DC. See also "Aunt Emma" to EC, 19 June 1941, Margaret Bourke-White Collection, Syracuse University, box one.

29. Hubert Bedenbaugh to WS, 23 June 1970, WS-UI; Helen Caldwell to WS, 6 September 1970, WS-UI; EC to WS, 12 December 1971, WS-UI. In all his autobiographical writings, Erskine laments his mother's refusal to allow him to attend school. See particularly *With All My Might*, p. 11.

30. It is critical to remember that Carrie was not solely responsible for her son's upbringing. Therapists are careful to avoid "mother bashing" in instances

when a father's absence has placed the entire burden of child-rearing on the
mother. This objectivity, understandably, is often not shared by the child
himself.

31. In his novels, Caldwell's insecurity is apparent in the host of female characters who bow helplessly to the overwhelming sexual magnetism of men.
In love letters, he filled pages with awkward boasts of previous sexual conquests. His wives were deluged with pleas for reassurance and demands for
total control. At the age of fifty, he was still serving as a judge for the Miss
Nude America Contest and taking swaggering satisfaction in entertaining
guests at Playboy Clubs. The love letters between Erskine and his first wife,
Helen Caldwell, are particularly revealing in this regard. See box marked
"Helen," EC-DC.

32. Interview with Miss Mary Maner, 21 January 1991. See also, R. C. Kennedy
to WS, 21 October 1970, WS-UI; EC to "Grandma Bell," 18 January 1911,
EC-DC.

33. Interview with Dove Connelly, 12 February 1991. Erskine describes both incidents in brutal, violent language in *The Sacrilege of Alan Kent*, pp. 8–9.

34. Interview with Miss Mary Maner, 24 January 1991. For the official account
of the fire see *Newberry Observer*, 12 January 1908.

35. JJ to DM, 9 January 1991.

36. *The Sacrilege of Alan Kent*, p. 11.

37. Caldwell's relationships, both personal and professional, would always be
characterized by his need to regulate the circumstances and people around
him. Fearful of the unknown around every corner, he sought desperately to
preempt betrayals of every kind. If his editors wrung their hands over his
obsessive involvement with publication details, if his children rebelled against
an unrelenting and at times sadistic demand for obedience, if friends laughed
when he sent notes to confirm a lunch date six months in advance—they
did not understand the history behind his behavior.

38. For an evocative account of how Ira's new job affected Erskine, see *Deep
South*, pp. 15–16. I am indebted to Dr. Ray King, professor of religious history
at Erskine College, for helping me better understand the function of the
Secretary of Home Missions.

39. The Staunton City Directory for 1912 lists the Caldwell's address as 16 Han-
cock Street, the Bell family home. For the remainder of this period, they
lived in residences attached to the church, and are therefore unlisted. I am
grateful to the pastors of the A.R.P. churches in Timber Ridge, Virginia;
Bradley, South Carolina; and Charlotte, North Carolina, for giving me access
to their church records in my effort to date the Caldwells' various stays in
these communities. I have also benefited from the chronology of Ira's career
in the *Sesquicentennial History of the A.R.P. Church*.

40. *With All My Might*, pp. 20–21. I am grateful to Virginia Caldwell for lending
me a photograph of Erskine at this age.

41. Even if Carrie had been enthusiastic about a more formal education for her
son, their frequent moves made it difficult to establish any consistent attendance. T. S. McSwain, Staunton Office of School Superintendents, to WS,
12 February 1971, WS-UI. Erskine attended school in Staunton from 13 November 1912 until 7 February 1913. The story of the Charlotte truant officer
became part of the Caldwell family legend. See WS interview with EC, 19
December 1971, WS-UI. For other information on the Caldwells' stay in

Charlotte, see Cy Hood to WS, 20 December 1970, WS-UI. The best example of Erskine's poor writing skills is a letter written to his aunt. See EC to "Aunt Sally," 12 May 1915, ISC-UGA.

42. *The Sacrilege of Alan Kent*, pp. 17–18; *With All My Might*, pp. 25–27. For a fuller description of his employment during these years see WS interview with EC, 19 December 1971, WS-UI.

43. *With All My Might*, p. 26. Ira's rather remarkable race liberalism was apparently a potent example to his young son. Erskine seems never to have absorbed the prejudices so common among his generation of white Southerners.

44. For descriptions of life in Atoka, Tennessee, I have relied on Tim Forbess, *Welcome Home Atoka!* (Memphis: Markham Reproduction, 1986). It is an excellent local history with dozens of photographs from the period. I have also benefited from a prolonged correspondence with Miss Lavinia Smith. Miss Smith has lived in Atoka since 1907.

45. C. T. Strong to WS, 29 November 1970, WS-UI; EC to WS, 5 August 1971, WS-UI; C. C. McCollum to DM, 27 April 1990; Miss Lavinia Smith to DM, 25 January 1991.

46. *With All My Might*, p. 36.

47. *With All My Might*, pp. 33–35.

48. EC to "Aunt Sallie," 12 May 1915, ISC-UGA.

49. M. G. Boyce to WS, 15 November 1970, WS-UI; C. T. Strong to WS, 29 November 1970; Miss Lavinia Smith to DM, 25 January 1991. For an excellent photograph and description of the Robison School, see *Welcome Home Atoka!*, pp. 6–7.

50. Nick Carter to WS, 29 November 1970, WS-UI.

51. Miss Lavinia Smith to DM, 25 January 1991.

52. For an enlightening interview with a boyhood friend, see *Augusta Chronicle*, 28 January 1973. M. G. Boyce to WS, 15 November 1970, WS-UI.

53. Wales Worthan to DM, 5 November 1990; Miss Lavinia Smith to DM, 20 November 1990 and 26 December 1990.

54. Miss Lavinia Smith to DM, 26 December 1990; Wales Worthan to DM, 5 November 1990. James Wright to WS, 29 November 1970, WS-UI; William Lucado to WS, 29 November 1970, WS-UI. As a boy, Caldwell was denied this kind of consistent limits on his behavior, and, as an adult, assaults on propriety would be a cornerstone of his most passionate fiction. Caldwell was indeed, as *Time* labeled him, a "naughty writer." *Time*, 30 September 1957.

55. In the following three pages I have attempted to summarize an exceedingly tangled and bitter situation. To this day, many residents of Atoka refuse to discuss the matter. On one occasion I was rebuked for "stirring up the coals." Erskine's own recollections of these events are largely misleading and represent his efforts to vindicate his father.

   I am indebted to Reverend Charles Todd, current pastor of the Salem A.R.P. church, for allowing me access to all the relevant church records. See also, CPC to EC, July 1953, EC-DC; CPC to EC, undated 1965, EC-DC; M. G. Boyce to WS, 29 November 1970, WS-UI. A petition for Ira's removal, from the seceding faction to the Memphis and Louisville Presbytery, details many of the congregation's complaints and is located in the ISC-UGA.

56. CPC to EC, July 1953, EC-DC.

57. The manse still stands, in much the same condition as in 1919. The Caldwells'
     arrival was noted in *The Jefferson County Reporter*, 25 July 1919.

58. The best published source on Wrens, Georgia, is *Tracking Wrens* (Thomson,
     Georgia: Luckey Printing Co., 1984). I conducted over twenty-five interviews
     with longtime inhabitants of Wrens, and all contributed to my understanding
     of that lovely town. I am particularly indebted to Miss Ruby Tanner, who
     has kept extensive notes on the people and history of Wrens over the last
     seventy-five years.

59. There are no extant photographs of Caldwell from this period. I have relied
     on the descriptions garnered in oral interviews with Miss Ruby Tanner, 22
     January 1991; Ralph Stephens, 16 January 1991; and Henrietta Boyce, 24 Jan-
     uary 1991.

60. Wrens Institute Catalogue, 1922, EC-DC.

61. Handwritten transcript from Wrens Institute, 1919–1920, EC-DC. Erskine
     would always have a reputation for behaving rudely when he was reading
     or working. This anecdote was related in an interview with H. P. Wren, 24
     January 1991.

62. In Wrens, as in Atoka, Erskine is remembered as a practical joker and trou-
     blemaker. These anecdotes were related in interviews with Mr. H. P. Wren,
     24 January 1991; Miss Ruby Tanner, 22 January 1991; Mr. Ralph Stephens, 16
     January 1991. I am indebted to C. C. McCollum, Jr. for information on
     Erskine's behavior in school. Mr. McCollum's father was the principal of
     Wrens Institute during the time that Erskine attended.

63. For information on the love affair, I am indebted to Miss Ruby Tanner, who
     was Sara Farmer's best friend during these years. Interview with Miss Ruby
     Tanner, 22 January 1991.

64. Interview with Miss Ruby Tanner, 24 January 1991. JJ to DM, 9 January 1991.

65. *With All My Might*, pp. 40–41.

66. Most of Erskine's friends recall his accounts of his trips with Dr. Pilcher.
     Interview with Miss Ruby Tanner, 22 January 1991; interview with Mr. H.
     P. Wren, 24 January 1991. See also *With All My Might*, pp. 40–41, and *Call It
     Experience*, pp. 23–24. For further discussion of conditions in that area of
     Georgia, see *Augusta Chronicle*, 10 March 1935. I am also indebted to Mrs.
     Henrietta Boyce for her recollections of her father's visits into these parts of
     Jefferson County. Interview with Henrietta Boyce, 24 January 1991.

67. *Call It Experience*, p. 25. Interview with Miss Ruby Tanner, 22 January 1991.

68. A similar challenge would someday motivate Erskine's most powerful writ-
     ing. He too would be frustrated by those who could not accept the harshness
     of his story, and he wrote with a fervent commitment inherited from his
     father. The beneficiaries of Ira's early welfare program would find their most
     compelling voice in characters like Jeeter Lester of *Tobacco Road* and Ty Ty
     Walden of *God's Little Acre*. Conrad Chatham to DM, 15 January 1991; Dor-
     othy McCollum to WS, 15 October 1991, WS-UI.

69. Interview with Miss Ruby Tanner, 22 January 1991; interview with Ralph
     Stephens, 16 January 1991. Both Tanner and Stephens visited Erskine during
     his night shift at the mill.

70. *Call It Experience*, pp. 14–15.

71. *With All My Might*, pp. 42–43; Interview with Miss Ruby Tanner, 22 January
     1991; Cy Hood to WS, 10 November 1970, WS-UI.

72. *With All My Might*, pp. 42–43.

73. *With All My Might*, pp. 49–50. Henrietta Boyce to WS, undated, WS-UI.

74. C. C. McCollum to DM, 27 April 1990; *The Douglas Enterprise*, 25 January 1973.

75. EC to CPC, 30 July 1920, box 1557, UGA-ISC; EC to CPC and ISC, 2 July 1920, box 1557, UGA-ISC. In both *Call It Experience* and *With All My Might*, Erskine incorrectly places his summer in Calhoun as following his freshman year of college. His memory of the work itself seems quite accurate.

76. EC to CPC, 30 July 1920, box 1557, UGA-ISC.

77. Unpublished manuscript entitled *In the Days of Our Youth* or *If Only to Remember the Flatlands*, undated, WS-UI. William Sutton found the manuscript in Margaret Bourke-White's window seat. It was written sometime between 1925 and 1928.

78. Ibid.; *With All My Might*, p. 50.

79. While the annual out-of-state tuition at the University of Virginia was $160 a year, and total expenses estimated at well over $500, the tuition at Erskine College was only $60, with yearly expenses estimated at less than $280. For an itemized expense sheet for these institutions, see *Handbook of the University of Virginia for 1920–1921*, pp. 111–114; *Erskine College Handbook for 1920–1921*, pp. 24–25. See also, EC to WS, 22 June 1971, WS-UI.

CHAPTER TWO: THE HOLY CITY AND BEYOND

1. For the discussion of life at Erskine College in the following pages I have relied heavily on the memories of alumni from those years. I have also benefited from *Erskine Mirror*, the school paper, and *Erskiniana*, the school yearbook, for the years 1920–1924. Both of these useful sources are housed in the Erskine College Library, Erskine College, Due West, South Carolina. For official college information I have relied on the Erskine College annual catalogues and bulletins, also housed in the school library. I am particularly indebted to Miss Edith Brawley, head librarian, Erskine College.

2. Mr. Lowry Ware, interview with DM, 15 January 1991. For additional information on the economy of this area in the 1920s I have profited from I. A. Newby, *Plain Folk in the New South* (Baton Rouge: Louisiana State University Press, 1989).

3. Jennings B. Reid to DM, 3 December 1990.

4. For the academic requirements of Erskine College, I have relied on the Erskine College *Course Catalogue* and Erskine College *Bulletin* for the years 1920–1924, located in the Erskine College Library, Due West, South Carolina.

5. John Marion to WS, undated 1970, WS-UI.

6. Cy Hood to WS, 10 October 1970, WS-UI. All transcript material is available through the Registrar's Office at Erskine College.

7. EC to "Mother and Father," 20 March 1921, Box 1557, ISC-UGA.

8. Erskine College course catalogues for these years are available at the Erskine College Library, Erskine College. These catalogues offer fairly detailed course descriptions and syllabi. See p. 18 of the *Course Catalogue* for the description of Professor McCain's course. T. E. Mabry to DM, 15 June 1991.

9. Ibid., p. 27.

10. Ibid.

11. EC to "Mother and Father," 20 March 1921, box 1557, ISC-UGA.

12. *With All My Might*, p. 52.

13. For information relating to Caldwell's football career, I have relied heavily

on the memories of his teammates. Joseph Woods to DM, 11 January 1991; Jennings B. Reid to DM, 3 December 1990; Paul Hanks to DM, 13 January 1991; William Pressley interview with DM, 16 January 1991; R. C. Kennedy to WS, 26 October 1970, WS-UI; Cy Hood to WS, 10 October 1970, WS-UI. See also *Erskiniana* for 1921 and 1922 for summaries of the team's season and photographs of the players.

14. Cy Hood to WS, 10 October 1970, WS-UI.

15. Paul Hanks to DM, 13 January 1991.

16. T. E. Mabry to DM, 15 March 1991; Jennings Reid to DM, 3 December 1990; Joseph Woods to DM, 11 January 1991.

17. EC to "Mother and Father," 20 March 1921, Box 1557, ISC-UGA.

18. Drinking had never been allowed on the Erskine College campus, but restrictions became even tighter with the advent of Prohibition in 1920. "Sneaking a nip," as one alumnus put it, was one of the central challenges of freshman year. *Erskiniana*, 1921, p. 75.

19. The incident with the lightbulb was witnessed by a number of students. The best account is found in a letter, Cy Hood to WS, 11 January 1970, WS-UI.

20. For an entertaining account of Caldwell and Murphy's weekend jaunts, see R. C. Kennedy to WS, WS-UI. Caldwell discusses these trips in *Call It Experience*, p. 22; *With All My Might*, p. 53.

21. Joseph Woods to DM, 11 January 1991; Ralph Blakely interview with DM, 16 January 1991; John Marion to WS, undated 1971, WS-UI. See also *Call It Experience*, p. 22; *With All My Might*, p. 52.

22. In 1919 a number of students in the sophomore class were suspended when a freshman was almost crippled by a severe paddling. Hazing was explicitly forbidden in the school handbook after that date, though it seems not to have diminished during Erskine's freshman year. It was, however, carried on with far greater secrecy. Caldwell described his hazing experience to his first wife. HLC to WS, 4 July 1970, WS-UI.

23. T. E. Mabry to DM, 15 June 1991.

24. Ruby Tanner interview with DM, 22 January 1991; H. P. Wren interview with DM, 23 January 1991.

25. Ruby Tanner interview with DM, 22 January 1991. I am indebted to Ralph Stephens for sharing his recollections. His father, Charles Stephens, was editor of *The Jefferson County Reporter* when Erskine worked there. Ralph Stephens interview with DM, 16 January 1991.

26. *With All My Might*, p. 59. In both autobiographies, Caldwell greatly exaggerates the extent and success of his early efforts at newspaper reporting. See *Call It Experience*, pp. 15–18, 26; *With All My Might*, pp. 46–48, 51.

27. For a description of the ravages of the boll weevil, see George B. Tindall, *The Emergence of the New South 1913–1945*, (Baton Rouge: Louisiana State University Press and the Littlefield Fund for Southern History, 1967), pp. 121–124. The weevil first hit Georgia in 1916 but caused the most damage in the early 1920s. The plummet in cotton prices is discussed in Tindall, pp. 111–112. Residents of Wrens still remember both calamities well. EC to WS, 19 December 1971, WS-UI. For excellent accounts of the Georgia chain gangs, see John Spivak, *Georgia Nigger* (New York, 1932), and Robert Elliot Burns, *I Am a Fugitive from a Georgia Chain Gang* (New York, 1932). The John Williams case is described in Tindall's *The Emergence of the New South*, p. 212. Many

citizens of Wrens well remember the cruelty and sadism of the town sheriff during this period.

28. *Deep South*, p. 12; Ibid., pp. 63–64. Erskine's impatience with Southern religion also stemmed, of course, from his negative experiences in Atoka.

29. EC interview with WS, 24 December 1970, WS-UI. For an unusually revealing interview with Caldwell concerning his childhood, see *Arizona Republic*, 24 October 1982.

30. For newspaper accounts, see, for instance, *Greenville* (S.C.) *Piedmont*, 19 November 1921. Most team members still vividly remember the Clemson game and the victory celebration that followed. I am particularly indebted to Ralph Blakely for his vivid description of the events. Ralph Blakely interview, 16 January 1991.

31. *With All My Might*, p. 56.

32. EC interview with WS, 24 December 1970, WS-UI.

33. *Erskine Mirror*, 2 June 1924.

34. The term "wickets" originates, reputedly, from the word "wicked." A great many alumni remember these amorous gestures quite vividly. Joseph Woods to DM, 11 January 1991.

35. Classmates who knew Erskine were well aware of his disdain for "wickets" and other courting rituals. See William Brice to WS, 28 October 1970, WS-UI.

36. Ralph Blakely interview with DM, 16 January 1991; Hugh Hoffman to WS, November 1970, WS-UI. Erskine evinced many of the classic symptoms of clinical depression.

37. T. E. Mabry to DM, 15 March 1991; Ralph Blakely interview with DM, 23 January 1991.

38. Cy Hood to WS, 6 November 1970, WS-UI; Gladys Cockran to DM, 30 September, 1970. Miss Cockran's mother ran the boarding house where Erskine lived following his dismissal from the college dormitory.

39. Cy Hood to WS, 2 February 1971, WS-UI; Andrew Murphy interview with WS, July 1970, WS-UI.

40. Many of Caldwell's classmates recall, above anything else, that Erskine took frequent trips away from campus. See R. C. Kennedy to WS, September 1970, WS-UI. See also *Call It Experience*, p. 22; *With All My Might*, p. 56. The school yearbook also contains references to Caldwell's frequent sojourns. *Erskiniana*, 1922, p. 80, Erskine College Library.

41. Andrew Murphy interview with WS, July 1970.

42. Erskine recalled his humiliation in *The Sacrilege of Alan Kent*, p. 20.

43. A full account of the wedding can be found in *Bogalusa Enterprise*, 27 January 1922. For Murphy's recollections of the trip, see Murphy interview with WS, 19 September 1971, WS-UI. Ruby Tanner interview with DM, 22 January 1991. Sara Farmer was kind enough to allow Miss Tanner to sample the pralines, "the first she'd ever tasted." For Caldwell's description of the Bogalusa trip see *Call It Experience* pp. 23–26; *With All My Might*, pp. 56–58.

44. Murphy interview with WS, 19 September 1971, WS-UI. *With All My Might*, pp. 56–57.

45. For an excellent description of the city of Bogalusa at this time, see Al Hansen, *Bogalusa Daily News*, to WS, 3 January 1972.

46. *Call It Experience*, p. 24. Caldwell's notice of arrest, dated 2 February 1922, is on file at the County Courthouse, Bogalusa, Louisiana.

47. In *Call It Experience*, his first autobiography, he lovingly recalls his bond with the prison's "middle-aged negro trusty" who sympathizes with his plight and points out their shared bondage: "I sure do know how you feel . . . because I feel like I've been locked up in here all my life my own self." *Call It Experience*, p. 24. In the first draft of this book Caldwell mentions only a "jailer," making no mention of the man's race. In the final edition of the text he changed "jailer" to the more evocative "negro trusty," and added the line of dialogue. In his second autobiography, Erskine invents a cell-mate, "an elderly black man who had white hair and an upper row of bright gold teeth," imprisoned because he had "failed to prevent his two rabbit hounds from barking at night and disturbing the peace." *With All My Might*, p. 57.

48. Erskine broke off his relationship with Sara for informing his parents of his whereabouts during his New Orleans escapade. Ruby Tanner interview with DM, 22 January 1991. For Caldwell's memory of the period, see *With All My Might*, pp. 47–48. Murphy's new moniker, "Bogalusa Murphy," appears several times in the 1922 *Erskiniana*, and was well remembered seventy years later by his classmates.

49. Ibid.

50. William Sutton, unpublished manuscript, unpaginated, WS-UI.

51. John Marion to WS, undated 1971, WS-UI.

52. When questioned by the Student Council, Caldwell and his accomplice claimed that they were only switching the players' belongings from one locker to the next. Caldwell does not acknowledge his expulsion from the school in any of his adult recollections.

53. See, for instance, *New Republic*, 27 June 1934, in which Caldwell lambasted "the dishonesty of the South Carolina college which taught by suppression and censorship."

54. That summer, Caldwell sought to ease his parents' financial burden by working as a string reporter for the Augusta papers—an experience he recalled in *With All My Might*. Wrens residents corroborate his recollection.

55. Janie Walthall interview with DM, 21 January 1991. Members of Ira's congregations throughout his career recall his willingness to forfeit his salary.

56. Although the scholarship had not been claimed in a number of years, its requirements were simple: "The applicant must be seventeen years old and in robust health, must be the lineal descendant of a confederate veteran, and must give suitable proof of his need for financial assistance." See *The University of Virginia Student Handbook for 1922–1923*, p. 120, Alderman Library, The University of Virginia, Charlottesville, Virginia. Also see "United Daughters of the Confederacy Minutes from the U.D.C. 13th Annual Conference in Washington, D.C.," 20 December 1924, p. 154, WS-UI. Erskine was only half in jest when, years later, he surmised that his "transcript dropped to the floor during the committee meeting on a rainy day and somebody inadvertently stepped on it with a muddy shoe . . . the resulting blur provided a providential improvement over the original." *With All My Might*, pp. 63–64. Ira Caldwell was notorious for his impatience with Southern "loyalists." "They haven't learned a new thing since Sherman marched through here," was one of his favorite expressions. Mary Maner interview with DM, 22 January 1991.

57. For a discussion of the admissions standards at The University of Virginia at the time Caldwell applied, see Virginius Dabney, *Mr. Jefferson's University* (Charlottesville: University of Virginia Press, 1981), p. 78. Professor Dabney's work is the single best source for understanding life at the university in the mid-1920s.

58. Registration materials for Caldwell are available in the Atcheson L. Hench Papers, Alderman Library, University of Virginia, Charlottesville, Virginia. In reconstructing Caldwell's first year at UVA, I have relied as much as possible on the recollections of his classmates. I am particularly indebted to Mr. Ralph M. Flynt, whose excellent memory and detailed knowledge of the university have been particularly helpful. Also see Virginius Dabney, *Mr. Jefferson's University*, ch. 2 *passim*.

59. Louis Ballou to WS, undated 1971, WS-UI. As an adult Caldwell refused to spend the night in anyone else's house, always preferring a hotel. Guests were discouraged from staying with him overnight. On one typical occasion, Caldwell's twenty-five-year-old son Dabney was greeted at his father's doorstep with the query: "Where do you plan to stay?"

60. The social life at UVA during these years is well covered in Dabney's *Mr. Jefferson's University*, ch. 2 *passim*. Drinking at the university did not seem constrained by federal Prohibition, and moonshiners made regular rounds of the fraternity houses. There was little danger of being caught, one alumnus recalled: "The president's secretary always called the frats when the federal men were in town." Nearby Shiflett's Hollow was only the most famous of several locations where undergraduates could buy illegal alcohol. For the dress code, see *With All My Might*, p. 65.

61. The elitism at the university is well remembered by many alumni. Ralph M. Flynt to DM, 25 May 1991; Mr. Howell C. Patton, Jr. to DM, 5 March 1991; J. R. Phillips to DM, 20 February 1991; James Carisery to DM, 22 March 1991. For a discussion of accepted social protocol, see also Dabney, *Mr. Jefferson's University*, p. 86.

62. Dabney, *Mr. Jefferson's University*, p. 61; *With All My Might*, p. 64; Ralph M. Flynt to DM, 25 May 1991; Carlton Von Lier interview with WS, June 1970, WS-UI. Von Lier operated LaRowe's poolroom after LaRowe's death.

63. *With All My Might*, p. 65; J. Gilbert Hinman to DM, 21 May 1991.

64. I am grateful to the Registrar's Office at the University of Virginia for access to Caldwell's transcripts while at UVa.

65. M. G. Boyce to WS, 15 November 1970, WS-UI; Andrew Smithers to DM, 12 February 1991.

66. Course catalogues for these years are available in the Alderman Library, University of Virginia, Charlottesville, Virginia. These catalogues provide fairly detailed descriptions of the classes and their syllabi.

67. WS to EC, 11 November 1970.

68. *With All My Might*, p. 71; EC to ISC and CPC, 5 September 1924, Box 1557, ISC-UGA.

69. For Caldwell's memories of his lunch counter job, see *With All My Might*, p. 70. See also EC to WS, 7 July 1970, WS-UI.

70. *The Sacrilege of Alan Kent*, p. 50; ibid., p. 47.

71. Ibid., pp. 50–51. In these poetic musings, Caldwell does not explicitly identify the setting as Philadelphia. It is clear from the ordering of the text, however, that he had the city in mind as he wrote.

72. *With All My Might*, p. 70; *The Sacrilege of Alan Kent*, p. 51.
73. For material quoted in these paragraphs, see EC to "Mother and Father," 5 September 1924, Box 1557, ISC-UGA.
74. For the material quoted in these paragraphs, see EC to "Mother and Father," 24 September 1924, Box 1557, ISC-UGA. For Caldwell's recollections of his time in Philadelphia, see *With All My Might*, pp. 70–73.
75. *With All My Might*, p. 71; EC to "Mother and Father," 24 September 1924, box 1557, ISC-UGA. For his employment record at the S. S. Kresge Company, see C. K. Darnell to WS, 13 November 1970. According to employment records in the Kresge files in Detroit, Michigan, Erskine was employed from 23 September 1924 until 11 November 1924. His pay was $22 a week.
76. Ibid.
77. *With All My Might*, p. 74; EC to "Mother and Father," 24 September 1924, Box 1557, ISC-UGA.
78. For an interesting discussion of the Anthracite League, and Caldwell's participation, see *Wilkes-Barre Times Leader*, 4 June 1977. See also *With All My Might*, p. 73, for Caldwell's embellished recollection of his experience on the Wilkes-Barre Panthers.
79. For the material quoted in the following paragraphs, see EC to "Mother and Father," 10 November 1924, Box 1557, UGA-ISC.

CHAPTER THREE: AWAKENINGS

1. H. P. Wrens interview with DM, 23 January 1991.
2. For an excellent discussion of the reception of female undergraduates at the University of Virginia, see Virginius Dabney, *Mr. Jefferson's University*, pp. 67–68. So changed were the courting rituals during these years that the school paper warned that the chaste "lure and lilt of the lawn" was giving way to the "love-making atmosphere of the mid-Western campus." Quoted in *Mr. Jefferson's University*, p. 68.
3. *Kent*, pp. 22, 54.
4. Ibid., p. 31. Erskine's first wife was convinced that "Erskine's aversion to 'good women' was rooted in the smothering attentions he received growing up from the upright Bell family women." It does seem that the moralistic, chaste dogma of Carrie, her mother, and her sisters encouraged in Caldwell, from a very early age, a preoccupation with anything and everything they tried so hard to repress. HLC interview with WS, 4 July 1970, WS-UI. "Grandma Bell" habitually washed Erskine's mouth out with ashes and water if he used improper language. Mary Maner interview with DM, 23 January 1991.
5. For Erskine's recollections of the prostitutes in Memphis, see *With All My Might*, pp. 29–32.
6. H. P. Wren interview with DM, 23 January 1991. Erskine's deep insecurities about his masculinity probably contributed to his reluctance to sleep with the prostitutes.
7. A classmate refers cryptically to Erskine and Murphy's trip to Greenwood, where they "entertained and were entertained until about 2:00 a.m." See R. C. Kennedy to WS, 26 October 1970, WS-UI. *Kent*, p. 19.
8. Erskine's fascination with sexually oriented entertainment was lifelong. In

later years he served as a judge for the Miss Nude America Contest and other, similar competitions. He preferred Playboy Clubs to any other night spot. *Kent*, p. 32. In later recollections, Erskine blamed the theft on a random streetwalker rather than a woman he admired and pursued. See *With All My Might*, p. 71.

9. *Kent*, pp. 27, 34, 54, 57. J. R. Phillips to DM, 20 February 1991.

10. Louis Ballou to WS, undated 1971, WS-UI.

11. For the best discussion of "Pop" Lannigan, see *Mr. Jefferson's University*, p. 118. Most alumni remember both Lannigan and the "pits" with affection.

12. Mrs. Foster Beal interview with DM, 17 November 1990.

13. Mrs. Matilda Whitehouse to DM, 3 May 1990; Mrs. Ruth Ritchie to WS, undated 1971, WS-UI.

14. HLC interview with Harvey Klevar, 28–29 June 1977, DC-EC. Helen's recollections have proved to be remarkably accurate. I have found no reason to doubt her version of the events surrounding the meeting and marriage.

15. *Kent*, p. 55; Ibid., pp. 54–55; J. Gilbert Hinman to DM, 21 May 1991.

16. HLC interview with WS, 4 July 1970, WS-UI; HLC interview with Harvey Klevar, 19 July 1977, DC-EC.

17. For Erskine's account of the wedding night, see *With All My Might*, pp. 76–78. See Louis Ballou to WS, undated 1971, WS-UI.

18. *With All My Might*, pp. 79–81. HLC interview with WS, 4 July 1970, WS-UI. By exhibiting his familiarity with the seedy underworld of strip joints, Erskine hoped to emphasize his own virility, experience, and sexual expertise. Erskine's fascination with the burlesque and his behavior on his wedding night also betray a significant misogyny.

19. Mrs. Foster Beal interview with DM, 17 November 1990.

20. HLC interview with WS, 4 July 1970, WS-UI.

21. Even had Erskine wanted to, he could not have returned to school that fall. He had been suspended for poor grades the preceding quarter.

22. In both autobiographies, Erskine describes an interview with the tough city editor Hunter Bell, who hired him because "he looked like he could handle it." See *With All My Might*, pp. 81–83; *Call It Experience*, pp. 35–36. In reality, Erskine's father, a friend of Bell's, wrote the editor and "asked him to give the young man a chance." See Hunter Bell to WS, July 1970, WS-UI. The *Atlanta City Directory* for 1926 lists the Caldwells' address.

23. For information on Atlanta during this period, I relied on Franklin M. Garret, *Atlanta and Environs: A Chronicle of Its People and Events* (Athens, Georgia: The University of Georgia Press, 1954); Clifford M. Kuhn, Harlon E. Joye, and Bernard West, *Living Atlanta: An Oral History of the City 1914–1948* (Athens, Georgia: The University of Georgia Press, 1990); Howard L. Preston, *Automobile Age Atlanta: The Making of a Southern Metropolis* (Athens, Georgia: The University of Georgia Press, 1979).

24. Atlanta's largest paper, the *Atlanta Constitution*, was a morning paper.

25. *With All My Might*, pp. 83–84. For an excellent description of the *Journal* offices during these years, see Anne Edwards, *Road to Tara: The Life of Margaret Mitchell* (New Haven and New York: Ticknor & Fields, 1983), pp. 90–103.

26. Erskine recalls his days at the *Journal* in an unpublished essay entitled "The Young Days of Newspapering." The manuscript is still in the possession of Mrs. Virginia Caldwell Hibbs, and I am indebted to her for allowing me

access to this source. He described his clothing in *With All My Might*, p. 85. Also see Frank Daniel to WS, undated 1970, WS-UI.

27. *Call It Experience*, pp. 29–30.

28. Centered on and around Auburn Street was a pocket of cultural and social energy that matched New York City's Harlem in intensity, if not in size. See *Living Atlanta*, pp. 9–32. Caldwell described witnessing a lynching to Virginia Caldwell Hibbs. VC interview with DM, 15 July 1991.

   Ten years after the Leo Frank case had brought Atlanta's anti-Semitism to national attention, religious prejudice in the city was also still very much alive. Jews as well as blacks were victims of the Klan. Bricks shattered storefront windows, and prominent southside businessmen were terrorized by nightriders and burning crosses. See *Living Atlanta*, p. 9.

29. *Call It Experience*, pp. 37–40. Erskine loved telling (and surely exaggerating) the story of his "initiation" at the *Journal*—a hoax whereby a group of journalists phoned in a fictitious report of a riot while Erskine was alone in charge of the city desk. The account appears in both autobiographies. See *With All My Might*, p. 86. Erskine also described his initiation in "The Early Days of Newspapering" and in *Call It Experience*, pp. 43–44. For a discussion of the migration of displaced farmers into Atlanta, see Arthur Raper's *Preface to Peasantry: A Tale of Two Black Belt Counties* (Chapel Hill, The University of North Carolina Press, 1936).

30. Erskine describes his experience as a book reviewer in *With All My Might*, pp. 86–87; *Call It Experience*, pp. 42–43. See also the correspondence of his close friend Frank Daniel. Frank Daniel to WS, 11 May 1970, WS-UI; EC to Frank Daniel, 9 October 1950, DC-EC. See also EC to Manuel Komroff, 19 July 1949, Komroff Collection, Butler Library, Columbia University.

31. Cora Harris is quoted in *With All My Might*, p. 86. EC to Mrs. May L. Becker, 27 August 1925, May L. Becker Papers, Temple University Library, Philadelphia, Pennsylvania.

32. Erskine Caldwell, review of *The Hunter's Moon*, by Ernest Poole, in *Atlanta Journal*, 20 December 1925; review of *Christina Albert's Father* by H. G. Wells, in *Charlotte Observer*, 6 December 1925; review of *The Selmans*, by V. R. Emanual, in *Charlotte Observer*, 6 December 1925. Because Caldwell had little time to proofread these reviews, there were many typographical as well as stylistic and grammatical errors.

33. Erskine Caldwell, review of *Passion and Glory*, by William Cummings, in *Atlanta Journal*, 13 December 1925; review of *A Modernist and His Creed*, by Edward Mortimer Chapman, in *Charlotte Observer*, 28 February 1926. Caldwell later claimed to have never read Lewis or Dreiser, two authors who obviously influenced him a great deal.

34. Erskine Caldwell, review of *Shepherds*, by Marie Conway Oemler, in *Charlotte Observer*, 25 April 1926.

35. Erskine Caldwell, review of *Folk Beliefs of the Southern Negro*, by Newbell Niles Pucket, in *Charlotte Observer*, 15 August 1926.

36. Money was so tight that Helen's parents had to pay for the hospital expenses relating to the birth of Erskine, Jr.

37. A collection of twenty-four unpublished poems is still in the possession of Mrs. Virginia Caldwell Hibbs, and I am indebted to her for access to this valuable material. The quotations in the following paragraphs are taken from this collection. For a discussion of the poetry, see Guy Owen, "The Unpub-

lished Poems of Erskine Caldwell," *The South Atlantic Bulletin* (May 1978): 53–57.

38. For a discussion of the racial climate on campus, see *Mr. Jefferson's University*, pp. 66–67.

39. A few years later Erskine mailed his collected verse to the well-known poet Louis Untermeyer for an appraisal. Untermeyer, not surprisingly, encouraged Erskine to pursue other forms of expression. Years later, Erskine scrawled on the cover sheet of this collection: "Never published and rightly so!"

40. *Call It Experience*, p. 41; Ibid., p. 40. For a full description of Margaret Mitchell's tenure on the *Journal* staff, see Anne Edwards, *Road to Tara: The Life of Margaret Mitchell* (New Haven and New York: Ticknor & Fields, 1983), pp. 91–103. Newman's novel was published in 1926. Frances Newman, *The Hard-Boiled Virgin* (New York: Boni & Liveright, 1926).

41. *Call It Experience*, p. 41. Given the quality of Erskine's prose evident in his published reviews, these rebuffs are hardly surprising.

42. Bean's course is listed in the university's course catalogue for that year.

43. The University of North Carolina at Chapel Hill was at the forefront of this movement. Only a few months before his return to Virginia, Erskine reviewed North Carolina professor Howard Odum's *Systems of Public Welfare* for the *Journal*. He had high praise for a "study given us by men who know the South and her problems." See Erskine Caldwell, review of *Systems of Public Welfare* by Howard Odum and D. W. Willard, in *Charlotte Observer*, 6 December 1925. Caldwell recalled Bean's course in *Call It Experience*, p. 34.

44. A. K. Davis interview with WS, June 1970, WS-UI; EC to Paul Weiss, 30 October 1926, Paul Weiss Papers, Rare Books and Manuscripts, Southern Illinois University Library, Carbondale, Illinois. For excellent descriptions of Professors Bean and Davis, I am indebted to Mr. Ralph M. Flynt. Ralph Flynt interview with DM, 20 July 1991. Caldwell's recollections are in *Call It Experience*, p. 34.

45. The Atcheson T. Hench Papers, Alderman Library, University of Virginia, Charlottesville, Virginia, offer an excellent picture of this outstanding teacher. Particularly useful is a long interview conducted with Hench, accession number 9800 Oh1, also located in his papers at Alderman Library. I am indebted to Mr. Ralph M. Flynt for his recollections of Professor Hench. Ralph Flynt interview with DM, 20 July 1991.

46. Hench interview, Atcheson L. Hench Papers, accession number 9800 Oh1, ATH-UVA; EC to WS, 25 May 1970, WS-UI.

47. A few years later, Hench wrote a letter in support of Erskine's application for a Guggenheim fellowship. Hench's notes for this letter are housed with his papers, box 9150-B, ATH-UVA. The social apathy at the university is described in *Mr. Jefferson's University*, p. 86.

48. Hench kept exhaustive files on his students' work. These records are part of the Hench papers, box 9150-B, ATH-UVA.

49. Erskine Caldwell, "Georgia Cracker," *The Haldeman-Julius Monthly*, 4 (November 1926): 39–42.

50. Caldwell, "Georgia Cracker," pp. 39–40.

51. Ibid., p. 41.

52. Ibid.

53. EC to Hench, 26 April 1937, EC-DC.

54. Metcalfe is eulogized in *Mr. Jefferson's University*, p. 401. I am indebted to a

number of Virginia alumni for their recollections of the English Department. Ralph M. Flynt interview with DM, 20 July 1991; Raymond Bice to DM, 6 June 1991. For the best picture of the department at that time, refer to Michael Plunkett's interview with Atcheson Hench, box 9150-B, ATH-UVA. For Caldwell's impression of Sandburg, see HLC interview with Harvey Klevar, 29–30 June 1977, EC-DC.

55. *Virginia Quarterly Review*, 2 (Spring 1925). The quotation is taken from the back cover of the journal.

56. As quoted in *Mr. Jefferson's University*, p. 100.

57. Stringfellow Barr, "Shall Slavery Come South," *Virginia Quarterly Review*, 6 (October 1930): 488.

58. For the best general history of these magazines, see Frederick J. Hoffman, Charles Allen, and Caroline Ulrich, *The Little Magazine: A History and a Bibliography* (Princeton, New Jersey: Princeton University Press, 1946).

59. *With All My Might*, p. 65. As quoted in *The Little Magazine*, pp. 10–11.

60. Erskine kept neatly tabulated lists of all the reading he did for Hench's class. In the margins of these lists he recorded his reactions to each piece. See box 9150, EC-UVA.

61. Carl Christian Jensen, "Life Is All a Variorum," *The Atlantic Monthly*, 176 (December 1926), p. 733. For Caldwell's comments on Lawrence, see "Reading Lists," Box 9150, EC-UVA.

62. Wilson D. Wallis, "Race and Culture," *Scientific Monthly* (October 1926): 321.

63. Carl Van Doren, "Why I Am an Unbeliever," *Forum*, 176 (December 1926), p. 864; Ibid., p. 869.

64. Caldwell, "Georgia Cracker," p. 40. See Hench's margin notes in the ATH-UVA. Erskine's impatience with the "lassitude" and deficient "intellectual vigor . . . in deep South life" was also rooted in personal experience. Frances Newman, one of his inspirations at the *Journal*, left the South when her stark pictures of the region met with a decidedly lukewarm reception. Erskine's expulsion from Erskine College was still fresh in his mind—to him, ample evidence of the South's narrow-minded persecution of an artistic temperament. EC to Mr. Edwin Coover, 26 July 1965, EC-UVA.

65. In a review of the issue, Stringfellow Barr was more restrained than the irate President Alderman. Barr remarked with wry condescension that "the suggestion that local flappers have Negro blood, while not very interesting, was one of the few suggestions not yet advanced about them." As quoted in *Mr. Jefferson's University*, p. 98.

In *With All My Might*, Erskine claimed that his jokes were not only published in the college humor magazine, but, on occasion, in the nationally distributed *College Humor*. Since jokes in both publications appear without bylines, there is no way to validate such a claim. Several of Erskine's friends remember him working on "dirty jokes" for submission, however, and Ballou recalls some of them appearing in the college paper. See Louis Ballou to WS, undated 1971, WS-UI; VC to DM, 2 August 1971; J. Albert Hinman to DM, 21 May 1991.

66. I am indebted to Gordon Lewis's son for his memories of his father and the New Dominion Bookstore. F. Sherwood Lewis to DM, 25 January 1991. Also see EC to Joseph Johnson, 2 November 1978, Rare Books and Manuscripts, Louisiana State University Library, Louisiana State University, Baton Rouge, Louisiana. Caldwell described his time at the bookstore in *Call It Experience*,

p. 35. Charles Wertenbaker, *Boojum* (New York: Boni & Liveright, 1928).

67. F. Sherwood Lewis to DM, 25 January 1991; EC to AM, 15 December 1932, AM-HU.

68. VC interview with DM, 22 July 1991. Several of Erskine's friends at the bookstore remember this incident.

69. HLC interview with Harvey Klevar, 29–30 June 1977, EC-DC; Albert Francis to DM, undated March 1991.

70. HLC interview with Harvey Klevar, 29–30 June 1977, EC-DC.

71. *With All My Might*, p. 90; unpublished poem in the possession of Mrs. Erskine Caldwell.

72. *With All My Might*, p. 90. Erskine described his writing as "holding up a mirror" on many occasions. See, for instance, an interview in *Bridgeport Post*, 1 April 1940, EC-DC.

CHAPTER FOUR: APPRENTICESHIP

1. For information on Mount Vernon, I am indebted to Mr. Clayton Dolloff, the town's official historian. Clayton Dolloff interview with DM, 17 November 1990. I have also profited from conversations with a number of other longtime Mount Vernon residents. Foster Beal interview with DM, 17 November 1990; Robert Cushman interview with DM, 15 November 1990.

2. I am grateful to Mr. Clayton Dolloff for access to his excellent photographs of the Caldwell house.

3. *Call It Experience*, p. 40.

4. VC interview with DM, 4 November 1990. See also HLC interview with WS, 4 July 1971, WS-UI. Residents of Mount Vernon still recall Caldwell's rudeness. Foster Beal interview with DM, 17 November 1990.

5. HLC to ISC and CPC, 15 August 1927, box 1557, ISC-UGA.

6. DC interview with DM, 1 November 1990. Ira had also encouraged Erskine to go without shoes and shirt as a boy, a parenting technique more defensible in Georgia, perhaps, than in Maine.

7. For his recollections of childhood, I am indebted to Dabney Caldwell. DC interviews with DM, 1 November 1990, 27 February 1990, 15 October 1991. See also DC to EC, 6 January 1946, EC-DC; Virginia Boyle to WS, 4 February 1971, WS-UI.

8. Virginia Boyle to WS, 4 February 1971, WS-UI; Clayton Dolloff interview with DM, 17 November 1990. See also AM to EC, 9 February 1939, AM-HU.

9. Clayton Dolloff interview with DM, 17 November 1990; Mrs. Dorothy Morang to EC, 17 December 1983. This and other letters sent to Caldwell on his eightieth birthday are in the possession of Mrs. Virginia Caldwell Hibbs. Caldwell recalled the terrible cold inside the house in *Call It Experience*, pp. 42–44; *With All My Might*, pp. 92–95.

10. EC to CPC and ISC, 27 November 1928, box 1557, ISC-UGA.

11. EC to HLC, 25 March 1931, EC-DC; EC to HLC, undated 1931, EC-DC.

12. Many Wrens residents recall the family's yearly visits and the fishing cabin where Erskine worked. See also *Call It Experience*, pp. 44–45.

13. Helen recalled their hours discussing Erskine's work as among the happiest of their marriage. See HLC to EC, 23 January 1939. For the influence of D. H. Lawrence on Caldwell's work, see Guy Owen, "Erskine Caldwell and D. H. Lawrence," *Pembroke Magazine*, XI (1979), pp. 18–21.

14. HLC to WS, 6 September 1970, WS-UI; HLC to WS, 30 July 1970, WS-UI;

EC to HLC, 12 July 1933, EC-DC; EC to HLC, undated 1937, EC-DC. Most close friends of the Caldwells remember Helen's involvement with Erskine's writing; many mistakenly concluded that she secretly authored much of the work.

15. EC to AM, 12 January 1933, AM-HU; EC to AM, 5 February 1934, AM-HU.

16. EC to Richard Johns, 4 December 1929, RJ-UD; JHW to EC, 12 November 1930, EC-PU. As quoted in EC to RJ, 27 April 1929, RJ-UD.

17. EC to CPC, 27 November 1928, Box 1557, ISC-UGA.

18. For Caldwell's apocryphal account of the Longfellow Square Bookshop, see, for instance, *With All My Might*, p. 99. The manuscript of "The Bogus Ones" is located at the D. H. Hill Library, North Carolina State University, Raleigh, N.C. "The Bogus Ones," p. 26.

19. "The Bogus Ones," p. 26.

20. Francis O'Brien interview with DM, 13 October 1990. O'Brien, a longtime book dealer in Portland, recalls Caldwell's botched efforts in the book business. EC to ISC, 13 March 1929, ISC-UGA.

21. EC to ISC, 13 March 1926, ISC-UGA.

22. I am indebted to Marjory Montgomery (not her real name) for recollections of her employment at the bookstore. Interview with DM, 13 April 1990.

23. HLC interviews with HK, 19 July 1977, EC-DC. See also two undated letters, Marjory Morse to HLC, EC-DC. Caldwell treated the dalliance with the schoolteacher in a story he titled "A Very Late Spring."

24. Marjory Morse interview with DM, 13 April 1990.

25. EC to HLC, undated 1931, EC-DC.

26. I am grateful to Francis O'Brien, Ray Skofield, and Leon Tibbetts for their recollections. All three men were members of Portland's artistic community at this time, and remember Caldwell well. Ray Skofield interview with DM, 17 November 1990; Francis O'Brien interview with DM, 13 October 1990; Leon Tibbetts interview with DM, 17 November 1990.

27. For an excellent description of Morang, see "The Ghost of Alfred Morang," *Maine Times*, 3 October 1987. Virtually every person interviewed recalled the eccentric, flamboyant Morang.

28. The relationship between Morang and Caldwell is well documented in their correspondence. Over 150 letters between the two men are located in the Alfred Morang Papers, Houghton Library, Harvard University, Cambridge, Mass.

29. "The Bogus Ones," p. 70.

30. Ibid., p. 70.

31. EC to ISC, 19 March 1929, ISC-UGA.

32. "The Bogus Ones," p. 126.

33. "The Bogus Ones," p. 73; Clayton Dolloff interview with DM, 1 November 1991. Erskine Caldwell, "July," *transition*, Nos. 16–17 (June 1929), pp. 170–173.

34. "Midsummer Passion" and "Tracing Life With a Finger" appeared in *The New American Caravan* (New York: The Macaulay Company, 1929), pp. 96–107. For Caldwell's account of the publication mix-up, see *Call It Experience*, pp. 56–57.

35. The other two writers who first published in the 1929 *New American Caravan* were Robert Cantwell and James Henry Sullivan. By far the best treatment of Caldwell's fiction is in Sylvia Cook, *Erskine Caldwell and the Fiction of Poverty* (Baton Rouge and London: Louisiana State University, 1991).

36. John Gould Fletcher to Lewis Mumford, 30 October 1929, John Gould Fletcher Papers, Special Collections, University of Arkansas Library, Little Rock, Ark. For Fitzgerald's remarks, see Andrew Turnbull, ed., *The Letters of F. Scott Fitzgerald* (New York: Charles Scribner's Sons, 1963), p. 219. Less than a year later, Fitzgerald would refer to Caldwell's work far less charitably as "more crimes committed in Hemingway's name." Ibid., p. 223.

37. The quotations are taken from Mumford's letter of recommendation for Caldwell's application for a Guggenheim fellowship, 11 October 1931. I am indebted to the John Simon Guggenheim Foundation for access to Caldwell's application folder.

38. EC to Richard Johns, 4 October 1929, RJ-UD.

39. "The Strawberry Season" appeared in *Pagany*, Volume 1, Number 1 (Winter 1930), pp. 34–37. For an excellent history of *Pagany*, see Stephen Halpert and Richard Johns, *A Return to Pagany: The History, Correspondence, and Selections from a Little Magazine, 1929–1932* (Boston: Beacon Press, 1969). EC to RJ, 7 January 1930, RJ-UD.

40. Erskine Caldwell, "The Automobile That Wouldn't Run," *Hound & Horn*, vol. 4 (October–December 1930), 75–81. "Saturday Afternoon," *Nativity*, no. 1 (Winter 1930), 12–16.

41. As quoted in Sylvia Cook, *Erskine Caldwell and the Fiction of Poverty*, p. 42. Ms. Cook had written the first book-length study of Caldwell's fiction, and I am indebted to her analysis for deepening my understanding of Caldwell's work. Malcolm Cowley, "Two Judgments of *American Earth*," *New Republic*, 67 (June 17, 1931), 130–132.

42. T. K. Whipple, "Two Judgments of *American Earth*," *New Republic*, 67 (June 17, 1931), 130–132.

43. EC to MP, March 1930, EC-PU; EC to RJ, 7 January 1930, RJ-UD.

44. EC to RJ, 7 January 1930, RJ-UD.

45. EC to RJ, 12 July 1930, RJ-UD; EC to RJ, 15 May 1931, RJ-UD. The description of *Contact* is quoted in Hugh Ford, *Published in Paris: American and British Writers, Printers, and Publishers in Paris, 1920–1939* (New York, 1975), p. 89. For an excellent overview of Williams's involvement in *Pagany*, see *A Return to Pagany*, passim.

46. EC to RJ, 15 May 1931, RJ-UD.

47. EC to RJ, 12 July 1930, RJ-UD; EC to RJ, 30 January 1930, RJ-UD. The best discussion of the left-wing literary culture of the 1930s is still Daniel Aaron's classic text *Writers on the Left*. Daniel Aaron, *Writers on the Left* (New York: Harcourt, Brace & World, 1961).

48. Erskine Caldwell, *The Bastard* (New York: The Heron Press, 1929); Erskine Caldwell, *Poor Fool* (New York: Rariora Press, 1930). The Heron Press, which stayed in business only a few years, was taken over and renamed Rariora Press in 1930.

49. There has been almost no critical attention to Caldwell's early novels. The single best treatment is in Cook, *Erskine Caldwell and the Fiction of Poverty*, pp. 17–32. See also Guy Owen, " 'The Bogus Ones': A Lost Erskine Caldwell Novel," *Southern Literary Journal*, XI (1978), 32–39; Guy Owen, "The Apprenticeship of Erskine Caldwell: An Examination of *The Bastard* and *Poor Fool*," in Jack D. Durant and M. Thomas Hester, eds., *A Fair Day in the Affections: Literary Essays in Honor of Robert B. White, Jr.* (Raleigh, N.C., 1980), p. 199.

50. *The Bastard*, pp. 145–146.

51. *Poor Fool*, p. 172.
52. *The Bastard*, p. 1.
53. Ibid., p. 21.
54. Ibid., p. 16.
55. Ibid., pp. 14, 15, 17.
56. Ibid., pp. 192–193.
57. *Poor Fool*, p. 115.
58. Ibid., p. 107.
59. Ibid., p. 143.
60. EC to Frank Daniel, 2 October 1929, Frank Daniel Papers, Special Collections Library, Emory University, Atlanta, Ga.
61. Marjorie Morse interview with DM, 13 April 1990; EC to AM, 23 November 1933, AM-HU; Edward O'Brien interview with WS, 3 July 1970, WS-UI. A week before *The Bastard* was banned, Caldwell was forced by the county attorney to remove a window display of the work of Mary Baker Eddy on the grounds that it was "obscene." In letters to friends Caldwell often referred to Portland's "Hitlerized government." See, for instance, EC to AM, 10 October 1933, AM-HU. Caldwell inscribed Van Vechten's copy of *The Bastard* with these words. The book is located in the Caldwell Papers, Beineke Rare Books and Manuscripts Library, Yale University, New Haven, Conn.
62. The one-page document, entitled *In Defense of Myself*, is located in EC-DC. All quotations are taken from this document.
63. Ibid..
64. EC to MA, 7 March 1932, MA-UT. For the rest of his life, Caldwell would depict Erich Posselt, the owner of Heron Press, as a fly-by-night shyster. See, for instance, the obviously exaggerated, though revealing, treatment of Posselt in *Call It Experience*, pp. 56–58.
65. MP to EC, 13 February 1930, EC-PU.
66. MP to EC, 26 February 1930, EC-PU; HLC interview with Harvey Klevar, 29–30 June 1977, EC-DC.
67. EC to MP, March 1930, EC-PU. See, for instance, *Call It Experience*, pp. 65–68. The myth of Caldwell's naïveté is perpetuated by Scott Berg in his excellent biography of Perkins. Berg understandably took Caldwell's own remembrances as factually correct. See Scott Berg, *Maxwell Perkins: Editor of Genius* (New York: E. P. Dutton, 1978), pp. 155–156. For Wheelock's more accurate impression of Caldwell's business savvy, see JHW interview with WS, undated 1970, WS-UI. Erskine Caldwell, "The Mating of Marjory," *Scribner's*, vol. 87 (June, 1930), pp. 639–642; Erskine Caldwell, "A Very Late Spring," *Scribner's*, vol. 87 (June 1930), pp. 636–639.
68. *Call It Experience*, p. 60; MP to EC, 13 March 1930, EC-PU; MP to EC, 20 May 1930, EC-PU; MP to EC, 20 May 1930, EC-PU; MP to EC, 26 February 1930, EC-PU.
69. MP to EC, 20 May 1930, EC-PU; EC to MP, 23 May 1930, EC-PU.
70. Caldwell's dubious recollections of his wildly eventful journey west fill five pages of his first autobiography. See *Call It Experience*, pp. 77–81. EC to AM, 18 November 1930, AM-HU. Erskine Caldwell, *American Earth* (New York: Charles Scribner's & Sons, 1931).
71. JHW to EC, 12 November 1930, EC-PU.
72. EC to MP, 23 May 1930, EC-PU; MP to EC, 2 June 1930, EC-PU. Ezra Pound

to Richard Johns, as quoted in Cook, *Erskine Caldwell and the Fiction of Poverty*, pp. 41–42. For this, and other discussions of Caldwell's short fiction, I am indebted to Sylvia Cook's *Erskine Caldwell and the Fiction of Poverty*, ch. 2, *passim*.

73. Erskine Caldwell, "Saturday Afternoon," in *American Earth* (New York: Charles Scribner's & Sons, 1931).

74. MP to EC, 2 June 1930, EC-PU; JHW to EC, 12 November 1930, EC-PU.

75. For a discussion of Caldwell's use of repetition, see Scott MacDonald, "Repetition as Technique in the Short Stories of Erskine Caldwell," *Studies in American Fiction*, 5 (1977), pp. 213–225.

76. JHW to EC, 26 February 1931, EC-PU.

77. EC to JHW, 7 August 1930, EC-PU. In the years to come, other editors, with an eye firmly on the bottom line, would allow Caldwell to indulge his own worst instincts for the promise of increased sales and greater royalties.

78. MP to EC, 28 July 1931, EC-PU. William Soskin, *New York Herald Tribune*, 27 April 1931. Though he could ill afford it, Caldwell hired a clipping service in 1931 to keep track of the reviews of *American Earth*. The reviews for this, and most of his subsequent books, were pasted carefully in scrapbooks. These volumes are now located in the EC-DC.

79. Horace Gregory, "Tom Sawyer's Children," *New York Herald Tribune*, 26 April 1931; Gorham Munson, *New York Sun*, 1 May 1931. Caldwell would later claim that the critical reception of *American Earth* was "contemptuous, and often sadistic," although this was far from the case. His angry appraisal of reviewers as "impotent lovers or unsuccessful authors" came as a result of their treatment of his later books, not his early ones. See *Call It Experience*, p. 85.

80. Malcolm Cowley, "Two Judgments of *American Earth*," *New Republic*, 67 (June 17, 1931), pp. 130–132; Vincent Wall, "Poor Whites," *Saturday Review of Literature*, 8 (March 19, 1932), p. 604.

81. T. K. Whipple, "Two Judgments of *American Earth*," *New Republic*, 67 (June 17, 1931), pp. 130–132.

82. Norman Macleod, "A Hardboiled Idealist," *New Masses*, 7 (July, 1931), p. 18.

83. Ibid.

84. "New Author Going Wrong," *Pittsburgh Sun Telegraph*, undated 1931, scrapbook I, EC-DC; *New Orleans Picayune*, 2 August 1931. A. B. Bernd, *The Macon Telegraph*, 9 August 1931. "The Automobile That Wouldn't Run," "The Mating of Marjory," and "Dorothy" were named to O'Brien's Roll of Honor. In the 1931 volume of *The Best Short Stories*, Caldwell appeared together with such notables as Ernest Hemingway and F. Scott Fitzgerald, as well as such rising stars as William Faulkner. Edward J. O'Brien, *The Best Short Stories of 1931* (New York: Dodd, Mead and Company, 1931), pp. 81–88.

85. EC to ISC and CPC, 24 March 1930, ISC-UGA.

CHAPTER FIVE: TOBACCO ROAD

1. Taylor Caldwell described her first meeting with Perkins in her novel *The Final Hour*. "There was an air about this man, in this casual room filled with stark sunlight, of greatness and simplicity," she wrote. "One knew instinctively that the veriest tyro of a frightened author would be accorded the same courtesy and consideration as the most gilded and popular writers who

could boast ten or twenty 'large printings.' " For Caldwell's recollections, see *Call it Experience*, p. 70.

2. *With All My Might*, p. 119.

3. Caldwell recalled his lunch in *Parade*, undated, Dartmouth Scrapbook, vol. 3. He later remembered the meal as "peanut butter and watercress sandwiches on whole wheat bread." See *With All My Might*, p. 119. EC to RJ, 6 October 1930, RJ-UD.

4. *Call It Experience*, p. 80. EC to Frank Daniel, 15 December 1930, Atlanta Historical Society Library, MSS 77, Box 1, Folder 2; EC to JHW, 15 December 1930, EC-PU.

5. For life in Wrens during the Depression, I have benefited from discussions with Leroy Lewis, 25 January 1991; Miss Ruby Tanner, 22 January 1991; Mr. H. P. Wren, 24 January 1991.

6. Caldwell's preface to the 1940 edition of *Tobacco Road* is extremely revealing. Caldwell, *Tobacco Road* (New York: Duell, Sloan & Pearce, 1940). For two of Caldwell's more accurate recollections of his inspiration for *Tobacco Road*, see *New York World Telegram*, 2 September 1942; *Washington Post*, 1 March 1987.

7. Boyce Wideman to WS, 24 May 1971, WS-UI; ISC to Charles Scribner's Sons, 15 March 1931, EC-PU.

8. I. S. Caldwell, "Let's Think This Over," *Augusta Chronicle*, 16 January 1931. Ibid., 13 July 1931; Ibid., 7 September 1931.

9. Ibid., undated 1931. A number of undated "Let's Think This Over" columns are located in WS-UI.

10. Many citizens of Wrens remember Ira's efforts on behalf of the local family. See Dorothy McCollum to WS, undated 1970, WS-UI; DM interview with Miss Ruby Tanner, 21 January 1991; DM interview with R. P. Wren, 24 January 1991.

11. Everyone who knew Ira remembers his use of this expression. See also *With All My Might*, p. 112.

12. I. S. Caldwell, "The Bunglers," *Eugenics*, vol. III, October 1930, p. 383. Ira's piece ran in five consecutive monthly issues of *Eugenics: A Journal of Race Betterment*. See Vol. III, nos. 6–10, June 1930 through October 1930.

13. Caldwell, *Eugenics*, Vol. III, October 1930, p. 334.

14. Ibid., p. 337; ibid., p. 378. Caldwell, *Eugenics*, Vol. III, August 1930, p. 296.

15. Caldwell, *Eugenics*, Vol. III, September 1930, p. 336.

16. Caldwell, *Eugenics*, Vol. III, September 1930, p. 334; Caldwell, *Eugenics*, Vol. III, October 1930, p. 377.

17. The exact chronology of Caldwell's frustrated efforts to begin *Tobacco Road* is difficult to ascertain. For the best accounts of the process, see *Call It Experience*, pp. 80–84; *With All My Might*, pp. 111–116. See also WS interview with EC, 26 December 1970, WS-UI.

18. *With All My Might*, p. 114; *Call It Experience*, p. 81.

19. From the sign posted by the Georgia Historical Society. See also *Call It Experience*, pp. 24–25.

20. Helen Caldwell later recalled that Erskine wrote only a small part of *Tobacco Road* in New York. See HLC to WS, 25 October 1970 and HLC interview with WS, 2 November 1970, WS-UI. Erskine, however, adamantly insisted that the bulk of the novel was written in New York. See EC to Atcheson Hench, 26 May 1970, WS-UI; EC to WS, 23 May 1970, ISC-UGA. Caldwell's

account in *Call It Experience* is more plausible than Helen's. In a letter to Perkins dated 14 January 1931, Caldwell wrote that he was "trying to get a novel started." EC to MP, 14 January 1931, MP-PU. Caldwell gives a vivid description of the writing process in *Call It Experience*, pp. 82–83.

21. EC to RJ, 12 April 1931, EC-DC.

22. Ibid.

23. See Verna Potter to WS, 15 March 1971, WS-UI; Wilo Anderson to Thelma Taliaferro, 20 September 1971, WS-UI; Amy Taliaferro to WS, 10 September 1971, WS-UI. For information about *Tobacco Road*'s real-life models in Wrens, I have relied on the memories of several local citizens. See interview with Sarah Wren Lively in *Atlanta Constitution*, 1 February 1982; interview with Jimmy Wren in *Douglas Enterprise*, 29 April 1987; William Beal to WS, 5 August 1971, WS-UI; C. C. McCollum to DM, 14 October 1990; Leroy Lewis to WS, undated 1971, WS-UI.

24. William Byrd wrote two narratives, *History of the Dividing Line Betwixt Virginia and North Carolina* and *A Secret History of the Dividing Line*, sometime between 1728 and 1738. The first of these was intended for a British audience, the second—a far more satirical and humorous work—was directed to other Southern readers. *History* was published in 1849 while *A Secret History* remained unpublished until 1929. William Byrd, *Histories of the Dividing Line Betwixt Virginia and North Carolina* (Raleigh, N.C.: North Carolina Historical Commission, 1929). See, for instance, Augustus Baldwin Longstreet, *Georgia Scenes* (New York: Harper Bros., 1835); George Washington Harris, *Sut Lovingood: Yarns Spun by a "Natural Born Durn'd Fool"* (New York: Dick and Fitzgerald, 1867).

25. For a discussion of Caldwell's relationship to the Southwest humorists, see Richard J. Gray, "Southwestern Humor, Erskine Caldwell and the Comedy of Frustration," *Southern Literary Journal*, 8 (Fall, 1975), pp. 3–26.

26. Interview with EC, *New Orleans Picayune*, 14 November 1939. Caldwell expressed his admiration for Wolfe on a number of occasions. See John Selby to EC, 25 September 1940, DC-EC.

27. EC to Milton Abernethy, 8 November 1932, EC-MA. Caldwell praised Faulkner in an interview for *Bridgeport Post*, 1 April 1940. Faulkner returned the favor a few years later when he named Caldwell one of America's five greatest authors.

    Sanctuary was published in February 1932, during the period when Caldwell was deeply immersed in the writing of *Tobacco Road*. Caldwell deleted from the final manuscript version of *Tobacco Road* a reference to Dude sexually molesting his sister with a "corncob." In *Sanctuary*, the story's heroine is raped by Popeye with a corncob. Malcolm Cowley was only one of a number of critics who recognized Faulkner's impact on Caldwell. See Malcolm Cowley to "Bruccoli," 30 December 1975, Waller Barret Papers, University of Virginia, Charlottesville, VA.

28. EC to MP, 11 June 1931, EC-PU.

29. EC to MP, 17 April 1931, EC-PU.

30. EC to CPC and ISC, 4 May 1931, Box 1156a, ISC-UGA.

31. EC to CPC and ISC, 4 May 1931, Box 1156a, ISC-UGA; EC to AM, 3 June 1931, AM-HU.

32. EC to RJ, 12 April 1931, RJ-UD; EC to RJ, 13 July 1931, RJ-UD; MP to EC, 10 June 1931, EC-PU. Ironically, "A Country Full of Swedes" was published by

the *Yale Review* the following year and won a $1,000 award as best story of
the year.

33. WS interview with JHW, 6 August 1970, WS-UI. In a discussion of the firm's
legendary conservatism, John Hall Wheelock jested that "Charles Scribner
would no sooner allow profanity in one of his books than he would invite
a friend to use his parlor as a toilet room." As quoted in Scott Berg's *Maxwell
Perkins: Editor of Genius*, p. 80.

34. JHW interview with WS, 6 August 1970, WS-UI.

35. MP to EC, 10 June 1931, EC-PU.

36. MP to EC, 10 June 1931, EC-PU; MP to Laurence Pollinger, 5 January 1932,
EC-PU.

37. There is an extensive and tangled correspondence between Caldwell and
Perkins regarding the publication controversy with Harcourt, Brace & Company. For a rough summary of events, see EC to MP, 11 January 1931,
EC-PU and MP to EC, 26 February 1932, EC-PU. Caldwell's complete unwillingness to recognize his own responsibility for the mix-up was typical.

38. EC to RJ, 15 June 1931, RJ-UD.

39. EC to RJ, 15 June 1931; EC to MP, 11 June 1931, EC-PU.

40. MP to EC, 12 June 1931, EC-PU; MP to EC, 13 June 1931, MC–PU.

41. WS interview with JHW, 6 August 1970, WS-UI.

42. MP to EC, 26 June 1931, EC-PU. As with *American Earth*, it fell to Wheelock
to suggest that Caldwell "soften" some of the more explicit language and
sexual antics. Although Wheelock sympathized with Caldwell's artistic goals,
he felt sure "that it would be a mistake to antagonize people when very
slight changes would obviate the danger." JHW to EC, 21 November 1931,
EC-PU.

43. James Southall Wilson, "Back-Country Novels," *Virginia Quarterly Review*,
March 1932, pp. 466–471.

44. J. Raiford Watkins, *Augusta Chronicle*, 14 February 1932; H. L. Bradshaw, "A
Tragedy of the Soil," *Richmond News Leader*, 29 February 1932; *Gastonia Gazette*, 28 April 1932.

45. *Louisville Courier*, 28 February 1932; *Baltimore Sun*, 20 March 1932.

46. Edward Dahlberg, "Raw Leaf," *New Republic*, 70 (March 23, 1932), 159–160;
James Gray, "New Realist Depicts South's Poor White's Pitiable Existence,"
St. Paul Dispatch, 16 February 1932.

47. Jack Conroy, "Passion and Pellagra," *New Masses*, 7 (April, 1932), pp. 24–25;
Edwin Seaver, "Poor Whites in Georgia," *New York Sun*, 26 February 1932.

48. Conroy, "Passion and Pellagra." Seaver, "Poor Whites."

49. *Saturday Review*, 5 March 1932. James Gray, *St. Paul Dispatch*, 16 February
1932. *Forum*, May 1932. *Philadelphia Enquirer*, 27 February 1932.

50. Horace Gregory, "Our American Primitives," *New York Herald Tribune*, 21
February 1932.

51. *Saturday Review*, 5 March 1932; Kenneth White, "American Humor," *Nation*,
135 (July 6, 1932), pp. 16–17.

52. *Portland Express*, 13 February 1932; EC to AM, 1 March 1932, AM-HU.

53. MP to EC, 28 July 1931, EC-PU. All quotations are taken from Perkins's letter
of recommendation to the Guggenheim Prize Committee, written sometime
between 2 October and 4 November 1931. The letter is in EC–PU.

54. Ibid.

55. For an account of the unsuccessful attempt to ban *Tobacco Road* from the

local library, see *Augusta Chronicle*, 9 March 1932. For community reactions to the novel, I have relied on the memory of people who were there. See W. E. Wren to DM, 13 April 1990; DM interview with Janie Walthall, 21 January 1991; DM interview with Leroy Lewis, 25 January 1991; Nancy Bowers to DM, 21 January 1991; Lucy Anne McCluer to WS, 27 May 1970, WS-UI; DM interview with Mary Maner, 27 January 1991; DM interview with Miss Ruby Tanner, 22 January 1991; W. J. Wren to WS, 7 October 1970, WS-UI.; W. W. Stone to WS, undated 1970, WS-UI; DM interview with Lowry Ware, 15 January 1991.

56. Miss Nancy Bowers to DM, 21 January 1991.

57. *Richmond News Leader*, 13 June 1936; EC to AM, 9 March 1933, AM-HU.

58. DM interview with Miss Janie Walthall, 21 June 1991; Miss Fannie Strauss to WS, 4 November 1970, WS-UI; J. S. Pittcairn to CPC, 11 November 1935, ISC-UGA.

59. DM interview with Lowry Ware, 15 January 1991. I. S. Caldwell, "The Menace of the Moron," *Augusta Chronicle*, undated 1931, EC-DC. R. B. Kennedy to EC, 21 December 1959, EC-DC.

60. I am indebted to Minna Lieber, Maxim Lieber's wife, for information on her husband.

61. EC to MP, 5 February 1932, EC-PU; HLC to WS, 30 July 1970, WS-UI.

62. EC to MP, 7 March 1932, EC-PU.

63. MP to EC, 4 March 1932, EC-PU; MP to EC, 10 March 1932, EC-PU.

64. EC to RJ, 7 March 1932, RJ-UD. EC to MP, 27 May 1932, EC-PU, EC to AM, 10 June 1932, AM-HU.

65. MP to EC, 18 June 1932, EC-PU.

66. For Caldwell's recollection of the failed publication of "Autumn Hill" and Lieber's role in the negotiations, see Caldwell, *Call It Experience*, pp. 94–98; EC to RJ, 7 March 1932, RJ-UD.

67. Caldwell, *Call It Experience*, p. 96. EC to MP, 5 March 1932, EC-PU.

68. EC to Gordon Lewis, 23 September 1932, GL-UVA.

CHAPTER SIX: GOD'S LITTLE ACRE

1. EC to WS, 26 December 1970, WS-UI.

2. EC to Gordon Lewis, 23 September 1932, GL-UVA. See also HLC interview with WS, 4 July 1970, WS-UI.

3. DM interview with Dabney Caldwell, 1 November 1990.

4. HLC to CPC, undated 1929, ISC-UGA.

5. Elizabeth Ames to JHW, 19 February 1932, EC-PU. See also JHW to Ames, 26 February 1932, EC-PU.

6. EC to Milton Abernethy, 17 September 1933, MA-UT. While Caldwell's statement was true enough when he made it, eventually all of these writers did produce books.

7. The most complete biography of Nathanael West is Jay Martin's *Nathanael West: The Art of His Life* (New York: Carroll & Graf Publishers, Inc.). For the literary culture at the Sutton Hotel, see p. 159.

8. *Call It Experience*, p. 88.

9. EC to GL, 23 September 1932, GL-UVA; EC to RJ, 20 June 1932, RJ-UD.

10. EC to Johns, 3 April 1932, RJ-UD; EC to Joseph Vogel, 18 September 1933, EC-DC; EC to RJ, 3 April 1932, RJ-UD.

11. EC to RJ, 1 November 1932, RJ-UD; EC to IOS, 3 September 1932, ILS-LOC.

12. Maxwell Perkins's Guggenheim recommendation letter, John Simon Guggenheim Foundation Archives, New York, New York.

13. EC to AM, 1 November 1932, AM-HU. Bennett Cerf was annoyed by collectors' interest in Caldwell's "inexcusable junk" and hoped Caldwell "ha[s] the grace to be ashamed" of both *The Bastard* and *Poor Fool*. See Bennett Cerf, "God's Little Acre," *Contempo*, 15 March 1933.

14. EC to AM, 15 November 1932, AM-HU.

15. EC to AM, 15 September 1932, AM-HU; Bennett Cerf, "God's Little Acre," *Contempo*, 15 March 1933.

16. EC to AM, 4 January 1933, AM-HU; EC to RJ, 18 January 1933, RJ-UD. See also EC to AM, 11 September 1932; 15 September 1932; 1 November 1932; 1 December 1932; 4 January 1933, AM-HU; EC to Milton Abernethy, 28 November 1932; 13 February 1932, MA-UT; EC to RJ, 18 January 1933, RJ-UD. Embarrassed by his failure, Caldwell later asserted that he had printed the pamphlets "merely for fun . . . not trying to sell them." See Caldwell's rebuttal to Bennett Cerf in *Contempo*, 15 March 1933.

17. Matthew Josephson also recalled Caldwell's trips to the *New Republic* offices. See Matthew Josephson, *The Infidel in the Temple* (New York: Knopf, 1967) pp. 140–143.

18. Jay Martin, *Nathanael West: The Art of His Life*, p. 160.

19. As quoted in Daniel Aaron's *Writers on the Left* (New York: Harcourt, Brace & World, Inc., 1961), p. 150. For my understanding of the left-wing literary culture in New York in the early 1930s, I am indebted to Daniel Aaron's classic text *Writers on the Left* and to discussions with Professor Aaron himself.

20. For an explanation of the appeal of Communism to intellectuals in the early 1930s, see Aaron, *Writers on the Left*, pp. 149–160. Koestler is quoted in Aaron, *Writers*, p. 153.

21. Caldwell's letter to Villard was never published in the *Nation*. EC to Oswald Garrison Villard, 6 June 1927, Oswald Garrison Villard Papers, Houghton Library, Harvard University, Cambridge, MA 02138. The "man who lived by the side of the railroad in a rented house," found fictional representation in the character of Lov Bensey in *Tobacco Road*.

22. Caldwell, *Poor Fool* (New York: Rariora Press, 1930), p. 149. In the final draft of *Tobacco Road*, located in the EC-DC, Caldwell added the following passage:

> An intelligent employment of his lands, stock, and implements, would have enabled Jeeter, and scores of others who had become dependent upon [the absentee landlord], to raise crops for food and crops to be sold at a profit. Co-operative and corporate farming would have saved them all.

23. HLC interview with WS, 4 July 1970, WS-UI.

24. EC to Mrs. R. B. Shipley, Director of the Passport Office of the United States, 14 November 1953, EC-DC; EC to AM, 5 October 1933, AM-HU; Matthew Josephson, "Some of the Younger Novelists," *Virginia Quarterly Review*, 9 (April 1933). EC to MA, 8 November 1932, MA-UT.

25. EC to JHW, 4 May 1931, MP-PU. Michael Gold, *New Masses*, VI (September 1930). Aaron, *Writers*, p. 205. For information on Mike Gold and his rela-

tionship with young writers, I have relied on Aaron, *Writers*, pp. 162–164.

26. At least five novels dealing with the Gastonia and other Southern mill strikes were published before Caldwell began work on *God's Little Acre*. See, for instance, Mary Heaton Vorse, *Strike!* (New York: Horace Liveright, 1930); Fielding Burke, *Call Home the Heart*, (New York: Longmans, Green and Company, 1932); Grace Lumpkin, *To Make My Bread* (New York: The Macauley Company, 1932); Myra Page, *Gathering Storm* (New York: 1932); Sherwood Anderson, *Beyond Desire* (New York: Liveright Inc., 1932). For a discussion of the Communists' interest in the South, see Aaron, *Writers*, pp. 177–182.

27. The quotation is taken from Caldwell's 1931 Guggenheim proposal located in the John Simon Guggenheim Foundation Archives, New York, New York. Richard Wright's fiction dealing with the black, Southern, rural poor would not be published for another few years.

28. Daniel Aaron credits Caldwell, above all other Southern writers, with creating "the South of *The New Masses*," where "the bodies of Negroes swung from gaunt trees and fat-bellied sheriffs and mean-looking gangsters presided over hellish rites." Aaron, *Writers*, pp. 178–179.

29. EC to AM, 3 June 1931, AM-HU. Orrick Johns is quoted in Aaron, *Writers*, p. 159. A flyer for the debate is in the Caldwell Collection at Dartmouth College, EC-DC.

30. *Culture and Crisis: An Open Letter to the Writers, Artists, Teachers, Physicians, Engineers, Scientists and Other Professional Workers of America* (League of Professional Groups for Foster and Ford, 1932). As quoted in Aaron, *Writers*, pp. 196–198.

31. EC to RJ, 5 December 1932, RJ-UD; Erskine Caldwell, "Ripe For Revolution," *New Masses*, (December 1932).

32. Ibid.

33. All quotations are taken from Caldwell's Guggenheim Foundation application, John Simon Guggenheim Foundation Archives, New York, New York.

34. Caldwell described the writing of *God's Little Acre* in the Foreword to the Modern Library edition of the novel. See Caldwell, *God's Little Acre* (New York: Random House, 1934), pp. vii–ix.

35. Ibid.; Erskine Caldwell, *Call It Experience*, pp. 99–100.

36. EC to I. L. Salomon, 3 September 1932, ILS-LOC.

37. Erskine Caldwell, *God's Little Acre* (New York: Viking Press, 1933). All page citations are taken from the Modern Library edition (New York, 1934). In his Guggenheim proposal, Caldwell had proposed a novel that told the story of " 'po' white trash' and the 'lint heads' "—"the tenant farmer, the textile mill operative, and all those living somewhere in between. . . ."

38. Ibid., p. 69; ibid., pp. 213–214. Caldwell wrote his Guggenheim proposal for *God's Little Acre* at virtually the same time that the Scottsboro Boys case first came to national attention. It is possible that he named the mill town in his novel "Scottsville" in their honor. Horse Creek Valley is the actual name of the area just across the South Carolina border from Augusta. In the 1920s and 1930s almost every town along this valley had a cotton mill, and Caldwell visited all of them with his father at one time or another. There is no evidence that Caldwell was particularly inspired by the Gastonia, N.C., textile mill strike, and in fact, his novel has little in common with the numerous fictional treatments of that event that were published between 1930 and 1934.

39. Ibid., pp. 217, 221.

40. Ibid., p. 242.
41. Ibid., pp. 242, 236–237.
42. Ibid., pp. 250–252.
43. Michael Gold, *New Masses*, VI (September, 1930); EC to AM, 1 June 1933, AM-HU. EC to ILS, 26 March 1933, ILS-LOC.
44. A few years later, in a review of Grace Lumpkin's proletarian novel *A Sign for Cain*, Caldwell lamented "the tendency of a propaganda author to stack the cards against the villains so hopelessly that the outcome of the conflict is never in doubt." Dartmouth Scrapbook, no. 4.
45. Caldwell, *God's Little Acre*, p. 99. The image of "beaten women" in both passages is noteworthy, although there is no evidence that Caldwell ever *physically* abused Helen.
46. James Devlin describes Ty Ty Walden as a "Dionysian" figure. See James E. Devlin, *Erskine Caldwell* (Boston: Twayne Publishers, 1984), pp. 55–74, *passim*.
47. Ibid., 298–299. For an excellent discussion of the thematic content of *God's Little Acre*, see Sylvia Jenkins Cook, *Erskine Caldwell and the Fiction of Poverty*, pp. 121–130.
48. EC to HLC, 12 July 1933, EC-DC. *God's Little Acre*, p. 23.
49. Caldwell's remarks are in *Argosy: Fiction-Fact Magazine for Men*, April 1958.
50. Caldwell, *God's Little Acre*, p. 128.
51. Ibid., pp. 80–81. In the final manuscript version of the novel, this scene is even more explicit and Darling Jill even more desperate for Will's attentions.
52. Ibid., p. 226.
53. Ibid., p. 222.
54. EC to Milton Abernethy, 26 April 1933, MA-UT; EC to Milton Abernethy, 27 November 1932, MA-UT. Caldwell's Guggenheim application essay, John Simon Guggenheim Foundation Archives, New York, New York. Caldwell's characterization of Ellen Glasgow as a romantic Southern writer is unjust. On other occasions he acknowledged an appreciation for Glasgow's *Barren Ground*, a bleak evocation of life on a Southern farm.
55. Mike Gold, *New Masses* (September 1930).
56. Erskine Caldwell, "Ripe for Revolution," *New Masses* (December 1932).
57. Ibid., pp. 251–252.
58. Lieber to EC, 5 July 1940, Box 5, MBW-SU; EC to AM, 3 July 1932, AM-HU.
59. EC to AM, 15 September 1932, AM-HU; EC to AM, 15 September 1932, AM-HU; EC to AM, 15 September 1932, AM-HU. Later, Caldwell would suggest that he had been wooed by the editors at Viking, who wined and dined him at an opulent downtown restaurant. For Caldwell's recollection of his first meetings with the editors at Viking, see *Call It Experience*, p. 97.
60. Ibid.
61. EC to MA, 19 September 1932, MA-UT; EC to MA, 19 October 1932, MA-UT; EC to AM, 1 November 1932, AM-HU. Some years later, Caldwell noted dryly that while he "had not gained the principal objective by changing publishers," he quickly came "to be pleased with my new association." Caldwell, *Call It Experience*, p. 98.
62. EC to Milton Abernethy, 19 October 1932, MA-UT. One reader at Viking suggested in the margins of the *God's Little Acre* manuscript that Caldwell delete a particularly explicit sentence in order to "avoid censorship." Cald-

well complied. The final manuscript with Caldwell's handwritten changes is located in EC-DC.

63. EC to Milton Abernethy, 19 October 1932, MA-UT. EC to Johns, 5 December 1932, RJ-UD.

64. EC to GL, 26 February 1933, WB-UVA.

65. Jonathan Daniels, *Raleigh News & Observer*, 5 March 1933; Louis Kronenberger, "God's Little Acre and Some Other Recent Works of Fiction," *New York Times Book Review*, 5 February 1933; *New Republic*, 8 February 1933; *Forum*, 19 March 1933.

66. Horace Gregory, *New York Herald Tribune Books*, 5 February 1933. *New Republic*, 8 February 1933; *Forum*, 19 March 1933.

67. James T. Farrell, "The Author of 'Tobacco Road,' Takes Us Again to Georgia," *New York Sun*, 7 February 1933.

68. Edward Dahlberg, "Erskine Caldwell and Other 'Proletarian' Novelists," *Nation*, 8 March 1933. Years later, in his memoirs, Dahlberg described *God's Little Acre* as a dual charade. On the one hand, Dahlberg argued, the novel was a sensational "humbug cash novel," on the other a transparent appeal to the reigning leftist literary critics. "He purported to be a palmy denizen of Philistia," Dahlberg wrote; "and at the same time tithe[d] his soul by giving a farthing of his fortune to 'the cause.'" See Edward Dahlberg's *The Confessions of Edward Dahlberg* (New York: George Braziller, 1971), pp. 264–266.

69. Edwin Rolfe, *New Masses*, 8 (February 1933).

70. Ibid.

71. *Springfield Republican*, 12 February 1933. Fanny Butcher, "Soil of South Yields Spring Crop of Novels," *Chicago Daily Tribune*, 4 March 1933. John Peale Bishop to Allen Tate, Allen Tate Collection, Box 12, Folder 4, Firestone Library, Princeton University, Princeton, N.J.

72. Carl Van Doren, "Made in America: Erskine Caldwell," *Nation*, 18 October 1933.

73. Letter from G. Bruce Wilson (Gordon Lewis's son) to DM, 19 November 1990.

74. EC to ILS, 26 March 1933, ILS-LOC.

75. EC to MA, February 1933, MA-UT. EC to ILS, 26 March 1933, ILS-LOC. EC to Gordon Lewis, 6 February 1933, GL-UVA.

76. William Soskin, "D. H. Lawrence and Erskine Caldwell—An Unusual Association," *New York Post*, 7 February 1933.

77. EC to Mike Gold, 11 April 1933, Joseph Freeman Collection, Butler Library, Columbia University, New York, N.Y.

78. EC to AM, 17 July 1933, AM-HU. Caldwell's juxtaposition of "going to the bathroom, or kissing your wife," is revealing.

79. EC to AM, 10 August 1934, AM-HU.

80. EC to AM, 10 August 1934, AM-HU; EC to AM, 5 October 1933, AM-HU; EC to AM, 10 August 1934, AM-HU.

81. The complete transcript of the court decision is appended to the 1933 Modern Library edition of *God's Little Acre*. Caldwell, *God's Little Acre* (New York: Random House, 1934). For additional information on the trial, see Marshall Best to WS, 7 July 1971, WS-UI; telegram, Marshall Best to EC, 24 May 1933, EC-DC; EC to Milton Abernethy, 26 April 1933; telegram, ML to HLC, 26 May 1933; EC to GL, 16 May 1933, WB-UVA.

82. EC to MA, 26 April 1933, MA-UT. EC to GL, 16 May 1933, WB-UVA.

83. Lieber's manifesto, released 23 April 1933, is located in the Caldwell Collection at Dartmouth College, EC-DC.

84. Judge Greenspan quoted extensively from Sumner's brief in his decision. For the complete text of the decision, see the appendix to the Modern Library edition of *God's Little Acre* (New York: Random House, 1934).

85. Ibid.

86. JHW to EC, June 1933, EC-PU; Marshall Best to EC, 24 May 1933, EC-DC. ML to EC, 15 June 1933, EC-DC.

87. EC to GL, 17 March 1933, GL-UVA; EC to AM, 11 June 1933, AM-HU; EC to AM, 22 January 1933, AM-HU; EC to GL, 17 March 1933, GL-UVA.

88. Harvey Klevar interview with HLC, 29–30 June 1977, EC-DC.

CHAPTER SEVEN: FAME AND GUILT

1. Helen saved all of Caldwell's letters from Hollywood in spite of his instructions to destroy them. Found years later in the Mount Vernon house's attic, the collection of correspondence offers the single best insight into their turbulent relationship. See the box labeled "Helen, Letters," in the EC-DC.

2. EC to HLC, 8 May 1933, EC-DC; EC to HLC, 6 July 1933, EC-DC.

3. EC to HLC, 9 May 1933, EC-DC.

4. EC to HLC, 9 May 1933, EC-DC.

5. EC to HLC, 11 June 1933, EC-DC; EC to HLC, 12 July 1933, EC-DC.

6. EC to HLC, 2 June 1933, EC-DC; EC to HLC, 29 May 1933, EC-DC.

7. EC to HLC, 7 May 1933, EC-DC; EC to HLC, 9 June 1933, EC-DC. Caldwell never forgot the trauma of his own house burning down in Prosperity, South Carolina, and he retained lifelong a fear of fire.

8. EC to HLC, 23 June 1933, EC-DC.

9. EC to HLC, 8 May 1933, EC-DC; EC to HLC, 11 May 1933, EC-DC.

10. EC to HLC, 2 July 1934, EC-DC.

11. EC to HLC, 23 May 1933, EC-DC.

12. EC to HLC, 6 July 1933, EC-DC.

13. EC to HLC, 9 June 1933, EC-DC; EC to HLC, 29 July 1933, EC-DC.

14. Ibid; EC to HLC, 8 May 1933, EC-DC; EC to HLC, 15 May 1933, EC-DC.

15. EC to HLC, 22 July 1933, EC-DC; EC to HLC, 20 July 1933, EC-DC; EC to HLC, 20 July 1933, EC-DC.

16. EC to HLC, 23 July 1933, EC-DC; EC to HLC, 18 July 1933, EC-DC; EC to HLC, 6 July 1933, EC-DC; EC to HLC, 19 June 1933, DC-EC; EC to HLC, 7 July 1933, EC-DC.

17. EC to HLC, 12 July 1933, EC-DC.

18. EC to HLC, 22 July 1933, EC-DC.

19. EC to HLC, 19 June 1933, EC-DC.

20. For an excellent discussion of Hollywood in the 1930s, see Nancy Lynn Schwartz, *The Hollywood Writers' Wars* (New York: Alfred A. Knopf, 1982). The best study of the Hollywood Left is Larry Ceplair and Steve Englund, *The Inquisition in Hollywood* (Garden City, New York: Doubleday, 1980). See also Victor Navasky's *Naming Names* (New York: Viking Press, 1982); Bernard F. Dick, *Radical Innocence: A Critical Study of the Hollywood Ten* (Lexington, Ky.: University of Kentucky Press, 1989). The article in *Fortune* is quoted in Schwartz, *The Hollywood Writers' Wars*, p. 20.

21. EC to HLC, 26 May 1933, HLC-DC; EC to HLC, 29 May 1933, EC-DC; EC to HLC, 2 June 1933, HLC-DC.

22. EC to HLC, 11 May 1933, HLC-DC; EC to HLC, 10 May 1933, EC-DC; EC to HLC, 26 May 1933, EC-DC. Caldwell's fears that the movie business might "blow up" were not entirely irrational. Ticket sales had dropped during the Depression, labor disputes were raging, and several studios were in serious financial difficulty. See Schwartz, *The Hollywood Writers' Wars*, pp. 5–15.

23. EC to HLC, 8 July 1933, EC-DC; EC to HLC, 12 July 1933, EC-DC; EC to AM, 1 August 1933, AM-HU; EC to HLC, 17 June 1933, EC-DC.

24. Schwartz, *The Hollywood Writers' Wars*, p. 3. EC to HLC, 17 June 1933, EC-DC. EC to AM, 11 June 1933, AM-HU; EC to AM, 11 July 1933, AM-HU.

25. EC to AM, 29 May 1933, AM-HU. Caldwell's boast that the studio "would pay, or else," was repeated in dozens of letters, in a dozen variations. See EC to HLC, 11 May 1933, EC-DC.

26. EC to GL, 16 May 1933, WB-UVA.

27. EC to HLC, 15 May 1933, EC-DC; EC to HLC, 15 May 1933, EC-DC; EC to HLC, 11 May 1933, EC-DC.

28. EC to HLC, 1 June 1933, EC-DC.

29. EC to HLC, 9 June 1933, EC-DC; EC to AM, 25 May 1933, AM-HU.

30. EC to HLC, 21 July 1933, EC-DC. C to AM, 11 June 1933, AM-HU. Caldwell's description of a harried, day-in-the-life of a Hollywood screenwriter makes clear that he found the demands of the job almost intolerable.

> I got a phone call asking for an original story noon Friday! That was all; no other information. I got hold of Harry Behn, an experienced scenario writer; I then reached up and pulled a tale out of the blue sky, told it to him, retold it twice; Harry churned it in his head for half an hour, and then told me the story in terms of continuity. At one o'clock we called in a girl, and Harry started dictating. While he was dictating, I was writing out a draft of the next sequence of scenes; that continued until Friday morning at ten o'clock. At 10:15 the girl wrote FADE OUT and dashed across the lot with it to the mimeograph plant; at 1:20 the thing was mimeographed, bound, and distributed. And now that we've worked the hair off our heads, we probably will never hear of the story again.

31. EC to HLC, 26 May 1933, EC-DC; EC to HLC, 12 June 1933, EC-DC.

32. EC to HLC, 12 June 1933, EC-DC; EC to HLC, 2 June 1933, EC-DC; EC to AM, 23 June 1933, AM-HU; EC to AM, 11 June 1933, AM-HU.

33. EC to AM, 11 July 1933, AM-HU; EC to AM, 23 June 1934, AM-HU; EC to AM, 11 July 1933, AM-HU.

34. EC to AM, 29 May 1933, AM-HU.

35. EC to HLC, 1 June 1933, EC-DC; EC to HLC, 18 July 1933, EC-DC.

36. EC to ILS, 28 May 1933, ILS-LOC. EC to AM, 11 June 1933, AM-HU. EC to HLC, 1 June 1933, EC-DC.

37. EC to HLC, 3 June 1933, EC-DC; EC to AM, 25 May 1933, AM-HU; EC to AM, 11 July 1933, AM-HU.

38. EC to AM, 1 August 1933, AM-HU; EC to HLC, 2 June 1933, EC-DC.

39. EC to AM, 25 May 1933, AM-HU.

40. EC to AM, 1 August 1933, AM-HU; EC to HLC, 1 June 1933, EC-DC.

41. EC to MA, 3 August 1933, MA-UT.
42. EC to AM, 1 August 1933, AM-HU.
43. EC to ILS, 29 August 1933, ILS-LOC; EC to ILS, 28 May 1933, ILS-LOC; EC to MA, 3 August 1933, MA-UT.
44. Caldwell employed a clipping service during the eight years of *Tobacco Road*'s run. The carefully composed scrapbooks are located in the Caldwell collection at Dartmouth College. In cases where the by-line, date, or newspaper title is missing, I have noted the volume and page number of the scrapbook where the article is located.
45. Undated article by Bernard Sobel in unknown New York paper (Dartmouth clipping book "1933 II"). Kirkland repeated this account on dozens of occasions.
46. EC to HLC, 26 July 1933, EC-DC. Caldwell thought *God's Little Acre* would make a better play than *Tobacco Road*. "If a play was to be made at all," he told Morang, "I would much rather it be about the other book." EC to AM, 5 October 1933, AM-HU.
47. EC to AM, 29 October 1933, AM-HU.
48. EC to AM, 23 November 1933, AM-HU.
49. Mrs. Gordon Lewis to WS, undated 1970, WS-UI; Mrs. Alfred Morang to EC, 17 December 1980, privately held letter in possession of Mrs. Virginia Caldwell.
50. Percy Hammond, *New York Herald Tribune*, 5 December 1933; Brooks Atkinson, *New York Journal*, undated, Dartmouth Scrapbook, volume II.
51. Ibid.
52. Walter Winchell, *New York Times*, 5 December 1933; John Mason Brown, *New York Post*, undated, Dartmouth Scrapbook, volume II; Richard Lockridge, *New York Sun*, undated 1933, Dartmouth Scrapbook, volume II; Burns Mantle, *New York Daily News*, undated 1933, Dartmouth Scrapbook, volume II. Most of the first reviews appeared on December 6, the day after opening night.
53. EC to AM, 14 December 1933, AM-HU; EC to ILS, 9 December 1933, ILS-LOC.
54. Undated clipping from *The New Yorker*, Dartmouth Scrapbook, volume II, p. 25; unsigned letter to *New York Times*, 5 December 1933; unsigned editorial, *New York Post*, 25 January 1934.
55. EC to AM, 5 February 1934, AM-HU; EC to AM, 15 February 1934, AM-HU; EC to AM, 1 March 1934, AM-HU.
56. EC to AM, 1 March 1934, AM-HU.; EC to AM, 22 February 1934, AM-HU.
57. *New York Times*, 10 March 1940. Unfortunately, Gershwin died before he could complete the work, which he planned to debut at the 1939 World's Fair. The hundreds of clippings in Volume II of the Dartmouth Scrapbooks communicate the New York press's fascination with the play.
58. A copy of Dreiser's letter is located in the Dartmouth Scrapbooks, Volume II, p. 22, and was reprinted on the jacket of the Viking Press 1934 edition of the dramatization. Lieber wrote letters to, among other people, the Governor of Connecticut, asking him to endorse the play for the Pulitzer Prize. Maxim Lieber to "Governor Cross," 2 February 1934, Beineke Library, Yale University, New Haven, CT. Percy Hammond, *New York Herald Tribune*, Dartmouth Scrapbook, Volume II, p. 48. EC to AM, 22 February 1934, AM-HU. Grisman was interviewed in *New York Post*, 6 May 1936.
59. Interview in *Washington Star*, 25 February 1941.

60. Robert Benchley, *The New Yorker*, June 1934, Dartmouth Scrapbook, vol. II.
61. Possibly, Caldwell arrived late on the play's opening night to avoid—albeit unconsciously—witnessing "the scene."
62. Kelly's comments were carried in newspapers nationwide. See, for instance, *New York Herald Tribune*, 21 October 1935.
63. As quoted in *New York Times*, 21 October 1935.
64. Letters, both for and against the play, were carried in the *Chicago Daily News*. See Dartmouth Scrapbook, Volume III, p. 48.
65. EC to AM, 13 November 1935, AM-HU.
66. As quoted in *New York Daily News*, 6 November 1935.
67. EC to AM, 3 April 1936, AM-HU; EC to Frank Daniels, 2 December 1938, Frank Daniel Papers, Special Collections, Emory University, Atlanta, GA.
68. EC to Brooks Atkinson, 28 February 1938, MBW-SU, box 1.
69. Marshall Best to Maxim Lieber, 15 October 1934, EC-DC. Erskine Caldwell Editorial Correspondence from Marshall Best. Used by permission of Viking Penguin, a division of Penguin Books USA Inc.
70. EC to HLC, 18 November 1934, EC-DC; EC to AM, 24 October 1934, AM-HU; EC to AM, 24 October 1934, AM-HU.
71. EC to HLC, undated 1934, EC-DC; EC to AM, 24 September 1934, AM-HU; Marshall Best to EC, 10 November 1934.
72. Kenneth Burke, "Caldwell: Maker of Grotesques," *The New Republic*, 82 (April 10, 1935); William Troy, *Nation*, 13 February 1934; Hamilton Basso, *New Masses*, 11 June 1935; James Farrell, *New Masses*, 2 April 1935; Horace Gregory, *New York Herald Tribune Books*, 3 February 1935.
73. Charles Wagner, *New York Mirror*, 7 June 1935. Louis Gannett, *New York Herald Tribune*, 7 June 1935. Harold Strauss, *New York Times*, 9 June 1935.
74. Hamilton Basso, *New Masses*, undated, Dartmouth Scrapbook, vol. 5, p. 63.
75. HLC to ILS, 26 February 1934, ILS-LOC; EC to Whit Burnett, 29 September 1937, EC-DC.
76. Lieber to EC, 11 December 1933, EC-DC.
77. Lieber to EC, 26 February 1951, EC-DC. All the letters appeared in *Time* and are located in Dartmouth Scrapbook, Volume V, p. 48.
78. Deen's speech was reprinted in a number of newspapers, including *New York Herald Tribune*, 7 April 1936.
79. *Monroe Georgia Tribune*, 1 December 1939; B. W. Middlebrook of Barnesville, GA to EC, 18 June 1959, EC-DC; *Gainesville Georgia News*, 20 March 1940.
80. Mrs. Russell Taylor to EC, undated, EC-DC.
81. Mrs. Russell Taylor to EC, undated, EC-DC; William T. Freeman of Asheville, North Carolina, to EC, 18 March 1940, EC-DC.
82. Unsigned letter to EC, undated, EC-DC. "C.Y.A." to EC, 13 February 1938, EC-DC. Caldwell was so disturbed by this letter that he contacted the F.B.I. and asked them to investigate the threat.
83. Years later, Caldwell wrote to McGill to thank him for his support. EC to Ralph McGill, 19 December 1966. EC-DC. W. J. Cash, *Charlotte News and Observer*, 26 November 1939.
84. In the mid- to late 1930s, for example, *Tobacco Road* was the most requested novel at public libraries in Greenwood, S.C., Atlanta, Ga., and Charlotte, N.C. *Greenwood Journal*, 8 January 1939; *Atlanta Georgian*, 27 December 1938; *Charlotte North Carolina News*, 29 March 1941.
85. *New York Times*, 1 December 1940. In 1940, Grisman estimated that the play

had grossed almost seven million dollars in New York and on the road. Caldwell's income is estimated on the basis of the percentage of royalties guaranteed by his contract with Kirkland and Grisman.

86. EC to Bob Brown, 10 December 1934, Special Collections, Southern Illinois University.
87. Caldwell's stock transactions and correspondence with his brokers are located in the EC-DC.
88. EC to AM, 23 April 1934; EC to AM, 10 June 1934, AM-HU; EC to AM, 23 June 1934, AM-HU.
89. EC to Frank Daniel, 8 March 1934, FD-EU. EC to AM, 5 July 1934, AM-HU.
90. EC to AM, 5 July 1934, AM-HU; EC to AM, 16 July, 1934, AM-HU.

CHAPTER EIGHT: "KIT"

1. For general information on sharecroppers and the New Deal policies that affected them, see David Eugene Conrad, *The Forgotten Farmers: The Story of Sharecroppers in the New Deal* (Urbana, Illinois: University of Illinois Press, 1965).
2. The figure of 7,000 letters was reported in *Time*, 4 March 1935.
3. Hugh Russell Frazier's article appeared in *Memphis Press-Scimitar*, 26 February 1935. See also *New York Times*, 11 March 1934.
4. Caldwell's four articles appeared in *New York Post*, on four consecutive days, from 18 to 21 February 1935.
5. Erskine Caldwell, *New York Post*, 18 February 1935; Caldwell, *Post*, 19 February 1935; Caldwell, *Post*, 20 February 1935.
6. Caldwell, *Post*, 18 February 1935.
7. Caldwell, *Post*, 18 February 1935; Caldwell, *Post*, 21 February 1935.
8. *Time* reprinted excerpts from the *New York Post* articles on 4 March 1935. The first local response appeared in *Augusta Chronicle*, 4 March 1935. For an excellent selection of the letters that appeared over the ensuing weeks, see Scott MacDonald, *Critical Essays on Erskine Caldwell* (Boston: G. K. Hall & Co., 1981), pp. 107–118.
9. J. T. Avret to *Augusta Chronicle*, 17 March 1935; L. E. Holmes to *Augusta Chronicle*, 17 March 1935.
10. These letters to *Time* were reprinted on 25 March 1935.
11. Ibid.
12. Erskine Caldwell, *New York Post*, 20 April 1935. The letters are located in Volume V of the Caldwell scrapbooks, EC-DC.
13. I. S. Caldwell, *Time*, 25 March 1935.
14. The *Augusta Chronicle* published the five-part article from 10 March 1935 through 14 March 1935. The quotation is taken from the final article on 14 March 1935.
15. I. S. Caldwell, letter to the editor of the *Augusta Chronicle*, 17 March 1935; *New Republic*, 82 (27 March 1935).
16. The second *New York Post* series appeared every day from 17 April 1935 through 20 April 1935. The photographs and captions were printed on 17 April 1935.
17. *New York Post*, 21 April 1935.
18. As quoted in a letter to the *New York Post*, 19 April 1935. For an understanding of documentary literature during this time period, I have relied heavily on William Stott's *Documentary Expression in Thirties America* (New York: Oxford

University Press, 1973). For the journalistic coverage of the sharecroppers that followed Caldwell's *Post* series see Stott, pp. 216–218. See also John Herling, "Labor and Industry: Field Notes from Arkansas," *Nation*, 10 April 1935; "Bootleg Slavery," *Time*, 4 March 1935. Henry A. Wallace, *New York Times Magazine*, 31 March 1935; Cecil Holland, "The Tenant Farmer Turns," *Survey Graphic*, May, 1935. See Stott, p. 218, for examples of the sharecropper's growing notoriety. Stephens is quoted in Stott, p. 217.

19. Granville Hicks, Michael Gold, Isadore Schneider, Joseph North, Paul Peters and Alan Calmer, eds., *Proletarian Literature in the United States* (New York: The Left-Wing Book Union, 1935). The most complete record of Caldwell's political activities can be found among the hundreds of clippings in the Volume V, 1935, Caldwell scrapbook at the EC-DC. The "Call for an American Writers' Congress" appeared in *New Masses*, 22 January 1935. For the best description of the event see Daniel Aaron, *Writers on the Left*, pp. 282–292.

20. Erskine Caldwell, *Tenant Farmer* (New York: Phalanx Press, 1935); Ella Winter, undated, in *Pacific Weekly*, Scrapbook Vol. V, EC-DC. Pound's quotation is taken from an unmarked clipping in the Waller Barrett Papers, WB-UVA.

21. W. T. Couch, *Raleigh* (N.C.) *Observer*, 4 August 1935.

22. Although Caldwell's assignment in New Bedford was reported in *New York World Telegram*, 9 August 1935, the article did not appear in *Fortune*. The article on the "Okies" was reported in an undated clipping in the ISC-UGA.

23. EC to Frank Daniel, 3 May 1934, FD-E.

24. The five-part article appeared in *Daily Worker* on 2, 4, 5, 6, and 7 June 1934.

25. *Daily Worker*, 4 June 1934; ibid., 5 June 1934.

26. Erskine Caldwell, *Some American People* (New York: Robert M. McBride & Company, 1935).

27. Caldwell, *Some American People*, p. 72.

28. John Spivak, *America Faces the Barricades* (New York, 1935). An exception to the regional or polemical tone of most travel books of this time was Sherwood Anderson's *Puzzled America* (New York, 1935).

29. Anonymous reviewer, *New York News*, "Horrors of Life in the U.S.A.," 20 October 1935; Louis Joseph Haloff, *Atlanta Constitution*, 8 December 1935; Ernest Sutherland Bates, *New York Herald Tribune*, undated clipping in 1935 Dartmouth Scrapbook.

30. Albert Halper, *New Masses*, 10 December 1935.

31. Travel books following *Some American People* included James Rorty, *Where Life Is Better: An Unsentimental American Journey* (New York, 1936); Louis Adamic, *My America* (New York, London: Harper & Brothers, 1938); Archibald MacLeish, *Land of the Free* (New York: Harcourt, Brace and Company, 1938); Dorothea Lange and Paul Taylor, *An American Exodus* (New York: Arno Press, 1939).

32. Caldwell, *Call It Experience*, p. 128.

33. For my understanding of Margaret Bourke-White, I have benefited a great deal from Vicki Goldberg's outstanding biography, *Margaret Bourke-White: A Biography* (New York: Harper & Row, Publishers, Inc., 1986). Citations in my text refer to the paperback edition (New York: Reading, Mass., 1987). Bourke-White's autobiography, *Portrait of Myself* (New York: Simon & Schuster, 1963) is also revealing. The best single source on Bourke-White is the

extensive collection of her letters and papers located at the George Arents
Research Library at Syracuse University.

34. Goldberg, *Bourke-White*, chs. 9 and 10, *passim.*

35. As quoted in Goldberg, p. 99.

36. Bourke-White describes the dream in *Portrait*, p. 112.

37. Bourke-White traveled to Russia three times between 1930 and 1932 on *Fortune* assignments, and her romantic, majestic photographs of the newly built factories were devoured by American readers fascinated with the Communist experiment. While her interests in Russia were more artistic than political, during these trips she began to take greater notice of Russian workers as well as the newly built machines they operated.

38. Lieber to MBW, 13 January 1936, Box 26, MBW-SU.

39. MBW to "Mr. Caldwell," 9 March 1936, Box 1, MBW-SU.

40. Lieber to MBW, 18 February 1936, Box 1, MBW-SU.

41. Lieber to MBW, 13 January 1936, Box 26, MBW-SU. For Goldberg's description of the trip see *Margaret Bourke-White*, Chapter 14, *passim.* Caldwell described the trip in both autobiographies. See *Call It Experience*, pp. 128–130, and *With All My Might*, pp. 144–151. Bourke-White's recollections are in *Portrait*, pp. 120–141.

42. EC to Helen, 17 July 1936, EC-DC.

43. MBW to EC, undated 1936 (probably 17 July), Box 1, MBW-SU.

44. EC to HLC, 20 July 1936, EC-DC.

45. EC to HLC, "Helen Caldwell Papers," undated 1936, Special Collections Library, Colby College, Waterville, Maine.

46. Ruth Carnell kept notes of the events before her departure. They are reprinted in William Sutton's unpublished manuscript located in the WS-UI. Bourke-White recalled Caldwell's frustration with being a "tourist guide" in *Portrait*, p. 125.

47. EC to HLC, 25 July 1936, EC-DC.

48. Carnell's notes in William Sutton's manuscript, WS-UI.

49. For Goldberg's interpretation of Bourke-White's seduction of Caldwell, see *Margaret Bourke-White*, p. 167. HLC interview with WS, 30 July 1970. Lieber's comments are quoted in Goldberg, p. 167.

50. Bourke-White, *Portrait*, p. 114.

51. Many of Bourke-White's lovers were married. She seemed drawn to men whose work or wives kept them from expecting too much of a commitment.

52. Caldwell, *With All My Might*, p. 146. Caldwell described the project's goals in an interview in *Popular Photography*, March 1938.

53. Bourke-White, *Portrait*, pp. 125–126.

54. Bourke-White described her photographic method in *You Have Seen Their Faces*. Erskine Caldwell and Margaret Bourke-White, *You Have Seen Their Faces* (New York: Viking Press, 1937), p. 51. Goldberg describes Caldwell's and Bourke-White's techniques in *Margaret Bourke-White*, pp. 168–169.

55. As quoted in Goldberg, pp. 168–169.

56. Bourke-White, *Portrait*, p. 125–126.

57. Ibid., pp. 133–134.

58. Bourke-White, *Portrait*, p. 132. Also see MBW to Earl Bell, 11 November 1937, Box 8, MBW-SU; MBW to EC, 20 August 1936, Box 1, MBW-SU.

59. Caldwell and Bourke-White, *Faces*, unpaginated preface. The photographs in the book are not paginated.

60. Caldwell and Bourke-White, *Faces*, p. 5.
61. For a full discussion of the photo-text medium in the 1930s, see Stott, *Documentary Expression*, ch. 12, *passim*. There is a brief discussion of the precursors to *You Have Seen Their Faces* in Goldberg, *Margaret Bourke-White*, pp. 192–193.
62. Roy Stryker thought Bourke-White's pictures were too "theatrical." See Goldberg, *Margaret Bourke-White*, p. 192.
63. Herschell Brickell, *New York Post*, 8 November 1937; Robert Van Gelder, *New York Times Book Review*, 28 November 1937; Margaret Marshall, *Nation*, 4 December 1937. A summary of the book's critical success was printed in *New York Herald Tribune*, 18 December 1937. Bourke-White quoted the *Philadelphia Record* review in *Portrait*, p. 138.
64. Edwin Seaver to EC, 9 December 1938, Box 6, MBW-SU.
65. Frank Daniel, *Atlanta Journal*, 19 December 1937; Hudson Strode, *New York Herald Tribune Books*, 21 November 1937; Lillian Smith to EC, 3 January 1937, EC-DC.
66. Cowley's comments and Bourke-White's response to them are included in *Portrait*, p. 138.
67. Caldwell treasured these angry Southern reviews. They are located (but undated) in the "1938" Scrapbook in the EC-DC.
68. W. T. Couch, "Landlord and Tenant," *Virginia Quarterly Review*, Spring 1938.
69. Donald Davidson, "Erskine Caldwell's Picture Book," *Southern Review*, IV (1938–1939), pp. 15–25.
70. H. C. Nixon, *Forty Acres and Steel Mules* (Chapel Hill: The University of North Carolina Press, 1938); Dorothea Lange and Paul Taylor, *An American Exodus* (New York: Arno Press, 1939).
71. The best comparison between *You Have Seen Their Faces* and *Let Us Now Praise Famous Men* is in Stott, *Documentary Expression*, pp. 218–222.
72. As quoted in Stott, *Documentary Expression*, pp. 222–223.
73. EC to MBW, undated, Box 1, MBW-SU; EC to "Kit," 7 April 1937, Box 1, MBW-SU; EC to MBW, 8 February 1937, Box 1, MBW-SU.
74. Malcolm Cowley, *And I Worked at the Writer's Trade: Chapters of Literary History, 1918–1978* (New York: Viking Press, 1978), p. 116. Maxim Lieber never forgot reading Bourke-White's explicit telegram. Minna Lieber interview with DM, 1 August 1993.
75. See Goldberg, chapters 16 and 17, *passim*.
76. EC to MBW, undated 1936, Box 1, MBW-SU; EC to MBW, undated 1936, Box 1, MBW-SU; EC to MBW, 8 February 1937, Box 1, MBW-SU.
77. EC to MBW, undated 1936, Box 1, MBW-SU.
78. EC to MBW, March 1937, Box 1, MBW-SU.
79. EC to MBW, February 1937, Box 1, MBW-SU. Bourke-White discussed Caldwell's moods in *Portrait*, p. 170.
80. EC to MBW, 7 November 1937, Box 1, MBW-SU. I am grateful to Peggy Smith Sargeant, Bourke-White's secretary, for her recollections of the relationship. Sargeant interview with DM, 17 October 1992. Bourke-White also discussed Caldwell's violent moods in an interview with William Sutton. MBW interview with WS, 30 June 1970, WS-UI.
81. EC to "Kit," 7 April 1937, Box 1, MBW-SU; EC to MBW, 20 February 1937, Box 1, MBW-SU; EC to MBW, undated 1937, Box 1, MBW-SU; EC to MBW, undated 1938, Box 1, MBW-SU.

82. CPC to EC, 27 July 1937, MBW-SU; CPC to EC, 9 August 1937, MBW-SU.
83. Bourke-White, *Portrait*, p. 171.
84. EC to MBW, undated 1938, Box 1, MBW-SU; EC to MBW, 23 July 1937, Box 1, MBW-SU.
85. Dr. Harry Stack Sullivan to MBW, 28 October 1937, MBW-SU.
86. MBW to EC, 31 October 1936, Box 1, MBW-SU; MBW to EC, 10 November 1936, Box 1, MBW-SU; MBW to EC, 15 November 1936, Box 1, MBW-SU. Goldberg describes Caldwell's wooing of Bourke-White in *Margaret Bourke-White*, ch. 17. Copies of Caldwell's telegrams are located in Box 1, MBW-SU.
87. EC to HLC, 19 May 1937, EC-DC.
88. EC to HLC, 28 April 1937, EC-DC.
89. EC to HLC, undated 1937, EC-DC.
90. EC to HLC, 23 May 1937, EC-DC.
91. EC to HLC, 1 March 1937, EC-DC. Helen discussed her feelings for Caldwell very candidly with William Sutton. HLC to WS, 16 January 1970, WS-UI.
92. Dr. Harry Stack Sullivan to MBW, 28 October 1937, MBW-SU. HLC interview WS, 4 July 1970, WS-UI.
93. HLC interview with WS, 4 July 1970, WS-UI.
94. The divorce papers are located in EC-DC.
95. Residents of Mount Vernon remember Helen as a charismatic and valued member of their community.
96. EC to HLC, undated 1938, EC-DC. HLC to EC, undated, EC-DC.

CHAPTER NINE: TROUBLE IN JULY

1. *New York World Telegram*, 30 August 1938; *New York Post*, 29 August 1938; *New York News*, 29 August 1938. Winchell is quoted in Goldberg, p. 214.
2. For information on Caldwell's efforts to change for Bourke-White's sake, I am indebted to Mrs. Maxim Lieber. Minna Lieber interview with DM, 11 July 1993.
3. Telegram, EC to "Miss Lalani Bourke White," 9 February 1939, Box 1, MBW-SU; Telegram EC to "Sugar Babe Bourke White, 9 February 1939, Box 1, MBW-SU; Telegram, EC to "Honeychile Bourke-White, 8 February 1939, Box 1, MBW-SU.
4. Bourke-White, *Portrait*, pp. 171–172.
5. Bourke-White, *Portrait*, p. 172; Caldwell, *With All My Might*, pp. 167–169. The wedding is also described in Goldberg, *Margaret Bourke-White*, p. 217.
6. "Kit" to "you adorable" [EC], 26 July 1939, Box 1, MBW-SU.
7. Quoted in Goldberg, *Margaret Bourke-White*, p. 220.
8. Telegram, EC to MBW, 23 July 1939, Box 1, MBW-SU; telegram, EC to MBW, 27 July 1939, Box 1, MB-SU; EC to MBW in Santa Fe, 25 November 1939, Box 1, MBW-SU.
9. Telegram, MBW to EC, 24 July 1939, Box 1, MBW-SU; MBW to EC, 3 November 1939, Box 1, MBW-SU; MBW to EC, 6 December 1939, Box 1, MBW-SU.
10. EC to MBW, November 1939, Box 1, MBW-SU; telegram, EC to MBW, 24 November 1939, Box 1, MBW-SU.
11. Telegram, MBW to EC, 12 December 1939, Box 2, MBW-SU. Dabney Caldwell provided excellent information on Bourke-White's desire to be a mother. Dabney Caldwell interview with DM, 27 February 1990. Goldberg

discusses Bourke-White's wish for a child in *Margaret Bourke-White*, pp. 219–220.

12. MBW to "Suzy, Fluffy, Lottie, and Johnnie," 2 November 1939, MBW-SU.

13. EC to MBW, 26 October 1939, Box 2, MBW-SU; EC to MBW, 4 December 1939, Box 2, MBW-SU; EC to MBW, undated 1939, Box 2, MBW-SU.

14. EC to MBW, 20 November 1939, Box 2, MBW-SU; EC to MBW, 5 November 1939, Box 2, MBW-BU.

15. MBW to EC, 11 November 1939, Box 3, MBW-SU; MBW to EC, 13 November 1939, Box 3, MBW-SU.

16. Telegram, EC to MBW, 2 August 1940, Box 2, MBW-SU.

17. As quoted in *Atlanta Georgian*, 25 November 1938. Caldwell's political activities were noted in the left-wing press. See, for instance, *Daily Worker*, 12 January 1939 and 27 December 1937; *New Masses*, 16 May 1939.

18. Caldwell's participation was noted in *New Masses*, 16 May 1939. Caldwell happily accepted his post as an honorary vice-president of the League of American Writers. See EC to "Miss Blake," 16 June 1937, EC-DC.

19. Caldwell was praised in *Daily Worker*, 5 November 1940. The 1939 Congress was Caldwell's last high-profile gesture of political sympathy with the Left. The American economy was on the mend, and the American government seemed as committed as most leftists to the fight against fascism. When, only a few months after the Third Congress, Hitler and Stalin signed a nonaggression pact, the mythic view of Soviet Communism that had sustained so many American leftists for so long was fatally tarnished.

20. These, and most other activities Caldwell undertook in the late thirties, were covered in the New York press. The Dartmouth Scrapbooks for 1937 and 1938 contain many of these articles. The lecture course was covered in *New York Herald Tribune*, 7 January 1938.

21. The possible sale of *Tobacco Road* to the movies was covered in *Albany Times Union*, 21 April 1938; *Newsweek*, 27 November 1939; *New York Post*, 6 December 1939. See Stanley Rose to EC, 4 January 1940, Box 6, MBW-SU; EC to CPC, 17 January 1940, ISC-UGA.

22. *New York World Telegram*, 1 February 1938; *Brooklyn Citizen*, 31 January 1938; *New York Evening Journal*, 31 January 1938; Robert Coleman, *Daily Mirror*, 31 January 1938.

23. Erskine Caldwell, *Southways* (New York: The Viking Press, 1938).

24. Arnold Shukotoff, *New Masses*, 28 June 1938; Robert Goldsmith, *Daily Worker*, 28 June 1938; Otis Ferguson, *New Republic*, 6 July 1938; Dorothy Van Doren, *Nation*, 25 June 1938.

25. Lewis Gannett, *New York Herald Tribune*, 17 June 1938.

26. William Soskin, *New York Times*, 19 June 1938.

27. For Bourke-White's recollection of the book see Bourke-White, *Portrait*, p. 170. Goldberg includes an excellent discussion of the project in *Margaret Bourke-White*, pp. 210–214.

28. Erskine Caldwell and Margaret Bourke-White, *North of the Danube* (New York: Viking Press, 1939).

29. EC to CPC and ISC, undated 1938, ISC-UGA; EC to AM, 11 May 1938, AM-HU; EC to AM, 30 May 1938, AM-HU; EC to AM, 16 June 1938, AM-HU; EC to Frank Daniel, 12 October 1938, FD-EU. Caldwell and Bourke-White's trip was followed in the press. See, for instance, *New York World Telegram*, 30 August 1938; *New York Herald Tribune, Paris Edition*, 10 April 1938.

30. EC to AM, 30 May 1938, AM-HU; EC to AM, 16 June 1938, AM-HU; EC to Frank Daniel, 19 May 1938, FD-EU. Bourke-White's father was Jewish, although she rarely mentioned the fact.

31. ML to EC, 11 May 1939, EC-DC.

32. Bertram Gale, *New Masses*, 25 April 1939; Leland Stowe, *New York Herald Tribune*, 2 April 1939; Maurice Hindus, *New Republic*, undated clipping, "1939" Dartmouth Scrapbook. Hurban's comments are contained in a letter from Robert L. Hatch to EC, 8 May 1939, EC-DC.

33. Bourke-White discussed her dissatisfaction with the book in *Portrait*, p. 170. EC to CPC and ISC, 28 December 1938, ISC-UGA.

34. *New Yorker*, 25 June 1938; Charles Poore, *New York Times*, 18 June 1938.

35. ISC to EC, August 1939, Box 2, MBW-SU.

36. Caldwell recalled his father's race liberalism on numerous occasions. For a thorough and intimate recollection, see Erskine Caldwell, *Deep South: Memory and Observation* (New York: Weybright and Talley, Inc., 1968).

37. For Caldwell's memory of Moses Coffee, see *Deep South*, pp. 207–220.

38. Nick Carter interview with WS, 29 November 1970, WS-UI; EC to Ben Farley, 5 July 1978, EC-DC.

39. For an excellent overview of racial violence in Georgia during this time period, see George Brown Tindall, *Emergence of the New South: 1913–1945* (Baton Rouge: Louisiana State University, 1967) chapter V, passim. These statistics are cited in Tindall, *Emergence*, p. 179.

40. Tindall, *Emergence*, p. 212.

41. Caldwell recalled the incident on numerous occasions. See, for instance, an interview in *New York Times*, 17 July 1965.

42. Ibid.

43. Cy Hood interview with WS, 20 December 1970, WS-UI; Mrs. H. A. Phagan to WS, 11 October 1970, WS-UI.

44. A number of Wrens residents recall lynchings and racial violence during these years. Ruby Tanner interview with DM, 22 January 1991; Cy Hood to WS, 23 October 1970; Leroy Lewis interview with DM, 25 January 1991. Ira S. Caldwell, "Civilization Is Only Skin Deep," *Augusta Chronicle*, 16 January 1931.

45. Lowry Ware interview with DM, 15 January 1991. Caldwell described the incidents to Virginia Caldwell Hibbs.

46. Erskine Caldwell, "Georgia Cracker," *The Haldeman-Julius Monthly* 4 (November 1926), pp. 39–42.

47. Caldwell's remarks on "The End of Christy Tucker" are contained in *Jackpot: The Short Stories of Erskine Caldwell* (New York: Duell, Sloan and Pearce, 1940), p. 226. Caldwell, "The People vs. Abe Lathan, Colored," *Esquire* 12 (August), pp. 26–27, 145; Caldwell, "Candy-Man Beechum," *Esquire* 3 (February), pp. 39, 146.

48. Caldwell, *The Sacrilege of Alan Kent* (Falmouth, Maine: Falmouth Book House, 1936), p. 29; Caldwell, "Savannah River Payday," originally published in *American Earth* (New York: Charles Scribner's & Sons, 1931).

49. Erskine Caldwell, *God's Little Acre* (New York: Viking Press, 1933), p. 278; Ibid., p. 13.

50. Caldwell, *Tobacco Road*, p. 107.

51. Howard Kester, "The Lynching of Claude Neal," pamphlet dated November 30, 1934. *New Masses*, 16 January 1934.

52. Caldwell, " 'Parties Unknown' in Georgia," *New Masses*, 23 January 1934.
53. Caldwell, "A Story That Got Lost," *New Masses*, 16 January 1934.
54. *New Masses*, 6 February 1934; EC to AM, 5 February 1934, AM-HU.
55. Caldwell, *New York Post*, 21 April 1935.
56. Caldwell and Bourke-White, *You Have Seen Their Faces*, pp. i–ii.
57. Bourke-White described the incident in an undated clipping in the EC-DC.
58. Tindall, *Emergence*, chapter XVI, *passim*. As quoted in Tindall, p. 553.
59. Erskine Caldwell, *Trouble in July* (Duell, Sloan & Pearce, 1940), p. 179.
60. Caldwell, *Trouble*, p. 177; ibid., p. 125; ibid., p. 122.
61. Ibid., pp. 223–224.
62. Ibid., pp. 98–99. Richard Wright, *New Republic*, 11 March 1940.
63. Caldwell, *Trouble*, p. 80; ibid., p. 190.
64. EC to MBW, undated 1939, MBW-SU.
65. For the strain between Caldwell and his publishers, see EC to AM, 25 September 1934, AM-HU; Marshall Best to EC, 17 April 1934, Box 7, MBW-SU; Lieber to EC, 11 May 1939; Best to EC, 26 May 1939, Box 7, MBW-SU.
66. Marshall Best to EC, 26 May 1939, Box 7, MBW-SU.
67. Lieber to EC, 26 February 1951, EC-DC; Marshall Best interview with WS, 3 March 1971, WS-UI.
68. Caldwell's increased cost of living is evidenced in the canceled checks from this period, located in the EC-DC.
69. The formation of DS&P was noted in *New York Times*, 7 December 1939.
70. Charles Duell to Lieber, 6 November 1939, Box 2, MBW-SU; EC to MBW, 3 November 1939, Box 2, MBW-SU.
71. Charles Pearce to EC, 2 February 1940; Bob Hunt to EC, 29 November 1939, 1 January 1939; ibid., 2 February 1940; ibid., 21 February 1940, EC-DC.
72. Beverly Shaw to EC, 12 September 1942, EC-DC.
73. Anonymous, "To the Letter Opener," undated, EC-DC. Much of Caldwell's hate mail was undated and unsigned.
74. Clifton Fadiman, *New York Times*, 25 February 1940; Harold Strauss, *Nation*, 17 August 1940.
75. Edwin Berry Bergum, *Newsweek*, 19 March 1940; Milton Rugoff, *Booklist*, 15 March 1940.
76. Richard Wright, *New Republic*, 11 March 1940.
77. Walter White to EC, 13 February 1940, EC-DC.
78. Telegram, MBW to EC, 24 February 1949, Box 1, MBW-SU.

CHAPTER TEN: ALL OUT ON THE ROAD TO SMOLENSK

1. The statement was reprinted in *New Masses*, 17 June 1941.
2. There are dozens of newspaper accounts of the founding of the American Folkways Series in the 1941 scrapbook in the EC-DC. See, for instance, *New York Times*, 19 January 1941; *St. Paul Dispatch*, 23 March 1941; *Camden, New Jersey Publishers Weekly*, 3 May 1941. Also see Charles Pearce to Mrs. Lucy Bailey, 17 March 1947, EC-DC.
3. Caldwell kept copies of most of his editorial correspondence—material now located in the EC-DC. EC to Gertrude Atherton, 16 June 1943, EC-DC. The comparison to Mencken is contained in a letter from Charles Pearce to EC, 16 March 1942.
4. Stetson Kennedy, *Palmetto Country* (New York: Duell, Sloan & Pearce, 1942);

Meridel Le Sueur, *North Star Country* (New York: Duell, Sloan & Pearce, 1945).

5. Caldwell described the purpose of the series in an interview for *St. Paul Dispatch*, 23 March 1941. Otto Ernest Rayburn, *Ozark Country* (New York: Duell, Sloan & Pearce, 1941); Edwin Corle, *Desert Country* (New York: Duell, Sloan & Pearce, 1941); Herbert Croy, *Corn Country* (New York: Duell, Sloan & Pearce, 1947); Jean Thomas, *Blue Ridge Country* (New York: Duell, Sloan & Pearce, 1942); Clarence Merton Webster, *Town Meeting Country* (New York: Duell, Sloan & Pearce, 1945); Gertrude Atherton, *Golden Gate Country* (New York: Duell, Sloan & Pearce, 1945). Caldwell was very proud that "one of the most important courses at Harvard, in the Department of Social Relations, [is] being built around the Folkways series." EC to Helen Worden, 3 February 1947, H. W. Erskine Collection, Butler Library, Columbia University, New York, N.Y.

6. Caldwell and Bourke-White granted newspaper interviews throughout the journey. *Tucson Arizona Citizen*, 3 December 1940; *Texarkana Texas Gazette*, 7 December 1940; *Tampa Florida Tribune*, 13 December 1940. That year, Caldwell and Bourke-White sent Christmas cards picturing themselves seated on top of a freight car.

7. The following quotations are taken from Erskine Caldwell and Margaret Bourke-White, *Say, Is This the U.S.A?* (New York: Duell, Sloan & Pearce, 1941).

8. Ralph Thompson, *New York Times*, 26 June 1941; *Boston Herald*, 2 July 1941. The sales figures were reported in *Dayton News*, 20 July 1941.

9. Articles on the proposed film adaptation of *Tobacco Road* appeared in *Newsweek*, 27 November 1939; *New York Post*, 6 December 1939. See also Stanley Rose to EC, 4 January 1940, Box 6, MBW-SU; EC to CPC and ISC, 17 January 1940, ISC-UGA. There are hundreds of newspaper clippings describing every aspect of the film in the "1940–1941" scrapbook in the EC-DC.

10. *Hollywood Daily Reporter*, 23 February 1940. Zanuck was quoted in *New Film Daily*, 21 February 1941; *New York Daily Mirror*, 1 March 1940. EC to MBW, 15 December 1939, Box 2, MBW-SU.

11. Mitchell wrote Caldwell and gently requested that he do something about the advertising. Margaret Mitchell to EC, 13 February 1941, EC-DC. The casting of the film was discussed in *San Francisco People's World*, 23 October 1940; *Los Angeles Evening News*, 24 February 1940; *New York Times*, 1 September 1940.

12. *Movies*, April 1941; *CUE*, 1 March 1941. Also see Janey Ann Place, *The Non-Western Films of John Ford* (Secaucus, New Jersey: Citadel Press, 1979), p. 71.

13. The New York premiere was covered in *New York Daily News*, 21 February 1941. For the film's profits, see Harry Oshrin to "Twentieth-Century Fox," 26 August 1952, EC-DC.

14. *Time*, 10 March 1941; *New York Herald Tribune*, 21 February 1941. Caldwell expressed his disgust with the film in an interview with *Seattle Post*, 17 October 1957.

15. *Chicago American*, 18 November 1959.

16. Goldberg, *Margaret Bourke-White*, p. 236.

17. Caldwell, *With All My Might*, p. 178.

18. Ibid.

19. Goldberg, *Bourke-White*, p. 237. For Caldwell's recollections, see Erskine Cald-

well, *All Out on the Road to Smolensk* (New York: Duell, Sloan & Pearce, 1942), pp. 1–16.

20. Caldwell and Bourke-White's incredible journey from New York to Moscow is described in several places. See Goldberg, *Margaret Bourke-White*, p. 237; Caldwell, *With All My Might*, pp. 178–183; Bourke-White, *Portrait*, pp. 174–175. An itinerary of the trip is located in the EC-DC. Caldwell's unpublished recollections are located in Box 2, MBW-SU. Also see *South China Morning Post*, 10 April 1941; EC to CPC and ISC, 19 April 1941, ISC-UGA.

21. Caldwell, *Call It Experience*, pp. 154–155. Goldberg, *Margaret Bourke-White*, p. 238. MBW to Wilson Hicks, 4 June 1941.

22. Caldwell, *Call It Experience*, pp. 154–155; EC to Rhoda Lynn, 19 May 1941, EC-DC.

23. Goldberg, *Margaret Bourke-White*, pp. 238, 244.

24. With the assistance of the Soviet Writers' Union and the Society of Cultural Relations with Foreign Countries, Caldwell and Bourke-White were afforded an unusual freedom. They were, for instance, allowed to visit the Ukraine and the Black Sea, areas forbidden to most Western journalists. Goldberg, *Margaret Bourke-White*, p. 239.

25. For these basic facts on the German invasion, see John Toland, *Adolf Hitler*, (Garden City, N.Y.: Doubleday and Company, 1976, pp. 674–675. Also Richard B. Morris, ed., *The Encyclopedia of American History*, 6th ed. (New York: Harper & Row, Publishers, 1982), pp. 435–436.

26. Goldberg, *Margaret Bourke-White*, 240; Caldwell, *With All My Might*, pp. 186–187.

27. For Bourke-White's recollections, see Bourke-White, *Portrait*, pp. 176–178; for Caldwell's, see Caldwell, *With All My Might*, pp. 186–189. Goldberg describes the events in Goldberg, *Margaret Bourke-White*, pp. 240–244.

28. Caldwell's correspondence with American editors is located in Box 5, MBW-SU. See Wilson Hicks to EC, 30 July 1941; "Billings" to EC, 30 July 1941; Noel Busch to EC, 26 August 1941. Caldwell *With All My Might*, p. 188. Caldwell's unedited and unpaginated ms. of *Call It Experience* in the EC-DC is the most honest account of his negotiations. He describes the hotel suite in *Call It Experience*, p. 160.

29. Caldwell's broadcasts were described in *Burlington News*, 10 July 1941; *New York World Telegram*, 30 June 1941; *New York Times*, 30 June 1941. Caldwell, *With All My Might*, pp. 188–189; Goldberg, *Margaret Bourke-White*, pp. 243–244; Bourke-White, *Portrait*, p. 179. Also see Erskine Caldwell, *All Out on the Road to Smolensk* (New York: Duell, Sloan & Pearce, 1942), pp. 65, 67. A few days after Caldwell's maiden broadcasts, the Soviets allowed Herman Hagicht of NBC to transmit after three years of refusal. *Petersburg, Massachusetts Progress Index*, 2 July 1941.

30. Caldwell, *Call It Experience*, pp. 160–161. Caldwell, *All Out on the Road to Smolensk*, pp. 27, 133; Caldwell, *With All My Might*, pp. 188–189.

31. Caldwell, *All Out on the Road to Smolensk*, pp. 68–69. Goldberg, *Margaret Bourke-White*, p. 244. Bourke-White provides an excellent account of the radio broadcasts in *Shooting the Russian War* (New York: Simon & Schuster, 1942), pp. 125–127. Caldwell's parents were very upset when they had trouble understanding his voice in the early broadcasts. See Rhoda Lynn to CPC and ISC, 6 August 1941, ISC-UGA.

32. *PM*, 18 July 1941. Transcripts of Caldwell's broadcasts for CBS radio are lo-

cated in Box 6, MBW-SU. Copies of his articles for *PM* are located in Box 8, MBW-SU.

33. *PM*, 14 July 1941. The League of American Writers criticized the war before the Nazi invasion, but reversed their position just six weeks later and signed a statement that declared, "A world free of fascism is essential to the democratic institutions and culture of the United States."

34. Caldwell, CBS Broadcast, 7 August 1941, Box 6, MBW-SU.

35. EC to Rhoda Lynn, 1 June 1941, EC-DC; EC to Rhoda Lynn, 28 March 1941, EC-DC.

36. Telegram, Noel Busch to EC, 3 August 1941; telegram MBW to Noel Busch, 9 September 1941, Box 5, MBW-SU.

37. Caldwell, *With All My Might*, pp. 189–194; Bourke-White includes the telegram in *Portrait*, pp. 188.

38. Bourke-White's schedule is extensively covered in *Goldberg*, pp. 249–250. Caldwell's contract with Columbia Lecture Bureau, 3 April 1941, EC-DC.

39. EC to CPC and ISC, 9 November 1941, ISC-UGA.

40. Caldwell's lectures are summarized in materials distributed by the Columbia Lecture Bureau, "1941" scrapbook, EC-DC. Caldwell also offered a lecture entitled "The South: America's Number One Social problem."

41. Transcript of *We The People* broadcast, 4 November 1941, "1941" scrapbook, EC-DC; Marjorie Griesser to EC, 2 December 1941, EC-DC; Edwin Seaver to EC, 19 January 1942. Clippings describing Caldwell's public engagements, including lectures and radio broadcasts, are located in the "1941" scrapbook.

42. Shirley Burke, supervisor of the Script Department at the Treasury Department to EC, undated 1942, EC-DC; Vincent F. Callahan, Director of Press and Radio, Defense Savings Staff, Treasury Department to EC, 8 April 1942, EC-DC. Transcripts of Caldwell's radio announcements are in the "1942" scrapbook, EC-DC.

43. Caldwell was quoted in *St. Louis Star-Times*, 21 February 1942; *New Orleans Picayune*, 1 March 1942; *Cincinnati Enquirer*, 21 February 1942.

44. Caldwell interview in *Chicago Sun*, 25 February 1942.

45. Lieber to EC, 6 November 1941, EC-DC; Bruce Bliven to EC, 5 November 1941; *New York Herald Tribune*, 1 November 1942. Lieber reported the sale to *Redbook* in Lieber to EC, 22 December 1941, EC-DC.

46. Erskine Caldwell and Margaret Bourke-White, *Russia at War* (London and New York: Hutchinson, 1942); Erskine Caldwell, *Moscow Under Fire* (London: Hutchison, 1942); Erskine Caldwell, *All Out on the Road to Smolensk* (New York: Duell, Sloan & Pearce, 1942). Caldwell described the writing of these four books in *Call It Experience*, pp. 163–164. Also see Lieber to EC, 22 January 1942, EC-DC; Lieber to EC, 28 January 1942, EC-DC; EC to CPC and ISC, 9 November 1941, ISC-UGA; EC to CPC and ISC, 13 January 1942, ISC-UGA.

47. Caldwell and Bourke-White were finally allowed the rare privilege of a trip to the front, just before their departure. See Goldberg, *Margaret Bourke-White*, pp. 246–248.

48. *The New York Herald Tribune*, 1 March 1942; Lillian Smith to EC, 21 May 1942, EC-DC; anonymous soldier to EC, 22 July 1942, EC-DC. For other positive reviews nationwide, see *Dallas Morning News*, 22 February 1942; *Cincinnati Enquirer*, 21 February 1942; *New York News*, 22 February 1942.

49. Samuel Sillen, *New Masses*, 10 March 1942. Many on the left found delicious

irony in the U.S. government's praise of the Soviet Union once the wartime alliance was in effect.

50. Erskine Caldwell, *All Night Long* (New York: Duell, Sloan & Pearce, 1942). For the sale to *Redbook*, see Lieber to EC, 10 August 1942. *Redbook* ran the story, complete with a picture of Caldwell in a combat helmet, beginning in November of 1942.

51. Caldwell, *All Night Long*, p. 58; ibid., p. 266.

52. William DuBois, *New York Times Book Review*, 6 December 1942; Anne F. Wolfe, *Saturday Review of Literature*, 19 December 1942; Howard Fast, *Nation*, December 1942; *Augusta Herald*, 16 December 1942; Sterling North, *New York Post*, 2 December 1942.

53. Caldwell summarized the sales history of *All Night Long* in a detailed letter to Bourke-White. EC to MBW, 9 September 1942, Box 4, MBW-SU.

54. William James Fadiman to Lieber, 5 May 1942, EC-DC; Lieber to EC, 5 June 1942, EC-DC; Lieber to EC, 6 July 1942, EC-DC; EC to AM, 15 July 1942, AM-HU; Al Manual to EC, 9 October 1942, EC-DC.

55. For an excellent discussion of the Davies book and its film adaptation, see David Culbert, *Mission to Moscow* (Madison, Wisc.: University of Wisconsin Press, 1980.) Also see *New York Herald Tribune*, 13 September 1942; *Los Angeles Times*, 20 July 1942. Caldwell discussed the project with Bourke-White. EC to MBW, 15 August 1942, Box 2 MBW-SU. Robert Sherwood was the first choice to write the screenplay, but he turned it down.

56. Culbert, *Mission*, p. 21.

57. EC to MBW, July 1942, Box 2, MBW-SU; EC to MBW, 15 August 1942, Box 2, MBW-SU.

58. EC to MBW, 18 August 1942, Box 2, MBW-SU. Quotations from the screenplay are taken from Culbert, *Mission*, pp. 19–20.

59. For Caldwell's explanation of his firing, see *With All My Might*, pp. 198–199.

60. EC to MBW, 15 August 1942, Box 2, MBW-SU. Caldwell's remarks are contained in a speech given on the "American Forum of the Air Program," 13 September 1942. A transcript is located in the "1942" scrapbook, EC-DC. Caldwell told his parents he might enlist, EC to ISC and CPC, 2 October 1942, ISC-UGA.

61. Caldwell's income tax returns for 1942 and correspondence with his accountant are located in Box 5, MBW-SU. Martin Mermelstein, to EC, 23 February 1943, EC-DC. Caldwell's salary as a screenwriter was $1,250 dollars a week.

62. Caldwell carried on an extensive correspondence with his accountant. Mermelstein to EC, 29 November 1941, Box 5, MBW-SU.

63. EC to Manual, 24 June 1942, EC-DC; EC to Lieber, 23 July 1942.

64. Burton Roscoe, *New York Herald Tribune*, undated clipping, "1942" scrapbook, EC-DC; *Lynchburg, Virginia*, 23 February 1942; Margaret Marshall, *Nation*, 26 December 1942.

65. Caldwell's comments are from an interview he gave to the *Honolulu Star-Bulletin*, 29 March 1941.

66. The five stories published previously were Caldwell, "The Night My Old Man Came Home," *The New Yorker*, 11 December 1937; "Handsome Brown and the Aggravating Goats," *New Republic*, 23 September 1940; "Handsome Brown and the Shirttail Woodpeckers," *Stag*, February 1942; "My Old Man and the Grass Widow," *Coronet*, February 1941; "Days Off," *Collier's*, 30 May 1942.

67. Bourke-White described Caldwell's unwillingness to leave the hotel room in two undated notes, MBW-SU. Goldberg describes Bourke-White's frustration in *Margaret Bourke-White*, p. 239. Caldwell described the writing process in *With All My Might*, p. 201.

68. EC to Lieber, 21 October 1942, EC-DC; EC to Lieber, 22 October 1942, EC-DC. Erskine Caldwell, *Georgia Boy* (New York: Duell, Sloan & Pearce, 1943).

69. For the best discussion of the text, see Sylvia Cook, *Erskine Caldwell and the Fiction of Poverty*, pp. 84–91.

70. Charles Pearce to EC, 5 January 1943, EC-DC. Sloan to EC, 5 January 1943, EC-DC; Charles Pearce to EC, 20 April 1943, EC-DC. DS&P's publicity flyers are located in the "1943" scrapbook, EC-DC.

71. Stanley Walker, *New York Herald Tribune*, 25 April 1943; Mark Schorer, *Yale Review*, summer 1943.

72. *Time*, 3 May 1943; Diana Trilling, *Nation*, 15 May 1943; William DuBois, *New York Times*, 25 April 1943; *New Yorker*, 1 May 1943; *Atlanta Journal*, 2 May 1943.

73. *Columbus Citizen*, 25 April 1943.

CHAPTER ELEVEN: TRAGIC GROUND

1. Erskine Caldwell, *Jackpot* (New York: Duell, Sloan & Pearce, 1940). Milton Rugoff, *New York Herald Tribune Books*, 1 September 1940; Clifton Fadiman, *New Yorker*, 31 August 1941.

2. Theodore Dreiser to EC, 15 October 1940, EC-DC; Waldo Frank to EC, 14 August 1940, EC-DC; Manuel Komroff to EC, 23 September 1940; John Steinbeck to EC, 12 August 1940; H. L. Mencken to Lieber, 29 July 1940, EC-DC; Carl Van Doren to EC, 29 July 1940, EC-DC. Saroyan listed Caldwell along with Thomas Wolfe, Faulkner, Dos Passos, and himself. The interview was reprinted in *Providence, Rhode Island Journal*, 8 June 1941.

3. William Blake and Christina Stead, *Modern Women in Love* (New York: The Dryden Press, 1945); Arnold Gingrich, *The Bedside Esquire* (New York: R. M. McBride & Co., 1940); David Greenberg, *Furrow's End* (New York: Greenberg, 1946); Somerset Maugham, *Great Modern Reading* (New York: Doubleday, Inc., 1943); Bucklin Moon, *Primer for White Folks* (Garden City, New York: Doubleday, Doran and Co., Inc., 1945); Allen Tate and John Peale Bishop, *American Harvest* (Garden City, New York: Garden City Publishing Co., 1943). *The Best Short Stories from the New Yorker* (New York: Simon & Schuster, 1940).

4. Cowley was quoted in *PM*, 16 February 1947; Carl Van Doren, *Nation*, 10 February 1940. Also see *Nation*, 1 June 1940 for their appraisal of Caldwell. Joseph Warren Beach, *American Fiction 1920–1940* (New York: The Macmillan Company, 1941), pp. 291–348. The seven other authors Beach included were John Dos Passos, Ernest Hemingway, William Faulkner, Thomas Wolfe, John P. Marquand, James T. Farrell, and John Steinbeck.

5. There are several excellent discussions of Caldwell's reception abroad. See Stewart H. Benedict, "Gallic Light on Erskine Caldwell," *South Atlantic Quarterly*, August 1961, pp. 390–397; Sidney D. Braun and Seymour Lainoff, eds., *Transatlantic Mirrors: Essays in Franco-American Literary Relations* (Boston: Twayne Publishers, 1978); Deming Brown, *Soviet Attitudes Toward American Writing* (Princeton: Princeton University Press, 1962); Sylvia Cook, *Erskine Caldwell and the Fiction of Poverty*, pp. 272–278. Mikhail Landor, "Erskine Caldwell in the Soviet Union," *Soviet Literature*, III (1969), pp. 183–186. Caldwell's

correspondence with Lieber in the EC-DC is also revealing. See, for instance, Lieber to EC, 1 February 1943, EC-DC; Lieber to EC, 13 November 1944, EC-DC. Caldwell's popularity abroad was also reported in the American press. See *Daily Worker*, 19 August 1941; *New York Times*, 7 January 1943; *New Yorker*, 17 May 1941.

6. See Cook, *Fiction of Poverty*, pp. 275–279 for an excellent summary of Caldwell's reception in France. Also see *Tout L'Edition*, 10 March 1936; *Vendredi*, 16 October 1937; *Populaire*, 9 February 1937, for examples of French appreciation of Caldwell's work.

7. As quoted in Goldberg, *Bourke-White*, pp. 238, 248, 251. MBW to Julius Weiss, 19 November 1942, MBW-SU.

8. Bourke-White, *Portrait*, pp. 170–171. Goldberg describes Bourke-White's frustration with Caldwell's interference in her work in *Margaret Bourke-White*, p. 214.

9. There are a number of photographs of Caldwell and Bourke-White in the scrapbooks in the EC-DC. For Caldwell's efforts to please Bourke-White, I benefited from conversations with Mrs. Maxim Lieber. Minna Lieber interview with DM, 12 July 1993.

10. Lieber interview with WS, 29 May 1971, WS-UI. Alice-Leone Moats is quoted in Goldberg, *Margaret Bourke-White*, p. 237. Caldwell often urged Bourke-White to be more frugal. See EC to MBW, 12 January 1940, MBW-SU.

11. Bourke-White commanded between $500 and $750 a lecture; Caldwell usually received between $250 and $400.

12. I am grateful to Peggy Smith Sargeant and Lee Scott, two of Bourke-White's secretaries, for their recollections. Peggy Sargeant interview with DM, 17 October 1992; Lee Scott interview with DM, 17 October 1992.

13. *Redbook*, September 1942.

14. For Caldwell's efforts to secure a screenwriting contract for Bourke-White, see Manual to EC, 30 May 1942, EC-DC; Manual to EC, 3 June 1942, EC-DC; EC to MBW, July 1942, Box 2, MBW-SU. For the purchase of the house in Arizona, see Julius Weiss to EC, 6 April 1942. For Bourke-White's interest in having children, see Goldberg, *Margaret Bourke-White*, p. 222.

15. EC to MBW, undated 1942, MBW-SU. For Caldwell's recollection of his efforts to convince Bourke-White, see *With All My Might*, pp. 193–197.

16. EC to MBW, undated, Box 2, MBW-SU; EC to MBW, 15 July 1942. The article was carried in the *Tulsa, Oklahoma Tribune*, 20 August 1942.

17. EC to MBW, undated 1942, MBW-SU; telegram, EC to MBW, 21 July 1942, Box 2, MBW-SU.

18. Bourke-White's radio interview is quoted in Goldberg, *Margaret Bourke-White*, p. 252. MBW to Julius Weiss, 19 November 1942, MBW-SU.

19. MBW to Julius Weiss, 19 November 1942, MBW-SU. Bourke-White, *Portrait*, pp. 196–197.

20. EC to MBW, 29 August 1942, Box 2, MBW-SU. Caldwell's gift of chipped beef was reported in the *Los Angeles Herald Express*, undated clipping, "1942" scrapbook, EC-DC.

21. EC to MBW, 29 August 1942, Box 2, MBW-SU.

22. EC to MBW, 29 August 1942, Box 2, MBW-SU.

23. EC to MBW, 9 October 1942, Box 2, MBW-SU.

24. Bourke-White's activities in Europe are described in Goldberg, *Margaret Bourke-White*, pp. 253–254. MBW to Julius Weiss, 19 November 1942.

25. Telegram, EC to MBW, 10 November 1942, Box 2, MBW-SU.

26. EC to MBW, 11 November 1942, Box 2, MBW-SU. Bourke-White quoted her telegrams in a letter to Julius Weiss. MBW to Julius Weiss, 9 November 1942, Box 2, MBW-SU.

27. For a summary of the evidence that Bourke-White had an abortion, see Goldberg, *Margaret Bourke-White*, pp. 221–224. Lee Scott interview with DM, 17 October 1992; Peggy Smith Sargeant interview with DM, 17 October 1992. Mark Saha to DM, 9 December 1990.

28. MBW to Julius Weiss, 19 November 1942, Box 2, MBW-SU. Bourke-White's letter to Hicks is quoted in Goldberg, *Margaret Bourke-White*, p. 255.

29. MBW to Julius Weiss, 19 November 1942, Box 2, MBW-SU. Bourke-White, *Portrait*, p. 210.

30. Harry Behn interview with WS, 30 May 1971, WS-UI. I am grateful to June Johnson Caldwell Martin for her cooperation. JJ to DM, 11 November 1990.

31. EC to AM, 8 January 1943, AM-HU.

32. Wedding announcements appeared, for instance, in *Washington Post*, 27 December 1942; *Phoenix Republic*, 27 December 1942; *Denver Post*, 22 December 1942, *PM*, 2 April 1943.

33. Caldwell was sued by his lecture agency for breaking the contract, and the dispute was settled out of court a few years later. Telegram, Charles Duell to EC, 5 August 1943, EC-DC. For his work in Hollywood in 1943, see EC to "20th-Century Fox," 13 January 1943, EC-DC; EC to AM, 4 February 1943, AM-HU; EC to AM, 18 February 1943, EC-DC, AM-HU; EC to AM, 9 March 1943, AM-HU. Also see *Showmen's Trade Review*, 16 January 1943; *Daily Variety*, 2 September 1943; *New York Sun*, 25 August 1943.

34. Letter from EC to AM, 18 February 1943, AM-HU. Receipts for rent, clothing, and other miscellaneous expenses are located in the EC-DC.

35. EC to AM, 24 September 1943, EC-DC; EC to ISC and CPC, 26 October 1943, ISC-UGA.

36. Lieber to EC, 24 May 1943, EC-DC.

37. There is extensive correspondence dealing with the failed adaptation of *Georgia Boy*. See Lieber to EC, 27 January 1943, EC-DC; EC to ISC and CPC, 31 March 1943, ISC-UGA; Lieber to EC, 5 April 1943, EC-DC; EC to Lieber, 14 September 1943, EC-DC.

38. For Caldwell's angry recollection of Jed Harris's role in the play, see *With All My Might*, pp. 206–207.

39. For Caldwell's interest in the *Augusta Chronicle*, see Earl Bell to EC, 14 January 1938, Box 1, MBW-SU. Ira Caldwell explained the purchase of the newspapers in a long, detailed letter, ISC to EC, 9 March 1944, EC-DC. Also see Julius Weiss to EC, 24 August 1942, EC-DC; ISC to EC, 9 March 1944, EC-DC. The purchase of the papers was covered in *Washington Star*, 28 February 1944.

40. ISC to EC, 9 March 1944, EC-DC.

41. Katherine Maner to EC, 24 November 1944, EC-DC. There is a great deal of correspondence dealing with the newspapers in the EC-DC. See, for instance, ISC to EC, 30 March 1944, EC-DC; ISC to EC, 21 April 1944, EC-DC.

42. EC to ISC and CPC, 14 December 1943, EC-DC.

43. EC to AM, 17 July 1944, AM-HU; EC to ISC to CPC, 31 March 1943, ISC-UGA.

44. Bourke-White recalled Caldwell's statement as being "one of his favorites." See Bourke-White, *Portrait*, p. 196.
45. Erskine Caldwell, *Tragic Ground* (New York: Duell, Sloan & Pearce, 1944).
46. Requests, suggestions, and invocations for new work made up a large part of the correspondence from Manual, Lieber, and the editors at Duell, Sloan & Pearce. See, for instance, Manual to EC, 23 February 1944, EC-DC; Lieber to EC, 1 February 1944, EC-DC; Sloan to EC, 15 June 1944, EC-DC. Lieber's quote is from Lieber to EC, 27 March 1944, EC-DC.
47. Manual to EC, 24 February 1944, EC-DC; Lieber to EC, 1 February 1944, EC-DC; Lieber to EC, 24 September 1943; Sloan to EC, 28 March 1944, EC-DC.
48. DS&P publicity materials are located in the "1944" scrapbook, EC-DC.
49. For an excellent discussion of *Tragic Ground*, see Sylvia Cook, *Fiction of Poverty*, pp. 155–160.
50. *New York Post*, 14 November 1944; Jack Conroy, *Chicago Sun*, 22 October 1944.
51. Herbert Kupferberg, *Weekly Book Review*, 15 October 1944; Malcolm Cowley, "The Two Erskine Caldwells," *New Republic*, 6 November 1944.
52. Samuel Sillen, *Daily Worker*, 19 October 1944; Bernard DeVoto, *New York Herald Tribune*, 13 October 1944; Jonathan Daniels, *Saturday Review of Literature*, 14 October 1944.
53. Sloan to EC, 10 May 1944, EC-DC; Pearce to EC, 3 May 1944, EC-DC.
54. Pearce to EC, 3 May 1944, EC-DC; Pearce to EC, 12 May 1944, EC-DC; Sloan to EC, 10 May 1944, EC-DC.
55. Lieber to EC, 10 April 1944, EC-DC.
56. Lieber to EC, 19 April 1944, EC-DC.
57. EC to AM, 16 October 1944, AM-HU; EC to AM, 23 October 1944, AM-HU.
58. EC to AM, 16 October 1944, AM-HU.
59. EC to AM, 16 October 1944, AM-HU.
60. EC to MBW, undated, Box 2, MBW-SU.
61. Residents of Wrens still recall Ira's loyalty to his son. Boyce Wideman to WS, 24 May 1971, WS-UI; Ruby Tanner interview with DM, 22 January 1991. Ira's involvement with the DS&P edition of *Tobacco Road* was described in *Colorado Springs Evening Telegram*, 16 February 1940. His involvement with the film was recorded in the *Boston Globe*, 30 October 1940.
62. Ira's neighbors still remember him sitting on the porch and listening to his son's reports. Henrietta Boyce interview with DM, 24 January 1941; *Augusta Chronicle*, 31 July 1941, also reported on Ira's dedication to his son. Bourke-White and Caldwell's visit to Wrens after their trip to Russia was noted in *Augusta Herald*, 30 December 1941.
63. EC to CPC and ISC, 23 December 1940, ISC-UGA; EC to Rhoda Lynn, undated 1941, EC-DC.
64. ISC to EC, undated, EC-DC.
65. EC to ISC and CPC, 14 December 1943, ISC-UGA.
66. ISC to EC, 21 April 1944, EC-DC; ISC to EC, 14 April 1944, EC-DC; ISC to EC, 22 April 1944, EC-DC.
67. ISC to EC, 4 August 1944, EC-DC; ISC to EC, August 1944, EC-DC.
68. There are five folders of condolence letters in the ISC-UGA. Mr. Henry Kittie to Ira's brother and sister-in-law, 23 August 1944, ISC-UGA; MBW to CPC, 19 August 1944, ISC-UGA.
69. Dallas Caldwell to EC, 23 August 1944, ISC-UGA.
70. Caldwell worked on the screenplay of *Look Homeward, Angel* for four months

and received more than $20,000 for his failed efforts. See Manual to EC, 19 January 1945, EC-DC; Manual to EC, 7 March 1945, EC-DC; Arthur Ripley to EC, 14 April 1945, EC-DC; Rudolph Monter to EC, 27 April 1945, EC-DC. For the negotiations around the failed production of *Tragic Ground*, see Lieber to EC, 5 January 1945, EC-DC; Lieber to EC, 14 February 1945, EC-DC; Lieber to EC, 11 March 1947. The sale of Ira's beloved newspapers is discussed in Earl Bell to EC, 27 January 1945, EC-DC; Earl Bell to EC, 18 October 1945, EC-DC.

71.   For an excellent discussion of the New American Library, see Thomas Bonn, *Heavy Traffic & High Culture: New American Library as Literary Gatekeeper in the Paperback Revolution* (Carbondale and Edwardsville: Southern Illinois University Press, 1989).

72.   For information on paperback books in America, I benefited from Thomas Bonn, *Under Cover: An Illustrated History of American Mass Market Paperbacks* (New York: Penguin Books, 1982); Ray Walters, *Paperback Talk* (Chicago: Academy Chicago Publishers, 1985); Frank L. Schick, *The Paperbound Book in America* (New York: R. R. Bowker, 1959); John Tebbel, *Between Covers: The Rise and Transformation of Book Publishing in America*, New York: Oxford University Press, 1987). These statistics are from Tebbel, *Between Covers*, pp. 161–166, 421–422, 424–425.

73.   The formation of Pocket Books is nicely summarized in Tebbel, *Between Covers*, pp. 294–295. As quoted in Tebbel, *Between Covers*, p. 295.

74.   Tebbel, *Between Covers*, p. 295; as quoted in Walters, *Paperback Talk*, p. 4.

75.   Tebbel, *Between Covers*, p. 296.

76.   Quoted in Tebbel, p. 345. *God's Little Acre*'s status as the most-read book of the Armed Services Editions is mentioned in a letter, Victor Weybright to Philip Yordan, 23 November 1955, EC-DC. In the Tony Award–winning play *Mr. Roberts* (and later in the movie), *God's Little Acre* is used as an example of a book that could interest even the most anti-intellectual sailor.

77.   Sloan to EC, 24 October 1944, EC-DC; Duell to EC, 24 April 1945, EC-DC.

78.   DS&P and Lieber had not yet figured out how best to represent Caldwell's financial interest in these deals. While Avon Books printed 50,000 copies of *Georgia Boy*, for instance, Caldwell received only $250. Duell summarized Caldwell's reprint editions as of 1946. Duell to EC, 15 February 1946, EC-DC; Sloan to EC, 24 January 1945, EC-DC; Lieber to EC, 3 December 1947, EC-DC.

79.   The American branch of Penguin, run by Victor Weybright and Kurt Enoch, split off to become the New American Library in 1948. For an excellent summary of the early years of Penguin in the United States and the subsequent creation of NAL, see Bonn, *Heavy Traffic*, ch. 2, *passim*. 79. Also see Victor Weybright's memoirs, *The Making of a Publisher* (New York: Reynal & Company, 1966), ch. 7, *passim*. Weybright, *The Making of a Publisher* p. 164.

80.   I am indebted to Allan Adams, circulation manager for Fawcett Publications during these years. Allan Adams to DM, 2 November 1990. Tebbel, *Between Covers*, ch. 15, *passim*, is also very helpful.

81.   I am grateful to Liza Mundy for access to her unpublished research analyzing the covers of Caldwell's paperbacks. For information on the cover art of American paperbacks, I also profited from Bonn, *Under Cover*, p. 49, 106.

82.   Caldwell kept exact sales figures for all his paperback editions in carefully

tabulated charts that are now located in the EC-DC. For sales of *Trouble in July*, also see *Publishers Weekly*, 7 June 1947.

83. Caldwell's sales records were rivaled only by detective-fiction writers like Mickey Spillane, also an NAL author. EC to AM, 13 April 1947, EC-DC; EC to AM, 30 April 1948, EC-DC. For Caldwell's phenomenal sales, also see Bonn, *Heavy Traffic*, pp. 174–175, 196–205.

84. For the influence of Jonas's cover design, see Bonn, *Under Cover*, p. 102.

85. Allan Adams to DM, 27 February 1991.

86. For a summary of censorship efforts against *God's Little Acre*, see Anne Lyon Haight and Chandler B. Grannis, *Banned Books 387 B.C. to 1978 A.D.* (New York & London: R. R. Bowker Company, 1978), pp. 83–84.

87. The story was covered in *PM*, 2 May 1946. Edward Lewis, National Sales Manager for Fawcett Books to WS, 23 May 1971. The Denver ban was covered in *New York World Telegram*, 20 January 1947; *Rocky Mountain News*, 21 January 1947; *Time*, 3 February 1947.

88. Sales charts, EC-DC.

89. Quoted in Weybright, *Making of Publisher*, pp. 182, 215.

90. Bonn, *Heavy Traffic*, Chapter 2, *passim*.

91. Sales charts, EC-DC. Lieber to EC, 11 March 1947, EC-DC. The papers of the New American Library are located in the Elmer Holmes Bobst Library, New York University, New York, New York. Caldwell's royalties are summarized in Victor Weybright to Arthur Thornhill, Box 17, File 278-15, NAL-NYU.

CHAPTER TWELVE: SLOWING DOWN

1. Caldwell, *With All My Might*, p. 205.

2. I benefited greatly from interviews with both Dabney and Erskine Caldwell, Jr. DC interview with DM, 27 February 1990 and 1 November 1990; Erskine Caldwell, Jr. interview with DM, 22 July 1992.

3. The Dartmouth Scrapbooks contain a number of scattered and unidentified press clippings noting Pix's first marriage and his scrapes with the law.

4. Manual kept Caldwell up to date on Pix's progress. Manual to EC, 18 July 1949; Manual to EC, 1 August 1949; Manual to EC, 9 August 1949. Erskine Caldwell, Jr. to EC, 27 January 1952, EC-DC.

5. For Helen's appraisal of Dabney, see HLC to EC, 12 February 1942; HLC to EC, 7 April 1946, EC-DC. For the general tone of the correspondence between Dabney and his father, see DC to EC, 8 September 1950, EC-DC; DC to EC, 30 December 1952, EC-DC; DC to EC, 6 January 1946, EC-DC. Telegram, DC to EC, 21 January 1950, EC-DC. For Dabney's recollection of being beaten, see DC to EC, 6 January 1946, EC-DC.

6. Helen discussed Caldwell's relationship with Janet in an interview with William Sutton, 4 July 1970. Also see EC to Janet Caldwell, 13 July 1949, EC-DC; HLC to EC, 4 July 1946, EC-DC; EC to Janet Caldwell, undated 1950, EC-DC.

7. EC to Janet Caldwell, 8 April 1951, EC-DC.

8. I benefited from conversations with Jay Caldwell, Jay Caldwell interview with DM, 24 December 1990. Jay calls his father the "gentlest man I ever knew." June Johnson Caldwell Martin was also extremely helpful. JJ to DM, 22 August 1993. For Jay's personality as a very young boy, see a letter from Jay Caldwell's kindergarten teacher to EC, 27 October 1949. Caldwell's

affection for his son is evident in a number of undated cards to him in the EC-DC.

9. As she grew older, Carrie became more eccentric and more difficult. Always meticulous and penurious, she began ironing and folding her money before putting it in her wallet. For descriptions of Carrie during these years, I benefited from the recollections of June Johnson Caldwell Martin and Miss Mary Maner. JJ to DM, 9 January 1991; Mary Maner interview with DM, 17 July 1990. See also CPC to EC, undated July 1953, EC-DC.

10. JJ to DM, 11 November 1990; JJ to DM, 14 October 1990. See also Oliver Drachman, temporary secretary of the Tucson Country Club to EC, 6 March 1947, EC-DC.

11. For information on the Press Club, see Don Phillips to EC, 5 April 1945, EC-DC; Gene Lindsey to WS, 28 August 1970, WS-UI. For Caldwell's description of the club, see *With All My Might*, pp. 210–211.

12. Jay Caldwell interview with DM, 24 December 1990; JJ to DM, 11 November 1990; JJ to DM 14 October 1990. For June's interest and involvement in Caldwell's career, see her long letters to book reviewer Harry Hansen. JJ to Harry Hansen, 31 August 1948; JJ to Harry Hansen, 8 September 1948, located in the Harry Hansen Papers, The Newberry Library, Chicago, Illinois. See also Charles Pearce to EC, 27 March 1951, EC-DC.

13. There is a great deal of correspondence relating to Caldwell's involvement in the radio station in the EC-DC. Of particular use were John P. Southmay to EC, 25 June 1947, EC-DC; Harry Behn to EC, 17 July 1946; EC to "The Catalina Broadcasting Company Directors," 19 September 1946, EC-DC; EC to William A. Small, 21 October 1946; George Chambers to EC 31 May 1954; Donald Davis to EC, 26 July 1954; Wayne Sanders to EC, 30 August 1954. The opening of the station was also covered in *Variety*, 13 February 1946.

14. EC to AM, 13 April 1947, AM-HU.

15. Allan Adams to DM, 2 November 1990. I also received assistance from Donald Demarest, publicist at NAL. Donald Demarest to DM, 14 December 1990. For other examples of Caldwell's heavy involvement in promoting his work, see Kurt Enoch to EC, 12 October 1948, EC-DC; Mary Kay Bent to EC, 16 November 1948, EC-DC; Charles Duell to EC, 18 October 1946, EC-DC; Allan Adams to EC, 9 November 1958, EC-DC; Donald Demarest to EC, 19 August 1949, EC-DC.

16. Edward E. Lewis, manager of the Signet Book Department of Fawcett Publications to EC, 10 November 1948, EC-DC.

17. For publication information on Caldwell's books, I am greatly indebted to Virginia Caldwell Hibbs for allowing me access to her private files. Mrs. Hibbs kept extensive records of Erskine's sales and translations abroad.

18. Lieber to EC, 31 May 1945, EC-DC; Lieber to EC, 23 October 1947, EC-DC.

19. The Caldwell papers at Dartmouth contain many letters regarding Caldwell's meticulously planned trips. Of particular use were Lieber to EC, 7 March 1949, EC-DC; Lieber to EC, 29 April 1948, EC-DC; EC to AM, 5 May 1949, AM-HU. I also benefited from Caldwell's itineraries compiled by the Thomas, Cook & Sons Travel Agents, also in the EC-DC. The Central and South American press coverage of Caldwell's visit is preserved in the Dartmouth Scrapbooks. See also EC to AM, 23 April 1946, AM-HU.

20. EC to AM, 26 July 1945, AM-HU; EC to AM, 13 April 1947, AM-HU. For

Caldwell's comparison of writing to smoking, see his interview in *London Daily Express*, 20 November 1963.

21. Caldwell described his work schedule during these years in a number of places. See *Call It Experience*, p. 188. He first broached the concept of a "cyclorama" in the introduction to *This Very Earth*.

22. For a far more complete and generous treatment of these novels see Cook, *Erskine Caldwell*, ch. 5, *passim*.

23. EC admitted his disinclination to read in EC to Kurt Enoch, 8 November 1948, NAL-NYU.

24. Caldwell compared writing to ditch-digging in an interview for the *Contra Costa Times*, 10 February 1963. Lieber to EC, 23 October 1947, EC-DC.

25. EC to AM, 26 August 1945, AM-HU. Caldwell's relationship with the editors at DS&P is well documented in the extensive correspondence located in the EC-DC. See, for instance, Lieber to EC, 12 November 1947; Pearce to EC, 9 August 1949; Duell to EC, 1 December 1948, EC-DC.

26. For sales figures of paperback editions, I have relied on the carefully tabulated NAL records in possession of Mrs. Virginia Caldwell Hibbs. Copies of these records are also located in the EC-DC and the papers of the New American Library, Elmer Holmes Bobst Library, New York University. For hardcover sales during the late 1940s see Duell to EC, 29 May 1946; Duell to EC, 14 October 1947, EC-DC; Duell to EC, 11 November 1948.

27. Duell to EC, 2 March 1948, EC-DC; Lieber to EC, 12 May 1947, EC-DC; Lieber to EC, 5 April 1950, EC-DC; Pearce to EC, 7 April 1950, EC-DC; Weybright's remarks are quoted in the letter from Duell to EC, 11 March 1948, EC-DC.

28. Hamilton Basso, *The New Yorker*, 11 May 1946; Joy Davidman, *New Masses*, 9 July 1946.

29. *American Mercury*, February 1948; *Time*, 30 August 1948; Lon Tinkle, "Crumbled Georgia Crackers," *Saturday Review of Literature*, 28 August 1948; V. P. Hass, *Saturday Review of Literature*, 21 October 1950.

30. James Baldwin, "The Dead Hand of Caldwell," *New Leader*, 6 December 1947.

31. Sterling North, *Chicago Sun*, 5 May 1946; James Aswell to EC, 23 November 1948, EC-DC; AM to EC, undated 1946, EC-DC. Roland Gant thought *A Place Called Estherville* was "one of the very finest books [Caldwell had] ever written, and one of the most moving I have ever read." Roland Gant to EC, 27 September 1949, EC-DC.

32. Most of DS&P's support came from Charles Pearce. See Pearce to EC, 1 September 1948; Pearce to EC, 19 July 1949, EC-DC; Pearce to EC, 16 October, 1947, EC-DC.

33. EC to AM, 13 April 1947, AM-HU.

34. Minna Lieber interview with DM, 11 July 1993. Also see Minna Lieber to EC, 6 September 1951, EC-DC; EC to Minna Lieber, 11 September 1951, EC-DC.

35. See *Daily Worker*, 11 February 1947 and 25 March 1947, for a description of Caldwell's involvement in the Progressive Writers Group. Also see Joseph North to EC, 15 September 1947, EC-DC.

36. ML to EC, 26 March 1948, EC-DC. Pearce is quoted in ML to EC, 21 March 1948, EC-DC.

37. EC to ML, 9 January 1950, EC-DC.

38. Kurt Enoch to EC, 25 July 1951, EC-DC; Victor Weybright to EC, 8 January 1951, EC-DC; Kurt Enoch to EC, 18 July 1951, EC-DC.

39. EC to Minna Lieber, 11 September 1951, EC-DC.

40. Victor Weybright to EC, 11 September 1950, EC-DC; JOB to EC, 9 December 1952, EC-DC.

41. JJ to DM, 11 November 1990; JJ to DM, 14 October 1990; JJ to DM, 9 January 1991. Also see JJ interview with WS, 28 August 1970, WS-UI.

42. Unsigned, undated letter from a cultural attaché in Buenos Aires to WS, WS-UI.

43. JJ to Harry Hansen, 31 August 1948, Newberry Library, Chicago, Illinois. Sloan to June, 26 June 1945; Donald Demarest to EC, 28 January 1946; EC-DC; JOB to EC, 8 June 1953, EC-DC; Pearce to EC, 16 March 1948, EC-DC; Duell to EC, 5 April 1951, EC-DC.

44. Katherine White, editor at *New Yorker*, to JJ, 15 November 1952, EC-DC; James Aswell to JJ, 10 February 1952, EC-DC.

45. JJ to her parents, 25 September 1952, EC-DC; JJ to Ralph Bunche, 20 July 1952, EC-DC; JJ to Barry Goldwater, 26 November 1952, EC-DC; JJ to DM, 11 November 1990; JJ to DM, 14 October 1990.

46. For Caldwell's recollection of June's psychotherapy, see *With All My Might*, p. 228.

47. Caldwell summarized his grievances with June in *With All My Might* p. 228. EC to AM, 28 May 1951, AM-HU.

48. EC to JJ, undated 1952, EC-DC.

49. JJ to EC, undated 1954, EC-DC.

50. Duell to EC, 7 November 1952, EC-DC; Weiss to EC, 7 December 1951; Duell to EC, 1 December 1948, EC-DC; JOB to Manual, 18 April 1952, EC-DC.

51. Bernard Geis, editor of Grosset and Dunlap, to Arthur Thornhill, 10 March 1952, EC-DC.

52. JOB to Manual, 18 April 1952, EC-DC; JOB to EC, 11 November 1957, EC-DC.

53. Lieber to EC, 8 May 1950, EC-DC; JOB to EC, 6 November 1951, EC-DC; JOB to EC, 13 December 1951, EC-DC. Erskine Caldwell, *A Lamp For Nightfall* (New York: Duell, Sloan & Pearce; Boston: Little, Brown and Company, 1952).

54. Caldwell, *Where the Girls Were Different* (New York: Avon Books Co., Inc., 1948); *Midsummer Passion and Other Stories* (New York: Avon, 1948); *A Woman in the House* (New York: New American Library, 1949); *A Swell Looking Girl* (New York: New American Library, 1950).

55. Caldwell, *The Humorous Side of Erskine Caldwell*, edited and introduced by Robert Cantwell (New York: Duell, Sloan and Pearce, 1951); *The Courting of Susie Brown* (Boston: Little, Brown and Co., 1952); *The Complete Stories*, Boston: Little, Brown and Co., 1953). Caldwell put together two other anthologies in the mid-1940s: *Stories by Erskine Caldwell*, selected and introduced by Henry Seidel Canby (New York: Duell, Sloan & Pearce, 1944) and *The Caldwell Caravan* (Cleveland and New York: World Publishing Co., 1946).

56. James Aswell, 14 January 1951, EC-DC; Aswell to EC, 7 April 1951, EC-DC.

57. For an excellent bibliographical listing of Caldwell's short fiction, see Scott MacDonald, "An Evaluative Check-List of Erskine Caldwell's Short Fiction," in *Studies in Short Fiction*, 1978, pp. 81–97. EC to Lieber, 26 March 1951, EC-DC.

58. JOB to EC, 20 November 1951, EC-DC. There are hundreds of letters from NAL to EC detailing his contractual arrangements in the EC-DC. For an excellent summary of NAL's support of Caldwell, see Weybright to Arthur Thornhill, 19 August 1954, EC-DC.

59. All sales figures are taken from Caldwell's sales' charts located in the EC-DC. JOB to EC, 19 March 1954, EC-DC.

60. JOB to Arthur Thornhill, 6 May 1954, EC-DC; JOB to EC, 14 March 1954, EC-DC; Weybright to Thornhill, 9 August 1954, EC-DC; JOB to EC, 3 October 1956, EC-DC.

61. Weybright to Arthur Thornhill, 19 August 1954, EC-DC.

62. A copy of the divorce agreement is located in the EC-DC. JOB to EC, 25 August 1954, EC-DC.

63. Erskine Caldwell, *Love and Money* (New York: Duell, Sloan & Pearce, 1954). The Hillman editions of *Poor Fool* and *The Bastard* sold poorly, largely because many distributors and merchants were afraid of potential censorship efforts. Caldwell received $8,000 for both books. JOB to EC, 27 April 1953, EC-DC; JOB to EC, 4 May 1955, EC-DC; Walter Wriggens to JOB, 27 August 1957, Box 17, Folder 281, NAL-NYU.

64. Weybright to JOB, 10 November 1954, EC-DC. The correspondence between Caldwell and the Passport Division is located in the EC-DC. See, for instance, Mrs. R. B. Shipley, director of the Passport Office, to EC, 16 November 1954. Ibid., 14 November 1954, EC-DC. The F.B.I. file on Caldwell is available through the Freedom of Information Act.

65. *The American Legion Firing Line*, 15 May 1955. The article is located in the "1955" scrapbook in the EC-DC. The statements of the Protect America League are taken from a letter from Nel E. Wetterman, president of the league, to Mr. J. Louis Motz, 17 May 1955, EC-DC.

66. Weybright to EC, 1 June 1955, EC-DC. EC to Mrs. R. B. Shipley, director of the Passport Office, 14 November 1953, EC-DC.

67. There are a number of photographs from this period in the EC-DC.

CHAPTER THIRTEEN: WITH ALL MY MIGHT

1. From an interview in *Wake Forest Gold and Black*, 18 January 1965.

2. For the best chronology of Caldwell short stories, see Scott MacDonald's "An Evaluative Check-List of Erskine Caldwell's Short Fiction." Caldwell did publish four pieces in 1953, although it is unclear when they were written. The review of *Gretta* is located in *The Spectator*, 10 February 1956.

3. Interview with Virginia Caldwell Hibbs, 15 June 1990.

4. Ibid.

5. The undated flyer is located in the EC-DC. For Caldwell's new contract at NAL, see Julius Weiss to JOB, 30 September 1955, EC-DC; JOB to EC, 1 October 1954, EC-DC.

6. The correspondence between Manual and Caldwell relating to the film versions of *God's Little Acre*, *Gretta*, and *Claudelle Inglish* are located in the EC-DC. For favorable reviews of the film *God's Little Acre*, see *Los Angeles Mirror*, 15 May 1958; *Life*, 5 May 1958; *Newsweek*, 2 June 1958. The review of *Claudelle Inglish* was published in *Publisher's Weekly*, 1 December 1958.

7. Virginia Caldwell Hibbs's sales figures are located in the EC-DC.

8. Dabney Caldwell interview with DM, 1 November 1990.

9. The itineraries for these trips are located in the EC-DC.

10. For an accounting of Caldwell's accumulated rubles, see JOB to EC, 3 July 1958. Caldwell's tours for the U.S.I.A. are described in *With All My Might*, pp. 292–293; JOB to EC, 10 March 1955, EC-DC. Virginia has fond memories of Caldwell's warm reception overseas.

11. Erskine Caldwell, *Jenny By Nature* (New York: Farrar, Straus and Cudahy, 1961); *Close to Home* (New York: Farrar, Straus and Cudahy, 1962); *Last Night of Summer* (New York: Farrar, Straus and & Company, 1963); *Miss Mama Aimee* (New York: The New American Library, 1967); *Summertime Island* (New York and Cleveland: The World Publishing Company, 1968); *The Weather Shelter* (New York and Cleveland: The World Publishing Company, Times Mirror, 1969); *The Earnshaw Neighborhood* (New York: The World Publishing Company, 1971); *Annette* (New York: New American Library, Times Mirror, 1973). *St. Louis Globe Democrat*, 4 August 1968; *Chicago Daily News*, 10 November 1973.

12. Erskine Caldwell; drawings by Virginia M. Caldwell, *Around About America* (New York: Farrar, Straus & Company, 1964); Erskine Caldwell; drawings by Virginia M. Caldwell, *Afternoons in Mid-America* (New York: Dodd, Mead & Company, 1976); Erskine Caldwell with illustrations by William Sharp, *Molly Cottontail* (Boston and Toronto: Little, Brown and Company, 1958); Erskine Caldwell with illustrations by Ben Wohlberg, *The Deer at Our House* (New York: Collier Books; London: Collier-Macmillan Limited, 1966).

13. Erskine Caldwell, *In Search of Bisco* (New York: Farrar, Straus and Giroux, 1965).

14. Erskine Caldwell, *In the Shadow of the Steeple* (London: Heinemann, 1966). The book was reissued in the United States with the title *Deep South: Memory and Observation* (New York: Weybright and Talley, 1968).

15. For an excellent overview of Caldwell's disappearance from the critical canon, see Sylvia Cook, *Fiction of Poverty*, ch. 7, *passim*. Also see VC to Frank Daniel, 14 July 1965, FD-E.

16. As quoted in Frederick L. Gwynn and Joseph L. Blotner, eds., *Faulkner in the University: Class Conference at the University of Virginia, 1957–1958* (Charlottesville: University of Virginia Press, 1959), p. 143.

17. Caldwell recalled the unpleasant experience at the writers' conference in *With All My Might*, pp. 211–213. Willard Thorp, *American Writing in the Twentieth Century* (Cambridge, Massachusetts: Harvard University Press, 1960), p. 261.

18. Carl Bode, "Erskine Caldwell: A Note for the Negative," *College English* 17 (March 1956), 357–359.

19. JOB to EC, 11 May 1959, EC-DC. Caldwell is quoted by Edwin T. Arnold in *Erskine Caldwell Revisited* (Jackson, Miss., and London: University Press of Mississippi, 1990), p. 4.

20. Virginia Caldwell Hibbs provided detailed information on Caldwell's declining health. See her interview with Edwin T. Arnold in *Erskine Caldwell Revisited*, pp. 99–110. In 1971, the year before his first cancer diagnosis, Caldwell underwent surgery to repair a blocked artery in his left leg—a condition also resulting from his years of heavy smoking and drinking.

21. I am grateful to information provided by Dr. Llewellyn P. Howell, one of Caldwell's attending physicians at the Mayo Clinic. Dr. Llewelyn P. Howell to DM, 10 December 1990.

22. For Caldwell's popularity in Japan, see Fujisato Kitajima, "Caldwell in Ja-

pan," reprinted in *Erskine Caldwell Revisited*, pp. 42–49. Virginia Caldwell Hibbs kept careful records of all of Caldwell's awards and honors.

23. *Atlanta Constitution*, 9 April 1973; *New Yorker*, 6 February 1978; *New York Times*, 18 December 1978. The Erskine Caldwell Museum in Moreland, Georgia, is now open for visitors.

24. James Korges, *Erskine Caldwell* (Minneapolis: University of Minnesota Press, 1969); Scott MacDonald, ed., *Critical Essays on Erskine Caldwell* (Boston: G. K. Hall & Co., 1981); James E. Devlin, *Erskine Caldwell* (Boston: Twayne Publishers, 1984); *Pembroke Magazine* 11 (1979). William Sutton's as-yet-unpublished manuscript was completed in 1980. The first draft of Harvey Klevar's biography was finished in 1979, and the book was published by the University of Tennessee Press in August of 1993.

25. Caldwell describes the trip to the White House in *With All My Might*, p. 321. John Hersey, "Tribute to Erskine Caldwell at the American Academy of Arts and Letters," first published in the *Proceedings of the American Academy and Institute of Arts and Letters*, Second Series, Number 38, Spring 1988.

26. The two leather-bound volumes are in the possession of Mrs. Virginia Caldwell Hibbs.

27. Interview with Virginia Caldwell, 15 June 1990. Two of Caldwell's final interviews appeared in *Scottsdale Progress*, 15 November 1986 and *Washington Post*, 1 March 1987. The introductions to both pieces comment on his poor health.

28. Caldwell's final months are eloquently described in the VC interview with Edwin T. Arnold, reprinted in *Erskine Caldwell Revisited*, pp. 99–110.

29. Ibid., p. 107.

30. Charles Truehart, *Washington Post*, 19 April 1987.

31. VC interview with Arnold, p. 108.

32. Ibid.

33. Virginia Caldwell Hibbs interview with DM, 11 July 1991, 20 August 1993. The quotation in the epilogue is taken from Caldwell, *With All My Might* (Atlanta: Peachtree Publishers, Ltd., 1987), p. 330.

EPILOGUE

1. Erskine Caldwell, *With All My Might* (Atlanta: Peachtree Publishers, Ltd., 1987).

2. Caldwell, *With All My Might*, p. 330.

INDEX

A NOTE ABOUT THE AUTHOR

Dan B. Miller was born in 1962 and grew up in Delmar, New York. He graduated
from Amherst College in 1985, and received a master's degree in history in 1989
and a Ph.D. in the history of American civilization in 1993, both from Harvard
University. He is now a teacher and Dean of Students at the Riverdale Country
School in the Bronx.

A NOTE ABOUT THE TYPE

This book was set in Monotype Dante, a typeface designed by Giovanni Mar-
dersteig (1892–1977). Conceived as a private type for the Officina Bodoni at Ve-
rona, Italy, Dante was originally cut only for hand composition by Charles Malin,
the famous Parisian punch cutter, between 1946 and 1952. Its first use was in an
edition of Boccaccio's *Trattatello in laude di Dante* that appeared in 1954. The
Monotype Corporation's version of Dante followed in 1957. Although modeled
on the Aldine type used for Pietro Cardinal Bembo's treatise *De Ætna* in 1495,
Dante is a thoroughly modern interpretation of the venerable face.

Composed by PennSet, Bloomsburg, Pennsylvania.
Printed and bound by Quebecor Printing Martinsburg,
Martinsburg, West Virginia.
Designed by Robert C. Olsson

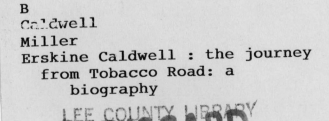